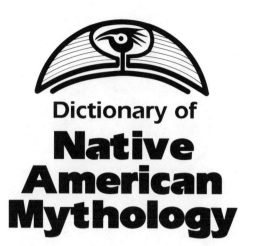

Dictionary of
Native
American
Mythology

Dictionary of
Native
American
Mythology

Sam D. Gill
Irene F. Sullivan

ABC-CLIO

Santa Barbara, California
Denver, Colorado
Oxford, England

Library of Congress Cataloging-in-Publication Data

Gill, Sam D., 1943–
   Dictionary of Native American mythology / Sam D. Gill, Irene F.
Sullivan
     p.   cm.
   Includes bibliographical references and index.
   1. Indians of North America—Religion and mythology—Dictionaries.
I. Sullivan, Irene F. II. Title
  E98.R3G46 1992 299'.7'03—dc20 92-27053

ISBN 0-87436-621-6

99 98 97 96 95 94 93   10 9 8 7 6 5 4 3 2

ABC-CLIO, Inc.
130 Cremona Drive, P.O. Box 1911
Santa Barbara, California 93116-1911

Contents

Illustrations

The following appear as captioned illustrations within the text.

Illustrations

The decorative illustrations on the first page of each chapter are from Dorothy Smith Sides's 1961 volume, *Decorative Art of the Southwestern Indians*. Each of these illustrations, listed by chapter and position on the page, is briefly described below, together with the original source of the art cited by Sides.

A

Top   Painted pottery decoration from Sikyatki ruin, Arizona [Fewkes 1901]

Middle   Pottery decoration, American Southwest [Chapman 1916]

Bottom   Pottery decoration from Sikyatki ruin, Arizona [Fewkes 1901]

B

Top   Painted ceramic decoration, Sikyatki ruin, Arizona [Fewkes 1901]

Middle   Pottery decoration from Sikyatki ruin, Arizona [Fewkes 1901]

Bottom   Pottery decoration from Four Mile Ruin, Arizona [Fewkes 1904]

C

Top   Painted snake design on pottery, Shongopovi ruin, Arizona [Fewkes 1904]

Middle   Pottery decoration from Pecos Pueblo, New Mexico [Kidder 1931, 1936]

Bottom   Prehistoric pottery decoration from the Mimbres River Valley, New Mexico [Southwest Museum specimen]

D

Top   Painted bird design on pottery, Shongopovi ruin, Arizona [Fewkes 1904]

Middle   Papago basket design, Arizona, Sonora [Kissell 1916]

Bottom   Stylized bird on painted pottery, Chevlon (Shakwabaiyki) ruin, near Winslow, Arizona [Fewkes 1904]

E

Top   Pottery design from Homolobi Ruin No. 1, near Winslow, Arizona [Fewkes 1904]

Middle   Pottery decoration from Santo Domingo, New Mexico [Southwest Museum specimen]

Bottom   Design on painted pottery, Homolobi Ruin No. 1, Arizona [Fewkes 1904]

F

Top   Pima basket design, Arizona [Russell 1908]

Middle   Pottery design from Acoma, New Mexico [Stevenson 1883]

Bottom   Pima basket design, Arizona [Russell 1908]

G

Top   Pottery design from Zuni, New Mexico [Stevenson 1883]

Middle   Pottery decoration from Chevlon (Shakwabaiyki) ruin, Arizona [Fewkes 1904]

Bottom   Pima design, Arizona [Russell 1908]

H

Top   Pima basket design, Arizona [Russell 1908]

Middle   Hopi pottery decoration, Arizona [Chapman 1916]

Bottom   Pima basket design, Arizona [Russell 1908]

I

Top   Pottery design from San Ildefonso, New Mexico [Chapman 1933]

Middle   Bird design on painted pottery, Pecos Pueblo, New Mexico [Kidder 1931, 1936]

Bottom   Pottery design from Sikyatki ruin, Arizona [Fewkes 1901]

J

Top   Pottery decoration from the Mimbres River Valley, New Mexico [Southwest Museum specimen]

Middle   Pottery decoration, Sikyatki ruin, Arizona [Fewkes 1901]

Bottom   Prehistoric Mimbres pottery design, New Mexico [Southwest Museum specimen]

K

Top   Papago basket design, Arizona, Sonora [Kissell 1916]

Middle   Pottery design from Sikyatki ruin, Arizona [Fewkes 1901]

Bottom   Papago basket design, Arizona, Sonora [Kissell 1916]

L

Top   Papago basket design, Arizona, Sonora [Kissell 1916]

Middle   Stylized bird on painted pottery, Zuni Pueblo, New Mexico [Chapman 1916]

Bottom   Papago basket design, Arizona, Sonora [Kissell 1916]

M

Top   Pottery decoration from Pecos Pueblo, New Mexico [Kidder 1931, 1936]

Middle   Hopi kachina, Arizona [Southwest Museum specimen]

Bottom   Painted design on pottery, Pecos Pueblo, New Mexico [Kidder 1931, 1936]

N

Top   Pottery decoration from Four Mile Ruin, Arizona [Fewkes 1904]

Middle   Bird design on Hopi painted pottery, Arizona [Bunzel, 1930]

Bottom   Painted pottery decoration from Four Mile Ruin, Arizona [Fewkes 1904]

O

Top   Decoration on painted pottery, San Ildefonso, New Mexico [Chapman 1933]

Middle   Papago basket design, Arizona, Sonora [Kissell 1916]

Bottom   Navajo rug design, Arizona, New Mexico [Southwest Museum specimen]

P

Top   Navajo rug design, Arizona, New Mexico [Specimen from collection of Mrs. Kenneth Worthen]

Middle   Pottery decoration, Homolobi Ruin No. 1, Arizona [Fewkes 1904]

Bottom   Navajo rug design, Arizona, New Mexico [Southwest Museum specimen]

Q

Top   Geometric pottery design from Four Mile Ruin, Arizona [Fewkes 1904]

Middle   Pottery design from Shongopovi ruin, Arizona [Fewkes 1904]

Bottom   Pima design, Arizona [Russell 1908]

R

Top   Mimbres pottery decoration, New Mexico [Hewett 1930]

Middle   Pottery decoration from Sikyatki ruin, Arizona [Fewkes 1901]

Bottom   Pottery decoration from Four Mile Ruin, Arizona [Fewkes 1904]

Preface

In preparing this dictionary we honor the richness and diversity of mythology and ritual of the hundreds of cultures in native North America, the region from northern Mexico to the Arctic Circle. The traditions of these cultures—the forms and substances that give each culture its identity and vitality—are transmitted through stories and rites; indeed, mythology and ritual constitute the traditions of a culture. By and large, Native Americans transmit culture, history, values, hopes, and dreams through what they say and do. The mythology and ritual are the heart, the lifeblood, of every Native American culture.

Mythology is a term that has received much attention by academic communities. Many have wanted to separate myth from tale, legend, and other forms of story. Some argue that myth refers primarily to "religious" stories or to stories that tell or describe the creation and origin of the world. We have not made any such distinction. We have considered as myth any story that reflects the quality and character of a specific Native American culture, or of Native American cultures more generally. We have given more attention to stories that distinguish a particular culture and these stories often deal with origins, with establishing patterns and paradigms. But we have not systematically excluded consideration of stories that are told primarily for entertainment or for fun, for these too establish and bear the imprints of a culture.

Ritual is not easily separated from mythology, though it has been common to consider it a set of actions, usually nonverbal. Many stories describe the origin or establishment of rituals. Many rituals are performed according to models and patterns described in stories. Mythology and ritual are often so interwoven as to be virtually inseparable. Stories, or story lines told through song, are common elements of ritual performances. The descriptions of rites performed by mythic characters occur frequently in stories. We have made no effort to establish hard distinctions between mythology and ritual. Rather we have seen them as necessarily complementary. Some descriptions and discussions of rites and rituals are made without reference to stories, but many interconnect with stories.

In the most primary way we want to respect the integrity and distinctiveness of each and every Native American culture and to do so in its own terms. Consequently, many entries are presented under titles in specific Native American languages. Still there are common themes, issues, ideas, motifs, and patterns that may be found interwoven among the traditions of these many cultures. These many commonalities need to be identified and discussed; indeed, they are likely the most familiar elements to those outside specific tribes and especially to non-Native Americans. They are presented under English entry titles that identify these comparative and common categories with cross-references presented to direct the reader to a variety of relevant culture-specific entries. Using the dictionary in this way makes the entries with native-language titles easily accessible. Readers are encouraged to read beyond the general entries discussing themes, motifs, figures, and such to the culture-specific entries, for it is these entries that reveal the great richness of Native American cultures.

There are thousands of publications on Native American mythology and ritual. The stories and descriptions of rites found in these published sources are removed from the living cultures, freezing in print what the cultures themselves never intended as anything other than the acts of culture part and parcel to living meaningful and fruitful lives. Most of the published sources are in English, with too little attention given to the translation processes that result in the virtual elimination of the Native American languages. We have attempted to exercise the utmost care in using only sources that have the highest reliability in translation and presentation. Still, when dealing with hundreds of native languages and hundreds of translators and collectors, there remains much reason for concern. Even with the very best of translations, we recognize that translation is always interpretation. Interpretation is always based on theory. And theory is held, often tacitly, by the translator. Thus no translation is a perfect replication of the source.

All mythology and ritual are inseparable from the performance of culture, the enacting of tradition. Clearly the qualities and characteristics of the performance are essential to understanding any myth or ritual. Stories are almost always told to select audiences in restricted cultural contexts. The stories are intended to *do* something at least as much as they are intended to *say* something. Rituals are performed to cure, to prepare for hunts, to assure agricultural fertility, to bring in a new year, to move one along the cycle of life. It is for their power to do something that rituals are performed. When rituals are observed and descriptions of them are recorded, this power inherent in them is almost always lost or obscured. Even when descriptions indicate that a ritual is intended to have an effect, the distance from its per-

formance may wrongfully make such intentions appear to be mere superstitions, or unscientific misconceptions. We are well aware that Native American mythology and ritual must be seen as part of the essential tapestry of life; it must be understood as existing only through its performance. Stories and rites are never frozen in Native American cultures as they are when published in books and pictures. Indeed, in Native American cultures, every story, every rite, is always on the verge of extinction. If it is not transmitted from one generation to the next, even from one performance or enactment to the next, it will be irretrievably lost. Native Americans bear the awesome responsibility for maintaining and continuing the creative process of the entire history and tradition of their culture. Native Americans may look at this responsibility somewhat differently. To at least some Native Americans, the stories and rites are revealed or entrusted to humans by beings in a more permanent and powerful level of reality, a reality we often term spiritual. If stories or rites can no longer be told accurately or performed properly, they may become dangerous to humans. Viewed in this way, it is the responsibility of humans to retire entrusted knowledge of stories and rites under certain circumstances, with the faith that this knowledge is held permanently in the spiritual world and can be revealed again if needed.

Native American mythology and ritual are part of history. All Native American myths and rituals have histories. No part of any culture is without change. Often stories and rites undergo extensive change from generation to generation, even from telling to telling, from one performance to the next. Many myths and rituals are powerful precisely because they can be adapted and applied to so many situations. Myths and rituals may be thought of as tools used by human beings to create and maintain community, health, identity, family, and self. Individuals who know stories and who know how to do rites are often considered wealthy, certainly much more so than on the basis of compiling material goods. The adaptability of stories and rituals has not often been appreciated by those who have recorded them. In most cases a single recording has been considered sufficient. Almost no recorders have appreciated the fact that a story and ritual only really exists in its application. Consequently, there are few records of the cultural contexts to which stories and rituals are applied. Most of the published records of myth and ritual present the stories and rituals without their histories and without their applications. As a result, and with regret, we have been unable to incorporate much history. We have adopted the use of the present tense in the summarization of stories, because we believe that this places the reader more directly into the action of the story and we want to remind readers that these stories do not tell of ancient history, but rather are a necessary part of life in the present. Where we know that a ritual is no longer practiced, we use past tense. Where we have been unable to determine the present practice of a ritual, we use the present tense because we know of a number of Native American rituals still practiced that have been proclaimed by some to be extinct.

As we have considered the selection and presentation of Native American mythology and ritual we have felt something of the awesomeness of this responsibility. We have had to acknowledge that, even at the best, the many sources on which we depend bear the imprint of non-Native Americans. We have had to reckon with the fact that our presentation of Native American mythology and ritual based on this mass of material requires a reduction, through selection and condensation, on such a scale as to cause us great concern. In summarizing, in describ-

ing, and in selecting we have further removed these forms from their living cultural performances; we have greatly simplified what is almost always unbelievably complex and intricate. This is a violation to these materials that we acknowledge and finally, with much regret, accept because we believe that so few people, even among modern Native Americans, know how truly rich and diverse are the traditions of Native American mythology and ritual.

It is a hope and intention in the design of this dictionary to encourage and assist readers in finding more information than, due to the limitations of a single volume, we are able to present. We want to tantalize and generate interest in the far greater resources to be found in published works that constitute the greatest ethnographic accomplishment in human history. For most entries there are designations of relevant bibliography items. Readers are encouraged to explore the richness of these materials. There is an index to the substantive entries and to the bibliography in the dictionary by tribe or tribal group. This index permits a culture-by-culture reading of the dictionary and facilitates culture-specific research beyond the limitations of the book.

The dictionary form as it has been developed here—with its cross-referenced entries, the bibliography, and the cultural index to the entries and bibliography—offers a fascinating way of presenting Native American mythology. It provides an alternative to the anthology, which selects whole stories but necessarily in limited number. In anthologies it is difficult to acknowledge themes and ideas along which readers might pursue comparison. The dictionary form used here allows many ways of integrating the materials presented, clues to how the many cultures and stories interrelate and differ. We hope that the form we have developed will encourage browsing and will stimulate much thought, beyond being useful for direct-lookup reference. Though the dictionary is miniscule in contrast with the extent of the material it attempts to present, it has been designed to help make accessible a wide range of resources that otherwise can be overwhelming.

Readers should know that though some of the cultures whose mythology and ritual we describe no longer exist, and though some of the stories and rites we describe may no longer be performed, Native American cultures all over North America are alive and well. It is to the respect for and appreciation of the people of these many cultures and their living traditions, and to their powerful and beautiful heritages, that we dedicate this work.

Acknowledgments

I wish to acknowledge gratefully the University of Colorado Graduate Committee on the Arts and the Humanities for a grant to develop and prepare the bibliography. Kelley Grimes and Corbin Gill did many hours of bibliographic research and typing. Judy Gill helped edit and typed, both at the most crucial times. The University of Colorado Religious Studies Department staff and faculty supported the project. Professor Allan Taylor of the University of Colorado Department of Linguistics provided essential insight on linguistic matters. Many thanks to all.

It has been a special pleasure to work with the ABC-CLIO staff: Heather Cameron, Jeffery Serena, Martha Whitt, Susan Ficca, Matthew Archer, and Tracey Butler. I appreciate their enthusiasm and sensitivity, their patience and amiability.

As always Judy, Corbin, and Jenny provided their good humor and love throughout, and I hope always to return the same to them.

Sam Gill

No undertaking such as this would have been possible without the support, love, and humor of many good friends. Thank you: Sue Regan and Lalit Roy; Andria Bronsten and Mike Gurrola; Judy, Jim and Caleb Oldendorf; Sandy and Jim Grundy; Chief Alice Cook; Pilar Bacca; and Dennis, Dorothy and Marty Whelan. To my friends and colleagues at the University Health Sciences Center Employee and Access Clinic, yes, it is finally finished.

To my mother Bernice Tarcynzski Sullivan who gave me a love of books and learning and to my father Edmund and his wife Nancy, thank you.

Last, but in no way least, thank you to my husband Will Reller, whose support in all my endeavors makes my life rich beyond words.

Irene Sullivan

User's Guide

Entry Format

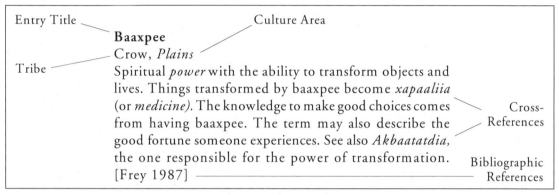

Entry Title: Every entry in the dictionary is headed with a word or phrase that is intended to most fully and accurately reflect the content. Because of the diversity and complexity of the information in many entries, an adequately representative title is not always possible. To provide readers access to the significant information in entries not adequately reflected in the titles, we provide entries under other significant titles that direct the reader, by means of cross-references, to these entries. Many of the entry titles are in Native American languages. We recognize that many of these terms will be unknown to most users of this work. Still it is by this means that we are able to retain cultural identity and integrity of the information presented. The information in these entries is intended to be accessible through other entries with more familiar entry titles by following the cross-reference suggestions. Often users of this work will want to follow a series of cross-references, even chains of cross-references, to find the information they seek. We also hope that, for many users, this cross-referencing technique will stimulate a process of exploration. We

hope that readers will be interested in comparisons, compilations, and connections among the entries in the dictionary.

Tribe and/or *Culture Area:* Entry titles are followed by the identification of the tribe and/or culture area where relevant. Typically a tribe, a list of tribes, or a tribal grouping is listed first followed by the culture area (identified in italic type) in which this tribe, list of tribes, or tribal grouping is located. The culture areas are in turn keyed to a set of detailed maps, as explained on p. xviii.

Cross-References: These are terms found in the text of the entries that are also the titles of other entries where related information is presented. These cross-references are in italic type.

Bibliographic References: Because the information in this dictionary represents only a small fraction of a veritable mountain of available material, bibliographic suggestions are provided for most entries. This feature, along with the extensive bibliography, enhances the usefulness of this dictionary for scholars and specialists, as well as for the general reader.

Maps

Maps are provided for the ten culture areas to assist in locating tribes. Tribe and/or culture area designations are given in entries where relevant. Map 1 can be used to locate each of the ten culture areas within North America; Maps 2–11 present the culture areas in detail.

Bibliography

The bibliography is in alphabetical order by the last name of the author. Works by the same author are organized chronologically by the year of publication. Multiple publications for the same year for a given author are arranged alphabetically by title and an alphabetic character is appended to the year. Brief references to the bibliography are made throughout the dictionary by reference to the author's last name and the year of publication.

Index by Tribe

An index to the entries and to the bibliography has been provided to facilitate research on specific tribes or tribal groupings. It is organized alphabetically by tribe, with entry titles followed in italic type by bibliographic references. Note that in addition to specific tribes, the index also contains headings for culture areas as well as a "General" heading that lists entries and references not specific to any one tribe.

Native American Languages

More than 150 Native American languages are represented in the titles of entries in this dictionary. Native American languages have come to be written primarily through the introduction by linguists and others of orthographic systems that assign a symbol or alphabetic character to the phonemic structure—the distinguishable sounds—of a language. For many Native American languages several different orthographies have been used. Further complexity is introduced by the abilities and eccentricities of various persons who have recorded these Native American terms. Some hear a "b" sound where others hear a "p" sound; some hear "ts" where others hear "s." The linguistic and orthographic complexities of any Native American language are fully understood only by the specialist in that language. Though ideally every Native American word used in the dictionary would be presented so that the orthography would most closely reflect Native American pronunciations, this is not even possible, much less practical, and it would require readers to engage a mini-course in phonetics to use the dictionary. We have decided to do all we can to avoid misrepresentation and confusion, yet we recognize that is is essential for the dictionary to be "user-friendly." Native American words are presented either in the most commonly used Anglicized forms, where known, or exactly as they appear, less most diacritical markings, in the sources we have used. The principal diacritic retained is the glottal stop ("?") when it appears between vowels. Readers should be aware that pronunciations of the terms based on the simplified presentation likely only generally resemble how the word would sound if pronounced by a speaker of the language. Many of the ethnographic documents contain discussions of language and orthography. Readers interested at this technical level are encouraged to consult these works, as well as writings on the relevant languages.

Maps

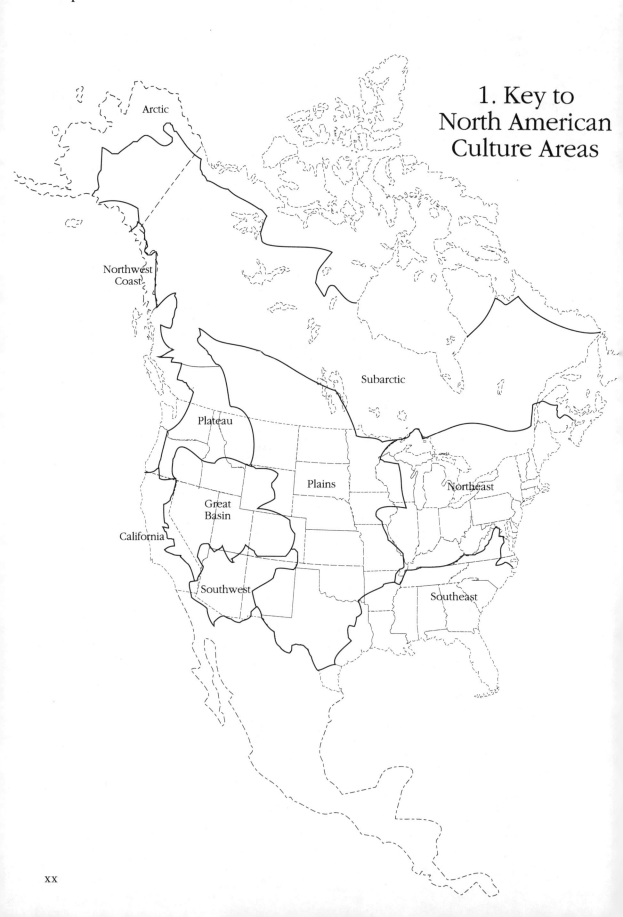

1. Key to North American Culture Areas

Arctic

Northwest Coast

Subarctic

Plateau

Plains

Northeast

Great Basin

California

Southwest

Southeast

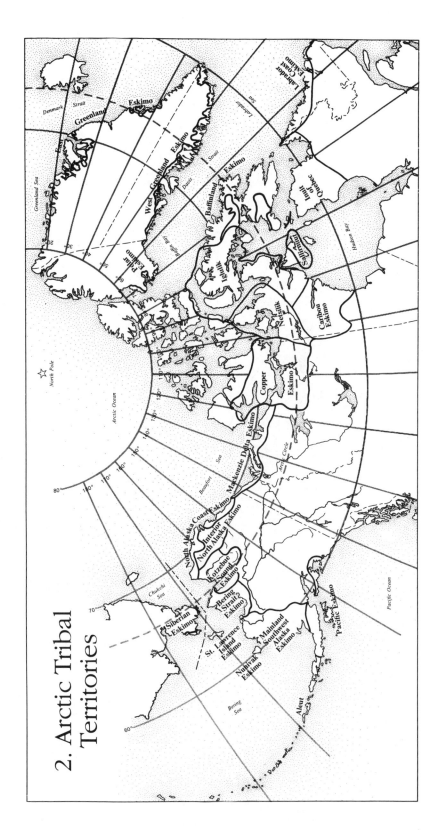

2. Arctic Tribal Territories

3. California Tribal Territories

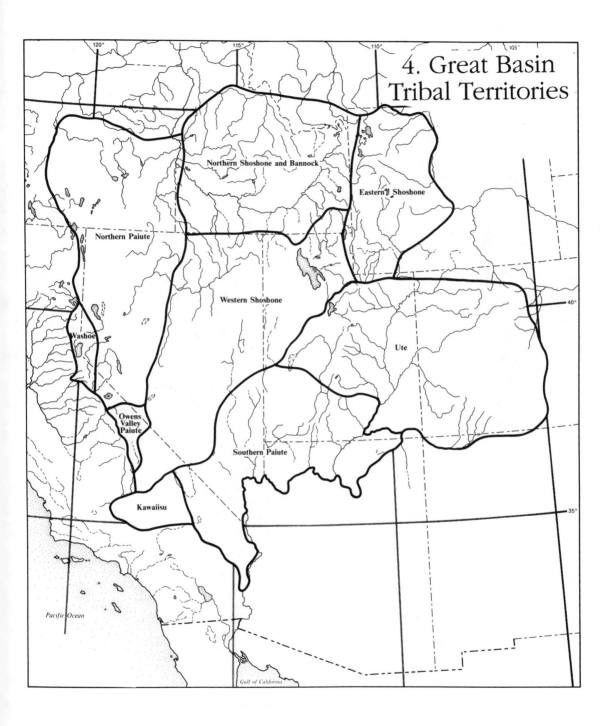

4. Great Basin
Tribal Territories

Northern Shoshone and Bannock

Eastern Shoshone

Northern Paiute

Western Shoshone

Ute

Washoe

Owens
Valley
Paiute

Southern Paiute

Kawaiisu

Pacific Ocean

Gulf of California

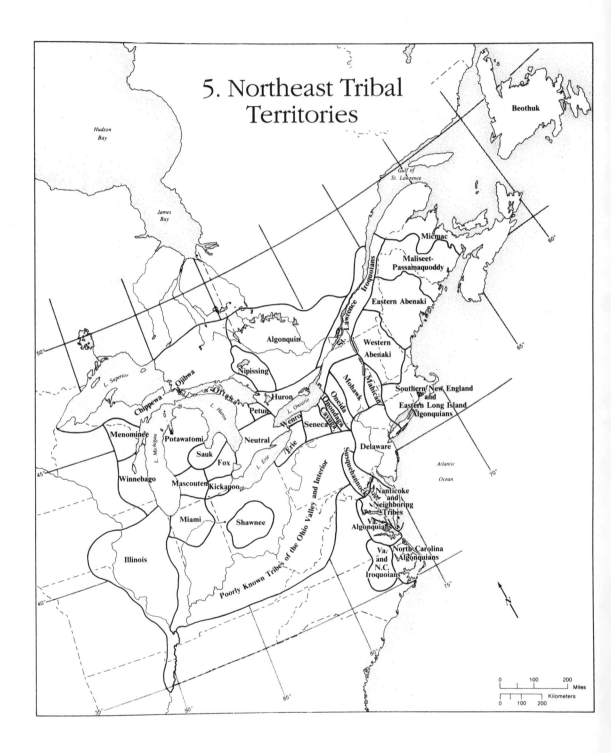

5. Northeast Tribal Territories

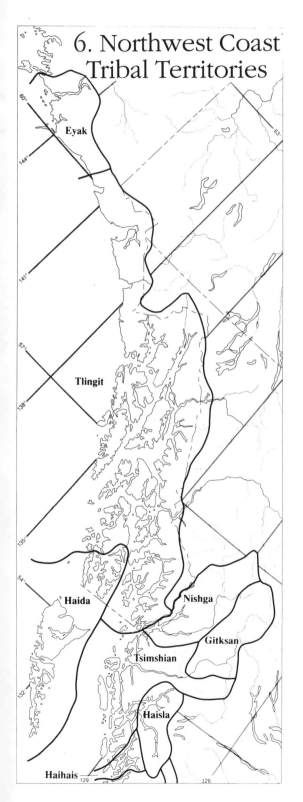

6. Northwest Coast Tribal Territories

Eyak

Tlingit

Haida

Nishga

Gitksan

Tsimshian

Haisla

Haihais

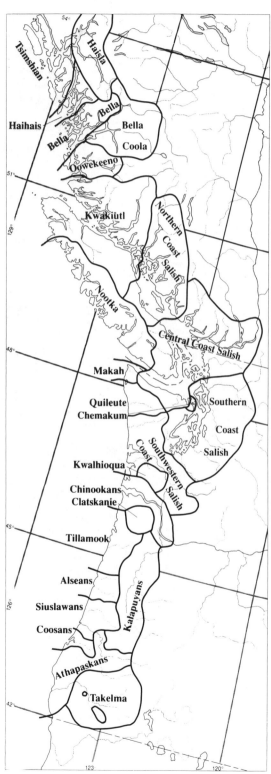

Tsimshian

Haisla

Haihais

Bella

Bella

Bella Coola

Oowekeeno

Kwakiutl

Northern Coast Salish

Nootka

Central Coast Salish

Makah

Quileute
Chemakum

Southern

Coast

Salish

Southwestern Coast Salish

Kwalhioqua

Chinookans
Clatskanie

Tillamook

Alseans

Siuslawans

Coosans

Kalapuyans

Athapaskans

Takelma

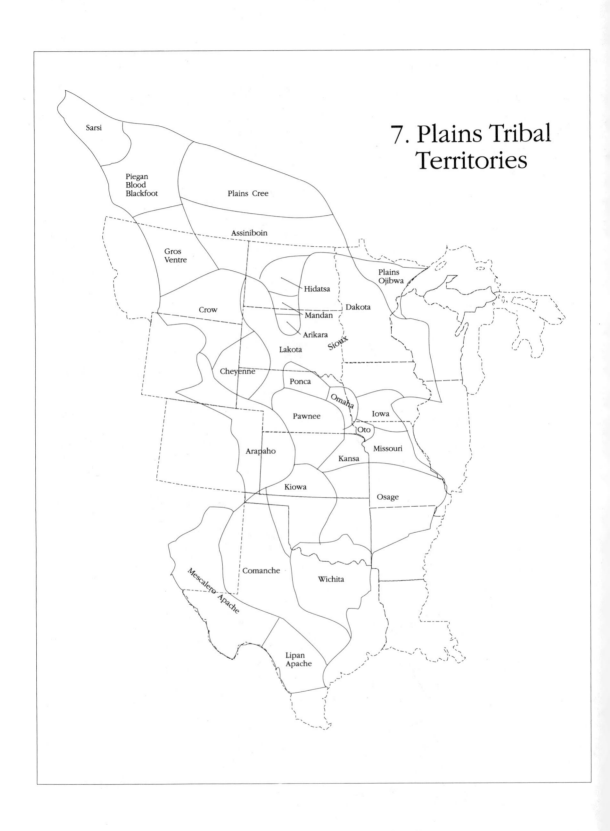

7. Plains Tribal Territories

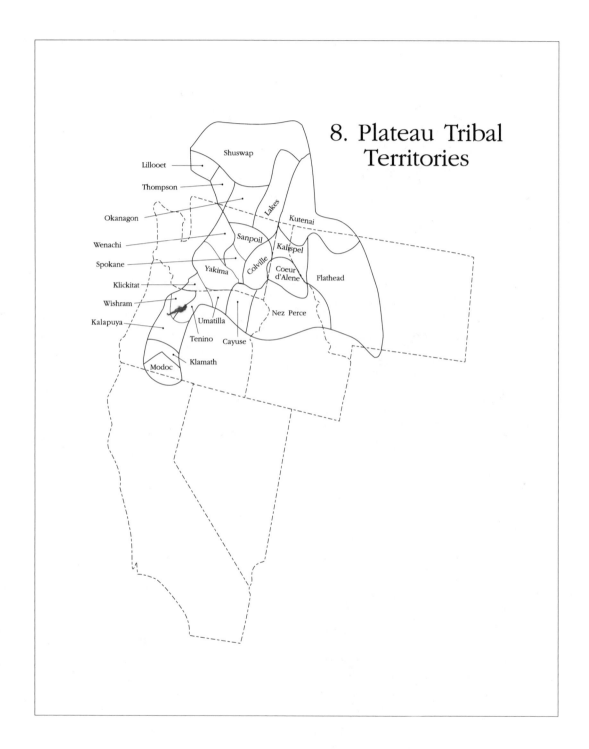

8. Plateau Tribal Territories

Shuswap

Lillooet

Thompson

Okanagon

Wenachi

Spokane

Klickitat

Wishram

Kalapuya

Lakes

Kutenai

Sanpoil

Kalispel

Yakima

Colville

Coeur d'Alene

Flathead

Nez Perce

Umatilla

Tenino

Cayuse

Klamath

Modoc

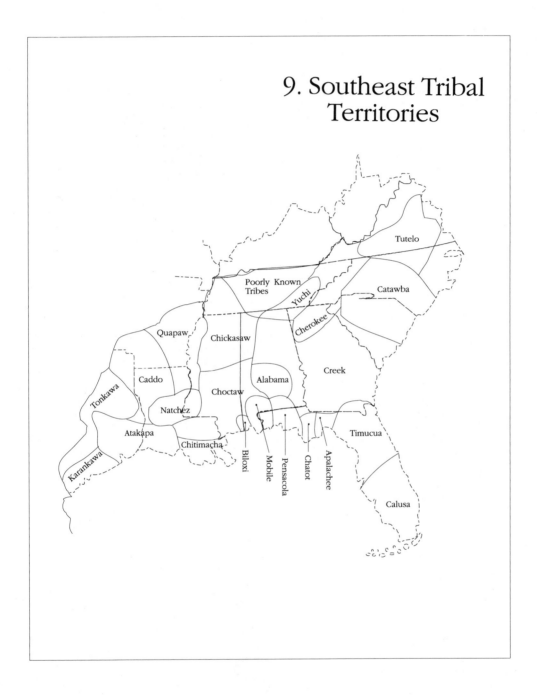

9. Southeast Tribal Territories

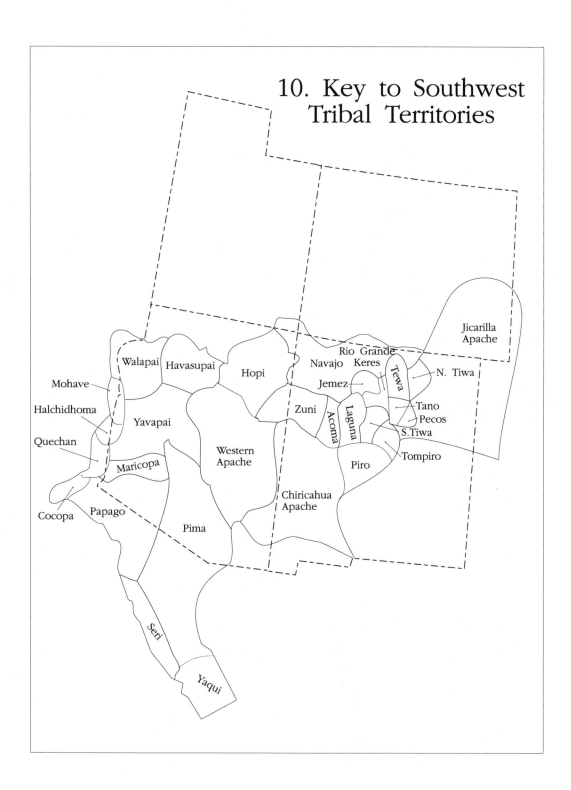

10. Key to Southwest
Tribal Territories

Jicarilla
Apache

Walapai Havasupai

Hopi

Rio Grande
Navajo Keres

N. Tiwa

Mohave

Jemez

Tewa

Halchidhoma

Zuni

Tano
Pecos

Yavapai

Acoma

Laguna

S.Tiwa

Quechan

Western
Apache

Tompiro

Maricopa

Piro

Cocopa Papago

Chiricahua
Apache

Pima

Seri

Yaqui

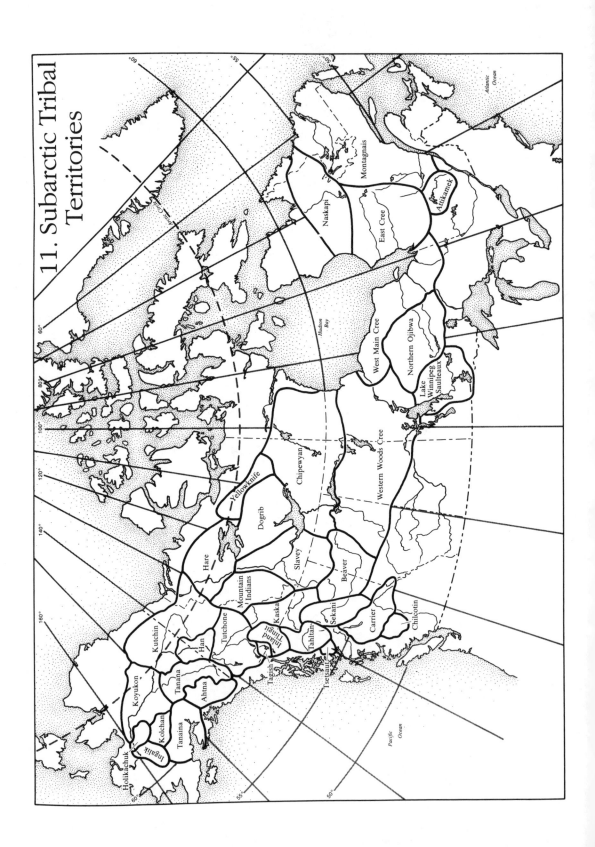

11. Subarctic Tribal Territories

Dictionary of
Native
American
Mythology

Aassahke

Crow, *Plains*

Clan (ashammaleaxia) aunts and uncles. An aassahke is a person involved in a special exchange relationship with a "son" or "daughter" who is not necessarily a blood relative. The aassahke relationship is based on the eight matrilineal clans of the Crow. Aassahke offer their "sons" and "daughters" praise, prayer, and protection. In return for these, people show respect for their aassahke in a variety of ways, such as giving them gifts and showing them special courtesies. For example, a "son" or "daughter" never walks in front of his or her aassahke. An individual who has received special honors, graduated from school, returned from war, or won a contest will host a giveaway (ammaakee) and honor his or her aassahke with special gifts. Aassahke are usually present on special occasions, such as birthdays, to offer prayers for continued health and wisdom of the "son" or "daughter," whose family thanks the aassahke with a gift of clothing, cigarettes, or some other item. [Frey 1987; Lowie 1956, 1960]

Aataentsic

Huron, *Northeast*

The mother of humankind; *Woman Who Fell from the Sky.* The pregnant Aataentsic falls from the sky while chasing a bear to obtain medicine for her husband. She lands softly on the earth piled on Tortoise's back. Eventually she becomes the maternal grandmother of two boys, *Iouskeha* and *Tawiskaron.* Iouskeha, the good grandson, creates lakes and rivers, releases animals from a hidden cave, causes corn to grow, and provides good weather. From Tortoise he learns how to make *fire,* passing the information on to humankind. The malevolent Aataentsic tries to undo Iouskeha's works. She breeds epidemics and causes men to die, taking charge of the dead souls. Tawiskaron is malevolent like his grandmother. He fights with his brother, shedding drops of blood that become flint, which is used to make spears and hatchets for warfare. See also *Earth Diver* and *Oehda.* [Tooker 1962; Trigger 1978]

Aawonaawilona

Zuni, *Southwest*

See *Ones Who Hold Our Roads.*

Ababinili
Chickasaw, *Southeast*
"Sitting above." The spirit of *fire* as separate from the Sun. Ababinili provides warmth and light, as well as being responsible for all plant and animal life. [Swanton 1928a]

Above-Old-Man
Wiyot, *California*
The *creator (Gudatri-Gakwitl)* of the world. Above-Old-Man decides to destroy his creation because the people, who are furry and cannot speak clearly, are more like animals than humans. The hero Condor, knowing that Above-Old Man plans to destroy the world by a *flood*, hides with his sister in a basket. When the waters finally recede, Condor finds only birds and a raccoon. He marries his sister and they have a human child, beginning a lineage of people who can talk and are not furry. [Kroeber 1925; Voegelin 1940]

Achayongch and Achgoyan
Aleut, Kodiak Island, Bering Sea, Alaska, *Arctic*
Two men who live together and, although they are both extremely noisy in their movements, speak to each other only when absolutely necessary. One day they go to a nearby island to visit a man named Petingyuwock, who spends his days taking sweat baths and catching codfish. When they arrive, Petingyuwock invites them to take a sweat bath with him. While they are in the bath, Petingyuwock ties together dried sea kelp to make a long rope. Then he invites his guests to feast on roasted codfish. While they are eating he ties the rope to the end of their boat. After the meal, Petingyuwock notes that the wind is blowing hard and warns Achayongch and Achgoyan they had better be getting back. When they are halfway home, Petingyuwock pulls the boat back to the island. "Why are you delaying," he asks them, "when the wind is getting stronger by the minute?" Twice more they start out and twice more find themselves back on the island. The third time the boat is overturned by the wind. Achayongch and Achgoyan are thrown ashore

and become two capes on the shoreline. Because they are so noisy, there is never any quiet weather on the capes. [Golder 1903]

Acoma Emergence and Migration
Acoma, *Southwest*
The people come out of *Iatiku,* their mother, at the *emergence* place, *Shipap,* in the north. They crawl out like grasshoppers; their bodies are soft and naked. There is no sun yet; it is dark. The people do not even have their eyes open yet. Iatiku lines up all the people, facing them to the east. When the sun rises, it shines on their eyes, causing them to open. At first they crawl around like babies, but soon they grow bigger and stronger.

At Shipap there is a lake with an island in the middle of it, and on this island there is a house. After Iatiku tells the people how to get food and that *kachinas* will soon come, she leaves them to live in this house. Among the people are twin brothers, *Masewa and Uyuyewa,* who are strong and become leaders. They show the people how to prepare for the arrival of the kachinas by making prayersticks (see *Prayer and Prayersticks)* and explain how to make offerings of bread and game. The kachinas come, bearing many gifts for the people: bows and arrows, clothing (for the people are still naked), pottery, flints, buckskins, and tools. They teach the people how to use these things. The kachinas dance in the plaza all day and the people are very happy.

After a time the people decide they must leave this place—it is so precious they fear they will defile it. Led by Masewa, they travel south to a place called Kacikatcutia (White House), where they settle (see also *Migration).* They call the kachinas to perform for them. They prepare prayersticks and make the proper offerings. The kachinas come and dance and everyone is happy. In the evening, after the dancing, one man shows the others how the kachinas dance, exaggerating their movements. This comic imitation causes great merriment among the people (see also *Humor).* But one of the kachinas has remained behind and observes this *comedy.* He tells the other kachinas and they prepare to make war on the village.

The next morning the people prepare to defend themselves. Thousands of kachinas run toward the village, raising a huge dust cloud. The people fight all day, but most are killed. Whenever a kachina is killed, it immediately comes back to life. When the kachinas finally leave, only a few people remain alive.

The next day scouts come to tell the people that they will never see the kachinas again. If they wish the kachinas to come, they must dress to look like the kachinas and pray as they have been taught. In time the people want the kachinas to return, so Masewa and his brother begin to make masks, engaging a few of the men to assist them. The men impersonating the kachinas respond when the people call them. They come to the village and dance in the plaza all day. Many people feel it is inappropriate to impersonate kachinas, and arguments and factions occur. Some groups abandon the others and migrate to another location. Iatiku causes the people to speak different languages so it will not be as easy for them to quarrel (see *Language)*.

Masewa has two eggs—a parrot egg and a crow egg. The people decide to go to the south where they hope to raise parrots. They head for a place called Aako. As they travel they come upon different places they suspect might be Aako. To test each one, Masewa calls out in a loud voice, "Aaaakooooooo!" If the echo resounds, the people stay to test the place further. If the echo is not good, they simply pass it by.

At a place just east of Acoma, the echo is perfect, and Masewa announces that this is Acoma. Not knowing which egg is the parrot egg and which the crow, the people divide themselves into groups. Some believe the white egg is the parrot egg, others think it is the blue one. Masewa throws the blue egg against the cliff and swarms of crows fly out. Those people who had chosen the blue egg are very disappointed, but agree to remain at Acoma. The others take the white egg and travel on to the south.

The people who remain at Acoma establish a village at the foot of the mesa. They call for the kachinas, and by means of impersonations the kachinas come and dance in the plaza. Because their prayers for *rain* are answered, the people consider the ceremony powerful and they carefully preserve the masks (see *Masks and Masking)*. In time it becomes dangerous to live at the base of the mesa, so they establish a new village on the mesa top. Some of those who survived the great fight with the kachinas are still living. In order to teach the people about this important event, they decide to reenact the fight. This ceremony continues to be enacted periodically at Acoma, although it has not been done now for many years.

Some versions of the story, told among other pueblos, feature female twins. [White 1932]

Adaox
Tsimshian, *Northwest Coast*
A *story type* in which animals appear as agents in human form. Adaox contain incidents describing the origins of features of the present world. [Boas 1902, 1916]

Adlet
Eskimo, Labrador Coast, west Hudson Bay, *Arctic*
Blood-drinking *monsters,* the children of an Eskimo woman who marries a red dog (see *Dog Husband)*. Five of the woman's ten children are dogs, which she puts into a boat that drifts across the sea. The dogs eventually become the parents of white people. The other five children become the Adlet. See also *Humans, Origin of.* [Boas 1888a]

Adlivun
Eskimo, central Canada, *Arctic*
"Those beneath us." The *underworld,* where all who disobey *Sedna* go after death (see *Dead)*. Murderers never leave Adlivun, but others may eventually go to Adliparmiut (those farthest below). Although Adliparmiut is darker and more remote than

Adlivun, people there are allowed to hunt in relative peace. See also *Anguta* and *Master/Mistress of Animals.* [Boas 1888a]

Affliction
See *Oh-gee-nay,* afflictions caused by wrongful conduct.

Afterlife
See *Yagatunne.*

Agriculture
Many Native American stories describe the origin of agriculture. The Iroquois credit the Husk Faces (see *False Faces).* In Pawnee stories *Cannibal Grandmother* stops eating flesh when given seeds, and *Moon Woman* releases corn and buffalo for her people. *Kokyan wuhti,* the Hopi spider woman, spins webs of rain clouds. The Keresan creator, *Iatiku,* scatters seeds. The origin of agriculture is also told in stories of *Navajo Emergence* and the *Whirling Logs' Sandpainting* story. [Hill 1938; Lawton 1974; Means 1960; Underhill 1938]

Ahayuta
Zuni, *Southwest*
The collective name of the warrior twins, sons of the Sun Father *(Yatokka taccu),* who came from the foam of a waterfall when struck by the sun's rays. When named separately they are Ahayuta and Matsilema. They led the people out from the interior of the earth *(Zuni Emergence).* Active mostly in winter, they are diviners and guard the six shrines that designate the directions.

The Ahayuta are central figures in an extensive cycle of stories revolving around ridding the earth of *monsters* and the twins' acquisition of the powers to make *rain.* Historical consideration of this cycle reveals that, while some of these stories have long been told (not only by the Zuni but also by other Pueblo peoples), some appear to be acquisitions from early in the twentieth century, perhaps from contacts with the Navajo and Apache. The strongest parallels with Navajo and

Apache mythology are the stories of the killing of monsters (see *Monsterway)* and the visits of the warrior twins to their father the Sun to obtain power (see *Twins' Journey to Sun Father* and *Monster Slayer and Born for Water).* For other Pueblo stories on warrior twins, see *Masewa and Uyuyewa.*

One story tells how the Ahayuta obtain rainmaking implements. Disobeying their grandmother's warning, the twins go to the place where the Saiyathlia (kachina warriors) live. There they find the Saiyathlia initiating their youth. The twins enter the kiva and are whipped along with the initiates. They die from their whipping, and the Saiyathlia cut off and cook their arms and legs to feed the new initiates. The voices of the twins remain alive, residing in all the objects surrounding the Saiyathlia. Their voices call out, accusing the Saiyathlia of eating dung. The Ahayuta enter the noses of the Saiyathlia, causing them to sneeze. The twins then jump out of the Saiyathlia's noses, steal their bows and arrows, and kill all the Saiyathlia who, upon dying, turn into *deer.* The Ahayuta are now free to steal the rainmaking things of the Saiyathlia: their lightning frame, arrows, and thunder stones. In many of the Ahayuta stories the twins play the role of *culture hero.*

In another story, the bow priest's daughter stays at home grinding cornmeal and weaving baskets. Although her father urges her to marry so that he might have a son-in-law to share his work, she refuses all suitors (see *Unwilling Bride).* The bow priest sponsors competitions and dances to interest his daughter in the young men, but she spurns everyone. Ahayuta, one of the warrior twins, appears at the bow priest's. Although he appears as a *dirty boy* with matted hair, the daughter quickly accepts him as her husband, angering the other young men. They challenge him to a series of footraces, the winner to receive the bow priest's daughter. With help from spiritual beings, Ahayuta wins the races. The new bride grinds cornmeal and takes it to Ahayuta's grandmother at Corn Mountain. The happy newlyweds return to the village with gifts of venison. Eventually Ahayuta, being a supernatural, returns to his shrine.

See also *Corn Maidens, Hopi Children Become Birds, Kanaakwe, Pyuykonhoya, Women's Ways, Worm and Turtle as Warriors,* and *Zuni Emergence.* [Benedict 1935; Boas 1922b; Bunzel 1933; Cushing 1896; Handy 1918; Parsons 1923d, 1930b; Stevenson 1905; Tedlock 1979]

Aikren

Karok, *California*

Duck-Hawk. Aikren lives on top of a mountain called Sugarloaf and is *guardian spirit* to the village below, called Katimin. One day Aikren comes to two young girls weeping over the loss of their dead lovers. He takes them to their lovers, who are happily dancing and eating salmon. After a time the girls reluctantly leave to return to their village. Before they go, they are given a piece of salmon backbone and shown how to smear it on the lips of the *dead* to revive them. As long as the salmon backbone lasts, death does not come to the village. Even when the backbone is gone and death returns to the Karok people, they do not grieve because they know the dead are dancing and happy.

Aiyaguk

See *Asking Stick.*

Ajilee

Navajo, *Southwest*

A body of stories known variously, and probably erroneously, as Prostitutionway and Excessway, having to do with *love* magic and hunting magic. Their hero is an orphaned boy who is adopted and raised by a woman; alternatively, he is born of a plant made pregnant by Sun, whose grandmother is Vegetation Woman. The hero and his grandmother travel about as he grows up, spending most of their time in the proximity of Pueblo people. Through gifts or processes of personal transformation the hero acquires love magic and hunting magic. In one

version he is ugly and offensive to girls. His sisters, born of butterflies, help him undergo physical transformation by patterning him after themselves. This version describes the origin of the differences between male and female *genitals.*

The hero meets non–sunlight-struck Hopi girls (girls who never go into the light of the sun) as they go for water in the early morning. He uses his love magic to attract them, and they are unable to resist his sexual advances. Taking the sisters as his wives, he uses his hunting magic to kill a dozen antelope, which he gives to their family as payment. The girls' father then accepts him as his son-in-law.

In one version of the story the hero attempts to abandon his Pueblo wives. In another, *Ma?ii (Coyote)* exchanges skins with him in order to enjoy the hero's wives. He is debilitated by being trapped in Coyote's skin until he is rescued and restored by a *Hoop Transformation Rite,* returning home to find his wives pregnant by Coyote. Although he does not blame them, since they thought they were having sex with him, he remains angry. Ignoring their pleas, he leaves them and goes to Canyon de Chelly with his grandmother. There he commands the plants and *diyin dine?e* to engage excessively in sex and learns that his wives have given birth to hairy monsters.

Wherever the hero goes, he seduces attractive women. In another conquest of Pueblo non–sunlight-struck girls, he uses his magic to transform himself into a beautiful *butterfly* and enters the chamber where the girls live. Attracted by his beauty (in one version they want to capture the butterfly to copy its designs in their weaving), they follow as he leads them far away from their home. Finally, he reveals his own male form to them. Realizing they have traveled a great distance and will be punished if they return home, the maidens decide to take the hero as a husband and live with him.

When he leaves to visit his grandmother, White Butterfly steals his new wives. On the hero's return he engages White Butterfly in a series of contests to regain his wives, succeeding despite his opponent's knowledge of witchcraft. In many versions these fights lead to White Butterfly being struck in the head with an ax. When his head splits open, a cloud of butterflies emerge, accounting for their origin. Depending on the version, the hero then either rejoins his wives or rejects them. One story portrays the girls as becoming afraid to live with him and returning to their Pueblo homes. Another ends dramatically with the wives drinking from the same stream as the hero. Telling them to look carefully at their reflections, he drowns them, collects his belongings, and leaves for good. [Haile 1978; Kluckhohn 1944; Luckert 1978; Pepper 1908; Wheelwright 1946a]

Akahcape
Pawnee, *Plains*
A conical tipi built for use as a temporary shelter while hunting in winter. [Dorsey 1906a; Murie 1989]

Akaririwis
Pawnee, *Plains*
"Side dwelling." A temporary shelter built while on the summer hunt. The akaririwis was shaped like a half-bowl, open in the front. It was made of bent saplings covered with skins. [Dorsey 1906a; Murie 1989]

Akbaalia
Crow, *Plains*
"One who doctors." Medicine person (see *Medicine People*) who exercises the most important use of *xapaaliia* (medicine). An akbaalia has the power to doctor (baalia) and cure (hawassee) a variety of problems, both psychological and physiological. The akbaalia prays at the *Sun Dance,* opens *medicine bundles,* and often works in conjunction with Western medical healers. Although any man or woman may become an akbaalia, it requires more than the mere possession of medicine. An akbaalia's reputation stems from the trust given him or her by the community. [Frey 1987; Lowie 1960]

Akbaatatdia
Crow, *Plains*
"The One Who Has Made Everything." Also known as "the First Doer" (Iichikbaaalee), "the One Above" (Baakukkule), "Father" (Axee), "Old Man Coyote" (Isaahkawuattee), or the "Old Man" (Isaahka). Akbaatatdia is responsible for the spiritual power of *transformation* (or *baaxpee)* and is also responsible for and part of all natural forces. See also *Wakan Tanka* and *Chiwakiia* (prayer). [Frey 1987]

Akhlut
Eskimo, Bering Sea coast, Alaska, *Arctic*
A *killer whale* who roams the land in the shape of a *wolf,* killing humans and animals. Wolf tracks leading to the sea ice indicate where he changes back into a killer whale. [Tennant and Bitar 1981]

Akhrendoiaen
Huron, *Northeast*
A ritual performed specifically to free someone from insanity. The Akhrendoiaen involved *dances* that were always prescribed in a *dream.* As they danced around the patient, the dancers gave one another *poison,* which they ingested in order to find the cause of the insanity. This initial dance concluded when the patient fell backward and vomited, after which the patient was declared a member of the medicine society Atirenda (see *Medicine Societies),* and another dance was begun. The second dance, known as *Otakrendoiae,* was intended to cure the insanity. [Tooker 1962]

Akicitas
Lakota, *Plains*
Police societies, responsible for maintaining order during camp travels and communal buffalo hunts *(Wani-sapa).* Akicitas usually originated with a *dream* or *vision* that told the dreamer how to organize a society. The dreamer was also required to test a whip or lance in battle to prove the society's viability. Any young man who had participated in a war party might be

invited to join one of the akicitas. Men who came from distinguished families, had killed enemies, or had sought visions were especially welcomed as members of the akicitas. See also *Vision Quest* and *Kolas* (male friends). [DeMallie 1984; Walker 1982]

Akutaq
Eskimo, Bering Sea coast, Alaska, *Arctic*
"Eskimo ice cream" made from whipped caribou fat or shortening, berries, sugar, and frozen snow. Akutaq is prepared for special communal feasts, to celebrate a boy's first catch, and to initiate babies into the importance of feast celebrations. It is mentioned in story traditions across Arctic Canada. See also *Irraq* and *Nakaciuq,* the Bladder Festival. [Lantis 1947; Riordan 1983]

Alarana and Aligunaluk
Eskimo, Point Barrow, Alaska, *Arctic*
During a time when humans are sometimes animals as well as people, Alarana and her brother Aligunaluk are left alone after famine and death destroy their village. While searching for caribou hunters, the children are killed and eaten by wolves (see *Wolf*). An old she-wolf who is also a medicine woman warns the other wolves not to break or eat any of the children's bones. After eating the children, the wolves turn into humans and take the bones back to the old she-wolf/medicine woman's house. She lays Alarana's bones on the skin of a young caribou cow and Aligunaluk's on the skin of a bull calf, covering them with stitched walrus intestine. Then she walks around the skins and sings over the bones. Soon Alarana's bones begin to move and come together, but Aligunaluk's bones remain motionless because some of them are missing. With the help of a red-and-white fox who has been watching her as she sings, the medicine woman recovers the missing bones and sings the children back to life. Dressed in beautiful caribou skins, they are able to transform themselves into caribou. The other caribou teach them how to dig for lichen under the snow, move quickly in deep snow, and avoid deceitful hunters. See also *Animal-Human Transformation.* [Chance 1990]

Alektca
Creek, *Southeast*
Doctors, *medicine people*. Alektca are initiated into a group known as the isti poskalgi (fasting men) by drinking a strong *emetic.* They seek visions and treat high-risk injuries such as gunshot wounds. They also keep secrets about conducting warfare. See also *Hilis-haya,* medicine maker, and *Kilas,* diagnosticians. [Swanton 1928a]

Aliil
Navajo, *Southwest*
Special or extraordinary *power* connected with the cause of an illness as well as its cure. Ritual cures must have aliil to be effective. [Haile 1943a; Reichard 1974]

All-Smoking Ceremony
Blackfoot, *Plains*
See *Kanochisisin,* the ceremony held when counting coup.

Amala
Tsimshian, *Northwest Coast*
The one who supports the world. Amala lies on his back holding a pole on which the world spins. He has a slave who strengthens him by rubbing his back once a year with wild-duck oil. The oil is nearly used up; when it runs out, Amala will die and the world will come to an end. [Boas 1902, 1916]

Amulet(s)
An object worn or carried to protect one from harmful spirits, malevolent medicines, and dangers such as *witchcraft. Love* charms sometimes take the form of amulets. Amulets are used in many Eskimo and other Native American tribes. They may be pieces of stone, grasses, animal parts, or human body parts such as dried pieces of navel cord or placenta. Amulets made of animal parts

are often used to transfer a particular quality of the animal to the wearer. For example, the Chickasaw put deer's feet into their pouches to give them speed when hunting. Hidatsa girls wear necklaces of beaver teeth to improve their industriousness. Members of the Dogrib tribe carry deer and moose antler points in hopes of bringing these animals within close range for hunting.

Amulets may be actual body parts, or objects found or made to resemble them. In western and northern Alaska the *Doll Festival* originated from the story of a powerful *shaman* who kills his granddaughter and uses the preserved parts of her body as divination objects to ensure good hunting. The Seneca story about *Othegwenhda,* the Flint chief, tells how his amulet, a flint finger, gives him directions.

Some amulets are associated with the wearer's *helping spirits.* The power of an amulet is guarded by its wearer. Amulets are often meant specifically for one individual and can be worn only by that person. Among some tribes, amulets are used to temporarily house souls. In the Arctic, for example, a medicine person may conjure the *soul* of a sick child into an amulet for safekeeping while the child fights off the disease. To the Maliseet, *Keskamsit* is the power of amulets.

Amulets are also used as ritual objects. The Hopi use *Tiponi* in major ceremonies. In the Iroquoian *Midwinter Festival,* amulets representing spirits or animals are given to people who guess the identities of spirits or animals in the dreams of others. Lakota grandmothers-to-be make amulets representing *sand lizards* for their daughters as protection for the unborn children. The mythic Seminole amulets of brightly colored animated stones known as *Sapiya* were fed squirrel blood and given water to drink.

Anal Snakes

Pawnee, Lakota, Kiowa, Crow, Blackfoot, *Plains*

A theme found in many hero tales, in which snakes enter the bodies of their sleeping victims in order to kill them. The heroes may outwit the snakes by covering their rectums with flat stones that have been rubbed against the heads of sleeping snakes, which explains why many snakes have flat heads. [Dorsey 1906a; Murie 1989]

Ancient People

Cree, *Subarctic*
See *Kayas-ioiniwak.*

Andaokut

Nootka, *Northwest Coast*

A transformer figure (see *Transformation)* born from the tears and nasal *mucus* of a woman grieving because her only child has been stolen by Woman of the Woods, Malahas (see *Dzoo-noo-qua).* The mucus child appears on the fourth day of the woman's grief and quickly grows to manhood. Taking a bow and two arrows the woman has made for him, Andaokut goes in search of Woman of the Woods. He tricks her into thinking he can make her beautiful and will marry her. Instead he kills her and rescues all the children she has stolen, reviving their dried, roasted bodies by urinating on them. He climbs a string of arrows to return to his father in the sky, stopping on the way to give sight to two old and blind mallard duck women.

Andaokut's father is delighted to see him, but tells him of the many things that remain to be changed on earth, such as people who look like humans but have the hearts of animals. The father changes his son's name to Qanexe nazw and gives him a blanket filled with herring and different types of salmon, telling him to put a male and female fish in each river that does not yet contain fish. Qanexe nazw returns to earth and fills the rivers with fish. He transforms Raccoon Man into a raccoon, Beaver Man into a beaver, Marten Man into a marten, Black Bear Man into a black bear, and many other human-animals into their present animal forms. Qanexe nazw meets a man and woman with their *genitals* on their foreheads. The man tells Qanexe nazw he has been trying to get his wife pregnant without success. Qanexe nazw realizes that if he does not relocate the genitals there will soon be no people left in the world. [Sapir and Swadesh 1939]

Andicicopec
Crow, *Plains*

"Dance-Four-Times." A mythic hero who is a great *warrior*. He is invincible to bullets and known for his kindness to others. As a young boy, he follows a bird while hunting and wanders over a ridge away from his camp. There he meets a strange man on horseback, who batters him by causing a strong wind and hailstorm. The horseman sings a war song stating that he is looking for battle, and the hailstones turn to bullets. The horseman gallops away, followed by the storm. Dance-Four-Times watches as the horseman, unharmed by the bullets, does battle with the storm. Eventually the storm clouds scatter, and the horseman returns to Dance-Four-Times, saying he will give the boy the power to fight in the same way. [Frey 1987; Lowie 1960]

Anerneq
Eskimo, western Alaska, *Arctic*

Breath, spirit, *soul.* People are thought to have different souls, or attributes, that separate from the body at death (see *Dead*) and follow the pathway to the underworld. A living person has a body, body warmth, visibility, breath, personality, and voice. Puqlii, an invisible spirit that keeps a person alive, is body heat and warmth. *Tarneq,* or tarenraq, is the visible ghost that is the likeness of the person seen after death. The personality or way one lives is yuuciq (life). The voice, avneq, identifies the dead person and, in the days of powerful *shamans,* could be summoned.

Angalkuq
Eskimo, Bering Sea coast, Alaska, *Arctic*

Eskimo *shaman.* Most but not all angalkuq were males whose shamanic powers were acquired through apprenticeship, in a dream, or by surviving a life-threatening event. Their primary responsibility was to ensure plentiful game. To do this, they performed *spirit journeys* under the sea to release animals and invite them to come to the hunters. To keep dry during these journeys, the angalkuq wore a seal-gut raincoat that made noises when rattled. Alternatively, the angalkuq could fly to *Moon Man,* who was responsible for keeping game. Other angalkuq responsibilities included healing, holding hearings on taboo violations, and battling other angalkuq in contests of power. See also *Orpingalik,* a famous shaman and poet; *Ivivarshuk and Nisguvaushaq,* the first two shamans; *Sea Woman,* who is visited by shamans; and *Tarneq,* a shaman's helping spirit. [Lantis 1947; Nelson 1899; Riordan 1983]

Anguta
Eskimo, central Canada, *Arctic*

"His father." Anguta lives with *Sedna* in *Adlivun.* He is responsible for carrying the *dead* down to Adlivun, where they must sleep next to him for a year. [Boas 1888a]

Ani Hyuntikwalaski
Cherokee, *Southeast*

Thunder Beings who cause a lightning *fire* in a hollow sycamore tree. The world is cold and fire is needed for warmth, but the animals cannot reach the fire because the tree is on an island. Various birds try to procure the fire. They fail, but as a result of their efforts they obtain distinctive physical features. The heat scorches Raven's feathers black. Little Screech Owl's eyes turn red from the heat. Hooting Owl and Horned Owl are burned and blinded by the fire, and the ashes make white rings around their eyes. Finally Water Spider skates along the water surface to the island, places a small coal of fire into a woven web bowl, and thus brings fire to the world. [Hudson 1976; Mooney 1888, 1900]

Animal Characteristics, Origin of
Native American stories often include some explanation for characteristics and body markings

of animals. The Seneca story *Weeping of the Corn* tells how Raccoon's split lip and stripes resulted from his stealing corn. *Aqonidzaba,* the Paviotso centipede, is responsible for Crow's black feet. The Seneca say *Chipmunk's stripes* are bear scratches. The spots that form a necklace around the necks of loons represent the burnt hearts of the children of *Loon Woman,* which she gathered after they died. Bears distrust humans because of the cruel trickery of the Inupiaq hunter *Pisig-sordleq.* Robin's red breast (see *Robin, Origin of Red Breast)* is the result of smearing her body with her own blood. The Zuni reflect on Worm's small size (see *Worm and Turtle as Warriors).*

Among many tribes a particular *trickster* or *culture hero* is the cause for a variety of animal characteristics. The Kawaiisu *Coyote* is responsible for the bill of *Hummingbird* and the appearance of tearstains on the face of *Mountain Lion. Ishjinki,* the Iowa culture hero, makes the buzzard bald. The Passamaquoddy and Micmac relate how *Glooscap* teaches *Winpe,* the loon, to cry, and gives *Frog* his voice, as well as boiling and disemboweling his uncle *Mikchich,* the turtle, to make his skin hard and give him longevity. The Klamath story of *Nikciamtcac* accounts for the size and shape of animals' tails.

Animal Spirit(s)

See *Kuksu-hesi* and *Wamaka nagi.*

Animal-Human Transformation

Animals, especially *tricksters* and *culture heroes,* frequently turn into humans and/or other animals in stories throughout North America. *Chulyen,* the Tanaina Crow, can transform into many different kinds of animals. Several Pawnee stories include transformations. *Bright Eyes* is a young man who becomes a prairie dog, then a human again; in the story of *Clam Shell,* Hawk becomes human; in *Four Beings of the North,* a bird becomes a woman; and in *Dog Boy,* a dog becomes a boy. *Grouse Girl* (Aleut) transforms into a beautiful young woman. *Qanekelak,* the Bella Bella figure who is half human and half

whale, becomes human. The Navajo *Hoop Transformation Rite* cures those suffering from being trapped in an animal form and restores them to human shape. In the Inupiaq story about *Alarana and Aligunaluk,* wolves become human. See also *Human-Animal Transformation.*

Animals, Creation of
Jicarilla Apache, *Southwest*
See *Black Hactcin Creates Animals and Humans.*

Animals, Proper Treatment of
See *Gitnagunaks.*

Animals, Release of
See Apache *Mountain Spirits* and Huron *Iouskeha.*

Aniwye
Ojibwa, Canadian Great Lakes, *Subarctic*
A giant monster skunk who travels all over searching out human beings and spraying to make them sick. Aniwye roots out people hiding underground and sprays into caves to get the people hiding there. One day a group of people flee their village to escape from Aniwye, except for one very old woman who decides to remain in her hut because she cannot keep up with the others. Aniwye finds the old woman and bites off the top of her hut. He asks her where the rest of the villagers are. She says everyone has left and that she stayed behind because she is old and crippled. Aniwye tells the old woman his spray will cure her. He turns, lifts his tail, and sprays her. She is annihilated.

Aniwye continues to follow the tracks left by the people of the village. In the meantime, the villagers reach Fisher Lake where Giant Fisher lives. They explain that Aniwye is after them and ask for Giant Fisher's help. Giant Fisher agrees and says, "Stay where you are until Aniwye finds you. Then, just as he is turning his back and lifting his tail to spray you, run away as fast as you can." When Aniwye approaches, the people stand still. As Aniwye lifts his tail, Giant Fisher leaps forward and pinches Aniwye's anus closed so that Aniwye cannot release his spray. The monster skunk screams in pain, but Giant Fisher will not let go. The poison builds up inside and kills him. After Aniwye dies, Giant Fisher tells the people to build a fire and roast the body. As the carcass burns, ashes fly into the sky. Each small ash that lands becomes a skunk like those found today. Because there is a strong wind, ashes are blown far and wide; thus skunks are found in many places. [Overholt and Callicott 1982]

Anog Ite
Lakota, *Plains*
Double Faced Woman, originally known as Ite, wife of *Tate* (the Wind) and daughter of First Man and First Woman (see also *Wohpe),* the daughter of *Skan,* the Sky. Because she attempts to seduce Wi, the Sun, Ite is condemned by Skan to live with two faces—one beautiful, one ugly—hence her name, Anog Ite (Double Face). See also *Ta Tanka Lowanpi.*

Some sources refer to Double Faced Woman as a figure appearing in the dreams of young women, in which she teaches crafts, particularly *quilling.* The skill of quilling is considered to be in conflict with the traditional roles of wife and mother, leading the dreamer to choose a lesbian lifestyle (which would leave her free to develop her skills as a craftswoman).

In Lakota stories Double Faced Woman teaches quilling to the people after she learns about it in a *vision.* She sets up a tipi and asks that a *porcupine* be brought to her. She develops a system of sorting and dyeing quills and makes the first quilled robe, a highly prestigious garment. Double Faced Woman hosts the first quilling contest.

Apache Bear Dance
Jicarilla Apache, *Southwest*
During the emergence, two girls remain in the underworld, refusing to follow the others (see *Apache Creation and Emergence).* Holy Boy makes two butterflies (see *Butterfly)* from flowers and sends them on a sunbeam into the underworld. The girls chase the butterflies and are led up the sunbeam into this world.

As soon as the girls emerge, the malevolent *Bear* and *Snake* steal them. Not knowing what has happened, the girls' relatives seek the help of Holy Boy and other *hactcin.* The hactcin ask all the animals if they know the whereabouts of the girls, but none do. All the animals assemble, and the hactcin send Small *Wind* to locate the girls. Small Wind finds them with Bear and Snake, who refuse to give them back. The hactcin send Small Wind back once again with a warning to Bear and Snake about what will happen if they do not give back the girls. Bear and Snake finally agree to return their captives.

That night Bear, Snake, and the two girls arrive. One girl is very fat and the other is but skin and bones, symptoms of Bear and Snake illness. For five days and nights the hactcin perform rituals to cure the girls of these illnesses. The rituals include singing, dancing, and other acts performed by the Tsanati *(medicine people)* and the clowns (see *Clowns and Clowning Societies).* This establishes the model on which the *Bear Dance* healing ceremony will be performed.

Apache Creation and Emergence
Jicarilla Apache, *Southwest*
It is dark in the *underworld* before the *emergence* (see *Hactcin* and *Black Hactcin Creates Animals and Humans).* Dissatisfied, Holy Boy decides there should be *light.* He tries without success to make the sun and moon, using specular iron ore and pollen. He tries again and again, using many different materials, but is unsuccessful. *Whirlwind,* who spies on the hactcin, tells Holy Boy that White Hactcin has the sun, and he should get it from him. Holy Boy convinces White Hactcin to give him the sun, although it is only the size of a pinhead. White Hactcin tells Holy Boy that Black Hactcin has the moon, and Holy Boy is able to acquire it as well. The hactcin instruct Holy Boy in the ritual acts of creating the

sun and moon. When the song rituals are complete the sun and moon rise, bringing light to the underworld. The many *medicine people* living in the lower world immediately claim responsibility for creating the sun and moon, arguing fiercely with one another. The hactcin warn them to be silent for four days, but the medicine people ignore the warning. On the fourth day, the sun rises to the center of the sky. Because the medicine people continue to argue, it goes through the hole in the center of the sky into the present earth. Only faint light comes through into the lower world. The Jicarilla identify this incident with solar eclipses.

The hactcin challenge the boasting medicine people to bring back the sun and moon. The medicine people demonstrate their considerable abilities, but nothing they do brings back the sun and moon. Next, all the birds and animals are challenged to try. Each animal comes forward and offers some kind of food. The hactcin accept all their offerings as useful items, but the sun and moon remain in the world above.

Finally, the hactcin direct the representation in sand *(sandpainting)* of a world bordered by four mountains. The mountains are represented by four differently colored piles of sand. On each mountain are placed leaves of the trees and seeds of the fruits that will grow upon it. The people sing and pray as the mountains begin to grow. Eventually the mountains grow together, forming a single mountain. The hactcin choose 12 medicine people, painting and costuming them so that six represent summer and six represent winter. The hactcin choose six more medicine people as clowns (the Jicarilla word for clown translates "striped excrement"). The clowns (see *Clowns and Clowning Societies)* are painted white all over with black stripes across the face, chest, and legs. Their hair is formed into two horns, painted white with four black stripes. Jicarilla clowns are powerful healers.

When the mountain has grown nearly to the sky, Fly and Spider are sent to the world above. They bring back four rays of the sun, from which the hactcin construct a ladder of 12 steps. Animals sent up the ladder report that the world above is full of water. The hactcin go up into the world and prepare the earth for others to enter. The emergence proceeds from this point, the clowns first, laughing (see *Laughter)* to scare away anything that will cause illness. Then the hactcin emerge, followed by First Man and First Woman. Next come the 12 medicine people, followed by all the people and animals. Finally two old people try to enter the world, but the ladders are now worn out and they cannot climb them. They call for help, but there is no way for them to emerge. The old people angrily proclaim they will remain in the underworld, but that those who have emerged must some day return, thus designating the underworld as the place of death (see *Dead)*.

The Lipan Apache have a similar emergence story. In the Lipan version *Killer-of-Enemies,* identifed as the *Sun,* is a principal *creator* and *culture hero.* Killer-of-Enemies seems to be synonymous with *Child-of-the-Water,* the child of *Changing Woman,* who is identified as the *Moon* and *Thunder.* Child-of-the-Water is a name rarely used. In Lipan stories Killer-of-Enemies has a younger brother known as Wise One.

The Chiricahua and Mescalero Apache do not have an emergence story. Their creation story begins with the flooding of a world that seems in retrospect to have fallen into malevolence. These stories proceed to the creative efforts of *White Painted Woman* and Child-of-the-Water who, rather than Killer-of-Enemies, is the dominant culture hero.

The western Apache seldom tell the emergence story. More commonly they begin with a brief account of the creation of the earth, moving on quickly to the slaying of monsters. Naayenezgane (Slayer of Enemies) is the most important male figure in western Apache religion other than the Sun. See also *Apache Bear Dance, Monster Slayer and Born for Water,* and *Prophecy.* [Goodwin 1939; Hoijer 1938; Opler 1938b, 1940, 1942]

Apanuugak
Eskimo, Nelson Island, Bering Sea coast,
Alaska, *Arctic*
A *culture hero.* Although occasionally portrayed
as a villain, Apanuugak is a strong, courageous,
and ingenious warrior and defender. He can
jump higher than any of his enemies, and has a
tremendous voice like a crane. He dies an old man
in the *qasgiq* in his village. [Riordan 1983; Tennant and Bitar 1981]

Apicilnic
Montagnais, Labrador, Canada, *Subarctic*
Little people who live in remote areas and steal
human children. They are only as tall as a human's
knee and can disappear instantly. Their presence
portends danger. [Fisher 1946; Helm 1981]

Apikunni
Blackfoot, *Plains*
A poor young man responsible for the first death
(see *Dead)* and the bringing of *tobacco* seed.
Apikunni is raised by his grandmother in a scantily furnished lodge. A young woman loves
Apikunni, but because his parents cannot pay her
bride price she is given to the chief as the youngest
of his three wives. After the marriage, Apikunni
and the girl continue to meet secretly. When the
chief discovers their love for one another,
Apikunni is publicly humiliated. He wanders
away and sits down next to a beaver dam where
he cries himself to sleep.

In his dream a very old, white-furred *beaver*
comes to him and invites him into the beaver
house. The beaver teaches Apikunni a song and
encourages him to spend the winter and learn the
many powers of the beaver. Meanwhile,
Apikunni's friend Wolf-Tail has been looking for
him. Wolf-Tail comes to the lake and calls out for
Apikunni, who responds that he is in the beaver
house for the winter and cannot leave. He asks
Wolf-Tail to come back in the spring and bring
food and moccasins. In the spring Wolf-Tail
returns. As Apikunni prepares to leave, the old
beaver gives him a long piece of aspen and tells

him to carry it into war. He also gives him a sack
of medicines, including some tobacco seed, and
instructions for their use.

The friends leave together, traveling at a distance behind the village war party. During the
night an enemy scout tries to cross a river into the
Blackfoot warriors' camp. Apikunni dives into
the water, swims underneath the enemy, and
pierces him with the aspen wood stick. This is the
first man ever killed in war. Apikunni returns to
his village a hero. The chief retires and makes
Apikunni the new chief. Apikunni marries his
lover, the youngest of the old chief's three wives,
and is given the other two wives as servants. He
calls a village council and tells the people everything the old beaver taught him, including how
to plant and offer the tobacco seed. [Grinnell
1892a; Thomas 1986; Wissler 1911]

Apotamkin
Maliseet-Passamaquoddy, *Northeast*
A *bogey* monster with long hair and huge teeth.
Fear of him keeps small *children* from straying
onto thin, newly frozen ice in the winter and
unguarded beaches in the summer. [Fisher
1946; Prince 1921]

Apsaalooke
Crow, *Plains*
The term the people of the Crow tribe use when
speaking about themselves as a group or culture.
[Frey 1987; Lowie 1956, 1960]

Aqalax
Kathlamet, Oregon/Washington coast,
Northwest Coast
The *Sun,* carried across the sky by an old woman
who lives in the sky with her granddaughter. The
old woman leaves her house early in the morning
and returns late at night. [Boas 1901b]

Aqonidzaba
Paviotso, *Great Basin*
Centipede, a notorious *gambler.* Aqonidzaba
keeps a large fire burning, tossing into it anyone

who gambles with him and loses. A young boy, with the help of *Crow,* outsmarts Centipede and tosses him into his own fire. In the process, Crow burns his feet, which is the reason crows hop about as they do. [Lowie 1924; Swanson 1970]

Archer
See *Pisigsordleq.*

Architecture
See *Akahcape,* the Pawnee tipi; *Kararata?u,* the Pawnee earth lodge; *Akaririwis,* the Pawnee temporary summer shelter; *Longhouse* (Iroquois); and *Qasgiq,* the Alaskan Eskimo men's house. See *Blessingway* for the cosmic significance of the Navajo hogan.

Arendiwane
Huron, *Northeast*
Medicine people. "Arendi" is thought to be a cognate of the word *orenda,* meaning a power or force innate in all objects from stones to deities. The suffix "wane" is from the word "wanen," meaning large, great, or powerful. Arendiwane gain their power through visions, fasting alone, depriving themselves of certain material possessions at a spirit's request, and observing certain periods of sexual abstinence. The arendiwane possesses an *oki,* a powerful spirit that enters the medicine person's body in dreams or immediately after the person awakens. The oki may be in the form of an eagle, raven, crow, flame, or ghost. The oki carries ondinoc (knowledge), which is the secret to recovery. Arendiwane are different from the *saokata,* who examine others by seeing, and the *ontetsans,* who extract spells. [Tooker 1962]

Arrow
See *Black Lightning Arrow* (Pawnee), *Bright Eyes* (Pawnee), and *Gutginsa* (Tsimshian).

Arrow Boy
Pueblo, *Southwest*
Arrow Boy is a standard hero figure whose character can vary considerably among different sto-

ries. He is commonly depicted as a dirty, lazy boy who refuses to hunt, instead spending all of his time courting girls. See also *Dirty Boy.* [Benedict 1931]

Asdiwal
Tsimshian, *Northwest Coast*
A *culture hero* and famous *hunter.* Several stories tell of Asdiwal's birth as the son of Ho, a supernatural being. During a time of famine, Ho disguises himself as a young man and sends animals to a young girl. Eventually he marries her and they have a son. Ho makes special snowshoes for his son, says that the boy is to be named Asdiwal, then disappears.

As a young man, Asdiwal uses the snowshoes to pursue a white *bear* up a steep mountain to the sky. Asdiwal discovers that the bear is actually a beautiful woman dressed in a white bearskin. Asdiwal marries the woman, who is the daughter of the Sun.

Other stories tell of the tests set for Asdiwal by the Sun, Asdiwal's adventures back on earth, and his marriages. Stories about Asdiwal are the subject of a much-discussed structural interpretation by anthropologist Claude Levi-Strauss. See also *Waux,* the son of Asdiwal. [Boas 1902, 1916; Levi-Strauss 1976; Moore 1975; Thomas, Kronenfeld, and Kronenfeld 1976]

Ash Blowing Rite
Iroquois, *Northeast*
A private rite of *thanksgiving* that may also involve *healing.* The *False Faces* gather in the evening during *Midwinter Festival* in response to a dream directing thanks to the False Faces. During the rite, the host of the event stands before the fire in his or her home. A singer accompanies masked dancers who blow ashes everywhere, reminding people of the activity of one of the first False Faces (see *Hodigohsosga?a).* If a patient is present, a False Face will rub the affected area of the patient's body with hot ash. See also *Faces of Forests, Godiont, Hadu?i,* and *Traveling Rite.* [Fenton 1987; Wallace 1972]

Ashammaleaxia
Crow, *Plains*

"As driftwood lodges." Term used for *clan*. Crow country has several rivers in which pieces of driftwood cling together as they float downstream in fast-moving and often dangerous currents. Just as a solitary piece of driftwood would have difficulty making it down the river, so a person does not travel well alone. Thus an individual's relationship to his or her clan is crucial for survival. This metaphor for relationships as driftwood lodging together is believed to have been given to the Crow people by *Old Man Coyote* (Isaahkawuattee).

There are eight matrilineal clans in Crow society. Old Man Coyote gave each clan a name that reflected an event or particular characteristics associated with members of the clan. For example, the Uuwuutasshe (Greasy Mouth) clan is so named because its members always ate the fattiest parts of their meat. See also *Aassahke*. [Frey 1987]

Ashiwi
Zuni, *Southwest*

The Zuni name for themselves. [Wright 1985]

Asin
Alsea, *Northwest Coast*

A fearful *monster*-girl who lives in the woods and carries people off, especially unattended *children*. If *medicine people* dream of Asin, she empowers them with bad medicine. Asin's laughter echoing in the mountains foretells the impending death of a person (see *Dead*). See also *Dzoo-noo-qua* and *Snee-nee-iq*. [Frachtenberg 1920]

Asking Stick (aiyaguk)
Eskimo, Bering Sea coast, Alaska, *Arctic*

A long, slender wand used to invite a selected village to the *Inviting-In Feast* and the *Messenger Feast* held in January. Three globes made of strips of wood are attached to the wand; these hold the types of gifts wanted by the village

issuing the invitation. The messenger swings the globes in front of the person chosen to receive it. During the subsequent ceremonies people show their respect for the asking stick by hanging it over the *qasgiq* entrance. [Lantis 1947; Morrow 1984; Nelson 1899]

Assin
Ojibwa, *Northeast, Subarctic*

The *Stone*. A potential *shaking tent* visitor honored with a song at the beginning of the shaking tent ceremony. Stones have the potential to become animate and can help people defend themselves against *witiko* encounters. [Overholt and Callicott 1982]

Astcatstudab
Puyallup-Nisqually, southern Puget Sound, *Northwest Coast*

Secret *power* (see *Sqalalitut*). A person with astcatstudab does not practice as a *shaman,* and never in public. Although people with astcatstudab can participate in ceremonies like anyone else, they can never initiate or lead a ceremony because of the power's secret nature. People with astcatstudab are able to identify all the powers held by others and can use this knowledge to kill people. A person who kills in this way cannot reveal that his or her astcatstudab was used to cause a death (see *Tudab*). [Smith 1940]

Atacokai
Kutchin, Alaska, Yukon Territories, *Subarctic*

"He paddled the wrong way." The *culture hero* of three major myth cycles. Originally able to communicate with both humans and animals, he lost this ability when he was shunned and isolated as punishment for accidentally killing his brother. [Damas 1984]

Atisokan
Ojibwa, *Northeast, Subarctic*

"Grandfather." *Midewiwin* stories (see *Story Types*) that are told only in the winter, when things are resting, in order to avoid disturbing the potential for transformative power connected with the stories. The ordinary familial term for grandfather is ni mico mus. [Landes 1968]

Atoshle
Zuni, *Southwest*
See *Women's Ways.*

Atseemath
Lillooet, *Plateau*
After the time when people and animals were the same, these humanlike characters arrive to put the world in order for the coming humans. These beings, known as transformers (see *Transformation),* are helped by Mink and Coyote. Their attempt to transform Mink into a rock fails because Mink's power is equal to theirs. Subsequently Mink and Coyote work as transformers, Mink among the Lower Lillooet people and Coyote among the Upper Lillooet people. Although transformers help to put the world in order, they are mischievous and greedy. They are often killed, but come back to life. [Kitanmax School 1977]

Atsitsi
Blackfoot, *Plains*
Screech *Owl,* a young warrior known for his great deeds on the warpath. As a child, Atsitsi does not want to play with other children and is always alone. He prays to birds and animals for the strength to become a great warrior. When Atsitsi is 14, a large band of Cree threaten war against the Blackfoot. Atsitsi asks his father for permission to go on the warpath. His father offers him a fast horse and many weapons, but Atsitsi takes only a small hatchet. His father also gives him a headband of small Thunderbird feathers because the Thunderbird is the father's medicine. As the war party approaches the band of Crees, Atsitsi removes his clothes and puts on the headdress. Thinking he is making fun of them, the older warriors tell Atsitsi to remain behind. Instead, he leads the war party into battle, where they tri-

umph. Atsitsi becomes a legendary warrior and, reflecting this, his name is changed to E-kuskini (Low Horn). [Grinnell 1913; Thomas 1986]

Atungaq
Eskimo, *Arctic*
One of the early people who, with his wife and child, travels around the world by dog team. En route they meet many strange people, including the Unngirlaat, the "laced ones," a happy people who wear their clothes all laced together, and the Inugagulligait, a group of friendly dwarfs. Throughout the trip, Atungaq's shy wife pretends she is snowblind in order to avoid meeting people. The Kuutsitualiit, *shamans* with only one hipbone, laugh at her because they know she is pretending. The three come to the home of the Kukkiayuut, the clawed ones, humans with nails like the claws of the snowy owl. The Kukkiayuut convince Atungaq's daughter to remove her coat, then scratch her to death and eat her. When Atungaq finds his daughter's heart bouncing around on the floor, he kills the Kukkiayuut with a knife. Atungaq and his wife return home thinking they have gone around the world. [Nungak and Arima 1988]

Augitsisiaq
Eskimo, eastern Hudson Bay, *Arctic*
A *culture hero* who is banished to an island along with his mother and left to starve because of her sexual indiscretion. They survive, and Augitsisiaq's mother teaches him to swim and dive like a polar bear. When two kayakers try to kill them, Augitsisiaq swims under the water and capsizes the kayaks, leaving the men to drown. He and his mother return to the mainland. [Nungak and Arima 1988]

Aurora Borealis
Algonquian tribes, *Subarctic;* and Eskimo, *Arctic*
Northern lights, seen in the higher northern latitudes. The flashing lights are believed to be the dancing spirits of the *dead. Children* are warned not to make noise while the lights are dancing,

lest they be stolen by the spirits. See also *Waziya* (Lakota).

Awaeh Yegendji
Seneca, *Northeast*
Mother Swan, a wise old woman who instructs her daughters to marry Big Earth's son, a successful hunter, so that she will be provided for. Mother Swan lives alone with her three beautiful and clever daughters. After many years of living on nothing but bread and beans, the old woman desires meat to eat. After several failed attempts to deliver *marriage bread,* a female-initiated form of marriage proposal, the eldest and youngest daughters successfully make their way to the lodge of Big Earth, whose son takes both of them as his wives. [Curtin and Hewitt 1918]

Awakkule
Crow, *Plains*
Dwarf people who live in the mountains in Wyoming and Montana and act as *helping spirits.* Often portrayed in stories as helpers, awakkule are very strong. They are known to play practical jokes (see *Jokes and Joking*) on people who camp near their villages. [Frey 1987]

Awataerohi
Huron, *Northeast*
Dancing and feasting performed in order to cure illness (see *Healing*). The term also refers to a disease-causing spirit. Ontarraoura, an animal resembling a lion, is a good hunter and a friend of the wolves. He is killed, but Owl predicts he will come back to life if a feast is performed. This is done, and becomes the exemplar for awataerohi, the practice of holding feasts to heal the sick.

During the curing ceremony, dancers dance around the patient, bringing him or her requested gifts. As many as 12 different dances are used for curing. The dances are illness-specific and are determined by the diagnosticians *(saokata)* or in a *dream* of the sick person.

The Awataerohi spirit causes a disease known as awataerohi. This fist-sized spirit takes up residence in a victim's body. The cure requires holding a specific feast in the dark with only invited guests present. [Tooker 1962]

Awusek
Crow, *Plains*
The *sweat lodge. Old Man Coyote* tells Red Fox (Ci raper k) to build a lodge using ten sticks and to cleanse himself with sagebrush in order to cure himself. Together Coyote and Red Fox fast and dream in the Awusek. They instruct others to do the same, and the Crow have used the sweat lodge ever since. [Lowie 1956, 1960]

Ayaxaus
Puyallup-Nisqually, southern Puget Sound, *Northwest Coast*
A malevolent *power* used out of meanness. Fits of violent temper are attributed to ayaxaus. Places where a person receives ayaxaus are said to have had landslides, with the trees being twisted in strange ways. The *transformation* of an animal into another kind of animal is considered to be a sign of ayaxaus. For example, a deer manifesting ayaxaus might turn into a snake while being skinned. For a person to see such a transformation means death. [Smith 1940]

Azeban
Western Abenaki, *Northeast*
Raccoon, a prankster who deceives animals and attempts to outwit other beings for food. Often classified as a *trickster.* [Trigger 1978]

Baaxpee
Crow, *Plains*
Spiritual *power* with the ability to transform objects and lives. Things transformed by baaxpee become *xapaaliia* (or *medicine*). The knowledge to make good choices comes from having baaxpee. The term may also describe the good fortune someone experiences. See also *Akbaatatdia,* the one responsible for the power of transformation. [Frey 1987]

Badger's Limitations
Kathlamet, Oregon/Washington coast, *Northwest Coast*
Because of his jealousy and anger, *Coyote* limits Badger's hunting skills. While catching birds, Coyote and Badger devise a scheme to kill animals. Badger pretends to be ill. Coyote asks the first victim, Sturgeon, to help him carry Badger into the house. While they are carrying him, Badger farts, and the smell kills Sturgeon. Badger manages to kill many animals this way. Coyote becomes jealous and asks Badger if he can borrow his anus. Badger agrees and the two trade anuses, but Coyote does not know how to use Badger's anus. Badger gets angry and throws Coyote's anus in the river. When Coyote finally retrieves his anus, it is all torn up. He curses Badger and says that the smell of Badger's farts will cause fear, but that Badger will not be able to kill anyone with weapons. [Boas 1901b]

Bagucks
Ojibwa, *Northeast, Subarctic*
A *spirit* of misfortune in the form of a small bird skeleton. As a small child, Bagucks starves because he is stubborn. Helping spirits pity him and give him powers believed to be even greater than those of the mide priests. See *Midewiwin.* [Overholt and Callicott 1982]

Baldhead
Kawaiisu, *Great Basin*
See *Pikagoyu,* Coyote's traveling companion.

Basamacha
Yavapai, *Southwest*
From ba ("person") and samacha ("medicine power")—a medicine person (see *Medicine People*) or *shaman.* Curing is done at nighttime song rituals, during which the

entranced basamacha diagnoses the illness by locating the place of malevolence in the sufferer's body. Cutting a cross in the flesh, the basamacha sucks the malevolence from the body. He demonstrates the effectiveness of the cure by producing from his mouth a bloodcovered, worm-shaped object. [Gifford 1932]

Basket Dice Game
Pawnee, *Plains*

A *game* played with a basket representing the *moon* and seven plum-seed dice representing stars (see *Stars and Starlore*). Its origin is told in a story. Moon, who has many female children, lives in a lodge with an altar guarded by four old men: Wind, Clouds, Lightning, and Thunder. One of Moon's daughters, *Evening Star,* dances in the west and is responsible for the storms. Whenever the four old men wish to create bad weather, they must receive permission from Evening Star. Basket Woman, the mother of all the stars and Moon, gives permission for earth to be created (see *Creation*). The first man and woman created enter Moon's lodge and are taught songs, games, and dances by her daughters. They are also given corn to eat and to plant. Basket Woman gives the pair a basket and plum seeds, telling the woman to gather plum seeds and put marks on them to represent the stars.

In the game, a woman representing Evening Star carries a basket representing Moon. The basket reminds people that *Tirawahat,* the creator, sent the stars in a basket, the moon, and that they fell to earth to teach the people all that they were to do. Four other women, representing the daughters of Big Black Meteoric Star of the northeast skies, also dance with baskets. Two of these baskets hold swan necks and the other two hold fawn skins, representing the four sky beings. Twelve sticks, used as counters in the game, represent 12 other stars. [Dorsey 1906a; Murie 1989]

Basket Woman
Pawnee, *Plains*

See *Basket Dice Game.*

Bead Spitter
Creek, Alabama, *Southeast*

Turkey-Killer, a figure who makes valuable beads and spits them out for people to collect. For the Creek, bead decorations on clothing signify the wearer's status. In one story, Turkey-Killer puts two young girls to a test of truth after they are fooled by Rabbit into thinking he is Bead Spitter. Rabbit tricks the girls into spending the night with him. The next morning he spits out beads he has stolen from Turkey-Killer's children. [Swanton 1928a]

Beadway
Navajo, *Southwest*

A mythology and ritual curing complex. The hero of Beadway is identified as the oldest of two sons of Bead Woman. She is one of five daughters, each born from a different body part of *Changing Woman.* The hero is presented as a beggar held captive by the Pueblos, who feed him poorly and force him to work hard.

The captors lower the hero over the side of a cliff into an eagle's nest containing two eaglets. The Pueblos command him to throw the eaglets down to them, after which they plan to abandon him. Warned by *diyin dine?e* of the plot, he refuses to throw down the eaglets. The Pueblos threaten him and finally shoot fire arrows into the nest. But the eaglets recognize him as a friend and help by throwing dust from their feathers onto the Pueblos, causing skin irritations. At night, the young birds cover him with their wings for warmth.

When they return, the grateful *eagle* parents carry the hero up to a hole in the sky, through which he is taken into the eagles' house. Here also are four pueblos, each housing various birds. The hero suffers on several occasions because he disregards warnings, but he also encounters and defeats a number of the eagles' enemies. In return the eagles offer him marriage to a beautiful eagle daughter and teach him both *Eagleway* and Beadway. In time he is returned to his home, either on a sunbeam or dressed in eagle plumage. He teaches these ceremonials to his brother, thus initiating the ceremonial lineage. He also is able to retaliate for the ill-treatment he received from the Pueblos. [Hill and Hill 1943b; Matthews 1897; Reichard 1939; Wheelwright 1945]

Bean Dance
Hopi, *Southwest*
See *Powamu.*

Bean Woman
Seneca, *Northeast*
Bean Woman stands by a stream and sings a song inviting someone to marry her. The first to approach Bean Woman is Panther. When she asks him what he would feed her, he replies, "Fresh meat." Bean Woman rejects Panther's offer because eating meat would kill her. Next, Deer offers to marry her, saying he would feed her the buds and tender bark of trees. Again she declines, being unfamiliar with that food. Then Bear offers to marry her and feed her nuts, but Bean Woman refuses. Wolf proposes marriage and a diet of meat and venison, but Bean Woman declines because she will not eat stolen meat. Finally Corn comes and promises to feed her sweet corn. Bean Woman agrees to marry him, and since that time the bean vine is always found entwined around the cornstalk. [Curtin and Hewitt 1918]

Bear
One of the most frequently appearing characters in Native American stories, the bear is revered in hunting practices and considered to be a powerful ally in healing. The Cree call Bear *Maskwa.* The Lakota refer to him as *Mato* and *Hu Nonp.* The Alsea culture hero is a black bear *(Suku).* The Osage *Wacabe* is a powerful black bear helping spirit. The *polar bear snout* is used in Alaska as a shaman's amulet, and *Qumu?uc* (Ute) is medicine owned by Bear. The great Pawnee medicine person known as *Smoking-with-the-Bear* received his power from the bear. The Inupiaq hunter *Pisig-sordleq* mistreats the bear. In a Tsimshian story, Bear teaches *Gispawaweda* how to fish. *Torngar-*

soak (Labrador) is a great white bear who is the master of animals. *Magucan* is the Naskapi feast held after a bear hunt. *Asdiwal* (Tsimshian) follows a beautiful woman who becomes a bear. Bear is the protagonist in the Seneca stories *Big Dipper, Gaha,* and *Ganiagwaihegowa. Changing Bear Maiden* (Navajo) is a woman who becomes a bear, and the malevolent *Great White Bear* (Menominee) lives underground. Several stories involve the *Great Bear Constellation.* The Bear clan is a powerful Hopi clan (see *Hopi Clan Grouping or Phratry);* see also *Wemaawe* (Zuni). [Dangel 1929; Deans 1889; Hallowell 1926; Michelson 1938; Mischler 1984; Morris 1976; Rockwell 1991; Speck 1935a]

Bear Ceremony
Delaware, *Northeast*
See *Linkan,* the Men's Dance, and *Pick-welaneokan,* the Nighthawk Dance, both done during the Bear Ceremony.

Bear Dance
A *dance* performed in many tribes by members of *medicine societies* for the purposes of curing (see *Healing)* and petitioning for long life. It involves imitating the bear's shuffling footsteps. Bear Dancers often wear bearskins and bear masks. Among the Pawnee, dancers of the Bear Society receive their healing powers from the *Sun.* When they dance the Bear Dance they place their palms up to catch the Sun's rays. Among the Fox and the Iroquois, women take part in the Bear Dance by waddling like a bear. *Mamakoni-nitkap* is the Ute spring dance celebrating the end of hibernation. *Mesing Keo* are Delaware dancers who wear bearskins. The Iroquois *Midwinter Festival* includes a Bear Dance. The Cherokee Bear Dance is called *Yona.* See also *Bear Parent, Bear Woman and the Fawns, Bear Medicine Woman,* and *Apache Bear Dance.* [Opler 1938b]

Bear Dreamer Society
Lakota, *Plains*
See *Mato Okolakiciye.*

Bear Medicine Ceremony
Pawnee, *Plains*
See *Bear Medicine Woman.*

Bear Medicine Woman
Pawnee, *Plains*
Originator of the Bear Medicine Ceremony. While Bear Medicine Woman is still in her mother's uterus, her father kills a bear, causing his daughter to be born with the spirit of the bears. She grows to womanhood and has three children. The first two die as infants, but the third, a boy, lives. When he is about ten years old, he returns ill from a hunting trip. The *medicine people* fail to cure him and he dies. Bear Medicine Woman mourns at her son's grave, cutting her hair and gashing her arms.

Later, after her son's grave is robbed and she finds his body exposed, Bear Medicine Woman continues to mourn by the grave for four days. At night she takes shelter under a cedar tree, where she hears bears growling. On the fourth day a bear tells her to follow him to his lodge to meet his wife and six cubs. "Chase the cubs," the bear tells her. "The number you catch will be the number of children you will have." Bear Medicine Woman catches two cubs, and the bear tells her to take them home with her. Then he blows colored *breath* on her face and says that she now has the *power* to heal the wounded with the Bear Medicine Ceremony. The female bear hugs her and coughs up pieces of cherry, hackberry, and bullberry, saying, "You will use these berries for *healing.*" The male bear gives her red paint and a red feather, and the female bear gives her yellow paint and a yellow feather. When the bears finish teaching Bear Medicine Woman, she returns home and builds and decorates a tipi of buffalo hides according to their directions.

Whenever Bear Medicine Woman is touched she growls like a bear. From this her husband recognizes her power. For his protection and bravery when fighting, Bear Medicine Woman gives her husband red paint and red feathers.

When a wounded man is brought to her for healing, Bear Medicine Woman sings bear songs and growls like a bear. In the morning she inhales power from the *sun* while her husband smokes to the sun. She breathes different colored breaths on the wounds of the injured man, and the wounds become fresh and start to bleed. Then cedar leaves are burned while Bear Medicine Woman becomes angry like a savage bear. After four days she and her husband repeat the healing and the wounded man gets well. In his dreams the wounded man sees Bear Medicine Woman as a cinnamon bear. He wants to repay her, but she tells him that she does not need any compensation. Instead she feeds him cherries from her mouth to make him a member of the Bear Society.

Bear Medicine Woman and her husband have many children, but only the first two, a son and a daughter, survive. Her husband kills many buffalo and they live well. During an enemy attack on the camp, Bear Medicine Woman's husband sustains multiple wounds and she cannot save him. Bear Medicine Woman mourns many months for her husband. She teaches her son the bear mysteries and performs in medicine lodges. She also originates the *Bear Dance,* which is part of the Bear Medicine Ceremony. She lives to be quite old, and her son becomes one of the four leaders of the Bear Ceremony. [Dorsey 1906a; Murie 1989]

Bear Parent
Kutenai, *Plateau*
A female bear discovers a boy lost in the woods and rears him along with her cubs. She teaches the child to eat bear food and to hibernate in cold weather. One winter night the bear wakes up and tells her children to follow her to a village where people are performing the Bear Ceremony. The people are smoking their *pipes* and praying for food and good health. The bear gathers up the pipe stems, each of which represents a prayer (see *Prayer and Prayersticks),* and brings them back to the cave. She sorts through

them, piling the sincere prayers in one group and the insincere ones, offered by people who mock bears, in another. Then the bears return to hibernation until the spring. The following winter, the female bear again hears the songs and prayers of the village people. She awakens the boy and gives him the power to hear his people singing and dancing. Together they go to the village and return with the pipe stems, which she teaches the boy to sort so that the sincere prayers are separated from the insincere ones. In the spring the bear returns the boy to his parents, and he tells his people that the bears know the difference between the prayers of sincere and insincere people. [Barbeau 1946; Boas and Chamberlain 1918; Schaeffer 1947]

Bear Society
Pawnee, *Plains*
See *Bear Medicine Woman,* who originated the Bear Medicine Society.

Bear Sweat Lodge
Ojibwa, *Northeast, Subarctic*
The curing ritual (see *Healing*) of Bear visionaries, or people who dreamed of the bear. The Bear Sweat Lodge is an intense ordeal that bestows great honor on the visionaries. The heat is much stronger and the time spent inside the lodge much longer than in other types of sweats.

Bear Wife
Carrier, *Subarctic*
A *hunter* meets a black bear woman and kills a grizzly bear that has been threatening her people. The hunter and the woman marry and live together happily. When salmon fishing season starts, the man returns to his village with his wife and they have a child. Because the wife does not help with the communal activities of drying fish and picking berries, the people resent her. When the winter supply of fish and berries is nearly gone and the people face starvation, the hunter's wife saves the village by showing them a large underground cave filled with dried salmon and berries.

The next summer all the families go fishing and the hunter meets an old lover. The bear wife is heartbroken and goes home and cries all night. The next morning she changes herself and her child into their bear form and they leave. The distraught husband follows their tracks but cannot find them. See also *Wife Mistreated.* [Boas and Chamberlain 1918]

Bear Woman
Pueblo, *Southwest*
See *Yellow Woman,* who becomes a bear. [Jenks 1902; Opler 1938b]

Bear Woman and the Fawns
Lassik, *California*
Various stories about these characters are told among tribes in California. Grizzly Bear and *Deer* are the wives of Chicken Hawk. One day while pretending to delouse Deer's head, Grizzly Bear kills her. She takes Deer's head home to roast. Deer's two children, the fawns, are horrified when they see their mother's head being roasted for dinner. They cry, but Grizzly Bear tells them to be quiet and go out to play. While they are out playing with Grizzly Bear's children, the fawns hear the hair on their mother's head cry out to warn them they are in danger. The fawns smother Grizzly Bear's children in a fire, then take the dead cubs home and give the meat to Grizzly Bear. When she eats the meat they tell her she is eating her own children. Grizzly Bear chases the fawns to a river, where Old Grandfather Crane stretches out his neck so the fawns can get across. When Grizzly Bear tries to cross, the crane twists his neck. She falls into the river, which carries her away. [Kroeber 1925]

Beast Gods
Zuni, *Southwest*
See *Wemaawe.*

Beast-Man
Choctaw, *Southeast*
See *Kashehotapolo.*

Beauty
Navajo, *Southwest*
See *Hozho*.

Beautyway
Navajo, *Southwest*

A myth and ritual healing complex. Beautyway runs parallel with *Mountainway,* beginning with the situation presented at the end of *Enemyway,* where two sisters have been fooled into marrying two old men, Bear and Snake. Beautyway follows the adventures of the younger sister, who has married Snake.

Both sisters flee from their dreaded husbands, going separate ways. Younger Sister gains help in her flight, but eventually winds up in a subterranean place that turns out to be the home of her snake husband's people. The Snake People, who appear to her in human form, warn her not to make a fire during the night, but she does so anyway in order to examine her sore feet and swollen legs. In the firelight, she sees that she is surrounded by snakes. She extinguishes the fire, but is unable to sleep. The next day the Snake People go out, leaving Younger Sister alone to prepare food. She uses ordinary measures of corn and beans, but these expand, filling all the containers and finally the entire house. Upon their return the Snake People admonish her for not knowing she should use just two kernels of corn and two beans.

For each of the next five days, the Snake People warn her against certain actions without explaining why she should not do them. Each time curiosity leads her to ignore the warning. Told not to touch certain water jars, she opens them and releases *storms* of all kinds. Warned on three successive days not to go to the east, south, and north, she does so anyway and gets into situations from which the Snake People must save her. Each rescue amounts to a ceremonial performance of Beautyway. Thus, through suffering the consequences of her curiosity, Younger Sister learns the songs, prayersticks, sandpaintings, and ceremonial paraphernalia and processes of Beautyway. She returns home to meet her older

sister and teaches Beautyway to her family. [Wheelwright 1951; Wyman 1957]

Beaver
Algonquian tribes, *Northeast*

The origin of the beaver is told in the story of a traveling family, the mother and children of which are lost in a river during a crossing. The grief-stricken husband and father returns to the river and finds his family changed into beavers and calling to him. They pull him into the water and he is changed into a beaver. For stories of Beaver in other tribes see *Apikunni* (Blackfoot), *Capa* (Lakota), and *Glooscap* (Micmac and Maliseet). [Fisher 1946]

Beaver and Porcupine at War
Haida, *Northwest Coast*

Porcupine steals Beaver's food supply, but denies it when questioned. Beaver (Tc!in) eventually learns Porcupine is responsible and the two start fighting. When Porcupine throws his spines into Beaver, Beaver seeks his parents' help.

Beaver's father calls the Beaver People together to fight Porcupine. They destroy Porcupine's house, capture him, and put him on an island with only two trees. Porcupine calls for help, but no one responds. Near starvation, he calls Cold Weather by singing songs of North Wind. When it begins to get cold, the water freezes, and his friends come and get him. By this time he is barely able to walk.

Porcupine's father calls all the forest people to retaliate against the Beaver People. The Porcupine People and the Beaver People go to war. The Porcupine People capture Beaver and leave him in a tall tree. Since beavers cannot climb trees, Beaver's only escape is to gnaw away from the top down. Beaver mysteriously disappears, and the Porcupine People and Beaver People end their war. [Swanton 1905b]

Beaver man
Dunne-Za (Beaver), *Subarctic*

Also known as Beaver Doctor, he travels the earth reducing the giant human-eating animals to their current size. Beaver Man also figures prominently in many healing stories in which a sick person might find him or herself in the beaver's lodge. Individuals who dream of beavers often hold the knowledge of the beaver's healing powers. [Turner and Edmonds 1968]

Beaver Tribe
Subarctic
They call themselves *Dunne-Za.*

Bee
See *Poison.*

Begocidi
Navajo, *Southwest*
"One-Who-Grabs-Breasts." A figure appearing in *emergence* and *creation* stories. Spoiled by his father, the *Sun,* he is put in control of game and domesticated animals. Begocidi has intercourse with everything in the world, giving birth to many monsters (see *Monster Slayer and Born for Water*). He can move about without being seen and is able to change at will into such forms as rainbow, wind, sand, and weather. His name comes from his practice of sneaking up on young girls, touching their breasts and shouting "be'go be'go." He is similarly annoying to hunters, whom he grabs by the testicles just as they are ready to shoot. Begocidi is described as being a blond- or red-haired, blue-eyed *transvestite* who dresses like a woman (see also *Gender Crossing*). He is also the first potter. Some versions of the creation story identify Begocidi as the *creator,* even equating him with the Christian God. See also *Christianity.* [Hill 1938; Matthews 1897; Reichard 1944b; Wheelwright 1942; Wyman 1947]

Berdache
See *Gender Crossing.* See also *Minquga,* the Omaha term for berdache, and *Winkte,* the Lakota term for transvestite. [Blackwood 1984; Callender and Kochems, 1983; Hauser 1990; Lee 1982; Medicine 1983; Thayer 1980; Whitehead 1981]

Big Bellies
Lakota, *Plains*
See *Naca Ominicia,* the tribal administrators.

Big Black Meteoric Star
(U pirit raruhu ru katikucu) Pawnee, *Plains*
"Big black star scattered about." *Tirawahat* placed this star in the sky northwest of *Morning Star* and made him second in power to *Evening Star* (see *Stars and Starlore*). Through Big Black Meteoric Star, human beings receive knowledge of all things. He rules all the animal beings, especially the *buffalo* (see also *Master/Mistress of Animals),* and also controls the coming of *night.* He is represented as having black streaks on his face and wearing a soft down feather on his head. [Dorsey 1906a; Murie 1989]

Big Dipper
Many Native American cultures tell stories of the origin of the constellation Ursa Major. For the Kawaiisu of south-central California, the story features *Coyote.* Desiring his beautiful daughter for himself (see also *Incest),* Coyote tricks his wife, son, and daughter. Feigning imminent death, he asks his family to burn his body and instructs them to give his daughter in marriage to someone resembling himself who lives on the other side of the mountain. Coyote escapes from his funeral pyre and quickly builds a house on the other side of the mountain. In time his unsuspecting daughter is given to him and he copulates with her, causing an instant pregnancy.

One day while Coyote is away, his wife and son discover the deception. They squeeze the pregnant belly of Coyote's daughter, releasing several babies, which they bake. They take some of the baked babies and leave the earth for the sky, where they become the stars of the Big Dipper. When Coyote returns looking for his family, he finds the baked objects and unknowingly eats his own babies. While quenching his thirst in a spring, he sees his family reflected from the sky above. He misses them and wants to join them but, unable to reach his family, Coyote dies of loneliness. See also *Trickster*.

For the Seneca of upstate New York and southern Ontario, the origin of the Big Dipper is told in the story of six *hunters*. One of the six is very lazy. He pretends to be ill, forcing the other five to carry him as well as their provisions. The hunters cross the path of a bear. Dropping their companion and provisions, they chase the bear. Because he has been carried, the lazy hunter has a great deal of energy and runs faster than the others. He catches the bear and kills it.

As they chase the bear, the hunters do not realize they are going upward. By the end of the hunt they have reached the sky, where they and the bear remain, visible as the stars of the Big Dipper. The bear is the star at the lower outside corner. It is said that in autumn, after the first frost, the leaves of the oak tree show blood and oil, believed to be those of the bear killed by the lazy man. See also *Great Bear Constellation* and *Stars and Starlore*. [Haeberlin 1900; Zigmond 1980]

Big Fish of Iliamna
Tanaina, *Subarctic*
A strong *monster* fish belonging to a class of strange, powerful creatures with limited supernatural powers. Big Fish is capable of biting out the bottoms of boats. [Turner and Edmonds 1968]

Big Fly (dotsoh)
Navajo, *Southwest*
Big Fly is apparently associated with the Tachnid flies of the species Hystricia pollinosa, which often alight on people's shoulders or chests. Big Fly serves as a guardian to many heroes in Navajo mythology. He typically sits on the hero's shoulder, guiding him through dangers and toward his goal. See also *Chiricahua Wind Way* and *Hailway*. [Haile 1938a; Matthews 1902; Newcomb and Reichard 1937; Reichard 1939]

Big Heads
Seneca, Iroquois, *Northeast*
"Our Uncles." Unmasked men from opposite moieties who announce the Seneca *Midwinter Festival,* a New Year's ritual complex. These men impersonate uncles who founded the tribes. They are dressed in buffalo robes and cornhusk anklets by two women from opposite moieties. They carry corn pounders (mallets used to grind corn) striped with red paint with which they stir the ashes in the fireplaces of the houses they visit. During the morning of the *New Year,* the Big Heads make three circuits of the village, visiting homes to announce the New Year. [Fenton 1987; Wallace 1972]

Big House Ceremony
Delaware, *Northeast*
See *Nkamwin* and *Mesing Keo.* [Speck 1931]

Big Man-Eater
Alabama, *Southeast*
A *cannibal* who, because of his poor hunting skills, orders his wife to amputate parts of her body for him to eat. The wife escapes to her brothers, who kill Big Man-Eater and cremate him. Bees, wasps, mosquitoes, flies, and crows rise from his ashes. [Hudson 1976]

Big Snake
Navajo, *Southwest*
See *Big Star Way* and *Shootingway.*

Big Star Way
Navajo, *Southwest*
A myth and ritual healing complex. A poor family offers their daughter as wife to a stranger who knows hunting magic. The stranger, the son of Big Snake, helps them. After his wife bears a son, the snake husband leads the family in the direction of his home. Unable to keep up, they lose track of him and camp by a lake. The baby disappears, swallowed by Big Snake, who lives in the lake. The wife and her brother are taken by *Talking God* into the lake where, in response to offerings, the winds perform a *Hoop Transforma-*

tion Rite, removing the snakeskin to reveal the baby, now grown to manhood. The wife and her brother learn medicines and taboos against such actions as eating the intestines, heart, or lungs of deer; sleeping in an arroyo; and lying with their heads close to a tree.

Central to Big Star Way are stories of the family's younger brother, who is married and has two sons. On a hunting trip the brother fails to heed the taboos and becomes sick after eating deer intestines. He is cured through the performance of *Navajo Wind Way.* Later, when a small whirlwind crosses his path, he becomes angry and shoots it. Because the whirlwind is the son of Cyclone, he fears the consequences of his act. The hunter protects himself by building a hogan of cactus and shielding himself with fire and arrows stuck in the four directions. Eventually he cooperates in restoring Whirlwind Boy.

Coyote (Maʔii) desires Younger Brother's wife and tricks him into climbing up a rock on which Coyote has painted a nest of eagles. Coyote blows on the rock, causing it to rise into the sky and strand Younger Brother, leaving his wife for Coyote. Wandering about in the sky, Younger Brother is confronted with angry people, but Star People (see *Stars and Starlore)* find him and offer help. Big Star teaches him the knowledge of Big Star Way and how to interpret dreams and omens. After performing the ceremonies in the sky, Younger Brother is sent through the sky hole and carried on clouds back to earth. Finding that Coyote has taken his place in his family, he exacts revenge by offering Coyote a piece of fat in which he has wrapped a star. Coyote greedily swallows the food, only to suffer great agony and die. In other versions Big Star Way is taught to Younger Brother's wife and sons, an extensive process involving sky journeys and the assistance of Big Star and the Star People. [Wheelwright 1940]

Big Twisted Flute
Lakota, *Plains*
A magical *flute* used in conjunction with specially composed songs as part of a powerful *love* charm used by a young man to entice a young woman. Carved of two grooved cedar halves glued together and tied with thin rawhide lashings, the flute was shaped like a headless horse with a twisted body and had five finger holes. It was made by a *shaman* according to instructions received from *Buffalo* in a *dream.* The shaman also composed the special music to be played on the flute in order to activate the love charm. A Big Twisted Flute produced a haunting melody. It was considered a dangerously powerful instrument and very expensive, usually costing as much as a fine horse. [DeMallie 1984; Powers 1975; Walker 1982]

Big-Tail
Haida, *Northwest Coast*
An important *shaman* through whom many supernaturals speak. Big-Tail visits the great shaman, Supernatural Being-at-Whose-Voice-the-Ravens-Sit-on-the-Sea, also known as Qonatac, who lives in a house under the sea. From Qonatac, Big-Tail obtains a dance headdress with a hawk carved on it and weasel skins decorating the back. Qonatac also teaches him how to make and decorate the headdress. Big-Tail returns to his village with the headdress and imitates the dances he learned under the sea. These dances bring many sea otters for his people to hunt.

Supernatural-Being-at-Whose-Voice-the-Ravens-Sit-on-the-Sea invites Big-Tail to a feast attended by all the other supernatural beings. He puts Big-Tail in his armpit so that he can see but will not be detected by the others. All the supernaturals come into the great shaman's house. Pestilence comes in a European ship, out of which disease-causing sparks fly. The other supernaturals fear that the sparks might strike them. Supernatural-Being-at-Whose-Voice-the-Ravens-Sit-on-the-Sea's nephew opens the container carried by Tidal-Wave, releasing a sudden wave against Pestilence. The supernaturals, wearing their many masks, dance until the masks split crosswise and snow falls out of them. There are a number of such composite masks in the Haida ritual.

One time Big-Tail's village is near starvation. Yayu, Supernatural-Being-Looking-Landward, who has the most whales of all the supernaturals, sends the whales to Big-Tail's village so the villagers will have food. [Swanton 1905b]

Biigistiin
Navajo, *Southwest*

"One who lies within it." Inner life-form. The Navajo understand life as consisting of the conjunction of an outer physical form and an inner life-form. The outer form may take any shape—human, mountains, streams, solar bodies—while the inner form (biigistiin) is invariably humanlike. This concept is essential to understanding Navajo mythology and religion, which center on creation and curing. See also *Biisiziinii; Blessingway; Hozho; Inua; Mountains, Four Sacred; Nilchi?i; Sa?ah naghai bikeh hozho; Soul; Talking God;* and *Ye'ii.* [Haile 1943b]

Biisiziinii
Navajo, *Southwest*

Literally "in-standing one," inner life-form, an alternative term to *Biigistiin.*

Birchbark Scrolls
See *Midewiwin.*

Bird
See *Wuchowsen,* the Passamaquoddy bird responsible for severe storms, and *Uchatngiak,* the only son of an Aleut chief, who disappears and causes geese to come to earth to nest and lay their eggs.

Birds, Origin of Colors
Kathlamet, *Northwest Coast*

One day two daughters of a village chief spear a piece of bright copper, which holds many different shades of color. The girls cut the copper into pieces and share it with the villagers, who are the birds. Each bird person receives a different color. [Boas 1901b]

Birth from Dead Mother's Uterus
Shoshone, *Great Basin;* Plains tribes, *Plains*

A theme found in several Plains tribes tales. In one story, *Wolf* asks the geese to find him a dead woman with a baby. The geese locate two such women, and Wolf takes a boy from one woman and a girl from the other. The baby girl walks immediately and becomes Wolf's traveling companion. In another version, Wolf kills his pregnant wife by decapitating her. He finds within her several babies fathered by other men and kills all of them except his own son. In another variant a woman goes to visit a snake and does not return. Her sons look for her and find her dead. They cut open her swollen stomach, releasing two snakes, a lizard, and, finally, their baby sister. [Lowie 1924]

Bison Calf Pipe
Lakota, *Plains*

See *Pipe.*

Black God (haashcheeshzhini)
Navajo, *Southwest*

Fire god, representing fire making and control of fire rather than fire itself. A frequent figure in Navajo mythology, Black God is the creator of stars, particularly constellations. His mask is black with the constellation Pleiades on the left forehead. Fearless and often feared, he is quick to anger and not easily called to one's aid. He is usually depicted as old and slow-moving. See also *Navajo Starlore* and *Ye?ii.* [Haile 1938a; Matthews 1897; Wheelwright 1942]

Black Hactcin Creates Animals and Humans
Jicarilla Apache, *Southwest*

A figure known as Black Hactcin plays a major role in the Jicarilla story of *emergence* and *creation.* In the beginning there are only *hactcin.* Everything that is to be has a hactcin: the mountains, the fruits, everything. All dwell in a world below the present earth. Their existence is like a dream; they have no flesh and blood and are like shadows. Black Hactcin decides to make an animal. He molds clay into a shape with four legs and sets the object on the ground to see how it will walk. From this first animal Black Hactcin brings forth all sorts of animals. He talks with each animal, often teasing them, in a process of determining how they will look, where they will live, and what they will eat.

When it comes time to make human beings, Black Hactcin draws an outline of a figure on the ground, making it like his own body. He outlines the figure in pollen and places precious stones in the middle of it; these become the flesh and bones. The veins are made of turquoise, the blood of red ochre, the skin of coral, the bones of white rock, the fingernails of opal, the pupil of the eye of jet, the whites of the eye of abalone, the marrow in the bones of white clay, and the teeth of opal. The hair is fashioned of dark cloud. Wind is made to blow through the body of the figure, giving it breath. In this way Black Hactcin creates the first human. The human is a man, and although he can speak and laugh, he is alone. In his sleep he dreams of a woman. When he awakes his dream has come true. This is the origin of the first man and woman, the ancestors of all human beings (see *Humans, Origin of*). Everything takes place in the underworld. See also *Apache Creation and Emergence* and *Mountain Spirits*. [Opler 1938b]

Black Lightning Arrow
Pawnee, *Plains*

A small, black arrow point given to a fasting warrior during a vision. The warrior returns to his war party and tells his companions about his fast, offering smoke to the arrow and vowing that if he ever neglects to honor the arrow it should disappear. Wearing the flint arrow around his neck, the warrior is successful against enemies in battle. Hunting buffalo one day, he forgets the arrow. A terrible lightning, thunder, and wind storm results, during which the arrow escapes and becomes part of *lightning*. The mourning warrior is visited by a mysterious being, who reminds him of his promise to honor the arrow at all times. The being says that, although he

will be a great warrior, because of his neglect he will never be chief. [Dorsey 1906a; Murie 1989]

Black Meteor Star
Pawnee, *Plains*

See *Squash Medicine*.

Blackening (anteec)
Navajo, *Southwest*

A rite in which soot blackened with the ashes of specific plants is rubbed on the body of the person being treated. It is identified with the armor of *Monster Slayer and Born for Water,* thus serving as protection against malevolent forces. It is often interpreted as having exorcistic powers. [Haile 1938a; Reichard 1974]

Black-Tailed Deer Dance Society
Piegan, *Plains*

A dance society (see *Societies)* used for hunting *deer* and *healing* the ill. The society, introduced to the Piegan by the Kootenai, is open to both men and women. The location of deer is revealed to its members in dreams.

The Black-Tailed Deer Dance Society is said to have originated when a very sick man dreamed of a deer that took pity on him. The deer tells the man to grasp her neck as they travel to the top of a hill. If he does not crush her windpipe, he will recover his health, but if he does crush it, he will die. When they reach the top of the hill, the deer tells the man where to find four other deer. Then she tells him how to care for a deer carcass: Never sever the windpipe. Remove the lungs, heart, and windpipe from the carcass. Never allow a dog to eat the heart of a deer. Never eat the head of a deer, and do not allow children to play with the hooves.

The *dance* may be held at any time and can last from one to four nights. Each member has his or her own special *song*. When the dance is held for a sick relative of a society member, all the dancers pray for the sick person (see *Prayer and Prayersticks)*. Each dancer wears a string of deer anklebones painted red, in hopes of having the speedy and graceful feet of a deer. Any person who does not believe in or ridicules the dance is put into a hypnotic trance by a member of the dance. The dancer takes a skin from his or her bundle and places it on the nonbeliever's head, then looks directly into the person's eyes and sings four special songs. The dancer finishes by making a sudden upward movement with his or her hands. The nonbeliever awakens and becomes an undoubting member of the Black-Tailed Deer Dance Society. [Thomas 1986; Wissler 1911]

Bladder
See *Poke.*

Bladder Festival
Eskimo, *Arctic.* See *Nakaciuq.*

Blessingway (hozhooji)
Navajo, *Southwest*
Essentially, that which makes the goal of life—long life—possible; also a song and prayer ceremony, usually lasting one night, performed for the purpose of acquiring good fortune and a long and healthy life. It takes numerous forms, such as house blessings, girls' puberty rites *(kinaalda),* weddings, *rain* ceremonies, travel blessings, and *childbirth* rites.

As the story of the *creation* of the Navajo world, Blessingway is incorporated into many other Navajo myths and ceremonies. Essentially a rite or enactment of creation or re-creation, it is often the first mythology and ceremonial a Navajo singer *(hataalii)* or medicine person learns. Navajos understand it as the backbone of Navajo religion or, alternatively, as the trunk of the branching tree of Navajo mythology and ceremonials. Sequentially, Blessingway comes after the *emergence* events, the stories of the journey up through worlds below the present world.

Blessingway is itself a complex of many extensive stories. Upon emerging onto the present earth surface, *First Man and First Woman* and the others who ascend with them enter a sweat lodge to plan the world they are about to create. They also demonstrate the creative powers of the *medicine bundle* (jish) brought from the lower worlds. In the first ritual act, they open the bundle. From it step two groups of human forms. These persons, identified with various semiprecious jewels, represent the materials from which will be created the inner life-forms *(Biigistiin)* of all things. In a second rite a beautiful young girl and boy arise from the bundle. They are Long Life Boy and Happiness Girl, who represent the means by which all life will proceed through time.

The creators build a hogan, the first house, where they will perform the acts of creating Navajoland. Like all Navajo houses, the hogan has four main support pillars identified with the cardinal directions. It is oriented with the door to the east, the direction of the rising sun. On the floor of the creation hogan, First Man constructs representations in human form of the life-forms of things to be created, using the colored semiprecious stones from the medicine bundle in a manner resembling a sandpainting. He dresses these human life-forms so that they take the physical appearance they will have in the created world: mountains, plants, animals, and other physical features of the earth. These acts of creation are inseparable from acts of *song* and *prayer* (see *Prayer and Prayersticks).*

At dawn, in final acts of song and *breath* (blowing), this microcosmic world created in the hogan is expanded to the present size of the Navajo world. First Man and First Woman send the human-shaped life-forms of dawn and evening twilight on a tour to inspect this newly created world. Ascending each of the mountains to survey the new world, they find it extremely beautiful (see *hozho).* First Man and First Woman return to the lower worlds where they will oversee death (see *Dead)* and *witchcraft,* negative and fearsome attributes associated with this subterranean domain.

The other stories of Blessingway are those of the birth of *Changing Woman,* her puberty rites *(kinaalda),* the birth of her twin sons *Monster Slayer and Born for Water,* their slaying of monsters, the origin of Navajo clans (see also *Humans, Origin of),* the teaching of Blessingway to the Navajo people, and the departure of the *diyin dine?e* or Holy People.

See also *Monsterway; Mountain Soil Bundle; Mountains, Four Sacred; Navajo Ritual Process; Sa?ah naghai bikeh hozho;* and *Tadidiin.* [Wyman 1970]

Blind Boy
Eskimo, eastern Hudson Bay, *Arctic*
See *Iumaaq.*

Blind Man
Tsimshian, *Northwest Coast*
See *Gitqada.*

Blood
See the Yuchi story of *Cedar Tree,* which explains why the sap is red. See also *Menstrual Blood.*

Blood Clot Boy
Cherokee, *Southeast*
The adopted son of *Kanati and Selu.* See also *Long Tooth Boy* (Pawnee).

Bloody Hand
Seneca, *Northeast*
See *Small Dose,* the medicine made by the animals to cure the hero Bloody Hand.

Blue-Jay
Chinook, Tillamook, Coos, *Northwest Coast*
A figure who plays a role similar to *Raven* in northern Pacific tribes and to *Mink* among the British Columbia tribes. Tales about Blue-Jay contain extensive accounts of his trying to outdo other animals. See also *Trickster.* [Jacobs 1959]

Bmola
Western Abenaki, *Northeast*
Wind Bird, a fearful flying creature that is responsible for fiercely cold weather. [Trigger 1978]

Bogey
The bogey is a rather common figure in Native American mythology. Children are warned not to do certain things for fear of being captured by this bogey. *Owner-of-Bag* is an Arapaho owl figure who frightens children. The Ponca bogey is named *Indacinga;* the Maliseet call him *Apotamkin. Hagondes* is the long-nosed Seneca cannibal clown. See also *Children.*

Bole-Maru Cult
See *Ghost Dance of 1870.*

Bone Keepers
Lakota, *Plains*
See *Hohu Yuha,* a malevolent medicine society.

Born for Water
Navajo, *Southwest*
Brother of Monster Slayer. See *Monster Slayer and Born for Water.* See also *Ye?ii.*

Bravery
Omaha, *Plains*
See *Hethuska,* the society responsible for stories of bravery.

Bread
Hopi, *Southwest*
The Hopi make a paper-thin bread called *piki.*

Breath
Breath is commonly associated with power and spirit. *Anerneq* is the Yupik term for breath, which is called *Ni* in Lakota and *Nilchi?i* in Navajo. In the Pawnee story of *Bear Medicine Woman,* breath is the means of conveying power. In the Navajo *Blessingway* account of creation, the world takes its size through blowing. *Hisagita-imisi* (Creek) is the preserver of breath. The Zuni believe the human spirit *(pinanne)* is lodged in the breath.

Breath Feather
Hopi, *Southwest*
See *Paho.*

Breath Maker
Seminole, Oklahoma and *Southeast*
See *Hisagita misa,* the culture hero.

Breath of Life
Keres, *Southwest*
A name for *Iatiku,* the female creator.

Breathing In (aji yidjij)
Navajo, *Southwest*
A ritual act often referred to in prayer and story as well as physically performed. To perform breathing in, one faces the sun or dawn, stretches out the hands with palms up, then pulls the power of the sun toward the body, finally sucking it in from cupped hands. This is usually done four times. At the conclusion of a ceremonial, the *one-sung-over* (the person for whom the ceremonial was performed) goes to the east and breathes in the dawn, signifying acceptance of all that has been done in the ceremonial and a willingness to carry out all requirements placed upon him or her. [Haile 1938a; Reichard 1974]

Bright Eyes
Pawnee, *Plains*
A handsome young boy who, when rejected by his lover, marries a prairie dog and transforms himself into one (see also *Human-Animal Transformation*). Bright Eyes is in love with a girl and waits for her every spring. When she says she does not love him, he goes to the prairie dog town near his home and marries a young prairie dog. Grieving for her son, Bright Eyes's mother follows his tracks and his trail of tears to the prairie dog town. There she has a dream in which a beautiful young woman says that her son is happy and has forgotten about everyone except his mother. The dream woman tells her to take a black arrow and quiver to the hole where her son is living. When Bright Eyes leaves his hole he jumps at the arrow and becomes human again.

Bright Eyes returns home, followed by his pregnant prairie dog wife who rolls in the dust and becomes human (see *Animal-Human Transformation*). They live happily together and have many children. Bright Eyes becomes a great man. His wife warns him, however, not to associate with the girl who rejected him. One day

Bright Eyes meets the girl, who apologizes to him. He accepts her apology and has sexual intercourse with her. When he returns home, he finds that his wife and children have returned to the prairie dog town and become prairie dogs. From that point on Bright Eyes has bad luck and dies a brokenhearted man. [Dorsey 1906a]

Bright-Cloud Woman
Tsimshian, *Northwest Coast*
A Salmon woman who is the provider and protector of salmon. Bright-Cloud Woman marries Txamsem *(Raven),* who greatly loves her. She turns his ugly black hair blond and makes his rough skin soft and white. She also brings many salmon to the rivers for him to catch. One day, while getting ready to smoke the salmon, Txamsem leaves his eyeball behind to guard the salmon from scavenging ravens. When he returns, both the salmon and his eye have been eaten. Bright-Cloud Woman makes him a new eye, with which he can see better than ever. Prospering with an abundance of salmon in his storehouses, Txamsem starts to gamble. When he accuses his wife of infidelity, Bright-Cloud Woman becomes so angry she leaves and takes her tribe, the salmon, with her. Txamsem's blond hair turns black and his skin becomes rough. He is scorched when he places his arms around Bright-Cloud Woman in an attempt to stop her. She turns to smoke and vanishes. See also *Wife Mistreated.* [Boas 1902, 1916]

Buffalo
Plains
The buffalo is the most important animal in most midwestern and Plains tribes. Many stories and ceremonies celebrate the buffalo's generative powers. To the Lakota, all buffalo descend from *Ta Tanka,* the great buffalo bull and special friend (kola) to the Sun. Buffalo and Sun sit in council together every night.

Buffalo is responsible for giving game to the Lakota (see also *Master/Mistress of Animals*). He rewards generosity and punishes those who are stingy. Buffalo is also responsible for the fertility of woman, rewarding women he likes with many children. Buffalo acts as protector for unmarried women and controls all affairs concerning love. Young women are often given the Buffalo's mark, red paint at the parting of the hair, in a special ceremony.

In the Lakota story *Big Twisted Flute,* buffalo gives a magical flute to a shaman as a love charm. Buffalo villagers are prominent figures of the Pawnee story *Cannibal Grandmother.* The Arapaho figure *Found-in-Grass* has the power to call the buffalo. During the *Sun Dance,* the buffalo is honored as a central figure. Kisenapew-mostos (Cree) is the guardian spirit Kind-Old-Man-Buffalo, and *Mostos* (Cree/Ojibwa) may appear as a visiting spirit in shaking tent ceremonies. See also *Medicine Bundle, Moon Woman, Mostos,* and *Napioa.* [Laird 1974]

Buffalo Bull
Lakota, *Plains*
See *Ta Tanka,* the Buffalo Bull spirit.

Buffalo Bull Ceremony
Lakota, *Plains*
See *Ta tanka Lowanpi,* the girls' puberty rite.

Buffalo Dance
Lakota, *Plains*
Part of the preparation for the buffalo hunt *(Wani-sapa).*

Buffalo Dance Cult (Cesahkows)
Menominee, *Northeast*
Members of the Buffalo Dance Cult *dance* to capture the lost *soul* of a sick person. The captured soul is placed in a wooden cylinder and attached to the patient's breast for four days so that it will return to the body. See also *Waipanows.* [Wissler 1913]

Buffalo Hunt
Lakota, *Plains*
See *Wani-sapa.* See also the Pawnee *Crow Lance Society,* which is responsible for successful buffalo hunting.

Buffalo Pipe
Pawnee, *Plains*
See *Long Tongue.*

Buffalo Rock
Blackfoot, *Plains*
A small fossil that gives power. See *Iniskim.*

Buffalo Skull
Lakota, *Plains*
Used in the adoption ceremony *(Hunkayapi).*

Buffalo-Gaming Sticks
Pawnee, *Plains*
Scorekeeping devices for the *hoop and pole game* given to the people by *Tirawahat.* After the first time this game was played, a young man went to a nearby field and had sexual intercourse with a young woman who was really Buffalo

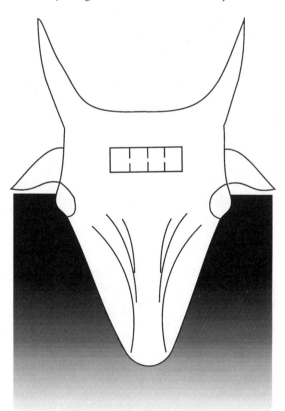

Pawnee buffalo skull. Markings indicate red paint symbolizing sun's rays.

Woman. She later gave birth to a buffalo calf. One day the young man and others from his village went hunting for buffalo, led by a snow bird. The young man came to a ridge and saw a large herd of buffalo. In the herd were Buffalo Woman, transformed back into a buffalo, and her buffalo calf son, who was always crying for his father. When the other calves cried for their fathers they came, but Buffalo Woman told her son that if his human father came to him the bulls would kill him. The young man approached the buffalo, and the bulls challenged him to identify the young calf and its mother. With his son's help, he won both contests, and the bulls let him go, promising to come to the hunters in four days. The young man returned to the hunting party and told the others that the buffalo would come and that there would be plenty of buffalo fat to grease the sticks for their game. Then the hunters played the game to thank Tirawahat for the game and the buffalo.

This story of the game's origin as a gift from Tirawahat and its importance in buffalo hunting is told only in a lodge where *medicine bundles* are held or during a buffalo hunt so the spirits of the buffalo will know they are being honored and will be more willing to give themselves to be killed for food. Songs are sung before and after playing the game. [Dorsey 1906a; Murie 1989]

Buffalo-Woman and Corn-Woman
Pawnee, *Plains*
Buffalo-Woman from the east and Corn-Woman from the west cause the scattering of buffalo herds and the growth of corn. The two women are the wives of the hunter Without-Wings. Buffalo-Woman gives birth to a boy and Corn-Woman a girl. One day the two children anger their mothers by fighting over a spoon and an ear of corn. Corn-Woman and her child disappear underground and Buffalo-Woman leaves with her son, who is now a calf.

Without-Wings turns into an *eagle* and follows Buffalo-Woman. Every evening Buffalo-Woman stops and builds a camp. Each night

Without-Wings finds the camp, transforms into a human, and plays with his son, but when he tries to reconcile with his wife she refuses him. After many nights of this, Without-Wings's son tells his father how to find Buffalo-Woman among a herd of buffalo. Following his son's directions, Without-Wings goes to the buffalo herd. He is invited into a *sweat lodge* by bull buffalo, who try to kill him by blocking his exit as the heat intensifies. He survives by turning first into a badger and then into a magpie. He kills the angry old bull chief of the buffalo and finds Buffalo-Woman. After the chief's death, the buffalo divide into many herds and scatter, and Without-Wings returns to his people. [Dorsey 1906a; Murie 1989]

Bundle
See *Medicine Bundles.*

Bundle Societies
Pawnee, *Plains*
Each Pawnee village has a medicine bundle filled with specific objects. Their significance is related in the story of the bundle's origin, which often declares that the founder of the village was created by a star or group of stars (see *Stars and Starlore*). Bundle societies construct an altar and perform rituals honoring the bundle. The wife of the bundle keeper or another female relative safeguards the bundle when it is not in use. When the owner of a bundle dies, it is passed on to his son.

Membership in a bundle society is usually gained through kinship. The two types of bundles are the cuharipi, "rains wrapped up," which belong to the village and band, and karu su, "sack," warrior bundles belonging to an individual, who uses them to gain success in war. Warrior bundles are opened before a war party sets out. [Dorsey 1906a; Murie 1989]

Bungling Host
A type of story character common throughout North America, distinguished by his inability to imitate other animals in getting food. For example, Coyote watches animals produce food by

letting oil drip from their hands, cutting their hands and feet, or killing their children for food. He sees birds produce food through song, and wood being transformed into food. When he attempts to use these methods, not only does he not obtain food, he often ends up injuring himself. See also *Trickster* and *Woodtick* (Coeur d'Alene).

Burnt Face
Crow, *Plains*

A young boy who is responsible for creating the *medicine wheel.* As a child, Burnt Face falls into a fire while playing. Because his scarred face is the cause of much ridicule and shame, the boy stays in his lodge and cries most of the time. When Burnt Face grows to manhood he takes a journey to the high mountains, where he fasts. During the daylight hours he moves large stones to form a large circle, the medicine wheel.

One day Burnt Face sees a tornado. As it approaches, it becomes a great *eagle.* The eagle asks Burnt Face why he is crying, and the man explains that he hates his scarred face. The eagle takes Burnt Face back to his lodge where two young eagles ask him to make bows and arrows for them. When Burnt Face is finished, the eagles bring him a mirror, which shows the reflection of his new scarless face. The large eagle asks Burnt Face to help him rid the river near the eagle lodge of Long Otter, an animal that eats baby eagles. Burnt Face feeds Long Otter rocks, and the fast-moving river water carries Long Otter far downstream. The eagle promises to stay close by and help Burnt Face, who returns to his village, marries, and lives to be very old. Since then, many people go to the medicine wheel to fast during their vision quests. [Lowie 1960]

Burnt-Belly
Pawnee, *Plains*

A beggar who is ridiculed because of his poverty. Burnt-Belly wants to marry a certain woman. When he begs food from her lodge, her brother makes fun of him and teases his sister by telling her she will marry Burnt-Belly. Humiliated, Burnt-Belly retreats to a stream where he meets a finely dressed young man whose power comes from the sun, and who tells Burnt-Belly how to become a great warrior.

Burnt-Belly follows the old man's instructions and joins a war party, despite the protests of the other warriors. He takes a scalp and gives it to the leader of the war party. Then he returns and fasts for four days. At the end of his fast he dives into the water four times, emerging the last time beautifully clothed. Afterward he meets the woman he desires. Not recognizing him, she falls in love with him. They spend the night together in the lodge of her brother, who is pleased with the marriage. Later Burnt-Belly repels an enemy attack and leads a successful war party. The village wonders who he is, and he finally reveals his identity to the surprised and ashamed villagers. See also *Dirty Boy.* [Dorsey 1906a; Murie 1989]

Bushy Heads
Seneca, *Northeast*

See *False Faces.*

Busk
Seminole, Oklahoma and *Southeast;* Creek and southeastern Iroquoian tribes, *Southeast*

See *Green Corn Dance.*

Butterfly

In the story of the *Apache Bear Dance,* butterflies entice girls from the underworld. The Hopi Butterfly clan is linked with the Badger clan in their migration story, *Honannyamu.* The Zuni kachina *Paiyatemu* creates butterflies by playing a flute. In the Navajo *Ajilee* the hero uses a butterfly disguise. This story cycle also tells of the origin of butterflies. [Fewkes 1910]

Caballeros
Yaqui, *Southwest*
See *Yaqui Easter Ceremony.*

Calling God
Navajo, *Southwest*
See *Talking God.*

Calumet
See *Pipe.*

Cannibal(s)
Cannibals are among the most common and widespread figures in Native American mythology. *Big Man-Eater* (Alabama) is a hunter who eats parts of his wife's body. *Cannibal Woman* appears in Seneca stories. *Cannibal-at-the-North-End-of-the-World* captures the initiate in the Kwakiutl *Hamatsa* dance. *Deadoendjadases* and *Ongwe Ias* are Seneca cannibal monsters. *Dzoavits* (Shoshone) is a cannibal giant. The Pawnee figure *Gambler* is a cannibal. *Hagondes* (Seneca) is a long-nosed clown who frightens children, as do the Ute *Siats. Irraq* (Inupiaq) is a baby cannibal much like the Arapaho *Raw Gums.* The Maliseet ice giant cannibal is called *Kiwahkw. Nauyavinaaluk* (Povungnituk) dies of a stomachache from eating women and children. The Ute have the cannibal water monster *Paiyuk. Pulekukwerek* is a Yurok figure who kills a cannibal. *Saya* is the Beaver culture hero who has adventures with a cannibal. *Stonecoats* (Seneca) and *Witiko* (northern Canada) are cannibals. In the Zuni stories of *Women's Ways,* a girl acting as a man gets caught by a cannibal (see also *Zuni Ritual Cycle). Hantceciitehi* (Arapaho) are cannibal dwarfs. The Bella Coola have a *Winter Ceremonial Season* where cannibals are an important part of the performances. See also *Cannibal Grandmother.*

Cannibal Grandmother
Pawnee, *Plains*
A powerful old woman who lives alone on the prairie with a poor boy and four vicious dogs. The largest dog is called Afraid-of-Nothing. Whenever *buffalo* come near the cannibal grandmother's tipi, the dogs scare them away. The boy wears black moccasins and leggings and a buffalo robe painted yellow. The old woman does not like the tough deer and buffalo meat the boy eats. Preferring tender

human flesh, she sends him out to kill humans for her. The knowledge that the old woman is eating human flesh angers the buffalo. They hold a council and decide to kill the boy. Suspecting the danger he is in, the boy prepares for a long journey. He gives into the old woman's begging and reluctantly kills four humans for her to eat while he is away, although he feels sorry for the humans and beseeches her to stop eating them. He then tells her to tie up the dogs and to release all of them except Afraid-of-Nothing after he is gone.

After traveling many days without seeing any game, the hungry boy finally kills a buffalo. As he is cutting into its back to get one of its kidneys, he hears a woman's voice telling him to take the kidneys, but to walk away and not look back. He sees a woman dressed in a new buffalo robe, the mate of the dead buffalo. She revives her husband and tells the boy to wait for them on a hill. They come to him and ask, "What is your secret for killing humans?" He shows them his magic bow, which is really a black snake. They take him to their village, where an old buffalo warns the boy he is about to be killed. The buffalo villagers challenge the boy to a number of contests. Although he wins them all, the buffalo chase him, trying to kill him. He flees to a high tree and calls for his dogs to help him. Hearing his cry, the old grandmother releases Afraid-of-Nothing, who leads the other dogs in driving away the buffalo and rescuing the boy.

At home, the boy implores the old cannibal grandmother to stop eating human flesh. He gives her a bag of seeds and sends her north to plant the seeds and live off them. The old cannibal grandmother and her descendants become agriculturalists (see *Agriculture*). The boy goes south and becomes known as a great *warrior*. His descendants are warriors who never plant seeds. [Dorsey 1906a]

Cannibal Woman
Seneca, *Northeast*

A woman who becomes a *cannibal* as a result of mistreating her husband's three dogs whenever he hunts. After the husband leaves to go hunting, the woman prepares a piece of meat for herself but offers nothing to the dogs. As she slices the meat, the dogs use their powerful *orenda* to make the woman cut her finger badly. She sucks the blood to stop the bleeding. She likes the taste of the blood so much that she sucks all the blood out of the finger and proceeds to cut each of her fingers to suck the blood out of them. By this time she no longer cares for the taste of animal meat and forgets about her cooking. She cuts each of her limbs and sucks out all the blood from them. She cuts off and eats pieces of her flesh. Then she kills and eats her young child.

The dogs run to warn the husband not to return home, telling him that his wife has become a cannibal. The man and the dogs find refuge with a poor elderly couple, and go hunting to provide the couple with meat. The old man tells the visitors the history of his people, and adopts the man as his own. Because of the faithfulness of the dogs, it is believed that when a person loves a *dog*, she or he receives great power. Dogs know all that is said, but do not have the power to speak. If a person is cruel to his or her dog, the dog's orenda can cause that person harm. See also *Ongwe Ias*. [Curtin and Hewitt 1918]

Cannibal-at-the-North-End-of-the-World
(Bakbakwakanooksiwae)
Kwakiutl, *Northwest Coast*

A *cannibal* spirit who abducts novices at the beginning of the *Hamatsa* dance and takes them to the far north, where they develop a desire to eat human flesh. When the initiates return, their spirits are often associated with masks of great bird monsters who live off human flesh. See also *Tsetseka*. [Boas 1921, 1930]

Cannibalism

The Tsimshian dance *Gather-on-the-Water* features cannibalistic activity. After *Taikomol*, the Yuki creator, created people they began to eat one another. For a similar account see *Tcu-unnyikita*, the Pima creation story. Cannibalism is believed to be practiced by Navajo skinwalkers *(Yenald-looshi)*. [Calkowski 1975; Walens 1981]

Cansasa

Lakota, *Plains*

"Red, red wood," from canhasa, "red bark." Dried willow or dogwood tree bark mixed with tobacco and smoked ceremonially. Also known as Kinnikinic. [Powers 1975]

Capa

Lakota, *Plains*

Spirit of *Beaver,* considered responsible for work, provisions, and domestic faithfulness. [Powers 1975]

Cardinal Directions

Designated in rituals, they serve as a means of orientation for nearly every Native American culture. For examples, see *Green Corn Dance* (Southeast) and *Horse Dance* (Plains).

Caskyet

Potawatomi, *Northeast*

A *shaman* who uses ventriloquism and juggling to prepare for a ceremony to locate lost possessions. [Landes 1968]

Cat

See *Sleep* and *Underwater Cats.*

Catamenia

Seneca, *Northeast*

The menstrual period. During *menstruation,* a woman is considered to have the power to overcome the hunting power of men as well as male spiritual power to heal. For this reason, menstruating women are warned not to touch hunting implements and to avoid certain healing ceremonies. [Curtin and Hewitt 1918; Hewitt 1902]

Cautantowwit

Narragansett, *Northeast*

The *creator* honored in regular rituals. Cautantowwit lives in a house in the southwest part of the known world. When heroic men and women die, at least one of their two souls dwells in Cautantowwit's house. [Fisher 1946]

Cawacnenitan

Arapaho, *Plains*

"Rising people." The name the Arapaho use to distinguish themselves from European-Americans. *Nihansan* gives the people this name after he creates them, explaining that they are to lie on the ground at night and rise in the morning. [Dorsey and Kroeber 1903]

Cedar

Nootka, *Northwest Coast*

Cedar is considered to have powerful properties. In stories supernaturals use shredded cedar bark as *medicine.* Cedar necklaces are often worn by participants in a variety of ceremonies. People also use *urine* stored in containers of red cedar to wash their hair and to gain effective power. [Sapir and Swadesh 1939]

Cedar Tree

Yuchi, *Southeast*

The cedar tree gains its red color and medicinal powers from the blood of the decapitated head of a wizard slain by two young men. The wizard plays tricks on the sun, making her dash quickly across the sky. The heroes stop him by cutting off his head. See also *Neshanu,* the Pawnee creator who transforms Mother Corn into a cedar tree. [Hudson 1976]

Cetan

Lakota, *Plains*

Spirit of *Hawk,* considered responsible for swiftness and endurance. [Powers 1975]

Chahnameed

Pequot, *Northeast*

"The great eater, the glutton." A *giant* who lives alone on an island. Chahnameed lusts after a beautiful young woman walking along the beach of the mainland. He paddles to the mainland and convinces her to live with him as his wife. Eventually the wife grows tired of being left alone while Chahnameed hunts to satisfy his voracious appetite, and she decides to escape from the island. She makes several *dolls,* decorating them with paint and shells. putting bits of her own feces on them to empower them (see *Fecal Power).* When Chahnameed returns, he finds his wife gone and his house full of dolls. Each time he turns his back, the dolls scream at him. He rushes to the shore of the island and sees his wife paddling rapidly toward the mainland. When he pursues her, she pulls a long hair from her head. The hair becomes a stiff spear that she uses to kill Chahnameed, after which she returns to her people. [Speck 1903]

Changer
Quileute, *Northwest Coast*
A culture hero who kills Wolf. See *Wolf Society.*

Changing Bear Maiden (tcikee cac nadleehe)
Navajo, *Southwest*
The female apotheosis of evil. The sister of many brothers, Changing Bear Maiden first appears as the model female, a good housekeeper and cook. Her brothers, hunters and controllers of game, are good providers.

Coyote (or *Ma?ii*) lusts after Changing Bear Maiden and is jealous of her brothers. He woos her, but she has been warned about him. She is very demanding and requires that he pass test after test (see also *Test Theme),* including being killed four times by her. Not only does Coyote pass these tests, he is the model gentleman throughout, and succeeds in winning her love. Through their intimate conversations during lovemaking, Coyote learns the secrets of the family and begins to exploit them. Changing Bear Maiden remains passionately in love with Coyote, causing her brothers to turn against her. This leads to her physical transformation into a vicious bear in front of her horrified brothers.

Day after day Changing Bear Maiden seeks her enemies, returning home every night battered and wounded. During the night she magically extracts the arrows that have penetrated her skin and heals her wounds. In time she defeats her enemies and directs her attention to destroying

her brothers. All but one of the brothers flee, heading in each cardinal direction. The youngest hides beneath the fire in their hogan. Each morning, Changing Bear Maiden pours water on the ground and watches to see which way it runs. She sets off in that direction, catching and killing the brothers who have fled that way. After four days she kills all her brothers save the youngest.

Changing Bear Maiden searches for and eventually finds her youngest brother. But he has a wind guardian (see *Nilchi?i*) who directs his actions. Changing Bear Maiden tries many methods to destroy him, but Wind always helps him avoid her attack. Finally, while running with Changing Bear Maiden in pursuit, he finds the plant in which she has hidden her vital organs (a technique some figures like Coyote use so they cannot be killed). He shoots the hidden organs, and Changing Bear Maiden falls down, her blood spouting in two directions and running across the ground. Wind instructs the brother to keep the two rivers of blood from meeting, for if they do Changing Bear Maiden will revive. See also *Mountainway.* [Haile 1943a; Luckert 1979; Matthews 1897]

Changing Masks Song(s)
Nootka, *Northwest Coast*
A category of *songs* sung during rituals involving masks (see *Masks and Masking).* The song is the cue for the dancers to change masks. Dancers hold their masks in place with their teeth. On hearing the Changing Masks song, each dancer drops his mask into a blanket. He puts on another mask lying ready for him nearby, turns quickly, and continues dancing. [Amoss 1978; Clutesi 1969; Kenyon 1977; Sapir and Swadesh 1939]

Changing Woman
Navajo, *Southwest*
The daughter of Long Life Boy and Happiness Girl (see *Sa?ah naghai bikeh hozho*), reared by *First Man and First Woman.* Receiver of the *mountain soil bundle* containing the powers of *creation* (including the life-forces represented by

her parents), Changing Woman is synonymous with life and the power of creation. She grows to maturity and old age only to endlessly repeat the life cycle. She is the foundation for and the measure of time. No other Navajo figure is so singularly beneficial, although with the Navajo penchant for pairing even Changing Woman is occasionally given an evil twin. She is known variously as *Whiteshell Woman,* Turquoise Woman, Abalone Woman, and Jet Woman, acknowledging the various dresses into which she changes. Her name may be understood as referring alternatively to her changes of dress, her correspondence with the change of seasons, and her repetitions of the life cycle.

Changing Woman is the mother of the twins *Monster Slayer and Born for Water,* whose father is *Sun.* She is central to *Blessingway* and its girls' puberty rite, *kinaalda.* Changing Woman is credited with giving origin to the Navajo people (see *Navajo People, Origin of).* She also appears in *Beadway, Eagleway, Monsterway,* and *Shootingway* mythology and ritual. Counterparts to Changing Woman include the Apache *White Painted Woman* (see also *Apache Creation and Emergence),* the Keresan *Iatiku,* and the Pawnee *Moon Woman.* [Goddard 1933; Matthews 1897; Newcomb 1940; Newcomb and Reichard 1937; Reichard 1939; Wyman 1970]

Chapayeka
Yaqui, *Southwest*
Costumed figures portraying common soldiers who belong to the fariseo society, representing the evil ones who persecuted and executed Christ (see *Yaqui Easter Ceremony).* The chapayekas wear helmetlike masks (see *Masks and Masking)* and old pants tied at the ankle. Blankets wrap their upper bodies, over which old coats are worn. They wear deer hoof–rattle belts and strings of cocoon rattles about their ankles. They carry a long wooden sword in their right hand and a wooden dagger in their left, making a distinctive sound by clacking the dagger on the sword.

New chapayeka masks are secretly made every year, using cow or goat hide, or sometimes card-board. The mask covers the head, with almost imperceptible openings for vision. The masks are either humanoid in appearance, with long ears, or resemble animals or birds that may or may not have long ears. The masks often portray an identifiable character: a policeman, a Mexican soldier, an Indian, an Anglo tourist, an Oriental, a hobo. The masks have potential for both good and evil. They are identified with Jesus by means of a cross painted inside the mask where the forehead touches it. This, along with any red paint used on the mask, represents the blood of Christ. The Chapayekas' function, however, is to portray the evil ones who captured and crucified Christ. The maskers carry the crosses of their rosaries in their mouths as long as they wear their masks, as protection against the evil power of the masks and the presence they invoke. The masks, swords, and daggers, along with the materials left over from making these objects, are consumed in the fire that burns Judas. [Painter 1986]

Charm
See Cudak, a Puyallup woman's charm, and Keskamsit (Maliseet), a power found in objects. See also *Amulet.*

Chepi
Narragansett, *Northeast*
Spirits of the *dead.* They give information to entranced *medicine people.* [Fisher 1946]

Chiefs
Omaha, *Plains*
See *Nikagahi.*

Childbirth
Navajo *Blessingway* is a rite of childbirth. The Zuni story *Flood Subsided by Sacrifice* describes a place associated with blessings for childbirth.

Child-of-the-Water
Apache, *Southwest*
See *Apache Creation and Emergence; Europeans, Origin of; Na ih es;* and *White Painted Woman* for

information about this Apache culture hero. He is similar to the Navajo *Born for Water.*

Children

All over North America stories are told in which children are abducted, frightened, eaten, or treated in some terrifying or horrible manner. Likely these stories are told to children as a means of disciplining them. But they are also stories that perhaps slightly older children tell one another, relishing, and maybe embellishing, the terror. Adults surely find some enjoyment in telling these stories as well. Since many of these stories are about punishing the offenses of misbehavior, they may serve as reflections of cultural values.

Bogey figures are numerous: *Apotamkin* (Maliseet), who frightens children; the monster *Asin* (Alsea); the giantess *Dzoo-noo-qua* (Kwakiutl), who steals children; *Haakapainizi* (Kawaiisu), a grasshopper who eats children; the long-nosed cannibal clown *Hagondes* (Seneca), who frightens children; *Indacinga,* the Ponka bogeyman; *Kwanokasha,* a Choctaw spirit kidnapper; the Cree water lynxes *(Michi-Pichoux),* who steal children; *Nahgane* (Slavey), a bush giant; the frightening owl *Owner-of-Bag* (Arapaho); *Seatco* (Nisqually), who makes children into slaves; *Siats* (Ute), kidnapping cannibals; *Snee-nee-iq,* a Pacific northwest coast child-eating female monster; and *Tammatuyuq* (Povungnituk), who specializes in killing infants.

Some stories feature special abilities of children. For example, the Seminole *little people* can be seen only by children and medicine people. Other stories describe the remorse and agony suffered by adults when children have been stolen. The story of *Hadentheni and Hanigongendatha* (Seneca) warns that children must never be mistreated. In the Algonquian stories of the *Aurora Borealis,* children are cautioned not to make noise lest they be stolen by spirits.

Children themselves are avid storytellers. Examples include the Eskimo *Story Knife Tales* and the Navajo skinwalker *Yenaldlooshi.*

Many Native American rituals involve children. From the time of conception through puberty, ritual occasions effect movement along the cycle of life. Birth is often the occasion of ritual. In many cultures names are formally bestowed. Sometimes the first laugh is an occasion marked by ritual. Puberty rites mark the end of childhood. Even the discipline of children takes a ritual form, consistent with the stories mentioned above; see Apache *Mountain Spirits* and the Hopi *Soyoko,* masked figures who help discipline children.

Chimikyanakowa
Zuni, *Southwest*
"That which was the beginning." Men devote years of their lives to learning these stories of origin (see *Story Types),* which are formally recited once every four or eight years by *Kiaklo,* a masked *kachina* figure. [Tedlock 1083]

Chingichnich
Juaneño, Luiseño, Chumash, *California*
The most important of four brothers responsible for *earthquakes.* Chingichnich taught the ritual practices of *initiation* by drinking a jimsonweed medicine (see *Datura).*

Chipmunk's Stripes
Seneca, *Northeast*
Chipmunk challenges Bear to prove the power of her *orenda* by preventing the sun from rising. When the sun comes up as usual, Chipmunk taunts Bear, who becomes angry and chases Chipmunk to his hole. Chipmunk slips by Bear's outstretched paw, but three of her claws catch in his back. Since that time, Chipmunks have borne three marks across their backs. [Curtin and Hewitt 1918]

Chiricahua Wind Way
Navajo, *Southwest*
A mythological and ceremonial complex of the Holyway classification, believed to have been adopted from the Chiricahua Apache during the time Navajos and Apaches were confined at Fort Sumner, 1864–1868. It is related to Navajo Wind Way.

The hero of this cycle of stories is a good hunter who lives with his mother, father, and sister. One day on returning from hunting, the hero comes upon the home of Wind and laughs because it is so filthy. Wind believes the hunter is laughing at the fawn meat hanging in his house. In retaliation Wind withholds game. From this time on the hero cannot find so much as a field rat to hunt, and his family suffers from hunger.

Wind Man and Wind Woman finally release a deer, Wind Deer. The hero tracks it for four days, but each time he attempts to shoot it he is unable to release the arrow (see the Visionary version of *Nightway*). He continues to follow the deer, which leads him over four different kinds of cacti. As he jumps over each cactus, the hunter feels increasing pain. Finally he falls unconscious, his body all twisted up. When his family learns of his injuries from *Big Fly*, the father undertakes a series of efforts to get help to cure his son. Eventually Wind comes to his aid and uses varieties of cactus to revive the hunter.

Although Wind has yet to release the game, the hero again goes hunting, this time finding himself in the home of Snake People. Impressed with the women because of their slimness and way of walking, he marries a snake woman and she gives birth to his children. In time he grows

Navajo ritual curing performed upon a sandpainting in the Chiricahua Wind Way ceremonial. Photograph by John B. Breed. © National Geographic Society.

tired of his snake family and announces he is leaving them. In revenge his father-in-law sends a lightning storm to prevent his return home. With the advice given him by Big Fly and the power he has acquired, he is able to survive the storm and finally arrives home.

In a dream the hero is instructed to make offerings and say a prayer on the top of a hill, then look on the south slope. When he does so, he discovers a cave and investigates it. Inside he finds a man and woman who control the deer (see *Master/Mistress of Animals*). They treat him to venison, then release enough deer for him to live on. He becomes a successful hunter once again.

The next episode involves the hunter shooting a whirlwind (see *Big Star Way* and *Navajo Wind Way* for similar episodes). In a dream he is warned to avoid a particular hill. At first he does, but when his hunting success declines he questions the importance of the dream and goes to the forbidden hill. There he meets male and female Big Dippers who ask him questions he cannot answer about the Wind Way ceremony. He pleads with them to provide him further instructions. They perform a ceremony for him during which he learns taboos on eating certain parts of deer. Finally, he acquires full knowledge of Chiricahua Wind Way, initiating the ceremonial tradition. See also *Nilchi?i*.

Chiwakiia
Crow, *Plains*

"To ask repeatedly." Prayer, the act of prayer (see *Prayer and Prayersticks),* considered the most basic act of the *Sun Dance.* For chiwakiia, dancers state their intentions and repeat their vows before *Akbaatatdia* ("the one who has made everything"), giving their reasons for dancing the Sun Dance. See also *Dissuua.* [Frey 1987]

Choctaw Emergence
Choctaw, *Southeast*

Human origins attributed to *emergence* from subterranean regions. According to the Choctaw, humans emerged at the well-known mound

Nanih Waiya, near Philadelphia, Mississippi. The Creeks, also known as the Muscogees, emerged first. They dried themselves in the sun and went east. The Cherokees emerged next. After they dried themselves, they tried to follow the trail of the Muscogees but got lost and ended up settling in the north. The third to emerge were the Chickasaws, who followed and settled near the Cherokees. The Choctaws came last and made their home at the place where they emerged.

Christianity
During much of the last 500 years Native Americans have contended with the presence of Christianity. Often their first contact with Americans of European ancestry was with Christian missionaries. Today a great many Native Americans are Christians; doubtless a whole mythology of Native American Christianity exists that is virtually unknown to non–Native American peoples.

Certainly the presence of Christianity has had a significant impact on Native American mythology and ritual. Much of this influence has led to changes in worldview, which in some cases is obvious. Particularly in earlier centuries missionaries identified many Native American mythological figures with the Christian devil, such as the Seneca *Hanisheonon.* This identity came to be incorporated into Native American identities of themselves. Native Americans, perhaps as a transition to Christianity, or to defend themselves against the presence of Christianity, have identified certain mythological figures with the Christian God: the Navajo *Begocidi; Hawenniyo,* the Iroquois False Face; the Yavapai Widapokwi (see *Widapokwi and Amchitapuka*—Amchitapuka is identified as Jesus); and the Okanagon creator, *Qoluncotun.* The Arapaho use the term *Hixtcaba Nihancan* to name the Christian God. The Seminole culture hero *Hisagita misa* is identified as Jesus Christ. The establishment of the figure broadly known as the Great Spirit may have resulted from the process of identifying specific Native American figures as equivalent to the Christian God.

The *Prophet Dance Movement* developed in the Great Basin area under Christian influences, as did the *Shaker Religion*. The *Yaqui Easter Ceremony* (see also *Talking Tree*) weaves Christian symbolism into a traditional Yaqui religious fabric. [Parmentier 1979; Ramsey 1977]

Chulyen

Tanaina, *Subarctic*

Crow, known for his ability to transform himself into any type of creature. Also classified as a *trickster*. Chulyen transforms himself into a handsome young man (see *Animal-Human Transformation*) and tricks the giant of Lake Iliamna into lending him his canoe. He travels about in the canoe, tricking animals and eating them. At one point Chulyen is devoured by a beluga whale but manages to kill the whale and escape through its blowhole.

Still disguised as a young man, Chulyen comes to a village. He deceives the villagers into thinking he is homeless because his family has eaten poisoned beluga whale meat. He charms the people so well that he ends up marrying the chief's daughter. When the villagers discover his true identity, they beat him to death before he can fly away. An old woman finds his discarded body and cuts off his beak to keep in her needlecase. Magpies defecate all over Chulyen's body, which is lying in the trash heap. This makes Chulyen so angry he comes back to life. He is furious with the magpies' lack of respect because he is considered to be the uncle of the magpies. Chulyen recovers his beak, but in his haste he puts it on crooked.

To get his revenge, Chulyen announces he has created a magic bridge to his home and invites all the animals to come over it. As Chulyen crosses the bridge he turns into a man. Impressed, the animals gather their families and prepare to follow him. As the last group of animals reaches the middle of the bridge, Chulyen jumps into the air and flies about. He tells the animals the magic bridge will enable them to fly also, and that all they have to do is jump off. They follow his instructions and plunge to their deaths. He watches them die and then eats their eyes. He leaves the country, vowing that from now on he will do good deeds.

Chulyen flies to a village where it is very cold. The people tell him that a rich man stole the sun and the moon. Chulyen goes to the rich man's house and watches until he sees the man's daughter fetching water, then drops one of his feathers into her bucket. The girl drinks the water and the feather and becomes pregnant. Soon she bears a healthy baby boy. As the child grows, he keeps crying for the sun and moon to play with. Finally his devoted grandfather gives them to him. When the child is alone with his new toys, he changes into a crow, having been Chulyen in disguise the entire time. Chulyen flies back to the village with the sun and the moon. The rich man feels so badly about losing his only grandson that he changes his ways. He is kind to his neighbors and never again tries to steal the sun and moon. The villagers thank Chulyen and accept him into the village. See also *Light* and *Guguyni* (Raven). [Nelson 1974; Turner and Edmonds 1968]

Ciciyogozi

Kawaiisu, *Great Basin*

Earthworm. A large, brown, shiny worm that attracts the attention of *Coyote*. Coyote attempts to wear the shiny worm, first as a belt and then as a bracelet, but he is not pleased with either effect. He ties the worm around his neck like a scarf. As Coyote admires himself, the worm tightens around his neck and chokes him to death. [Zigmond 1980]

Cimmis

Nootka, *Northwest Coast*

A supernatural being who gives power for obtaining wealth. [Clutesi 1969]

Cinauau

Paiute, *Great Basin*

Creator brothers who meet to decide the fate of the Ute people. At first the younger brother wants food to be abundant for the people, but his brother convinces him that if things are too easy people will become lazy and restless and begin to fight. Consequently people have to work to produce and gather food.

The brothers also argue about death. The younger brother wants a *dead* person to come back the morning after dying, but the older brother disagrees and mandates that once people die they are gone forever. The younger brother is filled with sorrow about death. One day while he is out walking, he comes across his brother's son playing. He shoots and kills the boy. When he returns to the village, his brother is inquiring about the whereabouts of his son. No one knows where the boy is, and the younger brother says nothing. The father finally finds his son's body and mourns for a long time. The younger brother reminds him it was he who mandated that the dead should never return. He says he is glad the older brother is the first to suffer because of his mandate. At this point the older brother knows who killed his son. Enraged, he wants to kill his brother. As his anger increases, the earth rocks and makes groaning sounds, and darkness falls. Fierce storms rage, lightning flashes, and thunder roars. In terror the younger brother flees to his father, *Tavwots,* for protection. [Lowie 1924]

Cipyapos
Potawatomi, *Northeast*
Twin brother of the culture hero *Wiske.* Cipyapos guards the afterworld and receives souls of the *dead.* [Densmore 1929]

Clairvoyance
Divination, the power to see things not apparent to the ordinary eye, is incorporated into and essential to many Native American religious cultures. Clairvoyance has developed into full rites, as in the northern Plains *Yuwipi* rites and the widely practiced *shaking tent* rites. Clairvoyance is also often used to diagnose the cause of ill health. *Syowoe* designates the power of clairvoyance

among the Nooksack and other Pacific northwest tribes. An Abenaki person with the power to divine lost objects is called *Medawlinno.* The Nootka have divining songs *(Nana csyak).* Divination is often a technique of diagnosing illness, as in the *Navajo Ritual Process.* See also *Medicine.*

Clam Shell
Pawnee, *Plains*
A woman who has outer skin like that of a witch, but inner skin that is smooth and delicate. A story tells how a young woman named Young Duck came to be Clam Shell. A man captures a diving duck but releases it at his wife's request. The wife later gives birth to girl whom she names Young Duck. As a child, Young Duck likes to imitate a duck by sitting in a hole filled with water. In a dream she is given a stick with the power to help her collect firewood.

Young Duck grows into a long-haired beauty. Many young men court her with games and flutes, but she ignores them, until one day she invites Hawk to visit her. Hawk changes himself to human form so he can marry Young Duck (see *Animal-Human Transformation).* After the marriage, a jealous old woman kills Young Duck by thrusting a fire-hardened stick into her ear. The old woman blows into Young Duck's mouth and removes her skin down to the waist. She exchanges skins with Young Duck and throws the girl's body into the water. In the village she pretends to be Young Duck. As time passes, however, her skin begins to rot. The efforts of many medicine men to heal her skin are unsuccessful. Finally Crow Doctor is summoned. He recognizes the old woman, and she is thrown into the water.

At the river, Hawk hears his wife singing. Becoming a hawk again, he flies up and down the shoreline for four days. Finally he sees smoke coming from a tipi and flies down to investigate. Inside the tipi are four girls, a woman, and his wife. At first Young Duck refuses to see her husband, because her body appears as that of an old woman. She asks Hawk to take her up to the sky and drop her to the ground. He agrees, and flying upward he lets her fall. When she lands, the old woman's skin cracks and comes off, and Hawk discovers that his wife has become Clam Shell. See also *Dog Boy* and *White-Sun.* [Dorsey 1906a]

Clan(s)

Clan is a common social unit marking lineage from a common ancestor through the female (matrilineal) or male (patrilineal) sides. Rules concerning marriage and residence (within or outside the clan) define basic social relationships. Clans and clan groupings, called phratries, often have stories of their origins and their relations with other clans. Frequently, admission to secret societies or other ritual organizations is restricted by clan.

Among the Crow, *Aassahke* is the term for clan aunts and uncles, and *Ashammaleaxia* is the term for clan. The Haida Eagle clan is called *Djilaqons. Qanekelak* (Bella Bella), a killer whale, is a clan ancestor. *Wiske,* the Potawatomi culture hero, originated clans. See also *Hanga* (Omaha), *Hopi Clan Grouping or Phratry,* and *Navajo People, Origin of.*

Cloud(s)

Pueblo, *Southwest*

As Cloud People *(Shiwanna),* clouds are associated with *rain,* rainmakers, and *rain priests* (uwanammi), hence with the fertilization of the earth. Humans who live good lives become clouds or Cloud People after death. Pueblo funerary practice commonly utilizes a cotton mask (see *Masks and Masking)* to cover the face of the deceased. The Hopi hold Spider Woman *(Kokyan wuhti)* in high esteem because her web looks like clouds. Prayer feathers and the *pahos* to which they are often attached (see *Prayer and Prayersticks)* are physically associated with the lightness of clouds and are used as offerings to the *dead.* The dead, who are closely associated with *kachinas,* eat the essence or odor of food rather than the substance. If properly remembered and fed, the dead serve the living as clouds and rain bringers, bringing rain and life. See also *Palulukon,* the Hopi horned water serpent who is the pet of clouds. [Parsons 1930a]

Clowns and Clowning Societies

Clowning societies are common to Pueblo cultures, most of which have clowns and clowning societies. Perhaps most well known are the mudhead clowns *(Koyemshi)* of the Hopi and Zuni and the distinctive black-and-white-striped clowns known as Koshare and Koyala (see also *Kacale).* The Zuni *Newekwe,* paricularly known for its defiling acts, is a curing society (for the story of the origin of the Newekwe, see also *Paiyatemu).* A group called the Black Eyes are clowns at Taos. At Jemez most people belong to one of two clown societies, Tabosh and Tsuntatabosh. At Hopi there are a great many clowns (see *Tsuku).* The Keresan creator *Iatiku* produces a clown from her epidermal waste.

Generally, Pueblo clowning consists of gluttony, including eating the inedible; simulating sexual activities; playing games and teasing onlookers; begging; joking; burlesquing ritual and ceremony; performing skits satirizing individuals or elements of one's own society, or, more likely, other societies (other pueblos, Navajos, and especially European-Americans); acting and speaking in opposites; inverse or backwards behavior; and doing virtually anything to make people laugh. Settings for clowning are frequently the most serious and important of ceremonial and ritual occasions. Clowns often perform at the same time as *kachinas.* See also *Plaza Dances* and *Shalako.*

Clowning has commonly been interpreted as comic relief from otherwise overly serious and extensive ritual activities. This is at best a partial understanding, and not at all satisfying. Because clowning tests boundaries by breaking taboos, reversing the normal, and performing the unthinkable, great power is unleashed. The power invoked by clowns is none other than the power of *creation,* that is, the power that orders the world and gives value to its many parts. The way the world is created and ordered, as well as the way a society is organized and human behavior established, finds its meaning through clowning because clowning demonstrates how ludicrous and dangerous are the alternatives. The power generated in clowning is surely why clowns are often identified as the most powerful *healers.*

For other clowns and clowning activities in the southwest U.S., see also: *Mountain Spirits, Apache Bear Dance,* and *Apache Creation and Emergence* (Apache); *Water Sprinkler* (Navajo); *Yaqui Easter Ceremony* (Yaqui); *Kuksu Cult* and *Kuksu-hesi* (California); as well as *Hagondes* (Seneca long-nosed cannibal clown), *Nolemahigan* (Penobscot Clown Dance), and the Seminole *Soup Dance,* where men dress as women. [Bourke 1886; Hieb 1972; Makarius 1970; Parsons 1930a; Parsons and Beals 1934; Sekaquaptewa 1979; Steward 1930, 1931; Tedlock 1975; Titiev 1971]

Color

Color is widely used by Native Americans in mythology and ritual. Rarely is the presence of color simply incidental. Color designates values and correlates with place designations like the

Pueblo striped clowns. Courtesy, Museum of New Mexico, T. Harmon Parkhurst, photographer.

directional orientations. See also *Birds, Origin of Colors* (Kathlamet) and *Cedar Tree* (Yuchi), which tells why cedar sap is red. [Applegate 1979]

Comedy

See *Clowns and Clowning Societies, Humor, Jokes and Joking,* and *Joking Relationships.*

Comet

Catawba, *Southeast*
See *Ugni.*

Coming-Sun

Pawnee, *Plains*

A young man who, with the assistance of North Wind, becomes a powerful buffalo hunter, prophet, and medicine man, only to lose his powers because he cannot resist *women.* North Wind entrusts Coming-Sun with a bag of medicine and gives him knowledge of birds, animals, grasses, and trees. He also gives Coming-Sun buzzard feathers; when worn on the heads of warriors, they cause great clouds of dust to rise and hide the warriors. Coming-Sun is given the power to summon buffalo with an eagle feather fastened to a pole. One night a woman comes to Coming-Sun's tipi, makes love to him, and steals the eagle feather. Because he prefers women to power, Coming-Sun loses all his power, becomes blind, and dies. [Dorsey 1906a]

Common Faces

Iroquois, Northeast
See False Faces.

Conception

Zuni, Southwest
See *Flood Subsided by Sacrifice.*

Conjuring

The practice of summoning a spirit for purposes such as finding lost objects or people, seeing into the future, determining guilt, or diagnosing disease. Conjuring is the special purview of the *shaking tent rites* (see also *Mistapew,* a figure with conjuring power; *Mostos,* a helping spirit; and *Witiko,* a cannibal monster overcome by conjuring). *Tcikapis,* the Montagnais culture hero, is skilled at conjuring. See also *Clairvoyance.* [Fogelson 1980; Hallowell 1940, 1942]

Cooked People (akna aahi)
or Daylight People (tekohannan aahoi)

Zuni, Southwest

Human beings, those who emerged from the earth (see *Zuni Emergence).* They are dependent upon cooked food. See also *Raw People* and *Sipofene.* [Tedlock 1979]

Copper

Tsimshian, Tlingit, *Northwest Coast*

A metal associated with the *Sun* and revered for its rarity, brilliance, and resilience as a tool or weapon. In some areas copper was used only for ornamentation. Some tribes used copper to make particular shieldlike objects, which they referred to as "coppers." Others used copper as a crest. Among tribes along the Great Lakes, copper was treated as a gift from beings who lived under the water. [Boas 1916; Swanton 1909]

Copper Woman

Chipewyan, Dogrib, *Subarctic*

The first female. She has sex with a dog who transforms into a man at night. Their children are the Chipewyan and other northern Athapaskans, known as the dog-ribbed people. The Dogrib are one of the largest indigenous populations in the Northwest Territories. They use the self-designation "Dogrib" when contrasting themselves to other Athapaskan groups such as the Chipewyan. See also *Dog Husband.* [Sheppard 1983]

Corn

Corn is grown by Native Americans throughout much of the area of the current United States, playing key roles in mythology and ritual among virtually all corn-growing cultures. In mythology, corn is usually personified as a woman, for example, the Cherokee *Selu;* the beautiful Seneca woman *Kanenhagenat;* the Pueblo *Corn Maidens* (as described in *Zuni Ritual Cycle* and *Flood Subsided by Sacrifice),* among whom *Yellow Woman* is perhaps best known; and the Pawnee *Corn Woman* (see *Grain-of-Corn Bundle).* Corn is not always female, however. The husband of the Seneca *Bean Woman* is Corn.

Many stories describe the origin of corn and its cultivation. The dwarf *Fas-ta-chee* brings corn to the Seminole, *Iouskeha* to the Huron, *Kanenhagenat* to the Seneca, and *Moon Woman* to the Pawnee. The Ute figure *Tavwots,* a rabbit, steals corn. The Pawnee creator *Neshanu* turns good people into corn when he destroys the world by flood. The Navajo *First Man and First Woman* find the powers of creation in ears of corn. *Okabewis* teaches the Ojibwa how to use corn. A common theme attributes the origins of cultivation to the mistreatment or killing of *Corn Woman,* as told in the story of *Selu.* A Seneca story tells of the *Weeping of the Corn* when it is unable to grow.

Corn, cornmeal, and corn pollen commonly symbolize fertility and *medicine.* Ritual uses of corn are manifold. The Navajo use *cornmeal* and corn pollen *(tadidiin)* widely in ritual (see *Sandpainting* and *Navajo Wind Way* for examples). Pueblo cultures use corn as important ritual objects (see *Mili* and *Honani).* Planting and harvest ceremonies occur in most corn-growing cultures. See, for example, *Green Corn Dance, Onenha* (Seneca corn dance), *Gondagonwisas* (Seneca corn harvest ceremony), and *Mesing Keo* (dancers who perform at the Delaware corn harvest Big House Ceremony).

Corn and Squash Medicine
Seneca, *Northeast*
Potent *medicine* for wounds. A Seneca hunter learned of this medicine from bears, beavers, and foxes who had transformed into humans and danced in the woods. These animals branded the hunter with a heated stick, instantly curing his wound with corn and squash medicine. They taught the hunter how to make the medicine, and

he used it to heal many people. Before his death, he made enough medicine to last 100 years. [Curtin and Hewitt 1918; Wallace 1972]

Corn Maidens
Zuni, *Southwest*
During the Corn Dance the six Corn Maidens stay in a shelter of boughs in the plaza. One of the bow priests desires the eldest sister and attempts to touch her. Offended, the Corn Maidens depart for the ocean in the southeast, taking all the corn in the village. Duck aids the maidens by tucking them under her wings and diving under the water. Without corn, the people endure famine for seven years. Every night the priests hold council, seeking help in finding the Corn Maidens. Finally, Newekwe Youth agrees to search for them, but demands that the priests keep strict retreat and make prayersticks for him while he is gone (see *Prayer and Prayersticks).* With the power gained from the retreating priests, Newekwe Youth is able to find the Corn Maidens, and returns with them. They come into Zuni Village, thus setting the precedent for the arrival of the Corn Maidens in the molawai ceremony (see *Zuni Ritual Cycle)* on the last day of *Shalako.* One version of the story includes the calling of the *Ahayuta,* the warrior twins, to search for the Corn Maidens. Although they are unsuccessful, their travels all over the world create the *Milky Way.* [Benedict 1935; Bunzel 1932; Cushing 1896; Parsons 1916; Stevenson 1905]

Corn Woman
A character found in many stories in which maize or corn is grown. Often she is murdered, sometimes decapitated, and her body dragged around a field; the first corn plants originate from her blood. Other stories tell of a beautiful female figure who appears as a single green stalk of corn and teaches *hunting* secrets and the importance of generosity before disappearing. In some Iroquoian traditions, Corn Woman is one of three sisters responsible for corn, beans, and squash. See also *Selu.*

Corncob Boy
Cochiti, *Southwest*

Cochiti *culture hero.* Beginning as a poor *orphan* who is often mocked and mistreated, Corncob Boy proves his worth in the successful management of the ceremonial rabbit hunt. His powers are many and directed to healing, hunting, weather forecasting, and warfare. He foretells the coming of European-Americans. Corncob Boy is the protagonist of many Cochiti tales. [Benedict 1931]

Cornmeal (naadaakaan)
Navajo, *Southwest*

Corn (naadaa) designates fertility and life. Cornmeal is used extensively in rituals to bestow health and life. It is sprinkled on sandpaintings to bless them, rubbed on the body after a ritual bath to dry the skin and bestow health, and used to mark the cardinal posts in a hogan during a hogan blessing, thus sanctifying a dwelling. Cornmeal is often used as a substitute for pollen *(tadidiin)* since it is more readily available. [Haile 1938a; Reichard 1974; Sapir and Hoijer 1942]

Cotsipamapot
Moapa, southern Nevada, *Great Basin*

The old woman *creator.* In the beginning, Cotsipamapot lives with her son and daughter on the only spot of earth not covered with water. She scatters earth all around her like seed, extending the land. Several times she sends her daughter out to see how much water still covers the earth. When the earth is large enough, she sends her daughter to look for people. The girl finds only one man. Cotsipamapot tells her to bring him to their lodge and take him as her husband. Not wanting to marry the man, the daughter attempts to drown him. But when she gets home, he is waiting for her.

Cotsipamapot tells the man to use a deer vertebra to file down the teeth of his wife's vagina so he can have intercourse with her (see also *Vagina Dentata).* The daughter beomes pregnant with many children. When she delivers them,

Cotsipamapot puts them in a bag and tells her son-in-law to take the bag to the center of the world. Each child receives a tribal name, and the children soon scatter around the earth. Cotsipamapot uses mud to make deer, rabbits, bears, and every type of animal. She creates all the *languages.* It is believed that Cotsipamapot lives eternally. She is responsible for all new human life, and people go to her when they die. [Lowie 1924; Swanson 1970]

Council of the Gods
Zuni, *Southwest*

See *Shalako.*

Coup
Lakota, Cheyenne, Iowa, *Plains*

From the French "coup," a blow, the basis of the *war* honor system. Coup were points awarded for striking an enemy and for acts of bravery and daring. The first man to touch an enemy was awarded "first coup" and gained the right to wear a golden eagle feather upright at the back of his head. The second man to touch the same enemy was entitled to wear an eagle feather tilted to the left. The third warrior to touch the enemy wore the feather horizontally. Accomplishing the fourth coup entitled one to wear a buzzard feather vertically from his head. Coup could also be indicated with face paint or painted stripes on leggings and on one's horse.

Coup were granted for touching a man, woman, or child and for stealing horses. Credit was given for touching—not killing—an enemy. To "count coup," one could touch with a hand, a lance, bow, rattle, or whip. All coup had to be witnessed. See also *Kanochisisin,* the Blackfoot ceremony to count coup, and *Scalping.* [Frey 1987; Grinnell 1962; Hassrick 1964; Lowie 1963; Powers 1975]

Coyote

Coyote is the figure who appears most widely in Native American stories; he is without doubt the best known. The preeminent *trickster,* he may also take the role of *culture hero,* although the aspects of culture and life he introduces often have a negative side to them. To the Chinook he is *Italapas.* The Navajo term for Coyote is *Ma?ii;* the Lakota word, *Mica.* He is *Skinkuts* in Kutenai and *Isil* in Cupeño. The Crow call him *Old Man Coyote.*

Coyote's origins are not often told, but the Pima consider him the offspring of the moon (see *Tcu-unnyikita*). He often travels with a companion, sometimes a brother, or with his family. Perhaps his most common companions are *Fox* (see also Achomawi *Silver Fox,* who is a cocreator with Coyote) and Wolf (see *Wolf Creates the Earth,* Paiute; and *Sunawavi,* Ute). Coyote also travels with the Alsea creator *Suku,* a bear, with whom he names all the things created. Coyote plays an important role in the *Navajo emergence.* The Kawaiisu team him with the bald-headed *Pikagoyu,* the Cheyenne with *Wihio,* the Kutenai with *Yaukekam. Woodtick* (Coeur d'Alene) wants to marry Coyote. The Kiowa figure *Sendeh* is capable of transforming into Coyote. Coyote often mistreats his companions (see *Ciciyogozi,* Kawaiisu), but is himself often tricked, as in the Huron tar baby story that depicts Pitch *(Sanopi)* as Coyote's antagonist. His trickery leads to *Badger's limitations.* When Coyote offends *Rolling Rock,* as told in a Pawnee story, the rock crushes him.

Coyote is always male, and his masculinity is exaggerated through frequent references to his penis, often depicted as being so large that it requires a pack to carry it in. Coyote's lust is expressed in his desire for *Changing Bear Maiden* and by his efforts to have sex with women by becoming a baby (see *Penis Baby),* although he forgets to transform his penis. Coyote's sexual desires even lead him to have incest with his mother-in-law or his daughter (see *Hummingbird*). In the Kawaiisu story this act leads to the departure of his children, who go to the sky and become stars in the *Big Dipper.* In the Navajo story of *Big Star Way,* Coyote tricks Younger Brother in order to sleep with Younger Brother's wife. He often exchanges skins with an unsus-

pecting hunter so that he may sleep with the hunter's wife (see *Ajilee*). Coyote is often credited with making *pleasurable sexual intercourse* by removing the teeth of *vagina dentata* (see *Korawini?i,* Paiute) or by moving the genitals to their present locations on the body. Coyote's appetite for menstrual blood determines practices in the Lakota girls' puberty rite, *Ta Tanka Lowanpi.* In a Kawaiisu story, Coyote chooses to eat carrion (see *Food Choices of Animals*).

As a culture hero, Coyote is widely held to be responsible for the finality of death (see *Nagaicho*). According to the Maidu, he also introduces work and suffering (see *Earth-Initiate, Earth-Maker*). The Apache believe Coyote had a role in the origin of Europeans (see *Europeans, Origin of*). The Kawaiisu tell a story in which Coyote gambles for the release of game (see *Inipi*), and he figures strongly in stories that tell of the release of *salmon.* In a Nez Perce story he kills Mosquito *(Wawa)* by gorging him with nose blood. The Zuni credit him with creating pubic hair (see *Paiyatemu*), while the Kawaiisu refer to Coyote's hair by the name used for moss *(Pazimora).* The Kawaiisu describe his creation of the Pazimora, a people who live to the north of them. He accompanies the Maidu creator *Kodoyanpe,* and is credited by the Pomo with stealing the sun, thus making the world dark (see *Madumda,* who is Coyote's brother, the creator).

Coyote is often depicted as a curious fellow who wants to do what everyone else does, regardless of his limitations. This often gets him into trouble, as in the widely told Eye Juggler story (see *Eyes, Substitution of*). In some cultures, Coyote is not only the wily trickster or the unpredictable culture hero, he is also a feared, malevolent shape shifter, as in the Navajo *Yenaldlooshi.* See also *Coyote and Eagle Steal Light, but Cause Winter* and *Coyote and Moon.* [Blue Cloud 1982; Bright 1977, 1980; Callaghan 1977; Chamberlain 1893, 1894; Chandler 1905; deAngelo 1973; Dixon 1900; Geertz 1987; Goodwin 1939; Kendall 1978, 1979; Laird 1978a; Lopez 1977; Milford 1941; Mourning Dove, 1933; Opler 1938b,

1940, 1942; Parks 1984; Pitkin 1977; Ramsey 1977; Shaul 1987; Silver and Wicks 1977; Trejo 1974]

Coyote and Eagle Steal Light, but Cause Winter

Zuni, *Southwest*

Coyote and *Eagle* are hunting companions. Coyote complains it is so dark he is unable to find any game and suggests to Eagle that they travel west in search of light. Coyote nearly drowns trying to cross a river over which Eagle easily flies. Eventually they come to *Kachina Village,* where the *kachinas* have light. They keep it in a box, opening it whenever they want light. Coyote and Eagle decide to borrow the box so they can have light with which to hunt. Eagle carries the box, but Coyote argues that as a chief, Eagle should not carry it. Eventually Eagle entrusts Coyote with the box. Curious to examine its contents, Coyote hides in the grass and opens it. The moon and sun slip out, taking the heat of the earth with them to the sky. This is why there is winter (see *Winter, Origin of).* See also *Light.* [Benedict 1935]

Coyote and Moon

Coeur d'Alene, *Plateau*

Coyote is originally chosen by the first humans to be the *Moon,* but they become dissatisfied because he takes advantage of his position in the sky to watch people on earth and divulge their secrets. He is replaced in the sky by Old-Man Chief (SpoxanitcElt), who travels about the world inspecting things Coyote has left undone. Coyote becomes angry because the *Sun* has killed some of his children. He cuts out the Sun's heart, and at once the earth becomes completely dark. Coyote attempts to carry the Sun's heart home in the dark but keeps falling. Finally he realizes he is getting nowhere. He puts Sun's heart back and light returns to earth. [Swanson 1970]

Coyoteway

Navajo, *Southwest*

See *Ma?ii.* [Luckert 1979]

Crazy Buffalo (Tatankan gnaskinyan)

Lakota, Plains

One who deceives young people in love.

Crazy Woman

Cree, Subarctic

A fearsome spirit believed to be present when the shaking tent is used. If for any reason Crazy Woman becomes annoyed she will carry off conjurers. [Clay 1938]

Creation

Although few Native American cultures tell stories of the world's creation from a void, most have stories about the beginning of the world, particularly about how the world gained its present shape and character. Often the stories account for the creation of human beings, plants and animals, clans, social relations, and even such attributes as hunger, sleep, disease, and malevolence.

An analysis of Native American creation stories suggests several types: (1) In stories of the *Earth Diver,* found all over North America, various beings attempt to dive to the bottom of the primordial waters and bring back a bit of mud from which to create the earth. Many animals fail before one finally succeeds. (2) The world parent myth is not so widespread as might be thought. The simple example of Father Sky and Mother Earth rarely occurs among tribal cultures, although it is often referred to in contemporary Native American spirituality (a cross-cultural identity). Many creation stories, particularly in the southwest, feature a strong celestial creator such as the Zuni Sun Father *(Yatokka taccu)* and Moonlight-Giving Mother. (3) The *emergence* weaves stories of the creation on the theme of a journey through lower worlds, eventually leading to the emergence onto the present earth. These stories are most common in the southwest, but can occasionally be found in the Plains and even the southeast. (4) Two creators or heroes occupy important creation roles in stories told widely in North America. Often these are *warrior twins,* but other related pairs are also common: father and son, sisters, uncle and nephew. Sometimes these creators are cooperative, but often the world takes its shape through their arguments and fights. (5) In southern California, Spider weaves the earth foundations and serves as the first being. (6) *Trickster* often plays a role in creation, despite—and sometimes as a result of—his foolishness.

This volume contains many examples of creation stories. The Pawnee story of the *Basket Dice Game* tells of creation. Navajo creation stories are told in *Blessingway*, in which *Changing Woman* is a central figure, but variations occur in stories of the figure *Begocidi* and the conceptions of Wind *(Nilchi?i)*. Apache creation is described in *Black Hactcin Creates Animals and Humans*. Conflict between antagonistic brothers results in the origin of Iroquois *False Faces*. The Pima story of creation is called *Tcu-unnyikita*. Clowns and clowning (see *Clowns and Clowning Societies)*, as practiced by the Pueblos, can perhaps best be understood as invoking the powers of creation. *Directional orientations* replicate and mark the order established in creation. The Paiute creation story appears in *Fish-Eater and Hawk Create the Earth*. Some Plains cultures attribute creation to oxenlike figures *(Unktehi)*. See also *Creator*.

Creator(s)

Native American stories of *creation* take a variety of forms. Often these stories attribute creation to figures with specific identities. Beyond these stories, however, a great variety of figures play creator. The variety may be appreciated in the following examples.

The Navajo tell of many creator figures: *First Man* and *First Woman, Changing Woman, Begocidi* (the breast-grabber), and Wind *(Nilchi?i)*, among others, are all considered diyin dine?e, the Holy People (see also *Navajo Emergence)*. Creation stories of the Apache share many similarities with those of the Navajo, to whom the Apache are related (see Apache Creation and Emergence).

A number of cultures consider sky-dwelling male figures as creators, yet these figures vary considerably from one culture to another. They include *Above-Old-Man* (Wiyot); the Maidu *Earth-Initiate, Earth-Maker,* who descends from the sky on a rope, as does another Maidu figure, *Kodoyanpe,* along with his companion Coyote; *Ehlaumel* (Yuki), the Thunderer; *Madumda* (Pomo); *Mukat* (Cahuilla), who is especially associated with the creation of plants; the Seminole *Es-te fas-ta; Sky-Holder,* a Seneca creator; *Iouskeha* (Huron), who created lakes and rivers; the Blackfoot Old Man *(Napioa);* and the Zuni Sun Father *(Yatokka taccu).* The Onondaga speak of *Sapling* as one name of the creator. Among the Crow, *Old Man Coyote* is portrayed as creator.

Examples of creator brothers include the Paiute *Cinauau* and Serrano *Pakrokitat.* Various *warrior twins* have roles in creation. See also the Arikara and Mandan creator pair, *First Creator and Lone Man.*

Female creators also play a prominent role in Native American cultures. The Moapa *Cotsipamapot* is a strong female creator, as is *Iatiku* (Keres). See also *Moonlight-Giving Mother* (Zuni). Kokumthena is the sky-dwelling Shawnee grandmother creator. *Nayaanxatisei,* the Arapaho Whirlwind Woman, created the earth from a ball of mud. Various corn women, animal mothers (see *Master/Mistress of Animals),* and creators of humans (see *Changing Woman* and *White Painted Woman)* have roles in creation, as do various culture heroines (see *Culture Hero).*

Although *tricksters* may be destructive, they frequently play a role in creation. They often serve as a creator's companions, such as *Italapas,* the Chinook Coyote; the coyote helper to the Kato/Sinkyone creator *Nagaicho;* and the Achumawi creator *Silver Fox.* Coyote is fully elevated to creator in the Crow figure *Old Man Coyote.*

The creation of human beings (see *Humans, Origin of)* and *clans* are important works of Native American creators. See the Modoc creator of humans, *Kmukamch.* Creation is often accomplished through naming (see *Names and Naming),* as exemplified by the Kutenai creator

Nalmuqtse, who crawls about naming things. Related to the creation of human beings is the determination of the duration of life and the finality of death, issues widely represented in Native American mythology (see *Dead).*

In a number of creation stories, the world in its primordial state is peopled with mythological characters, but lacks light. Someone has entrapped light or fire, thus making life impossible. Stories often tell of the heroic theft of *fire* or *light,* allowing the world to come fully into existence.

For other creators see *Cautantowwit* (Narragansett), *Hisagita-imisi* (Creek); *Kuksu Cult* (California), centered on the creator Kuksu; the Yuma creator of life *Kwikumat,* born at the bottom of the ocean; *Neshanu* (Pawnee), who destroyed the people he created who turned out badly, but preserved the good ones in the form of corn; *Qoluncotun* (Okanagon); *Quawteaht* (Nootka), who created earth and animals; *Sapling* (Onondaga); the Abenaki creator of humans and owner of the world, *Tabaldak; Taikomol* (Yuki); *Tirawahat* (Pawnee); *Wolf Creates the Earth* (Paiute), in which Wolf creates the world by piling up dirt; and the Joshua creator *Xowalaci,* whose name means "the Giver."

Cremation

A funerary practice of burning the body of one who has died. The Mohave practice of cremating the dead began when *Mastamho,* the culture hero, was cremated. For the Pima story of the origin of cremation, see *Tcu-unnyikita,* the creation story.

Crest(s)
Northwest Coast
A physical representation of the important lineages, made of *copper.* Ownership of a crest carries considerable prestige. See *Gispawaweda* (Tsimshian), *Qaslanas* (Haida), *Sisaok* (Bella Coola), and *Tsetseka* (Kwakiutl).

Crier
Pawnee, *Plains*
See *Pattikus,* the old one who announces ceremonies to the village.

Crippled Boy *(Tsauz)*
Salish, Northwest Coast
A story of a boy who looks ugly but is actually beautiful.

Crisis Cult(s)
The generic term for movements, usually short-lived, that arise in response to crises. Since Native Americans suffered major crises as the American frontier advanced upon them with all its transformations, these movements have been common. Such cults were usually inspired by prophetic figures such as Neolin (the Delaware prophet); Tenskwatawa (Shawnee); Kanakuk (Kickapoo); Handsome Lake (Seneca); and Wovoka, whose prophecies inspired the *Ghost Dance of 1890.* See also *Ghost Dance of 1870* and *Smohalla Cult.*

Cross-Dressing
The practice of dressing as the opposite gender. See *Gender Crossing; White Faces* (Miami), males who dress as women; *Begocidi,* the Navajo figure who sometimes dresses as a woman; and *Matoki,* a Blackfoot cross-dressing women's society.

Crow
A common and often prominent mythological character. A few examples are *Chulyen,* a trickster of the Tanaina of Alaska. A Paviotso story about the centipede, *Aqonidzaba,* explains why Crow's feet are black. *Gaqga* is the Seneca term for crow. For the Nootka, Crow *(Keninqas)* is a woman who owns fresh water. See also *Inua* (Alaska) and *Raven.*

Crow
Plains
The people of the Crow tribe call themselves *Apsaalooke.*

Crow Lance Society
Pawnee, *Plains*
A society (see *Societies)* concerned with success in *war* and buffalo hunting. A lance representing the *North Wind* helps hunting parties by driving

buffalo to them. The origin of the society and the lance is told in the following story. The members of a war party are advised by their chief to sacrifice a raccoon before getting too far into enemy country. A scout finds a raccoon, and the warriors kill it and burn its carcass. Some of the warriors, however, believe the raccoon should have been roasted and eaten instead of burned. They become afraid and return to their village. The scout who found the raccoon continues on until he is killed by a group of warriors. When his comrades look for him, they discover he has been killed by crows and coyotes. The warriors inform the chief of the scout's death, which is attributed to the improper sacrifice of the raccoon. When the chief retrieves the dead scout, he finds only scratches on the body. He covers the body with his robe and returns to the village.

That night, the dead scout hears people dancing. He sits up so he can see the dancers, but he does not know any of them. They are all painted black, and one of them carries a lance covered with crow feathers. The scout travels with the dancers to the mountains, where he is told to lie down under a tree on the mountainside. When he awakes, he sees a number of deer, antelope, and fawns. He wants to follow them, but the crows warn against it. Suddenly the crows disappear, and the scout hears singing inside the mountain. A crow leads him to a cave in the side of the mountain where the other crows are seated in a circle. The crow-feather lance is standing in the west. The crow people sing songs, ending each song with a crow imitation. They dance and sing all night.

For three nights the man dances with the crows during the night and sleeps during the day while the crows are gone. On the fourth night the crow leader gives him the crow-feathered lance and tells him to start the Crow Lance Society. The one who carries the lance is to be known as the "old man" *(kurahus)*. Any young man who belongs to the Crow Lance Society can take the lance into battle, but the kurahus has to carry it when hunters are looking for buffalo. The crows

can see where the buffalo are and help the hunters find them. The crow explains that the coyotes wanted to eat the scout when he was scared to death by Coyote barking and Crow cawing, but the crows intervened and revived the scout so they could teach him the Crow Lance Dance. The scout is to teach the people that fright from the sound of coyotes and crows can sometimes kill people, but if people remain unafraid they will not be killed. [Frey 1987; Lowie 1956, 1960]

Crown Dancers
Apache, *Southwest*
See *Mountain Spirits.*

Crow-Water Society
Piegan, Crow, *Plains*
A Crow society (see *Societies)* introduced to the Piegan in 1903 by a Piegan man named Iron, who learned of it while living among the Crow. Iron was initiated into the society and dreamed of six dwarfs who gave him power to obtain horses, property, food, and long life. Power to obtain material property was one of the benefits of the society. The power of the society could be transferred to others. Iron transferred some of his power to Curly-Bear when he returned to the Piegan and initiated the society among them.

Membership in the Crow-Water Society enhances personal wealth and power. Unmarried women may join the society alone, but if a married woman joins, so must her husband. A person joins the society by going to an established member and requesting some Crow-Water power. The petitioner gives many quilts and horses to the member, who then shares the gifts with others in the society. Each of these recipients must contribute a song, medicine power, or other object to a *medicine bundle* to be given to the new member. These bundles, unlike other medicine bundles, may be opened at any time. When a person is taken into the society, he or she is given the skin of an otter, weasel, or beaver, along with a *song* that has been dreamed by one of the members.

Meetings of the Crow-Water Society are usually held on the first day of the new moon. The meetings are not considered secret; anyone may watch the initiation ceremony, but only members may come into the tipi and ceremonial circle. [Lowie 1960]

Crow-Woman
Arapaho, *Plains*

The jealous first wife of a water monster (hi-intcabiit). Jealous of her husband's second wife, *River-Woman,* whom he has rescued from *Wanou,* Crow-Woman drowns her. But River-Woman is resuscitated by her brother, Beaver-Foot, and returns to Crow-Woman's lodge. One day while Beaver-Foot and the water monster are out hunting, River-Woman takes Crow-Woman to the river and drowns her. When she tells her husband, he says he understands, but then he begins to cry for Crow-Woman, causing the river water to rise. Beaver-Foot saves the village by painting his body and stretching out his hands and feet, causing the waters to recede.

Cudak
Puyallup-Nisqually, *Northwest Coast*

A *charm* whose knowledge and use is confined to *women.* Cudak is said to have come from the *sun.* It is sometimes referred to as talking medicine because of the secret words spoken when it is used. A woman uses cudak when she wants to keep her husband's attention focused on her and not on another wife or woman. Cudak is also used in curing (see *Healing),* in conjunction with certain herbs.

Culture Hero(es)

A type of character responsible for establishing distinctive features of a culture. Culture heroes may take diverse forms. They almost always have proper names and distinct transformational abilities. They are often clearly differentiated from trickster characters, even though some trickster characters are also understood to be culture heroes.

The culture hero may appear in stories of creation but usually enters a world already cre-ated. The culture hero is frequently responsible for conditions in nature and culture. Primarily a wanderer, he or she is able to talk with and transform living things into animals as well as to change the shape of the landscape. Like the trick-ster, the culture hero may have a fierce appetite for sex, food, and gambling. The culture hero's birth may be of an unusual nature, sometimes with a nonhuman parent. Often he or she grows quickly and may be raised by an isolated grand-mother figure. Some culture heroes have animal siblings, such as a wolf or moose.

Native American mythology features hundreds of culture heroes. The following examples demon-strate the range and richness of these characters.

Culture heroes are often the first people on earth, such as the Cree *Pine Root and Beaded Head.* Culture heroes are responsible for estab-lishing distinctive elements of culture and the world. For example, *Kliatata* (Kaska) teaches people how to make fishnets, the Haida *Sin* brings snow, and Spider Woman *(Kokyan wuhti)* brings weaving. The *hoop and pole game* is a gift from a culture hero. The Milky Way is created by the Seminole culture hero *Hisagita misa.* Virtually every aspect of culture may be attributed to culture heroes, including the ex-istence of *light* and *fire, clan* origins, the loca-tion of genitalia, the origin of *agriculture,* the finality of death (see *Dead),* and the origin of funerary practices (see *Cremation).* Culture he-roes serve as *Master/Mistress of Animals.* Some-times the culture hero destroys the world as it exists in order to transform it. Such is the case of the Pima *I?itoi,* who destroys the world by flood.

One of the most common tasks of the culture hero is to slay or transform monsters who appear after creation and make life impossible for human beings. *Beaver Man* (Yukon) transforms giant animals to their present size. The Takelma drag-onfly *Daldal* kills monsters, as do various *warrior twins,* such as the Zuni *Ahayuta,* the Apache Killer-of-Enemies (see *Apache Creation and Emergence), Monster Slayer and Born for Water* (Navajo), *Old Woman's Grandchild* (Crow),

Pulekukwerek (Yurok), *Yimantuwinyai* (Hupa), and *Masewa and Uyuyewa* (Keres).

Culture heroes are often indistinguishable from *tricksters. Coyote, Gugyni* (Tanaina), *Raven, Glooscap, Winabojo,* and *Wesucechak* (Cree) are important examples of such figures. Sometimes a trickster-type culture hero makes sex pleasurable by destroying vaginal teeth (see *Vagina Dentata).*

Other culture heroes include: *Asdiwal* (Tsimshian); *Atacokai* (Kutchin); *Apanuugak* (Yupik); *Augitsisiaq* (Povungnituk); *Corncob Boy,* a Cochiti orphan; *Ganyadjigowa,* the Seneca mud hen; *Hadentheni and Hanigongendatha* (Seneca); the Iowa *Ishjinki;* the Chinook creator *Italapas,* also a culture hero; *Kwatyat,* who creates all of Nootka culture; *Mastamho* (Mohave); the Cherokee *Stonecoat (Ocasta),* who helps with creation; *Okabewis* (Ojibwa); *Saya* (Beaver); the black bear Suku (Alsea); *Sunawavi,* the Ute wolf; a dwarf called *Tcikapis* by the Montagnais; the Alaskan figure *Vasaagijik* (which means greasy mouth), a Canada jay; *Wegyet* (Gitksan); the Yavapai *Widapokwi and Amchitapuka; Wiske* (Potawatomi); and *Yamonhdeyi,* the most important culture hero of the Dene Dhaa. [Hultkrantz 1984; Jones 1901; Wake 1907]

Cunawabi
Moapa, southern Nevada, *Great Basin*

A figure responsible for making sickness and for naming mountains, waters, rocks, and bushes. Cunawabi is often characterized as a *trickster.* He is a *gambler* who has many adventures. Often killed, he is then resuscitated by Bat and other animals. When Cunawabi's brother Tobats dies, he leaves Cunawabi a *medicine bundle.* Cunawabi opens the bundle, causing *darkness* and bringing night into the world.

In one story Cunawabi wants to have intercourse with his daughter (see *Incest).* He has an extra penis, which he uses to attack his daughter. The penis gets stuck in the daughter and makes her very ill. Duck, a powerful medicine person, is summoned to find the cause of the illness. He finds the penis, removes it, and burns it in a fire, thus curing the girl. [Lowie 1924]

Cure and Curing
See *Healing.*

Cyclone
Alsea, *Northwest Coast*
See *Wind-Woman.*

Dagwanoenyent

Seneca, *Northeast*

Daughter of the *Wind,* who often takes the form of a whirlwind. She is a dangerous *witch* who lives in the north. She is destroyed by the father of her child and his nephew with the help of Mole.

The uncle hunts every day, but there is never any meat in his lodge. Although forbidden to do so by his uncle, the nephew journeys to the north. He discovers Dagwanoenyent sitting quietly in a *longhouse* filled with bear meat, venison, and bags of bear's oil. A young boy toddles about. The nephew plays with the child, but Dagwanoenyent ignores them. The nephew steals a piece of meat, then returns to his uncle's home. The nephew continues his visits to the longhouse for many years. Each time he plays with the youngster while Dagwanoenyent sits quietly, then steals a piece of meat as he leaves.

When the young boy of the longhouse turns 15, he informs the visiting nephew they are really cousins—the nephew's uncle is the boy's father and the husband of Dagwanoenyent. When the nephew returns home, his uncle questions him. He admits visiting the longhouse for many years and stealing meat. He tells his uncle he has punctured the bag of bear's oil that hangs over Dagwanoenyent's head. The uncle angrily reveals that he is the one who has been supplying the longhouse with meat all these years. He tells his nephew that by breaking the bag of bear oil the nephew has put them in great danger, because Dagwanoenyent is a violent witch who cannot be killed.

Soon Dagwanoenyent comes as a *whirlwind,* destroys the uncle's lodge, and carries him away. After the wind has gone, the nephew goes to the longhouse and finds Dagwanoenyent sitting quietly in the corner as if nothing happened. He asks his cousin what Dagwanoenyent has done with his uncle, but the boy does not know. The boy warns the nephew that Dagwanoenyent will return the next day to get him. With the help of his guardian, the mole, the nephew escapes Dagwanoenyent's fury by hiding in Mole's belly. Eventually, however, Dagwanoenyent finds Mole, tosses him in the air, and kills the nephew. Mole resuscitates him.

The mole and the nephew find the uncle under a great elm tree, which is standing on his chest. The nephew pushes the tree aside and gives his uncle a smoke, reviving him. The nephew returns to Dagwanoenyent's lodge and kills her, burning her body in a fire of bear oil. But Dagwanoenyent comes back to life and arrives at the nephew's lodge in a terrible rage. She exhausts herself chasing him and finally walks back to her lodge. The nephew follows her, kills her, and burns her body once again. This time his uncle helps him by removing her bones from the fire and pounding them into a fine powder. They divide the powder into three separate bags, and the uncle, the nephew, and the mole each keep a bag. They decide that whenever there is a storm they must keep the bags apart so the force of the powders cannot unite and revive Dagwanoenyent. [Fenton 1987]

Dahdahwat
Seneca, *Northeast*
Mythical animals that could take many forms. The Dahdahwat appeared in the dreams of *Gan-yadjigowa,* a mud hen and culture hero who travels about. According to stories, the Dahdahwat chase Ganyadjigowa and catch him. Then they bite him, causing his sweat to pour out like rain. See *Shodieonskon,* the brother of death, who is killed by Dahdahwat. [Fenton 1987]

Daldal
Takelma, *Northwest Coast*
Dragonfly, the *culture hero* of numerous stories, who introduces benevolent behavior as a way of life. Daldal appears after traveling east up the Rogue River. He has multiple adventures, killing *monsters* and wicked beings, after which he turns into a mountain. [Sapir 1909a]

Dance(s)
Much of Native American ritual is virtually synonymous with dance. Dancing is important in grand ceremonials and for private curing rites. Many dances are transmitted from generation to generation, while others are newly created for each performance. Some originate in vision experiences. Many societies are organized around dancing. Both women and men dance, sometimes

together, but often separately. The following catalog represents only a few Native American dances and dance occasions.

Dances associated with healing include those of the Iroquois *False Faces* (see also *Faces of Forests; Akhrendoiaen,* a Huron dance prescribed in a dream; and *Hodigohsosga?a).* The *Awataerohi* and *Otakrendoiae* are Huron curing dances, as are the Menominee *Buffalo Dance Cult* and the Piegan *Black-Tailed Deer Dance,* which is also done in association with war. The Seneca do a naked dance to counteract the malevolent act of *heart squeezing.* The *Matoki,* a Blackfoot women's medicine society, held an annual four-day dance during the *Sun Dance* ceremony. The Quileute *Wolf Society* is a healing society that does the Wolf Dance for curing.

Masks are often worn by Native American dancers. Masked dances include the Iroquois *False Faces* (see also *Longhouse Ceremony);* the Pueblo *Kachina* (see also *Hopi Ritual Cycle, Plaza Dances, Night Dances, Niman, Tewa Ritual Cycle,* and *Zuni Ritual Cycle);* the various dances of the *Yaqui Easter Ceremony* (see also *Deer Dancers* and *Pascola);* the Navajo *Yeibichai;* the Nootka masked dance done to *Changing Masks Songs;* and the many masked dances of the Pacific northwest coast (see *Hamatsa Society* and *Tsetseka).*

Many Native American cultures do animal dances such as the widely performed *Bear Dance* (see also *Mamakoni-nitkap,* the Ute dance to celebrate the end of hibernation; *Linkan,* a Delaware men's dance done during their Bear Ceremony; and *Yona,* the Cherokee Bear Dance). Other animal dances include *Ganegwa?e,* the Iroquois Eagle Dance; the Oglala *Horse Dance;* the Plains Owl Dance (see *Owl);* the Delaware Nighthawk Dance *Pickwelaneokan;* the Menominee *Rabbit Dance;* the Hopi *Snake Dance;* and the Penobscot Snake Dance *Yuneha.*

Dancing is often related to agriculture and hunting. All Pueblo dances address the growing season. The *Green Corn Dance* is practiced widely in the southeastern United States (see also

Pascolas dance and clown at ceremonies, such as children's funerals, saint's day fiestas, weddings, and Holy Week ceremonies. Courtesy, Arizona State Museum, The University of Arizona, George Iacono, photographer.

Onenha), and during the Yupik Bladder Festival *(Nakaciuq).*

Dancing societies include: *Crow Lance Society* (Pawnee); the Blackfoot women's medicine society, *Matoki;* the Bella Coola *Sisaok;* and the Quileute *Wolf Society,* a curing society.

Dances may be performed to open ceremonies; an example is the Penobscot greeting dance known as *Skawehe.* Nootka women have a dance known as *Great-Favorite.* The Bella Coola have a group of five dances, the *Kusiotem,* performed during midwinter ceremonies. *Ka?espai* is the Blackfoot Grass Dance (see also *Grass Dance*). *Kuksu-hesi* is the dance group that performed in the *Kuksu Cult* (California). The *Hulkilal wok* is the Yuki Dance of the Dead, and the Shawnee celebrate the one-year anniversary of a death with the *Kaukiwawakauwa.* In the *Kawenho,* known as the Arikara Hot Dance, dancers immerse their hands in boiling kettles of dog stew. Nootka men do the *Lover-Signaling Dance* to meet women. *Nolemahigan* is the Penobscot Clown Dance, and *Nulmal* are Kwakiutl fool dancers (see also *Clowns and Clowning Societies*). *Omiigiwen* is the Ojibwa Drum Dance. The Seminole do the *Soup Dance,* which includes a Drunken Dance and the *Stomp Dance. Taikomol,* the Yuki creator, gave the people *Taikomol wok,* a dance to honor him. In a Pawnee Orpheus story, *Whistle Dance* is done as a reminder of the dead. *Dissuua* is the Crow term for dancing. The Ghost Dance crisis cults of the late nineteenth century were known for their trance dancing (see *Ghost Dance of 1870* and *Ghost Dance of 1890*).

Dark Corral Ceremony

Navajo, *Southwest*
See *Mountainway.*

Darkness

The existence of darkness may be explained in stories. For example, *Cunawabi,* the Moapa trickster, causes darkness. The Lakota story *Day, Following Night* also explains darkness.

Datura (Datura stramonium)

Jimsonweed, one of the principal psychoactive plants of North and Central America. Jimsonweed was once a man who told people that when he died he would be changed into a plant, from whose roots they could obtain health and *visions.* Among the Plains tribes of North America the visionary effects of jimsonweed are used to induce a trance state for diagnosing illness. The Cherokee believe the root of the jimsonweed has power to improve memory and promote a stable personality. The Luiseño use datura as an anesthetic for setting bones and surgery, as well as in initiation rites. The leaves of the jimsonweed are used medicinally to treat internal sores and injuries. See also *Chingichnich.* [Dobkin de Rios 1984]

Day, Following Night

Lakota, *Plains*

Han, the black of *darkness* that existed before any thing or any time, was banished by *Skan,* the Sky, to the regions under the world because *Maka,* Earth, complained about sharing space with her. After Skan created Anp, the red of light, and Maka saw how naked and cold she was, she complained to Skan, who then created *Wi,* the sun. The sun constantly heated everything. Maka had no comfort from Wi and begged Skan to return Han so she would have some comfort in Han's shadows. Finally, Skan commanded Anp and Han to follow each other so that each would remain for a certain time upon the earth, and Maka was finally content. See also *Wiyohiyanpa.* [Powers 1975]

Daylight People

Zuni, *Southwest*
See *Cooked People.*

Dead

Death and the dead are common subjects in many Native American stories. Perhaps the most common are stories about the origin and finality of death. For examples of these stories see the following: *Aikren* (Karok), *Apikunni* (Pawnee),

Cinauau (Ute), *Hixtcaba Nihancan* (Arapaho), *Kukitat* (Serrano), *Kwikumat* (Yuma), *Ma?ii* (Navajo), *Nagaicho* (Kato, Sinkyone), *Pikagoyu* (Kawaiisu), *Roasting-Dead-People* (Takelma), *Sitec* (Nooksack), *Sunawavi* (Ute), *Takwe* (Juaneño), *Taikomol* (Yuki), *Tcu-unnyikita* (Pima), and *White Painted Woman* (Apache). The Kathlamet hold that death is caused by a spirit named "Famine." The Tsimshian believe that witches (see *Haldawit*) can cause death.

A number of signs foretell death. Among the most common is the presence of an *owl*. The Maliseet tell stories of *Kehtakws,* creatures who foretell death. For the Haida understanding of the timing of death see *Power-of-the-Shining-Heavens.*

Many stories refer to the place of the dead, the land where they live. For an elaborate account of this place in Zuni tradition, see *Dead, Land of.* See also *Adlivun* (Eskimo); *Anerneq,* the Yupik destiny of the soul; *Apache Creation and Emergence,* which tells of the underworld place of the dead; and Navajo *Blessingway,* which tells why the dead live in the lower worlds, an ugly *(hocho)* place. *First Man and First Woman* oversee the lower worlds after the *Navajo Emergence.* See also *Underworld* (Yupik); *Hadentheni and Hanigongendatha* (Seneca); *Qudlivun, Qudliparmuit* (central Eskimo); and the Pawnee *Whistle Dance.* The land of the dead and its inhabitants are overseen by such figures as *Cipyapos* and his brother *Wiske* (Potawatomi), who receive souls; *Pana* (Eskimo), a woman who keeps souls; and *Pakrokitat,* the Serrano creator.

Funerary practices and conducting the dead to their new home are other common story motifs. For examples, see *Anguta* (Eskimo); *Cloud,* represented by cotton masks placed on the dead; the Lakota *White Buffalo Ceremony,* which is followed by a four-day grieving period *(Wacekiyapi);* the Haida potlatch *(Gia is su);* and the story told by the Beaver tribe about the dead who walk a trail to heaven *(Yagatunne).*

Native Americans perform a variety of ritual events to honor the dead. The Huron *Ohgiwe*

Society honors the dead as one of its functions. Elriq is the Yupik feast of the dead. The Yuki do a dance of the dead *(Hulkilal wok).* The Shawnee dance to honor the dead at the one-year anniversary of death *(Kaukiwawakauwa).* The Lakota honor the dead in a *Spirit Keeping Ceremony.*

The dead are conceived of as having many forms, some of which remain helpful to the living. Pueblo *kachinas,* who are associated with the dead, are essential to ongoing life. They bring rain and essential food. Much of Pueblo religion pertains in some way to the dead. *Masau?u* (Hopi) presides over the house of the dead. The Zuni figure *Pautiwa* receives the spirits of the dead *(pinanne),* who become Cloud People *(Shiwanna;* see also *Rain Priest).* Many cultures consider the dead to be *ghosts.* The Algonquians believe that the dancing lights of the *Aurora Borealis* are spirits of the dead. The Narragansett dead *(Chepi)* may give information to medicine people. To the Yupik, bladders *(Nakaciuq)* represent the souls of the animals hunted throughout the year. They are honored in annual Bladder Festivals. The Cree identify a helping spirit that is a skeleton *(Pakahk).*

A story type Native Americans share with cultures the world over goes by the term *Orpheus.* In these tales, a husband attempts to thwart the finality of death by retrieving his wife from the land of the dead. His eventual failure makes death final.

The crisis cult Ghost Dance and the *Prophet Dance Movement* prophesied the return of the dead. See *Ghost Dance of 1870* and *Ghost Dance of 1890.* See also *Shodieonskon,* the Seneca brother of death; and *Wiyohipeyata,* the West, whose spirit is present at the death of humans and animals.

Dead, Land of
Zuni, *Southwest*

A widely told story featuring a man who goes to the sky with a sky maiden and dies for breaking some taboo related to corpses or skeletons. Several versions of the story center on a youth who travels to the home of the eagles. In one version, the son of a priest has a pet *eagle*. His sisters are jealous of the bird and plan to kill it. The eagle departs, taking the boy with her. In her home, she removes her eagle garment, revealing her human form. The young man is given an eagle garment and taught to fly. Although warned not to, he flies to the pueblo of the dead in the west. As a consequence, two corpse girls come to him in the guise of beautiful maidens. Although warned not to laugh at them, he does. They capture him and take him to their village. With spiritual help, the young man is able to move the corpse village far away to the other side of the ocean. After he is purified, he is sent back to Zuni Village with new clothes and presents. See also *Kachina Village*. [Benedict 1935; Bunzel 1933; Cushing 1896]

Dead, Resuscitation of

A common story motif. The body of the dead person may be rubbed or beaten, stepped on or jumped over. It may be boiled or placed in a body of water such as a stream or river. Parts of the body, usually bones and intestines, may be scattered in a river or desert. Survivors and a *shaman* may do a *sweat lodge* and then reassemble parts of a body that has been torn to pieces. Only people with the strongest spiritual power have the ability to resuscitate the dead. Animals and monsters may also be resuscitated. In one Shawnee story a monster is destroyed by fire. Only one drop of its blood remains on a leaf. Ants find the blood and use their power to restore the monster to life.

Deadoendjadases

Seneca, Iroquois, *Northeast*

"The Earth-Circler." A *cannibal* monster who lives with his three witch sisters in a longhouse in the middle of a forest. Every day the sisters prepare human flesh and pound green corn for their brother to eat. The lodge of Deadoendjadases lies in the north-south direction instead of the proper east-west direction. A large and luscious strawberry patch surrounds his lodge,

guarded by the inflated skin of a man known as *Hadjoqda*. Deadoendjadases is killed by a young male hero from the Turkey clan with the help of Hadjoqda. Eventually the Turkey, Quail, and Partridge peoples settle around the rich strawberry patch. [Fenton 1987]

Deagahgweoses

Seneca, *Northeast*

"Long upper eyelids." The maker and keeper of *tobacco,* so named because he was able to process tobacco by hammering it with a mallet and singing over it. The tobacco processed by Deagahgweoses was believed to have special curative powers. Deagahgweoses was eventually killed by *Hodadenon,* a culture hero. [Fenton 1987]

Deanodjes

Seneca, *Northeast*

"He who has two long teeth." The name for Walrus. [Fenton 1987]

Deer

A common character in stories. Although it may be portrayed as male or female, Deer usually is cast as the wife, mother, or sister of another animal character. In some stories, Deer Woman marries a human man but is eventually offended by remarks made about her eating habits. She leaves her husband, taking their son with her. See also the Zuni twins, *Ahayuta,* who create deer by killing Saiyathlia; *Bear Woman and the Fawns* (Lassik); *Black-Tailed Deer Dance,* a Piegan dance done in preparation for hunting deer; the Pawnee *Dog Boy,* who is protected by deer; *Heluta* (Cochiti), the creator of deer; and *Kanaakwe* (Zuni), who hide deer from hunter kachinas. *Hustoyowanen* is a Seneca name for a deer. [Dangel 1929; Martin 1978; Morris 1976]

Deer Dancers (maso yeome)

Yaqui, *Southwest*

"He who dances deer." A *dance* group associated with deer that commonly performs at fiestas. In earlier eras, before the late–nineteenth-century defeat and dispersal of the Yaqui people, deer were the most important source of food and skins, as well as the most feared and admired animal. The special relationship the Yaqui people have with the deer is danced and mimed to song by this group of dancers. Deer dancers dance solo in alternation with the *pascola.*

The deer dancer wears a rebozo (scarf) wrapped around the waist and secured with a woven belt over which a deer hoof–rattle belt is worn. The dancer is bare above the waist and wears a necklace with a carved cross. Cocoon rattles are worn around each ankle. A deer head

A cedar deer mask recovered from an archaeological site in Key Marco, Florida. Courtesy, The University Museum, University of Pennsylvania (neg.#13256-7).

that includes a few inches of neck and is furnished with glass eyes is worn as a headdress. A white cloth covers the head of the dancer and the face down to the eyes. The deer head sits on this cloth, slightly forward on the head, its antlers decorated with red ribbon. The dancer holds a large gourd rattle in each hand while dancing. The dance is quite effective in miming the characteristic postures and movements of deer. Yaqui believe that deer dancers are born to their role. Unlike pascolas, deer dancers never tell jokes or stories. The deer dancer tends to remain silent, aloof, and distant. See also *Seataka* and *Yaqui Easter Ceremony.* [Evers and Molina 1987; Painter 1986]

Deer Hunting
Kawaiisu, *Great Basin*
In this story tradition, an old man prevails upon a small boy to let himself be turned into a deer (see *Human-Animal Transformation*) so that people will have deer meat. Against the wishes of his two sisters, the boy agrees. The people put horns on his head, dress him in a deerskin, and glue hooves to his feet with pitch. Then they send him up to the hills to eat grass. Many tribes try to hunt this deer, but none succeed in killing him. Finally the old Kawaiisu man kills the deer. He skins it and shares the meat with all the tribes. Because it has no fat, the meat is very dry. The old man cuts a piece of fat from his own body and wraps it around the deer's heart. This is why there is fat around a deer's heart. Another relevant Kawaiisu story deals with *Food, Choices of Animals.* [Zigmond 1980]

Dehodyatgaieweh
Onondaga, Iroquois, *Northeast*
"His body split in half." *False Face* masks of this figure are divided into two parts. One half of the mask (see *Masks and Masking*) is painted red, designating the east; the other half is painted black for the west. These masks represent half-human bodies and have the power and freedom to wander wherever they choose. See also Ohswedogo.

Dehotgohsgayeh (Dehotgohsga:yeh)
Onondaga, Iroquois, *Northeast*
"Split-faced being" or Wry Face. This *giant* lives in the south along the margin of the earth in total

darkness. One side of his body is red, the other black. He protects human beings against malevolence. He carries a staff made of the whole peeled trunk of a hickory tree and wears a belt made of a large hickory tree. Wry Face is dressed in the skin of a monster bear, and when he shakes his rattle everyone on earth hears it. [Fenton 1987]

Delaware Prophet
Delaware, *Northeast*

The name given to a man who appeared among the Delaware people in 1762, telling of a vision in which he had seen the union of all tribes and a return to old lifestyles. Pontiac described the vision in a meeting in 1763 during which a French missionary wrote down the chief's words.

This document came to be known as the Pontiac Manuscript. Its message of a peaceful life and unity was the underpinning of the grand confederacy of tribes that, under Pontiac's leadership, were opposed to the further encroachment of the English on Native American land. [Voegelin and Voegelin 1954]

Dentalium Shell Money
Yurok, *California*
See *Pelintsiek.*

Deoyadastathe
Seneca, *Northeast*

"He whose body is bright." The youngest son of Hadjowiski, the thousand-legged worm. As a child, Deoyadastathe never goes outside. Instead he stays in the house under his bed, playing with his dog, which is a flea. When his six older siblings fail to return after going to search for their missing father, Deoyadastathe finally leaves the house to hunt for him. Deoyadastathe becomes a hero to his people by killing dangerous and malevolent enemies. He saves his mother from the torture of Chief Dihdih and kills the malevolent Toad People. See also *Hadjowiski.* [Fenton 1987]

Desini
Chilcotin, *Subarctic*

Strangers, rarely seen, who steal women. Desini are found in the vicinity of camping places. [Ruby and Brown 1986]

Devil

With obvious origins in *Christianity,* the term devil has often been misused to identify a wide variety of Native American figures, such as the Alaskan figure *Tarneq.* Perhaps as a result of this unfortunate and oppressive practice, some figures have come to be identified by Native Americans with this English term. *Donogaot* is a Seneca mask sometimes characterized as a devil. The Yaqui use Christian terms creatively to express their religious views of the struggle between good and evil. *Morea* is the Yaqui term for witchcraft, which they sometimes identify as the work of the devil. The first *pascola* is considered to have been the son of the devil.

Diagnosticians

Figures common among Native American traditions who use a variety of mystical and clairvoyant methods to determine the cause of illness. See Huron *Saokata* and *Navajo Ritual Process* for examples. [Hill 1935a]

Directional Orientations

The designation of meaningful correlations with cardinal and semicardinal directions, including zenith, nadir, and center. To designate or acknowledge directional orientations is equivalent to an act of creation or a founding of the world. Creation stories are given concrete reference in terms of directional orientations. Ritual is invariably enacted within directional orientations, which may be linked with colors, animals and birds, seasons, clans, and certain helping spirits. Most groups have extensive local terminology for directional orientations.

Tate, the Lakota Wind, established the directions. The Zuni recognize six directions plus the center; these divide the Zuni cosmos accordingly.

Even some figures such as the Beast Gods *(We-maawe)* are numbered and identified in terms of these directions. The four great winds (see *Winds, Four Great)* of Tsimshian mythology are the chiefs of the corners of the world. See also *Cardinal Directions.*

Dirty Boy

A figure appearing under various guises common to stories throughout North America: a boy who appears dirty (a disguise of one of the Zuni twins, *Ahayuta),* crippled *(Tsauz,* Salish), lazy *(Arrow Boy,* Pueblo), or poor *(Burnt-Belly,* Pawnee), and who is shunned or mistreated. In actuality he is a powerful and often handsome young man. When treated with kindness by a person—often one who has been overlooked or ignored—Dirty Boy reveals his power and true appearance to the person and lavishes his benefits on him or her.

The Jicarilla Apache (southwestern U.S.) tell the following story of Dirty Boy. A young man who lives with his grandmother trains as a runner. He runs all night, returning to his grandmother's home each morning, and sleeps all day. The people in the village despise the boy because they think he is lazy and dirty. However, he always brings his grandmother game he has caught and supplies her with buckskin.

One day this young man learns that the chief is leading a party of men into enemy territory after some horses. Dirty Boy asks his grandmother to sew him two pairs of double-soled moccasins and prepares his club. As the party leaves Dirty Boy follows, but they refuse to let him travel with them, beseeching him to return home. Nonetheless Dirty Boy persists and eventually is permitted to join the group.

In time the party runs out of food. Dirty Boy sees buffalo; because of his training at running he is able to run after them. He kills several buffalo and his tribesmen feed on them. When they arrive at the enemy camp, it is Dirty Boy who runs into the camp to steal the horses. When the others leave, Dirty Boy remains behind to protect the group from enemy attack.

When the enemy catch up, he runs down their chief, killing and scalping him.

Despite these deeds, Dirty Boy's running skill is so great that he arrives home several days before the others. Once home, Dirty Boy makes no claim for his accomplishments, and everyone believes he returned home early because he never caught up with the party. When the rest of the group returns, they honor Dirty Boy's grandmother with gifts and tell everyone about his accomplishments. The chief offers him riches and marriage to his daughter and niece. When Dirty Boy cleans up and combs his hair, he is a handsome young man. See also the Arapaho story of *Found-in-Grass.* [Opler 1938a, 1938b]

Disease

Healing is a major concern of most Native American religions. Disease may be caused by spirits, such as the Huron *Awataerohi;* by witches, such as the Tsimshian *Haldawit;* or by other means such as the Nootka practice of *Disease Throwing.* The Onondaga figure *Haduʔigona* controls disease.

Disease Throwing
Nootka, *Northwest Coast*

A form of malevolent medicine by which *disease* is made to enter the victim's body through a secret ritual. The disease entities are thought to be invisible. Supernatural beings may also cause disease by throwing "air-worms" to harm humans. [Amoss 1978; Elmendorf 1977; Sapir and Swadesh 1939]

Dissuua
Crow, *Plains*

Dancing (see *Dance).* A crucial part of the *Sun Dance,* highly individual in its performance. See also *Chiwakiia.* [Frey 1987]

Diyin dineʔe
Navajo, *Southwest*

Often referred to as Holy People. Figures in Navajo mythology who are *creators, culture heroes,* and persons of power. Although often criticized, the term "Holy People" remains a common rendering of the Navajo phrase, which is nonetheless preferred.

For reference to diyin dine?e in Navajo ceremonials see also *Ajilee, Beadway, Blessingway, Eagleway, Hailway, Mountainway, Navajo Wind Way, Nightway* (as well as *Whirling Logs' Sandpainting,* which is part of Nightway), and *Shootingway.* Diyin dine?e are particularly associated with the ceremonials classified as *Holyway.* The *ye?ii,* such as *Talking God* and *Water Sprinkler,* are types of diyin dine?e. Prayersticks *(keetaan)* are vehicles used to communicate with the diyin dine?e. The *rainbow* is a bridge to their domain, while pollen, *tadidiin,* is their food. See also *First Man and First Woman* and *Ma?ii.* The Apache *hactcin* is similar.

Djieien

Seneca, *Northeast*

A six-foot-tall monster *spider.* Djieien's heart is kept buried in the ground under the lodge, so the spider is able to live through the most devastating physical attacks. Djieien is killed when *Othegwenhda,* Flint, thrusts a limb from a tree into the ground, splitting the spider's heart. See also *Hagowanen,* the hunter whose son kills Djieien. [Fenton 1987]

Djigaahehwa

Seneca, Iroquois, *Northeast*

Little people who are *Husk Faces* (see also *Hadjihsa Thokste?ah).* They are responsible for the healthy and peaceful growth of medicinal plants. [Fenton 1987]

Djilaqons

Haida, *Northwest Coast*

Ancestress of the Eagle clan, she lives in the water. Because some fishermen have insulted her, Djilaqons causes a fire that burns an entire village. After the fire, she emerges from the water to sing a mourning song and discovers the sole woman survivor, Yelukxinang. Djilaqons

appoints Yelukxinang to be the mother of the Eagle *clan.*

Djilaqons is also a figure in stories of the tribes' migration across the Aleutian Islands. She may be portrayed as Copper Woman, Volcano Woman, or Frog Woman. She comes out of the sea with six canoe loads of people and marries Ka?iti, chief of the *Grizzly Bears.* [Swanton 1905b]

Djoeaga

Seneca, *Northeast*

Raccoon. The raccoon, a figure common in stories, is prized for his fat, which is burned to produce an oil used in grooming one's hair. Djoeaga is hunted with great respect. [Fenton 1987]

Djogeon

Seneca, *Northeast*

"Dwarf Man." A young man with special power. While hunting, Djogeon meets Elk Woman, who convinces him to rest. Djogeon lays his head in Elk Woman's lap and she searches his hair for head lice. The stroking of her fingers puts him to sleep. When she is confident Djogeon is sleeping soundly, Elk Woman puts him in a basket, places the basket on her back, and runs quickly until sunset. Djogeon awakens when she puts the basket down. He recognizes the spot as a place where he hunted as a boy.

Elk Woman has a canoe the size of a walnut. When she hits it with her hand, it grows large enough to hold them both. They travel to Elk Woman's home, where Djogeon is welcomed as Elk Woman's husband by her mother and three sisters. Djogeon and Elk Woman live happily until one night when the mother-in-law has a terrible nightmare. She rolls around on the floor, screaming. Djogeon and his wife cannot get her to respond. Finally Djogeon brings her to her senses by hitting her on the head with a pestle. She tells them she dreamed that Djogeon will kill a giant monster bear. The next morning Djogeon kills the bear and brings the carcass to his mother-in-law. The following evening the mother-in-law dreams that Djogeon will give a feast for the whirlwind beings, providing such great amounts of food that it will not all be eaten. The next morning Djogeon fills the lodge with deer, elk, and bear he has killed for the feast. He calls together all the whirlwind beings, who fill every corner of the house. The mother-in-law urges them to eat more, hoping there will not be enough food and they will become angry and kill her son-in-law, whom she secretly dislikes.

While the whirlwind beings are eating, Djogeon, his wife, her three sisters, and their husbands get more food. The Dagwanoenyent eat until their jaws and tongues can no longer move. They plead with Djogeon's mother-in-law to stop feeding them. When Djogeon hears their pleas and realizes his mother-in-law's intentions, he instructs the walls and floors of the lodge to become flint, trapping them all in the house. The whirlwind beings fly about, begging for mercy. Djogeon refuses to listen and commands the house to become red-hot. As the house heats up, the whirlwind beings fly faster and faster, knocking around the walls and creating a noise heard around the world.

When the lodge finally becomes silent, Djogeon and his wife and her family travel back to where they first met. When they come to the lake, it is not frozen thick enough to support their weight. Djogeon takes eight puffballs from an oak tree and transforms everyone into a miniature size. Then he lines up the puffballs on the lake and commands the west wind to blow them across. When they reach the other side the travelers regain their natural size. Eventually they make their way to Djogeon's home. [Curtin and Hewitt 1918]

Dodanohgaweh
Seneca, *Northeast*

"Protruding Tongue." A type of False Face mask (see *False Faces* and *Masks and Masking*) distinguishable by its protruding tongue. It is used to portray pain. [Fenton 1987]

Dog(s)

The dog plays a significant role in Native American mythology. The Seneca *Cannibal Woman* gains power through her love of dogs. The Lakota consider the dog (*Sunka*) to be the spirit responsible for friendship and faithfulness. The Killer Whale (*Qanekelak*) is, according to the Bella Bella, the creator of dogs. *Qiqirn* is an Eskimo creature that looks like a dog. A common motif is marriage between a woman and a dog (see *Dog Husband*). Dogs are eaten in ritual settings among many Native American peoples. At one time dog was eaten at the Blackfoot Grass Dance (*Ka?espai*); in the Arikara Hot Dance (*Kawenho*), dancers immersed their hands in boiling dog stew to retrieve pieces of meat.

Dog Boy
Pawnee, *Plains*

A human boy, born as a dog and thrown into a creek by a witch. *Clam Shell* rescues Dog Boy from the water and shows him how to follow the trail back to his people. As Dog Boy looks around, he realizes he has turned into a boy (see *Animal-Human Transformation*). Eventually he finds the village and tells the villagers he is the son of the hunter/warrior White Moccasins. The chief of the village takes Dog Boy into his lodge. Dog Boy leads a buffalo hunt, and on his return marries the chief's daughter.

Dog Boy and the chief's daughter have many children. One day while Dog Boy is hunting, he comes across a *deer* who tells him that White Moccasins is trying to kill him. The deer offers him her protection. When Dog Boy returns home, he invites all the village men to his lodge and challenges his father to a contest, which Dog Boy wins. Then Dog Boy waves his hand and White Moccasins starts butting his head against everything in sight. Seeing that Dog Boy has placed White Moccasins under some sort of magic, the other men attempt to kill Dog Boy with clubs, but Dog Boy yells and all the men, including his father, fall dead. [Dorsey 1906a]

Dog Husband

The marriage of a female mythological figure to a dog. The dog husband is a common motif in Native American stories. For Eskimo examples see *Adlet, Marriage, Sea Woman,* and *Sedna. Copper Woman* is the Chippewa woman who marries a dog. Their offspring are the Dogrib people of northern Canada. [Sheppard 1983]

Doll Festival

Western and northern Alaska, *Subarctic*

A festival to provide good *hunting* and renewal of game animals. The Doll Festival is believed to have originated after an old *shaman* killed his grandchild at birth and used its body as a powerful *amulet.* Another shaman, troubled by the dead child's ghost, had a vision and went to visit the third sky world, where he learned how to hold the Doll Festival. The festival was held in a *qasgiq* decorated with small wooden figures and moving wooden devices. Food and drink offerings were made in an attempt to please the sky spirits, who transformed the small wooden *figurines* into animals for the humans to hunt. The dolls used in the festival were also used to divine future hunting success. [Lantis 1938a, 1947; Nelson 1899]

Doll(s)

Native American religions make occasional use of dolls. Although sold as objects of art, the spectacular *kachina* dolls retain a valued religious role, particularly in educating children. The Seneca use dolls in divination *(Dream Divining).* The Nooksack consider a person's soul to look like a doll (sitec) image of him or her. *Wanagemeswak* (Penobscot) are dwarfs that leave lucky dolls to be found by people. A Pequot woman used a doll to overcome a giant (see *Chahnameed).* The Tlingit hold that sickness is caused by witches, who use dolls to inflict it (see *Master of Sickness).*

The Seminole of Oklahoma and Florida used clay human effigies to avenge murders. Four male relatives of a homicide victim participated in this ritual. The doll maker, joined by the other three men, placed the doll in the center of a hot fire. If the clay figure fell over as it turned red, the murderer would die in four days. If the effigy remained erect, the murderer had strong counterpowers and would probably become ill but not die. [Fewkes 1894a; Haile 1947b; Sturtevant 1987]

Donogaot

Seneca, *Northeast*

A horned mask (see *Masks and Masking)* that appeared in the nineteenth century. It may have been a caricature of the devil described by Christian missionaries. [Fenton 1987]

Dooehdanegen

Seneca, Iroquois, *Northeast*

"He-Who-Has-Two-Feathers-Placed-Side-by- Side." A powerful medicine person (see *Medicine People)* who held sole custody of his family's medicines. Dooehdanegen raises his nephew, *Hathondas,* and teaches him about the medicine. While Hathondas is still a child, a powerful sorceress seeks to marry him to her daughter. Dooehdanegen protects his prepubescent nephew from the marriage advances by smoking a pipe filled with tobacco and potent medicines. After puberty, Hathondas marries the sorceress's daughter and uses the powers he inherits from his uncle to survive many adventures. [Fenton 1987]

Doonongaes

Seneca, *Northeast*

"He has two long horns." A *horned serpent* who lives in deep rivers, lakes, and springs of water, coming onto land to sun himself and capture prey. Doonongaes has the power to assume human form and faculties, and even to marry humans. Stories about Doonongaes are told only in winter, when he and other reptiles are hibernating and thus unable to hear what is being said about them.

The power of the Doonongaes is harmful to humans, as are the waters where the serpents live. If a human limb comes into contact with the water where a Doonongaes is living, the limb will disappear. *Hinon,* the Thunderer, and his sons are enemies of Doonongaes and other reptiles. Doonongaes should not be confused with *Gaasyendietha,* meteor fire dragons, who also live in deep bodies of water. See also *Skahnowa,* a turtle, who is Doonongaes's servant. [Fenton 1987]

Double Faced Woman
See *Anog Ite.*

Dream(s)
In the religious views of many Native American cultures dreams, like visions, provide access to the spiritual world. Rarely are dreams considered merely dreams. They may give origin to rituals and to mythology. Dreams may cause, or suggest the cause of, illness. The Huron diagnostician *Saokata* receives information from dreams. *Ononharoia,* the dream-guessing healing rite, effects cures. *Hitebi,* the Yaqui curer, diagnoses with dreams, and the Yaqui believe that witchcraft *(Morea)* can be augmented by dreams. See also *Dream Doctor.*

The following examples illustrate the role of dreams and dreaming in Native American culture. *Akhrendoiaen* (Huron) is a healing ritual in which the dances performed have been prescribed in dreams (see also *Awataerohi*). Dreams were responsible for the creation of *akicitas,* the Lakota police society. Membership in the Ojibwa *Bear Sweat Lodge* is restricted to those who have dreamed of Bear; the Lakota have a similar society *(Mato Okolakiciye).* In the Yukon, those who dream of Beaver gain power (see *Beaver Man*). Iroquois masks are revealed in dreams, as are the *Faces of Forests.* The Lakota magical *Big Twisted Flute* was revealed to a shaman in a dream. Some Native Americans decide to change gender on the basis of dreams (see *Gender Crossing*). The Chippewa refer to the knowedge gained through dreams as Inkoze. During the *Ghost Dance of 1870* and the *Ghost Dance of 1890,* dreams prophesied the return of the dead. The Zuni spirits of the dead *(pinanne)* can communicate

with the living through dreams. The Pawnee *Grain-of-Corn Bundle* originated in a dream. One may become a *heyoka* (Lakota) only by dreaming *(Hanmdepi)* of Thunderbird. The Ojibwa refer to the spirits who visit the shaking tent as dream visitors *(powatakan).* Ojibwa fire handlers *(wabeno)* use fire to interpret dreams. People of northern Canada believe they can be possessed by *witiko* in dreams. See also *Dreamed Stories, Medicine,* and *Sleep.* [Applegate 1978; Eggan 1971]

Dream Dance, Drum Dance (ni mihetwan)
Menominee, *Northeast*
A dance and ceremonial organization carried from the Plains to Wisconsin in the 1870s. The Dream or Drum Dance is based on the revelations received by a young Lakota woman as she hid among lily pads after a battle between whites and Indians. After she had been alone and without food for several days, a spirit came to her. The spirit gave her a drum, taught her the rituals, and instructed her in the organization of the Drum Dance, whose purpose was to create *peace* between Whites and Native Americans. The Menominee Drum Dance organization still meets weekly and holds seasonal rites. Membership is open to those who have met their *guardian spirits* and are able to care for and properly use the drum. [Vennum 1982]

Dream Divining
Seneca, *Northeast*
The gaining of knowledge from dreams. Divining is accomplished with the use of a small female *doll* kept in a bark case and consulted by an older relative of the dreamer or a medicine person. [Curtin and Hewitt 1918; Wallace 1972]

Dream Doctor
Ahtna, *Subarctic*
Sleeper, gyenen/diyenen. A *shaman* who acquired power to heal by dreaming of an ancestor performing a shamanic healing. The dreamer awakened singing the song of the deceased shaman, having also dreamed of the equipment essential

to ritual healing. Although fewer women than men became dream doctors, the women doctors were the more powerful. The older the doctor the more powerful he or she was. Dream doctors were secretive and jealous of each other. In addition to healing, dream doctors located game and entertained at seances by showing off their power.

During a healing performance, the spirit soul (ye gi) of the dream doctor would take flight as the patient dreamed of his or her own spirit soul. When the patient awakened, the dream doctor could predict his or her recovery. Illness could also be attributed to loss of the life soul due to fright. In such cases the dream doctor covered the patient's head along with his or her own. While the audience remained quiet, the doctor retraced the patient's travels to the place where the soul had been lost. Malevolent dream doctors could think misfortune upon others, possibly even resulting in death. [Lantis 1947]

Dreamed Stories
Mohave, *Southwest*
Dreaming is of major religious importance to the Mohave. Some stories, particularly those dealing with clan *migrations,* are said by their narrators to be dreamed, that is, the narrator is shown the events of the story in dreams. Such stories are epic in proportion. A. L. Kroeber, who recorded some of these stories, referred to them as historical to distinguish them from stories of creation and the culture hero (see *Tumanpa and Kwa?akuyisavepone* and *Mastamho*). [Kroeber 1925, 1948, 1951]

Dreamer Cult
A movement that developed from the Earth Lodge Movement. See *Ghost Dance of 1870.*

Dreamers
See *Naachin,* the prophets of the Dunne-za and *Smohalla Cult.*

Dreaming
See *Dream.*

Drum
A powerful ritual object often associated with shamanism. *Medawlinno,* the Abenaki person of spiritual power, uses a drum. The Ojibwa term *Omiigiwen* refers to giving a gift of friendship, usually a drum. Drum sounds inform the Haida that salmon are plentiful (see *Qolqalg Odai*). [Hoffman 1974; Vennum 1982]

Duajida
Papago, *Southwest*
Curing. See *Mumkidag.*

Duck
Zuni, *Southwest*
A wise creature carried by *Kiaklo.*

Dunne-za
Subarctic
"Real People." The name the people of the Beaver tribe call themselves. Early ethnographies list the Dunne-za as Tsat-tine, an Athapaskan word meaning "Beaver People." For the Dunne-za, humans, animals, wind, rocks, and all natural forces are "people." Humans are constantly in contact with these other-than-human people. See also *Yagatunne* and *Saya.* [Ridington 1988]

Dwarf(s)
Little people and dwarfs are found in mythology throughout North America, fulfilling a variety of roles. The following are some examples.

The *Awakkule* (Crow) are dwarf people who live in the mountains and serve as helping spirits. *Fas-ta-chee* is the name of a Seminole dwarf character. The Huron identify *Ondoutaehte,* who appears either as a woman or a dwarf, as the perpetrator of war. *Sea Woman* (Eskimo) sometimes lives with a dwarf. *Tcikapis* is a helping-spirit dwarf of the Montagnais. Dwarf-Man *(Djogeon)* is a Seneca character. *Hantceciitehi* is the Arapaho term for dwarf. The Snohomish story *Killer Whales* tells of dwarfs living on an island. *Wanagemeswak* (Penobscot) are dwarfs who live in rivers.

Dyoyoqgwahacyon
Seneca, *Northeast*
"Striped rump." A partridge. [Fenton 1987]

Dzelarhons
See *Djilaqons.*

Dzoavits
Shoshone, *Great Basin*
The *cannibal* giant who steals Dove's two children. Eagle helps Dove rescue her children and gives her some fat, the stomach, and feathers from an animal he has killed. Dzoavits chases after Dove and her children, who escape with the help of Crane, Chickadee, and Weasel. When Dzoavits begins to gain on Dove, she throws the fat Eagle gave her. It becomes a deep gulch and briefly stops Dzoavits from getting closer. Next Dove throws the stomach, which becomes a steep cliff that Dzoavits has trouble climbing. Last she throws the feathers, and they become a thick fog in which Dzoavits gets lost. When he emerges from the fog he continues to track Dove and her children. Badger helps by digging a deep hole and hiding them in it. Dzoavits questions Badger, who directs him to the wrong hole. When Dzoavits goes into the hole, Badger throws hot rocks on him and plugs up the hole, finally freeing Dove to return home with her children. [Lowie 1924]

Dzoo-noo-qua
Kwakiutl, *Northwest Coast*
An ugly giantess (see *Giant*) who steals children. She lives across a river in a remote area of the forest and keeps her life spirit in a hole in the floor of her house. Sky Boy shoots an arrow through the hole in the floor, killing her and freeing all the captive children. See also *Asin* and *Snee-nee-iq.* [Boas 1921, 1930; Rohner and Rohner 1970]

Eagentci
Seneca, *Northeast*
"Old woman" or "ancient bodied one." Known as the First Mother. See also *Aataentsic*. [Fenton 1987]

Eagle
This powerful bird appears frequently in Native American mythology and ritual, perhaps most commonly as *Thunderbird*. For other examples of the roles and characters of Eagle see the following: *Beadway* and *Eagleway* (Navajo); *Buffalo-Woman and Corn-Woman* (Pawnee), in which a hunter becomes an eagle; *Burnt Face* (Crow), in which a tornado becomes an eagle; *Coyote and Eagle Steal Light, but Cause Winter* (Zuni); *Dead, Land of* (Zuni); *Mastamho*, the Mohave culture hero who becomes an eagle; *Tinmiukpuk* (Yukon), the great Thunderbird; and *Wambli* (Lakota), the eagle spirit responsible for hunts and wars. [Rasmussen 1932; Wilson 1929]

Eagle Clan
Haida, *Northwest Coast*
Djilaqons is the ancestress of the Eagle clan.

Eagle Dance
Iroquois, *Northeast*
See *Ganegwaʔe*.

Eagleway
Navajo, *Southwest*
A mythological and ritual curing complex. The stories of Eagleway are set in the period after *Changing Woman* has been born, but before her twin sons (see *Monster Slayer and Born for Water*) rid the world of the monsters created by adulterous relations of the Sun (see *Monsterway*).

Whiteshell Woman and Turquoise Woman, who were created from epidermis rubbed from beneath Changing Woman's breasts, live atop a mountain in an attempt to avoid the monsters. *Talking God* gives each woman an ear of corn, warning her never to give it away. Traveling to the south in search of food, the women meet a young man, identified as Monster Slayer, who leads them to food and helps them avoid a number of monsters. He offers to take them to his home in the south. There they bathe and he provides them with beautiful garments and ornaments. From him they also acquire long hair and eyebrows, bright eyes, and shining mouths. He persists in asking what they carry with them, inquiring whether it is corn. After repeatedly refusing to answer they finally yield to his request for a single grain from each ear. As they grind these grains on two rows of metates, the corn magically increases and fills a basket. For four nights the women grind the corn, which continues to increase.

Two Corn Maidens come to the man's house and win him from Whiteshell Woman and Turquoise Woman in a meal ball–tossing test (see *Test Theme*). The Corn Maidens' maternal grandfather, Cornsmut Man, is angry with them for bringing home the man, whom he considers an earth person. He awaits a chance to get rid of this intruder. In the meantime the four travel to the home of the Eagle People, whose headman is Hair Turning White. Together Cornsmut Man and Hair Turning White engage the hero in all sorts of tests, the failure of which would mean his destruction. With the help of *Little Wind*, the hero survives these trials. As a reward he is taught the prayers and songs of Eagleway and shown the ritual of catching eagles, which is done from a pit using a live rabbit as bait. The eagle feathers procured in this way are offerings to *diyin dine?e*. See also *Beadway*. [Newcomb 1940; Wheelwright 1945]

Ear Piercing
Lakota, *Plains*

A practice used to identify a person as a Lakota man, woman, or child who will live according to Lakota custom and obey Lakota laws. Children often have their ears pierced during the *Sun Dance,* but anyone may have it done at any time. The ear piercing is done by a *wicasa wakan*, the religious leader.

A new name (see *Names and Naming*) may be given at the ear piercing. The one giving the name becomes the child's godparent and is responsible for teaching the child Lakota customs. If ear piercing is done at a time other than during the Sun Dance, a feast is held, during which presents are given to the child and to the person doing the piercing. [Powers 1975]

Earth
The earth is sometimes personified in mythology; examples include the Tlingit *Hayicanako,* the woman who supports the earth, and *Maka* (Lakota).

Earth Diver
Earth diver is a type of creation tale found widely throughout North America. In the beginning the entire world is covered with water. The earth diver, portrayed as Beaver, Duck, Mink, Muskrat, Turtle, or Loon, dives to the bottom of the water and brings up a small bit of soil that the creator transforms into land. In some stories a contest is held among animals to bring up the soil. In the Iroquois origin story, Turtle succeeds after various other animals try unsuccessfully to bring up soil to support Woman Who Fell from the Sky (see also Aataentsic). Among the Blackfoot, many animals try, but only Muskrat returns to the surface with mud under his claws. In the Beaver (Dunne-za) version of the story, Muskrat surfaces with a speck of dirt under his claws and commands it to grow. See also *Earth-Initiate, Earth-Maker* (Maidu); *Lone Man* (Mandan); *Muskrat* (Crow), who is directed by *Old Man Coyote* to dive for mud to make the earth; and the Haida story of animals diving for earth after *Nikciamtcac* abandons Beaver and makes him cry tears that cause a flood. *Oehda* is the Iroquois term for the bit of mud from which the earth is made. [Dundes 1962; Kongas 1960; Weigle 1987]

Earth Lodge(s) *(Kararata?u)*
Pawnee, *Plains*

Moon Woman shows the Pawnee anthills as models for earth lodges. See also *Evening Star.*

Earth Lodge Cult
See *Ghost Dance of 1870.*

Earth Shaman
Pima, *Southwest*

A creator. See *I?itoi* (the culture hero) and the Piman creation story *Tcu-unnyikita.*

Earth-Circler
Seneca, *Northeast*
See *Deadoendjadases.*

Earth-Initiate, Earth-Maker
Maidu, *California*
The *creator* who descends from the sky on a rope of feathers to join *Turtle* and Father-of-the-Secret-Society as they float in a boat on the water-covered earth. Earth-Initiate's face is covered and cannot be seen. He sends Turtle to bring up some soil for land and calls forth Turtle's sister, the Sun, and his brother, the Moon. Turtle's brother and sister are Earth-Makers.

Coyote, the only one able to see and understand Earth-Initiate, opposes the creator's plan for a gentle and easy world. Before he is brought under control, Coyote introduces work, suffering, and death to the Maidu. Although he continues to shape people, he cannot give them life, and he is unable to join Earth-Initiate in the sky. [Kroeber 1925]

Earthquakes
Chingichnich is responsible for earthquakes in southern California. *Hayicanako* (Tlingit), the woman who supports the earth, causes earthquakes. According to the Iroquois, the turtle who supports the world causes earthquakes (see *Oehda*). The *One-Standing-and-Moving* is the Haida land spirit who causes earthquakes.

Easter
See *Yaqui Easter Ceremony.*

Ecan
Coos, *Northwest Coast*
A *ghost* that reenters a corpse, causing it to reanimate and escape to the forest to do malevolent things to poor people. [Beckham, Toepel, and Minor 1984]

Echo
Paiute, *Great Basin*
Turtle Dove, I-o-wi, leaves her baby son, U-ja, under the sage bush (ti-ho-pi) while she works.

The sage bush asks its younger sister, the summer Yellow Bird, O-ho-tcu, to watch over the baby. One day a witch (tso-a-vwits) comes to Yellow Bird and asks about the baby boy. Knowing that witches prefer to steal little boys, Yellow Bird lies and says that U-ja is a little girl. But the witch knows Yellow Bird is lying. She transforms into a terrible-looking creature, and Yellow Bird is paralyzed with fright. The witch steals baby U-ja and takes him to her home. She stretches his limbs so that he is physically an adult, although his heart remains that of a baby. She has sexual intercourse with him, making him her husband.

When Turtle Dove returns and discovers the witch has stolen her son, she sets out to find him with the help of her brother, Eagle (Kwi-na). They find U-ja, but Turtle Dove does not recognize him because of his adult size. When U-ja hears his mother's voice he cries out for her, but the witch laughs at him and convinces him to hide with her in the belly of a mountain sheep she has killed. When the witch comes out to get food, Eagle swoops down and carries U-ja away, creating a severe windstorm to hide his trail from the witch. He takes U-ja back and carefully lays him under the sage bush, and U-ja returns to the size of a baby.

Frightened, the witch goes to her grandfather, Rattlesnake (To-go-a), for help and protection against Eagle. When she hears Eagle approaching she crawls into Rattlesnake's stomach to hide, making him very ill. He begs her to crawl out of his stomach, but she refuses because she is so afraid. Rattlesnake tries unsuccessfully to vomit the witch. Finally, near death, Rattlesnake crawls out of his own skin, leaving the witch imprisoned in it. Stuck in the snakeskin, she rolls around and finally hides in the rocks. When Eagle approaches and calls for the witch, she repeats his words in mockery. Since that time witches have lived in snakeskins and hidden among rocks, from which they take great delight in repeating the words of passersby. See also *Acoma Emergence and Migration,* in which Echo decides the location of Acoma; and *Tumbianoobi* (Moapa) for the story of how a woman got the name Echo. [Lowie 1924]

Edzo
Dogrib, Great Slave Lake, *Subarctic*
The leader noted for making *peace* with Yellowknife Chief Akaitcho. He is a character in many Dogrib stories. [Damas 1984]

Effigies
See *Dolls* and *Inviting-In Feast.*

Egg
See *Acoma Emergence and Migration,* in which the choice between two eggs determines who will settle at Acoma.

Ehlaumel
Yuki, *California*
Thunder, who acted as the *creator* for the Yuki. [Foster 1944]

Eʔican
Nootka, *Northwest Coast*
A category of stories from old times, sometimes referred to as legends. These differ from oyaqhmis, stories considered to be news or narrations of events. See also *Himowico.* [Sapir and Swadesh 1939]

Elder Brother
Pima, *Southwest*
One of the names of *Iʔitoi,* the culture hero, whose adventures are told in the creation story *Tcu-unnyikita.*

Elriq (ihl-u-g-i)
Eskimo, *Arctic*
"Throwing away." The Feast of the Dead, held to feed, clothe, and give gifts to the dead through their living namesakes. Elriq provides an opportunity to ensure the continuity of relationship between living namesakes and deceased relatives. Each year one of the five participating villages plays host, so that each village holds the feast once

every five years. In addition, each village holds a smaller annual memorial feast.

The Yupik Eskimo believe that the *dead* depend on living relatives for food, water, and clothing. A small crumb of food offered to the dead becomes a large basket of food in the underworld. Water is an essential offering, as the dead are thought to be constantly thirsty. During Elriq the namesakes of the honored dead are dressed in new parkas and boots. The number of parkas given away is significant. Usually 20 are given away, since the Yupik word for 20 means "a complete person" (counting all fingers and toes).

The dead have a direct relationship with their namesakes. In stories, when a dead person returns to life his or her namesake immediately dies. Thus the feast is a dangerous time because of the proximity of the dead. During the feast, the honored namesakes sit on grass mats as a protection against being passed down through the ground to the underworld. Elriq was one of the first ceremonies suppressed by Christian missionaries. [Morrow 1984; Nelson 1899]

Emergence
Southwest
Throughout the southwest, the population of the present world is attributed to an emergence by the inhabitants of one or more worlds below the present surface of the earth. Many stories describe the era of existence in the lower worlds and the inhabitants' complicated and often strife-filled efforts to find a world suitable for life. The emergence often incorporates an explanation for the diversity of cultures and languages in this world. The emergence is often followed by descriptions of *migrations* from the emergence place to the present location of the culture.

For Apache entries related to emergence see *Apache Bear Dance, Apache Creation and Emergence,* and *Black Hactcin Creates Animals and Humans.* For Hopi entries see *Kokyan wuhti, Masauʔu,* and *Sipapu.* For Keresan (Acoma and Laguna) entries see *Acoma Emergence and Migration, Iatiku,* and *Masewa and Uyuyewa.* For

Navajo entries see *Begocidi, Blessingway, First Man and First Woman, Ma?ii, Nilchi?i, Separation of Men and Women,* and *Ye?ii.* For Tewa see *Sipofene.* For Yavapai see *Widapokwi and Amchitapuka.* For Zuni see *Zuni Emergence.* For a more general discussion see *Pueblo Emergence and Migration.*

Emergence is not exclusive to the southwestern United States, as is evident from the story of the *Choctaw Emergence.* [Bahr 1977; Haile 1942, 1981a, 1981b; Hudson 1976; Vecsey 1983; Weigle 1987; Wheeler-Voegelin and Moore 1957; Wheelwright 1942, 1949]

Emergence Place (hazhiinai)
Navajo, *Southwest*
The place where, after an arduous journey through worlds below the present surface of the earth (see also *Navajo Emergence),* the predecessors and creators of the Navajo world emerged. See also *Sipapu.* [Haile 1947a]

Emetic
A cause of vomiting, or a medicine that causes vomiting. In Native American religions, emetics are often associated with preparation for ritual. An emetic is drunk at the initiation of a Creek medicine person *(alektca).* A black emetic drink is consumed during the *Green Corn Dance* and the *Stomp Dance.* Huron healers *(ontetsans)* use emetics to exorcise spells.

Emogoalekc
Kathlamet, *Northwest Coast*
The son of a chief who falls in love with a slave girl. Disciplined by his father, the boy leaves his people and jumps into a lake, becoming a *water monster* (see also *Monster).* His friend finds him and weeps, but Emogoalekc warns his friend not to tell the village where he is. The friend keeps the secret, but the villagers find out anyway and try to catch him and kill him with arrows. Emogoalekc escapes and comforts his friend, saying he is not dead and that anyone who sees him will become a chief. [Boas 1901b]

End of World
Tsimshian, *Northwest Coast*
See *Amala*

Enemyway (anaaji)
Navajo, *Southwest*
A mythology and ritual healing complex, familiarly known as the *Squaw Dance* because of the female-choice public dance that is part of the concluding portions of the ceremonial. Enemyway is one of the few Navajo ceremonials performed in the summer. It is directed toward any Navajo whose illness is attributed to contact with an enemy (that is, non-Navajo) *ghost.*

A young man of the Corn People visits a family of Rock Crystal People. He marries the beautiful daughter, but then learns she is also married to her father. The father becomes jealous of the young couple and follows them around, spying on them. The father-in-law proposes a raid on Taos to the young husband. During the raid the father-in-law captures a Taos boy in a manner inexplicable to the young husband. This is repeated on another raid. Finally, the young man learns his father-in-law is a *witch* and that his powers are contained in a *medicine bundle.* The young couple plot to exchange medicine bundles in order to trick the older man and acquire his powers. They succeed and the tables are turned, but the father-in-law is able to switch the bundles back. This time he invites the young man to ask all his Corn People relatives to join them in a raid on Taos. Without the medicine power almost all the Corn People are killed by the Taos People.

The young man has two nieces of marriageable age. He refuses to allow any of their suitors to marry them. Coyote *(Ma?ii),* known by his name First Scolder, insists on marrying the girls, so their uncle devises a test (see *Test Theme)* that will also give him revenge on the Taos People. In order to marry the girls, First Scolder must obtain the scalps of two non–sunlight-struck Taos maidens, that is, maidens who never go out into the sunlight.

Monster Slayer (see *Monster Slayer and Born for Water*) is called upon to lead the raid, joined by various warriors and two old men, Bear and Snake. *Talking God,* who upholds the cause of peace, tries unsuccessfully to avert the war. The party attacks Taos Pueblo and fighting continues all day. At the end of the day, although it is believed the raid was unsuccessful, it turns out that the two old men, Bear and Snake, have captured the sought-after maidens. The old men pass the many tests necessary to win the maidens, but they are not allowed to marry them.

While the other warriors are performing rituals to cleanse themselves of war activities, the old men camp at a distance and smoke a magical tobacco that transforms them into handsome young men and attracts the maidens to their camp. The girls ask to smoke this tobacco, and by this means Bear and Snake seduce them. The next morning Bear and Snake are again shriveled old men. From this point the story branches to *Beautyway* and *Mountainway.*

The balance of Enemyway mythology concerns itself primarily with the ceremonials performed for the Corn People and others who took part in the raid on Taos and who, because of their proximity to death and the dead, were sick and weak. This is the origin of the Enemyway ritual process. [Curtis 1907; Haile 1938a; Wheelwright 1951]

Errand Men
Pawnee, *Plains*
Ones who assist at all ceremonies, *Tarucuhus.*

Eskimo
Alaska, *Arctic*
The name designating an inhabitant of the circumpolar Arctic, believed to have originated with the Montagnais (eastern Canada). The word most likely diffused into English and French from Basque whalers who learned it from the Montagnais. The word has had various spellings since the first ethnographic accounts in 1584 presented it as "Esquimawes."

The most widespread self-designation used by Eskimo speakers in Canada, inuk (pl. inuit), means simply "person, people." In accordance with the International Circumpolar Conference Resolution of 1978, "Inuit" is used to refer to Eskimo people of Canada and Alaska. The central Alaska Bering Sea coast Eskimos call themselves Yupik (sing. yuk) meaning "real, genuine person." People who live in north and northwest coast Alaska use Inupiaq (sing. and adjective) meaning "real people."

Es-te fas-ta
Seminole, Oklahoma and *Southeast*
"Gives everything." The son of Sa-kee (breath), tom (everybody), mas-see (make it). The Old Man *creator* who dwells in the sky. Es-te fas-ta gave the Seminoles the three *medicine bundles* that designate the divisions within the Seminole tribe. They are guarded by an appointed medicine person (see *Medicine People)* and kept "alive" by the annual celebration of the *Green Corn Dance.* When new and different medicines are needed to meet changing needs in the Seminole community, Es-te fas-ta reaches down during the Green Corn Dance and gives the people the needed medicines. Es-te fas-ta gave the Seminoles land, rice, and the coconut-shell rattle. He appointed Tiger and Wind as the first two medicine people and prepared the people for the coming of *Fastachee,* "Little Give," the bringer of corn. [Sturtevant 1987]

Es-te mat-tee
Seminole, Oklahoma and *Southeast*
"Person Look All Over." An old monkeylike person who lived before the Seminole people came into being. He prepared the first Seminole *medicine bundle.* Es-te mat-tee comes upon Rattlesnake and Owl after they have survived a five-month bet on who could go the longest without food. Rattlesnake wins the wager and offers Owl's claws to Es-te mat-tee, who convinces Rattlesnake to give up two of his four fangs for the bundle.

Ettowe
Zuni, *Southwest*
Medicine bundle, often referred to as *fetish,* consisting of an object or objects, often stone, considered to have great power. The most powerful belong to Zuni *rain priests,* and the welfare of the community depends on them. Ettowe are carefully stored and, like masks, fed regularly. See also *Mili.* [Bunzel 1932]

European-Americans
Americans of European ancestry are sometimes included in Native American mythology. American southwest emergence mythology occasionally includes stories describing the diversity of peoples. Spanish and "White" Americans may be included with other native peoples as originating at that time. Other stories, such as one told by the Apache (see *Europeans, Origin of),* specifically describe the origin of European-Americans. Most Native American cultures have developed a distinctive name by which to call European-Americans. Along the Bering Coast the term is *Kassaq.* The Haida call them *Iron People.* The Hopi term "Bahana" refers to a mythological tradition about a lost White brother who will someday return. The Lakota term is *Wasicun.*

Europeans, Origin of
Jicarilla Apache, *Southwest*
Coyote teases Cyclone and runs away from him. Coyote goes to *Child-of-the-Water* and, pretending to be a great friend of Cyclone's, invites him to visit Cyclone. When they find Cyclone, Coyote plays tricks on him and runs away. Child-of-the-Water is not very swift and is caught by Cyclone and torn to pieces.

A woman finds blood on leaves and takes them home to cook for soup. From the cooking pot she hears someone crying. It is Child-of-the-Water. Rescued from the soup, Child-of-the-Water travels to the east and walks upon the ocean. Finding a kind of fish with blue eyes, he captures a female and a male. With the help of *White Hactcin,* Child-of-the-Water uses the fish

to make White people. He makes a tracing of himself on the ground and places the fish within it. In stages, White Hactcin progressively transforms the fish into human beings. Many birds and animals are called forth to give these new human beings whatever they want, including buckskin clothing and square houses with windows. *White Shell Woman* is their stepmother.

From here the story predicts the coming of Europeans and how they will relate to the Apache people. [Opler 1938b]

Evening Star (Cu-piritta-ka)
Pawnee, *Plains*
"Female white star." The wife of *Morning Star.* Both are known by westerners as the planet Venus. She is referred to as a star (see *Stars and Starlore)* because of her place in the western sky, not because she is astronomically present as a star. Evening Star keeps her husband's *medicine bundle,* which includes a war club. She sends her daughter to earth with the rains-wrapped-up-bundle to rule over the *earth lodge* in the west, where all the animals are kept. She sends the four sky beings of the west to guard her daughter. Because Evening Star wants women to be superior to men, she tells her daughter to kill any young man who courts her, so that all women will do the same to overcome men.

The daughter has already killed a number of suitors when she is approached by a poor boy from a village in the east. The boy has been sent by Morning Star, who gave him his power and war club and told him how to overcome the obstacles Evening Star's daughter will put in his way. Thus armed, the poor boy overcomes a deep canyon, a raging stream, and a thick forest, then releases the animals being held in the earth lodge ruled by Evening Star's daughter (see *Game, Release of).*

The poor boy marries Evening Star's daughter, but is unable to have intercourse with her until he has accomplished a number of feats, which he does with the help of various animals (see *Test Theme).* Evening Star's daughter tries to protect herself from him by turning loose snakes, bears, and wildcats to attack him, but he kills them all with Morning Star's war club. The daughter has a toothed vagina (see also *Vagina Dentata*) like the mouth of a rattlesnake. Morning Star tells the poor boy to file the vagina with a stone while having intercourse with her, thus making intercourse possible and transforming her into his wife. Then Morning Star gives the poor boy and Evening Star's daughter two bundles. She tells them to offer a sacrificial ceremony with a young woman captured from an enemy, so that all the obstacles overcome with Morning Star's power will be remembered. Thereafter all newborn children are placed in cradle boards with a picture of Morning Star on the top. The infants are covered with buffalo and wildcat skins and tied in with otter-skin string.

For related Pawnee entries see also *Big Black Meteoric Star; Grain-of-Corn Bundle; Kurahus,* the Pawnee priests responsible for the Evening Star Bundle; *Long Tongue,* in whose cave the daughter of Evening Star is trapped; and *Basket Dice Game.* [Dorsey 1906a; Murie 1989]

Everlasting Man
Tillamook, *Northwest Coast*
A name for the south wind *(Tkahyal).*

Evilway
Navajo, *Southwest*
See *Uglyway.*

Excessway
Navajo, *Southwest*
See *Ajilee.*

Excrements, Swallowing of
Serrano, *California*
Activity based on the belief that having possession or use of another's excrements can give one power over that individual. See *Kukitat.* In most stories the excrements of the creator become *culture heroes* or are swallowed, usually by *Frog,* who hides in the ocean, thus bringing about the creator's

death. See also *Fecal Power, Mastamho* (Mohave), and *Takwe* (Juaneño). [Kroeber 1925]

Excreta
Among the Eskimos, people who have traveled under the sea or to the moon are instructed to rub themselves with urine or feces in order to reenter their human community. Similarly, people who have had experiences with ghosts are supposed to roll in the village dump where human waste has been disposed of, in order to prevent the ghost from influencing others in the village.

In Pacific northwest tribes, urine is used to keep malevolent spirits from harming travelers who are journeying to supernaturals under the sea.

In northern Canada, *witiko* can be blinded by hurling feces at his face. See also *Fecal Power* and *Winter, Origin of* (Kathlamet).

Eye Juggler
See *Coyote* and *Eyes, Substitution of.*

Eyes
Eskimo, Bering Sea coast, Alaska, *Arctic*
Socially restricting sight and avoiding direct eye contact was thought to produce powerful supernatural vision. In a story told on Nelson Island, Alaska, a young aspiring hunter lives and travels with the seals for a year. They teach him how to make his sight strong and powerful by keeping his eyes downcast and using them sparingly, especially around women. [Lantis 1947; Riordan 1983]

Eyes, Substitution of
A story motif in which the hero exchanges eyes with another animal in order to accomplish a particular feat. In a Crow story, Old Woman's Grandchild enters a storytelling contest with some snakes. In order to appear awake throughout the contest, the boy exchanges eyes with Jackrabbit. In a related motif, *Coyote* learns to throw his eyeballs to look for something at a distance. He abuses this privilege and loses his eyes, having to replace them with pitch. [Lowie 1956, 1960]

F

Fabrics (or soft goods)
Navajo, *Southwest*
See *Yodi and Ntliz.*

Face
See *Inua* (Alaska), which may be represented in art as a face; and *Lone Bird* (Ojibwa), Moon's female lover whose face is reflected in the moon (see also *Moon* for other stories about the face in the moon).

Faces Alone
Iroquois, *Northeast*
A curing song and dance taught by *Hodigohsosga.*

Faces of Forests
Iroquois, *Northeast*
The common faces of spirits found in trees in the forest, who are under the leadership of the Great False Faces (see also *False Faces)*. Members of the Society of Faces claiming the power to control sickness represent these spirit faces in their masks (see *Masks and Masking)*. Although Faces of Forests are not considered as powerful as the False Faces, they are important in healing rituals.

The Faces of Forests have disembodied heads and long hair. They were initially encountered by Iroquois hunters who saw them moving from tree to tree in the forest. The Faces did not intend to hurt the hunters; they just wanted tobacco and white corn mush. Later the Faces gave instructions through *dreams* on how to carve masks of their likenesses and *dance* their healing dances. They also specified that the dancers were to carry *turtle rattles* and peeled hickory staffs. The Faces promised to give healing power whenever a feast is held in their honor, providing they are honored with the burning of tobacco and the singing of curing songs. The Faces of Forests speak a language of nasal grunting sounds and are able to pick up ashes with their bare hands without suffering burns. They cure the sick by blowing hot ashes on them (see also *Ash Blowing Rite)*. [Fenton 1987]

False Face(s)
Iroquois, *Northeast*
The English term generally used to designate any Iroquoian *masks and masking* practices. Such masks and/or the figures they personify are called the Gagohsa (mask)

among the Seneca; the Hadu?i (hunchback) among the Onondaga; and Gagu:wara (face) by the Mohawk. The term False Faces is most specific to the Society of Faces, which is one of three medicine societies; the other two are the *Husk Face* Society, also known as the Bushy Heads, and the Medicine Company or Society of Animals, the *Hadidos.*

The Society of Faces, also known as the Society of Wooden Faces and the False Face Company, is distinguished by its use of wooden masks with deep-set eyes highlighted with tin or brass, large noses that are frequently bent, deeply arched eyebrows, and wrinkled foreheads. The mouths on these masks vary. The masks are often divided longitudinally by a crease or comb of spiny protrusions. The figures represented by mask and costume may disguise themselves as hunchbacks and move about with a crawling gait. When they participate in the *Traveling Rite,* which occurs in spring and autumn, they are scantily dressed and known for their healing ability, which is effected by blowing hot ashes on the sick (see *Ash Blowing Rite).*

According to the Seneca, Shagodyowehgowah is responsible for *creation.* One Seneca leader considered Shagodyowehgowah to be "headman of all False Faces." This figure is also referred to as *Hadu?i* (Our Maker) among the Onondaga and Cayuga (see also *Hadu?igona,* "the Great Hunchbacked One"). Among the Cattaragus he is known as Gagohsa (First Man). Over time, Shagodyowehgowah came to be representative of the power of the mask or the mask's spirit.

All the other wooden masks used by the Society of Faces are known as Common Faces or "Only Faces." They are also known as the Beggar Masks and make their debut at the *Midwinter Festival.* The Common Faces live in the forest (see also *Faces of Forests)* and are crafted from trees by male carvers who may dream a specific face (see also *Hodigohsosga?a).* The spirit represented by the masking causes or relieves the *False Face Sickness.* Each mask has power of its own that is

transferred to the maskers during the healing ceremonies. Other faces are specifically dreamed about by a person who has been ill. False Face masks are classified into a variety of types based largely on the character of the nose and the shape of the mouth. For discussions of these mask types, see *Dehotgohsgayeh, Dodanohgaweh, Hanogagah, Hayondiha, Odogwa?shodo?, Hodesadoghdo,* and *Hosedo.* See also *Iroquois Masks, Storage of* and *False Face Medicine.*

A person who has been cured of False Face Sickness automatically joins the medicine society that assisted in his or her recovery. Although membership in the three orders of the False Faces is open to both men and women, women never wear the wooden mask of the Society of Faces. Other Common Faces have their origin in specific stories. They are often categorized by such facial features as straight lips or a long nose.

There are many origin stories for the wooden False Faces. A story told in the late nineteenth century relates how *Hawenniyo* went around inspecting creation and banishing evil. He divests the *Stonecoats* (jokao) of their stone shirts, but allows them to remain to help hunters cure illness. As Hawenniyo travels west to the edge of the world, he meets a huge man, the great False Face, leader of all the Faces, who is known as Shagodyowehgowah. Hawenniyo inquires about this great False Face's origins and is told that he comes from the Rocky Mountains and has lived on earth since its creation. An argument ensues about who created and owns the earth. Finally Hawenniyo and the great False Face decide to have a contest to determine who is the creator and rightful owner of the earth. They sit down with their backs to the west. Whoever causes the distant mountains to move closest to them will be the winner.

The great False Face shakes his large *turtle rattle,* frightening all the animals, and calls the mountain to him. The mountain moves only a short distance. Then Hawenniyo conjures and calls the mountain, which comes to rest immediately behind them. The great False Face is impa-

hagodyowehgowah, "Their Great Protector," the head of all
e False Faces, as portrayed by Sherman Redeye, wearing his
ther's mask, Allegany Reservation, 1933. From *The False
aces of the Iroquois,* by William N. Fenton. Copyright ©
987 by the University of Oklahoma Press.

tient to see how far the mountain has moved. He turns around so quickly that he smashes his face into the mountain, breaking his nose and distorting his mouth.

Although Hawenniyo has easily won the contest, he realizes the great False Face has tremendous power. He tells the great False Face that he must rid the earth of disease and help traveling hunters. The great False Face agrees that if humans will make portrait masks of him, call him "grandfather," make tobacco offerings, and feed him corn mush, he will give humans the power to cure disease by blowing hot ashes. Hawenniyo gives the great False Face a place to live in the west at the edge of the earth, and the spirit agrees to come whenever the people call him.

At Midwinter Festival, the Society of Faces comes to the *longhouse* in order to enable persons to fulfill particular dreams or to renew dreams. The Common Faces also participate by announcing the arrival of two maskers representing Shagodyoweh (the great rim dweller) or Shagodyowehgowah (the head of all the False Faces). This activity, along with guarding the door and keeping order, is known as the Doorkeepers Dance. See also *Longhouse Ceremony.*

The Husk Faces *(Hadjihsa Thokste?ah)* are a separate medicine society. The masks of these mythic figures are made of cornhusks. The male and female wearers of the Husk Face masks comprise a healing society with distinct curing songs and dances. Membership in the society is gained by dream or cure. According to Seneca stories, the Husk Faces live on the opposite end of the earth from humans, where the seasons are reversed. The Husk Faces till the soil in a ravine among high tree stumps. Every New Year they come from the east, visiting the longhouse during two of the eight nights of Midwinter Festival. The Husk Faces act as heralds for the Common Faces, door watchers, and police during ceremonies.

The Husk Faces are mute and require a speaker. Although not as well integrated into the Midwinter Festival as the Society of Faces, the Husk Faces have the power to cure anyone who gives a dance for them, by blowing hot ashes on the patient. The Husk Faces are responsible for teaching humans *hunting* and *agriculture*. Their appearance at the Midwinter Festival celebrates the gift of maize (corn) beans, and squash.

The Husk Face masks are distinguished by age and sex. Older women usually make them, using one of two methods. One method uses braided cornhusks; the other involves sewing the cornhusk braids together to form the eyes, mouth, and nose with a smoother looking surface. Husk Face masks with fringed hair, nose, and eyes designate females. Rougher unfringed masks are grandfathers, and smoother masks are youths. Another mask variation of the Husk Face society is the Wooden Bushy Heads. These have wooden heads with cornhusk fringe for hair, and distinctive red ceremonial markings on each cheek and vertical lines beneath the lower lip.

The Husk Faces participate in specific *dances:* the Fish Dance, the Women's Dance, and the *Great Feather Dance*. These dances are usually held on the eighth night of the Midwinter Festival to honor the Husk Faces. The Women's Dance is danced only by women, while the Fish Dance is danced by men and youths of both sexes. Since the 1930s, women have participated in the Fish Dance by dressing as men, while men dressed as women participate in the Women's Dance.

The Society of Animals is known as the Hadidos among the Seneca and the Hanahidos among the Onondaga. The masks of this society are distinctive animal masks such as Shadagea (Eagle) or Gahgagowa (Giant Raven). The masks represent the power of certain animals in healing. Members of the Hadidos do a *round dance* and juggle hot stones while wearing a blind mask (a mask without eyeholes). See also Godiont (woman chief known for her relationship with False Faces), *Idos* (the ritual of the Hadidos), *Mesing Keo* (Delaware False Faces), and *Sapling* and *Sky-Holder* (both names of Iroquoian creator figures). [Curtin and Hewitt 1918; Fenton 1987; McElwain 1980; Wallace 1972]

False Face Medicine
Iroquois, *Northeast*

A curing *medicine* prepared by older women members of the Society of Faces, using the roots of the Manroot plant and Ongwe (sunflower seed medicine). Plants that grow upright, such as sunflowers, are considered to be effective curing medicine. Plants growing horizontally are considered poisonous and used in *witchcraft*. See also *False Faces*. [Fenton 1987]

False Face Sickness
Iroquois, *Northeast*

Sicknesses caused by not properly respecting the *False Face* masks (see *Masks and Masking*). These include ailments of the head, shoulders, and joints. Symptoms can include swelling of the face, toothache, eye inflammation, nosebleeds, sore chins, earaches, and facial paralysis. The same masks that cause the illnesses can, when worn by the appropriate maskers, cure these afflictions. Red spots on the face, such as boils, measles, and bacterial skin infections, are also considered to be False Face Sickness. Their cure requires that red-painted masks dance before sunrise. The cure of black facial spots requires black-painted masks to dance at night. Older people are consulted to determine which False Face ceremony should be used. Ridiculing any mask is an invitation to False Face Sickness. [Fenton 1987]

Famine
Kathlamet, Oregon/Washington coast, *Northwest Coast*

The name of a female *helping spirit* who is responsible for people starving because she keeps the bones of beaver, raccoon, sturgeon, and bear, as well as the shells of seafood, rolled up in her mat. Because their bones have not been properly honored, none of these animals will allow themselves to be caught for food. Famine is the helping spirit of two young men. One of them, knowing she is causing death (see *Dead),* overcomes Famine and takes away her mat. He dumps its contents onto the floor of his house. The old men in the village rejoice when they see the animal bones, because they know food will be plentiful again. They honor the bones by placing them in the water, and game animals become abundant once more. [Boas 1901b]

Fariseos
Yaqui, *Southwest*
Evil ones who persecuted and executed Christ. See *Yaqui Easter Ceremony.*

Fas-ta-chee
Seminole, Oklahoma and *Southeast*
"Little Give." A small anthropomorph (see *dwarf*) *who brings corn* and *medicine* to the Seminoles. Little Give's hair and body are made of corn, and he carries a bag of corn. He teaches the Seminoles how to grow, preserve, and grind corn, as well as the songs that go with each of the other medicines. See also *Es-te fas-ta.* [Sturtevant 1987]

Fecal Power
Examples of the curative and preventive power of human and animal feces in dealing with illness are found in many stories. The Pequot (New England Coast) applied cow feces to the face to cure toothache; sheep feces mixed with the urine of the youngest child in a family was believed to prevent measles. The Iroquois *Husk Faces* smeared their arms and hands with human feces before shaking hands around the village in order to keep disease from affecting people.

Feces may also hold magical power. In several Plains stories about starvation, buffalo feces are spread over a field while repeating a prayer. The next morning many buffalo appear, ending the famine. Those characters typically classified as *trickster* are often talked to by their feces, which give advice or warn of danger. See also *Chahnameed,* a Pequot giant who empowers objects with his own feces; *Excrements, Swallowing of; Excreta; Keninqas* (Nootka), whom Raven tricks using feces; *Kukitat* (Serrano), the younger brother of the creator, killed when Frog eats his feces; *Mastamho* (Mohave), who is made sick when his feces are

swallowed by Frog; and *Newekwe* (Zuni), clowns whose performances include the consumption of excrement. [Beckwith 1938; Speck 1903]

Fetish
A term used to designate ritual objects believed to have power. Although widely used to designate Native American objects, particularly small carved birds and animals that appear in jewelry, the term should be used carefully to avoid its association with superstition and primitive magic. See *Ettowe* and *Mili,* terms related to Zuni medicine objects. See also *Amulet.* [Cushing 1883]

Figurines
Objects made in human or humanlike shape are common in Native American ritual and often referred to in mythology. Perhaps most common are the great variety of Pueblo *kachina* dolls. Navajos carve ritual dolls for secret use in some healing rites. Even Iroquois False Face figures have appeared in recent years. See *Dolls* and *Doll Festival.*

Fire
The qualities of fire—its resemblance to living things, its creation of light, and its relationship to the sun—make it an important element in many Native American stories and rituals. Some stories tell of the acquisition of fire. The Huron hold that fire making was learned from *Aataentsic* or from *Iouskeha.* The Cherokee obtained fire from *Ani Hyuntikwalaski,* the Thunder Being. *Black God* is the Navajo creator of fire. *Okabewis* (Ojibwa) teaches people how to make fire, and the Menominee received fire as a gift from *Winabojo. Masau?u* gave fire to the Hopi. When Frog rubs his hands on the back of *Mastamho,* fire is created for the Mohave. Fire entered the Pima world to resolve the issue of what to do with the dead (see *Tcu-unnyikita*).

Fire is often missing during the mythic era, having been locked up or hidden by some malevolent being. In many stories, a culture hero makes a dangerous journey to steal fire so that it may be released for use by human beings. In many traditions *Coyote* is the heroic figure who steals fire. The Nootka woodpecker *(Lehmamit)* and creator *(Quawteaht)* both appear in stories where they steal the fire. The Ute wolf *(Sunawavi)* and the Kawaiisu *Tocitumba* are also portrayed in this role.

Fire may be used to represent new life, as when the fire is renewed in the *Green Corn Dance.* In a Kathlamet story of *Grizzly Bear's Fire,* the bear prides himself in always having a fire. *Ababinili* is the Chickasaw spirit of fire.

Fire, Theft of
See *Fire.*

Fire Dogs (Totki fa)
Seminole, Oklahoma and *Southeast*
Animals about a foot tall, with pointed ears, bushy tail, and globular feet. Fire dogs always travel in mated pairs, and always north or south, never east or west. They are seen at the sources of streams. [Sturtevant 1987]

Fire God
Navajo, *Southwest*
See *Black God.*

Fire Handlers
Ojibwa, *Northeast, Subarctic*
Men who use fire to interpret dreams. See also *Wabeno.*

First Creator and Lone Man
Mandan, Arikara, *Plains*
Cocreators (see *Creator)* of the lands on either side of the Missouri River. First Creator made valleys, hills, mountain streams, springs, buffalo, elk, and deer. Lone Man created the level land and small lakes and streams, along with the animals living in them, such as beaver, otter, and muskrat. He also created multicolored cattle and moose. An argument arose among the two creators as to which creations were the most helpful to humans. They finally agreed that humans should first use what First Creator made; when that was exhausted, they could use what *Lone Man* had created. [Dorsey 1904b]

First Man and First Woman
(atse hasteen and atse esdzaa)
Navajo, *Southwest*
The first pair to exist in the first world. Some say they were transformed from two primordial ears of *corn.* They direct the *emergence* journey through the four lower worlds, culminating in the ascension to the present earth's surface. See also *Navajo Emergence.*

At emergence, the surface of this earth is featureless dried mud. First Man and First Woman build a sweat lodge, in which they plan what the world should be like, and display the powers of creation contained in First Man's *medicine bundle.* The couple also build a hogan and enter it, along with those *diyin dine?e* that emerged with them. There they construct the world in microcosm, later transforming it into the present Navajo world.

Although *Changing Woman* is not their child, they rear her. When she reaches maturity they give her the medicine bundle of creation, first building a copy of it to take with them as they return to the lower world, where they will serve as chiefs of *witchcraft* and death (see *Dead).* See also *Blessingway, Changing Woman, Ma?ii,* and *Navajo Emergence.* [Goddard 1933; Haile 1938a; Matthews 1897; Reichard 1974; Stephen 1930; Wheelwright 1942]

First Mother
Seneca, *Northeast*
See *Eagentci.*

First People
See *Wazi and Kanka* (Lakota) and *Woge* (Yurok).

First Scolder
Navajo, *Southwest*
One of the names of *Coyote.* See *Ma?ii* and *Enemyway.*

First-Worker
Crow, *Plains*
See *Old Man Coyote.*

Fish
The Tsimshian tell the story of a slave girl who is a codfish. She lives in an underwater house *(Gitnagunaks)*. The Seminole culture hero, *Hisagita misa,* teaches people how to fish. *Hogan* is the Lakota term for the fish spirit responsible for water powers. Navajo *Shootingway* mythology includes a story in which a man is swallowed by a fish. The Puyallup associate the loon *(Swoxqwad)* with fishing power. *Kliatata,* the Kaska culture hero, teaches people how to make fishnets.

Fish-Eater and Hawk Create the Earth
Owens Valley Paiute, *Great Basin*
The world is nothing but water except for Black Mountain where all the people live. Fish-Eater (probably Crane) is Hawk's uncle. Together they sing and shake a rattle from which dirt falls. All night they sing and shake the rattle, until there is so much dirt the water begins to recede. When the water is all the way down, Fish-Eater and Hawk construct the Sierra Nevada mountains to hold back the ocean. A river runs through the valley. When they finish, Hawk declares he will live on rabbits; Fish-Eater will live on fish. See also *Creation.* [Steward 1936; Swanson 1970]

Flint
Flint is personified by the Iroquois under the names *Othegwenhda* (Seneca) and *Tawiskaron* (Mohawk), and as brother to *Winabojo* (Menominee). See also Pawnee *Flint Man.*

Flint Man
Pawnee, *Plains*
A human who is given powers to turn to stone, bring *rain,* and cure sickness. Flint is able to transform himself into any creature and to see great distances. One day he becomes invisible by asking a wandering man to smoke around him. The human obliges, and Flint gives him the power to heal sick people by using pieces of flint. He also transforms the human into Flint Man. Flint shrinks into a small piece of blue flint stone with a picture of the sun on one side and the moon on the other. Flint Man returns to his home with the piece of blue flint and places it on an altar in his lodge. He uses the power of the piece of flint to kill a menacing monster by trampling on its spiny back, remaining unharmed because his feet have turned to flint. The fat from the monster's carcass is used for medicines. The stone also protects Flint Man from an attack by a bull buffalo, but during the attack he loses the magic piece of blue flint. Consequently, beings from the sky who control the weather send a rainstorm, and lightning strikes Flint Man. Since that time Flint Man lives in the sky. [Dorsey 1906a]

Flintway
Navajo, *Southwest*
A mythology and ritual curing complex of the *Lifeway* classification. The hero, a good hunter, is the older brother in a family. During his travels he meets a beautiful young woman and agrees to accompany her home. He spends the night with her, during which they have sexual relations. When he departs the next morning to continue his hunting he learns she is the wife of White Thunder. In time he kills a mountain sheep, but finds that the sheep has no left eye and its left horn is marked by lightning. While he is skinning the animal, a storm arises suddenly and he is struck by lightning. All that is left of him is a trickle of blood.

Talking God informs the family what has happened to their son, but cannot tell them what to do. Finally the family learns that Gila Monster can help. To demonstrate his powers, Gila Monster cuts himself to pieces and scatters the parts. Then he reconstructs and revives himself. He revives the hero in the same manner, and this performance initiates the Flintway ceremonial tradition.

In another episode, the hero follows four buffalo who lead him away from his home. At night they come to him and ask why he is following them. He sleeps with the two female buffalo, and they blow a buffalo hide on him so that he may travel with them to their home. There he is unwelcome and is attacked. In fending off the attacks he kills the angry Buffalo Who Never Dies, who embodies all the lives of the buffalo. All the buffalo except his two wives fall dead. The hero is instrumental in reviving the buffalo, and in return he receives medicines and sandpaintings to extend Flintway. [Haile 1943a; Newcomb and Reichard 1937; Reichard 1939]

Flood(s)

In several instances the creator (or a succeeding culture hero) is displeased with the world after it is created, usually because of some characteristic of the people. As a result, the world is destroyed by flood. The Wiyot creator *Above-Old-Man* destroys the world by flood because he is unhappy with the people he has created. The Arapaho creator *Neshanu* does the same. *I?itoi* floods the world in the Pima creation story *Tcu-unnyikita*. The Pawnee creator Tirawahat floods the world to destroy giants (see *Squash Medicine*).

Sometimes monsters or giants cause floods. *Hiintcabiit* is an Arapaho monster who can cause floods. The Navajo *Water Monster* causes a flood when his child is stolen by Spider Woman. Tears of grief commonly cause flood, as when Beaver (Kathlamet) cries for his lost wife (see *Nikciamtcac*). *Sun's Grief* (Cherokee) is another example. Floods may be caused by misbehavior, as in the Zuni story *Incest Causes Flood.* Causing a flood may be an act of revenge. *Wesucechak* avenges the death of his brother *Misapos* in this manner. *Tavwots,* the Ute rabbit, causes a flood when his head explodes upon being burned by Sun. After the Yavapai emergence, failure to close the hole to the lower worlds causes a flood (see *Widapokwi and Amchitapuka*). [Gilliland 1972; Reagan 1919, 1921; Sapir 1919; Schmidt 1948; Smith 1906]

Flood Subsided by Sacrifice
Zuni, *Southwest*

A despised boy who claims to be the grandson of *Paiyatemu,* the sun youth kachina, is tested by his father. As a reward for passing the tests, he is given the power to marry the daughters—*Corn Maidens*—of eight rain priests. The powerful songs known by these Corn Maidens cause so much *rain* that it floods, and the people retreat to Corn Mountain. The flood finally stops when the young son and daughter of the village chief are sacrificed (see *Sacrifice*). Dressed in ceremonial costume and carrying great bundles of prayersticks (see *Prayer and Prayersticks),* they step off the mesa into the flood—the boy to the west, the girl to the east. They become the Boy and Girl Cliffs of Corn Mountain, the place of a shrine considered to give blessings in conception and *childbirth.* [Benedict 1935]

Flower Woman
Yaqui, *Southwest*

A woman capable of understanding the *Talking Tree* that revealed the nature of the world.

Flute

The flute appears frequently in Native American mythology and ritual. Throughout the southwest, a humpbacked, flute-playing figure known as *Kokopelli* is etched and inscribed on rock walls. The Lakota associate the flute with a love charm *(Big Twisted Flute).* The sister of the Zuni kachina Paiyatemu uses a flute to make butterflies. In the *Hopi Ritual Cycle,* the *Snake Dance* and *Flute Dance* are performed in alternate years.

Flute Dance
Hopi, *Southwest*

An August ceremonial complex performed in alternating years with the *Snake Dance.* In addition to the concerns of the Snake Dance, it incorporates concerns for the productivity of springs. [Bradfield 1973; Fewkes 1894b; Parsons 1936; Stephen 1936; Titiev 1944; Voth 1902]

Food Choices of Animals
Kawaiisu, *Great Basin*

According to story tradition, after deer are created and found good to eat (see *Deer Hunting),* the animals come together to decide what their main sources of food will be. *Coyote* declares he will eat dead things. Then Eagle, Chicken Hawk, Falcon, and Squirrel Hawk all decide they will eat jackrabbits. Rattlesnake decides to bite people, but Gopher Snake resolves to be good and not bite human beings. Blue Jay and Ground Squirrel declare they will eat pinyons and acorns. Water Snake decides to eat gophers, and Wildcat states that he will eat cottontails. [Zigmond 1980]

Fool Dancer

See *Nulmal* (Kwakiutl).

Foot-Stuck-Child (Hasixtaciisan)

Arapaho, *Plains*

A girl child who is carried and given birth to by a man. The man is hunting with his six brothers when he sticks his foot on a thorn. The foot becomes severely swollen, and when the wound opens, a female infant emerges. The brothers name her Foot-Stuck-Child. They dress her in pieces of their own clothing and make a panther-skin cradle for her. When she grows older, they make her a beautiful dress decorated with elk teeth. The child grows to be quite beautiful, and the men love her greatly.

Bone Bull, a powerful buffalo skeleton, hears about the girl and sends Magpie to find out more about her. Bone Bull then asks to marry Foot-Stuck-Child. At first the brothers refuse, but Bone Bull persists, and eventually the brothers reluctantly send Foot-Stuck-Child to him. With her they send a dowry of gifts to flesh out Bone Bull's body: a woven blanket to become his paunch, a deerskin to become the fat of his intestines, an eagle feather to become his tongue, and a soft pumpkin filled with pith to be his skull and brains.

The brothers miss their daughter and are filled with remorse for letting her marry Bone Bull. They send many animals to rescue her, but all fail. Finally Mole and Badger dig down and travel under the ground to where Foot-Stuck-Child is sleeping. She slips out of her buffalo robe and

travels with them underground back to her fathers. Bone Bull pursues them and they escape up into a tree. Other buffalo come and help him butt the tree, but Bone Bull gets stuck in the tree and is killed by his wife's fathers. Then a stone demands Foot-Stuck-Child in marriage. Frightened, the young men surrender their daughter to him. Again Mole and Badger save her and she escapes with the brothers, pursued by the stone. This time Foot-Stuck-Child slows the pursuing stone by making a canyon. Then Foot-Stuck-Child and her fathers rise to the sky and become the *Pleiades,* which are known to the Arapaho as the buffalo bulls (banokuci). [Dorsey and Kroeber 1903]

Forked Tongue

A common English-language designation for speaking falsely. See *Two-Hearts.*

Fotease

Jemez, *Southwest*

In the mythic era, the chief of the War Society who plans the emergence as well as the way things will be in this world. Fotease leads the people out from Wawanatutu *(Shipap)* where they have been living in the underworld. Before leading the people out, Fotease plans and practices the agricultural ceremonials and medicine rites. As a consequence it rains and the crops are good. These acts establish the Jemez ritual cycle and the practice of medicine rites.

Fotease also teaches the people in matters pertaining to the sun, moon, and stars. Under his direction, they dress the *Sun* in order to make it cold, develop the ceremonies necessary to make spring return, and make four mountains in which to set up feathers as offerings for the spirits. After all these ceremonials are planned and tested, Fotease leads everyone onto the earth's surface. The people then repeat the ceremonies they had performed in Wawanatutu and begin their *migration* journey to the present location of Jemez pueblo. [Parsons 1930a]

Found-in-Grass
Arapaho, *Plains*

A well-known story character who calls *buffalo* for a successful hunt. One of two brothers, Found-in-Grass has many adventures as a result of his failure to heed his father's warnings. Everyone ridicules him because he is dirty and fat. One time Found-in-Grass is picked up by a whirlwind and carried off to a grass field, where he is found by an old woman cutting grass. The old woman makes bows and arrows for him, and he becomes a great hunter and warrior. Over time, Found-in-Grass becomes a handsome man, marries the woman he has long desired, and becomes chief. He is credited with resuscitating *Nihansan,* the culture hero. See also *Dirty Boy.* [Dorsey and Kroeber 1903]

Four Beings of the North
Pawnee, *Plains*

Responsible for the food supply of the people, they exist with the creator *Tirawahat* and are led by *Ready-To-Give,* also known as Wind. The Four Beings send buffalo and other game as well as rain for crop growth. The following story is told about the Four Beings. Tirawahat instructs First Man to put his thumbs together and point them north. First Man does this, and the faces of the Four Beings of the North are imprinted on his thumbnails. This gives First Man the power to create a mate for himself. The Four Beings send King-fisher to divide the earth into land and water. When Kingfisher has finished this task, First Man transforms Kingfisher into a human woman and takes her as his mate (see *Animal-Human Transformation).* The man and woman hold a ceremony to honor the Four Beings of the North. They teach this ceremony of honor to their offspring. [Dorsey 1906a; Murie 1989]

Fox

A common story character. Among western tribes Fox is usually male. He is often a companion of *Coyote,* yet he may deceive Coyote and steal his food. Among some Eskimo peoples, Fox is a beautiful woman who comes to the home of a hunter while he is gone. She cooks for him and ends up staying with him (see also *Mysterious Housekeeper).* When the hunter asks about the musky smell in the house, the beautiful woman admits it comes from her. She puts on the fox skin and disappears from the house. See also *Silver Fox,* the Achumawi creator.

Frog

Glooscap, the Micmac culture hero and trickster, gives Frog his voice. The Lakota consider Frog *(Hnaska)* responsible for occult powers. See also *Excrements, Swallowing of.*

Frost
See *Winter, Origin of* (Kathlamet).

Gaasyendietha
Seneca, *Northeast*

"Traveling torch of light." Meteor fire dragons. *Monsters,* prominent in many stories, identified by their illuminated fiery bodies. They are forced to remain in the watery depths because their constant shedding of sparks would set the world on fire. Gaasyendietha can think, talk, and act like human beings except during their brief flights from one body of water to another. Although Gaasyendietha are powerful, they are not necessarily harmful to humans, and they have been known to befriend a human being chased by an enemy. Gaasyendietha are not to be confused with *Doonongaes,* the horned serpent, who also lives in deep water but is never helpful to humans. See also *Ganyadjigowa and Haiendonnis.* [Fenton 1987]

Gadjiqsa
Seneca, *Northeast*

An other-than-human being, represented by a *Husk Face* mask, who teaches Hadentheni (the Speaker) and Hanigongendatha (the Interpreter) how to overcome *Ganiagwaihegowa,* the bear monster. [Fenton 1987]

Gagixit
Haida, *Northwest Coast*

"Wild men." Humans who were made wild by the *Land Otter People.* The Land Otter People transformed themselves into insects and crawled into the anuses of their victims, usually those who were camped alone in isolated areas away from their home villages. [Swanton 1905b]

Gaha
Seneca, *Northeast*

The *Wind,* who often befriends humans and helps them in different quests. In one story, Gaha befriends an *orphan* boy who has been deserted by members of his tribe while hunting. Gaha hears the boy crying bitterly and comes to comfort him. Gaha tells the boy he need only think of the wind and Gaha will come to help him.

Meanwhile the hunters return to the village and tell the chief what they have done. Fearing the child will die, the chief sends a trusted man to retrieve him. As soon as the man leaves the village, he turns into a great bear in order to run faster. Gaha knows of this and warns the boy that the person coming is really a dangerous bear who wishes to kill him. Gaha instructs him to stab the bear in the forepaw, its only vulnerable spot. When the bear arrives, the boy does as he has been told.

Gaha tells the boy he will make him into a swift runner. He says if anyone asks about the great bear, he is to deny ever having seen it, saying only that he heard a great wind rush through the woods. Gaha warns the boy not to be proud or boastful about his running ability.

The boy returns to the village to live. He is treated well, but every time he sees others running he laughs, believing he can run faster than any other living human. One night he hears a knocking at his door and a voice challenges him to a race.

The boy prepares ten pairs of moccasins, along with flint for his arrow points and parched corn to eat. At the place where the race is to begin, he sees a large, dark mass and realizes it is a great sleeping bear. At dawn the bear awakes and tells the boy the race will begin. The bear speeds away, leaping from hilltop to hilltop. The boy runs through the valleys and soon falls behind. He thinks of his friend Gaha, and Gaha instantly arrives as a whirlwind that carries the boy far ahead of the great bear. The bear withdraws from the race and offers his life to the boy. The boy kills the bear and burns tobacco as an offering to his friend Gaha. [Curtin and Hewitt 1918; Fenton 1987]

Gahondjidahonk
Seneca, *Northeast*

"She who is burned in many places." The name of one of a group of ferocious *women* who attempt to destroy their daughters' new husbands on their wedding nights. The women throw themselves into the fire as a challenge to their new sons-in-law to save them. The women, however, are immune to fire. Husbands who are not aware of this trick are killed when they attempt to rescue their mothers-in-law. [Fenton 1987]

Gambler

Gamblers are frequent and colorful figures in Native American stories. *Aqonidzaba* is a famous

Paviotso gambling centipede. *Cunawabi* is the Moapa trickster who gambles. In the Navajo story of *Hailway,* the protagonist Rainboy has a weakness for gambling. *Inipi* (Kawaiisu) gambles in order to gain the release of game animals. *Thlakalunka,* the Alabama moccasin game, is an occasion for gambling. The Crow warrior *Tsisapuec* takes responsibility for the debts of his gambling brother.

The Pawnee have a wonderful story of Gambler, a male *cannibal* who seduces young men into gambling games. When Gambler's victims lose the games, his wife, *Witch Woman,* chops off their heads and hangs them in the lodge. One day the older of two brothers with magical power goes to Gambler's lodge to find out why young men are not returning to the village. Gambler feeds him human eyes, which causes him to lose his power. The brother gambles and loses. Gambler kills him, and Witch Woman cuts off his head and hangs it in the lodge.

Later the younger brother sends some birds to look for his brother. When Raven returns and tells him what has happened, the younger brother sets out for Gambler's village, taking along his own food supply. He stays at Gambler's lodge five nights. Gambler tries unsuccessfully to get him to eat human brains and human ears. On the fourth night, the younger brother goes to a buffalo wallow where there are many buffalo skeletons. He sits next to a buffalo skull and cries. The buffalo skull speaks to him and offers to teach him the *hoop and pole game,* which is played with a black and a white javelin. "You must give the white javelin to Gambler when you play this game with him," the skull warns.

The next day the younger brother challenges Gambler to the ring and javelin game. As Witch Woman watches, Gambler wins the first game. The younger brother stakes his life on the next game. On the next throw, the younger brother breaks Gambler's javelin. Gambler asks for a postponement, but the younger brother refuses. Gambler sends Coyote, his errand man, to get a new javelin, but Coyote is scared away by the buffalo spirits. Gambler then sends Blackbird, who soon returns with the new javelins. Gambler chooses the white javelin for last game. Then the players decide to raise the stakes. The winner will kill the loser and all his friends. By the final round, when it is apparent the younger brother is winning, Gambler tries to postpone the game by pretending he has a broken leg. But the younger brother taunts Gambler and forces him to keep playing. The younger brother wins the game, and on the last throw the javelins turn into buffalo and run away. Gambler and all his family and friends are killed. See also *Buffalo-Gaming Sticks.* [Dorsey 1906a; Matthews 1889]

Game

See *Basket Dice Game* (Pawnee); *Hihi ogashoon* (Seneca), which are dice made of owls' eyes; *Hodadenon,* a Seneca story about a game used to cure; *Hoop and Pole Game; Match Ball Game* (Seminole); and *Moon Woman,* who gave the Pawnee the hoop and pole game.

Game, Release of

During the mythic era, animals on whom human beings depend to sustain their lives may be held captive. Sometimes the animals are kept in storehouses so that hunting is unnecessary. Eventually the animals are released, sometimes by accident or through the foolishness of the curious. Stories of this type account for the origin of hunting, which is now necessary because the animals have scattered.

In other cases the animals are held by an overseer or a *Master/Mistress of Animals,* who must be persuaded to release them to the hunters. For example, the Eskimo shaman *Angalkuq* must seek this release of game. Other stories feature heroic figures who release game in the mythic era, making human life possible. For examples see *Evening Star* (Pawnee), *Inipi* (Kawaiisu), *Kanaakwe* (Zuni), *Marriage Test* (Zuni), *Moon Woman* (Pawnee), *Neshmuk* (Bering Sea coast), *Tcu-unnyikita* (Pima), and *Witch Woman* (Pawnee).

Ganegwa?e
Iroquois, *Northeast*

Striking-a-Fan or Eagle Dance. The eagle is believed to be able to restore life and to entice animals for hunting. The Eagle Dance is done to ensure good hunting. At the beginning of the Eagle Dance, songs are sung to the accompaniment of the water drum and the horn rattle. Then a water drum is presented to the first singer and a horn rattle to the singer's helper. Each dancer is given a small rattle and fan. After each dance song, a speech is given and small cakes are distributed to the dancers as gifts. [Fenton 1987]

Ganiagwaihegowa
Seneca, *Northeast*

A mythic *bear* who eats people. He has no hair, and his skin is like a human's. His only vulnerable spots are the soles of his feet. In one story Hadentheni, the Speaker, and Hanigongendatha, the Interpreter, travel to the underworld. There they meet Ganiagwaihegowa, who is tormenting people. *Hadentheni and Hanigongendatha* place manikins made of basswood in front of their lodge and lure Ganiagwaihegowa to them. Then they kill him by shooting him in the soles of his feet. They cut off his feet and burn his bones to ashes so he cannot come to life again. See also *Gadjiqsa.* [Fenton 1987]

Ganyadjigowa
Seneca, *Northeast*

"Mud Hen." As *culture hero* and *trickster,* Mud Hen travels around giving names to things and planting trees. She also shows off her strong *orenda* by killing different animals through trickery. At the end of her travels Ganyadjigowa starts a dangerous fire and is killed by *Gaasyendietha,* meteor fire dragon, who proves to have more orenda than Ganyadjigowa. See also *Dahdahwat, Gwiyee, Hongak,* and *Onoqgontgowa.* [Fenton 1987]

Gaqga
Seneca, *Northeast*

Crow, also known as Gagahgowa. In one of the many stories about him, Gaqga starts traveling, not knowing how he came to be, where he comes from, or where he is going. Presently he comes upon four Djodjogis (blackbird hunters). While they are away he steals their meat. Lonely, he travels on and comes upon a family of Djoniaik (Robin People). Although the parents try to drive him away, Gaqga eats the Robin children. He leaves the parents crying for their children and goes on his way. When he comes to the Gano-geshegea, Sparrow People, they gang up on him and beat him on the head until he flies away.

Gaqga travels on and finally finds his own people, the crows. He sits down and watches as they hold a great dance. Soon *Hanisheonon,* Muckworm, comes from the east. The Crow people stop dancing and run in every direction, but Hanisheonon catches one crow person after another by the neck, killing them. After killing many of the Gaqga People, Hanisheonon travels west, followed by Gaqga. After a time Hanisheonon asks Gaqga what he wants. Gaqga tells him he is lonely and only wants to be company for Hanisheonon. Hanisheonon not only refuses Gaqga's company, he attacks him. Gaqga screams so loudly that all his people who fled from Hanisheonon come to his aid and peck at Hanisheonon until they kill him. [Fenton 1987]

Gather-on-the-Water
Tsimshian, *Northwest Coast*
Gather-on-the-Water's father gives him to the companies of Cannibal Dancers at the time of the annual Cannibal Dance. (See *Cannibal.*) The dancers place the young man high in the trunk of a tree. He thinks he is going to learn the Cannibal Dance but instead, a cannibal being brings him a dead child and makes him eat it, lest he himself be eaten. The cannibal being then takes him to the village and tells him that whenever he feels hungry he is to catch and eat a person.

Gather-on-the-Water lives in his tree above the village, coming down twice a day to eat people, and the entire village is in terror of him. Finally the chief holds a council, where it is decided to build a huge wooden trap to catch Gather-on-the-Water. The dancers sing and beat their drums loudly until he comes along and is caught in the wooden trap. Everyone throws medicine on him and feeds him slaves until he is full. The village tries various ways to deplete his supernatural power and kill him, but his powers always save him. Eventually he escapes and resumes killing people in the village, although not as many as before, and he no longer eats his victims. [Boas 1902, 1916]

Gayegwanowasgona
Seneca, Iroquois, *Northeast*
Great *tobacco* planted by *Hawenniyo* to carry messages to *Hadu?i,* the Humpbacked. The smoke from smoking or burning tobacco offers thanks and ensures protection. [Fenton 1987]

Geldegwsets
Coos, western Oregon, *Northwest Coast*
Benign *giants* who live near streams and eat fish.

Gender Crossing
Also referred to as *berdache* (from the French, for "male prostitute"). The adoption of the dress, occupations, and behaviors of the opposite sex by anatomically normal persons. This activity occurs in both directions and is culturally defined. Berdache behavior occurs in varying degrees in most Native American cultures. Male and female berdaches usually conform to a social heterosexuality. The sexual partners of berdaches are always nonberdaches. Berdache marriages are usually secondary marriages occurring in addition to marriage with a nonberdache.

Gender is often strongly associated with occupational specialization. For example, women do *quilling* and hide making, and men hunt. Male berdaches are anatomically male, but in occupation and dress are considered to be women. In an earlier period, men attracted to the female sphere might have quit the battlefield and become successful women. Some Yurok (California) men crossed gender to become *shamans,* a lucrative position for women. In some tribes where the female sphere was perceived as leading to prosperity and distinction, male gender crossing was tolerated. Among the Navajo (southwest), Cheyenne (northern Plains), and Mohave (southern California), male berdaches are matchmakers, love magicians, and healers of sexual diseases. Among the Yokut in California they were the corpse handlers. Among the Crow, they were responsible for cutting the ritual lodge pole. Cheyenne berdaches officiated at scalp dances. (See also *Scalping.*)

Unlike male berdaches, women who gender-cross are not reclassified. They are considered to be women no matter what their dress or occupation. Women who cross the sex boundary are recognized and honored by their community. The female berdache often experiences transformation visions, sometimes involving a female helping spirit like the moon. A woman might experience a *dream* or a series of dreams that result in her crossing gender boundaries. In most such situations she receives the encouragement of her father and/or husband. She is encouraged to learn male skills and to act in the place of male family members in curing, ceremonial, and war activities. These experiences often result in complex and variable behavior—sometimes the woman acts and dresses like a man and other times she does not. Women may cross gender boundaries out of economic necessity. For example, a woman might hunt and raid so she could support herself. In some of the northern Plains cultures female berdaches, referred to as "manly hearted women," match successful men in prestige. See also *White Faces* (Miami) and *Winkte* (Lakota), transvestites. [Blackwood 1984; Hauser 1990; Kochems and Callendar 1983; Lee 1982; Whitehead 1981]

Genitals

Occasionally Native American stories explain the placement or sexual difference of genitals. For example, a Nootka figure, *Andaokut,* relocates the genitals from foreheads to make sexual intercourse possible, and the Navajo stories associated with the curing way *Ajilee* explain the origin of differences in male and female genitalia.

Genonsgwa

Seneca, *Northeast*

Stone skins, figures capable of transforming into any number of forms to capture and kill humans. A Genonsgwa possesses an animate finger that it uses to locate people who are hiding. In one story an elk hunter leaves his comrades, ignoring a warning about straying too far, and trails an elk farther than he intended. At nightfall he sees two women on the other side of a stream, and they ask him how they might cross. He tells them to cross at the shallow part just below their camp. Rather than following his instructions, the women keep asking him how he crossed.

Presently the hunter realizes they are not women but Genonsgwa, stone skins. One of the "women" crosses the stream in an attempt to capture him, but he doubles back and crosses to the side where the "women" are camped. Angry at being fooled, the stone skins become more determined to capture him. The hunter climbs a tree and hides in the thick branches above their heads, protected from their view. Then one of the "women" takes a small animate finger from its hiding place between her breasts. Placing it in her palm she asks it to find the hunter. The finger stands on end and points to the tree branches above her head. The "woman" is puzzled by this sign. Taking advantage of her bewilderment, the hunter slips down the tree and steals the animate finger. The Genonsgwa women chase him, begging him to return the finger, but he outruns them and uses the animate finger to locate his companions.

When the man tells the chief of his encounters, the hunters decide to leave the next day. At daybreak the stone skins stand across the river weeping and begging for the return of the finger. They promise the hunter constant good luck in hunting if he will return the finger. The chief insists that the young hunter return the finger, because he knows the Genonsgwa will only continue to bother them. The young hunter places the finger on his palm and stretches his hand over the stream toward the women as far as it will go.

When they reach for it, they lose their balance and fall into the stream, sinking to the bottom. The hunters leave immediately and arrive home safely. With the aid of the animate finger the hunter becomes noted for his skill in locating many types of animals. (See also *Stonecoat.*) [Curtin and Hewitt 1918; Fenton 1987]

Ghost(s)

Stories about ghosts, the return of the *dead,* and beings that help the dead are widespread throughout North America. In one story told among Plains and eastern woodlands tribes, a young mother who has drowned is cared for by a *water monster* who lives underwater and brings her to the surface so she can nurse her orphaned baby. In some of the Pacific northwest coast tribes, stories of *Raven* begin with the death of a young boy whose parents grieve for him. The grief causes the mother to discover a shining young boy in place of her son's corpse. The boy tells the parents he is the answer to their grief. As the story unfolds it is revealed that the shining boy is not their dead son, but a substitute.

Some stories tell of ghosts seen as shadows when the living visit the land of the dead (see also *Orpheus)* in search of their relatives. These shadow ghosts are seen only at night and rarely return to earth. Many eastern woodlands tribes believe that a person's ghost does not leave earth until four days after death. During this time the ghost frequents many places it traveled while living. Some northern Algonquian tribes believe that the ghost of a person who dies suddenly or violently wanders for four to six weeks.

Many tribes hold yearly feasts to honor the ghosts of the dead. The favorite food of the dead is placed in a darkened room before the living relatives and friends begin their feast. See also *Ecan,* the Coos term for ghost; Navajo *Enemyway* and *Uglyway,* in which ghosts are considered the cause of illness; *Hihankara,* the Lakota figure who guards the spirit road traveled by ghosts; and *Tarneq* (Alaska), an invisible ghost. [Dorsey 1888d; Millman 1987]

Ghost Dance of 1870
Great Basin, Oregon, *California*

A dynamic religious *revitalization movement* started by the Paviotso man Wodziwob (Gray Hair) in 1869. While in a trance, Gray Hair learned that a ruler was coming with all the spirits of the dead. He would change earth into paradise, bring eternal life, and eliminate all distinctions between races. Preparation for this event entailed dancing with only short rests, bathing daily, and decorating oneself with red, black, and white paint. It was thought that dancing would hasten the approach of the *dead.* Ghost Dancers were encouraged to faint and dream of the returning dead. In these Ghost Dance dreams, many people met and talked with dead relatives who were on their way back to join the living. Others saw that everyone in the land of the dead was happy.

Gray Hair's teachings were adopted by another prophet, Weneyuga (Frank Spencer), who converted the Washo and then traveled to the Paviotso in northeastern California and the Klamath in southern Oregon. A modified version of the Ghost Dance known as the Earth Lodge Cult developed in north-central California among the Wintun and Hill Patwin tribes. The Earth Lodge Cult emphasized the end of the world more than the return of the dead (see *Millenarian Movements).* The dances were held in semisubterranean structures to protect the cult's members from the holocaust that would occur at world's end.

The Earth Lodge Cult was carried to the Pomo tribe, who developed it into the elaborately expressive Dreamer Cult or Bole-Maru Cult. This cult consisted of dreamers inspired by the Christian God, who taught the revelations of their dreams and preached a highly moralistic code. They abandoned the idea of the impending end of the world and emphasized teachings about the afterlife and a supreme being. Modified forms of the Bole-Maru religion are still practiced by contemporary Pomo and Patwin peoples in north-central California.

Among the Tillamook of Oregon, the Ghost Dance became the Southwest Wind Dance. It was introduced in the 1870s by a man named

Yetcit, who taught that all the Native Americans would die if they did not become involved. The Tillamook who participated in the Ghost Dance believed that if they danced they would live, their dead relatives would return, and whatever they wished for while dancing would appear the next morning. Nothing in the Southwest Wind Dance promoted getting rid of Whites. See also *Smohalla Cult, Ghost Dance of 1890,* and *Shaker Religion.* [Beckham, Toepel, and Minor 1984; Jorgensen 1986]

Ghost Dance of 1890
Bannock, Shoshone, Arapaho, Cheyenne, Kiowa, Lakota, Paviotso, *Great Basin* and *Plains*
A religious *revitalization movement* started by the powerful healing medicine person Wovoka (Jack Wilson) among the Paviotso in Nevada. While experiencing a high fever, Wovoka saw the Christian God and was told to carry the message of end times to his people: the *dead* would soon return, and the intruding White people would be annihilated. The 1890 Ghost Dance spread primarily to tribes who lived east of those influenced by the *Ghost Dance of 1870,* never reaching western Oregon. Among the Plains tribes, the Ghost Dance of 1890 was a factor in the last clash with the U.S. Army at Wounded Knee, where hundreds of Lakota men, women, and children were massacred. The *Wounded Knee Massacre* effectively ended the millennial expectations of the movement, although Ghost Dancing has persisted to the present as a dance form among some tribes. See also *Shaker Religion.* [McLoughlin 1976, 1990; Mooney 1896]

Ghostway
Navajo, *Southwest*
See *Uglyway.*

Gia is su
Haida, *Northwest Coast*
"To give things away." The term used to designate any occasion where property is ceremonially given by a host group to a guest group (see also *Give-away Dance).* This *potlatch* activity marks such occasions as the death (see *Dead)* of a person, the succession of an heir, a girl's puberty, the accusation or justification of some wrongdoing, or the erasure of the memory of an embarrassing incident. See also *Walal Potlatch.* [Swanton 1905b]

Giant(s)
A remarkable variety of giants and *monsters* appears in Native American mythology. Almost all are malevolent, although occasionally a giant is friendly or even helpful to humans; examples include the Iroquois *Dehotgohsgayeh,* the Netslik *Inugpasugssuk,* and perhaps even the Coos *Geldegwsets.* Some giants specialize in stealing children, including *Dzoo-noo-qua* (Kwakiutl) and *Nahgane* (Slavey). Others, such as *Tsavoojok* (Paviotso), cause men to fight so the giant can steal their wives. *Iya* (Lakota) and *Tuurnngaq* (Povungnituk) are simply terms meaning giant. *Nulayuuiniq* (Povungnituk) is an infant who becomes a toothless giant. *Tall Man* is the Seminole giant who smells bad. *Waziya* (Lakota) is a giant in the north who blows cold wind. *Winalagilis* (Kwakiutl) is named "Warrior of the World." The Lakota tell stories of *Unktehi,* who look like giant oxen. *Witiko* (northern Canada) sometimes takes the form of a giant. Maliseet cannibal ice giants are known as *Kiwahkw.* See also *Chahnameed,* the Pequot giant, and *Raven.* [Simmons 1982]

Gichi-manitou
Ojibwa, *Northeast, Subarctic*
The Great Creator. See *Omiigiwen.*

Gifts
Gifts are commonly exchanged in Native American societies. Reciprocity is often the rule: one who receives a gift must give one in return. Gift-giving takes on grand proportions in the *potlatch* of the Pacific northwest coast. It also plays a major role in the Yupik *Messenger Feast* and in *Nakaciuq,* the Yupik Bladder Festival. Throughout the Plains

and in other regions, such occasions as vision seeking are accompanied by a *giveaway,* in which one gives away literally every possession.

Girls' Puberty Rite(s)

Rites to induct girls into womanhood are widely performed. These rites almost invariably occur at the onset of menstruation or soon after. In many cultures the initiate is isolated during the time of her first menstruation. The girl and anything with which she may come into contact are considered dangerous or so potent as to become dangerous. During this period of seclusion, girls are often taught the responsibilities and privileges of womanhood. The rite ends with the presentation of a new woman, often now eligible for marriage, to her community. The Lakota rite is the Buffalo Bull Ceremony *(Ta Tanka Lowanpi).* The Navajo rite is *Kinaalda* (see also *Changing Woman),* very similar to the Apache *Na ih es* (see also *White Painted Woman).* A Nootka girl's coming of age is celebrated with the *Nucil* potlatch. See also *Women.* [Driver 1941]

Gispawaweda

Tsimshian, *Northwest Coast*

A man who spends two years living with a black *bear,* who teaches him how to catch *salmon* and build canoes. When Gispawaweda returns to his village, everyone is afraid of him because he looks like a bear, cannot speak, and will not eat boiled meat. The people rub him with medicine until his human form returns. Afterward, whenever he has difficulties, he goes to the mountains to find his friend the bear. In the winter, when no one else can catch salmon, Bear catches salmon and gives it to him. Gispawaweda paints a picture of the bear on his house. His sister's dance apron is decorated with Bear's image, and all her descendants use the bear *crest.* [Boas 1902, 1916]

Gitnagunaks

Tsimshian, *Northwest Coast*

The name of the underwater house where Chief Nagunaks lives with his slave girl, a beautiful blue

codfish. Gitnagunaks also becomes the family name of the human chief Dzagam-sagisk, Dragging-along-Shore, after his adventures with Chief Nagunaks. One day Dzagam-sagisk is fishing with men from his village. When he drops his anchor stone for the night, it lands on Chief Nagunaks's house. The chief sends Blue Cod, his slave, to check on the noise. Blue Cod keeps Dzagam-sagisk from sleeping. He is so annoyed that he catches her, breaks off her fins, and tosses her back in the water.

The slave returns to Chief Nagunaks, weeping because her fins have been broken off. The chief brings Dragging-along-Shore's boat and his sleeping crew down to his underwater house. When the crew awakens, Mouse Woman tells them where they are and how to behave. Chief Nagunaks feeds them boiled seal and becomes quite fond of them. Dragging-along-Shore and his crew stay with the chief an entire year, although other chiefs taunt Chief Nagunaks and tell him to let his guests go. Finally the chief gives a great feast, to which he invites the other chiefs. Afterward he blesses Dragging-along-Shore and tells him that as long as no fish are hurt, he will have everything he needs to live on the land.

With Chief Nagunaks's blessing, Dragging-along-Shore becomes a great hunter. One day some young men who do not know the taboo against hurting fish torture a grounded bullhead fish and club it to death. The young men perish in the depths of the whirlpool, and Dragging-along-Shore goes to live with Chief Nagunaks, taking the name Gitnagunaks. [Boas 1902, 1916]

Gitqada

Tsimshian, *Northwest Coast*

A blind man who lives with his young son and deceitful wife. Although blind, Gitqada saves his son from an attacking grizzly bear by shooting an arrow through its heart. His wife ridicules him, takes their son and the bear meat, and leaves Gitqada to starve. Out of love for his father, Gitqada's son smuggles meat to him. Gitqada asks to be taken to a remote lake in the woods.

The boy takes him to the lake and reluctantly leaves him there alone.

As Gitqada sits by the lake and weeps, a loon asks him why he is weeping. Gitqada tells the loon about his abusive wife. Out of sympathy for his plight, *Loon* restores his vision. Gitqada returns home and hides until his wife leaves. When he enters his house, he finds his son mourning for him. The two seal the hut to keep out the wife. She returns and pleads to be let in, but they refuse. Before daylight, she is transformed into a hooting owl. In the morning the owl hoots at Gitqada, but he chases her into the woods.

Once again a great hunter, Gitqada often hears an owl hooting in the woods. One night he forgets he is talking to an owl and says to it, "Foolish woman, leave me alone! I do not want you near my camp!" The owl stops hooting. As Gitqada walks out of his hut the owl flies over his head and Gitqada falls dead. [Boas 1902, 1916]

Giveaway(s)
The distribution of all one's worldly possessions as *gifts* to the members of the community. Giveaways are widely practiced on ritual occasions in Plains cultures, including the Lakota *White Buffalo Ceremony,* Crow *Aassahke,* and Blackfoot Grass Dance *(Ka?espai).* Along the Pacific northwest coast the occasions for giveaways are formalized as the *potlatch* (see *Gia is su,* the Haida term for giveaway; *Nucil,* the Nootka potlatch; and the Haida *Walal Potlatch).*

Giveaway Dance
See *Pakahk,* the Cree helping spirit honored at the Giveaway Dance.

Glooscap
Northeast
A character of both benevolence and deception, also known as Gluskap, Kluscap, Gluskabe. In some stories he travels in a stone canoe and names the stars and constellations (see *Stars and Starlore),* as well as giving *Frog* its voice and Beaver its tail. Glooscap is also credited with creating rock

outcroppings and stream outlets along St. John's River in New Brunswick, Canada, and in the Chic-Choc Mountains along Gaspe Bay on the north Atlantic coast.

Glooscap disappeared after attempting to kill his twin brother Malsum (Wolf). His two pet dogs, named Loon (Paqueem) and Wolf (Molsum), are so fond of him they continue to mourn his disappearance with their haunting cries. Glooscap is credited with teaching humans how to tan hides, weave, beadwork, fish, and hunt. In Maliseet stories Glooscap disguises himself as *Kiwahkw,* the ice giant. The Maliseet identify Glooscap's older brother as *Mikumwesu.*

In Passamaquoddy stories *Mikchich,* the turtle, is Glooscap's uncle; *Nimakwsowes,* a sable who is a culture hero, is associated with Glooscap; *Pukjinskwes* is a witch whom Glooscap outsmarts; *Winpe* is a loon Glooscap teaches to cry; and *Wuchowsen,* the bird responsible for storms, is tamed by Glooscap. See also *Trickster* and *Culture Hero.* [Fisher 1946; Hamberger 1973; Helm 1981; Hill 1978; Leland and Prince 1902; Parkhill 1992; Prince 1921]

Goal of Life
Navajo, *Southwest*
See *Sa?ah naghai bikeh hozho.*

Godasiyo
Seneca, *Northeast*
The woman chief who lived during the time when the earth was new and everyone spoke the same tongue and lived in peace. Godasiyo's village occupies both sides of a large river. Every night her people cross the river to attend dances and exchange goods with the people there. Eventually Chief Godasiyo's large white dog begins to cause trouble. Fearing a fight, the chief decides to remove her loyal followers to another residence upstream.

The people construct two birchbark canoes with a platform between them for Chief Godasiyo to ride on. The people make canoes for themselves and paddle upstream on either side of

Chief Godasiyo's canoe. At the fork in the river the people begin to squabble about which way to go. The two men paddling Chief Godasiyo's canoe fight, causing her platform to split. Chief Godasiyo falls into the river and is transformed into a great fish. The people are upset, but when they try to talk they find they no longer understand each other. Their *languages* are no longer the same and they become a divided people. This is the reason so many languages are spoken by the various tribes on earth. [Fenton 1987]

Godiont
Seneca, *Northeast*
A woman chief elected by her people and known for her relationship with the *False Faces.* The False Faces want to settle permanently in the Genesee Valley at a place known as Dediotgeon, the mouth of a gully. Godiont encourages the False Faces to settle there. When anyone in her village is sick she goes to Dediotgeon to invite the False Faces to her lodge. She prepares a pot of corn pudding for them and presents the sick person. The False Faces blow ashes on the patient to cleanse him or her (see *Ash Blowing Rite),* then eat the corn pudding. The False Faces tell Godiont that whenever they are summoned they want the corn pudding ready and waiting, because it is important to begin the curing work without delay.

A man in the village wants to fool the False Faces. He calls on them, saying their help is needed. When the False Faces arrive at the appointed place, no one is there and nothing has been prepared. The False Faces know Godiont has not tricked them. They decide to kill the person responsible as a warning to others not to fool with the False Faces. Then the False Faces tell Godiont they are moving away from the Genesee Valley. They instruct her to make masks (see *Masks and Masking)* that resemble their faces. The men are to wear them so the False Faces can work their healing through the masks. Presently the man who fooled the False Faces comes running in a crazy fit. The oldest False Face tells Godiont to watch carefully so that all will know

never to make fun of the False Faces. The man runs to the gathering of the False Faces, begins to vomit blood, and soon dies. [Fenton 1987]

Godzadowi
Seneca, Iroquois, *Northeast*
Possession or hysteria overtaking a person, usually during the *Midwinter Festival* when an animal spirit can inhabit a human. For example, a person possessed by the bear spirit might demonstrate great strength, grunt, and clench his or her teeth, but be calmed by eating berries. [Fenton 1987]

Gondagonwisas
Seneca, *Northeast*
The Corn Harvest Ceremony taught by *Onenha,* Corn. At harvest time the corn is gathered in large piles in the middle of the field for husking. The husks are braided into ostensas (cornstrings), which are hung on poles. When the strings have dried, the corn is brought into the lodges and the Corn Dances are performed. [Fenton 1987]

Gonyahsgweont
Seneca, *Northeast*
"Her throat is swollen." The descriptive name given to Toad. [Fenton 1987]

Goyo
Takelma, *Northwest Coast*
Medicine person (see *Medicine People)* who practices medicine for malevolent purposes. Chicken Hawk once took vicious revenge on a goyo by slitting his neck because the goyo had caused the death of Chicken Hawk's wife. As a result Chicken Hawk is considered to be one of the guardian spirits of the somlohoxs (helpful medicine people), who recite the story of his revenge as a charm against the malevolent doings of the goyo. [Sapir 1909a]

Grain-of-Corn Bundle
Pawnee, *Plains*
A *medicine bundle* that originated when a man roaming the prairies heard a woman crying and

was guided to her in his *dreams*. The beautiful woman is a kernel of corn dropped by a group of buffalo. *Corn Woman* tells the man to pick her up and always carry her, because her spirit is that of *Evening Star*. When the man goes to *war,* he ties the kernel to the end of his quiver, and Corn Woman helps him overcome the enemy by warning him in a dream that the enemy is near.

In another dream Corn Woman tells the man to prepare the grain-of-corn bundle by covering the corn kernel with buffalo calfskins. She tells him to care for the bundle and not to marry for two seasons, the period needed to understand Corn Woman's spirit. Corn Woman says that his mother is to plant Corn Woman in a large hill of earth. When the resulting corn is ripe, she is to harvest it and then replant. When the man understands how the corn has multiplied, then he can marry. The man does as Corn Woman has told him. Eventually he marries. When his first child, a daughter, is born, Corn Woman comes to him in a dream and tells him to name the girl Woman-Carry-the-Leading-Corn. See also *Agriculture*. [Dorsey 1906a; Murie 1989]

Grand Medicine Society
See *Midewiwin*.

Grandmother
A figure, usually without a proper name, found in many stories about the adventures of culture heroes. The grandmother, portrayed as an old woman who lives alone, advises the hero how to kill threatening monsters, escape from danger, use magic, and follow safe trails. In many stories the grandmother can transform herself into an animal who gives advice or teaches humans how to become great hunters. In Eskimo stories, Grandmother is associated with knowledge of spiritual powers. She makes amulets for protection against malevolent spirits and teaches survival skills, hunting, and tracking. Grandmothers also teach girls how to relate to the spiritual world. See also *Old-Woman-Who-Never-Dies*.

Grass Dance,
Plains
A men's competitive social dance believed to have originated with the Pawnee dance known as the iruska (an early dance demonstrating an immunity to fire). The dancers wear large amounts of grass tied to their belts and perform either singly or in pairs. The dance is strenuous, involving much leaping and bending. Many songs are connected with the Grass Dance, which has come to be considered a dance of celebration as well as competition. The Blackfoot Grass Dance is *Ka?espai*. See also *Kawenho* (the Hot Dance). [Wissler 1913]

Greasy Mouth
See *Vasaagijik,* the Alaskan culture hero Canada Jay.

Great Bear Constellation
A story figure who ends up becoming the constellation Ursa Major, the *Big Dipper*. In an Iroquois story, a giant *bear* is eating all the game during the coldest part of the winter. Every time hunters find the bear it disappears, never leaving a footprint. One night three brothers dream they have found the bear. Taking their small dog, they follow it to the end of the earth where the earth touches the northern sky. In the icy mist they see the bear running up the snow-covered mountains. They climb the mountains and see the bear moving through the clouds. As he runs, he weaves a large invisible net. Finally the bear comes to a cave and goes inside to rest. Thinking they can trap him as he sleeps, the brothers follow, but the bear wakes up and catches them in his net. He throws the the net into the sky, where the brothers become the three stars in the handle of the Big Dipper.

In the Coeur d'Alene (Idaho) story, three brothers have a grizzly bear for a brother-in-law. The youngest brother loves the brother-in-law, but the older two brothers do not. One day the two older brothers tell the youngest they are planning to kill Grizzly Bear while they are out hunting. Invited to join them, he refuses. The older brothers prepare to shoot Grizzly Bear, but the youngest brother warns him. As the arrows are flying, the three brothers and the grizzly bear are all transformed into stars and go up to the sky to form the corners of the cup of the Big Dipper. Some stories identify the four stars in the square of the dipper as the bear and the three stars forming the handle as the three brothers. See also *Stars and Starlore.*

Great Feather Dance
Iroquois, *Northeast*
See *False Faces* and *Midwinter Festival.*

Great Hunchbacked One
Onondaga, *Northeast*
See *Hadu?igona.*

Great White Bear
Menominee, *Northeast*
Copper-tailed white *bear,* a Menominee ancestor who lives at the lowest level beneath the earth. Great White Bear is considered to be chief of the *underworld* and the source of malevolence. [Bloomfield 1928a]

Great-Favorite
Nootka, *Northwest Coast*
Women perform this *dance* to song as they enter a *potlatch* house. The dancers come in swaying and scratching their hair with both hands to one side. They circle the inside of the house and then kneel down. According to story tradition, the song and dance were taught to a young girl by *Salmon* when she was lost in her canoe. On her return she taught it to other women. [Sapir and Swadesh 1939]

Green Corn Dance
Seminole, Creek, southeastern Iroquoian tribes, *Southeast*
Also known as busk or posketa among the Creek and eastern Iroquoian tribes. The Green Corn Dance is a rite initiating the *New Year,* held during July or August when crops have matured.

It is the most important seasonal ceremony, celebrating the *corn* harvest, renewal of *fire,* and the power of the *medicine bundles.*

The Green Corn Ceremony usually lasts four to six days. It includes fasting and cleansing in preparation for the renewal of the fire, as well as eating the ripening green corn of mid to late summer.

For the Seminoles, the Green Corn Ceremony marks the time of renewal for the medicine bundle. During the dance, Es-te fas-ta, the creator, can renew the medicine bundle and add to it the medicines necessary to treat new diseases. The medicine bundle is the life and center of the Seminole tribe's strength and healing. The Green Corn Ceremony keeps the medicine bundle, and therefore the tribe, alive. Letting several years go by without holding the ceremony is thought to portend the death of the tribe.

For the *dance,* the ceremonial *Square Ground* is cleared, usually by two chosen young men. The Oklahoma Seminole have a well-established Square Ground used year after year. The medicine person for the Florida Seminole picks a new area every year or so to ensure privacy. Among the Iroquoian and southeastern tribes, the ceremonial area is surrounded by low log sheds with the openings facing inward, where the men stay while they fast and purge themselves with an *emetic* drink called Black. The Seminoles drink and wash in the emetic hoyvnijv after the initial *Stomp Dance.* There also may be a ball game between boys and girls each evening.

During the ceremony, food taboos are observed by the entire village. All homes and hearths are cleaned, and all fires extinguished. Most eastern and southeastern tribes observe a three-day fast, which ends when a new fire, known as "breath master," is ignited with a fire drill at the center of a square formed by four logs pointing to the four *cardinal directions.* The Iroquoian and Creek medicine people blow medicines onto the new fire and make offerings of green corn to it. Among the Seminole, old clothes, worn-out utensils, and grains remaining from the previous year's crops are gathered and burned. The women take fresh coals from the fire to start new fires in their homes.

The Green Corn Ceremonies end with feasting on new corn and other native foods. Friendships are renewed and previous wrongs between friends are forgiven. Before the closing feast and dances, there is a period of personal cleansing involving rubbing the skin with ashes, bathing, fasting, and drinking an emetic. Mock battles, singing, and costumed dancing celebrate the beginning of the New Year. See also *Hadentheni and Hanigongendatha* (Seneca); *Hisagita-imisi,* "preserver of breath" (Creek); *Locv-saukv,* women's leg rattles worn during Green Corn Dances; and *Pickwelaneokan* (Delaware), the Nighthawk Dance, and the Menominee *Rabbit Dance,* both performed during the Green Corn Dance. [Curtin and Hewitt 1918; Hudson 1976; Skye 1911; Sturtevant 1987; Swanton 1928a; Wallace 1972; Witthoft 1949]

Grizzly Bears
Haida, *Northwest Coast*
Dzelarhons is chieftess of the Grizzly Bears.

Grizzly Bear's Fire
Kathlamet, Oregon/Washington coast,
Northwest Coast
Grizzly Bear prides himself on always having a *fire.* Other animals keep watch on their own fires so they will not burn out. Panther and Lynx live together and take turns watching their fire. One day Lynx is responsible for watching the fire while Panther is out hunting. Instead of keeping watch Lynx plays, and the fire goes out. Lynx steals some fire from Grizzly Bear. When the old woman who watches Grizzly Bear's fire realizes that some of the fire is gone, she accuses her own vulva of eating it. Meanwhile Panther returns home and realizes from the smell that the fire in his house is new. Grizzly Bear arrives at Panther's house, Lynx hides under a dish, and Panther and Grizzly Bear get into a fight. The angry Grizzly Bear nearly

kills Panther, but at the last minute Lynx comes out of hiding and kills Grizzly Bear. Panther curses Lynx for causing so much turmoil and abandons him. [Boas 1901b]

Grouse Girl
Aleut, Kodiak Island, Bering Sea, Alaska, *Arctic*
A grouse flies into the camp of two men who live by themselves. One man is old and lame; the other, young and good-looking. The young man chases the grouse away, but when it returns the old man strokes it and speaks kindly to it. He decides to keep the bird as a pet.

In the morning the men leave as usual to go hunting. When they return there is a warm supper waiting for them and new sealskin mukluks (boots) are hanging above the old man's bed. No one is there except the grouse, who is sleeping on her bed with her head under her wings. Each day the men return to a clean hut, a warm meal, and new clothing hanging above the bed of the old man. When the weather turns bad and the men cannot go out, the grouse tries to befriend the young man, but he treats her roughly and does not let her come close to him. When good weather returns, the men set out to hunt. The old man waits until his companion is out of sight and goes back to the hut, where he sees a beautiful young girl step out of the grouse skin. He asks her to be his wife and hides the grouse skin over her protests.

When the young man returns and sees his partner's young wife, he is jealous. One night he kills the old man while he sleeps, then demands that the girl become his wife, telling her she will never be able to escape. She refuses and searches for the grouse skin, which she finally finds among her dead husband's tools. The young man continues to demand that she marry him, but she rejects him, saying that when she tried to be his wife he was mean to her. As she speaks she shakes the grouse skin three times, pulls it over her body (see *Animal-Human Transformations),* and flies out through the smoke hole, leaving the young man alone.

See also *Mudjikiwis* (Ojibwa), who like Grouse Girl is a *Mysterious Housekeeper.* [Golder 1903]

Guardian
Navajo, *Southwest*
Big Fly, one who guards and guides the culture heroes.

Guardian Spirit(s)
Plains
Across the northern Plains young men, and occasionally women, enter quests for vision. These ritual quests, directed by medicine people, vary from culture to culture. Most require the seeker to fast in isolation for a considerable time period. The power obtained through the vision experience is understood to appear in the form of a guardian spirit, on whom the visionary can call in times of need and on whom he can depend for guidance throughout life. Frequently a power object associated with the vision can be used to call the guardian spirit. Sometimes these spirits are referred to as *helping spirits.* They include Aikren (Karok), a duck-hawk, and *Kisenapew-mostos* (Cree), Kind-Old-Man-Buffalo. The Menominee *Dream Dance, Drum Dance* was restricted to those who had a guardian spirit. [Benedict 1923]

Gudatri-Gakwitl
Wiyot, *California*
See *Above-Old-Man,* the *creator.* [Kroeber 1925]

Guguyni
Tanaina, *Subarctic*
Raven, who released the *sun* and *moon* from captivity, enabling people to see. He is often classified as a *trickster* and *culture hero.* See also *Chulyen.* [Turner and Edmonds 1968]

Gutginsa
Tsimshian, *Northwest Coast*
The chief of the village known as House of Air, which is found beyond this world. In many stories, people travel to the village to meet with Gutginsa and gain shamanic *power.* Gutginsa owns a live *arrow* with the head of a reptile, which kills any enemy at whom it is shot. It is a long and arduous journey to the House of Air, which lies beyond the last of many villages, each a month's journey from the previous one. [Boas 1902, 1916]

Gwenhdaen nisedosyoden
Seneca, *Northeast*
A red-breasted bird known for its beauty, often found in stories. [Fenton 1987]

Gwiyee
Seneca, *Northeast*
Gull, who was named by *Ganyadjigowa,* Mud Hen, on her travels about the earth. Gwiyee presents himself as an old man living in the rocks and claims that whenever he talks everyone listens to him. After Ganyadjigowa names Gwiyee, she warns him not to chase people, which is the reason gulls do not chase after others. [Fenton 1987]

Haakapainizi

Kawaiisu, *Great Basin*

A giant grasshopper who came from Nevada. Haaka-painizi carries a large basket and sings as he hunts for human *children* to steal and eat. Haakapainizi is eventually tricked and killed by *Mouse,* who throws a hot coal in the giant grasshopper's mouth. Mouse's cave and Haaka-painizi are turned to stone. [Zigmond 1980]

Hactcin

Jicarilla Apache (Hacti for the Lipan Apache), *Southwest*

Supernaturals, personifications of the power of objects and natural forces (compare to Navajo *diyin dine?e* and *ye?ii*). See also *Apache Bear Dance; Apache Creation and Emergence; Black Hactcin Creates Animals and Humans; Hactcin, Departure of;* and *White Hactcin.* [Opler 1938b]

Hactcin, Departure of

Jicarilla Apache, *Southwest*

After the world has been made as it now appears, the hactcin all live together in one huge lodge. At this time all people look alike. One day the sky appears to be burning. The hactcin go to the sky to extinguish the fire. Before they leave, they make each person different from everyone else in appearance, intelligence, and character. The hactcin then depart, never to return to the earth. [Opler 1938b, 1940]

Hadentheni and Hanigongendatha

Seneca, *Northeast*

"The Speaker" and "the Interpreter." Two *culture heroes* who, shunned by their village, travel to their father, the *Sun.* They receive power, conquer enemies, and return to their people to teach and explain the meanings of the rituals they have learned.

Hadentheni and Hanigongendatha are shunned by their village because they do not know the identities of their parents. They move south looking for a place to live. One day they come to a large hemlock tree and climb it. From its top they see a beautiful trail leading from the tree through the air. Leaving their bows and arrows, they follow the unknown trail and soon reach a beautiful world. They come to the lodge of an old man, who invites them in. The old man is Kaahkwa, the Sun. He knows all about their troubles. He informs them that after a short stay with him they must travel on and visit the next lodge along the trail.

When they arrive at the second lodge they enter and see an old woman, the *Moon,* who welcomes them and feeds them boiled squash from a bark bowl. She tells them she is commanded by *Hawenniyo,* the controller of all things, to provide light for people on earth at night, and that only at certain times can all of her be seen. Moon warns Hadentheni and Hanigongendatha to be on guard, for the trail ahead of them is very dangerous. She warns them never to look at anything off the trail and to ignore anything they hear or see.

The two come to a third lodge and meet a man who calls himself their uncle. He welcomes them but says they cannot join the large gathering of people until they have been transformed. Transformation and purification are necessary for entrance to the land of the dead. The uncle transforms Hadentheni first, while Hanigongendatha watches. Hadentheni lies on a piece of bark. The uncle blows through his hand onto Hadentheni's head, separating the bones and flesh, which fall into two piles. He separates Hadentheni's bones, wiping each one clean and setting them aside in a pile. He blows forcefully on the bones and Hadentheni becomes a man again. Then it is Hanigongendatha's turn to be purified and reassembled. Hadentheni and Hanigongendatha are now able to chase any animal and catch it. They are welcomed to the great gathering of people.

After a short while they meet a man who is to be their guide. As they approach they smell flowers and hear people laughing. They come to the *longhouse* of Hawenniyo. Handentheni and Hanigongendatha watch the performance of the *Green Corn Dance* in honor of Hawenniyo. They are told that this is where people come when they die, and that they must return home to tell their people all they have seen and learned.

Back in their village, the two tell their people of the dances that Hawenniyo wishes them to know, especially the Green Corn Dance. Haden-

theni, the Speaker, is to sing the songs and teach the dances. Hanigongendatha, the Interpreter, is to explain the meaning of everything touching Hawenniyo. They also decide that *children* are never to be forsaken or anyone shunned. See also *Ganiagwaihegowa.* [Curtin and Hewitt 1918]

Hadidos
Iroquois, *Northeast*
A *medicine society* representing certain animals. Members of the Hadidos do a *round dance* and juggle hot stones while wearing blind masks (i.e., masks without eyeholes). See also *Idos* and *False Faces.* [Fenton 1987]

Hadjihsa Thokste?ah
Onondaga, Iroquois, *Northeast*
The eldest *Husk Face,* Chief of the Husk Faces. In an Onondaga story, Hadjihsa Thokste?ah meets a deer hunter deep in the forest. The Chief of the Husk Faces is guarding the meat of a deer the hunter killed, dressed, and hung in a tree the day before. Hadjihsa Thokste?ah tells the hunter that the Husk Faces live in a valley in the forest and bring success to hunters. He speaks of other Husk Face beings: the Great Hunchbacked One (*Hadu?i);* Whistler; the woman Voice in Water; Echo, the pet dog owned jointly by all the Husk Faces; and the little people (*Djigaahehwa).* Finally Hadjihsa Thokste?ah instructs the hunter in making cornbread offerings and explains the position and role the Husk Faces are to take when preceding the *False Faces* during the *Traveling Rite* (the spring and fall rite of purging illnesses). [Fenton 1987]

Hadjoqda
Seneca, *Northeast*
Skin Man, one of the Turkey People. *Deadoendjadases,* the Earth-Circler, captures Hadjoqda and flays his skin, which he inflates and uses to guard the strawberry patch around his lodge. Hadjoqda's skin is liberated and given back its flesh by a poor young boy from the Turkey clan who lives in the woods with his old grandmother.

The boy and his grandmother live alone, Deadoendjadases having taken all their people. Hadjoqda helps the boy by warning him that neither Deadoendjadases nor his sisters can be killed in the ordinary way because their hearts are not inside their bodies. Instead, they are kept under the wing of a loon who lives in a lake under Deadoendjadases's bed. Hadjoqda tells the boy that if the hearts are squeezed, Deadoendjadases and his sisters will fade away, but if the hearts are crushed they will die. The boy and Hadjoqda contrive a plan to steal the hearts and kill Deadoendjadases and his sisters. As the boy is killing Deadoendjadases, the bones and remains of many of the boy's cannibalized relatives arise and come together. Hadjoqda, the boy, and his relatives settle near the magnificent strawberry patch. Their relatives are the Partridge, Turkey, and Quail peoples. [Fenton 1987]

Hadjowiski
Seneca, *Northeast*
"Thousand-legged worm." Hadjowiski lives with his wife and seven children in a large lodge in the forest. Hadjowiski tells his wife he is a poor hunter because he has lost all his hunting *orenda*. She constantly berates him because he cannot provide for his family. Becoming suspicious when he comes home from hunting with blood on his back, his wife follows him and discovers he is providing for another wife in another lodge. She returns home and tells her children their father has another wife and she will not remain with them any longer. She puts on her panther-skin robe and runs away.

When Hadjowiski returns home, his children tell him what has happened. He searches for his wife, telling his children that if he is still alive in ten days he will return to them. Hadjowiski trails his wife to the lodge of an old man called Shagoi-yagentha ("he who tortures them"), who is one of the Toad People. The old man offers to help Hadjowiski by giving him a flint canoe that has great power and can sail through the air. Hadjowiski climbs into the canoe, which flies until it

lands and collides with some rocks. Hadjowiski is thrown out and killed, and the canoe returns to the old man.

Meanwhile, because Hadjowiski has not returned, his children leave one by one to search for him. The last to leave is the youngest son, *Deoyadastathe*. As he leaves the lodge, Deoyadas-tathe hears his mother weeping in the west. He travels west with his dog at his side. They stay several nights at the lodge of an old woman called Yeqsinye and her granddaughter, members of the Crow People. One day a messenger arrives to invite Yeqsinye and her granddaughter to attend the burning of a woman's feet (a form of torture) and pick up valuable *wampum* beads from the tears the woman will shed while her feet are burned.

Yeqsinye explains to Deoyadastathe that this torture is the doing of Shagoiyagentha, the wicked servant of Dihdih, chief of the Bluejay People. Deoyadastathe enters the lodge and sees his mother tied to a post. This is why he heard her weeping when he left his home. The two daughters of Chief Dihdih light torches and burn the bottoms of his mother's feet. Tears fall from her eyes to the ground, becoming beautiful beads of wampum. As the people gather the wampum beads, Deoyasdastathe unties his mother and escapes with her. He places a curse on the lodge, causing it to become like flint and heat up, killing everyone inside. The heads of the dead burst open and owls fly out, leaving the lodge through the smoke hole. Deoyadastathe, his mother, and his dog return to the lodge of Yeqsinye and live in peace. [Fenton 1987]

Hadu?i
Iroquois, *Northeast*
Among some Onondaga this humpbacked medicine being is known as *Hadu?igona* (the Great Humpbacked One). Hadu?i was met by *Hawenniyo* in some versions of the story that explains the origin of the *False Faces*. He loses a contest to Hawenniyo and tells him that humans will make likenesses of Hadu?i, offer

tobacco *(Gayegwanowasgona)*, and blow ashes (see also *Ash Blowing Rite)* on the sick. In return Hadu?i is to help cure the sick (see *Healing)*. See also Hadjihsa Thokste?ah. [Fenton 1987]

Hadu?igona

Onondaga, *Northeast*

"The Great Humpbacked One." A term used by the Onondaga to refer to *False Faces* (see also *Hadu?i)*. These masked beings have power to control high *winds* and *disease*. Masks representing Hadu?igona have long hair with black or red faces and broken, twisted noses (see also *Masks and Masking)*. [Fenton 1987]

Hagondes

Seneca, Northeast

A *cannibal* clown (see *Clowns and Clowning)* called Long Nose, whose buckskin mask has an elongated nose (see Masks and Masking). Hagondes threatens misbehaving children, who are told that he will carry them off in a basket. See also *Bogey*. [Fenton 1987]

Hagonsadji

Seneca, *Northeast*

Black Face, the name often used for *rattlesnake*. [Fenton 1987]

Hagowanen

Seneca, *Northeast*

A great *hunter* with powerful *orenda*. Hagowanen kills many animals and transforms his large catch into small packages so he can transport them easily. When he reaches his destination he transforms the game back to its original size. One day while Hagowanen is hunting, his canoe is stolen by Handjoias ("he spears fish"), one of the Turtle People. Handjoias then offers to retrieve the canoe in exchange for some of Hagowanen's catch. Handjoias returns the canoe, but Hagowanen sees through the trick and does not share his game as promised.

Hagowanen marries *Hongak* (Wild Goose) and has ten sons with her. The youngest is called *Othegwenhda*, Flint. Hagowanen eventually becomes tired of the responsibility of so many children and leaves his wife and family. Hongak searches everywhere for her husband but cannot find him. As her sons grow older, they also search unsuccessfully for their father. In time all but the youngest son, Othegwenhda, are killed by four old men called Hadiiades (Blacksnakes), who have great power. When Othegwenhda announces that he also wants to go and look for his father, Hongak gives him her orenda to protect him against the evil of the Hadiiades. She instills her power in a small piece of flint in the shape of a little finger. With this power Othegwenhda is capable of any transformation he desires.

Othegwenhda travels northward and finally finds his father, near death, being held captive by the monster spider *Djieien*. After killing Djieien, Othegwenhda rubs his father's skeleton with his flint amulet and saliva. Hagowanen recovers and returns to his wife Hongak. [Curtin and Hewitt 1918; Fenton 1987]

Haiendonnis

Seneca, *Northeast*

"Woodworker." Powerful sorcerer who helps his friends and harms his enemies. Haiendonnis travels north, sleeping in his bedroll and summoning game by pointing his finger. When he settles and builds his home, he summons wood for fuel by pointing his finger. He commands the skins off animals he has killed and instructs the carcasses to quarter themselves.

One day Haiendonnis meets *Gaasyendietha*, the meteor fire dragon. He kills the dragon by pointing his finger at him and makes a pouch of the dragon's skin. Haiendonnis also kills a panther and a fox by pointing his finger at them and makes pouches of their skins. He hangs all three pouches on the wall of his cabin. Growing bored, Haiendonnis commands the pouches to come to life. Gaasyendietha, the fox, and the panther all stand alive inside his cabin.

Near Haiendonnis's cabin lives a powerful *witch* named Yenogeaunus (Long-Tooth) and her three daughters. She convinces her eldest daughter, Deyondennigogenyons ("she who deceives as a habit") to take cornbread to Haiendonnis in an attempt to get him to marry her. As Haiendonnis sees the daughter approaching, he tells Gaasyendietha to stand behind a tree, the panther to stand close to the cabin, and the fox to stand in the doorway. When the girl passes the tree and sees Gaasyendietha, she is so frightened she drops the cornbread and runs home to her mother. Haiendonnis laughs. Yenogeaunus sends her second daughter Yonwithahon ("she who thrusts into apertures") to Haiendonnis with cornbread. Yonwithahon passes Gaasyendietha and the panther unafraid, but becomes frightened by the fox and runs home, dropping the cornbread. Again Haiendonnis laughs.

Finally Yenogeaunus sends her youngest daughter, Yenongaa ("the shingle-haired female") to the cabin of Haiendonnis. Realizing Gaasyendietha is only animated skin, she strikes him to the ground. She does the same to Panther and Fox. Seeing this, Haiendonnis tricks her into thinking he is an old man. In this guise he tells her that Haiendonnis will not be back for ten days. Yenongaa says she will return in ten days. When she does, Haiendonnis tricks her into thinking he is a small boy and again says that Haiendonnis will return in ten days. Once again Yenongaa says she will return in ten days. Upon her third return, Haiendonnis makes himself invisible. Not receiving any answer to her inquiry in his cabin, Yenongaa decides to sit and wait with her basket of cornbread at her side. The invisible Haiendonnis laughs out loud, frightening Yenongaa, who leaves her basket of cornbread and flees home to her mother.

Yenogeaunus sends Yenongaa back to Haiendonnis with another basket of cornbread. This time Haiendonnis accepts Yenongaa as his wife. Together they have vast magic power. When Yenongaa visits her mother, the witch works over her to enhance Yenongaa's power so she will be able to enslave her husband. Each time Yenongaa returns to her husband, he knows her intentions and nullifies her new powers.

Finally Haiendonnis tires of these attempts and decides to fight the witch Yenogeaunus face to face. She accepts his challenge, and the two fight fiercely with clubs. Yenogeaunus is killed, along with her two older daughters, Deyondennigongenyons and Yonwithahon. When Yenongaa appears, her husband sends her outside and sets fire to the lodge, burning Yenogeaunus and her two elder daughters inside. As the fire dies down, a horned owl, a common owl, and a screech owl fly up from the embers to a neighboring tree. The witches were owls in human form. Realizing that Haiendonnis has killed the malevolent Yenogeaunus and her two daughters, the entire world shouts with joy. Haiendonnis covers his hands with saliva and rubs the malevolent power out of his wife's head, then pulls and smooths her short hair, which becomes long and glossy. From then on the two live contentedly in Haiendonnis's cabin. [Curtin and Hewitt 1918; Fenton 1987]

Hailway
Navajo, *Southwest*

A curing ritual (see Healing) whose origin is described in a complex body of mythology. Rainboy, the protagonist of Hailway mythology, has a weakness for gambling. In various games with the Pueblos, he loses his clothing and his father's beads, which are the token of his leadership. His family locks him away to await punishment. Bat Woman helps him escape.

Rainboy lives alone. One day he discovers a house decorated with rainbows and enters it to find a beautiful girl. Ashamed of his poor moccasins Rainboy leaves, but the girl draws him back with zigzag lightning. Four times the shy and ashamed Rainboy attempts to leave, and four times the girl draws him back. She makes love to him by embracing him with lightning, rainbow, and sun ray. This girl is the wife of White Thunder. In a jealous rage, White Thunder shatters Rainboy with a lightning bolt (in some versions with a hailstorm). Big Fly informs other winds and thunders what White Thunder has done.

The winds and thunders gather Rainboy's bones and flesh, placing them between covers and stepping over them. Many other *diyin dine?e* are called upon to help revive Rainboy.

After this adventure, Rainboy starts home, only to discover a frog (or toad). Although warned against doing so, Rainboy accepts a challenge race with Frog around a mountain. Frog disables Rainboy by shooting hail at him. Frog wins Rainboy's feet, legs, gait, body, heart, nerves, mind, speech, face, nose, eyes, and head. Once again Rainboy is debilitated and requires help. Big Fly knows what gifts must be given to Frog. Thunders procure the necessary gifts and make the offering in order to acquire the lost body parts of Rainboy. In a ritual renewal, Rainboy is again re-created. With the help of the diyin dine?e, Rainboy challenges Frog to another race, which he wins, taking some of Frog's body parts. Rainboy gives back Frog's body parts, with the understanding that Frog will take charge of clouds, rain, and fog.

Several other stories follow. Thunders make war against Winter Thunder, who is considered evil. When peace is finally won, a peace ceremony is performed, with Rainboy as the principal ritual recipient. Rainboy then visits the homes of the diyin dine?e, riding on the magical vehicles of lightning, rain and sun streamers, and rainbows. The diyin dine?e teach Rainboy the Hailway rituals, and he returns to his family to introduce Hailway to the Navajo world. [Reichard 1944a; Wheelwright 1946a]

Hairy Hearts
Cree, Ojibwa, *Northeast,* and *Subarctic*
Ancient beings. See *Omemihoetehesiwak.*

Hairy Man
Tanaina, *Subarctic*
A large, harmless, hair-covered creature who lives in mountain villages. The eyes of this grayish, two-legged being have no pupils. He is helpful to humans unless injured. [Turner and Edmonds 1968]

Hairy-Face
Arapaho, *Plains*
A famous medicine woman who died in 1876. Hairy-Face had special knowledge of the *water monsters* (hiintcabiit) and refused to eat fish, water turtles, or other aquatic animals, or to allow them in her tipi. It is said that she died not long after her young grandson ignored her rule and brought her fish to eat.

As a midwife, Hairy-Face attended a young woman who had been impregated by a water monster while crossing a stream. During the last month of her pregnancy the woman became ill. Hairy-Face painted the woman's body and face with spots and made a special herb tea for her. The woman went into labor and passed a large amount of blood, followed by a great quantity of water that filled the tipi. When the water receded, Hairy-Face found the infant and covered it with a blanket. The other women in attendance were bewildered. When Hairy-Face removed the blanket, they saw not a human infant but a strange animal. It had a slender body covered with black and white spots, short legs, a long tail, and feet like a cow. Its face looked like a bulldog, with a short, broad forehead and no eyes. Frightened, the women went outside. When they returned, Hairy-Face had covered the infant water monster with the blanket. When she removed the blanket the infant had disappeared. [Dorsey 1903b]

Hakulaq
Tsimshian, *Northwest Coast*
A female water *monster* responsible for sea *storms.* Her child floats between two islands in a bay, inviting travelers to bring it aboard their canoes. At night, when the canoers camp on the land, Hakulaq comes out of the sea demanding her child and accusing the people of stealing it. She kills the travelers with waves from a fierce sea storm. [Boas 1902, 1916]

Haldawit
Tsimshian, *Northwest Coast*
Malevolent practitioners or *witches* who cause illness, *disease,* and even death (see *Dead)* for their

enemies, using a piece of corpse they keep hidden in a box. After a haldawit has caused a death he circles the house of the deceased. Later, disguised in an animal skin, he circles the grave where the corpse lies. If he fails to do this, he himself will die. Therefore the family of the deceased keeps close guard at the grave, and if they discover the haldawat he is killed. People caught spying on a group of haldawat are given the choice of immediate death or becoming haldawat themselves. [Boas 1902, 1916]

Half-Rock Woman

Haida, *Northwest Coast*

Half-Rock Woman teaches *Qolqalg Odai* about the taboos related to salmon.

Hamatsa

Kwakiutl, *Northwest Coast*

A *cannibal.* Everything the Hamatsa did, including his dance and his cry, referred to eating human flesh. Hamatsa songs talk about carrying corpses, swallowing people alive, and consuming different body parts. Earlier reports describe Hamatsa eating parts of corpses and

Crooked Beak Hamatsa Mask from the Kwakiutl tribe of the Pacific Northwest. Courtesy, Thomas Burke Memorial Washington State Museum, Eduardo Calderon, photographer (catalog #1-1669).

inflicting bloody bites on people. See also *Cannibal-at-the-North-End-of-the-World, Nulmal, Toxwid, and Tsetseka.* [Boas 1921; Goldman 1975; Holm 1977; Rohner and Rohner 1970]

Hamatsa Society

Kwakiutl, *Northwest Coast*

The most complex and important religious society of the Winter Ceremonial Season (see also *Tsetseka*). Hamatsa *(cannibal* dancers) are under the guidance of Bakbakwalanooksiwae (the powerful cannibal spirit). Members of the male Hamatsa Society are primarily responsible for making the community aware of the presence of spirit visitors during the Winter Ceremonial Season. The Hamatsa Society initiation rite enacts a fundamental belief that animals and

supernaturals give power to a community, and focuses the attention of the village on the power of the wild. At the end of the initiation the village participates in the taming of the wild initiate, thus completing the cycle of tame to wild to tame.

During the Winter Ceremonial Season, everyone in the village is aware of the activity of members of the Hamatsa society. A Hamatsa initiate is abducted from the village by society members. Alternatively the novice, wearing hem-lock boughs, is led to the woods, where he is captured by society members wearing red cedar bark about their heads and necks. In the evening, when the initiate is ready to reappear, the people of the village gather in the ceremonial house. Then the initiate, dressed in hemlock boughs, returns, coming through a hole in the roof of the house. He whistles to express wildness. His songs and cries tell of eating human flesh, swallowing people alive, and consuming different body parts. Early accounts of these dances report that Hamatsa ate parts of corpses and inflicted bites on people during this part of the ceremony. Attendants try to capture the Hamatsa, but he escapes.

The following morning, the people in the village finally capture the Hamatsa and bring him to the ceremonial house. His dances become increasingly tame. If wildness overcomes the Hamatsa again, he goes behind a curtain, and companions wearing great bird masks appear to calm him down. These companions *dance* a slow dance that involves squatting, jumping, and sitting. When this dance is finished, the Hamatsa returns, wearing a blanket and apron, to dance a final dance as a tame person. After this the female attendants and their relatives dance to symbolize his successful taming. [Boas 1921; Goldman 1975; Holm 1977; Rohner and Rohner 1970]

Hanblapi
Lakota, *Plains*

Vision quest, an activity undertaken to seek a vision, known as a hanble, a communication from *Wakan Tanka* or a spirit to a human. The vision may come at any time or in any manner to anyone. It may be of significance to the one who receives it or to another person. It may be communicated in the Lakota language or in *hanbloglaka*, language of the spirits understood only by a *wicasa wakan* (shaman). The message may consist only of sight or sounds without the use of language. It may come directly from a spirit or from an akicita (messenger).

A person seeking a hanblapi first takes an *inipi* (sweat). Then the person remains alone, concentrating on the vision desired. The seeker fasts and drinks no water. He or she may smoke the pipe under the direction of the wicasa wakan. The wicasa wakan will interpret the language of the spirits in the vision.

Traditionally, a young man whose voice is changing, indicating approaching puberty, goes on hanblapi to find direction in his life. A young *woman* seeks a hanble by wrapping her first menstrual flow (see *Menstrual Blood)* and placing it in a tree. Hanble frequently come without being sought to very old men and women and wicasa wakans. [Neihardt 1932; Walker 1982]

Hanbloglaka
Lakota, *Plains*

The *language* of the spirits spoken during a vision quest (see also *Hanblapi).* This language is understood only by a *wicasa wakan* (religious leader). [Neihardt 1932; Powers 1975; Walker 1982]

Hands
Eskimo, western Alaska, *Arctic*

In Yupik Eskimo stories and masks (see *Masks and Masking),* the thumbless hand with holes in the palms is a motif representing impaired grasp. On masks it also represents the spirit's *(tunghak)* willingness to release an abundance of animals for hunting. Hands are responsible for connecting the human world and the world where the *inuas* of the animals dwell. The inuas must know that the hunters respect them in order for the game to regenerate each year. See also *Inviting-In Feast.*

Hanehwa
Seneca, *Northeast*

The name for the human skin that was flayed whole and made to serve as a guard for a noted sorcerer or sorceress. These skin beings never slept. They would warn of a stranger's coming by giving three loud shouts. [Curtin and Hewitt 1918; Fenton 1987]

Hanga
Omaha, *Plains*

"Foremost." The first Hanga people were buffalo who lived under the water. The Hanga are the first of the two principal *clans* of the Omaha tribe. All the clans are exogamous groups that acknowledge descent only through the male and endorse marriage outside their respective clans.

Responsibilities for religious ceremonies are divided along strict clan lines, with the first tents and pipes (see also *Ninba jide)* being entrusted to the Hanga. Whenever the Omaha meet to discuss matters concerning the entire tribe, they pitch their tents in a tribal circle, with the families of the Hanga clan on the right of the circle and those of the Ictasanda clan on the left. Each family of the clan holds a specific position in the circle, with the Wejicte or Elk family being the first of the Hanga clan. [Dorsey 1888c]

Hanisheonon

Seneca, *Northeast*

Muckworm, (larvae of the beetle Ligryrus relictus) literally "dweller in the soil," the term some Iroquois storytellers applied to the Christian concept of Satan because of their common subterranean domicile. See also *Gaqga,* the crow. [Fenton 1987]

Hanmdepi

Lakota, *Plains*

To *dream,* to seek a *vision.* In preparation for hanmdepi, a person participates in a fast which may last for up to three days. After fasting, the person *sacrifices* some part of his or her body by cutting the arm, chest, or fingers with a knife, then waits in silence until a vision becomes clear. The bodily sacrifice further emphasizes the sincerity of the vision seeker. [Brown 1953; Walker 1982]

Hanogagah

Seneca, Iroquois, *Northeast*

"He is whistling." A *False Face* whistling mask (see *Masks and Masking)* with puckered mouth and wrinkles. Like many False Face masks, it has tobacco bags attached, indicating rewards for cures the mask has brought about. [Fenton 1987]

Hantceciitehi

Arapaho, *Plains*

Dwarfs. Dwarfs provide food and provisions for one another. They often try to capture or seduce young women in order to marry them. Long ago some dwarfs were *cannibals.* They were ugly and had voices like children. In order to keep their hearts from being pierced by hunters, they would hang them from rafters in their lodges. The cannibal dwarfs were eventually destroyed by a hunter who came across their lodge and pierced the hanging hearts with a sharp stick. [Dorsey and Kroeber 1903]

Hantitaeinici

Arapaho, *Plains*

"The beheaded ones." Seven very powerful and dangerous brothers. A lazy young man disguises himself as a woman, and seeks out and marries one of the Hantitaeinici. One day while the other brothers are hunting, the young man delouses the head of his spouse, kills him, and runs off with the head. Birds report the deed to the other brothers, who pursue the young man. He runs to the tent of an old woman who agrees to help him. Her tent is made of solid iron. When the brothers reach it, they demand the young man's release. The old woman invites them inside; as they enter, she chops off their heads with the iron door. The young man returns to his family with the scalps and is never again accused of being lazy. [Dorsey and Kroeber 1903]

Hanwi

Lakota, *Plains*

The *Moon,* created by *Wi,* the Sun, to be his companion. [Powers 1975]

Hataalii

Navajo, *Southwest*

"Singer." The conductor of Navajo healing ceremonials, a medicine person (see *Medicine People).* The hataalii must learn the entire mythology for each ceremonial he or she performs, as well as the remarkably complex ritual procedures. A person usually does not enter this activity until midlife. Learning a ceremonial requires an extensive period of apprenticeship, concluded by an initiatory performance of the ceremonial. Navajos distinguish singers from curers (aza?ooniligi), who have a much narrower range of ceremonial activities. See also *Blessingway, Navajo Ritual Process, Sandpainting, Waterway,* and *Yenaldlooshi.* [Mitchell 1978; Newcomb 1964]

Hathondas

Seneca, *Northeast*

"The listener." A poor boy who lives alone in the woods with his uncle, *Dooehdanegen,* a powerful medicine person. At puberty Hathondas is sent into a ravine with instructions to listen and report everything he hears to his uncle. After several trips to the ravine, Hathondas hears two women who are traveling through the air on their way to the lodge of Hathondas and Dooehdanengen. The women are singing of their intention to marry Dooehdanegan. Hathondas rushes home to tell his uncle what he has heard.

The women arrive with a basket of *marriage bread*. Dooehdanengen attempts to attract the women to himself, but they are more interested in Hathondas. At nightfall, the women seduce Hathondas, making the uncle angry. The women leave at dawn. When Hathondas awakes, he has become a full-grown, strong, and handsome man.

Dooehdanegen tells Hathondas to follow the two women. He tells Hathondas they are a mother-and-daughter team, and that the mother is a powerful sorceress searching for a husband for her daughter. The uncle explains to Hathondas that an eagle sits outside the sorceress's lodge. The man who kills the eagle will be chosen to marry the daughter. Dooehdanegen outfits Hathondas with protective clothing, including an otter-skin cap, a panther-skin coat, leggings of wildcat skin, moccasins of owl skin, and a fawn-skin tobacco pouch. The cap can become a live otter; the robe, a live panther; the leggings, a pair of live wildcats; and the moccasins, owls. The uncle teaches Hathondas how to spit out valuable *wampum* beads and warns him always to travel and sleep alone.

Hathondas meets a stranger on his travels. Ignoring his uncle's warning, he camps with the stranger for the night. The man steals Hathondas's special clothing and makes him ill by thrusting a dart of hickory bark down his spine. Hathondas is rescued by a poor girl, whom he discovers to be his niece, and her mother, who is his sister.

One day a group of people gather at the sorceress's house to attempt to shoot the eagle. The sorceress sits under the tree where the eagle is perched. Hathondas shoots the eagle and starts to pick it up, but the stranger who had stolen Hathondas's clothes emerges from the crowd and grabs it. The stranger then goes to the sorceress and claims the daughter for his wife. The daughter refuses to wed him, insisting he did not kill

the eagle. The sorceress, however, says the promise must be kept, and her daughter must marry the man who holds the dead eagle.

Hathondas's niece visits the sorceress and discovers that her daughter refuses to have sex with the stranger. That night Hathondas's sister steals back his special clothes. In the morning they find the stranger doubled up in pain, old and ill. The people know by this transformation that the stranger did not kill the eagle. Hathondas marries the daughter of the sorceress. [Curtin and Hewitt 1918]

Hauhau
Tsimshian, *Northwest Coast*
Extraordinary animals resembling bear cubs and dog puppies. *Raven* (Txamsem) creates a pair of these creatures to hunt for him when he decides to retire to the mountains. [Boas 1902, 1916]

Hawenniyo
Seneca, *Northeast*
"He is master or controller of it." The main character in the origin story of the *False Faces*. This term came to be used to refer to the Christian God (see *Christianity*). Hawenniyo was the first to plant tobacco (*Gayegwanowasgona*). For related Seneca figures see *Hadentheni and Hanigongendatha, Hadu?i, Kaahkwa, Sapling,* and *Sky-Holder*. [Fenton 1987]

Hawichyepam Maapuch
Chemehuevi, *California*
Old Woman *power,* which is not personified in the origin story. Because of Old Woman power, the waters covering the earth dried up and allowed Coyote and Puma to come down from a mountain and populate the earth. [Kroeber 1925]

Hawk
The Lakota Hawk *(Cetan)* is the spirit responsible for swiftness. The Kawaiisu tell stories of a hawk-like creature *(Nihniknoovi)* that eats people. The Shawnee story of White Hawk *(Waupee) tells the origin of hawks.*

Hayicanako

Tlingit, *Northwest Coast*

Old Woman Underneath Us, who supports the *earth* either by herself or by watching a pole made of a beaver leg to make sure the pole does not slip. *Earthquakes* are an indication of Hayicanako's hunger, which is satisfied when people throw grease in their cooking fires. [Swanton 1909]

Hayondiha

Seneca, Onondaga, Iroquois, *Northeast*

"He is smiling." A category of *False Face* masks known as smiling masks. The Hayondiha masks tend to be larger than other False Face masks. Used in curing, they are recognized by their pointed heads, sharp chins, and the presence of ears. Often they are recognizable caricatures of actual men and women. [Fenton 1987]

Healers

Healers, often referred to as medicine people or shamans, may be either male or female. Although they may be herbalists or perform other kinds of medical treatment, invariably they are religious figures who use ritual techniques. Because of their knowledge and power, they are highly respected and sometimes even feared members of the community. They may work alone or with others who are specifically designated as herb gatherers, medicine makers, and diagnosticians.

Following are a few examples of healers, which must be complemented by reference to the categories *medicine people* and *shaman. Tcikapis* is a Montagnais culture hero skilled in healing. Perhaps surprisingly, clowns often have great healing power (see Pueblo *Clowns and Clowning Societies, Newekwe,* and the Lakota *Heyoka).* Coos *talking doctors* heal by reciting the creation story. Many Native American cultures have societies whose primary task is healing, for example, the Quileute *Wolf Society* and the Lakota Bear Dreamer Society *(Mato Okolakiciye).* Terms for healer include *Hilis-haya* (Creek), *Hitebi* and *Morea* (Yaqui), *Kura?u* (Pawnee), *Nanandaw*

(Ojibwa), *Si?atcokam* (Pima), and *Ontetsans* (Huron). See also *Healing.*

Healing

Health and healing are among the most important concerns of Native American ritual. It is essential to understand the concept of health other than in the terms of Western medicine. Many Native American cultures understand illness not as the result of some biochemical, physiological, or psychological malady, but as a sign of disorder in society or the world, which is then reflected in the illness of an individual. Diagnosis thus consists of discerning the status of the community or the world. Healing requires repairing or restructuring these environmental concerns. See also *Disease.*

Among Native American religions, healing is perhaps most central to the Navajo religion (see *Navajo Ritual Process* and all Navajo healing rituals). Some examples of the many Native American healing rites are: the Pawnee *Lightning's Medicine Ceremony; Akhrendoiaen,* the Huron rite to cure insanity; the Ojibwa *Bear Sweat Lodge;* the Iroquois *Ash Blowing Rite;* the Pawnee *Loon Medicine Ceremony;* Ojibwa *Midewiwin;* the Huron dream-guessing healing rite *(Ononharoia);* the curing rites of *Shaker Religion;* and Apache *Mountain Spirits,* ritual healers.

Healing rites often take the form of or include dancing, such as the *Apache Bear Dance,* the Piegan *Black-Tailed Deer Dance,* the Cherokee Bear Dance *(Yona),* the Huron dances *Awataerohi* and *Otakrendoiae,* and the *Buffalo Dance Cult* of the Menominee.

Acquisition of the power to heal is often the subject of Native American stories. The Pawnee attribute healing power to *Flint Man* and *Bear Medicine Woman,* the Iroquois to *Hadu?i* and *Hodigohsosga?a* (see also *Faces of Forests* and *False Faces),* the Zuni to the Beast Gods *Wemaawe,* the peoples of the Yukon to *Beaver Man,* the Lakota to Bear *(Mato),* the Crow to *Miritatsiec* (Moon Woman), the Ojibwa to *Winabojo,* and the Kawaiisu to *Yahwera.* See also *Tcu-unnyikita,* the Pima creation story.

Curing is often done through spiritual intervention. This approach particularly distinguishes shamanism (see *Shaman*). For example, the Cree call on the helping spirits *Pakahk* and *Maskwa,* a bear ally, to cure.

Medicine is a term widely used to designate spiritual power. It sometimes refers to substances consumed by or applied to the body of a suffering person. More broadly, however, medicine refers to the healing power that may reside in physical objects or in the healing knowledge and techniques of healing rites. See *Small Dose* (Seneca); *Cudak* (Puyallup), a women's curing charm; and Pawnee *Squash Medicine.* Some tribes consider *menstrual blood* to have healing powers.

Health
See *Healing.*

Heart
See *Pinanne,* where the Zuni believe the human spirit lodges.

Heart Squeezing
Seneca, *Northeast*

Used by those practicing *Otgon* (malevolent power) to cause great pain in the chest and even death. The effects of this experience can be nullified by holding a naked dance in which people summoned for the *dance* undress, face a wall, and dance while an old man sings in the center of the room. In one story, a young man whose heart is squeezed by a powerful woman returns to his home where a naked dance is held for him. He then calls for a mole and makes himself small enough to crawl inside the mole. The mole is instructed to carry him underground to the feet of the woman. There he enters her body and begins squeezing her heart. A naked dance is held to cure the woman, but the young man inside her squeezes her heart again and she falls dead. The young man comes out of her body and is no longer tormented. [Curtin and Hewitt 1918]

Heat and Cold
Coeur d'Alene, *Plains*

Personified as two brothers. Heat is very handsome, but Cold is ugly. While Heat is away traveling, Cold gets angry at human beings and says he will kill them. He makes freezing *weather* and humans start to die. When Heat hears humans are dying, he rushes back to save them. He makes the weather so hot that he kills his brother. Because of this, heat melts ice and snow. Eventually Cold revives, and the two brothers agree to live in such a way that their powers will balance. If either Heat or Cold travels too far away from home, however, the remaining brother is left with the power to cause extremes in the weather.

Heaven
See *Yagatunne,* Road to Heaven.

Hehaka
Lakota, *Plains*

Male Elk, whose spirit is responsible for sexual relationships. [Powers 1975]

Helping Spirit(s)
Sometimes referred to as *guardian spirits,* these helpers guide, guard, and teach the humans who seek them. When the spirits decide to enter a relationship with a human, they teach the person curing songs as well as how to succeed in war, gambling, and love. In some tribes, helping spirits come to humans in dreams or isolated encounters with an animal. In many tribes, pubescent boys participate in some type of *vision quest* or fast that facilitates their first encounters with a helping spirit. Girls are isolated at the time of their first menstruation (see *Menstrual Blood),* during which they meet their first helping spirits. Instruction given by the helping spirit to a human at an early age is often not used until the person is older. Secrecy is an important part of the helping spirit's relationship with a human, and dreams or visions are discussed only with a few older wise people in the village.

Shamans have the special ability to call upon helping spirits to assist in their religious endeavors. See *Tarneq* (Alaska), a shamanic helping spirit; *Nanandaw,* an Ojibwa medicine person who cures with helping spirits; *Sati,* the Tlingit master of a dead shaman's helping spirit; and *Healers.* Helping spirits may be called upon in special conjuring and divination rites such as the *shaking tent.* Power objects or *amulets,* such as the *polar bear snout,* may be used to call helping spirits.

Helping spirits often take the form of animals, such as Bear (see Osage *Wacabe).* They may even take the form of *Famine* (Kathlamet), or the Cree skeleton *Pakahk. Awakkule* (Crow) are dwarf people who are helping spirits. The Creek helping spirits *Yahola and Hayuya* live in the sky and support health and healing. Helping spirits in some cultures correspond with *directional orientations.* See also *Spirit Powers* (Kalapuya); *Winter Berries,* a story of how a man gains spirit help; *Hoop and Pole Game,* considered to be a gift of the helping spirits; *Sleep,* which the Ojibwa believe allows the meeting of spirits; and *Quiyoughcosuck,* the Algonquian term for helping spirit. [Altman 1947]

Heluta
Cochiti, *Southwest*
Father of the *kachinas,* creator of *deer;* he lives in *Shipap.* As father of kachinas he is first to appear at kachina dances, announcing the kachinas to the people by means of signs. Heluta is a figure in many stories. [Benedict 1931]

Hemis Kachina
Hopi, *Southwest*
See *Niman.*

Heshwash Ceremony
Yokuts, *California*
A shaman contest lasting two nights; also known as the hiding ceremony. Shamans gathered from various Yokuts communities to hold spell-placing contests in which they attempted to project poi-

sons and disease-carrying objects into one another. A shaman who was unable to extract the poison placed on him had to pay the opponent to remove it. [Kroeber 1925]

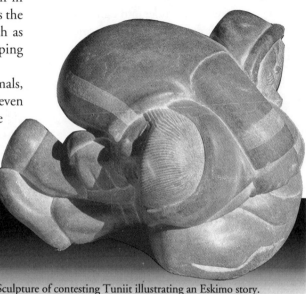

Sculpture of contesting Tuniit illustrating an Eskimo story. Courtesy, Canadian Museum of Civilization (neg.#J 14354).

Hethuska
Omaha, *Plains*
A society (see *Societies)* responsible for keeping alive memories of bravery in tribal history through *songs.* Members judged whether or not the activities of returning warriors were worthy of the creation of a new song. Hethuska was also responsible for instilling attitudes of heroism and for mocking the fear of death (see *Dead).* Many of the society's songs stress the transient nature of death in relationship to the longevity of the mountains, rivers, and earth. [Dorsey 1888a, 1888b]

Heyoka
Lakota, *Plains*
People who *dream* of the *Wakinyan (Thunderbird),* characterized by talking and acting in an opposite manner, such as dressing for cold weather in the middle of summer and walking backward when asked to come forward. They

purposely make people laugh with their speech and actions, and often act as healers. They dress shabbily, wearing skins inside out, and sometimes rub mud over their entire bodies. They also act as interpreters of dreams. Heyoka dreamers are extremely frightened of thunder and lightning. See also *Iktomi* (Lakota), the trickster, and *Sun Dance*. [Powers 1975; Walker 1982]

Hiding Ceremony

See *Heshwash Ceremony.*

Higu

Omaha, *Plains*

Humorous stories told for amusement, preferably on winter nights. [Dorsey 1888a, 1888b]

Hihankara

Lakota, *Plains*

The Owl Maker, an old woman who guards the Spirit Road (the Milky Way), which is the path taken after death by a human's spirit *(nagi)*. Hihankara examines each nagi for an identifying tattoo on the wrist, forehead, or chin. If she does not find the marks, she pushes the spirit from the trail and it falls to earth to become a wandering *ghost*. [Walker 1982]

Hihi ogashoon

Seneca, *Northeast*

Six owls' eyes used as dice in a game. See also *Hodadenon*. [Curtin and Hewitt 1918; Fenton 1987]

Hiintcabiit

Arapaho, *Plains*

Horned *water monster*. These underwater beings often take pity on humans who are in trouble or wandering in grief (see *Wanou*). They have an extra eye in their upper backs that enables them to see people approaching from behind. If wounded or killed, they can cause the body of water where they live to rise and *flood* surrounding areas. See also *Lime Crazy* and *River-Woman*. [Dorsey and Kroeber 1903]

Hilis-haya

Creek, *Southeast*

Medicine makers or *healers,* either male or female. Hilis-haya knew how to gather the necessary roots and plants for making medicines as well as how to prepare and apply the medicines. The Hilishaya were more numerous than the *Alektca* (medicine people). [Swanton 1928a]

Himowico

Nootka, *Northwest Coast*

The story category that tells of events occurring in the distant past, involving activities of a culture hero and supernatural beings. Himowico do not usually refer to particular persons or places. See also *E?icain,* another story type. [Sapir and Swadesh 1939]

Hinon

Seneca, *Northeast*

Thunderer, a powerful medicine person (see *Medicine People*) who dwells in a cave under Niagara Falls and acts as the protector of people afflicted by the malevolence of reptilian creatures. Hinon saves the life of a young woman who tries to kill herself by going over the falls in a canoe. She is distraught because an evil *snake* has crawled into her body and is killing her husbands at night. Hinon rescues the young woman and takes her to his cave. He shakes the snake out of her, and roasts and eats it. The young woman lives with Hinon for some time and conceives a son with him. When it is time for her to deliver, Hinon's companions return her to her people. The son of Hinon and the young woman can always tell when his father is coming because of a thunderous roar followed by hard rainstorms. Eventually the son goes to live with his father under Niagara Falls. Their voices are heard every time there is sharp thunder in the distance.

Hinon is also credited with teaching people to use *tobacco* for cleansing and for giving thanks to him by burying small amounts in the forests from time to time. See also the horned serpent *Doonongaes,* and *Hinon Hohawaqk*. [Curtin and Hewitt 1918; Fenton 1987]

Hinon Hohawaqk

Seneca, *Northeast*

The son of *Hinon,* Thunderer. Hinon Hohawaqk's mother dies while she is pregnant with him. One dark night Hinon Hohawaqk's grandmother, who is very poor, finds him naked and crying on top of his mother's grave. He has crawled up from the grave through a hole in the earth. The grandmother had no idea her daughter was pregnant when she died. She raises Hinon Hohawaqk, who grows rapidly.

One day when the grandmother returns from gathering wood, her grandson is gone. That night there is a raging thunder and lightning storm. The next morning Hinon Hohawaqk returns and tells his grandmother he has been to visit his father Hinon. Hinon Hohawaqk has many adventures and takes good care of his destitute old grandmother. [Curtin and Hewitt 1918]

Hisagita misa

Seminole, Oklahoma and *Southeast*

Breath Maker, the *culture hero* who taught people how to *fish* and dig wells for water. Breath Maker is credited with creating the *Milky Way* and the pumpkin plant. He is equated with *Jesus* Christ (see also *Christianity*). [Sturtevant 1987]

Hisagita-imisi

Creek, *Southeast*

"Preserver of *breath*." Also known as the One Sitting Above, the *creator*. Hisagita-imisi is related to, but should not be confused with, the Sun. He is honored on earth in the Busk ceremonial fire. See also *Green Corn Dance.*

Hitebi

Yaqui, *Southwest* and northwest Mexico

Curer or medicine person (see *Medicine People*) who treats illness resulting from witchcraft (see *Morea*). Curers, who may be either male or female, must possess *seataka* and perhaps also *utea.* The hitebi diagnoses illness through dreaming (see *Dreams*) in which he or she sees the witch causing the illness, often in the form of an animal. Assuming her or his seataka is stronger than the witch, the hitebi uses it to struggle with and overcome the witch. [Painter 1986]

Hixtcaba Nihancan

Arapaho, *Plains*

"Above-White-Man." The Arapaho term for the Christian God (see also *Christianity*). The son of Above-White-Man is born to a white woman who has kept her pregnancy secret. She delivers her child alone while her husband is out planting and then abandons both the baby and her husband. When the husband returns he finds the child running about. The boy grows very quickly. He is killed many times, including being burned to ashes. Each time he secretly returns to his mother. But when, as an adult, he is nailed to a cross he does not return. After this there is death and bloodshed among the Arapaho people (see *Dead).* [Dorsey and Kroeber 1903]

Hnaska

Lakota, *Plains*

Frog, whose spirit is responsible for occult powers. [Powers 1975]

Hochinagen

Seneca, *Northeast*

Medicine person (see *Medicine People*). See also *Small Dose,* medicine so strong that only Hochinagen could come into contact with it. [Curtin and Hewitt 1918]

Hocho

Navajo, *Southwest*

Ugliness and disorder, an important religious concept, paired and contrasted with *hozho,* order and beauty. Order and beauty have little meaning without the contrast of chaos and ugliness. Thus in Navajo thought, while order is defined in part by everything being in right relation with its complement, this is extended to the notion of beauty and order itself. Hocho is identified with the lower worlds, the domains of death (see *Dead)* and *witchcraft*. See also *Navajo Emergence* and *Uglyway*. [Gill 1979a]

Hodadenon
Seneca, *Northeast*

"He, the last." The younger brother of Yenyenthwus ("she, the planter"). Whenever Yenyenthwus goes out to plant, she locks Hodadenon in the lodge. To keep him amused, she gives him a raccoon's foot and a bow with arrows. Hodadenon tosses the raccoon's foot in the air and commands his arrows to strike the foot, which they do every time.

One day while he is alone in the lodge, Hadadenon hears the voice of his elder brother, Hadjigwas (mush eater), from the upper part of the lodge, asking for corn mush to eat. Hadjigwas is barely alive because a malevolent wizard has put a spell on him, causing a severe illness. Yenyenthwus keeps a special piece of chestnut hidden under her bed. Because of its powerful properties she is able to make cornmeal to keep her brother alive. Hodadenon finds the piece of chestnut and uses all of it to feed his brother. He also uses up all the specially hidden tobacco to give his brother a smoke. When Yenyenthwus returns and finds the chestnut and tobacco supply gone, she scolds Hodadenon, because without these two items Hadjiwas will die.

The chestnuts grow at the far eastern edge of the world. In front of the chestnuts grows tobacco. All of this is guarded by powerful medicine people. Hodadenon sets out to find more chestnut and tobacco. He has many adventures along the way, meeting and killing many animals. He meets his uncle, Hodiadatgon, a powerful and malevolent medicine man who is responsible for Hadjiwas's illness. They play a riddle and dice *game* that uses owls' eyes for dice (see *Hihi ogashoon*). The uncle loses the game, and consequently his head, to Hadadenon. Hadadenon frees a man named *Hotgoendaqsais* who is being tortured with fire, does battle with Ongwe Ias (the cannibal), and fights and kills Degohgweoses, who keeps the tobacco Hodadenon

needs to save his brother. Hodadenon gathers the chestnuts and tobacco, and returns home. See also the related Seneca mythological figures *Deagahgweoses* and *Ongwe Ias*. [Curtin and Hewitt 1918]

Hodesadoghdo
Iroquois, *Northeast*

"His mouth is straight." A *False Face* mask with a duckbill-shaped mouth (see *Masks and Masking*) used in curing. [Fenton 1987]

Hodigohsosga
Onondaga, Iroquois, *Northeast*

A *False Face* with a red face and long hair parted in the middle. One fall, two Hodigohsosga reveal themselves to two hunters. The hunters make a campfire every night and awake every morning to find their fireplace destroyed and the ashes strewn about the camp. On a nearby post they find a great dusty handprint.

The hunters hide in the bushes to discover the cause of the disturbance. They see a man with a red face, long hair parted in the middle, and eyes encircled with a shiny substance. He is carrying a mud *turtle rattle*. The Hodigohsosga looks around, then scatters the ashes about. The hunters are unable to intervene because they can see that the Hodigohsosga has great power. The hunters rebuild their campfire, go to sleep, and dream about the Hodigohsosga they have met. In the dream this False Face tells them it wants corn mush and tobacco. When the hunters awake, they put corn mush and tobacco into the fire for the False Face. As they do this, two False Faces arrive carrying turtle rattles. They teach the hunters the curing songs (see *Healing*) and the dance known as "the Faces Alone."

The False Faces tell the hunters that the Faces Alone Dance is to be the first dance of any False Face ritual and that the False Faces are to be fed corn mush. In a subsequent dream, the False Faces inform the hunters that the two Hodigohsosga a that appeared to them are to be honored by carving their likenesses in wood, giving offerings of corn mush and tobacco, and holding an annual dance for them. See also *Ash Blowing Rite*. [Fenton 1987]

Hogan
Lakota, *Plains*
Fish, whose spirit is responsible for ablution and for all the powers associated with *water*. [Powers 1975]

Hogan
Navajo, *Southwest*
Home, constructed on the model of the world with which it is identified in a form of *Blessingway*.

Hohu Yuha
Lakota, *Plains*
Bone Keepers, a medicine society (see *Medicine Societies)* composed of medicine men who practiced and met in secret because they did not want their malevolent deeds known. The Hohu Yuha could kill people with their medicine. They made love potions for unworthy young men who wanted to marry women who had refused them. The potions caused the young woman to become ill, so that her family pleaded with the Bone Keepers to heal her and eventually agreed to the marriage out of fear. The Hohu Yuha were feared and hated because of their malevolent power. [Powers 1975; Walker 1982]

Holy People
Navajo, *Southwest*
The common English translation of *diyin dine?e.*

Holyway (diyinkehji)
Navajo, *Southwest*
A classification of ritual healing ceremonials directed by the *diyin dine?e* or Holy People and intended to cure illnesses considered to be due to the anger of the diyin dine?e. Holyway ceremonials usually span a period of nine nights and the intervening eight days. The first part, bohochooji, focuses on removing the malevolence and sickness from the suffering person. Prayerstick

(keetaan) offering rites, unravelings, and ritual baths are common to bohochooji. The second portion, bohozhooji, which commonly includes *sandpainting* rites, is concerned with re-creating the person. See also *Ma?ii, Navajo Ritual Process, Navajo Wind Way, Nightway, Sandpainting,* and *Shootingway.*

Home Dance
Hopi, *Southwest*
See *Niman.*

Homosexuality
See *Gender-Crossing* and *Minquga* (Omaha).

Honani
Acoma, *Southwest*
The principal medicine object: a perfect ear of corn (i.e., completely kerneled to the tip) wrapped with native cotton. The base is sheathed with buckskin. The top is encircled with strings of beads, and parrot feathers are attached. The honani is placed in an upright position in front of the altar during ceremonies. (Honani is the Hopi word for badger.) [White 1932]

Honannyamu
Hopi, *Southwest*
Badger people or clan. After the emergence (see *Masau?u),* a group of people wandering about looking for a place to live (see *Migration)* find a man digging. They tell him they are heading for Walpi to settle, and ask what he is doing. He tells them he is a relative of theirs and will travel with them. He says he is a badger, and even though he looks like a person, when he puts on his skin he is like a badger. While traveling, they find a *butterfly* (establishing a link between the Badger and the Butterfly clans; see *Hopi Clan Grouping or Phratry).* A child becomes sick and Badger digs up medicine plants that are effective in curing the child, thus establishing the association of the Badger clan with plant growth and medicines. [Bradfield 1973; Dorsey and Voth 1901; Eggan 1950; Parsons 1933; Stephen 1936]

Hongak
Seneca, *Northeast*
Canadian Wild Goose, wife of *Hagowanen,* the great hunter, and mother of *Othegwenhda,* Flint. She became good friends with *Ganyadjigowa* (Mud Hen), a culture hero, but in the end fought with her and died because she became bloated with water while diving to the bottom of the lake. [Fenton 1987]

Hoop and Pole Game
A *game* played among many Native Americans, primarily by men and boys. A net-covered hoop is rolled along the ground as players attempt to shoot arrows or throw lances into it. In some areas the hoop and pole game is considered to be a gift from *helping spirits* or specific *culture heroes.* Thus it is often played in conjunction with annual ceremonies promoting crop growth and the re-generation of animals, as a reminder that these also originated with helping spirits.

Moon Woman gives the hoop and pole game to the Pawnee. See also the Pawnee story of *Gambler* and *Buffalo-Gaming Sticks.*

Hoop Transformation Rite
Navajo, *Southwest*
A rite appearing in *Big Star Way, Navajo Wind Way, Shooting Way, Ajilee,* and other healing ceremonials, especially of the *Uglyway* classification. The premise is that the person's ill health is due to an *animal-human transformation* that has left him or her debilitated by the unwanted outer form of some animal. Preparations for the rite include constructing a ritual trail of mountains (small mounds), *sandpaintings* (usually of animal tracks), and hoops set upright to form a tunnel. The suffering person, covered with an animal skin or a cloth representing a skin, is led over the mountains and barriers and through the succession of hoops. As the person passes through each hoop, the skin is pulled downward on his or her body, signifying the progressive removal of the unwanted outer form, which is completely re-moved by the last hoop. The rite is usually per-formed on four successive days, with the hoop arrangement placed in a different cardinal direc-tion each day. See also *Ma?ii.* [Reichard 1974]

Hopi Children Become Birds
Zuni, *Southwest*
The warrior twins, *Ahayuta,* are not fed when they visit the Hopi. Only one old woman offers them anything to eat. The twins grind blue paint and call all the Hopi children to dance with them. They paint the children and ask them to hold the ends of cottonwood branches. The twins sing and the children become chaparral jays. The rest of the people in the village are turned to stone. [Benedict 1935; Parsons 1930b]

Hopi Clan Grouping or Phratry
Hopi, *Southwest*
As with many other Native American cultures, Hopi clans or lineages are linked together into groupings. These groupings correlate ceremo-nial activities and influence the character of social relationships and responsibilities. Stories serve as the basis for how clan groupings were formed. For example, the Bear-Spider grouping is based on an episode in the *migration stories (see Masau?u).* As the clan groups travel about look-ing for a place to settle, one group of people comes upon a dead *bear* and takes the name Bear (honau) as their clan name. They are fol-lowed by another group, whose members cut straps from the skin of the bear and take the name Hide-Strap clan. Another group finds the bear, now covered with the web of spiders, and takes the name Spider clan. Another party finds a blue bird sitting on the dead bear; it takes the name Blue Bird. The next party finds that the eyes of the bear have been eaten by maggots, but in the eye cavity remains a little fat. They are the Fat Cavity clan. Finally, a group comes along and finds that a mole has dug his way up under the body of the bear. They call themselves the Mole clan. These six clans are linked by the authority of this story. See also *Honannyamu.* [Nequatewa 1936; Voth 1905b]

Hopi Ritual Cycle
Hopi, *Southwest*

Seven major ceremonial events *(wimi)* are performed annually by the Hopi. Each of the 13 Hopi villages maintains, more or less, an annual ceremonial cycle. The major division within the cycle is marked by the presence or absence of the *kachinas.* These appear at the winter solstice (see *Soyal)* and remain until shortly after the summer solstice (see *Niman).* In early February is the celebration of *Powamu,* which turns the attention of the community to the upcoming agricultural season. While these are the three major ceremonial events during the kachina portion of the year, the kachinas dance frequently: at the *night dances* in kivas during the winter and early spring, and at the *plaza dances* in the village plazas from the time it warms up in the spring until Niman. In addition to these three ceremonial events, there are the alternation between the *Snake Dance* and *Flute Dance,* performed in August; the *Marau* and *Oaqol,* women's societies events performed in the fall; and *Wuwutcim,* the male tribal initiation rites, performed in November. [Wright 1973]

Horn Society
Blackfoot, *Plains*

See *Transfer Ceremony,* the initiation ceremony.

Horned Serpent(s)

A figure appearing widely in Native American mythology, from North America into Central America. For examples of stories related to this figure, see *Doonongaes* (Seneca); *Old-Woman-Who-Never-Dies* (Mandan), who rides the serpent; *Kolowisi* (Zuni); *Misikinipik* (Cree); and *Thunderbird.*

Horse Dance
Blackfoot, Lakota, *Plains*

Also known as the Horseback Dance or Big Dance. Among the Blackfoot this event involved the decoration and painting of horses by their riders, who then rode them in a circle formed by members of the camp. This event occurred in preparation for *war* and functioned as a ritual to build courage and enthusiasm for battle. The decorations on the horses symbolized the number of guns the rider had captured, whether or not the horse had been wounded, and whether the horse's swiftness had overcome an enemy warrior. The horses' tails were tied and decorated, and

A manitou, perhaps representing the Great Horned Serpent, carved above the door of a Delaware house before 1731.

they wore beaded bridles. The riders dressed in their finery and warbonnets and carried war bundles, shields, and lances. The people in the camp sang special songs and the riders dismounted occasionally to *dance.*

The Oglala had a specific religious vision-questing ceremony, also known as the Horse Dance, that involved 16 horses and riders decorated and painted in groups of four to represent the four *cardinal directions.* While the person seeking the vision was fasting and sweating, the horses, their riders, and four female virgins surrounded the sweat lodge. Highly respected religious figures known as the Grandfathers sang songs about the four directions represented by the horses and their riders, and called for the renewal of the earth. Toward the conclusion of the ceremony, people who were ill approached the four women with offerings of tobacco and experienced healing. When the sweat ended, the horses were rubbed down with sage and the participant in the sweat gave thanks for the healing, the vision experienced, and the horses. [Brown 1953; Neihardt 1932; Walker 1982; Wissler 1913]

Hosedo
Seneca, Iroquois, *Northeast*

"Corners of mouth are hanging." A *False Face* mask (see *Masks and Masking)* identified by a crest of spinelike protrusions running vertically on the forehead. [Fenton 1987]

Hotgoendaqsais
Seneca, *Northeast*

A figure held captive and tortured by two women in the *longhouse.* His brother *Hodadenon,* a culture hero, is invited to witness the torture. Whenever a firebrand burns Hotgoendaqsais's skin he cries, shedding valuable *wampum* beads instead of tears from his eyes. The witnesses to this torture gather the wampum.

Hodadenon frees Hotgoendaqsais by blowing out the firebrands used for torture, casting all the occupants of the longhouse under a deep sleep,

and turning the entire lodge into red-hot flint. [Curtin and Hewitt 1918]

Hotho
Seneca, *Northeast*

"He, the cold one." Winter. In one story Winter is challenged by a hunter to a contest. The hunter claims that Hotho cannot make him freeze no matter how hard he tries. The hunter returns to his home and gathers enough firewood to burn all night. He also brews himself a large kettleful of hemlock tea. The hunter stays awake all night drinking his tea and turning first one side of his body toward the fire, then the other. The night grows colder and colder. At daybreak Hotho, naked, comes to the hunter's home and admits that the hunter has defeated him. At that moment it begins to grow warm and thaw, showing that humans can conquer Hotho. (See *Winter, Origin of.)* [Curtin and Hewitt 1918; Fenton 1987]

House Blessing
Navajo, *Southwest*

See *Blessingway.*

House of Air
Tsimshian, *Northwest Coast*

See *Gutginsa.*

Hozho
Navajo, *Southwest*

Beauty and order, a central religious concept. After the world is created (see *Blessingway),* the inner forms *(Biigistiin)* of the dawn and evening twilight are sent out to inspect the new world. They ascend each of the mountains that border this new world. From each vantage point they see an all-encompassing environment of beauty. This newly created world is one in which all things have places and are in those places. The order of this world is one in which inner and outer forms are in balance—east complements west, north complements south, men complement women, and so on. It is this newly created world that gives definition to the term hozho. See also *Hocho, Navajo Emergence, Sa?ah naghai bikeh hozho,* and *Uglyway.* [Witherspoon 1974, 1975, 1977; Wyman 1970]

Hu Nonp
Lakota, *Plains*
The *bear,* known for wisdom. See also *Mato.* [Powers 1975]

Hulkilal wok
Yuki, *California*
Hulkilal meaning "spirits," wok meaning "dance." The *dance* of the *dead,* given to the Huchnom by the creator *Taikomol* so people would live long and healthy lives. In this unmasked dance, the dancers' bodies are painted with black-and-white stripes and their hair is decorated with flowers. The dance is performed only by men; no women, children, or uninitiated men are allowed into the dance house during its performance. At puberty, boys are prepared for participation in the Hulkilal wok. They live in the dance house from fall to spring, participating in a program of strict discipline during which they learn the creation stories and songs, along with all the necessary aspects of the Hulkilal wok. [Voegelin 1940]

Human Effigies
See *Dolls.*

Human Sacrifice
Rarely practiced by cultures in North America. See *Evening Star* (Pawnee).

Human Snakes
Seminole, Oklahoma and *Southeast*
Malevolent creatures who can appear in either human or snake form. An ugly young man is seduced by a beautiful young girl at a *Stomp Dance.* He follows her to her home under a tree and discovers she is a *snake* woman who lives with huge blind snakes. Because of the malevolent power of the snake woman, the poor young man becomes so ill that even the medicine man cannot save him. Some men of the village follow his directions to the snake woman's home and see the den of giant snakes. The medicine man makes a strong *medicine bundle* to negate the power of the human snakes. The clothing of menstruating women is burned and the ashes wrapped in deerskin. Then a menstruating woman lowers the bundle into the snake den. The snakes hiss in agony, turn into human and semihuman forms, and die. The people fill the den with stones. [Sturtevant 1987]

Human-Animal Transformation
Just as transformations from animal to human often occur in Native American stories (see *Animal-Human Transformation),* so do transformations from human to animal form. These may occur for a variety of reasons. *Bright Eyes,* the boy in a Pawnee story, becomes a prairie dog because of failure in love. The Kawaiisu story *Deer Hunting* tells of a boy who becomes a deer. *Gaha* is a Seneca character who turns into a bear to catch a boy, and *Godasiyo* is a Seneca woman chief character who turns into a fish. A Snohomish story tells of humans becoming *killer whales. Old-Woman-Who-Never-Dies,* the Mandan witch, turns a young man into a serpent. *Qisaruatsiaq* is a Povungnituk old-woman character who turns into a wolf. *Qolqalg Odai* (Haida) becomes a salmon. *Skatene* is an old woman in a Choctaw story who becomes an owl. Among the Seminole are *Stikini,* people believed to have the power to turn into owls.

This transformational power is often connected with malevolence (see also *Witchcraft),* as with shape shifters and skinwalkers (see the Navajo figure *Yenaldlooshi).* The mistreated wife of *Sun-Ray* (Pawnee) becomes a mole. See *Sweat Lodge* for the Crow story of a man who becomes a reptile. *Buffalo-Woman and Corn-Woman* (Pawnee) turn a hunter into a buffalo. *Alarana and Aligunaluk* (Inupiak) are children who turn into caribou.

Humans, Origin of
How human beings were created, where they came from, how they got to their present habitat,

and how clans, families, or races relate to one another are important concerns in Native American mythology. *Blessingway* mythology tells how *Changing Woman* created the Navajo (see also *Navajo People, Origin of*). *Korawini?i* is the mother of the Paiute. The Ute creator *Kwikumat* made humans of clay. *Morning Star* made the Pawnee, *Nagaicho* the Kato, *Napioa* the Blackfoot, *Kmukamch* the Modoc, *Madumda* the Pomo, *Copper Woman* the Dogrib, *Quawteaht* the Nootka, and *Tabaldak* the Abenaki. *Tipiskawipisim,* the Moon, created the Cree; Yuchi people come from the blood of the female Sun *Tcho*. *Tirawahat* created the Pawnee, and *Unktehi,* powerful oxenlike beings, created people in some of the Plains cultures. *Xowalaci* created the Joshua, *Italapas* created the Chinook, *Taikomol* the Yuki, and Earth Shaman the Piman peoples (see *Tcu-unnyikita)*. The Yuchi came from a drop of *menstrual blood*. Eskimo people trace their origin to a woman and her dog husband (see *Adlet).*

Figures understood as *tricksters* sometimes have a hand in creating humans, for example, *Wesucechak* (Cree), *Old Man Coyote* (Crow), and *Raven*. See also *Black Hactcin Creates Animals and Humans* (Jicarilla Apache).

Hummingbird
Kawaiisu, *Great Basin*
The first curing *shaman,* summoned by *Coyote* to heal his daughter, who is ill because of being impregnated by her father. Hummingbird sings over Coyote's daughter, and Coyote pays him with awls, which become Hummingbird's bill. [Zigmond 1980]

Humor
Humor is prevalent throughout Native American mythology and ritual. Figures commonly known as *tricksters* appear in the story traditions of all Native American cultures. *Clowns and Clowning Societies* are present in many cultures, as are jokes (see *Jokes and Joking)* and joking relationships. In stories of *Acoma Emergence and Migration,* the humorous imitation of kachinas leads to the kachina wars. The Omaha designate stories of a humorous type as *Higu*.

Many occasions call for humor, among them Eskimo *song duels* performed in the *Messenger Feast* and joking in the Blackfoot women's medicine society, *Matoki*. Some *shaking tent* spirit visitors, including *Mank* (Loon) and *Nacwapew,* are known for their humor.

Humor is also an essential characteristic of such figures as *Memekwesiwak* (Cree water spirit), *Miskinahk* (Cree turtle), *Wegyet* (Gitksan culture hero), and *Wesucechak* (Cree). [Hill and Hill 1943a; Holden 1976; Keaveney 1983]

Humpbacked Flute Player
Southwest
See *Kokopelli*.

Hunka Lowanpi
Lakota, *Plains*
The *Sun Dance,* one of the central religious ceremonies of the Lakota people. This four-part ceremony involves everyone. It is conducted by a *wicasa wakan,* holy person, at a ceremonial camp. During the first part of the ceremony, the dancers and the people prepare for the dance. During the second part, everyone gathers at the place for the dance. The third part consists of the camp and the ceremonies prior to the dance, and the last part is the dance itself.

A person may vow to do the Sun Dance after a great trial, such as having experienced an illness of a child or spouse, or having participated in and survived a war. An individual who wants to become a wicasa wakan will also vow to make the Sun Dance. Any man, woman, or child may do the dance, although women do not traditionally pierce their chests as the men do. A person desiring to do the Sun Dance must let the wicasa wakan know far enough ahead so that he or she may be taught and prepared for the dance by the tunkansila, a person who instructs the Sun Dance candidate in such behavior as respectful silences and subjects to talk and think about. Once the candidate begins the Sun Dance, the tunkansila has nothing more to do for her or him. A person who has danced the Sun Dance becomes known as a Hunka and may be called upon to teach others about the Sun Dance.

Once someone has vowed to do the Sun Dance, the entire village knows, and everyone carefully watches that person's activities. The candidate is expected to act and speak properly at all times. When the Sun Dance leader decides it is time for the Sun Dance to take place, he goes with a filled pipe to select a place for it. Once the location is selected, the entire village comes together there and erects a ceremonial camp. The Sun Dance leader erects a Sun Dance lodge in the center of the camp for the Sun Dance candidates, using a specially cut tree as the center pole and covering the floor with sage. The candidates and their instructors then take an inipi, or sweat bath, to cleanse themselves. A buffalo bull head and pipe are placed inside the lodge. The candidates dress in fur robes and live within the lodge under strict rules; for example, no laughter is allowed. The candidates repeatedly paint themselves red, wear twisted sage around their heads, and have buffalo hair tied on both their wrists and ankles.

An old man announces that all skillful male and female singers are to assemble and sing during the feast, which lasts for four nights. At the end of the fourth night, a wakan (special) tree is sought for use as the center pole. Children whose relatives are candidates for the Sun Dance are sent to look for the tree, which has been chosen and marked by a person designated to find it. The wicasa wakan commands that the tree be forked at the top.

When the special tree is located, a song is sung. While a hole is dug in the ground where the pole will be erected, the rest of the village gathers with the leaders of the Sun Dance to cut down the tree. Songs are sung, and the children are given gifts. A woman of good character is selected to chop down the ceremonial tree and separate the branches from it. Then the tree is carried back

to the camp with care that it not touch the ground.

A bundle of red clay, buffalo loin, and the stem of a peeled chokecherry bush is prepared, along with tobacco, red-dyed porcupine quills, and a feather. These items are placed in the fork of the tree. Thongs made from hide are suspended from the fork. While the people shout with excitement, the tree is carefully pushed upright into the hole dug for it. The women sing, and the tree is painted on all sides to represent the four winds. A tree branch lodge is constructed around the center pole. All the young men paint themselves red and dance around the pole to smooth out the ground. When this is completed, the leader of the Sun Dance brings the buffalo head to the center of the lodge. He blesses the ground with tobacco and red clay, and places the pipe on a dried buffalo chip.

At noon the candidates approach the pole and fasten themselves to the suspended thongs by piercing the skin of their chests and running the thongs through the holes. They hang suspended from the pole as they dance and sing, watching the sun as it moves across the sky. They do not eat or drink while dancing. They dance until their skin tears loose from the pole. When the Sun Dance is completed, the candidates are considered Hunka and are responsible for caring for other Hunka if they are ever in need. Hunka are responsible for sponsoring other candidates to the Sun Dance ceremony and must show generosity to all village mates. See also Shirt Wearers and *White Buffalo Maiden*. [Powers 1975; Walker 1982]

Hunkayapi
Lakota, *Plains*

"Waving the horse tail." An intricate ceremony in which a young man is adopted by an older man who has already been through the Hunkayapi, creating a lifelong relationship that includes an obligation to share everything. Although it is understood that the Hunka relationship is mutual, the older man usually takes care of the younger one. Occasionally, a parent honors a son by sponsoring the ceremony so the son can adopt a less fortunate friend.

The Hunkayapi is coordinated by the Wicasa Itacan, who appoint an assistant and musicians, as well as two men to wave the horsetails used at the climax of the ceremony when the Hunka relationship is finalized. The Wicasa Itacan also instruct the two candidates on the responsibilities of the Hunka relationship. The ceremony takes place in a ceremonial tipi, where an altar holds a buffalo skull painted with red stripe marks to represent the Hunka. For the ceremony, the members of the Hunkayapi society dress in eagle down feathers and paint their faces with red stripes. The men sit at the right of the tipi and the women at the left. The prospective adoptee is placed in the tipi as a "captive" while his future partner is ritually interrogated as to whether he will accept the Hunka relationship. When the interrogators are satisfied, the older man "rescues" the captive, and the ceremony proceeds. [Neihardt 1932; Walker 1982]

Hunter(s)

For some examples of great hunters who are the subjects of Native American stories, see *Asdiwal* and *Waux* (Tsimshian), the Seneca hunter *Hagowanen,* and *Pisigsordleq* (Inupiaq). The Carrier story of *Bear Woman* includes a great hunter. Kanati, the mythological keeper of game, releases the game and thus originates hunting, as told in the Cherokee story of *Kanati and Selu. Naca Ominicia* refers to the Lakota "Big Bellies," who are retired hunters. See also *Hunting.*

Hunters, Female

Kawaiisu, *Great Basin*

Initially *women* did the *hunting* because men did not know how to hunt. Bluejay, who is unmarried and a fine huntress, lives on a mountain with many animal people. Coyote, who wants Bluejay as his wife, thinks he can hunt as well as she. He takes her arrows and gathers all the men to go hunting, proclaiming that the best hunter will

marry Bluejay. Red Bug (a small bug that eats into wood and skin and cannot be removed) goes along on the hunt, even though no one believes he will kill anything. The hunters come across a long line of deer going over the mountain. Red Bug shoots one arrow, which goes through every deer, killing all of them, and wins the right to marry Bluejay. Coyote is furious and jealous at being beaten by a lowly, unimportant insect. He vengefully decides that from now on only men will hunt. [Zigmond 1980]

Hunting

Virtually every Native American culture practices hunting, even those well known for being agriculturalists, like the Pueblo in the southwestern United States. It is thus no surprise that animals, hunters, and hunting fill Native American mythology, as shown by the following examples. In some cultures *Corn Woman* teaches hunting secrets. The Alaskan *Doll Festival* is performed to provide good hunting. The Iroquoian Husk Faces originated hunting practices (see *False Faces).* Although hunting is usually thought of as a masculine role, female hunters exist and appear in stories (see *Hunters, Female).* The Zuni *Kanaakwe* are enemies of hunters. The Hopi associate Spider Woman *(Kokyan wuhti)* with hunting and her web with a hunting net. The Hopi also consider *Tih-kuyi-wuhti* the mother of game animals, and they make an offering to her prior to hunting. The Cree call upon allies or helping spirits, such as *Maskwa* the bear and *Pakahk,* a skeleton, for help in hunting. The Crow believe that Moon Woman *(Miritatsiec)* makes hunting easier for them. The Tlingit carve wooden whales to help them fish (see *Whales, Carved Wooden).* See also *Hunter.* [Beckwith 1930a; Hill 1938; Luckert 1975, 1978; Nelson 1980; Sabo and Sabo 1985; Young and Cutsforth 1928]

Hunting Magic

Navajo, *Southwest*

See *Ajilee.*

Husk Face(s)

Iroquois, *Northeast*

See *False Faces, Longhouse Ceremony, Midwinter Festival, Fecal Power,* and *Traveling Rite.* For examples of Husk Faces see *Gadjiqsa, Djigaahehwa,* and *Hadjihsa Thokste?ah,* the oldest Husk Face.

Hustoyowanen

Seneca, *Northeast*

"Long snouted one." A name for buck or male deer, also known as Dodjenendogeni, "the cloven hoofed one" or Onogengow, "the great horned one." [Fenton 1987]

The beautiful Hemis Kachina, a favorite at Hopi Niman, the Home Dance. Painting by Cliff Bahnimptewa from Kachinas: A Hopi Artist's Documentary, by Barton Wright, copyright © 1973 by The Heard Museum. Published by Northland Publishing, Flagstaff, Arizona, with The Heard Museum, Phoenix, Arizona. Painting from the collection of The Heard Museum, Phoenix, Arizona.

Iatiku (Iyatiku)
Keres, *Southwest*
Female *creator* figure whose actions are recounted in the *emergence* stories of the Acoma, Laguna, Cochiti, and Zia tribes. Also known by the names Uretsete and Utshtsiti, Iatiku may be considered the mother of all Native Americans. Utsiti, considered the creator of the universe, made the earth from a discarded clot of his own blood, into which he planted Iatiku and her sisters. All the people live in a dark underworld. Iatiku lives with her sisters in *Shipap,* a village in this world. She has a son, Masewa (Laguna), or sons, *Masewa and Uyuyewa* (Acoma and Laguna). Iatiku sends her son(s) in search of the sun to bring *light* to the world (see also *Twins' Journey to Sun Father).*

After Masewa (and Uyuyewa) leads the people up into this world, *Spider Woman* gives the sisters a basket of seeds and images to assist in their creation and tells them what to do. Iatiku and her sister Nautsiti come up into this world and sing the creation song. As they sing, they reach into the basket and throw seeds and images that become the things of which they are singing. The sisters engage in contests, the nature of which differs among the Keresan traditions. Iatiku makes the *kachinas* and the *Kobictaiya* from the dirt left in her basket.

Desiring someone to make her laugh, Iatiku rubs epidermal waste from herself and makes it into a ball, which she covers with a blanket (see also *Changing Woman).* From underneath the blanket comes the clown Koshare, who is assigned the task of making fun to help the people forget their troubles (see *Clowns and Clowning Societies).*

Iatiku watches over human beings to promote their general welfare. She is sometimes identified as the breath of life. A short prayer and a bit of food are offered to her at meals. Prayersticks (see *Prayer and Prayersticks)* are also offered. See also *Acoma Emergence and Migration.* [Dumarest 1919; Parsons 1930a; Stevenson 1894; White 1932]

Ice Giants
Maliseet-Passamaquoddy *Northeast*
See *Kiwahkw,* cannibal monsters.

Ich-kanava
Mohave, *Southwest*
"Great tellings." (1) The name for the lengthy stories of the Mohave migration. (2) The term used to classify tales of *war.* [Kroeber 1948]

Idos

Seneca, Iroquois, *Northeast*

The ritual of the *Hadidos* medicine society (see also *False Faces),* in which members wearing masks (see *Masks and Masking)* without eye openings juggle hot stones and move cornhusk dolls on inverted corn mortars to demonstrate their power to see despite wearing the blind masks. [Fenton 1987]

Iʔitoi

Pima and Papago, *Southwest*

Culture hero made by Earth Shaman (or Earth Doctor). He ruins the world created by Earth Shaman by causing a *flood.* The Pima and Papago ancestors are saved by being sent to the underworld, while the deities save themselves by getting into things that float. After the flood, the gods give Iʔitoi the names Elder Brother (Seʔehe) and Elder Brother Shaman (Sis makat). He creates a new race of humans, but because he continues to be so obnoxious to Earth Shaman, these people sink into the underworld. Their residence is attested to by the many prehistoric ruins of the Hohokam found in southern Arizona. The Hohokam also dislike Elder Brother and engage Buzzard to kill him. Buzzard flies overhead in the place of the sun and shoots Elder Brother with rays of light. Elder Brother dies, but comes back to life. He journeys into the underworld, where he finds the ancestors of the Pima and Papago who have taken refuge from the flood. He leads them from the underworld as an army and they destroy the Hohokam. The Pima and Papago settle in this land, and Elder Brother leaves the world. See also the Pima creation story *Tcu-unny-ikita.* [Bahr 1975; Jose 1980; Russell 1908]

Ikalu nappa

Arctic

Half woman and half fish, not to be confused with *Sea Woman.* See also *Sedna.*

Ikanam

Chinook, *Northwest Coast*

Ikanam is one of the Chinook creators; the other is *Italapas.*

Ikonnokatsiyiks

Blackfoot, *Plains*

"All comrades." A series of men's *societies* grouped according to the age and experience of their members. Among these were the Mosquitoes (Sohskriss), the Kit-Foxes (Sahnipahks), and the Horn Warriors (Etsinaki). [Wissler 1913]

Ikosait

Kathlamet, Oregon/Washington coast, *Northwest Coast*

Mink. After Mink is abandoned by people with whom he has gambled, his brother, Panther, provides food for him and they travel together. Mink is attacked and killed several times. Each time Panther resuscitates him. When Mink and Panther reach the house of Panther's wife, her father also attempts to kill Mink, but Mink is stronger and blinds the old man. [Boas 1901b]

Iktomi or Unktomi

Lakota, *Plains*

The firstborn son of *Inyan,* the Rock, who was originally named Ksa. Iktomi is born full-grown from an egg and is the size of an ordinary human. He has a big round body like a spider, with slender arms and legs and powerful hands and feet. He dresses in clothes made of buckskin and raccoon.

Iktomi can speak with every living thing, as well as with rocks and stones. He is capable of making himself invisible, and often disguises himself as an old man. Iktomi is considered to be *heyoka* because he talks with *Wakinyan,* the Thunderbird. Iktomi rides dogs and causes their hair to fall off. He also rides wolves and coyotes. The one thing Iktomi fears is the *sweat lodge.*

Iktomi convinces the Lakota to scatter instead of living close together. When enemies come, the Lakota are alone without strong defenses. Iktomi laughs at these predicaments. As a result, the Lakota hold a council and decide to build their camps in a circle, with the door of each lodge pointing toward the door of the neighboring lodge. This way everyone will know if Iktomi comes into a lodge. See also *Ta Tanka Lowanpi* (the Bull Buffalo Ceremony), *Tate* (Wind), and *Trickster*. [Black Elk and Giago 1980; Powers 1975; Walker 1982]

Ikuutayuuq
Eskimo, eastern Hudson Bay, *Arctic*
"The one who drills." Ikuutayuuq and his brother kill people by pinning them down on their backs and drilling holes in them. Rock piles on the tundra, called inuksuut, mark the places where the brothers' victims are found. Ikuutayuuq is finally killed by a strong *tuniit* (early man) who cares greatly about his people. The tuniit fights Ikuutayuuq while tied to him with rope. When Ikuutayuuq is stabbed by the tuniit, his brother runs away. [Nungak and Arima 1988]

Illness
See *Disease* and *Healing*.

I-mukh-pi-mi a-klan-kun
Eskimo, Bering Sea coast, Alaska, *Arctic*
A sea weasel, who takes advantage of lonely, inattentive hunters. [Tennant and Bitar 1981]

Incest
Incest is a relatively common motif in Native American mythology. It may lead to the creation of the world, to the creation of humans (see *Above-Old-Man*), or to the birth of clowns *(Koyemshi)* or monsters. Figures classified as *tricksters* commonly engage in incest with their daughters or mothers-in-law. *Cunawabi*, the Moapa trickster, causes illness when he commits incest with his daughter. *Nehanimis* is seduced by his trickster father *Wesucechak* (Cree), disguised as a woman. Coyote sleeps with his daughter in the Kawaiisu stories of the *Big Dipper* and *Hummingbird*. In some stories incest produces animals with certain physical characteristics or markings. *Loon Woman* obtains her necklace as a result of incest. The marks on the moon reflect Sun, her brother, who is also her lover (see *Sun and Moon*). In the Yavapai story of *Widapokwi and Amchitapuka*, Widapokwi conceives a child with her father, the Sun. *Tumanpa and Kwa?akuyi-savepone* (Mohave) are a brother and sister who commit incest. The Lakota figure Rock *(Inyan)* commits incest with his mother, producing a beautiful but seductive woman. See also *Incest Causes Flood*. [Oosten 1983; Schmerler 1931]

Incest Causes Flood
Zuni, *Southwest*
The Corn clan is the largest of all Zuni clans. The beautiful young people of the clan are attracted to one another, and have sexual intercourse with one another in the kivas. Only one young man, a priest's son who is a member of the Corn clan, acknowledges that this is wrong. He contacts a deceased uncle by making a prayerstick offering (see *Prayer and Prayersticks*). Responding to the call, the uncle frightens the people with his apparition. Fearing an earthquake, the people flee to Corn Mountain. The earth rumbles and floods come. A priest tells the people they caused this destruction by their incestuous acts. This established the rule that people of one clan should be as brothers and sisters, and never desire one another.

Some versions of this story, collected earlier, include the *sacrifice* of the priest's incestuous son and daughter to make the *flood* subside. (See *Flood Subsided by Sacrifice.)* Their sacrifice accounts for the origin of the rock formations on the west side of Corn Mountain known as Boy and Girl Cliffs. Some versions do not attribute the cause of the flood to clan incest. One version even considers the flood a blessing in that the Ahayuta, the warrior twins, dry the foam from the floodwaters in their hair to form the war hoods worn by the bow priests.

See *Kolowisi*, the horned serpent, who appears during the flood. For related material see *Initiation Secrets*. [Benedict 1935; Cushing 1896; Parsons 1923e; Stevenson 1905]

Indacinga
Ponca, *Plains*
Beings with great physical strength who live in the forests and hoot like owls. Indacinga are

powerful enough to uproot trees and overturn lodges. Mothers use the threat of being caught by Indacinga to influence the behavior of their *children*. See also *Bogey*.

Inipi
Kawaiisu, *Great Basin*

A spirit of the *dead* who lives at the end of the world and keeps doves. *Coyote* gambles with inipi and wins the doves, thereby releasing them for the Kawaiisu people. During the seasons when no doves are seen, the inipi are believed to be winning the gambling match against Coyote. If inipi are seen by humans a disaster may follow. [Zigmond 1980]

Inipi
Lakota, *Plains*

Sweat bath taken in an inipi, *sweat lodge,* to gain strength before doing something of importance. Inipi is also taken for refreshment, as a *medicine* for healing, or as part of a ceremony. When the inipi is part of a ceremony it is conducted by a *wicasa wakan*. The inipi is also done prior to undertaking a *Hanblapi* (vision quest). See also *Hunka Lowanpi* (Sun Dance), *Ni* (breath), and *Ta Tanka Lowanpi* (Bull Buffalo Ceremony, a girls' puberty rite). [Neihardt 1932; Powers 1975]

Iniskim
Blackfoot, *Plains*

Buffalo Rock, small fossil-type stone found on the prairie. A Buffalo Rock is believed to give the person who finds it great power with buffalo, and thus finding one is always cause for celebration. In one story, a village suffers great hunger. A man goes hunting but finds only a rabbit, which he kills and takes home to his wife. When the wife goes to get water, she hears singing but cannot figure out where it is coming from. She looks at a split cottonwood tree and finds a strange rock jammed into it. She also finds buffalo hair on the trunk, as if a buffalo had rubbed up against it. She becomes frightened, but the rock speaks to her

and tells her to take it to her lodge and to teach the people the *song* she heard it sing. It also tells her to pray that her people will not starve and the buffalo will return. After she does so, the people hear the noise of buffalo coming over the prairie. They place the rock in a special place and pray to it regularly. [Grinnell 1892a; Thomas 1986]

Initiation

Entrance into societies or to a new stage of life is effected through ritual. Rites associated with coming of age or the passage into adulthood are widely practiced by Native Americans (see *Girls' Puberty Rite* and *Vision Quest*). The *Chingichnich* is a southern California rite of passage utilizing datura. The initiation of Eskimo children takes place during the *Inviting-In Feast* and is known at Hopi as the *Kachina Cult Initiation;* see also *Kuksu-hesi* for the initiation procedures of this cult. Initiation into the Winnebago *Midewiwin* involves being "shot" from a medicine bundle. The *Hamatsa* initiations of the Pacific northwest coast are among the most dramatic in North America. [Fewkes and Stephen 1892; Gill 1977; Steward 1931b]

Initiation Secrets
Pueblo, *Southwest*

The rites that initiate Pueblo children into their adult religious lives include the revelation that *kachinas* are humans wearing masks. This often-disenchanting experience is conjoined with the demand that initiated youth not reveal this knowledge to the uninitiated. Stories of what might happen to them if they tell are related to reinforce the importance of keeping this initiation secret.

The Zuni tell a story set at the time during the flood when the people are living on Corn Mountain (see *Incest Causes Flood*). An initiation is held and the initiates warned against telling the secret. While playing at making clay figures of kachinas, one youth reveals that the kachinas are the children's fathers and uncles dressed up in masks. Dangerous kachinas are summoned. They break open the boy's house where he is hiding, cut off his head and, leaving the body lying in his house, kick his head all the way to *Kachina Village*. [Benedict 1935; Bunzel 1932; Stevenson 1887]

Inkoze
Chipewyan, Athapaskan, *Subarctic*
Specific knowledge and *power* about the universe revealed in *dreams* to humans by other-than-humans. In Athapaskan culture, which does not acknowledge accidents, Inkoze is a complex theory of causality and explanation. This power and knowledge can be used in a positive way or, in cases of sorcery, malevolently to cause death. Kinship groups who hunt together are affected and defined by the Inkoze they hold. Inkoze may be used by hunters to call animals. Medicine people use it to locate medicine plants. Inkoze should not be talked about or sought, and may not be claimed.

In Chipewyan stories every human, regardless of gender, has Inkoze. Because of this, humans, animals, and other-than-humans can understand each other. The arrival of Christian missionaries influenced gender roles, resulting in the restriction of possession of Inkoze to men. [Mishler 1990; Nelson 1974]

Inner Life-Form
Navajo, *Southwest*
See *Biigistiin* and *Biisiziinii*. See also *Inua* and *Soul*.

Insects, Origin of
Insects come from the ashes of a cremated monster in the Alabama story of *Big Man-Eater*.

Intellect
Lakota, *Plains*
See *Sicun*.

Interpreter
Seneca, *Northeast*
See *Hadentheni and Hanigongendatha*. Hadentheni is known as the interpreter.

Inua(s)
Eskimo, *Arctic*
An inua is an independent humanlike entity, sometimes described as a *spirit*, which is possessed by all living things—not only plants and animals, but also mountains, bodies of water, and air. An inua enables a natural object or living thing to take on various physical forms. This ability to transform is central to west-coast Eskimo religions. Humans may appear as animals, animals as other animals, or animals as humans. The key action in many creation stories involving *Raven* or *Crow* is the ability of their inuas to take on other forms. In masks (see *Masks and Masking*), drawings, prints, and carvings, the inua is generally shown in the form of a humanlike *face* on the back, breasts, or eye of an animal. See also *Inviting-In Feast; Tunghak,* a malevolent spirit; *Underworld;* and *Hands.* [Lantis 1947; Nelson 1899; Riordan 1983]

Inugpasugssuk
Eskimo, *Arctic*
A *giant* who catches fish and seals with his bare hands and has lice as big as lemmings. Inugpasugssuk likes and protects human beings. He moves villages lying too close to the shore so that waves created when he wades out to get seals will not wash them away. Inugpasugssuk camps near human villages. He falls in love with a local woman, and he and the woman's husband agree to exchange wives. The human woman is split wide open when Inugpasugssuk has intercourse with her, and the human man falls into the genitals of Inugpasugssuk's wife. He dissolves inside her and his bones come out with her urine.

Inugpasugssuk feels great sorrow over killing the human woman and consoles himself by adopting a human son. The foster son grows to be larger than most humans and helps Inugpasugssuk with his work. One day Inugpasugssuk's foster son says he wants to visit his home village, now far away. Inugpasugssuk gives him a magic stick to help him find his way. When the boy arrives at home, he is far too large to get into any of the houses. He goes back to his foster father and neither is seen again. [Nungak and Arima 1988]

Inuquillit
Eskimo, *Arctic*

"Little people." Miniature human characters, capable of remarkable feats of strength and courage, found in the story traditions of the Inupiaq-speaking Eskimo. [Chance 1990]

Inviting-In Feast(s) (Kelek)
Eskimo, *Arctic*

The last festival of the year, usually held in spring. The Inviting-In-Feast featured masked dances honoring the *inuas* of other spirits and animals besides those of the seals. Neighboring villages were invited to the feast by a messenger carrying an *asking stick* requesting the guests to come bringing gifts, but these requests were small compared to the demands of Kevgiq *(Messenger Feast)*. *Shamans* composed songs and dances meant both to bring about and give thanks for the successful harvesting of animals and other resources. After the messenger left with the invitation, new masks, made according to the shaman's instructions, were carefully decorated, wrapped, and put away until the start of the dancing and pantomimes. Other large masks (see *Masks and Masking)* and moving figures were suspended from the *qasgiq* ceiling.

The helping spirits of the shamans and the inuas of many birds and animals were revealed in the masked performances. People who had been helped by spirits during the year also had masks made to help them perform, through song and dance, the story of the spiritual help they had received and their gratitude for it.

Some masks were purposely ugly or funny, such as one worn by a male cross-cousin whose female cousin was dancing in front of him, in order to upstage the usurper and make people laugh. These masks were meant simply to cover one's face and were not considered to be representative of inuas. Other masks were highly respected and used only at the beginning of the

dances. The shamans' helping spirits were revealed in large hanging masks that made noises as they were lightly struck. Then the masks were donned for slow dancing, and their stories told in *song*. Many masks representing the inuas of birds, animals, and other beings were worn in dances directed toward achieving a bountiful hunting season. The words of the songs empowered the request. Moving effigies and *puppets* helped tell stories about past incidents and supernatural encounters.

Children were often initiated into adult roles at the Inviting-In Feast. Initiate boys and girls danced for the first time wearing masks, often of birds and fish, which had been made especially for them to use during practice dances. Spiritual intervention by shamans and the importance of individual spiritual contacts were reinforced during Kelek. The enactment of former spiritual encounters through songs and masked dances evoked power for the future. See also *Hands* and *Nakaciuq*. [Morrow 1984; Nelson 1899]

Inyan
Lakota, *Plains*

The *Rock,* source of all things, existing before time or any other thing. Its spirit is *Wakan Tanka,* the great mystery. At first Inyan was soft and shapeless, although his powers are already fully developed. He carried his powers in his blood, which is blue. Because Inyan is lonely, he decides to create another being from a piece of himself. He creates *Maka,* the earth. Because it takes so much of his blood to create Maka, Inyan shrinks and becomes hard and powerless. His flowing blue blood becomes all the waters of the earth. Inyan also creates *Wakinyan,* Winged One, to be his active associate.

Inyan has two offspring. The first is Ksa, later called *Iktomi,* the mischief maker. Ksa is born full-grown from an egg laid by Wakinyan. He is supposed to be filled with wisdom, but he becomes mischievous. Inyan's second son is *Iya,* completely malevolent and responsible for all malevolent beings. Iya commits *incest* with his mother Unk. Their offspring is the beautiful, seductive, and deceitful Gnaski. [Powers 1975; Walker 1982]

Iouskeha
Huron, *Northeast*

Grandson of *Aataentsic,* the mother of human-kind. *Creator* of the lakes and rivers. Iouskeha frees all the animals from a great cave, makes *corn* grow, gives the Hurons *fire,* and is responsible for good weather. [Trigger 1978]

An Iroquois mask. All rights reserved, Photo Archives, Denver Museum of Natural History.

Iron People
Haida, *Northwest Coast*

The Haida name for *European-Americans.* Many Haida stories associate the advent of European-American traders with the introduction of iron. [Blackman 1977]

Iroquois Masks, Storage of
Iroquois, *Northeast*

Masks (see *Masks and Masking)* are usually owned by men, although women may be their temporary custodians. False Face masks are kept in individual *medicine bundles* along with a *turtle rattle* for protection. Each mask is decorated with bags of tobacco and stored facedown with its hair wrapped around it and the turtle-shell rattle nestled in the hollow back of the mask. The bundle is then wrapped in a cloth.

When masks are not in ritual use, their faces are always covered to prevent people from becoming frightened or possessed by accidentally seeing them. An unused mask can be a source of illness. Stored masks are regularly fed corn mush, offered tobacco, and have their faces rubbed with sunflower oil. If there are no heirs to receive a mask, it may be buried with its owner.

Among the Onondaga, matrons, who are members of the False Face Society, have the task of rubbing the masks with sunflower oil before the maskers leave the *longhouse* to make their travels around the village. [Fenton 1987]

Irraq
Eskimo, Alaska, *Arctic*

A baby who devours its parents and other villagers because it is not given the traditional *akutaq* (Eskimo ice cream) at a village feast. Even newborns are expected to have their mouths smeared with this ritual food. Irraq's mother neglects to do this, and later the infant is found hopping about with blood all over his mouth, having bitten his parents to death and eaten them. Irraq is finally confronted by a man who gives the child an armlet made of straw to play with and banishes him to the mountains. [Norman 1990]

Ishjinki
Iowa, *Plains*

A *culture hero* known for his deception and daring. One time Ishjinki begs Buzzard to take him flying. When they are airborne, however, Ishjinki screams in fright, and Buzzard dumps him headfirst into a dead tree stump. Ishjinki sings out, pretending to be a raccoon trapped in the tree, until some women free him. Then he lies on the ground pretending to be a dead elk, while crows peck away at his buttocks. Finally Buzzard lands and pokes his head into Ishjinki's anus. Ishjinki closes his anus around Buzzard's head and drags him around for a long time before releasing him. This is why the buzzard's head is bald and smells bad.

Ishtohoollo Aba Eloa
Creek, *Southeast*

The-big-holy-one-above-who-thunders. The being who is responsible for *thunder* and *lightning,* and who sends the rains as he pleases. [Swanton 1928a]

Isil
Cupeño, *California*

Coyote. There are many stories about Coyote. In one, he argues with Wildcat (Tukut) over who is older. Coyote wins because he was the first to speak. At that time humans were on earth, but they could not yet see. When they heard Coyote speak they rose from the mud. Ever since this event medicine people have been able to understand Isil. [Kroeber 1948]

Italapas
Chinook, *Northwest Coast*

Coyote, who acts as a cocreator with the *creator* Ikanam. Italapas is waiting in a tree for the water to subside after a great flood. He throws some sand in the water and it becomes land. Italapas then helps Ikanam make humans, and shows them how to catch salmon, make utensils, and weave. He also teaches them all the taboos. [Jacobs 1959]

Itiwana
Zuni, *Southwest*

"The middle place." The place name for Zuni Village, locating it equidistant from the four oceans. Also the designation of a 20-day ceremonial period coinciding with the solstices. In the stories of the Zuni migration, the people search for a place to live, finally settling at itiwana after its location is designated by a water strider, an insect that skates on the surface tension of water. The water strider stretches out its legs to the edges of the world. Where its heart touches down is the middle place, sometimes also identified as halona itiwana, the middle anthill of the world. See also *Zuni Emergence* and *Zuni Ritual Cycle.* [Tedlock 1979]

Iumaaq
Eskimo, eastern Hudson Bay, *Arctic*

A *blind boy,* abandoned by his wicked mother but kept alive by his sister, who smuggles food to him in her parka. Iumaaq asks *Loon* to help him regain his sight. Loon tells him to dive underwater and stay there without moving until he can no longer hold his breath. Iumaaq does this three times. Each time his sight improves, until he has excellent vision. After regaining his sight, Iumaaq provides for his mother and sister. One day, while harpooning white whales, he convinces his mother to help him with the harpoon line. She is cast out with the harpoon and sticks to the plunging whale. Her parka hood becomes the whale's tail. [Nungak and Arima 1988]

Ivivarshuk and Nisguvaushaq
Eskimo, *Arctic*

The first two *shamans (angalkuq)* who came from the sky to look for an earth woman to birth them. Ivivarshuk and his younger brother, Nisguvaushaq, search for a shining woman (nothing dark should cast a shadow on her body) because such women give birth to great hunters. The brothers search for a long time until Ivivarshuk finds a woman, all shiny except for her spine. He crawls inside her and grows there until he is born.

Because he is born of a shining woman he grows quickly and becomes a great shaman. He travels through the earth to agdlerpat, the place where worms and maggots live. There all the flesh is eaten off his bones and his brains become light. He returns to the earth to practice shamanism. His journey opens the path to agdlerpat and establishes the precedent for traveling to agdlerpat as an essential part of the initiation of great shamans. Ivivarshuk's spirit is also able to travel through the air (ilimarpoq) during a seance. Nis-guvaushaq also finds a shining woman to bear him. He becomes a shaman but is unable to travel to agdlerpat through the air. He teaches the people how to consult spirits. [Norman 1990]

Iya

Lakota, *Plains*

The malevolent *giant* created by *Inyan* (the Rock), after *Skan* (the Sky) and *Maka* (the Earth). See also *Ta Tanka Lowanpi* (girls' puberty rite) and *Wakanpi.* [Walker 1982]

Jesus

Some Native American mythological figures are identified with Jesus. See *Widapokwi and Amchitapuka* (Yavapai), and *Hisagita misa* (Seminole). See also *Christianity.*

Jewels (or hard goods)

Navajo, *Southwest*
See *Yodi and Ntliz.*

Jimsonweed

See *Chingichnich,* a California intiation rite in which jimsonweed is used, and *Datura.*

Jish

Navajo, *Southwest*
See *Medicine bundle.*

Jokes and Joking

Jokes are common occurrences in Native American mythology and ritual. Some ceremonial and feast occasions are particularly noted for the predominance of joking, such as the song duels held during Alaskan Eskimo *Messenger Feasts.* The Cherokee Bear Dance *(Yona)* is an occasion for sexual joking. Some spirit visitors to Cree *shaking tent* rites are known for their jokes; these include *Miskinahk* the turtle and *Nacwapew* the pike. The Crow tell of the *Awakkule,* a joke-playing dwarf people. *Clowns and Clowning Societies,* so common to Native American cultures, play their share of jokes. The many stories known for protagonists classified as *tricksters* are filled with tricks and jokes. See also *Humor* and *Joking Relationships.*

Joking Relationships

Also referred to as teasing relationships, these often involve sexual jokes. The joking relationship is usually found between people of the opposite sex who are related in some specific way. By contrast, certain types of relatives may not even speak to one another. For example, a man shows respect to his mother and sister, but in many tribes he is strictly forbidden to speak to his mother-in-law *(Mother-in-Law Taboo).* He may, however, have a joking relationship with his sisters-in-law and in some tribes with his wife's sister's daughters. A woman may have joking relationships with her brothers-in-law, as well as with her brother's sons.

Jugglers

Illinois, Menominee, western Great Lakes area, *Northeast*

From jongleurs, the name the French gave to male and female Menominee shamans. Jugglers defanged rattlesnakes to display their power. The process of overcoming and defanging the rattlesnake symbolized overcoming the death to which their patients had succumbed and the affliction over which the jugglers had power. Other jugglers handled hot coals and removed embedded objects from afflicted victims. See also *Wabeno* (Ojibwa) and *Caskyet* (Potawatomi). [Bloomfield 1928a]

K

Kaahkwa
Seneca, *Northeast*

The *Sun,* who lives in his lodge in the sky as an old man. Kaahkwa is commanded by *Hawenniyo,* the controller of all things, to give light. See also *Hadentheni and Hanigongendatha.* [Fenton 1987]

Kacale
Acoma, *Southwest*

A secret organization, now extinct at Acoma, with clown (see *Clowns and Clowning Societies)* and *war* functions similar to those of the Rio Grande Pueblo societies known as Koshare. Their distinctive appearance included a white-painted body with black horizontal bands, black rings around the eyes and mouth, cornhusk headdress, black breechcloth, and bare feet. [White 1932]

Kachina(s)
Pueblo, *Southwest*

The term kachina has come to be broadly used to refer to any masked figure among the Pueblo peoples and even among other southwestern cultures. Even when restricted to a single culture, such as Hopi, its meaning is far from simple. It may refer to anthropomorphic spirit beings who mediate between the human and spiritual worlds, to masked dancers who personify these spirit beings, or to elaborately carved and decorated *dolls* of these beings. Kachinas may be understood as spirits of the *dead.* The Hopi believe that, upon death, those who have lived the proper Hopi life go to the west, where they become kachinas, returning to Hopi villages as clouds. Yet there is no clearly direct link between specific deceased Hopi people and specific kachina appearances. Hopi kachinas have designated homes in the San Francisco Mountains near Flagstaff, Arizona, at the spring Kisiwu northeast of Hopi, and other places. The kachinas live in their homes half the year. During the other half, they live around Hopi villages where they dance and sing for the people (see *Hopi Ritual Cycle).*

Two distinct kinds of Hopi kachinas are recognized: the chief (mon) kachina and the ordinary kachina. Mon kachinas never dance in groups; ordinary kachinas do. The masks of ordinary kachinas are made by their owners and redecorated for each performance. Mon kachina masks are permanent and never duplicated. These masks, considered to be ancestors and objects possessing great power, are handled with care by the lineage to which they belong. Mon kachinas may compare to the *Ones Who Hold Our Roads* (honaa-wonaawillapona) of the Zuni.

The mask (see *Masks and Masking*), kuʔitu, is the basis for all kachina impersonations. Most masks are shaped like a bell jar and fit over the head and face of the wearer down to the neck. Each mask is elaborately painted in designs distinctive to the particular kachina, often incorporating common motifs representing corn, clouds, lightning, and falling rain. Commonly, feathers and other significant objects are attached to the masks. When a Hopi man places the mask over his head and wears the appropriate costume, he becomes the kachina he is representing. Every kachina is identified by name and recognized by distinctive features of mask and costume. There are several hundred different Hopi kachinas. New kachinas of the ordinary kind have been added from time to time.

The kachina *dance* is the most common setting for kachina appearances. By dancing in the villages, the kachinas summon their "cloud fathers" to come from the six directions and bring rain, the very symbol of life. This suggests that the kachinas, rather than being literally clouds, are the spirits standing in close relation to clouds and to the deities that control rain and give life. In the secrecy of the kiva, from 25 to 60 men belonging to a common society create, learn, and rehearse songs and dances in preparation for the public kachina dance. The dances are performed from daybreak to sunset, with intervals of rest. Each performer wears a kilt woven of white cotton and embroidered along the edge, a woven sash, and buckskin moccasins. Most wear fox skins hanging from the back of the waist with the tail barely touching the ground. Exposed skin is covered with paint. Each dancer wears a turtle-shell rattle tied to the calf of his right leg; often a band of sleigh bells is attached to the left calf. A gourd rattle held in the right hand is also used to accompany the singing. In line dances all the figures appear identical or with slight individual

distinctions. The dancers hold their bodies erect, with arms close to the sides and hands forward. The dancing is primarily a rhythmic stepping with occasional synchronized changes in rhythm executed with changes in the step. The songs and dances performed by the various kachinas are distinctive to the specific kachinas. See also *Acoma Emergence and Migration, Hopi Ritual Cycle, Initiation Secrets, Kokkookwe,* and *Zuni Ritual Cycle.* [Anderson 1955; Bradfield 1973; Colton 1947a, 1947b, 1959; Earle and Kennard 1938; Fewkes 1897b, 1903; Parsons 1930a, 1936; Wright 1973, 1985]

Kachina Cult Initiation
Hopi, *Southwest*

The *initiation* of children into their adult religious lives. These rites of passage occur during *Powamu* and include revealing to the children certain elements of esoteric knowledge, a ritualized whipping reminding them of the importance of secrecy, and the disenchanting revelation that the *kachinas* are actually the men of their own community—their male relatives—wearing masks. [Gill 1977]

Kachina Village (kothluwala)
Zuni, *Southwest*

The place at the bottom of a lake to the west of Zuni Village, where most kachinas (see *Kokkookwe*) live. It is also the home of the hoofed game animals who, when they die, return to Kachina Village to be restored. See also *Dead, Land of; Initiation Secrets; Kanaakwe* (the enemies of kachinas); and *Pautiwa* (chief of Kachina Village). [Tedlock 1979]

Kacim mumkidag
Papago, *Southwest*

"Staying sickness." See *Mumkidag.*

Kaʔespai
Blackfoot, Gros Ventre, *Plains*

The *Grass Dance,* also known as the Hair-Parters Dance. The Grass Dance has a variety of expressions

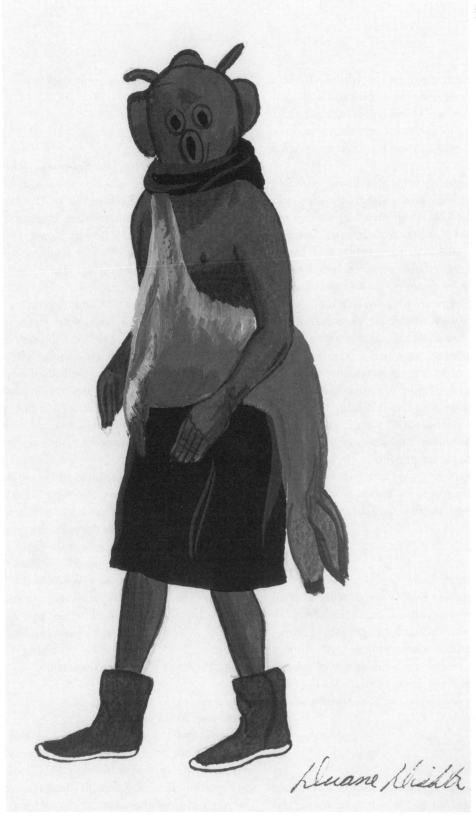

Zuni Kachina version of the Mudhead Clown, Koyemshi. Painting by Duane Dishta from the collection of The Heard Museum, Phoenix, Arizona.

within different tribal groups. Initially it was a massive *giveaway* (known also as a throwaway) of women, horses, and blankets. For each gift a stick was thrown into the crowd, and the person who retrieved the stick got the property for which it was thrown.

The ka?espai is held in a house especially constructed for the event, with many sides and a square smoke hole. Both men and women can belong to the Grass Dance Society (see *Societies*), but only selected male participants may handle the dance paraphernalia, which include a tomahawk, sword, warbonnet, drum, and dancing whip. These items are wrapped in bundles when not in use and purified with *sweet grass* before each dance. The owners of the dance whip or sword hold the ceremony, in which a member struck with a sword or whip is forced to dance. A person injured by such a strike is compensated by the owner of the whip or sword causing the injury. The women dance four at a time, taking turns wearing a warbonnet. The wearer of the warbonnet is responsible for presenting gifts to the visitors. In the past *dogs* were eaten at the ka?espai. These were furnished by guests, who were well paid in blankets, clothing, and occasionally a gun or horse.

Kaik
Salish, *Northwest Coast*
Mink, who marries Fog. While dancing with his bride and her sisters around the mountains, Kaik hurts his paws. He marries Eagle and, ignoring her advice, hurts himself trying to catch salmon. Kaik marries a number of animals, as well as Gum Tree and Sea Kelp. Each marriage leads to another injury. In the end, he is eaten by a whale. [Smith 1940]

Kan
Lakota, *Plains*
That which is established by custom and should not be changed, or that which is *mysterious* and cannot be understood. Also, anything that is old or has existed for a long time. The prefix a- with

kan, *akan,* means that the thing spoken of is kan. [Walker 1982]

Kanaakwe
Zuni, *Southwest*
A group of *kachinas* (see also *Kokkookwe)* who live to the south of Zuni and are the enemies of the kachinas who live at *Kachina Village*. The *hunting* territories of these groups overlap. The Kanaakwe decide to conceal all the *deer* by hiding them in their corrals. The kachinas of Kachina Village hunt without even seeing any game. Learning that the deer have been concealed, they challenge the Kanaakwe to a fight over hunting rights. The Kanaakwe string their bows with yucca fiber, while the kachinas string theirs with deer sinew. When it rains, the deer sinew stretches while the yucca fiber tightens, enabling the Kanaakwe to be victorious. As a result, the deer belong to the Kanaakwe, who are responsible for bringing them to the Zuni people, while the kachinas of Kachina Village bring the Zuni people corn, seed, and other things.

This story is often included in the stories of *Zuni Emergence*. In some versions the Kanaakwe are led by a giantess who keeps her heart in a rattle. Other versions account for the origination of the Ahayuta, the twin warrior sons of the Sun Father *(Yatokka taccu),* in response to the Kanaakwe concealing the deer. In some versions, the sons travel to their father to obtain weapons to kill the giantess leader of the Kanaakwe (see also *Twins' Journey to Sun Father* and *Game, Release of).* [Benedict 1935; Bunzel 1932; Cushing 1883, 1896; Parsons 1923d; Stevenson 1905]

Kanakuk
Kickapoo, *Northeast*
A *prophet* of the mid-1800s who advised the Kickapoo not to surrender to government demands to relocate from western Illinois to the Missouri mountains. Kanakuk's message, which he received from the Great Spirit, said that the Kickapoo were on their land by divine right. It also condemned medicine bags and witchcraft.

Heavily influenced by Methodist missionaries, Kanakuk introduced his followers to the use of prayersticks, which he carved, painted, and sold. The prayersticks, often referred to as Indian bibles, were inscribed with pictographs of prayers that people were to say twice a day, followed by a chant Kanakuk had taught them. [McLoughlin 1990]

Kanati and Selu
Cherokee, *Southeast*
"The Lucky Hunter" and his wife, "Corn," sometimes referred to as First Man and First Woman. Kanati and *Selu* live alone with their only son. One day while playing by the river, their son finds a small boy. Kanati and Selu realize the boy is their son's twin, who has sprung from the blood of the killed animals that Kanati brought home and Selu cleaned at the riverbank (see also *Blood Clot Boy*).

Although the river boy is wild, Kanati and Selu take him home and eventually tame him. They name him Inage Utasuhi, "He-Who-Grew-Up-Wild." Cherokee stories tell of the adventures of the twin sons of Kanati and Selu, Inage Utasuhi being responsible for leading his brother into many mischievous acts, including the killing of Selu. It is believed that Kanati and Selu live in the east where the sun rises and that their sons, known as the Twin Thunder Boys, live in the west. Whenever there is a thunderstorm, the boys are playing ball. [Mooney 1888, 1900, 1920]

Kanenhagenat
Seneca, *Northeast*
White *corn*, a major food source for the Seneca, given to them by a beautiful woman who lives atop a steep cliff and sings to the village below. The woman directs her song to a very old but highly respected man in the village whom she wants as her husband. At first the old man refuses, saying the climb to the mountaintop is too difficult. But the woman sings to him day and night, and the people become anxious. The village council meets and asks the old man to learn the reason for the woman's singing, and finally he agrees.

After a difficult trip up the side of the mountain, the old man finds the beautiful young woman standing at the brink of the cliff. She asks him to have sexual intercourse with her, but he replies that he is too old. She says she will make him potent again. She then tells him how to care for a young plant that will sprout and grow in the spot where they will lie together. She says the plant will be a chief source of food for his people and that it is called Kanenhagenat.

As the old man embraces the young woman he faints. When he revives, the young woman has vanished into the air. Thinking he has embraced a vision, he returns to his village. After five days have passed he returns to the mountaintop as the young woman directed. In the spot where he embraced her, a young corn plant is growing. He cares for the plant as she taught him, and when it ripens he picks three ears of corn. He carefully husks the corn and divides the grain among the community, teaching them how to plant and care for the corn. This is how white corn came to the Seneca people, who then shared it with the neighboring tribes. See also Onenha. [Curtin and Hewitt 1918]

Kanochisisin
Blackfoot, *Plains*
The *All-Smoking Ceremony,* held to count *coup* of all the different medicine rituals owned by the people attending. A kanochisisin celebrates the vast knowledge of the people gathered for it, highlights the successes of different medicine rituals, and generates enthusiasm for learning more rituals. It is considered a great privilege to lead a kanochisisin.

A person who wants to hold a kanochisisin makes payment of blankets and clothing to the designated leader and prepares a pot of animal tongue and berry soup, as well as a quantity of cut and mixed tobacco. During the ceremony, guests take turns singing songs from their own medicine rituals, ending with the people who own the most medicines. Each person sings a series of four songs, preceded by the shaking of four rattles. Before singing his or her song, the song's owner makes a smudge (a short purification ritual done with the smoke of burning sweet grass or sage), describes the medicine object to be sung about, and tells the amount paid for the song. The owner then says a short prayer.

After the songs are sung, four black smoking *pipes* are used. The pipes, which must not contain any metal, are filled and passed among the people present until all the *tobacco* is smoked. Then the leader makes an offering of smudge and tobacco to the sun and prays for the host, while the other participants offer prayers to the sun, moon, stars, and animals. At the close of the ceremony, the leader may give the host the privilege of leading the next kanochisisin. [Wissler 1911, 1913]

Kararata?u
Pawnee, *Plains*
Earth lodge. Large, dome-shaped structures of wood covered with packed sod and earth that served as permanent shelters. Earth lodges were roomy, often holding several families. Lodges of chiefs, healers *(kura?u),* and ritual leaders *(kurahus)* were large enough to host ceremonial gatherings. Kararata?u had long and narrow covered entrances. In the center of each lodge was a sunken fireplace, around which cooking and socializing took place. The west end of the lodge contained a rectangular altar of raised earth. If the family was responsible for keeping a medicine bundle, it was hung over the altar. Beds were raised off the floor along the north and south walls, with woven mat curtains for privacy. On either side of the outer doorway were corn mills where corn was ground. Also surrounding the kararata?u were sweat lodges, piles of firewood, underground food storage pits, and gardens for growing food. [Murie 1989]

Kasgig
See *Qasgiq.*

Kashehotapolo
Choctaw, *Southeast*
From kasheho, "woman" and tapolo, "call." A *beast-man* with a small shriveled head. Kashehotapolo lives in isolated, low, swampy places and is afraid of humans. When hunters come near its home, Kashehotapolo first screams to frighten them, then quickly runs away. See also the anthropomorphic beings *Nalusa Falaya.* [Hudson 1976]

Kashim
See *Qasgiq.*

Kassaq
Eskimo, Bering Sea coast, Alaska, *Arctic*
A white person.

Katydid
Nez Perce, *Plains*
An old woman, a katydid, who sings herself to death. One fall, the old woman, her daughter, and her son-in-law are out camping. The daughter has told her husband not to talk about any events of the day in front of her mother. One day after a hunting expedition he forgets the warning and tells his wife that the katydids make a great deal of noise this time of year. Overhearing, the old woman asks her son-in-law to repeat what he said. He refuses, but she badgers him until he gives in and tells her. At this the old woman throws on a cape and goes out to join the singing katydids. Saying she must catch up with them, she begins to sing out of tune. The other katydids listen for awhile, then go back to singing without her. The old woman dies of exhaustion from her attempts to catch up with the other katydids. [Phinny 1969]

Katyutayuuq
Eskimo, eastern Hudson Bay, *Arctic*
A female *monster* who has no body and whose large head is attached directly to her feet. Her breasts grow out of her cheeks. She can come through walls and often bangs her head against

empty houses. See also the tattooed creature *Tunnituaqruk*. [Nungak and Arima 1988]

Kaukiwawakauwa
Shawnee, Oklahoma and *Northeast*
A *dance* performed by both men and women one year after the death (see *Dead*) of a well-known and highly respected person. It is also known as the Turning Dance because the dancers move first in one direction, then turn and dance in the opposite direction. Kaukiwawakauwa is accompanied by a four-day feast that includes a gift exchange and contests to win goods. [Voegelin 1944]

Kautyayuq
Eskimo, eastern Hudson Bay, *Arctic*
A neglected orphan boy who, along with his sister, is rescued from drifting sea ice by the people of a village. After rescuing the children, the villagers treat them badly. Night and day the sister is forced to braid thread for trousers and kayaks, while Kautyayuq is kept in the entranceway of the house and given only walrus hide (usually fed to dogs) to eat. He is also forced to sleep with the dogs. When he is wanted inside the house, two large women pull him in by his nose.

One night the people hear bears outside. A man calls for Kautyayuq, planning to send him out in hopes that the bears will eat him and leave the villagers alone. When Kautyayuq refuses, the people chase him outside, where he grows quite big and kills the bears. Then he kills all the people in the village except the two large women, whom he abandons so they might suffer as he has. [Nungak and Arima 1988]

Kawenho
Arikara, *Plains*
The Hot *Dance,* so called because participants immerse their hands into pots of scalding water to retrieve ceremonially boiled pieces of dog meat, simultaneously claiming that the water is cold. Kawenho dancers wear headdresses of deer tails and turkey feathers. See also *Grass Dance.* [Walker 1982]

Kayas-ioiniwak
Cree, *Subarctic*
Ancient people, human in appearance, but without the intelligence of the modern-day Cree. Cree stories say the Kayas-ioiniwak lived before the advent of steel tools. [Bloomfield 1930]

Keetaan
Navajo, *Southwest*
Prayerstick (see *Prayer and Prayersticks).* Hollow reeds or wooden dowels of varying lengths, decorated and, if hollow, filled with such items as bits of feather, herbs, and semiprecious jewels. The decoration and the associated items are determined by the *diyin dine?e* to whom the prayerstick is directed. Often prayersticks are placed along with other offerings in cornhusk or cloth wrappers. Prayersticks have been referred to as "ritual cigarettes," because of their shape and the ritual practice of lifting the pollen-sealed end of the prayerstick to the light. It is perhaps more accurate to understand them as the vehicles of prayer. They have the power not only to cross between the human world and the world of the diyin dine?e but, by virtue of the way they are prepared, to obligate the diyin dine?e to respond.

In numerous Navajo ceremonial performances, bundled prayersticks are prepared in groups and stacked. The *one-sung-over* (the person for whom the ceremonial is being sung) holds them during prayers addressed to the diyin dine?e for whom the prayersticks have been prepared. Following the prayer, each bundle is deposited at a place associated with the diyin dine?e to whom it is directed. See also *Holyway,* a Navajo ceremonial classification in which prayersticks are commonly used; *Monsterway,* in which a prayerstick is used as a signal; *Shootingway;* and *Ye?ii,* to whom prayersticks are directed.

Kehtakws
Maliseet-Passamaquoddy, *Northeast*
Creatures, sometimes called ghosts, who bring warnings of coming death (see *Dead).* During storms, the sound of a scream followed by a

mournful laugh is understood by the entire village to be Kehtakws foretelling a death, while the appearance of a ball of fire forewarns of death and tragedy. The fire is thought to be the part of the person that leaves the body in dreams, capable of traveling great distances. [Fisher 1946]

Kelek
See *Inviting-In Feast.*

Keninqas
Nootka, *Northwest Coast*
Crow, the woman who owns the fresh water. Crow will not give a drop of water to anyone unless she is paid for it. Many people are dying of thirst, and their chiefs are complaining. Seeing this, *Raven* summons all the chiefs to his house and asks them to help him take the water from Crow. The chiefs say that if Raven succeeds in getting the water, they will make him chief over all of them. Raven asks one chief to make him a small mat. He takes the mat home and defecates into it.

Hiding the rolled mat under his arm, Raven goes to Crow's house and asks for a drink. Crow will not give him so much as a drop, even though he pretends to be dying of thirst. He tells her he is cold and asks if he might warm himself by lying next to her, but she refuses. Raven pleads to be allowed just to smell the water. Finally he casts a sleep spell on Crow. While she is in a deep sleep, he lifts her bedclothes and places the feces near her buttocks. He calls her by her spirit name. "Wake up, Gesgosamaga!" Crow awakes, smells the feces, and asks, "What smells so bad?" Crow accuses Raven of smelling bad, but he shows her the feces in her bed and says that if she does not give him a drink of water he will tell everyone she soiled her bed. Crow relents, but when she opens the box where she keeps the water, Raven tips it over and lets it all run out. He commands the water to turn into a large lake he names Litsit (Green Lake). He leaves Crow and returns to the people, telling them to drink from Green Lake. Raven makes a stream that runs from the lake to the sea. Finally he takes some of the water and carries it all over the world, turning each drop into a river. [Sapir and Swadesh 1939]

Keskamsit
Maliseet-Passamaquoddy, *Northeast*
Power found in objects that are believed to bring good luck. Such objects may become treasured *amulets* once they prove to bring good fortune. A person can also have keskamsit for certain tasks such as hunting, fishing, trapping, or lovemaking. [Fisher 1946]

Kevgiq
See *Messenger Feast.*

Keya
Lakota, *Plains*
Turtle, whose spirit is the guardian of health and the patron of healing rituals involving the removal through surgery of foreign objects such as arrows. Keya also tries to prevent accidents. [Walker 1982]

Kiaklo
Zuni, *Southwest*
The keeper of Zuni history. During the *migration* after the Zuni emergence, Kiaklo is sent to search for the middle place where the Zuni will settle. He gets lost and wanders far to the north where it is cold and covered with snow. His face turns white with frost from his breath, and he is blinded by the snow. His cheeks become grooved from the flow of tears, and his voice cracks, making the sound of a duck. Duck, considered a wise creature, answers his call and listens to his story. Duck guides Kiaklo by means of the sound made by the ceremonial shells worn around the duck's neck. After being given prayersticks (see *Prayer and Prayersticks),* Rainbow Worm carries Kiaklo across a great body of water, leaving the imprint of the *rainbow* on his cheek; the Kiaklo kachina mask bears these distinctive markings. Kiaklo is stranded until the *Koyemshi* carry him to *Kachina Village.* The deities restore his sight and decide he

Kiaklo kachina (Zuni) carrying his guide, Duck. Painting by Duane Dishta from the collection of The Heard Museum, Phoenix, Arizona.

is the one to keep the story of the creation. They tell him Duck must always accompany him.

Kiaklo returns to the Zuni every four years for the initiation of young boys. He chants the Zuni history *(Chimikyanakowa)*—a two- or three-hour performance—in each of the six kivas. The performance is repeated, this time in abbreviated form, eight days later. See also *Zuni Ritual Cycle.* [Benedict 1935; Cushing 1896; Stevenson 1887; Wright 1985]

Kilas
Creek, *Southeast*

The knowers, individuals who combined both medical and ritual leadership functions. A kila diagnosed the cause of an illness by examining a piece of clothing from the sick person, who was then treated by the *alektca* (the doctors). The kilas were also clairvoyants. Some kilas claimed to have power over the weather, contending they could cause rain or blow clouds away. They usually did this by wallowing in shallow muddy water for four mornings and then singing while drinking an emetic. See also *Megillis Hadjo,* a well-known kila. [Swanton 1928a]

Killer Whale(s)
Snohomish, Puyallup, Klallam, *Northwest Coast*

Four brothers who are deceived by a vengeful fifth brother and end up as killer whales. The four brothers go out to sea in pursuit of a seal that the fifth brother has made out of wood in order to trick them. They become lost in the sea fog and drift toward an island inhabited by powerful dwarfs. The brothers grow very hungry and steal a halibut from the canoe of one of the dwarfs. The dwarfs are so powerful that it is easy for them to get another halibut. Since they eat only the maggots that gather on rotted fish, the dwarfs let the brothers camp beside them, cooking and eating all the fish they want. Shortly after the brothers' arrival, ducks and cranes arrive and attack the dwarfs, many of whom are killed. The four brothers defend the dwarfs and revive some of the dead before leaving the island. The brothers decide to transform themselves into killer whales so they can travel faster through the water. They return home and take revenge on the fifth brother. Then they go out to sea and remain as killer whales forever. See also *Akhlut* (the Bering Sea coast term for killer whale) and *Qanekelak,* a Bella Bella mythological figure whose upper body is human and lower body whale. [Smith 1940]

Killer-of-Enemies
Apache, *Southwest*

A creator and culture hero, son of *White Painted Woman,* and son of Sun (in Lipan Apache culture), similar to the Navajo *Born for Water.* See also *Apache Creation and Emergence.* [Opler 1938b]

Kinaalda
Navajo, *Southwest*

Girls' puberty ceremony; also the girl undergoing the ceremony. A version of *Blessingway* performed at the onset of *menstruation* and modeled upon the coming of age of *Changing Woman.* The four-day ceremony serves to educate kinaalda about her roles and responsibilities as a Navajo woman, as well as to transform her into a woman (see *Women*). Each day kinaalda runs three times to the east, each time running farther than the time before, to strengthen herself physically. For days she grinds corn in preparation of a huge corncake (alkaan), which she bakes in a pit and serves to the community on the final day of the ceremony. Dressed as a woman, kinaalda is molded (through a mild massage) into the form of a beautiful woman. She practices numerous taboos and restrictions, all focused on reinforcing desired adult female qualities. Blessingway songs, which tell the story of Changing Woman, are sung frequently during the kinaalda ceremony. [Frisbie 1967]

Kinap
Micmac, *Northeast*

Men who performed remarkable feats of strength in order to surprise non-Micmacs making fun of them because of their funny shape. Kinap could uproot trees and move boulders. The Micmacs appreciated the considerable power of the Kinap, which was used in pranks, but always for good. [Fisher 1946]

Kinnikinic
Lakota, *Plains*
See *Cansasa*.

Kisenapew-mostos
Cree, *Subarctic*
Kind-Old-Man-Buffalo, a *guardian spirit* of the Plains Cree. [Bloomfield 1934]

Kisikohkew
Cree, *Subarctic*
A malevolent spirit (see *Malevolent Creatures)*, subordinate in power to *Wesucechak*.

Kiva
Pueblo, *Southwest*
Partially subterranean ceremonial chamber, either circular or rectangular.

Kiwahkw
Maliseet-Passamaquoddy, *Northeast*
Cannibal ice giants. The corpse of a *witch* killed by another witch does not rot, but transforms into a Kiwahkw, capable of eating any human who ventures too close. In order to become Kiwahkw, a corpse has to eat at least three people. A Kiwahkw's power is based on the size of its heart. Female Kiwahkw are more powerful than males. A family of Kiwahkw usually consists of a father, two sons, and a daughter.

In one story, *Glooscap*, the culture hero, disguises himself as an ice giant and is adopted into an ice giant family. He performs great feats of

Kiva in the large circular style of the Rio Grande Pueblos. The ladder leads through a hatchway into the subterranean room. Courtesy, Denver Public Library, Western History Department, H.S. Poley, photographer (P856).

magic for them, gains their trust, and invites them to smoke his pipe with him. Then he stomps on the ground, causing water to rise and foam, and sings a song of transformation. The Kiwahkw are transformed into fish and carried away by the water. [Prince 1921]

Kiwetin
Cree, Ojibwa, *Northeast, Subarctic*
The north *wind,* associated with bringing misfortune. Kiwetin is said to be the grandfather of *Wesucechak.* He is an opponent of *Nehanimis,* Wesucechak's son. See also *North Wind* and *North Wind Man.* [Norman 1982]

Kliatata
Kaska, *Subarctic*
A *culture hero* who teaches the Kaska how to make fishnets (see *Fish*) from willow bark, and brings them bows and snowshoes. [Chandler 1905]

Kmukamch
Modoc, *California*
"Ancient old man." *Creator* of humans. [Kroeber 1925]

Knowers
Creek, *Southeast*
The Creek medical and ritual leaders, known as *kilas.*

Knowledge
Chipewyan, Athapaskan, *Subarctic*
Inkoze is the knowledge revealed in dreams.

Kobictaiya
Acoma, *Southwest*
Powerful spirit beings similar to *kachinas.* A story tells how it was determined that they would never know sexual intercourse. The daughter of a war chief dies. Her body is stolen by witches (kanadyaiya) who revive her in order to seduce her. The Kobictaiya come to her rescue.

Rather than fight for her, they decide to play a game with the witches. If the witches win, they will get the girl to use as they desire. If the Kobictaiya win, they get the girl but must forgo sexual intercourse forever. The Kobictaiya are the victors.

The Kobictaiya appear in masked personated form only at the winter solstice ceremony, during which they promote fertility and aid the sick. They live either in the east at the sunrise or in a crater southeast of Acoma. See also *Iatiku.* [White 1932]

Kodoyanpe
Maidu, *California*
"Earth namer." *Creator* who descended from the clear sky with *Coyote.* Kodoyanpe and Coyote are floating in a canoe and discover earth before it has any people. The two prepare the earth for the arrival of the first people, who are eventually transformed into the present-day animals before the arrival of the first humans. With the help of the culture hero Conqueror, Kodoyanpe attempts to kill Coyote, who escapes to the east just as the first humans arrive on earth. [Kroeber 1925]

Kogukhpuk
Eskimo, Bering Sea coast, *Arctic*
A huge animal who lives underground and burrows from place to place, emerging one night each year to roam the earth. If Kogukhpuk breaks through the earth at any other time, it dies immediately. Mammoth bones found in the area of the Alaskan coast are said to be the remains of these untimely emergences. [Tennant and Bitar 1981]

Kokkookwe
Zuni, *Southwest*
Kachinas, Raw People who wear masks and dance. Most live at *Kachina Village,* at the bottom of a lake west of Zuni. There they sing and pray for rain. The chief kachina is *Pautiwa.* The term "kachina" is widely used to refer to all Pueblo masked impersonations and spirit beings. See also *Kanaakwe.* [Benedict 1935; Tedlock 1979]

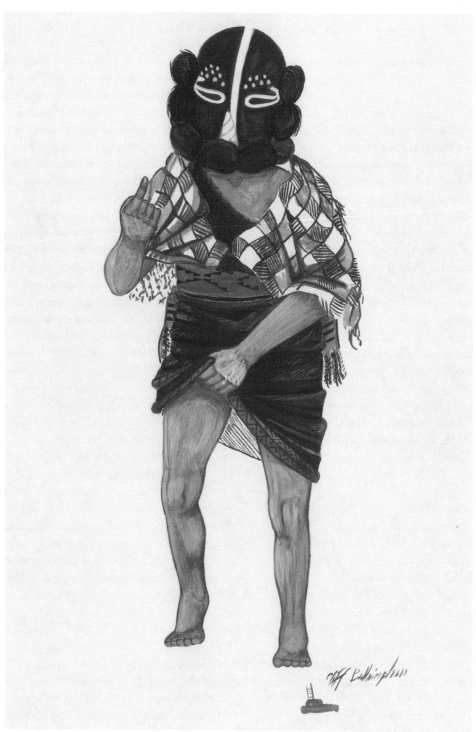

Kokopelli Mana (Hopi) extends a sexually suggestive invitation. Painting by Cliff Bahnimptewa from *Kachinas: A Hopi Artist's Documentary,* by Barton Wright, copyright © 1973 by the Heard Museum. Published by Northland Publishing, Flagstaff, Arizona, with The Heard Museum, Phoenix, Arizona. Painting from the collection of The Heard Museum, Phoenix, Arizona.

Kokomat
Yuma, *California*
Brother to the Yuma creator *Kwikumat.*

Kokopelli
Southwest
The Humpbacked Flute Player who appears widely in rock art and ancient pottery throughout the southwestern United States. Often humpbacked, carrying a flute, and ithyphallic, this figure has become a widely used motif on pottery, jewelry, and other Native American items. Although his origins and the significance of his prehistoric appearances are speculative, he has contemporary presence as a figure in Hopi stories and as a Hopi *kachina,* where he is characterized as a seducer of girls, a bringer of babies, and a hunting tutelary.

The Hopi also have a female Kokopelli kachina (Kokopelli Mana) who, impersonated by a man as are all kachinas, uses sexually suggestive actions to entice someone to race with her. She overtakes her opponent, throws him to the ground, lifts her skirts, and simulates copulation with him, to the amusement of the onlookers. See also *Zuni Ritual Cycle.* [Berckefeldt 1977; Titiev 1939; Wright 1973]

Kokumthena
Shawnee, Oklahoma and *Northeast*
"Our grandmother." Also referred to as Snaggle Tooth Woman or Cloud. The female *creator* responsible for creating humans, putting the world in its present-day order, and giving the Shawnee their way of life. Kokumthena is depicted as either large or normal in size with gray hair. At one time she and her grandson lived on earth, but now they reside somewhere near the land of the dead, along with a small dog and some other young men who are cannibals. She can be seen bending over her cooking pot during a full moon. She occasionally attends the annual Bread Dances, where she can be heard singing in a high clear voice. See also *Moon, Faces in.* [Voegelin 1936]

Kokyan wuhti
Hopi, *Southwest*
Spider Woman, a powerful deity associated with the Spider clan; she is, on the whole, supportive of Hopi people. She often serves in the capacity of culture heroine (see *Culture Hero*). She helps Hopi people during the *emergence* and their wandering *migrations.* She spins a mantle of white cotton to form the *moon.* She teaches Hopi people how to spin and weave (see *Weaving*). Hopis offer prayers to Spider Woman for long life because she has the power to give and take life. She has connections with hunting by virtue of her ability to snare and entrap in her web. She has connections with *agriculture* and *rain* by association with her webs, which resemble *clouds,* and the dew collecting on her webs. Thus, as a figure capable of mediating many oppositions, she is extraordinarily powerful. [Cushing 1923; Nequatewa 1936; Stephen 1929, 1940; Titiev 1942; Voth 1905b; Wallis and Titiev 1944]

Kola(s)
Lakota, *Plains*
Male friends who pledge exclusive devotion to each other, usually as an outgrowth of childhood friendship. Men who agree to be kolas agree to share material possessions and assist each other to the point of death in war and hunting. Kolas often marry sisters and occasionally exchange wives. If a man dreams about starting an *akicitas* (police society), he shares the dream with his kola and they start the society together. See also *Buffalo.*

Kolowisi
Zuni, *Southwest*
Water Snake or Horned Water Serpent. Kolowisi appears during the flood (see *Incest Causes Flood).* When the waters finally recede, Kolowisi takes residence in a spring. A girl washing at the spring finds a little baby. Attracted to it, she takes it home, nurses it, and sleeps with it. Her mother suspects something is not right. During the night, the baby turns into a huge serpent (see *Snake*)

Zuni puppet appearance of Kolowisi, the Horned Water Serpent. Painting by Duane Dishta from *Kachinas of the Zuni*, by Barron Wright, copyright © 1985 by Barron Wright. Published by Northland Publishing, Flagstaff, Arizona, in cooperation with the Southwest Museum. Painting from the collection of The Heard Museum, Phoenix, Arizona.

who wraps the girl in his coils. Kolowisi returns to the spring with the girl as his wife. The waters open for them to enter. This story is one of those told by Zuni parents to their daughters as a warning not to enter water to bathe. In some versions, the girl who enters the water to bathe is impregnated while in the water.

During the initiation of boys, Kolowisi appears in the form of a stick puppet protruding through a screen and carried by two men. He comes from the west, leading a procession of *kachinas.* He later appears in a kiva, where he disgorges water and other materials connected with the fertility of corn, which have been collected by the initiates. See also *Palulukon* for the Hopi counterpart and *Horned Serpent.* [Benedict 1935; Cushing 1896; Stevenson 1887]

Korawini?i
Owens Valley Paiute, *Great Basin*
Mother to all Native American peoples. Korawini?i goes around visiting all the people. The men fall in love with her and follow her home. During sexual intercourse she kills them because she has teeth in her vagina (see *Vagina Dentata*). Eventually all the men are killed except *Coyote,* who is so ugly Korawini?i does not want him. One day Coyote sees Korawini?i and decides to follow her. She moves very swiftly, and he is unable to catch her until she comes to a lake. She agrees to pack Coyote on her back as she crosses the lake. In the middle of the lake Coyote fondles her and she drops him. That night at her house they eat a feast with food provided by Coyote. As Korawini?i eats, she places the bones under the table and Coyote hears a crunching sound, which he thinks strange.

When they go to bed, Coyote is determined to have intercourse with Korawini?i, but he is frightened. He makes one attempt and quickly withdraws his penis when he hears the snap of teeth. He changes his penis into a hard, knotty wooden stick and tries again. This time the teeth in Korawini?i's vagina snap on the stick and get stuck. In this way Coyote rips out all the teeth. The rest of his evening is pleasant.

Korawini?i is pregnant with children from all the men she has killed. Preparing to give birth, she sends Coyote for water. Once at the lake, Coyote forgets his task and plays in the water. Eventually he sees a great many people who have been born from Korawini?i. They are the people who will make all the tribes in the world. Coyote wants to claim a group as his children, but by the time he returns to his wife only the poorest looking people are unclaimed. He still agrees to be their father and declares they will be superior to all others. [Lowie 1924; Steward 1936; Swanson 1970]

Koshare
Pueblo, *Southwest*
Black-and-white-striped clown. See *Clowns and Clowning Societies, Iatiku,* and *Kacale.*

Koyemshi
Hopi, Zuni, *Southwest*
Mudhead clowns. According to the Zuni migration stories, while the people are stopped at Tenatsalin Spring, the son and daughter of the village chief venture ahead. The girl is hot and tired, and lies down to rest. The boy goes ahead to scout. When he returns, his sister is still sleeping, and he becomes so enamored of her that he has sexual intercourse with her. When she awakens she is angry with her brother. When she tries to talk, she sounds like Kachina Old Woman; when he tries to talk, he sounds like koyemshi. They cannot understand one another. That very night, as a result of this incestuous relationship (see *Incest),* the girl gives birth to ten children. These are the koyemshi, who are witless, impotent, and grossly misshapen with bulbous lumps on their heads. Knowing they can never return to the others, the boy seeks a place where they can be alone. He creates the Zuni and Little Colorado rivers by marking the sand with his foot.

While the ten koyemshi are similar in appearance, they have quite distinctly individual identities and names. Their actions are in opposition to the attributes associated with their names. For example, Eshotsi, the Bat, is afraid of the dark and avoids every shadow. He is able to see remarkably well in bright daylight, but not at all at night. Koyemshi are among the most frequently appearing figures throughout the *Zuni Ritual Cycle,* often playing the roles of clowns (see *Clowns and Clowning Societies*). See also *Kiaklo, Shalako, Zuni Emergence,* and *Zuni Ritual Cycle.* [Wright 1985]

Ksa
Lakota, *Plains*
The first name of *Iktomi,* the Spider, before he used his wisdom for mischief and cunning. [Walker 1982]

Kukitat
Serrano, *California*
The destructive younger brother of the creator *Pakrokitat.* Kukitat creates death (see *Dead*). After his brother created human beings, Kukitat teaches them to speak differently and to make *war.* Frog kills Kukitat by hiding in the ocean and swallowing his excrement. See also *Excrements, Swallowing of* and Takwe. [Kroeber 1925]

Kuksu
See *Kuksu Cult.*

Kuksu Cult
Patwin, Miwok, Yuki, Pomo, Maidu, *California*
A men's secret society that held ceremonies in winter (between October and May) to initiate boys into the cult in order to make them strong, healthy, and fast-footed. The *dances* performed during these ceremonies were thought to bring rains and nourish the earth so there would be healthy crops and plentiful game. They were also believed to keep epidemics from the villages as well as prevent floods and earthquakes. The ceremonies were held in a semisubterranean dance house and involved masked (see *Masks and Masking*) dances accompanied by a foot drum (a drum beaten with one's foot). They were organized by the village shaman, who acted as ritual leader. The central and most important dance of the ceremony was the dance of Kuksu, the creator, who

was represented by a dancer wearing a headdress made of a large ball of feathered sticks. The complete ceremonial cycle varied from village to village, with new cult members being taught by adult members. Among the Maidu, the cult clown (see *Clowns and Clowing Societies*) held his position for life and named his successor. [Voegelin 1940]

Kuksu-hesi
Maidu, Pomo, Miwok, *California*
The *dance* group of a secret men's society. Kuksu-hesi have power over the spirits of game animals and crops. Each tribe has different variations of the dance, which features complex *initiation* stages. At each stage, members learn a new dance to honor specific slatu (animal spirits). The most important spirit is Kuksu, the creator. The spirits are honored with dances and masks (see *Masks and Masking*) made of paint, feathers, and rushes, although certain dances, called weng-kamini, do not use masks. The Maidu include a female impersonation known as lole. The Miwok group includes woochi, the clown (see Clowns and Clowning Societies), and uzumati, the grizzly bear. See also *Taikomol wok,* the dance of the dead. [Voegelin 1940]

Kukuweaq
Eskimo, Barrow, Alaska, *Arctic*
A *monster* in the shape of a ten-legged polar bear. During a time of hunger in a northern village, a man kills a walrus but goes against custom by not sharing it with his neighbor, a man named Kucirak who has many children to feed. Upset at his neighbor's selfishness, Kucirak goes hunting for food for his family. While on the glacier, he finds the lair of the Kukuweaq. Although frightened, Kucirak waits by a hole in the ice, and when the Kukuweaq lifts its head he blinds it with his hunting spear. Kukuweaq roars in pain and jumps out of the water, chasing Kucirak by smelling his footprints. Kucirak tricks the Kukuweaq into following him into a narrow passage in the glacier, where the bear gets stuck. Kucirak kills

the Kukuweaq, cuts off one of its ten legs, and returns home with food for his family. When Kucirak's neighbor hears of the catch, he gladly shares his walrus meat. Kucirak returns to get the rest of the bear meat to share with his village. [Norman 1990]

Kurahus
Pawnee, *Plains*
"Old man." The word for priest (ritual leader) in Pawnee culture. The kurahus are responsible for ceremonial leadership and the overall welfare of the group. They have extensive knowledge of *medicine bundle* rituals, used to ensure abundant crops, successful hunts, tribal unity, and success during war. The organization of the kurahus is patterned after the bundles. The head kurahus is responsible for the *Evening Star* bundle. The next four ranking kurahus are responsible for the four leading bundles: Yellow Star, Red Star, White Star, and Black Meteor Star. All five kurahus are responsible for conducting rituals and expected to be present at all ceremonies. The kurahus are distinct in organization and function from the kura?u, the healers of the loosely organized medicine societies. See also *Crow Lance Society; Kararata?u*, the earth lodge; *Starisu*, the women's dance to celebrate the gift of buffalo; and the story *Warrior Bird and the Origin of Stars*. [Murie 1989]

Kura?u
Pawnee, *Plains*
Healers or *medicine people* who are members of medicine societies and medicine lodges. The kura?u are concerned with aspects of group welfare different from the *kurahus*, principally with *healing*. Their powers come from land animals, unlike the kurahus whose powers come from sky beings. The medicine societies are loosely organized. The members, who share certain curing powers, include several noted healers, novices in training, and a large number of associated members who take part in the dancing but do not know the curing secrets of the more tightly organized medicine lodges.

Each of the several medicine societies holds ceremonies in early spring and again in the fall to renew and purify their ritual objects. Besides the medicine societies, there are local medicine lodges, which include only the most skilled healers. The lodges were led by the kura?u who have mastered the secrets of all the medicine societies. The medicine lodges hold ceremonies lasting two days in the spring and 20 to 30 days in the early fall. During these ceremonies people are cured and the healers display their healing powers. See also *Kararata?u*, the earth lodge. [Murie 1989]

Kusiotem
Bella Coola, *Northwest Coast*
The five *dances* that comprise the midwinter *kusiut* (masked dancing society) ceremonies. The five dances include: (1) the Fungus Dance, performed by a woman holding a kanani (a shelf fungus that grows on the side of trees), which only a kusiut can gather; (2) the Burning Dance, involving the swallowing of hot stones; (3) the Drowning Dance, which uses a dummy and a box with a special trapdoor to simulate drowning; (4) the Beheading Dance, in which a false head is used to simulate decapitation; and (5) stomach-cutting by a person impersonating Kuldlkamidjut (who was capable of having his stomach cut). In this dance a false stomach of animal gut is cut, death is enacted, and the woman restorer, Snitsmana, brings the victim back to life. All the dances involve elaborate masks (see *Masks and Masking)* and wooden props. Participants are initiated after being called to join the society in a dream or vision. See also Winter Ceremonial Season. [Boas 1916]

Kusiut (pl. Kuskusiat)
Bella Coola, *Northwest Coast*
A masked dancing (see *Dance*) society; also a member of the society. Kuskusiat, who include both men and women, perform dances *(Kusiotem)* during the *Winter Ceremonial Season.* Members are initiated into the society based on an inherited name that entitles them to dance a

certain dance, or because of a name given to them by a helping spirit in a dream or vision. A person may also join after having his or her name changed by a chief. The female spirit, Anolikwotsaix, guards the names in a box; she also keeps up a running commentary during the dance performance. See also *Sisaok,* members of a dance society. [Boas 1916]

Kwanokasha
Choctaw, *Southeast*
A little *spirit,* no larger than a two- or three-year-old child, who lives in a cave under large rocks. Kwanokasha steals sick *children* and takes them to his distant home to test them (see *Test Theme).* Three ancient spirits offer the child a poisonous knife and two bunches of herbs, one of which is also poisonous. A child who takes the knife will become an evil person, and a child who takes the poisonous herbs will never be able to cure or help other humans. But a child who takes the nonpoisonous herbs will become a great doctor and an influential person in the community. Kwanokasha and the three old spirits teach such children curing methods and the use of herbs and medicines. Only when these children are grown can they claim their *power.* [Hudson 1976]

Kwatyat
Nootka, *Northwest Coast*
Culture hero, sometimes also classified as a *trickster,* who is responsible for creating everything known to the Nootka. Kwatyat has the ability to transform himself into anything (see *Transformation).* His dwelling place is not known. In various stories Kwatyat steals land from the chief of the wolves, turns grease into a lake, and swells up and explodes from overperspiring. He disappears to the south, taking a river with him. Although Kwatyat is credited with creation, prayers are not offered to him. See also *Tihtipihin,* Kwatyat's younger brother. [Sapir and Swadesh 1939]

Kwikumat
Yuma, *California*
Creator of life; born at the bottom of the ocean with his brother Kokomat. Kokomat, blinded by the salt water as he came out of the ocean, opposes Kwikumat and is the cause of death (see *Dead).* Kwikumat makes humans out of clay (see *Humans, Origin of).* When Kokomat attempts to imitate his older brother by making clay figures, all his creations turn out web-footed. From these arise all the web-footed birds of the earth. [Kroeber 1925]

Kyakyauna
Hopi, *Southwest*
An adjective meaning sacred or powerful. A related word, kyala, is an adjective meaning powerful, potent, full of mysterious power, causing dread to the touch, perilous to approach. The left hand is considered kyakyauna; it is used to place and remove masks (see *Masks and Masking)* and to place prayersticks, prayer feathers, and meal offerings (see Prayer and Prayersticks). The right hand, used for eating, is avoided for ceremonial use and considered kakyakyauna, or ceremonially defiled. [Bradfield 1973; Parsons 1936; Whorf 1936]

Lagua
Haida, *Northwest Coast*

The Haida name for a Tlingit supernatural being. Lagua spoke through a Haida *shaman,* who held onto Lagua with his teeth. Lagua helped the Haida discover iron, which they used to make spears and knives. [Swanton 1905b]

Lakota
Plains

Originally a linguistic dialectic category linked with Oglala. The Lakota are also known as the Sioux. The terms Dakota, Lakota, and Nakota originally applied to dialects of Oglala; eventually anthropologists began using these terms to define political and social units as well. [Powers 1975]

Lance
An object used in the Pawnee *Crow Lance Society.*

Land Otter People (Otter People)
Tsimshian, *Northwest Coast*

Beings who deceive survivors of capsized canoes by disguising themselves as humans who have come to their rescue. The unsuspecting victims go with the Land Otter People, who try to feed them fish and seaweed. Those who eat the offered food are transformed into Land Otter People, but victims who resist these deceptions are eventually rescued by humans. See also men made wild *(Gagixit)* by the Land Otter People. [Boas 1916; Shotridge 1922]

Language(s)
Until recently, Native American languages have not had written forms. Perhaps due to this primacy of the spoken word, Native Americans are acutely aware of the importance of language, the differences between languages, and special kinds of language such as that used by medicine people, the old ones, and shamans. Creation stories often include the creation of language (see for example *Acoma Emergence and Migration* and the Moapa *Cotsipamapot).* Some cultures have stories about the diversity of languages, such as the Serrano story of *Kukitat.* Other stories, such as the Seneca story of *Godasiyo,* tell how all peoples once shared a common language and reveal the events leading to the present diversity of languages. Many Native

Americans refer to the mythic era as the time when humans and animals spoke the same language. Shamans, medicine people, and children are often capable of speaking with animals. The Lakota term referring to the language of spirits is *Hanbloglaka*. [Nusbaum 1925; Powers 1986]

Laughter

Laughter is treasured by Native Americans, as it doubtless is by all human beings. *Clowns and Clowning Societies* bring laughter even on important ritual occasions. Tales of *tricksters* are considered essential to education. A child's first laugh may be marked with a ritual ceremony. In the *Apache Creation and Emergence* stories, laughter frightens away illness. The Keresan female creator *Iatiku* creates clowns to make her laugh. See also *Humor, Jokes and Joking*, and *Joking Relationships*.

Lawalawa

Coos, *Northwest Coast*

"Noisy ones." Miniature creatures (see *Little People*) covered with long hair, who can only be seen at night. They leave tracks along creekbeds and wrestled with any humans they encounter. They spend their time making noise by throwing rocks at people's houses. [Beckham, Toepel, and Minor 1984]

Lehmamit

Nootka, *Northwest Coast*

Woodpecker, chief of the wolves (see *Wolf*) and the only being in the world who has *fire* in his house. Woodpecker's rival is the wise chief Eebewayak. Having heard that a winter ceremonial is going to be held at Woodpecker's house, Chief Eebewayak's people have a secret meeting, and plan to go to the feast to steal Woodpecker's fire. When the chief asks who will try to steal the fire from Woodpecker's house, Deer volunteers. Woodpecker has many sharp pointed sticks on the doorway of his house so that people running out of it will hurt their feet. Chief Eebewayak puts hard black stones on Deer's feet so the sharp pointed sticks will not hurt him (this accounts for

the origin of deer hooves). He gives Deer some hair oil in a seaweed bottle, a comb, and a piece of stone. According to the plan, after Deer steals the fire, he is to run away, dropping the things Chief Eebewayak has given to him. The stone will turn into a large mountain, the comb into a thornbush, and the hair oil into a large lake. These obstacles should deter the pursuing wolves. When Deer comes to Periwinkle Shell (a type of seashell) on the beach, he will give the fire to the shell and then run to save his life.

Their plan ready, the people of Chief Eebewayak's tribe go to the ceremonial dance at Woodpecker's house. Against her father's wishes, Woodpecker's daughter admits the visitors because she wants to see Deer dance. Before the dance, Woodpecker has the door barred and guarded so that no one can steal the fire. Deer dances to the first dancing song, then asks if the smoke hole can be opened to let in some fresh air. Woodpecker agrees, thinking Deer incapable of jumping that high. Deer dances closer and closer to the fire. Halfway through the song he grabs the fire, jumps up through the smoke hole, and runs to the woods with Woodpecker's warrior wolves in pursuit. Following the plan, Deer drops the stone, the comb, and finally the hair oil. These transform into a mountain, a thornbush, and a lake, slowing down the wolves. Finally, Deer comes to the beach where Periwinkle Shell is waiting and hides the fire in Periwinkle's mouth. When the wolves come to Periwinkle Shell, they ask him if he has seen Deer. Unable to open his mouth, Periwinkle makes noises and points in all different directions. The wolves thus lose track of Deer. Soon *fire* is spread all over the world. [Sapir and Swadesh 1939]

Lesbian

See *Anog Ite* (Lakota) and *Minquga* (Omaha).

Lgum

Tsimshian, *Northwest Coast*

Raven (Txamsem) uses rotten spruce wood to make himself a slave, Lgum. One day Lgum tricks Txamsem and locks him in a box. While his master is in the box, Lgum feasts on codfish. Greedy Lgum is killed when he falls into a deep canyon and his belly bursts open. Txamsem escapes from the box and finds Lgum, surrounded by all the food he ate while his master was in the box. Transforming himself into Raven, Txamsem flies down to the bottom of the canyon and eats the contents of the slave's stomach. [Boas 1902, 1916]

Liar

See *Two-Hearts*.

Lifeway

Navajo, *Southwest*

A classification of healing ceremonials intended to cure illnesses caused accidentally or due to the normal waxing and waning of life. See *Flintway* and *Navajo Ritual Process*.

Light

Essential for life, light often signals the full achievement of creation. In this respect it is associated with *fire*. Consequently the tale of its origin is a common motif in Native American creation stories, such as that of the *Apache Creation and Emergence*. Often the creation of light is attributed to the creator of the world, as in the example of *Loak-Ishto-hoollo-Aba*, the Chickasaw Great-Holy-Fire-Above. The Keresans attribute the origin of light to the sons of the female creator *Iatiku*. The Tsimshian credit *Raven*.

As with fire, light is often entrapped or hidden by some malevolent being. It is then the task of some culture hero to make the dangerous journey to steal the light and release it to the world. This "theft of light" motif appears widely throughout Native American mythology, as shown by the following examples. *Chulyen* (Tanaina) is a Crow trickster who steals light. *Coyote* often takes this role, as in the Zuni story *Coyote and Eagle Steal Light, but Cause Winter* and the Pomo story of *Madumda,* the creator. Many animals work to free light from *Sun Trapper* (California).

Lightning

In an Achumawi (California) story, Lightning is the wife or younger brother of *Thunder*. Often believed to be a weapon of thunder or the flash of the eyes of *Thunderbird*. According to some stories, lightning takes the form of a *raccoon* or is caused by a mole, because moles are found wherever it strikes. In one story Lightning and Raven get into a contest. Thunder tells Raven that any woman pregnant in the spring who dreams she is struck by lightning will be killed. Only a shaman who knows how to discipline the cloud from which lightning comes will be able to save her.

See also *Black Lightning Arrow* (Pawnee); *Ishtohoollo Aba Eloa* (Creek), the one responsible for lightning; *Lightning's Medicine Ceremony* (Pawnee); and the Huron spirit of lightning, *Onditachiae*. [Voegelin 1940]

Lightning's Medicine Ceremony

Pawnee, *Plains*

A major curing ceremony whose origin is found in the following story. A girl is born with a birthmark on her forehead. She spends her childhood counting the stars and is allowed unusual freedom growing up. She develops into a beautiful young woman. One clear day she predicts that it will rain, and to the surprise of her village mates, it does. During the storm she takes shelter next to the fire in her lodge. The lodge fills with smoke. Suddenly lightning strikes, and all the people in the lodge are stunned. When her father recovers, he checks on his daughter and finds her dead. Smoke is rising from a hole that goes clear through her head and into the ground. The father digs down to the bottom of the hole, where he finds a multicolored stone that transforms into the miniature shape of a woman. The other people in the lodge bathe in cedar-nut tea, smear their faces with lightning-struck mud, and pray to the stone. They bury the girl on a hill.

Later the girl's father sees her in a dream. The birthmark on her forehead is as bright as a star, and she wears 11 eagle feathers around the back of her head in the shape of a crescent moon. She tells her father she lives with the moon, and that the stone, not the lightning, killed her. She tells him to sleep on the north side of the stone in the lodge, so that the stone will speak to him. He does as instructed; the stone tells him it always loved his daughter and that it killed her so she could be with it, but it has lost its place in the sky. Then it says it will teach the father medicine power and how to make a *medicine bundle* out of soft, downy feathers.

Following the stone's instructions, the father fasts in the rain. During his fast he learns the powers of many animals. The last animal to give him power is the skunk, who is able to make rainbows and cure people with lightning. The animals tell the girl's father to build a medicine lodge, which is to have two altars. One altar is for the stone; the other is for the beaver, who will teach him sleight-of-hand techniques and many songs that are part of the curing ceremony. [Murie 1989]

Lime Crazy
Arapaho, *Plains*

The lazy, unkempt brother of a powerful chief. As a result of Lime Crazy's indiscriminate liaisons with women, the chief is constantly having to pay large fines of horses and blankets. Finally the chief, at the end of his patience, abandons Lime Crazy while they are out hunting, leaving him wandering around a pile of buffalo carcasses. This act of abandonment causes the people to ostracize the chief, and in desperation he goes back to Lime Crazy to convince him to return. By this time Lime Crazy has worn a trench by pacing around the dead buffalo and is covered with flies. He refuses to accompany his brother, who returns home despondent. The chief's wife, who always cared for Lime Crazy, offers to try to persuade him to return. She succeeds, the chief's respect is restored, and he prospers once again.

In another story the chief again takes Lime Crazy hunting. This time they cross a dangerous river in thick woods, and the chief again deserts his brother. Lime Crazy is gathering eagle feathers when a hawk tells him to pray to the owner of the river. Soon the horned water monster

(*hiintcabiit*) surfaces. Lime Crazy ties the eagle feathers to the monster's horns so that it will carry him across the stream. Halfway across, the water monster tries to kill Lime Crazy, but he reaches the other side and returns to camp. In some story versions Lime Crazy is finally killed by lightning; in others he is killed by White Owl (*Nankubacein*). [Dorsey and Kroeber 1903]

Linkan
Delaware, *Northeast*

The men's *dance* done on the fifth night of the ten-day winter *Bear Ceremony*. This fast-moving dance originated with a group of boys who danced themselves into the sky and became stars (see *Stars and Starlore*). The men who perform this dance sing songs that repeat the going-away message sung by the boys as they disappeared into the sky. [Speck 1931]

Little Owl
Arapaho, *Plains*

A child whose misbehavior causes his mother to threaten him with being abducted by *Owner-of-Bag*, a large *owl*. She sends the child outside; Owner-of-Bag comes along and puts him in his bag, giving him food to make him stop crying. When Little Owl's mother comes out to look for him, he is gone. Thinking he has gone to stay with a relative, she does not worry until the next morning, when she realizes that Owner-of-Bag has taken him. Grieving, she vows to make a buffalo robe, moccasins, and leggings, and decorate them with porcupine quills. She wraps the items in a bundle and sets out to rescue her son. With the help of a bird she eventually finds him, and they escape by using the quilled clothing, which provides them with power, strength, and protection. [Dorsey and Kroeber 1903]

Little People (Fstilvpucki)
Seminole, Creek, Choctaw, Chickasaw,
Oklahoma and *Southeast*

Small human beings who can be seen only by *children* and *medicine people*. The Seminoles describe them as looking like Seminoles and speaking Muskogee. The Fstilvpucki live in trees and take care of children who wander from their homes, feeding them and teaching them how to use herb remedies before returning them to their parents. For examples of *dwarfs* in other cultures see *Apicilnic* (Montagnais), *Djigaahehwa* (Seneca), and *Lawalawa* (Coos). [Howard 1984; Sturtevant 1987]

Little Wind
Navajo, *Southwest*
A guardian or messenger wind. See *Wind's Child.*

Litsu
Nootka, *Northwest Coast*
A simple feast given by a chief or any other member of the community at any time. The purpose of a litsu, which differs from a *potlatch,* is to share abundance of any kind of food, celebrate a life crisis, or welcome visitors from another tribe. [Kenyon 1977]

Loak-Ishto-hoollo-Aba
Chickasaw, *Southeast*
The-Great-Holy-Fire-Above responsible for all *light* and warmth and, therefore, all animal and vegetable life. Connected with the *Sun,* but not the Sun, he can live in the sky as well as with people on earth. [Swanton 1928a]

Locv-saukv
Seminole, Creek, *Southeast* and Oklahoma
Leg *rattles,* worn by *women* in preparatory dances for the *Green Corn Ceremony.* The women who wear the locv-saukv are referred to as shell-shaker girls and are vital to many of the night dances. The medicine man makes the rattles from land *turtle* shells (terrapins). After the empty shells are dried, gravel is added to make the shells rattle. During the making of the locv-saukv, special prayers are said so the rattles will have voices.

Because of their bulk and weight, great skill is required to use the locv-saukv. In the *Stomp* *Dance,* the shell-shaker girls position themselves behind the male dance leaders and provide the rhythm accompaniment for the dance, using a toe-and-heel action to produce a beat matching the tempo of the leader's songs. The most adroit locv-saukv wearers can quickly change the sound of the rattles. The locv-saukv are women's property, passed down from mother to daughter. See also *Soup Dance.* [Howard 1984]

Logobola
Tsimshian, *Northwest Coast*
Raven's (Txamsem) brother, who causes all the fresh water to disappear and creates a fog in which *Raven* gets lost. [Boas 1916]

Lokha
Seminole, Oklahoma and *Southeast*
A type of spirit animal that lives within a human. At night the lokha emerges from the sleeping person's mouth and turns into a chicken, which steals and eats human hearts. People who host lokhas can be detected by their breathing, which sounds like a chicken. [Howard 1984; Sturtevant 1987]

Lone Bird
Ojibwa, Great Lakes area, *Northeast*
Lover of the *Moon,* in which her *face* can be seen. The only child of Dawn of Day and She Eagle, Lone Bird lives on the shores of Lake Superior. Beautiful and graceful, she has many suitors, but none interest her. To find Lone Bird a husband, her father holds a race and invites all the eligible young men. When two of the men tie repeatedly, Dawn of Day decides this means his daughter should not marry. Lone Bird continues to live with her parents until they grow very old. One spring night, as Lone Bird is helping her father gather maple syrup, the full moon comes up. Lone Bird finds the Moon very beautiful and stretches out her arms to him. The Moon reaches down and takes Lone Bird as his wife. Dawn of Day looks up, and to his satisfaction sees the

happy face of his daughter in the moon. See also *Unwilling Bride.* [Overholt and Callicott 1982; Squier 1848]

Lone Man
Mandan, Hidatsa, *Plains*

The traveling companion of First *Creator,* who goes with him across the surface of the water and helps with creation. While walking across the water, Lone Man and First Creator meet Duck. They ask her how she manages to live. Duck dives beneath the water (see *Earth Diver)* and brings back a small piece of earth. She explains that food grows on the earth and that is how she stays alive. Lone Man and First Creator create the earth and all the animals. They also make the soil produce food. Then Lone Man travels north and First Creator journeys south. Between them they leave a strip of water (the Missouri River). First Creator makes mountains, hills, valleys, rivers, streams, trees, buffalo, antelope, and mountain sheep. Lone Man creates the flatlands, ponds, lakes, beaver, otter, and cattle. When First Creator and Lone Man come back together, First Creator does not like what Lone Man has created. He tells Lone Man that the land is too flat, there are not enough trees, and that the water of lakes and ponds will stagnate.

The stories of Lone Man and First Creator have been significantly influenced by the stories of Jesus told by early Christian missionaries. After the initial creating of Lone Man and First Creator, humans multiply on earth and Lone Man is born to a Mandan virgin. He has many journeys with 12 men, whom he teaches certain ceremonies for overcoming evil. When he leaves earth, Lone Man sets up a cedar tree in the center of the village. He tells the people the tree is his body, and instructs them to pray and sacrifice to it. He also says he will return. In the Hidatsa version of the story, Lone Man created this side of the world and Jesus was born on the other. See also *First Creator and Lone Man.* [Beckwith 1938]

Long Ears (Hvcko capko)
Seminole, Oklahoma and *Southeast*

An ugly gray animal *(monster)*, three feet tall, with a horse's tail, the head of a wolf, and very long ears. Long Ears smell like stagnant, muddy water and prefer to live in rocky areas. They can cause severe illness. [Howard 1984]

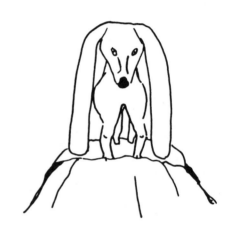

Long Ears, a smelly, gray mythological animal who causes illness, here as rendered by Seminole artist Willie Lena. From *Oklahoma Seminoles,* by James H. Howard. Copyright © 1984 by the University of Oklahoma Press.

Long Life Boy and Happiness Girl
Navajo, *Southwest*

See *Blessingway, Mountain Soil Bundle, Nilchi?i,* and *Sa?ah naghai bikeh hozho.*

Long Nose
Seneca, *Northeast*
The Seneca cannibal clown *Hagondes.*

Long Tongue
Pawnee, *Plains*
A fierce rolling skull that lives in a cave and guards a *medicine bundle* containing the Buffalo Pipe. When the bundle is unwrapped, it causes windstorms. Long Tongue can travel rapidly over great distances, but he creates tremendous noise while doing so. A young girl, the daughter of *Evening Star,* is trapped in Long Tongue's cave. *Raven* tells her how to escape and helps her steal the bundle from the cave. The girl stops Long Tongue's pursuit with arrows, knives, and turkey feathers. She escapes to a lodge where a man and his six hawk sons offer her protection from Long Tongue. The man kills Long Tongue by splitting his head in two with an ax. One piece of Long Tongue's skull flies west into the sky, where it becomes the *moon;* the other piece flies east and becomes the *sun.* Long Tongue's skull provides the human visages seen on the sun and the moon. [Dorsey 1906a]

Long Tooth Boy
Pawnee, *Plains*
A boy with magical *power* and long teeth who emerges from the placenta of his brother (see *Blood Clot Boy),* which was thrown into the water after the mother died in childbirth. The motherless older son is fed animal milk by his father. As he grows older, Long Tooth Boy comes to play with him. One day the father asks a buffalo for advice on how to catch the elusive Long Tooth Boy. The buffalo tells the father to kill him and remove his bladder. He is to fill the bladder with air and tie it to the head of Long Tooth Boy, so it will act as a buoy and keep Long Tooth Boy from slipping away under the water. The father does as the buffalo instructed and captures Long Tooth Boy to be a playmate for his son.

One day when the boys are playing together they disobey their father's instructions about doing dangerous things and end up as foam on the water. They try desperately to get back to their father, but instead float down the river and into the mouth of a monster. Long Tooth Boy shoots arrows inside the monster's mouth and the boys are able to escape. Thereafter the brothers have many adventures, and Long Tooth Boy often uses his magic power to get them out of scrapes.

One day an old witch hears about Long Tooth Boy's powers. She becomes jealous and decides to kill him. In the form of a yellow bird, she flies to their lodge. Recognizing the bird as a witch, Long Tooth Boy urges his father to shoot it. The father shoots and misses, and the bird picks him up by his hair and carries him away. The two brothers set out to rescue their father. Long Tooth Boy disguises himself, which enables him to cause a dust storm. The brothers enter the witch's lodge while she is sleeping, cut off her head, and rescue their father. When they return home, Long Tooth Boy places the witch's head on a pole outside the lodge to act as a guard. [Dorsey 1906a]

Longhouse
Iroquois, *Northeast*
The public place of assembly for meetings or councils. It also designates the traditional religion of the Iroquois people. Contrary to popular belief, the term never denoted the Iroquois League or Federation. [Cornplanter 1938; Fenton 1987]

Longhouse Ceremony
Iroquois, *Northeast*
A distinct rite culminating the *Traveling Rite,* involving the assembling of the *False Faces* in the longhouse after they have chased sickness away from each individual home in the settlement. In the presence of the gathered community, the Husk Face maskers announce the arrival of the False Faces, who soon enter the longhouse and crawl toward the fire, sliding on their hips and pulling themselves with upright poles held in their left hands, while simultaneously shaking their *turtle rattles.*

When they reach the center fire, the False Faces receive a pail of *medicine* made by specially appointed women. The leader gathers the *tobacco* collected by the False Faces on their journey around the settlement. The False Faces are requested to ask their guardian spirits to protect the people of the settlement from diseases and bad weather. The False Faces serve the medicine to the gathered people while the Husk Faces guard the door to make sure no one enters or leaves. *Dances* follow for each type of mask: common, husk, and doorkeeper (see *Masks and Masking*). [Fenton 1987]

Loon

The loon's distinctive appearance and haunting cry make it a popular character in Native American mythology. In a Tsimshian story, the blind Gitqada has his sight restored by Loon. The Povungnituk tell a similar story about a blind boy, *Iumaaq*. A Pawnee story of the *Loon Medicine Ceremony* tells how Poor Boy receives medicine power from Loon. *Mank*, the Ojibwa loon, is a visitor to the *shaking tent*. The Puyallup term for Loon is *Swoxqwad;* the Passamaquoddy term is *Winpe*. The most widely known story explains how Loon received her necklace, that is, the distinctive markings about the loon's neck. See *Loon Woman* for a California version of this story. [deAngelo 1973; Demetracopoulou 1933; Hamilton 1894]

Loon Medicine Ceremony

Pawnee, *Plains*

Ceremony given to Poor Boy, who raises two young loons as his children. According to story tradition, Poor Boy is befriended by a chief and his son. The chief's son is in love with the daughter of a chief of another village. Although he spends much time with her, he decides not to marry her. Instead he asks Poor Boy to have sexual intercourse with her, and tells the girl that if she refuses he will never marry her. She refuses anyway. The chief's son tries to deceive her again, this time disguising Poor Boy in his own clothing.

When Poor Boy meets the girl, he reveals the deception and asks her to marry him. She agrees, and the couple travel south. When the girl's family asks where she has gone, the chief's son realizes that Poor Boy and the girl have eloped.

Poor Boy and the chief's daughter build a grass lodge next to a pond. One day, while getting water, the girl sees Loon and discovers her nest, which contains two young birds. She tries unsuccessfully to capture the young loons. Later she hears them asking why their mother has not come back. She returns to the pond and this time the baby loons allow themselves to be caught. Thereafter the loons stay with the young couple at night, returning to the pond during the day. They tell the couple they will not have children, but that the loons will give them power. One day Poor Boy follows the loons. As they enter the water there is a tremendous noise and sparks fly into the air. Other water birds swim with the loons, and their downy feathers form the shape of an earth mound. Poor Boy spends time with the loons and other waterfowl. He learns the *healing* arts of the birds and is instructed to return to his people and start a medicine dance among them.

Poor Boy returns to his village with his wife, who carries the loons. At first the people in the village are frightened, because the couple has been gone for years. Poor Boy gives his old friend, the chief's son, several ponies, and the chief's son invites Poor Boy, his wife, and the loons to eat with him. Later, Poor Boy accompanies the chief's son on a war party, taking one of the loons with him as a guide and protector. While they are away a young man sleeps with Poor Boy's wife and mistreats the other loon. When Poor Boy returns, he finds that the loon is ill. The sick loon tells Poor Boy his wife has been unfaithful and that it has been mistreated by her lover. The other loon becomes ill and both loons die. Poor Boy banishes his wife from his lodge. He skins the loons and keeps the skins, which have medicine power. Poor Boy dies of a broken heart, leaving his loon medicines to his childhood friend, the chief's son. [Dorsey 1906a]

Loon Woman
Modoc, Shasta, Wintu, *California*
A family keeps one brother hidden. His sister, *Loon* Woman, discovers strands of his hair and wonders to whom they belong. She finally discovers her brother and insists they run away together. She wants to have intercourse with him, but he runs back to the family. Loon Woman threatens to start a great fire, and her family escapes to the sky in a basket. During their flight one child looks down, and as a result the entire family plunges to earth and into the fire. As they burn, their hearts burst from their bodies. Loon Woman gathers up the hearts and strings them together to make herself a necklace. Later she is killed and the members of her family resuscitated. See also *Incest.* [Demetracopoulou 1933]

Love
The physical and emotional attraction between male and female adds drama to many stories. Often matters of the heart are influenced by charms (see *Amulet)* or magic. The Lakota tell the story of *Big Twisted Flute,* which is used as a love charm. The Navajo have a ceremonial for love magic *(Ajilee).* The Seminole sing love songs during their *Soup Dance.*

Lover-Signaling Dance
Nootka, *Northwest Coast*
A *dance* done by men when they wish to meet a woman in the woods. During the dance each dancer makes a peculiar sound by placing the tip of his tongue against the inside of his lower lip and withdrawing his tongue with suction. [Clutesi 1969]

Lunar Eclipses
Tillamook, *Northwest Coast*
The result of spirits talking to the *moon,* interfering with its ability to shine. [Beckham, Toepel, and Minor 1984]

Made People
Tewa, *Southwest*
See *Tewa Ritual Cycle.*

Madumda
Pomo, *California*
Creator who lives in the sky. His younger brother, *Coyote,* is responsible for traveling the earth and creating humans. After creating the world, Madumda becomes passive, while Coyote steals the *sun* so there will be daylight (see *Light*) and transforms animal-monsters into the present-day animals. [Kroeber 1925]

Magic Herbs
Seneca, *Northeast*
Certain herbs that, when mixed with *tobacco* and smoked in the *pipe* of sorcerers, provide immunity from a spell or enchantment. Magic herbs are also smoked in the presence of strangers as protection against any malevolent power that might accompany them. This is the reason the pipe is smoked when any startling information is about to be announced. [Fenton 1987]

Magucan
Naskapi, *Subarctic*
The *bear* feast, held after a bear hunt to honor the bear's spirit. The bear skull is placed in a central location, and men dance in a specially constructed tent as the rest of the community watches. Special restrictions govern which parts of the bear can be eaten. [Helm 1981]

Ma?ii or *Coyote*
Navajo, Southwest
The quintessential *trickster* in Native American mythology. This view, however, severely underplays the complexity of the figure. His ceremonial name, atse hackee, means First-One-To-Use-Words-for-Force or, more simply, First Scolder, referring to war power.

Coyote's origin is accounted for in several ways. Often he is with First Man and First Woman in the lowest world during the *Navajo emergence* journey. Another account places his origin in the fourth world. During the emergence journey, there is a moment when the sky bends down and touches the earth. From this coming together spring Coyote and Badger. Another story says Coyote was born of Sky Maiden in the first world.

Coyote is always in motion. Stories of him begin: "Coyote was trotting along." He is able to change his color and appearance to blend in wherever he is, yet there is no place he calls home. During the meetings of the *diyin dine?e* about how the world should be created, Coyote always sits by the door of the hogan so he can easily ally himself with either side according to his whim.

Coyote is a liar, driven by greed, lust, and gluttony without constraint. He is often credited with the origin of death (see *Dead),* although he is also often the first to suffer grief for the death of a loved one. Death itself has no power over Coyote, who keeps his vital principle in the end of his nose and tail. Even when the rest of him is destroyed, as so often happens in stories, he can regenerate. He often exchanges his skin (that is, his appearance) with hunters, in order to have sex with the hunter's wife and be fed by her. He is always eventually discovered, despite his disguise, because he is lazy and smells of coyote urine. This skin shifting has a nefarious character in the Navajo *yenaldlooshi* or skinwalker stories. See also *Hoop Transformation Rite.*

Coyote is trickster, transformer, creator, entertainer, offender. There is no way of fully capturing or understanding his character; this is his nature. Navajos believe no one can grow up to be a true Navajo without being fully immersed in the story traditions of Ma?ii. The telling of Coyote stories is restricted to winter. Coyote is a central figure in a ceremonial complex known as Coyoteway (Ma?iiji), now rarely performed and not widely known, which has both *Holyway* and *Uglyway* versions. See also *Ajilee, Big Star Way, Changing Bear Maiden, Enemyway, Shootingway,* and *Navajo Starlore.* [Goddard 1933; Haile 1938, 1984; Hill 1936; Hill and Hill 1945; Keaveney 1983; Kluckhohn 1944; Kluckhohn and Wyman 1940; Luckert 1979; Matthews 1897; Roessel and Dillon 1974; Sapir and Hoijer 1942; Stephen 1930; Toelken and Scott 1981; Wheelwright 1942; Wyman and Bailey 1943]

Maka
Lakota, *Plains*

The *earth.* Maka creates Unk, Contention, to be her companion, but Unk is banished to deep water to be the head of all the waters and the ancestress of malevolent beings. See also *Day, Following Night, Inyan* (Rock), and *Iya* (Giant). [Melody 1977; Walker 1982]

Makai
Pima, *Southwest*

Medicine people, usually men, responsible for crops, weather, and war. See also *Si?atcokam.* [Russell 1908]

Malesk
Tsimshian, *Northwest Coast*

A *story type* told from individual experience, which may include animals as protectors and helpers. These tales often explain certain customs of a clan or group of people. [Boas 1916]

Malevolent Creatures
Native American stories contain a multitude of *monsters, cannibals,* and other malevolent beings. Danger in hideous guise lurks behind every tree and rock. Many of these beings are capable of transformation or shape shifting, like the Seminole *Human Snakes. Culture heroes* kill and control these malevolent creatures. See also the heavily tattooed creature *Tunnituaqruk* (Povungnituk), the child-stealing *Seatco* (Nisqually), *Kisikohkew* (Cree), and the malevolent beings known as *Tunghak* (Bering Sea coast), who live in the moon.

Mamakoni-nitkap
Ute, *Great Basin*

The *Bear Dance* held in the spring to celebrate the end of the bear's hibernation. In this four-day event men and women *dance* in parallel lines. The dancers imitate bears by taking slow, heavy footsteps, singing with low growls and grunts, and rubbing a notched stick to make sounds like a bear. On the last day of the dance the rhythm changes, and the women dancers chase the male dancers. [Powell 1881]

Mammoth Bones
Eskimo, Bering Sea coast, Alaska, *Arctic*
Mammoth bones found along the Bering Sea coast of Alaska are believed to be the remains of the huge mythological animals known as *Kogukhpuk*.

Mana
Hopi, *Southwest*
Maiden. Kachina mana are male representations of female *kachinas*. Wuhti denotes a married woman. [Bradfield 1973]

Man-Above
Arapaho, *Plains*
A famous Arapaho medicine person (see *Medicine People*) who learned from Bull how to heal using the bull tail and rattle. When another medicine person practicing witchcraft made him ill, Man-Above did not retaliate. Instead he developed his powers so he could cure people who were stricken with the bites of poisonous insects. The only payment he required was that a patient's family smoke a pipe filled with tobacco as an offering to the spirits before he came to cure. Every spring, Man-Above called people together to rehearse the healing songs, make more medicine, and discuss new ways of healing. Man-Above always fasted for four days prior to the *Sun Dance*. [Dorsey and Kroeber 1903]

Manabozho
See *Winabojo*.

Manabush
See *Winabojo*.

Manitou
Western woods Cree, *Subarctic;* Ojibwa, Great Lakes area, *Northeast*
Spirits that inhabit all living things, including wind, thunder, birds, animals, plants, rocks, all physical objects, and the sun and moon. The characteristics and animation of these living things are enhanced by the presence of the manitou. Even life circumstances like poverty and parenthood have manitou. The Ojibwa classify the manitou into different groups according to the types of living things in which they dwell. If one manitou of a group is insulted or hurt, the other manitou in that group are also affected. The manitou often appear in *dreams* to give special *power* or protection. There are many manitou, all of which are considered equal in power and rank. [Densmore 1929; Graves 1935; Preston 1975]

Mank
Ojibwa, Cree,*Northeast, Subarctic*
Loon, a humorous visitor to the *shaking tent* who calls out "nee-weah-wee-wey," meaning "I want to marry!" [Preston 1975]

Manly Hearted Women
Plains
The term for female *berdache*. See also *Gender Crossing*.

Marau
Hopi, *Southwest*
A mid-September harvest ceremonial complex performed principally by the Marau women's society. The nine-day ceremonial includes the preparation of special Marau *pahos,* boards painted with designs of clouds, corn, and representations of *Muyinwa* (the deity of germination and growth), to which feathers are attached. *Kiva* performances include women's dancing and the singing of songs whose subject is corn and rain. Marau is concerned with rain, the ripening of corn, and the fertility of *women.* Incorporated into the ceremonial complex are rites initiating new members into the society. See also *Hopi Ritual Cycle* and *Oaqol*. [Bradfield 1973; Stephen 1936; Voth 1903, 1912b]

Marriage
Eskimo, western coastal Alaska, *Arctic*
Marriage with a dog is a common theme in Yupik stories of the origins of different Eskimo groups.

The puppies born of the union eventually shed their dog skins and transform into humans, who travel to become the founders of the other Eskimo groups living in western Alaska. See also *Dog Husband.* [Murdoch 1887; Nelson 1889; Tennant and Bitar 1981]

Marriage Bread
Seneca, *Northeast*
Seneca women practiced the custom of carrying cornhusk-wrapped, dumbbell-shaped loaves of cornbread to the homes of their intended husbands as part of the woman-initiated marriage proposal. Marriage bread appears in the story of the marriages of the daughters of Mother Swan *(Awaeh Yegendji)* and the story of the poor boy *Hathondas.* [Curtin and Hewitt 1918]

Marriage Test
Zuni, *Southwest*
A common theme in Zuni mythology that applies to either a male or female prior to marriage. It may serve a number of purposes from punishing an *unwilling bride* to releasing game (see *Game, Release of)* for human use to demonstrating the importance of marriage. In one story, for example, a hunter does not want to marry the girls who are courting him. He tells them he will know they are virtuous if he kills a deer the next day. Although he does kill a deer, he prays for it to be hidden because he does not want to marry. Cactus Girl courts him and receives the same treatment as the others. She upbraids him and makes him ill by removing his heart. His family seeks the help of Cactus Girl and her family to cure him. They finally agree, and when he recovers he marries Cactus Girl.

In time Cactus Girl, a spiritual being, must return to her home. She tells the hunter to marry the first girl who asks him. Grieving over the loss of his wife, he follows her to a cave, where he finds only cactus plants. The Zuni tell this story to explain why they have only one wife. See also *Ahayuta.* [Benedict 1935; Bunzel 1933; Cushing 1896; Parsons 1917b]

Masau?u
Hopi, *Southwest*
The deity who first allotted the Hopi people their lands and gave them their first crops. He presides over the house of the *dead.* Masau?u gave *fire* to the Hopis. He is a figure common to Hopi mythology. As the first owner of the earth he is associated with the directional orientation "above," meaning the surface of the earth. When impersonated, Masau?u appears as a single figure in spring and fall ceremonies. Masau?u wears no mask. Rather than a kilt he wears an old woman's dress. His body is rubbed with ashes and he goes barefoot. He carries a digging stick in one hand and a woven basket in the other, which symbolize his close connection with agriculture. See also *Muyinwa,* to whom Masau?u often stands in contrast.

According to Hopi stories, the people who live in the *underworld* prior to emergence hear footsteps above them. When they reach the surface of the earth it is dark and cold. A messenger is sent out and returns with the news that he has found a field of corn, watermelons, and beans. There are fires burning all around the field, keeping it warm so the plants will grow. The messenger has also found a handsome man, Masau?u, here called Skeleton, who wears a grotesque death's head mask. Masau?u invites all the people to come warm themselves and gives them food.

The people travel on, wandering about in search of a place to settle (see *Pueblo Emergence and Migration).* The people of the Bear clan eventually settle at Oraibi, where Masau?u is living. He allots them a tract of land on which they are charged to live.

As peoples of the other clans arrive, they ask the Bear clan if they may settle there. Each new clan must demonstrate that they have some useful ceremonial knowledge. See also *Honannyamu* (Badger clan story) and *Hopi Clan Grouping or Phratry.* [Bradfield 1973; Malotki 1987b; Nequatewa 1980; Talashoma 1980; Titiev 1944; Voth 1905b]

Masewa and Uyuyewa

(var. Masewi and Oyoyewi)

Cochiti, Acoma, *Southwest*

Hero or warrior twins who led the people out from *Shipap* in the emergence to this world. They are considered sons of the sun (their mother was impregnated by sunlight), and stories tell of their journey to their father. They are credited with killing monsters, releasing the rains, and other feats common to *culture heroes.* See also *Acoma Emergence and Migration, Ahayuta, Monster Slayer and Born for Water,* and *Twins' Journey to Sun Father.*

In an Acoma story, Masewa and Uyuyewa dance every night at the house of Iatiku in front of her altar to ensure that the water in the medicine bowl does not dry up. This assures a sufficient supply of *rain.* But Iatiku tires of this nightly dancing. The twins decide to demonstrate that they, not Iatiku, hold the power to make it rain. They leave and go to the lower worlds for ten years. After their departure, Iatiku notices that the water in the medicine bowl on her altar is drying up. She seeks help from many, but only the twins can make it rain. Throughout the ten years, every effort is made to appeal to Masewa and Uyuyewa, but they refuse to return. Many people die of starvation and the earth becomes parched. At last the twins return. The rains begin, and the few seeds remaining sprout and grow. In this way the people learn of the power of Masewa and Uyuyewa. See also *Pyuykonhoya* (Hopi warrior twins) and *Acoma Emergence and Migration.* [Benedict 1931; White 1932]

Masks and Masking

Masks are used on religious occasions in many Native American cultures. Masks, as objects, are often considered living beings, as for example the Iroquois *False Faces,* which play a central role in the *Longhouse Ceremony.* These masks are carefully stored (see *Iroquois Masks, Storage of*) and regularly fed and cared for. They hold the power to cure as well as to entertain. Masks are worn in *Nkamwin,* the Delaware Big House Ceremony.

Pueblo *kachinas* are masked figures essential to the ceremonial cycle. They appear frequently in villages, bearing gifts, and serve to communicate with the spiritual world and the world of the dead. The deceased wear cotton masks, associated with *clouds,* to identify them with

Cherokee booger mask. Courtesy, The University Museum, University of Pennsylvania (neg.#13075).

these rainmakers. Navajo healing rites are occasions for masked *ye?ii* figures. *Mountain spirits,* or Crown Dancers, frequent Apache ritual. Yaqui communities have incorporated extensive masked performances in the *Yaqui Easter Ceremony.* In California, masking is done in the *Kuksu Cult.* In the *Northwest Coast* region, masked dancing occurs during the *Winter Ceremonial Season (Tsetseka).* Eskimo masks, which may represent the *inua* of some living thing, are present on such occasions as the *Inviting-In Feast.* See also *Clowns and Clowning Societies.* [Griffith 1972; Haile 1947a; King 1979; Levi-Strauss 1982; McElwain 1980]

Maskwa

Cree, Algonquian tribes, *Northeast* and *Subarctic*

Bear, the most intelligent and spiritually powerful land animal. He is a powerful ally for *hunting* and curing (see *Healing*). [Norman 1982]

Maskwamiy

Cree, *Subarctic*

Ice, personified as an unpleasant being associated with *witiko.* [Norman 1982]

Mastamho

Mohave, *Southwest*

Culture hero. All things are born of the union of sky (Ammaya) and earth (Amata), which took place across the ocean to the west. Matavilya, the first to be born, comes from the west. Along with him comes Mastamho (a little boy) and Frog (a girl who is Mastamho's daughter). Mastamho has no wife. He measures the earth and locates the middle, where he builds a house. At this time it is still always dark. Matavilya lies down in the house, Frog near the door. When Matavilya crawls out of the house to relieve himself, he puts his hand on Frog's genitals. While he is out, Frog travels along underground, coming up underneath him. Matavilya's feces drop into her gaping mouth and she swallows them, resulting in Matavilya's sickness. As Matavilya nears death, he tells Mastamho how to make the sun, moon, and stars. Frog originates *fire* by rubbing her hands against the backs of her thighs. With this fire Matavilya is cremated.

Now Mastamho becomes active as a culture hero. One episode of the story tells how Mastamho loads the Mohave, the Yavapai, the Yuma, the Maricopa, the Kamia, and the Kohoalche Paiute into a boat and floats with them down the Colorado River. The way he tips and rocks the boat gives character to the land along the journey. When they come to the sea, everyone gets out of the boat and Mastamho lets it float on into the sea. Mastamho creates all the features of these several cultures, from the items of their material cultures to their song and dance curing rituals. He sends the various tribes to new locations, except the Mohave, whom he lets settle in this place. Mastamho teaches the Mohave how to grow plants for food. Finally he transforms himself into an eagle and flies away. The Mohave people say that when they dream of Mastamho they see him in human form, not as a bird. See also *Dreamed Stories.* [Kroeber 1948]

Master of Sickness or Master of Pain

Tlingit, *Northwest Coast*

Tlingit *witches.* All witches, male and female, originate from the first witch, a man who obtains the power to punish his faithless wife by drinking from the skull of a *shaman.* Witches possess a "witch spirit" gained through repeated vigils in the graveyard and the handling of human remains. Witches also have sexual intercourse with the spirits of the dead.

Witches cause illness by making *dolls* in the likeness of their intended victims, using bits of hair, clothing, and leftover food. The dolls are placed in graves, and as the dolls rot with the corpses, the victims get sicker. Witches can be detected by shamans. An accused witch is bound painfully and left without food and water until he or she confesses. A confessed witch can cure a victim by removing the doll from the grave and then washing in salt water. [Swanton 1909]

Master/Mistress of Animals

Hunting cultures throughout North America believe game animals are controlled by a master or mistress. This figure may be a very large specimen of the animals he or she controls, or appear in humanlike form. *Hunting* is successful only if the hunters, often with the help of a shaman, contact the master/mistress of the animals and persuade this being to release game for them to hunt. Proper methods of hunting as well as respectful treatment of carcasses are essential to keeping the master/mistress happy. Often, bones from killed animals must be thrown into a lake or river so they may return to their home, where they will be regenerated into living animals.

Big Black Meteoric Star is the Pawnee star who controls the animals above the ground, as does *Moon Man* in Alaska. Known across the Arctic is *Sedna,* one of the identities of *Sea Woman,* who controls sea mammals (see also *Adlivun*). Shamans take spirit journeys to Sea Woman's home at the bottom of the sea to persuade her to release the animals. *Buffalo* gives the game animals to the Lakota. *Superguksoak* (Labrador) and *Tirawahat* (Pawnee) are masters of animals. *Tkahyal,* the Wind, is the Tillamook master of the salmon. The great white bear *Torngarsoak* (Labrador) is master of whales and seals. *Yayu* (Haida) is keeper of the whales. For Navajo examples see *Chiricahua Wind Way* and *Nightway.*

Mastop
Hopi, *Southwest*
A Hopi kachina. See *Soyal.*

Match Ball Game(s)
Seminole, Oklahoma and *Southeast*
A formal ball *game* played on a 150-yard field bracketed with goalposts. To initiate a game, one town gives a challenge invitation to another. Special clothing is worn and ceremonies performed to prepare for the game. Each team spends approximately a week at its *Square Ground,* dancing and drinking a black emetic. The players' ball sticks are hung in the arbor of the Square Ground. The players, who are male, fast for a day before the game. The women dance the night before the game to strengthen their team's medicine and weaken that of the opponents. Before the game, the medicine man helps the players paint their equipment and coat their arms and legs with medicine made from yellowjacket nest mud and

Choctaw match ball game. Courtesy, Smithsonian Institution, National Anthropological Archives (neg.#57,079).

hoyvniji. At the game site, the Ball Game Dance is performed around the fire at the center of the Square Ground. The players retire to the woods to dress and pick up their equipment before going to the ball field. During the game, two women stand at each goalpost. Whenever the ball nears their end of the field, they "call the ball" with water drums and rattles. The game is played to 12 points. [Howard 1984; Sturtevant 1987]

Mato
Lakota, *Plains*

Bear (Hu Nonp), whose spirit is responsible for love, hate, and bravery. Mato is also responsible for *healing* wounds and for many types of medicines. Mato is associated with mischief and fun. [Walker 1982]

Mato Okolakiciye
Lakota, *Plains*

Bear Dreamer Society. Its members are *medicine people* whose specialty is curing the severely wounded. Anyone cured by these medicine people becomes a member of the Bear Dreamer Society. The leader of the society is one who has had a *dream* about the bear and knows the use of the bear medicines. See also *Pejuta wicasa*, medicine person.

Bear Dreamer Society healing takes place in a tipi whose floor is covered with sage. Society members sing and beat round drums, while members who may have different types of medicine dance about the wounded patient. Suddenly the leader comes growling through the tipi entrance. He is painted red except for his hands, which are painted white. He carries a knife, and if a dog is present during the ceremony he may kill it and eat it raw. The leader faces all four directions as the other members move the wounded person to the place of honor at the rear of the tipi and apply healing roots to his body. [Walker 1982]

Matoki
Blackfoot, Blood, *Plains*

A female medicine society (see *Medicine Societies*), referred to as the Buffalo Cow Society, that held a four-day *dance* each year when camps came together for the *Sun Dance*. The Matoki erected a special tipi for their ceremony, using a center pole owned by the society's leader. Society members lived inside the tipi for the duration of the ceremony, during which no one was allowed to sleep. Six men were attached to the Matoki society; four did the singing and the remaining two acted as messengers and attendants.

Society members were organized into groups (signified by their head bonnets). Six women wore snake bonnets, four wore scabby bulls, and the remaining members wore buffalo-wool and feather bonnets. Each group had its own specific dance. Each woman wore a bone whistle, which she blew while dancing. During the ceremony, people who had made vows and promises during the year brought the Matoki a feast of berry soup. People with special needs brought tobacco and kettles of soup, which they offered to the Matoki leader while telling of their need. The soup was shared with all the members and prayers were said for the petitioner. At this time new members were brought into the society (see *Transfer Ceremony*). Membership could be bought for the price of a horse, gun, or other property. The most expensive membership was that of the tipi center pole owner, requiring a minimum fee of 12 horses.

At nightfall the six male members were sent home, and the women played and joked all night long. Some dressed like men and acted out male parts by giving orders to their "wives" (see also *Cross-dressing*). Others rolled up blankets like medicine bundles and held mock ceremonies (see also *Humor*). Before sunrise on the last day, the Matoki formed a line. Imitating buffalo going to water, they went outside and looked for a low place in the prairie. At their leader's command, they all laid down like buffalo. The women were followed by a man or boy who had made a special vow to drive in the Matoki and who had sacrificed a horse and given presents to the Matoki leader in return for the privilege. As soon as he spotted them, he built a fire with cow dung. When the Matoki smelled the smoke, they got up and ran back to the tipi, with the man riding beside them on horseback and the four scabby bull members trailing behind. Inside the tipi the women raced around in the direction of the sun until each was grabbed and led back to her seat. [Wissler 1913, 1918]

Maxpe
Crow, *Plains*
The term for the *mysterious,* unexplainable, and unpredictable. See also *Wakan.* [Lowie 1960]

Medawlinno
Western Abenaki, *Northeast*
A person born with the *spirit powers* to locate game, sink footsteps into rock, and cure people. The *drum* is the chosen instrument of the medawlinno. See also *Shaman.* [Trigger 1978]

Medicine
A term referring to the power of persons, objects, and activities. This power may be used for benevolent ends like *healing,* divination, or the control of game and weather, or for such malevolent purposes as sorcery. Medicine is given to *healers, medicine people,* or *shamans* by animals, spiritual beings, or empowered objects. It may be revealed in a *dream* or *vision,* sometimes accompanied by a song or medicine object needed to activate the medicine.

The Abenaki refer to medicine power as *baax-pee.* The Kawaiisu call it *so?oda. Xapaaliia* (Crow) is a physical representation of medicine power. Often medicine refers to tobacco or an herbal mixture that is drunk or rubbed on the body of a sufferer. *Cedar* is used as medicine by the Nootka. The Seneca use *Corn and Squash Medicine* for treating wounds. Iroquois women prepare *False Face Medicine* for the *Longhouse Ceremony. Small Dose* (Seneca) is a medicine made by animals. *Qumuuc* is Ute hot rock medicine.

The power and use of medicine often relates directly to its source. *Fas-ta-chee* is a dwarf in Seminole stories who brings medicine. The Cree/Ojibwa Thunderer *(Pinessi)* is a helping

spirit with powerful medicine. *Inipi,* the Lakota sweat, is done as medicine. The Seminole medicine *Stvkwvnaya,* used for hunting and love, comes from the tie snake. *Winabojo,* the Ojibwa trickster and culture hero, gives medicine to humans. The Catawba medicine *witi* is administered by blowing it through a tube. [deRios 1984; Dorsey 1903c; Haeberlin 1896; Howard 1984; Mooney 1891; Skinner 1920b]

Medicine Bundle(s)
A collection of objects and medicines wrapped in a bundle or held in a bag. The bag and its contents hold strong significance for a group or tribe's heritage, power, and identity. Bundles are often associated with special animal powers. These bags of skin or cloth may include such objects as feathers, herbs, stones, animal and bird parts, and pipes. Some medicine bundles contain scalps (see *Scalping*).

The origins of four medicine bundles (ettowe) are described in the stories of *Zuni emergence.* The Navajo have many medicine bundles *(jish).* Perhaps the most well known and widely used is the *mountain soil bundle,* whose origins are told in the *Blessingway* creation story. *First Man and First Woman* brought the components of this bundle from the lower worlds in the *Navajo emergence.* Bundles can contain medicines used for malevolence, as described in Navajo *Enemyway* mythology.

The Pawnees tell the story of creation by *Tirawahat* at the opening of bundles such as the *grain-of-corn bundle* and the bundle of the *Crow-Water Society.* Pawnee priests *(kurahus)* use medicine bundles. *Lightning's Medicine Ceremony* includes telling the creation story. *Evening Star* is a keeper of medicine bundles. The story of the mythological figure *Long Tongue* includes an incident involving a medicine bundle guarded by a rolling skull. Other information on Pawnee medicine bundles relates to the *Buffalo-Gaming Sticks.*

During initiation into the *Midewiwin,* the initiates are "shot" and "killed" by a medicine bundle. This type of bundle is made from the skin of a whole animal, as is the Seneca *skin pouch*. The Lakota *ozuha pejuta* is a bundle used to hold medicines.

At creation the Seminole received three medicine bundles representing the principal tribal divisions (see *Es-te fas-ta* and *Es-te mat-tee).* In one story, the power of medicine bundles is used to combat *human snakes.* The Potawatomi trace the origin of their medicine bundle to the culture hero *Wiske.*

The *Green Corn Dance* serves to renew the power of medicine bundles. Iroquois masks are stored in protective bundles (see *Iroquois Masks, Storage of).* Crow medicine people *(akbaalia)* are responsible for opening medicine bundles. *Wakan Wacipi,* the Plains mystery dance, uses medicine bundles. The Blackfoot women's society *Matoki* uses a mock medicine bundle. *Waruxawe* is the Winnebago medicine bundle. *Xapaaliia* is a Crow term that refers to the physical representation of spiritual power, such as the objects in a medicine bundle.

Bundles are commonly maintained and protected by select keepers. Some types of bundles are buried with their owners. The opening of a bundle is invariably a ritual occasion, and *songs* are sung as each item is handled or used. Specific bundles may be associated with different ritual and story events. For example, the Sarcee tribes associate their beaver medicine bundle with the *Sun Dance* and the growing of *tobacco.* In a Sarcee story, a hunter kills a large buffalo near a lake. While he is skinning the buffalo, a whale comes up from the lake and begs him for protection against Thunderbirds circling in the sky above. The hunter saves the whale by giving the buffalo meat to the Thunderbirds. The whale thanks him by showing him how to make a medicine bag from the buffalo's stomach, then fill it with the skin of every living creature and decorate it. The whale tells the hunter to keep tobacco and berries inside the bundle as food for the whale, and to make an offering to the lake whenever he is nearby. The whale also teaches the hunter the

beaver songs associated with the bundle. He says the medicine bundle should never be given to another tribe, and that it should be passed down through a lineage of trusted members of the Sarcee tribe. [Frisbie 1987]

Medicine Makers
Creek, *Southeast*

The Creek distinguish between medicine people and medicine makers *(Hilis-haya),* people responsible for gathering and making medicines.

Medicine People

A term generally applied by ethnographers and missionaries (and now also by Native Americans) to designate Native American *healers,* priests, *shamans,* ritualists, storytellers, wise elders, and even those involved in malevolent practices such as *witchcraft.* See also *Medicine.*

In many tribes, diagnosing and curing are separate activities, each undertaken by specifically trained people. In other tribes, healing activity is specialized according to the sex of the practitioner. In almost all activities concerned with diagnosing, healing, and maintaining health, the activity is intimately linked to spiritual powers and ritual practices. Many tribally specific terms for activities and people involved in curing and diagnosing have been lost or forgotten. Tribal terms designating medicine people include: *Kura?u* (Pawnee), *Akbaalia* (Crow), *Alektca* (Creek), *Arendiwane* (Huron), *Basamacha* (Yavapai), *Goyo* (Takelma), *Hataalii* (Navajo), *Hitebi* (Yaqui), *Hochinagen* (Seneca), *Nanandaw* (Ojibwa), *Pejuta wicasa* (Lakota), and *Si?atcokam* and *Makai* (Pima).

Medicine Societies exist in many cultures. The members of the Lakota Bear Dreamer Society *(Mato Okolakiciye)* are medicine people. Clowns are often considered powerful medicine people (see *Clowns and Clowning Societies),* as are those who cross gender lines (see *Gender Crossing* and Omaha *Minquga).* Figures known to be great medicine people in Native American mythology include *Dooehdanegen* (Seneca), *Bear Medicine*

Woman (Pawnee), *Hinon* the Thunderer (Seneca), the Arapaho *Man-Above,* the Bering Sea coast *Neshmuk,* and *Smoking-with-the-Bear* and *White-Sun,* both Pawnee.

Asin is a monster in Nootka stories. If Asin appears in dreams he gives bad medicine. The Narragansett believe the dead can give information to medicine people (see *Chepi).* Seminole medicine people and children are the only ones who can see the *little people.* In Cherokee stories the men who kill Stonecoat *(Ocasta)* become powerful medicine men. For information on Apache medicine people, see *Apache Bear Dance* and *Apache Creation and Emergence.*

Medicine Societies

Throughout North America, *medicine people* are members of societies. These societies are commonly distinguished by the functions they perform and the powers they maintain. Often they have esoteric knowledge and perform secret rites. Eligibility for membership in medicine societies may be determined by clan or lineage, by election, or by having been successfully treated by the society (in which case the society might be called a "cult of affliction"). Members of a culture may call upon medicine societies for healing or protection.

Zuni has an elaborate organization of 12 medicine societies (see *Wemaawe).* The Huron have a women's medicine society *(Ohgiwe Society).* The *Akhrendoiaen* is a medicine society specializing in treating insanity. *Matoki* is a Blackfoot women's medicine society. *Hohu Yuha* is a Lakota medicine society considered to be malevolent. The *bear dance* is widely performed by medicine societies of various cultures. For other references to medicine societies see also *Medicine People, Healers,* and *Shaman.*

Medicine Wheel

A wheel-shaped arrangement of stones at which ritual and meditation are performed. Medicine wheels are located at many places of power throughout North America. In a Crow story, *Burnt Face* originates the medicine wheel.

Megillis Hadjo

Creek, *Southeast*

A well-known *kilas* (knower) who lived in the village of Tukabahchee in the early 1800s. Megillis Hadjo is credited with bringing quenching rains during a severe drought and a spell of milder weather during a severe winter. [Swanton 1928a]

Memekwesiwak

Cree, *Subarctic*

Comical water spirits who are friendly to humans but play tricks on nonbelievers. They often exert a sexual and romantic influence. See also *Humor.* [Clay 1938]

Menapus

See *Winabojo.*

Menstrual Blood

According to a number of story traditions, menstrual blood is reserved for concocting powerful medicines. Because of the inherent power of menstrual blood, women lived in separate dwellings during menstruation and immediately after childbirth. Men, along with their hunting tools and dishes, were kept away from menstruating women because the power of the blood would drive away game and a man's helping spirits. During menstruation, particularly the first, a female might have a *vision* and receive *helping spirits* who taught her special songs and the power for *healing.* In Shawnee tradition, shamans used ashes from the menstrual hut (where a woman was isolated during menstruation) to capture a dangerous *water monster.*

According to Ojibwa, Menominee, and Potawatomi stories, menstruation was caused by *Winabojo,* who made his grandmother bleed and therefore decided that all women would bleed each month. The Yuchi attribute their creation to the Sun, who caused their ancestors to spring from a drop of menstrual blood in the sky and then sent them to earth.

Menstruation

The onset of menstruation often determines the timing of such *girls' puberty rites* as the Apache *Na ih es,* the Navajo *Kinaalda,* and the Lakota Bull Buffalo Ceremony, *Ta Tanka Lowanpi.* When a Lakota girl seeks a vision *(hanblapi),* she places her menstrual blood in a tree. *Ta Tanka* is the Lakota guardian of young menstruating women. *Catamenia* is the Seneca term for menstruation.

Menstruating women are often prohibited from contact with food that is to be eaten by hunters or medicine men. They may be barred from ceremonials and healing rites. In some instances this may be due to a belief that menstruation is polluting, but in many cases menstruation is associated with great power. The latter is reflected in the Cherokee story of Stonecoat *(Ocasta),* where Stonecoat is entrapped by menstruating women. See also the Seminole story of *Human Snakes.* See also *Tatahkesewen.* [Powers 1980]

Mesing Keo

Delaware, *Northeast*

The False Face Dancers of the Delaware, not to be confused with the *False Faces* of the Iroquois. These 12 dancers danced at the Midwinter *Bear Dance* of the Grand River tribal groups and at the Corn Harvest Big House celebration of the Oklahoma tribal group. Six dancers wore white masks (see *Masks and Masking)* to represent peace, while the other six wore red Wapanachki masks representing violence.

During the Big House Ceremony the mask, called mesing, could be worn only by a man who personified the power of mishinghalikun, a spirit whose malevolent power kept disease and evil away. This spirit was also responsible for ensuring good crops and plentiful game. The mask was half red and half black, with thick lips, tin eyes, and horsehair. The dancer wore a bearskin that reached to his toes and carried a tobacco pouch, a twisted wooden staff, and a turtle-shell rattle filled with corn. [Speck 1931]

Messenger

See the Ojibwa culture hero, *Okabewis.*

Messenger Feast (Kevgiq)

Eskimo, Yukon-Kuskokwim area and northern Alaska, *Arctic*

In the Yukon-Kuskokwim area, a feast held to celebrate a son's first kill or a daughter's first berry picking, usually after the Bladder Festival (see *Nakaciuq)* but sometimes in the summer. It is called the Messenger Feast because the host sends three sets of messengers to his male cross-cousin. The first two messengers, whose mission is to invite the cousin's entire village to the upcoming feast, carry a red-painted feathered wand called an *asking stick.* A second pair of messengers carries a list of gift requests to the invited village, returning home with a similar request list from the proposed guests. When the Kevgiq is due to start, a third pair of messengers is sent to bring the guests.

Upon their arrival in the village, even if it is winter, the guests sing and dance outdoors. Then the host villagers dance. The guests settle in the qasgiq and the hosts bring in the food. The hosts begin the feasting by singing songs meant to shame any individual who has done anything offensive during the year (see *Song Duels).* Many of the songs are filled with teasing, but some songs about the commission of offenses are serious. Kevgiq allows for the regulated expression of social tensions, helping curb the expression of potentially violent emotions. During these songs, a cross-cousin has special license to joke and tease (see *Jokes and Joking),* even to the extent of fabricating and exaggerating an incident.

Gift-giving follows. *Gifts* are given first to the qasgiq, then to the elderly and orphans. The hosts sing gift request songs as the guests dance the first of two main dances. Three people, called "pointers," lead the songs for gift requests. The pointers, naked above the waist except for dance headdresses and necklaces, know all the songs, initiate the verses, and pronounce special words while pointing feathered dance sticks at the audience. During the dances, the requested items are brought into the qasgiq. The redistribution of wealth within and between related villages that occurs during Kevgiq uses up food and goods stockpiled during the year and prevents waste. Kevgiq also ensures good hunting in the coming year by demonstrating respect to the animals. See also *Inviting-In Feast.*

The Messenger Feast performed in northern Alaska differs from the Yukon-Kuskokwim version described above. In northern Alaska it is an annual feast originating in the Kotzebue area. It is described in the story about a young hunter who kills a beautiful giant eagle. The eagle is big and powerful and can carry a large whale in its claws. After killing the eagle, the young hunter is taken to its parents, who tell him to hold a festival to return the dead eagle's spirit to its home. The young hunter returns to his village and instructs the people in the masked dances, face painting, and food and gift exchanges that are to occur at the festival.

This feast requires that a messenger dressed in new clothing go to neighboring villages to invite people for competitive dancing, gift exchanging, and the ritual finding of the eagle's home. The ritual includes drumming on a specially constructed box drum that reproduces the sound of the eagle's heart beating. Participants wear eagle skins and carry staffs of eagle feathers. Stuffed bird and animal heads are hung, and food and skins are given to the elderly people of the community who can no longer hunt for themselves. [Lantis 1947; Morrow 1984; Nelson 1899]

Meteor
See the Pawnee figure *Pahokatawa,* who appears in the form of a meteor.

Meteor Fire Dragons
See *Gaasyendietha* (Seneca).

Mica
Lakota, *Plains*
Coyote, whose spirit is responsible for thievery, cowardice, and all malevolent mischief. Mica constantly tries to outwit *Ta Tanka,* the great Bull Buffalo. See also *Trickster.* [Walker 1982]

Michi-Pichoux
Cree, *Subarctic*
Water lynxes who hold malevolent control over lakes and rivers, especially dangerous rapids. They are associated with unexplained deaths and believed to steal children. The Michi-Pichoux are antagonists of *Wesucechak* and responsible for killing his brother *Misapos.* See also the great horned water snake *Misikinipik* and *Underwater Cats.* [Norman. 1982]

Middle Place
Zuni, *Southwest*
See *Itiwana.*

Midewiwin
Lake Winnipeg Saulteaux, Winnebago, Ojibwa, Great Lakes area, *Northeast, Subarctic*
"Mystic doings." Also known as Grand Medicine Societies. Young men and women are trained in practical and ritualistic *healing* arts, as well as how to use herbs to prolong life. Training involves private and public ceremonies in which the initiate is ritually "shot" with small shells projected from a Mide (white shell) bag or pouch (see *Medicine Bundle*). The initiate feigns death and is revived by the Mide leader, who "sucks" the

Pictographs serving as mnemonics for a Midewiwin song, incised on a birchbark scroll.

intruding shells out of his or her body. Upon *initiation* a new member is licensed to prepare and administer plant remedies.

Mide priests supervise the training of initiates in the healing songs and secrets of the eight "degrees." Each degree correlates with a level of knowledge and with a particular Mide bag, which holds the medicines gained with that degree of knowledge. The Mide bag, made of a bird or animal skin, is the most valued possession a person can have. Songs are used to call medicine from the Mide bag. Mide bags are usually buried with their owners.

Mide lodges are usually large and open at one end. A large seashell, placed in the center of the lodge, is scraped during ceremonies for a curing powder. Right living and respect for women are primary Midewiwin tenets. Lying, stealing, and alcoholism are strictly forbidden. At the higher degrees of knowledge, practitioners learn the use of subtle herbal poisons to punish offenders of the Midewiwin code. Midewiwin history and stories are recorded in mnemonics inscribed on birchbark scrolls. These pictographed scrolls are used to tell the stories of the degrees and their origins. See also *Atisokan,* which refers to the Mide story type; *Bagucks,* an Ojibwa malevolent spirit; *Shell-Covered-One,* one of the Ojibwa originators of the Midewiwin; and *Sleep,* who assures order in the Midewiwin. [Hallowell 1936; Hickerson 1962; Hoffman 1891; Landes 1968; Radin 1945, 1950; Vecsey 1984]

Midwinter Festival

Iroquois, *Northeast*

Also known as the *New Year* Festival or the Feast of Dreams. This nine-day festival of thanksgiving and hope is held in January or February. Beginning at dawn on the fifth day after the first new moon, the festival designates the start of the New Year. Among the Seneca, two older men whose identities are revealed through dreams and two older women of opposite families meet in the *longhouse.* Each woman dresses the male cousin of her opposite moiety in a buffalo robe or old

blanket, tying the garment together with ropes of braided cornhusks. She places a wreath of cornhusks on the man's hooded head and gives him a wooden mallet used for mashing corn. The two men are sent around the settlement to announce the Midwinter Festival. These men are referred to as the *Big Heads.* The Canadian and New York Onondaga do not use masked figures to announce the New Year.

On the first day of the festival there is a public naming (see *Names and Naming)* of babies born since the last Midwinter Festival. The morning of the second day brings the Big Heads dressed in bearskin coats and Husk Masks to remind people that the New Year has started. The False Faces wander through the village, entering homes and stirring ashes in fireplaces, singing songs of thanksgiving, and blowing ashes on people who are ill (see also *Ash Blowing Rite* and *Traveling Rite).* This ash-stirring ritual is continued on the third day of the festival. Toward the middle of the day the False Faces return to the longhouse. The village joins them and the False Faces invite the people to guess their dreams.

The rituals of the secret medicine society are enacted on the fourth day of the festival. The *Great Feather Dance* precedes the public curing done by the different medicine societies. Dream guessing continues, and people who guess correctly are given miniature *amulets* representing the animal or helping spirit revealed in the dream. Nightfall brings the emergence of the Common Faces, also known as the Beggar Maskers, who go around to homes begging food. If they are not given what they want, they steal the food. On the fifth day public curing continues at the longhouse.

The sixth day brings the playing of games and the *Bear Dance,* where everyone eats specially prepared strawberry jam in honor of the bears. Public curing continues. In the evening the False Face maskers return, dressed in ragged clothes and making awkward gestures as they crawl and limp about requesting gifts of *tobacco.* They are followed by the *Husk Faces,* who cure and dance the Women's Dance honoring the gifts of corn, squash, and beans. Days seven and eight are a continuation of day six, with the people singing personal songs of thanksgiving. Day nine brings the conclusion of the festival, the time when new council members are presented to everyone gathered at the longhouse. [Curtin and Hewitt 1918; Fenton 1987; Wallace 1972]

Migration(s)
Southwest
Many southwestern cultures account for their origins through a process of emerging from worlds below the present surface of the earth, followed by often long and difficult journeys to the place of their present residence. For these stories, see *Pueblo Emergence and Migration, Acoma Emergence and Migration,* and *Fotease* (for the Jemez migration story). For Hopi accounts, see *Hopi Clan Grouping or Phratry; Pachavu,* Hopi rituals commemorating these migrations; and *Kokyan wuhti* (Spider Woman), who assists the Hopi in their migrations. See *Kiaklo* for part of the Zuni migration stories and *Dreamed Stories* for Mohave migration stories. [Dozier 1956; Fewkes 1902; Gatschet 1884, 1888a; Halbert 1894; Mason 1921; Utley 1974; Vennum 1978]

Mikapi
Blackfoot, *Plains*
Red Old Man, a *warrior* who avenges the deaths of members of a hunting party killed in a sneak attack. Mikapi fights alone bravely and is wounded. A bear rescues him, takes him to a deep mud hole near his cave, plasters him with mud, and sings over him to revive him. The bear accompanies Mikapi to his village and then leaves him. Mikapi has many scalps about his belt (see *Coup*). The villagers stops grieving because he has avenged the hunters' deaths. [Thomas 1986]

Mikchich
Maliseet-Passamaquoddy, *Northeast*
Turtle, the uncle of *Glooscap.* Glooscap cooks and disembowels Mikchich, makes his skin hard, and

gives him the gift of long life. For this reason the great turtle can live on both land and water and is able to roll through fire. [Prince 1921]

Mikumwesu
Maliseet-Passamaquoddy, *Northeast*
The older brother of *Glooscap.* Although Mikumwesu was smaller than his brother and did not have as powerful a bow and arrow, he was stronger and more skilled at archery. In some story variants Megumooweco is portrayed as the father of Glooscap and is known as Mekmues, a helpful spirit. Among the Passamaquoddy (Maine) he is known as Mickumwes, a miniature spirit who lives in the woods and is capable of increasing his size at will. [Fisher 1946]

Mili or Miiwe
Zuni, *Southwest*
Often referred to as *fetish,* these are feathered ears of *corn.* See also *Ettowe.* [Bunzel 1932]

Milky Way
The great river of stars spanning the sky is the subject of many Native American stories. Some consider it to be the road taken by the dead. *Hihankara* is an old-woman character in Lakota mythology who guards the Milky Way, believed to be the spirit road (see also the *Spirit Keeping Ceremony* honoring the dead). The *Corn Maidens* (Zuni) played a role in the creation of the Milky Way. The Seminole culture hero *Hisagita misa* makes the Milky Way. Stories in *Navajo starlore* tell how Coyote arranged the stars to create the Milky Way. The Pima creation story *Tcu-unny-ikita* describes the Earth Shaman making the Milky Way from ashes. See also *Stars and Starlore.*

Millenarian Movements
Movements of a religious character that seek the imminent destruction of the world, after which a new world will be created. The movements usually involve a ritual practice and the establishment of a right way of living. They are a type of *crisis cult.* Such movements occurred more frequently

after the initial contacts with Europeans, as suffering increased in Native American cultures. In the eastern United States, millenarian movements arose in the early nineteenth century and before. In the central and western portions, they more frequently occurred late in the nineteenth century. The most well known and widely practiced millenarian movement was the *Ghost Dance of 1890.*

Mink
Kwakiutl, Nootka, Kathlamet, *Northwest Coast*
A figure known for his erotic escapades and multiple marriages, best characterized as a *trickster.* Mink was clever at piling up stones to make mountains. Wherever he camped, rivers and lakes sprang up. He killed monsters, stole the sun, and transformed birds, fish, and trees for human use. Mink is credited with preparing the world for the coming of humans. See also *Blue-Jay* (Tillamook), *Ikosait* (Kathlamet), and *Kaik* (Salish). [Boas 1921]

Minquga
Omaha, *Plains*
Berdaches, or cross-gender people, considered to be mysterious because they have been affected by the *Moon,* usually during puberty. Moon holds out bows and arrows, used by men, and a pack strap, used by women. When the youth reaches for one object, Moon quickly crosses the items, thereby fixing the young person's lot in life. A young male who reaches for bows and arrows but ends up with the pack strap has no choice but to act as a woman, speaking in a high-pitched voice, dressing in women's clothes, and doing women's work. Stories tell of male minquga who take other men as their husbands. The minquga are publicly accepted by the tribes, and many are considered to be powerful *medicine people.* [Blackwood 1984; Dorsey 1888b]

Miqqiayuuq
Eskimo, eastern Hudson Bay, *Arctic*
An ancient, faceless, hairy *water monster.* In the winter, Miqqiayuuq prevents people from getting

water by tipping their buckets every time they are lowered under the ice. [Nungak and Arima 1988]

Miritatsiec
Crow, *Plains*
Moon Woman, who is known for taking pity on the lost and deprived. She also gives knowledge of *healing* and medicine bundles. Moon Woman is responsible for directing the movement of buffalo. She can make *hunting* easier. [Lowie 1960]

Misapos
Cree, *Subarctic*
Wesucechak's younger sibling, who is killed by the water lynxes *(Michi-Pichoux). Wesucechak* avenges his brother's death, leading to the great *flood.* See also *Okiskimanisiw,* the Cree kingfisher who tells Wesucechak about the death of his brother Misapos. [Norman 1982]

Misikinipik
Cree, *Subarctic*
A great *horned serpent* who lives under the world and water. Misikinipik is dangerous to humans. Eternally at war with *Thunder* Beings, he is also allied with the water lynxes *(Michi-Pichoux)* against *Wesucechak.*

Miskinahk
Cree, *Subarctic*
Turtle, a comic spirit who comes as a messenger during the *shaking tent* ceremony. He often jokes with those outside the tent, requesting tobacco and telling off-color jokes.

Missapos
Ojibwa, *Northeast, Subarctic*
Big rabbit or great hare, a figure who often transforms himself in order to deceive other animals and humans.

Mistapew
Cree, *Subarctic*
An ancient figure who performs great feats of strength and has magical powers. Mistapew can

see great distances and holds foreknowledge of hunters' kills. Mistapew is not a dream visitor (see *Powatakan),* but is encountered during waking hours, usually while alone in the bush. As the master of ceremonies in *shaking tent* performances, Mistapew makes his power available to any adult male. Only Mistapew can give permission to use the shaking tent. The eastern Cree believe Mistapew is the sole holder of *conjuring* knowledge. [Flannery, Chambers, and Jehle 1981]

Moccasin Game
See *Thlakalunka.*

Molawai
Zuni, *Southwest*
Ritual dramatization of the loss of the *Corn Maidens.* See *Zuni Ritual Cycle.*

Moldy-Forehead
See *Qolqalg Odai,* the boy in Haida stories who becomes Salmon.

Monster(s)
Cannibals and malevolent creatures join with hundreds of monsters in the horror tales of Native American mythology. They seem to appear in every size, shape, sex, and character. Adlet is a blood-drinking monster in Eskimo stories. *Asin* is an Alsea monster girl. *Emogoalekc* (Kathlamet) is a boy who becomes a water monster. The Tanaina *Hairy Man,* unless he is injured, is helpful to people. *Katyutayuuq* (Povungnituk) is a bodiless female monster. *Kogukhpuk* is a huge animal monster who appears in stories along the Bering Sea coast. *Kukuweaq* (Inupiaq) looks like a ten-legged polar bear. The Seminole *Long Ears* is an ugly gray animal that can cause illness. The Slavey bush giants *Nahgane* steal careless children. *Tammatuyuq* (Povungnituk) is an infant-killing monster. The Lakota monster *Unhcegila* resembles a dragon and causes disappearances and death. *Wakandagi* are monsters that live beneath bluffs on the Mississippi River. *Was* is a Tsimshian monster that protects shamans. Other monsters include *Big Fish of Iliamna* (Tanaina) and the meteor fire dragons *Gaasyendietha* (Seneca).

A common theme is the population of the world by monsters after creation, making it impossible for human beings to live. In some *Southwest* stories these monsters arise due to incest or sexual abuse (see *White Painted Woman).* Monster slayers, often *Warrior Twins,* eradicate these monsters. For examples of monster slayers see the Zuni

Uktena-like monster incised on a Moundville pot.

Ahayuta (see also *Zuni Ritual Cycle);* the Navajo twins *Monster Slayer and Born for Water* (see also *Monsterway);* the Takelma culture hero *Daldal;* the Crow figure *Old Woman's Grandchild;* the Yurok *Pulekukwerek; Saya,* the Beaver culture hero; *Suku* (Alsea); and the Hupa culture hero *Yimantuwinyai. Tihtipihin* (Nootka) is a culture hero who helps rescue his mother from the belly of a monster. [Fewkes 1895; Morris 1986]

Monster Slayer and Born for Water
(naaghee neezghani and to bajishchini)
Navajo, *Southwest*

After attaining womanhood, *Changing Woman* is made pregnant by the *Sun* (who shines in her vagina) and Dripping Water (spring water drips into her vagina). In some Navajo accounts *Begocidi* is their father. The children are Monster Slayer and Born for Water. Changing Woman refuses to tell them who their father is, but eventually they learn he is the Sun. Although Born for Water appears to have a different father, as the twin of Monster Slayer he is considered the son of the Sun. See also *Blessingway.*

In a long and dangerous journey, the twins travel to the home of their father, who refuses to acknowledge them as his children and sets about testing them (see also *Test Theme).* Assisted by knowledge and magic given them by guardians, the twins pass all these tests. Sun finally acknowledges his responsibility as their father and grants their requests for armor, weapons, and, in some versions of the story, horses, domestic animals, game animals, and many kinds of goods. The twins are *culture heroes* in this heroic journey that accounts for the origins of so many of the things on which Navajos depend. Upon their return, Monster Slayer and Born for Water destroy the monsters that make the earth uninhabitable for Navajos. With regard to this journey see also *Twins' Journey to Sun Father.* See also *Monsterway, Eagleway, Enemyway, Shootingway,* and *Ye?ii.* In some Navajo ceremonials a *blackening* rite is performed in which the person blackened is identified with the armor of these warriors.

For comparable warrior twins in other cultures, see: *Ahayuta* (Zuni), *Apache Creation and Emergence* and *White Painted Woman* (Apache), *Old Woman's Grandchild* (Crow), *Pyuykonhoya* (Hopi), *Masewa and Uyuyewa* (Keresan), and *Widapokwi and Amchitapuka* (southeastern Yavapai). [Tyhurst 1975; Wyman 1970]

Monsterway
Navajo, *Southwest*

One of the many complex bodies of stories belonging to *Blessingway.* The sun, a powerful figure in the created Navajo world, is married to *Changing Woman* and is the father of her twin sons. Sun travels across the sky daily, encountering a number of women with whom he enters into adulterous relations. The offspring of these relations are *monsters* who dwell upon the land, making it difficult if not impossible for human beings to live.

The twins, *Monster Slayer and Born for Water,* travel to their father's home to seek armor and weapons from him so they can fight the monsters (see *Twins' Journey to Sun Father).* Properly prepared, Monster Slayer, the more agressive of the twins, searches for the monsters and upon finding them, destroys them. Among the monsters he kills are Horned Monster, Rock Monster Eagle, Eye Killers, Kicks-Off-Rocks, and Overwhelming Vagina. Although he intends to kill all monsters he is persuaded to spare some: Sleep, Hunger, Poverty, Lice, and Old Age. Born for Water remains at home, but watches a prayerstick *(keetaan),* which glows whenever Monster Slayer needs his assistance. See also *Eagleway.* [Wyman 1970]

Moon

Of all the bodies in the sky, the moon is the most mysterious. It changes shape as it passes through its cycle, and on some nights it disappears entirely. It is bright, but not so bright as to preclude a clear view of its surface, the features of which appear to many people as a face or the body of an animal. Given these characteristics, it is not surprising Native Americans tell many stories about the moon, and that it is a prominent mythological character.

The Zuni *Moonlight-Giving Mother* is an important cocreator with the Sun Father. In the *Apache creation and emergence* stories, Killer-of-Enemies is identified as the moon. The Alaskan *Moon Man* is master of animals, and the Pawnee *Moon Woman* released the buffalo and corn. The grandmother of the Crow cuture hero *Old Woman's Grandchild* becomes the moon. The Kutenai tell a story of twin lynxes called *Short Faces,* who become the sun and moon. In the Pima creation story *Tcu-unnyikita,* Earth Shaman makes the moon from a block of ice. The Cree moon, *Tipiskawipisim,* is the sister of Sun. In the Pawnee *Basket Dice Game* the basket represents the moon. In a Coeur d'Alene story *Coyote and Moon,* Coyote is chosen to be the moon.

In some stories the moon, like *fire* and *light* in others, is stolen and hidden. *Guguyni,* the Tanaina raven, releases the moon. In Tillamook stories, *lunar eclipses* are understood as the theft of the moon by spirits. The Seneca tell the story of *Hadentheni and Hanigongendatha,* who visit the moon. *Kokyan wuhti,* the Hopi Spider Woman, spins a moon of white cotton. *Minquga,* the Omaha berdaches, are believed to be influenced by the moon. The son *(Wultcixaiya)* of Moon in a Haida story rescues his sister from marriage to Pestilence.

Many stories tell of faces in the moon. The Ojibwa tell a story of the moon's female lover, *Lone Bird,* whose face shines in his. See also an Arapaho story in *Moon, Origin of Shadows on.* The Pawnee story of *Long Tongue* accounts for the face in the moon. [Grinnell 1893a; Holm 1980; Oosten 1983]

Moon, Faces in

Many stories explain the patterns seen on the moon. Some western tribes see Frog, who is busy protecting the moon so Bear will not swallow it. Some tribes believe the patterns are teeth marks left when Bear bit the moon. In another story, Frog once swallowed Moon, but Moon in turn

swallowed Frog. Frog can now be seen in the center of the moon, busily weaving a basket. In another variant, two frog sisters repeatedly reject potential husbands. The disappointed men cry and start a flood. The sisters escape to the moon and jump onto its face, where they can be seen to this day. Other tribes state that the shadow on the moon is an oak tree from which the dead get their food. See also *Kokumthena.*

Moon, Origin of Shadows on
Arapaho, *Plains*

Sun and Moon are brothers who want to marry women on earth. Moon turns himself into a porcupine and entices a woman into climbing a tree that takes her to the sky. Sun brings back a frog as his wife. One day the woman and the frog engage in a chewing contest, and Frog uses charcoal to make chewing noises. Moon makes fun of her, and she jumps on his chest, causing the dark pattern seen on the moon. Moon's wife later gives birth to a male child who becomes a hero and a famous chief. This story has many versions. In one, Moon's wife digs for roots and falls through a hole in the sky. In another, an old woman takes pity on her and lets her down through the sky on a sinew rope. [Dorsey and Kroeber 1903]

Moon Man
Eskimo, Bering Sea coast, Norton Sound to Lower Yukon, Alaska, *Arctic*

A manlike being who lives in the moon and controls game animals (see *Master/Mistress of Animals*). *Shamans* make spirit journeys to him to ensure there are enough animals for hunting season. [Nelson 1899]

Moon Woman
Pawnee, *Plains*

The releaser of *buffalo* and *corn.* Moon Woman lives in a cave on the side of a hill. During a time of famine, when people know only how to live off roots, a young man fasts on a hill under Moon Woman's direction. Moon Woman commands him to quench his thirst, and in the water he sees first the reflection of an old woman (the last quarter of the moon), then the reflection of an older woman (the first quarter of the moon), and finally that of a middle-aged woman (the full moon). Moon Woman directs him to a cave, where he meets a young girl who proceeds to change herself into women of many ages, each representing a different phase of the moon (see also *Changing Woman*).

Moon Woman gives the young man the hoop and pole for the men's game (see *Hoop and Pole Game)* and a basket of dice for the women's game. She shows him small anthills that are to serve as models for the people's *earth lodges*. She provides him with buffalo meat and teaches him how to care for the buffalo hide and skull.

Finally she gives him a bundle, known as the Small Ant's Bundle, and a bowl of corn with which to feed the people. When the people perform the ceremonies Moon Woman taught the young man, the buffalo come from the cave where she lives. When the young man returns to the cave, the water where he saw her reflection has dried up, and the cave has disappeared. The people are disillusioned because they believe the young man no longer has access to the buffalo, even though he does. They go off in different directions and become the different bands within the Pawnee tribe. See also *Miritatsiec* (Crow) and *Witch Woman* (Pawnee). [Dorsey 1906a]

Moonlight-Giving Mother
(ya?onakka citta)
Zuni, *Southwest*
Wife of the Sun Father *(Yatokka taccu)*—although, as in the sky, they are always separated—and, with him, giver of light and life. See also *Ones Who Hold Our Roads* and *Raw People*. [Tedlock 1979]

Morea
Yaqui, *Southwest*
Witchcraft. Morea-kame is a person, male or female, who practices witchcraft, which is thought of only in the malevolent sense. Witchcraft is an inborn quality that is neither inherited nor ac-

quired, although its powers can be augmented through *dreams* and visions. Because Yaqui religious culture has long articulated itself in Christian terms, a morea may be identified with the *devil*. Envy and jealousy are the most common motivations for the malevolent actions of the morea. Morea make people ill or even kill them by thinking evil thoughts, giving evil looks, attacking people in their dreams, and poisoning their food. Morea can change shapes, sometimes appearing as ghosts or animals (see also *Shape Shifting*).

Wearing a cross of huchahko wood around the neck deters witchcraft. Certain curers specialize in healing those made ill by witchcraft. Suspected witches are placed on trial and burned if found guilty. Yaqui people tell many stories about witches and witchcraft that likely serve both to deter malevolent actions and to articulate Yaqui values and ethics. See also Hitebi and *Seataka*. [Painter 1986]

Morning Star
Pawnee, *Plains*
The first and most powerful figure to be placed in the sky by *Tirawahat*. Morning Star is considered by non-Pawnees to be the planet Venus. Morning Star stands in the sky on a bed of red-hot flint. He is dressed like a warrior and is painted all over with red dust. His head is covered with soft down, and he carries a war club. His greatest power is over all the stars. It is through Morning Star that people are created (see *Humans, Origin of)*. He then demands that a human *sacrifice* be made to him. Morning Star also replenishes the fire for his brother, the *Sun*. See also *Big Black Meteoric Star, Evening Star, Pahokatawa* (a meteor being), *Stars and Starlore*, and *Witch Woman*. [Murie 1989]

Mosquito
Pukjinskwes (Passamaquoddy) is a witch who becomes a mosquito. The Nez Perce tell a story of a mosquito, Wawa, who kills his grandmother by sucking her blood.

Mostos
Cree, Ojibwa, *Northeast, Subarctic*
Buffalo, a formidable alien spirit who often appears in the *shaking tent* and who speaks a language that only the conjurer can understand. [Preston 1975]

Mother Corn
A common figure identified with *corn. Neshanu,* a Pawnee creator, becomes an ear of sky corn. See also *Kanati and Selu* (Cherokee).

Mother of Game Animals
A figure identified in many Native American cultures, for example, the Hopi *Tih-kuyi-wuhti.* See also *Master/Mistress of Animals.*

Mother of Humankind
See the Seneca figure *Aataentsic* and *Humans, Origin of.*

Mother-in-Law Taboo
In some Native American cultures it is taboo for a man to see or talk with his mother-in-law. See also *Joking Relationships.*

Mountain Lion
Kawaiisu, *Great Basin*
The twin sons of Mountain Lion and his wife Cottontail are stolen by Coyote. Mountain Lion is so distraught he leaves his wife and grandmother and roams the mountains for years. He cries night and day, his tears causing the streaks seen on mountain lions' faces to this day. Mountain Lion discovers his sons when they are hunting deer. He tricks Coyote with their help and kills him. Reunited with his sons he wanders through the mountains. From then on, mountain lions have no homes and wander in the mountains. [Zigmond 1980]

Mountain Soil Bundle (jish)
Navajo, *Southwest*
A *medicine bundle* replicating the one First Man brought from the lower worlds, out of which the current Navajo world was created. This bundle is the central ritual object of *Blessingway.* Many Navajo families have these bundles. A mountain soil bundle consists of four pieces of *unwounded buckskin,* each containing soil from one of the four mountains in the cardinal directions (see *Mountains, Four Sacred),* along with corresponding jewels. Maintaining the directional correspondences, the bundles of mountain soil are arranged around images of Long Life Boy and Happiness Girl. This core is placed in a larger buckskin and tied into a bundle with a jewel attached in the appropriate place on the outside to designate the east. The bundle is microcosmic as well as containing the powers of cosmic creation. It lies in a basket during the Blessingway singing and is held in the hands during the intonement of prayer. See also *Changing Woman* and *Navajo People, Origin of.* [Wyman 1970]

Mountain Spirits (gahe)
Apache, *Southwest*
Representatives of the Mountain People, who appear among the Apache people in masked form (see *Masks and Masking)* and are often referred to as Crown Dancers. Apache people tell many stories of the Mountain Spirits, usually attesting to their power to cure and protect, or to the ill consequences of showing disrespect for the Mountain Spirits. Mountain Spirits perform healing rites, as well as dancing at *na ih es,* the girls' puberty rite. The masked dance performances may be used to protect against illness, to cure (even when witchcraft is the cause), and to control the weather. Apache stories attribute to the Mountain Spirits the freeing of the animals from a subterranean region where Crow kept them prisoners (see also *Animals, Release of).*

Apaches who perform Mountain Spirit healing rites acquire the masked images they personify through personal vision. Mountain Spirit masks are buckskin hoods, usually painted black, that fit snugly over the head and are secured by a drawstring gathered about the neck. Tiny holes are cut for the eyes and sometimes one is cut for the mouth. Attached to the top of the hood is a complex upright structure, brightly painted and decorated, sometimes referred to as horns. Its basic framework is a construction of wooden slats. On each side hang short wooden slats (earrings) that strike against one another, making the distinctive sound of the approaching Mountain Spirits. Feathers are attached to the ends of these earrings. The masker's upper bodies and arms are painted, and they wear yellow buckskin skirts and tall moccasins. The dance ground on which the Mountain Spirit dancers perform contains a large fire. When the dancers enter the dance ground, they circle the fire in preparation for the dance. Then, at a signal, singers and drummers begin the accompaniment and the dance begins.

Often appearing with the Mountain Spirit dancers is a clown figure (see *Clowns and Clowning*

Chiricahua Crown Dancers, San Carlos Reservation, Arizona, 1969. Courtesy, Arizona State Museum, The University of Arizona, Helga Teiwes, Photographer.

Societies) known variously as "Gray One," "Long Nose," or "White Painted." His mask differs from the others, being made of scraped buckskin and decorated with a big nose or big ears. He does not wear a skirt, only a breechcloth. The rest of his body remains bare, covered only with white paint. The clown is the servant and messenger for the other dancers. He carries messages between the masked dancers and the people. He makes fun of everything and creates fun by enacting foolishness as requested by the audience. The clown functions as an aid in disciplining *children,* who are threatened that Gray One will put them in his basket and carry them off. Parents may arrange to have Gray One frighten naughty children during the girls' puberty rite. Although it may appear that the clown is a pleasant but powerless addition to the Mountain Spirit dances, many Apache people identify the clown as the most powerful, particularly in the context of healing. See also *Black Hactcin Creates Animals and Humans.* [Opler 1941]

Mountains, Four Sacred
Navajo, *Southwest*

The four mountains standing theoretically, although not geographically, in the four cardinal directions, serving as the perimeter of the Navajo world. These mountains are important elements in the creation (see *Blessingway)* and are considered living beings in that they have inner forms *(Biigistiin)* and are identified with the communication powers of Wind *(Nilchi?i).* The eastern mountain (sisnaadjini), "the particular one that is black belted," has been variously identified as Abiquiu Peak, Pedernal Peak, Wheeler Peak, and Blanca Peak. The geographic location of this mountain is widely debated among Navajo singers. The southern mountain (tsoodzil), "tongue mountain," is uniformly identified as Mt. Taylor; the western mountain (dooko?osliid), "light shines from it," is Mt. Humphreys in the San Francisco Peaks. The northern mountain (dibentsah), "mountain sheep," is often considered to be Hesperus Peak or Mogollon Baldy in the White

Mountains in Arizona. See also *Mountain Soil Bundle.* [Reichard 1974; Wyman 1970]

Mountainway
Navajo, *Southwest*

A myth and ritual healing complex. The stories of Mountainway begin where *Enemyway* ends. At the conclusion of Enemyway, two sisters have been seduced by two old men, Bear and Snake, using magical smoke. The older sister, who is married to Bear, and her son are the protagonists in Mountainway.

Older Sister flees her bear husband and attempts to live on berries in the mountains. Chipmunk leads her to a cave where she meets First Earth People, who care for her. Here she gives birth to a baby bear girl. In time, Older Sister sees her first Mountainway ceremonial. The *diyin dine?e* take her on a long series of journeys, introducing her to many Holy People and teaching her many powerful things. On one of these adventures, Older Sister observes *Changing Bear Maiden* and Hunger (or Thin Woman), who appear with other maidens grinding corn. They are the prettiest among the women. The maidens play a game in which each tosses a cornmeal ball to the man of her choice. If the ball does not break, the man must marry the maiden. Only Changing Bear Maiden and Thin Woman are able to pass this test (see also *Test Theme).* However, the man who marries Changing Bear Maiden gets boils and sores, while Thin Woman starves her husband to death.

Taken to the home of the bears, Older Sister again meets her husband, who tries to reclaim her. With the help of the diyin dine?e she flees, but her bear daughter remains with the Bear People. Older Sister marries among her own people and soon has a son. One day a starving mother bear frightens away Older Sister and her husband, and takes the baby boy home with her to raise as her own. He is taught the secret knowledge of the bears, including how to hear the voice of the Wind *(Nilchi?i).* One day, warned by the Wind that his bear mother intends to eat him, the child flees and hides in a cave.

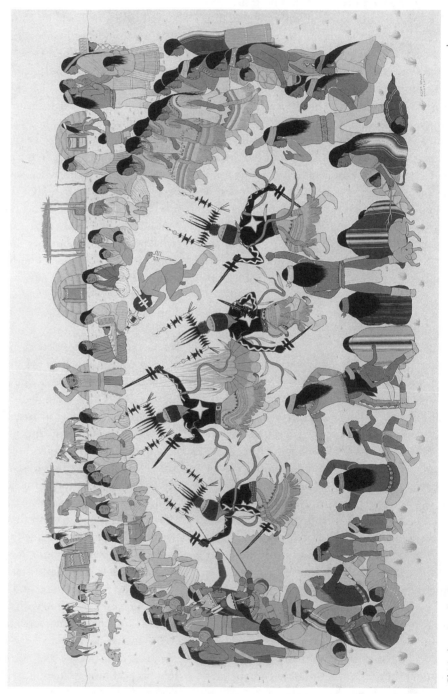

Chiricahua Apache Crown Dancers as represented in a painting by Chiricahua artist Allan Houser, 1953. Courtesy, Denver Art Museum.

Reunited with his family, the young man marries and has twin daughters. But he falls in love with his wife's younger sister, feigns death, and disguises himself as a stranger in order to marry her. When his identity is revealed, the new wife is shamed by her marriage and abandons the son born of it. Raised by Owl, this boy becomes a great hunter and acquires many powers. Fearing him, Owl sends the boy to find his own family. He does so with the assistance of a magical object, but his family is also threatened by him, and once again he is forced to flee.

Owl Boy's father (who is Older Sister's son) has another son named Reared-within-the-Mountain, whom he teaches how to prepare a mask for stalking deer. One day, having disobeyed his father's warning not to hunt to the south, Reared-within-the Mountain is captured by Utes and taken to their camp. The Utes want him to teach them how to prepare and use the deer-stalking outfit. Several helpers warn the boy the Utes will kill him if he does not save himself. Finally he makes his escape with the assistance of *Talking God* and many diyin dine?e. The Utes pursue him, but each time he is spared by the help of Holy People.

Reared-within-the-Mountain is taken on journeys to visit the diyin dine?e and learns many things related to being a warrior. Finally he is shown how to return home. His family greets him warmly and prepares to have a ceremony performed for him to remove the alien influence. Reared-within-the-Mountain finds that his family and their home smell intolerable to him. A dance, the dark corral ceremony, is performed to overcome this affliction. This ceremony, which includes a footrace between one representing Navajos and one representing an alien tribe, is a distinctive part of the performance of Mountainway. As with many Navajo heroes, Reared-within-the-Mountain teaches what he has learned to members of his family before returning to live permanently with the diyin dine?e. See also *Beautyway*. [Coolidge and Coolidge 1930; Matthews 1887; Wheelwright 1951]

Mouse

In a Kawaiisu story, *Haakapainizi,* a grasshopper, is killed by a mouse. *Ugjuknarpak* (Eskimo) is a giant mouse.

Mouse Woman

Bella Coola, Haida, Tsimshian, *Northwest Coast*
Mouse woman is a *spirit* being belonging to a group of beings called narnauks, or animal-people. Some of these creatures try to help humans. Mouse Woman, who often appears as a tiny grandmother, is disturbed by disorder and mischief makers. She works hard to keep the world orderly and undisturbed by troublemakers, who include both animal-people and selfish humans. She is notorious for disciplining and tricking hunters who kill more game than they need. Mouse Woman lives with underwater supernaturals and teaches humans how to behave while visiting them. Stories of Mouse Woman are traditionally told in the feast houses. See also *Narnauks,* Tsimshian animal-people, and the Tsimshian story set in the underwater house, *Gitnagunaks.* [Swanton 1905b]

Mucus

Andaokut is a Nootka figure born from mucus and tears. Nalq is the Tsimshian term for mucus.

Mudhead Clowns

See *Koyemshi*.

Mudjikiwis

Ojibwa, western Great Lakes area, *Northeast;*
Plains Cree, west-central Canada, *Plains*
The eldest of ten brothers, Mudjikiwis discovers a beautiful young woman who has been mysteriously cleaning the brothers' house while they are hunting (see also *Grouse Girl).* The middle brother marries the young woman and Mudjikiwis becomes jealous. He tries to seduce her, and when she refuses him he shoots at her with his arrows. She escapes and her husband goes in search of her. An old woman helps him follow a trail to the sky where his wife is living with the

Thunderer. He convinces his wife and her nine sisters to return with him. The eldest sister marries Mudjikiwis. In some versions of the story, Mudjikiwis's adventures continue. He kills a giant bear and is honored by having his name changed to Kabeyun, the West Wind. See also *Mysterious Housekeeper.* [Bloomfield 1928a; Overholt and Callicott 1982]

Mukat
Cahuilla, *California*

The *creator.* Mukat is killed with a spear, and in the place where his body is burned many useful plants begin to grow. A great Cahuilla *shaman* follows Mukat's spirit trail, hidden among the whirlwinds, to find out about the growing things. Finding Mukat's spirit leaning against a rock, the shaman learns about the plants. Tobacco grows from Mukat's heart, squashes from his stomach, and watermelons from the pupils of his eyes. His teeth are corn, his lice eggs become wheat, and his semen, beans. [Kroeber 1925]

Mumkidag
Papago, *Southwest*

Sickness. Papago recognize two types of real sickness: kacim mumkidag, or "staying sickness," and oimmeddam mumkidag, or "wandering sickness." Conditions due to such things as snakebite, indigestion, and broken bones are considered afflictions, not real sicknesses. Staying sickness is caused by the "ways" or "strengths" of dangerous objects associated with all sorts of animals, plants, birds, and even qualities such as "cold." The cause of wandering sickness is attributed to various noxious substances such as germs, heat, or pus. Staying sickness is treated in a shamanic event that includes diagnosis and curing (duajida), using both sucking and blowing techniques. See also *Shaman* and *Papago Ritual Cycle.* [Bahr et al. 1974]

Munsee
Delaware, *Northeast*

The guard of animals, represented by a mask in the Big House ceremony *(Nkamwin).*

Muskrat
Crow, *Plains*

Used as a man's personal name among various Plains tribes. Muskrat is the animal who, after other animals have tried and failed, succeeds at bringing up from the floodwaters a bit of earth that is used to create the world. See also *Earth Diver.* [Lowie 1956]

Muyinwa
Hopi, *Southwest*

"The maker of all life germs." The deity who controls growth of all plants. Muyinwa is associated with the direction "below," from which he sends up beans, squash, and melons for the Hopi to eat. Because he is one of the six directional chiefs or "cloud fathers," prayers for *rain* are directed to him. He is a figure common to Hopi mythology. Unlike *kachinas* who are impersonated in multiple masked representations, Muyinwa is impersonated only singly. He appears during *Powamu* in February and again during *Oaqol* in October (see *Hopi Ritual Cycle).* He wears an elaborate two-horned headdress, a buckskin kilt, and moccasins. A white line is painted down the front of his arms and legs. He carries a deer's horn in one hand and a stick in the other. See also *Marau,* the harvest ceremony; *Masau?u,* who is often contrasted with Muyinwa; and *Tih-kuyiwuhti,* Muyinwa's sister, who is the mother of game. [Bradfield 1973; Colton 1947a; Parsons 1936]

Mysterious
Kan (Lakota) and *Muxpe* (Crow) mean mysterious.

Mysterious Housekeeper
A story character in many tribal areas. A man or group of men find their house cleaned, food prepared, and even new clothing when they return from hunting. The mysterious helper may appear as an animal who comes to visit and then is seen to transform into a woman, or she may be a woman who later disappears when mistreated. In the Eskimo tale of Fox Wife (see also *Fox),* a hunter finds a young woman who is really a fox. He marries her

and she keeps house for him, but when he hurts her feelings she puts on her fox skin and leaves him. See also *Grouse Girl* and *Mudjikiwis*. [Golder 1903]

Mystery Dance

Wakan Wacipi, a dance given to humans by *Unktehi*.

Pima healing ritual. The sufferer is treated by the medicine person. Painting by Louis Valdez. Courtesy, Arizona State Museum The University of Arizona.

Na ih es

Apache, *Southwest*

Girls' puberty rite, often called the "Sunrise Dance," performed sometime after the onset of *menstruation* and lasting four days. The rite's origin is attributed to *White Painted Woman.* After *Child-of-the-Water* rids the earth of monsters and evil things, people begin to appear. When the daughter of one of the families reaches maturity, White Painted Woman gives the people instructions in the ritual process. The rite is conducted by a medicine man, and the initiate is tended and instructed by an exemplary woman who serves as a model for the girl. A full buckskin dress is made for the initiate and decorated with appropriate symbols. The initiate practices a variety of taboos, each focusing attention on attributes that define Apache womanhood. For example, she must not touch herself with her hands lest her skin be marred. The initiate dances many hours in a four-pole tipi frame enclosure, a considerable feat given the weight of her dress.

By virtue of her identification with White Painted Woman, the initiate has considerable power, even the power to cure. This power is distributed among the community in an event that concludes the rite. Candy and fruit are poured over the initiate, and everyone rushes forward to obtain some of these goodies that, through their contact with her, have become objects of power and good luck. The ceremony culminates with a feast offered to the entire community and guests invited from near and far.

Social dancing occurs during the evenings prior to, during, and following the rite. Masked dancers, representing the Mountain Spirits, dance in the evenings during the rite. Through the presentation of White Painted Woman and the Mountain Spirits, the girls' puberty rite serves not only to make a girl into a woman, but also to renew the entire community through the reenactment of the mythic events by which the world and community were created and defined. [Basso 1966; Opler 1941]

Naachin

Dunne-za (Beaver), *Subarctic*

"*Dreamers.*" Those among the Beaver tribe who experience the Trail to Heaven *(Yagatunne)* and return to tell about it. The English word for these people is *prophet.*

Dreamers dream for the entire community, leaving their bodies and "grabbing hold" of a *song* that carries them on a song trail to heaven and back.

The prophet tradition connected with the Dreamers began with the Sikanni chief named Makenunatane, meaning "his tracks, earth trail," who "dreamed ahead" and predicted the coming of the Whites. He also revealed a method of cooperative hunting involving every member of the community. The Dunne-za believe that animals will give themselves up to be killed only when people are generous and in right relationships with one another. Right relationships entail people respecting family members and duties toward them.

Dreamers follow the tracks of Makenunatane and the song tracks of animals. The swan has a special association with the Dreamers, because it is believed that swans can fly straight to heaven without dying. Swan is the original name of *Saya,* the first hunter and culture hero of the Dunne-za. Swan is in charge of everything that changes with the seasons. Dreamers are closely associated with Saya. [Ridington 1988]

Mask worn by Apache Crown Dancer to represent Mountain Spirits in girls' puberty ceremony. Courtesy, Denver Art Museum.

Naayenezgane
Apache, *Southwest*
Slayer of Enemies. See *Apache Creation and Emergence.*

Naca Ominicia
Lakota, *Plains*
"Big Bellies." A civil society (see *Societies)* composed of distinguished retired *hunters,* tribal leaders, and *warriors* who were members of the tribal council. Their name comes from the fact that their gatherings always featured much

food. They met to hear reports from scouts and to determine when to hold hunts, as well as to decide whether camp should be moved or a peace should be declared. The Naca Ominicia acted as a whole, reaching decisions by unanimous agreement. They had final control over tribal administration and appointed people to all positions of power. See also *Nacas* and *Shirt Wearers.* [Walker 1982]

Nacas
Lakota, *Plains*
Nonreligious societies made up of tribal leaders, famous hunters, warriors, and *shamans* all past their prime in terms of activity and considered to be retired. The most important of the nacas was the *Naca Ominicia* (Big Bellies), because of its members' power and experience. Nacas are very important in Lakota society, where both the accomplishments of youth and the wisdom of maturity are held in high esteem. See also *Wani-sapa,* the buffalo hunt. [Walker 1982]

Nacwapew
Cree, Ojibwa, *Subarctic*
Pike, a humorous *shaking tent* visitor who speaks French and exchanges jokes (see *Jokes and Joking)* with the audience. [Preston 1975]

Nagaicho
Cahto, Sinkyone, Yuki, *California*
"Great traveler." The *creator,* also known as Kyoi (spirit), a name applied to non–Native Americans and therefore nonhumans. Nagaicho made the earth and humans with the help of *Coyote,* who is also credited with introducing death. In Cahto stories, Nagaicho's cocreator is Ehlaumel *(Thun-*

der), who is stronger than Nagaicho and responsible for the creation of animals, mountains, trees, rivers, and humans. [Voegelin 1940]

Nagi
Lakota, *Plains*

A *spirit* distinct from, but attached to, a human (see also *Wanagi).* There are also spirits attached to animals (wamaka nagi) and to food (wo nagi). The nagi resides outside the human but cares for and warns its human of danger. It also helps its human when he or she is in trouble.

When a human dies, the nagi leaves the human. No longer responsible for a specific human, the nagi becomes wanagi. It may stay nearby for a short time and should be respected while lingering. If the detached spirit is not respected, it may cause trouble. After a while it goes with the human to show the way to the spirit world, *wamaka nagi.* The wanagi is most happy if another wanagi accompanies it. Sometimes the animal spirit of the dead human's deceased horse or dog will travel with the human's wanagi. When a spirit comes back from the spirit world after a death, it is referred to as wica nagi, the spirit of a deceased human who visits the living. See also *Hihankara,* the old woman who guards the spirit road taken by the nagi, and *Ni,* the life breath. [Powers 1975; Walker 1982]

Nagila
Lakota, *Plains*

The immaterial self of inanimate objects, a personal expression of one of the many aspects of "the great mystery," *Wakan Tanka.* [Walker 1982]

Nahgane
Slavey, *Subarctic*

Bush *giants* (see *Monster)* who steal careless young *children.* [Moore and Wheelock 1990]

Nakaciuq
Eskimo, western Alaska, *Arctic*

Literally, "pulling up, something done with bladders," i.e., *Bladder Festival.* This winter solstice

event was the pivotal point of the annual ceremonial cycle. It was held for five days, or eight days if a death occurred during the previous year. Preparations for the event began in October, when new songs and clothes were made. At Nunivak Island new food dishes, pails, and ladles were also made and decorated. At the beginning of Nakaciuq, bladders of seals killed during the year were inflated and hung in the *qasgiq* with honor and respect. The bladders were never left alone, and fresh water and food were continually offered to them.

Masks were not worn during Nakaciuq, and only the underground entrance to the qasgiq was used. In the qasgiq there was feasting, and men gave *gifts* to their male cross-cousins. Women danced and made special bowls of *akutaq,* Eskimo ice cream, for the men. On the last day of Nakaciuq, stalks of wild celery were lowered through the smoke hole and positioned in the qasgiq, one bundle across the other. Then the women brought gifts and danced. Each husband gave these gifts to the community qasgiq as his wife danced. In turn the gifts were given to those village people who could no longer care for themselves.

The next morning, the wild celery stalks were lit and used as torches to lead a procession of the bladders as they were lifted out of the qasgiq through the smoke hole. The bladders were tied to the hunters' spears and taken to a hole cut in the sea ice, where they were touched to the celery stalk torch, causing them to burst. Then the bladders were submerged in the sea, along with gifts directed to the *dead.* Finally everyone returned to the qasgiq, where the women danced as akutaq was served. This ritual honoring and disposition of the bladders of game killed during the previous year ensured abundant game in the coming season. See also *Inviting-In Feast, Messenger Feast,* and *New Year.* [Morrow 1984; Nelson 1899]

Naked Dance
Seneca, *Northeast*

A Seneca dance done to nullify *heart squeezing.*

Nalmuqtse

Kutenai, *Plains*

A figure who prefers crawling to walking. He crawls about in his headdress, which gives him power. He travels the countryside naming mountains, rivers, and valleys (see *Names and Naming*). His tracks form riverbeds. When Nalmuqtse finally stands up to stretch, his headdress touches the sky and is knocked off. With the loss of his power he dies. [Boas and Chamberlain 1918]

Nalq

Tsimshian, *Northwest Coast*

Mucus, the husband of North Wind Woman, who travels with her whenever the north *wind* blows hard. Nalq feels cold when traveling with his wife, and mucus drips from his nose, falling on the water to become ice. This is the reason that ice comes along with the north wind. [Boas 1902]

Nalusa Falaya

Choctaw, *Southeast*

Anthropomorphic beings with small eyes, pointed ears, shriveled faces, and human voices. Nalusa Falaya live in the woods and appear at dusk, calling to hunters, who faint upon seeing one of them. While a hunter is unconscious, the Nalusa Falaya bewitches him by sticking him with a small thorn. Hunters thus bewitched will do malevolence to others without knowing why. Nalusa Falaya children can remove their internal organs at night, becoming small luminous bodies that can be seen along marsh edges. See also *Kashehotapolo.* [Hudson 1976]

Names and Naming

To name is to create. To utter a name assumes a relationship. Native Americans typically have many names. Among the most important is the *clan* name. If the clan of another person is unknown it is almost impossible to communicate or relate properly with her or him. Even pronouns are determined by clan relatedness, sex, and age.

Many Native Americans receive a number of names throughout their lifetimes. At birth, or shortly after, baby names are given. Later, when a person is initiated into adulthood or into societies, other names are given. Names of honor or shame may be given throughout life. In some cultures the names of the deceased persons are never spoken. In other cultures the names of those deceased whose lives were exemplary are given to others so that their traits might be passed on. Ceremonial names are usually held secret—they are disclosed only to a person's closest relatives and friends.

In cultures of the Pacific northwest coast, a specific set of names constitutes reality. To exist with status in these cultures, one must inherit one of these names. One may think of this set of names as constant, with a flow of living human beings running continually through it, as people occupy the names during their lifetimes. These names are important family property and are used only on special occasions, and only during the ceremonial season *Tsetseka* (see also *Walal Potlatch*).

In some cultures a very sick or distraught person may be given a new name to fool the offending spirit. Warriors often receive new names to reflect their accomplishments. The Lakota accompany naming with *ear piercing*. Bella Coola names are received during dreams or visions (see *Kusiut*). Members of the Bella Coola dancing society *Sisaok* have special names. Salish *spirit dancing* is done to validate names. The Iroquois give public names during the *Midwinter Festival*.

Naming is also an act of creation. For example, the Yavapai culture heroes *Widapokwi and Amchitapuka* name the months and constellations. The Alsea black bear *Suku* names the rivers. The Kutenai figure *Nalmuqtse* is depicted as crawling about naming things. Of related interest are the Navajo figures *Long Life Boy and Happiness Girl,* who personify speech and thought. Names can be used for malevolent purposes, as in casting spells (see Nooksak *Siwin*). [Boas 1930; Johnston 1982; LeFlesche 1928; Nelson 1899; Pettit 1946]

Nana csyak
Nootka, *Northwest Coast*
Divining *songs* sung by a medicine person while in a trance. The medicine person (see *Medicine People)* sits and sings with eyes closed, occasionally shouting and waving his or her arms. The nana csyak enables the medicine person to see what has taken place or what is happening at a distance. Divining songs are also used to find lost objects. [Sapir and Swadesh 1939]

Nana Ishto-hoollo
Creek, *Southeast*
Good *spirits* who are the spirits of humans who have died after living a good life. They attach themselves to humans and forewarn them of danger, disease, and possible enemies. [Swanton 1928a]

Nanabozho
See *Winabojo.*

Nanabush
See *Winabojo.*

Nanandaw (pl. nanandawi)
Ojibwa, central Great Lakes region, *Northeast*
A medicine person (see *Medicine People)* who specializes in curing (see *Healing)* and diagnosing with the aid of *helping spirits.* The nanandaw applies small bones to the distressed area of a victim's body and blows or sucks on the area to extract the disease-causing agent. Nanandawi also use herbal healing preparations. See also *Shaman.* [Landes 1968]

Nanbozho
See *Winabojo.*

Nankubacein
Arapaho, *Plains*
White Owl Woman, also known as *Snow* Storm, who is responsible for snow. She is also believed to have caused the death of *Lime Crazy.* [Dorsey and Kroeber 1903]

Napioa
Blood, Blackfoot, *Plains*
Old Man *creator* who floats on a log in the water with Mameo, the fish; Matcekupis, the frog; Maniskeo, the lizard; and Spopeo, the turtle. Napioa sends each of the animals into the water to see what they can find. Only Turtle returns, bringing some mud, which Napioa uses to make the earth. Napioa creates women and men, but because the men fear the women they do not live together until Napioa encourages the men to take the women as wives. Napioa creates buffalo and gives the Blackfoot bows and arrows with which to kill them. Since Napioa did not create the two-headed people on the earth, no one knows where they came from. See also *Buffalo* and *Earth Diver.* [Grinnell 1892a]

Nariniiha
Arapaho, *Plains*
Badger, who beguiles a beautiful young woman into agreeing to marry him by disguising himself as a handsome young man. As part of the Arapaho marriage custom, she takes him a transparent goat-horn spoon filled with water. He drinks from it, thereby agreeing to take her as his wife. When Nariniiha leaves her to go to the *Sun Dance,* the woman discovers his real identity. She leaves him and marries a handsome Sun Dancer named Sasayi. [Dorsey and Kroeber 1903]

Narnauk(s)
Tsimshian, *Northwest*
A group of spirit beings who appear as animal people. Narnauks can be either helpful to humans, by aiding in hunting and traveling, or harmful to them, by discharging traps or causing accidents. The best-known narnauk is *Mouse Woman.* See also *Snee-nee-iq.* [Boas 1902]

Native American Church (Peyote Religion)
Peyote is a hallucinogenic, spineless cactus (Lophophora williamsii) eaten in ritual settings. Peyote rituals originated in Mexico and were

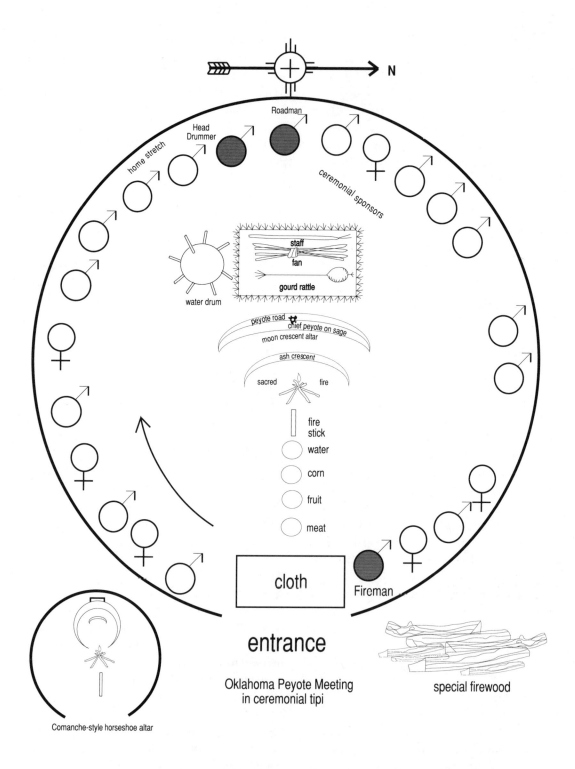

Schematic of Oklahoma peyote meeting performed in tipi.

introduced into the southern Plains in the nineteenth century. Itinerant leaders carried the ceremonies northward, encouraging their broader use among Plains cultures. Widely established by the early twentieth century, the religion was increasingly threatened by government efforts to make the use of peyote illegal. As a measure to gain protection under the principle of religious freedom, the movement incorporated as the Native American Church in 1918. Today it has some 30,000 adherents.

Peyote meetings are conducted for a variety of purposes, from healing the sick to celebrating birthdays. Misconceptions abound about the Native American Church, most likely because peyote is a hallucinogen. Peyote communities are often highly conservative and have demonstrated remarkable effectiveness in overcoming drug and alcohol abuse among Native Americans. Church meetings are serious, prayerful, singing meetings, usually held from dusk to dawn on Saturday nights. They are conducted by a Road Chief, assisted by a Fire Chief, who tends the fire, and a Water Woman, who brings water for the community to drink. A prominent form of meeting has as its focal point a crescent-shaped altar bearing a drawing of the peyote road of life. Centered on the road is a large peyote cactus button, representing the peyote spirit who leads the community.

A water drum is prepared for each meeting and used, along with gourd rattles, to accompany the singing. A beaded staff is passed from person to person; the one holding the staff serves as the singer. The Fire Chief tends the central fire throughout the night, scraping ashes against the concave side of the altar to form a peyote or water bird design. At dawn, when the meeting is complete, the members enjoy social intercourse and share a meal. The foods eaten often carry ritual significance.

The Native American Church is a distinctively Native American form of religion, practiced by people from many tribes. It enjoys the distinction of being indigenous, yet practiced across cultural and language boundaries. It includes numerous Christian symbols and trappings. The peyote spirit is sometimes identified as Christ. While eating peyote, a nineteenth-century Caddo leader experienced revelations that showed him the Christian connections with peyote religion. [Aberle 1966; Brito 1989; McAlister 1949; Stewart 1986, 1987]

Nauyavinaaluk
Eskimo, eastern Hudson Bay, *Arctic*
A man who turns *cannibal,* then kills and eats his wife and baby. In his travels, he kills and eats every woman and child he comes across, until a small boy whose mother and brother he has killed and eaten escapes him by pretending to be dead. The boy tells other people about the cannibal, and thereafter everyone stays away from Nauyavinaaluk. One spring, after he has been ignored for three or four years, Nauyavinaaluk dies of a horrible stomach ache while fishing on the ice. [Nungak and Arima 1988]

Navajo Emergence (haneelneehee)
Navajo, *Southwest*
Prior to the creation of the present Navajo world, a long and complex era takes place in worlds below the present earth's surface. This era is the subject of the emergence mythology. There are usually four of these lower worlds (more according to some accounts), stacked one on top of another. They are the setting for a series of stories beginning in the lowest world and concluding with the emergence onto the present earth's surface.

At the beginning, *First Man and First Woman* and sometimes *Coyote (Ma?ii)* exist along with various ant and insect peoples who speak, act, and live generally according to the rules and customs practiced by Navajo people. As they attempt to live on each of the worlds, they fall to quarreling, adultery, and strife. Warned repeatedly by "chiefs" of surrounding oceans that they are not living as they should, these peoples seem unable to mend their ways. Consequently, eventually the waters (sometimes fire) are released and their world is destroyed. They flee upward in search of a new home. Commonly, as they enter the next world above, the travelers meet new peoples of various identities, from birds to Pueblos, and settle down once again.

In most versions of the story the fourth world immediately precedes the emergence and is the most complex of the lower worlds. A series of stories taking place in this world accounts for the origin of *witchcraft*, the construction of the *medicine bundle* from which First Man draws the powers to create the Navajo world, the *separation of men and women*, and sometimes even the origin of *agriculture*, which is taught by Pueblos living in the fourth world. The emergence itself is motivated by the destruction of the fourth world and is usually accomplished by the peoples traveling upward through a reed. Often a hole must be made into the present world (see also *Emergence Place*). One story tells of the various animals who try and fail, and the one who finally succeeds in making the hole. The earth's surface is covered with water and cannot be entered until contests are won, often by Locust, leading to the draining and drying of the earth's surface.

The pattern of these stories is not necessarily based on a model of growth or emergence from a womb. Navajos likely adopted and developed this body of mythology as a result of their contact with Pueblo agriculturalists. In terms of the pattern of Navajo categories, the emergence stories present a demonstration of alternatives to an orderly creation, something of a precreation chaos. After the Navajo world is created, First Man and First Woman return to the lower worlds as chiefs of death (see *Dead*) and witchcraft. Thus the lower worlds are structurally associated with the Navajo term *hocho*, designating chaos and ugliness, in contrast to the term *hozho*, designating order and beauty defined in the very acts of creation. Blessingway is the story and ceremonial process dealing with this creation.

A healing ceremonial known as Upward Reaching Way, which is performed as an *Uglyway*-type ritual, is associated with the emergence mythology. [Haile 1981a]

Navajo People, Origin of
Navajo, *Southwest*

Changing Woman creates Navajo people by rubbing epidermal waste from her body into balls (see also *Humans, Origin of*). Using the powers of her *mountain soil bundle*, she uses the skin-waste balls to create four couples, the ancestors of the first four Navajo *clans*. Typically the clan identity of the storyteller influences which clans are acknowledged as being first. [Wyman 1970]

Navajo Ritual Process
Southwest

Most Navajo rituals are performed to restore health to someone who is ill; *Blessingway* is a notable exception. Techniques of divination are used to diagnose the illness's cause, which need not be physiologically related to its symptoms. The diagnosis leads to a recommendation for a specific ceremonial within a curing way. A "singer" *(hataalii)* is procured to perform the ceremonial, which may last from one to nine nights, including the intervening days. Singing is heard almost constantly throughout the event, yielding to prayer intonement (see *Prayer and Prayersticks)* at focal points in the ceremonial's ritual acts.

Hataalii are responsible for maintaining the traditional knowledge of the various ceremonial ways. Because learning the songs, prayers, and ritual procedures necessary to perform the many ways is an enormous task, singers normally specialize in only one or two ceremonials (see also *Holyway, Lifeway,* and *Uglyway)*. [Gill 1979a]

Navajo Starlore
Navajo, *Southwest*

Black God (haashcheeshzhini), also known as Fire God because he is credited with the origin of fire, is credited with the origin of stars, particularly the constellations, of which the Navajo recognize 37. The *Pleiades* constellation appears on the left forehead of Black God's mask. Many constellations recognized by Navajos have human form and are used to illustrate

Navajo stories. Constellations commonly appear in *sandpaintings,* on rattles, and on other ritual paraphernalia.

In one story, Black God is engaged in the careful process of placing the stars in the sky in meaningful constellations. He has the stars on a blanket (or in a bag). Coyote *(Ma?ii)* arrives and with typical impatience snaps the blanket, throwing the remaining stars all over the sky. This accounts both for the many stars that do not have names and are not in constellations and for the existence of the great river of stars, the *Milky Way.* [Haile 1947c]

Navajo Wind Way
Navajo, *Southwest*

A mythological and ceremonial healing complex of the *Holyway* classification. The oldest son of the "Woman Who Encircles the Earth" is chosen by the winds (see *Nilchi?i*) to race with *Talking God* and becomes a heroic adventurer. During a game of tag played between the Snake and Wind peoples, the Wind People become so absorbed that the Snake People are able to steal the boy and take him to the home of Big Snake beneath a lake. He is rescued with the help of several *diyin dine?e.*

Later the boy enters territory where he is forbidden to hunt. A storm gathers and he seeks shelter beneath a tree, making the mistake of placing his arrows tips down instead of up. Without this protection he is shattered by Thunder into small pieces and his flesh widely scattered. The Ant People are called upon to gather the pieces of the boy's flesh and place them on a buckskin. Thunder, who did the damage, sings for the boy and restores movement by striking him four times with lightning. His speech is restored by Dark Wind and Bluebird People.

The hero ignores a warning not to attend a *Shootingway* ceremony. When he arrives he finds many beautiful and friendly women, the bird maidens, grinding corn. They bless him by covering his body with *cornmeal.* He suggests a test (see *Test Theme*). Each maiden will throw a ball of meal into the air, and he will go home with the maiden whose ball rolls to him. Only one ball does not break, the one thrown by the "Woman Who Dries You Up." He accompanies her to her home on "the stone that extends into the sky." Warned by *Little Wind,* the boy avoids having sex with the maiden or eating the food she offers him. The next morning he finds she has turned into an old hag and that the meat she offered him is dried human flesh. He attempts to escape, but her home has been elevated into the sky. Finally he is rescued by two maidens, Jay and Dove. They give him food and tell him that Big Snake can take him down to earth if he places a turquoise between Big Snake's horns, grasps the horns, and closes his eyes. But Woman Who Dries You Up follows him. This time Toad saves him by challenging the woman to a race. She loses when she falls in a place that the toad has made muddy by urinating.

Traveling on, the hero kills a deer and again violates a taboo by eating its intestines. The deer is a decoy used by Big Snake, and the intestines turn into a snake and swallow the hunter. His younger brother learns what has happened and informs his family. The hero, now appearing as a snake, chases and threatens the members of his family who attempt to help him. After asking the winds for help, they finally catch him and throw him through hoops to remove the snakeskin (see *Hoop Transformation Rite*).

In another episode the hero is hunting in forbidden territory. He shoots at a *whirlwind,* resulting in the death of a human being. As punishment, the whirlwind twists him into the ground, leaving only his head showing. The winds pry him out of the ground with flints. Talking God and Calling God apply pollen to him and take him to their home. The hero cannot breathe or walk because his mind and speech have been stolen. After many failed efforts to restore him, Dark Wind retrieves his mind and speech from the restless prostituting Coyote People.

In these and other adventures into forbidden territory the hero learns many rituals of restoration that together make up the ways of Navajo

Wind Way. After returning to teach what he has learned to his family, the hero departs to become part of the wind. See also *Big Star Way, Chiricahua Wind Way,* and *Whirling Logs' Sandpainting.* [Hill and Hill 1943c; Wheelwright 1940, 1946b; Wyman and Bailey 1945]

Nayaanxatisei
Arapaho, *Plains*

Whirlwind Woman, whose name also means "caterpillar." The Arapaho believe whirlwinds are caused by caterpillars. During creation, Nayaanxatisei spins a small piece of mud until the earth reaches its present size and shape. She is also credited with the origin of quill embroidery, which she does as she circles around the earth. Whirlwind Woman's circular motions and pauses for rest are represented in Arapaho decorative patterns on objects such as rawhide bags.

In one story, *Nihansan* attempts to seduce Nayaanxatisei by asking her to be his sweetheart. When she says she is not accustomed to remaining in one place, Nihansan says that he also moves about quickly and has as much power as she. Eventually she grows tired of his persistence and they enter a challenge match to see who can spin faster and kick dust higher. She picks him up and tosses him headfirst into a stream. She announces that this is the nature of her power and vanishes. [Dorsey and Kroeber 1903]

Nehanimis
Cree, *Subarctic*

Nehanimis is the son of *Wesucechak* and an antagonist to North Wind and Hairy Beasts. Because Nehanimis is not interested in women, Wesucechak transforms himself into a beautiful woman and seduces his son. His *incest* and metamorphosis into a female gets Wesucechak in trouble with his mate, who even becomes angry with her son Nehanimis. See also *Kiwetin,* the North Wind, who is Nehanimis's enemy. The Hairy Hearts *(Omemihoetehesiwak)* fight with Nehanimis. [Norman 1982]

Neshanu
Pawnee, *Plains*

A creator figure who, shortly after the creation of the earth, realizes that some of the people he has created are fearless, disrespectful, and lack good judgment. Neshanu decides to get rid of these humans but desires to spare those he likes. He saves his favorites by turning them into grains of corn, planting some of them in the sky and some on earth. Then he destroys the wicked humans left on earth in a *flood.* After the flood, Neshanu harvests an ear of the sky corn and transforms it into *Mother Corn.* He sends Mother Corn to find and restore the good people left on earth. First, Mother Corn finds the hidden corn grains, releases them, and teaches them arts, ceremonies, agriculture, and bundle rituals. When she finishes her tasks, Mother Corn becomes a *cedar tree.* [Dorsey 1906a]

Neshmuk
Eskimo, Bering Sea coast, Alaska, *Arctic*

A legendary great medicine man of Hooper Bay, Alaska. According to the story, Neshmuk had himself burned alive in a fire to show the greatness of his powers. Within hours he reappeared unsinged. He could change the weather by throwing his knife into the air and singing. He walked the bottom of the sea to free mammals and to bring fish. [Norman 1990]

New Year

Native American cultures that practice agriculture must pay special attention to the sequence of seasons. They must plant at the optimal time in order to survive. This attention to the passing seasons is often formalized into a ritual annual calendar that begins and ends with the marking of the New Year. For many corn-growing cultures, the New Year falls at the time corn ripens. See, for example, the *Green Corn Dance.* For others it falls at or near the winter solstice, the time when the sun is turned back in its course (see Seneca *Midwinter Festival,* during which the *Big*

Heads make a circuit of the village; Zuni *Shi-tsukia,* the White Kachina who comes from the east bringing the New Year; and the *Tewa Ritual Cycle).* Even hunting cultures may celebrate the New Year, as in the Eskimo Bladder Festivals *(Nakaciuq).*

Newekwe
Zuni, *Southwest*
A clown group and curing society (see *Clowns and Clowning Societies),* no longer extant. This group is especially known for its practice of drinking urine; eating feces, sticks, and rags; and the bare-handed killing of dogs and other animals. Although these acts appear horrifying, the power invoked through such seemingly unthinkable actions was considered the very power of creation. Consequently the Newekwe was the most powerful society of curers. For the story of the origin of the Newekwe society, see *Paiyatemu.* [Bourke 1886; Parsons 1930a]

Ni
Lakota, *Plains*
Human life *breath* that gives strength and keeps everything inside the human body healthy. A weak Ni cannot clean the inside of the human body. If the Ni leaves, the human dies. Ni is caused by Niya, also known as *nagi,* the spirit given at the time of birth. One of the purposes of an *inipi,* a sweatbath, is to strengthen the Niya and thereby keep one's Ni healthy. [Walker 1982]

Niagara Falls
See *Hinon,* the Seneca Thunderer, who lives beneath the falls in a cave.

Night
Big Black Meteoric Star (Pawnee) is the star that controls night. *Taku Skanskan* (Lakota) is the powerful being whose messengers are dark spirits of the night. The Lakota hold that *Wiyohipeyata,* the spirit of the west, is responsible for what happens at night. See also *Darkness.*

Night Dances (ankwati or anktioni)
Hopi, *Southwest*
Dances held, usually on Saturday nights, in kivas (partially underground ceremonial chambers) during winter and early spring months. Each kiva (the ceremonial house for a particular society) prepares a masked dance performance. The village people enter the kivas during the evening. Throughout the night, the dance groups circulate among the kivas in the village, dancing for the people. These dances may feature a wide variety of *kachinas.* Occasionally *puppets* appear in a dance. See also *Hopi Ritual Cycle* and *Palulukon.* [Wright 1973]

Nighthawk Dance
Delaware, *Northeast*
Pickwelaneokan, a dance done during the Bear Ceremony.

Nightway
Navajo, *Southwest*
A myth and ritual healing complex of the *Holy-way* type, perhaps the most complex and elaborate Navajo ceremonial. Restricted to winter, the ceremonial performance is popularly known as *yeibichai,* which designates the outdoor public dancing done on the concluding two nights. There are two separate bodies of mythology for Nightway. The most well known is called "the Visionary," the other "the Stricken Twins."

The visionary version centers on the adventures of a hero named Bitahatini, meaning "his visions." The third of four brothers, Bitahatini is prone to visions, which are scoffed at by his brothers. The two older brothers and a brother-in-law go hunting, leaving the two youngest brothers at home. Bitahatini belatedly decides to follow. At the end of the first day he has yet to catch up with his brothers. He camps on a canyon rim, and during the night he has a vision in which he learns that the brothers have killed a crow and a magpie, the owners of game (see *Master/Mistress of Animals).* Consequently they will kill no more game.

The next day Bitahatini catches up with the party and shares his vision with the hunters. As usual, they discount the vision as Bitahatini's foolishness, but the prophecy turns out to be correct. On the way home, the party comes upon four mountain sheep. They send Bitahatini with a bow and arrow to kill them. He draws an arrow but is unable to release it. He follows the sheep and tries four times to kill one, each time unsuccessfully. The mountain sheep, who are actually *diyin dine?e* in disguise, lead him to a canyon rim away from the hunters. Revealing themselves, they give Bitahatini a mountain sheep disguise and lead him into their home in the canyon, where they teach him the rituals of Nightway. Eventually Bitahatini returns home to teach Nightway to his younger brother before departing to live permanently with the diyin dine?e. See also *Whirling Logs' Sandpainting.*

The "Stricken Twins" version of the story begins with an impoverished family who live in Canyon de Chelly. The daughter hears a strange voice while gathering food, but her family discounts her story. She hears the voice four days in a row; on the fourth day, *Talking God* reveals himself to her and asks her to marry him. She is shy because he is so fine and she so poor. She is afraid to even ask her parents for their permission. Talking God suggests a secret marriage and she finally agrees. They meet on four successive days and then no more. Soon the girl realizes she is pregnant, and nine months later she gives birth to twin boys. She refuses to reveal the father's identity to her family.

When the twins grow to boyhood they wander about and the family has trouble keeping track of them. On one occasion they wander off and do not return for days. The mother thinks they may be searching for their father. When they return, one is blind and the other lame, having met with accidents on their wanderings. They are now a burden on the family and are asked to leave. With the blind boy carrying his lame brother, the twins wander about aimlessly. Their father, Talking God, watches out for them and eventually

takes them to the home of the diyin dine?e so that they may seek a cure. But they do not know the proper offerings and the diyin dine?e repeatedly refuse to help them. They search repeatedly, yet unsuccessfully, for the proper offerings. Finally, the diyin dine?e engage the twins in a series of tests (see *Test Theme)* to determine whether they have a kinship with them. When it is finally revealed that Talking God is their father, the cure proceeds.

The twins are admonished not to talk in the sweat lodge, but when they realize they are being cured they cry out with joy. Immediately everything vanishes and they are left blind and lame once again. Navajos say that this is why ritual cures must be paid for. As the twins depart from the failed cure they cry, but their crying turns to *song.* The diyin dine?e are so moved by this that they call the twins back, vowing never again to turn away their own children. After the children are cured and taught the rituals of Nightway, they return home to teach it to their family before returning to live with the diyin dine?e. See also *Chiricahua Wind Way, Shootingway,* and *Water Sprinkler* (the Navajo clown). [Curtis 1907; Faris 1990; Matthews 1902a; Sapir and Hoijer 1942; Stevenson 1891; Wheelwright 1938]

Nihansan
Arapaho, *Plains*

A figure also called Niha can, known for his many adventures, his ability to transform, his large sexual appetites, and his many resuscitations after being mortally wounded (see also *Found-in-Grass).* In one story, Nihansan chases a group of mice out of an elk head lying on the prairie. In the process he gets his head stuck in the skull. Wearing the skull, he runs into several trees and finally falls into a river and floats downstream. Eventually a group of women bathing in the river see the skull floating by. Nihanasan tells them to free him by striking the skull with a rock. When they do, the skull shatters into fragments. These are the skin scrapers women use for scraping hair and fat when tanning hides. Nihansan gives the Arapaho the name *Cawacnenitan* after he creates them. *Found-in-Grass* resuscitates Nihansan, and he attempts to seduce Whirlwind Woman *(Nayaanxatisei)*. [Dorsey and Kroeber 1903]

Nihniknoovi

Kawaiisu, *Great Basin*

A hawklike creature (see *Hawk)* who carries people in its talons to its mountain home and eats them. When Nihniknoovi arrives home he washes off his victims' blood in a pond, giving it a red tinge. [Zigmond 1980]

Nikagahi

Omaha, *Plains*

Chiefs of the Omaha tribal groups who possessed the sole voice and authority. The *wanace* are their policemen, servants, and messengers.

Nikciamtcac

Kathlamet, Oregon/Washington coast, *Northwest Coast*

The girl who marries Beaver by mistake. When she discovers that Panther is more handsome than her husband, she leaves Beaver to marry him. The abandoned Beaver cries and produces a *flood.* The animals save themselves in a canoe and then dive into the water to bring up new land (see *Earth Diver).* As they dive, each animal knocks off his or her tail on the gunwale of the boat. The animals that do not return to get their tails end up with short ones. [Boas 1901b]

Nilchi?i

Navajo, *Southwest*

Wind, a person who appears in *Navajo emergence* and *creation* stories as the source of the means of life, based on the association of wind with breath, speech, thought, and even gait. In the lower worlds before the emergence and creation of Navajoland (dinetah), orientation in time and space is accomplished by means of mists of variously colored light that arise in the cardinal directions. Four winds emanate from these mists of light, giving figures (humanlike and creatures) in the lower worlds strength and the breath of life.

Although Navajo tradition is not unified, at least one strain identifies Wind, in the form of a person, as the *creator* of the Navajo universe. Wind emerges with the others onto the present earth's surface, where it continues to provide human beings and all living things with the means of life. Navajos point to the spiral patterns in the skin of human fingertips as evidence of the winds entering them.

In the Navajo concept of life, all living things have an "inner form" *(Biigistiin)* or "the one who lies within it." Wind is often identified as this inner form or as one of them. In Navajo creation stories, thought and speech are personified as male and female figures, *Long Life Boy and Happiness Girl.* This pair is also abstracted as one of the central religious concepts of the Navajo, *sa?ah naghai bikeh hozho.* Wind, being identified with speech and thought, is thereby associated with this concept.

Wind is associated with communication in other ways as well. The Navajo world is oriented by four designated mountains, one in each cardinal direction (see also *Mountains, Four Sacred).* As living beings, these mountains have inner forms. A wind is associated with each mountain and each cardinal direction. It is by means of the winds that the inner forms communicate with one another.

Indeed, it is through winds that the entire living universe is constituted as a community of discourse. In many stories, heroes or leaders are guided by a seemingly all-knowing wind that sits in the fold of the ear. This messenger wind is often identified as Wind's Child or *Little Wind.* Although there appear to be many winds, Navajos seem to agree that these are but many names for the one Wind. See also *Changing Bear Maiden, Chiricahua Wind Way, Mountainway, Navajo Wind Way,* and *Shootingway.* [McNeley 1981]

Nimakwsowes
Maliseet-Passamaquoddy, *Northeast*
Sable, the traveling companion of the culture hero *Glooscap*. Glooscap meets Sable in Newfoundland, teaches him to hunt, and gives him special powers that help him become a successful hunter. When Sable goes hunting with She-Bear and almost drowns in a river, Glooscap rescues them by singing magic songs. The three then become companions and helpmates. [Prince 1921]

Niman
Hopi, *Southwest*
Home Dance, the last appearance of *kachinas* at Hopi before they depart for their homes in the San Francisco Mountains. This early August event closes the kachina season (see *Hopi Ritual Cycle*). The most common masked dancers on this occasion are the Hemis kachinas, although others may appear. In its solemnity, this kachina *dance* differs from the *plaza dances* that precede it throughout the spring and summer. No clowns are present. [Wright 1973]

Ninba jide
Omaha, *Plains*
Pipes made from red pipestone (Catlinite). The stems of the pipes are nearly flat, and the mouthpiece is decorated with woven porcupine quills. Stories tell of a group of old men who make seven pipes and carry them around the tribal circle where all the Omaha clans have gathered. First they go to weji cte (a fearsome male elk representing one of the main families of the two principal Omaha clans). He is not found to be worthy, so he does not receive a pipe. Next the old men go to the Inke-sabe, the Black Shoulder or Buffalo who is the other central family of the two main Omaha clans, and give him a pipe. For this reason the Inke-sabe family keeps the Ninba jide, although it belongs to the main clan, the *Hanga*.

The old men continue distributing pipes around the circle. Not every family representing the two main clans receives a pipe, because some families are considered to be less responsible than others. The seventh and last pipe is given to the Ictasanda, even though they are a disobedient, wandering group who have no food. The ownership and privilege of having a pipe make them realize they must be more responsible in their behavior. In the tribal council circle, a man whose family is a member of the Ictasanda clan is responsible for filling and lighting the pipes. If such a person is not present, the pipes cannot be smoked. Pipes are passed down through male members of families in the respective clans. Whenever an heir receives a pipe, he undergoes a four-day initiation ceremony teaching him the history, use, and care of the pipes. [Dorsey 1888b]

Nixant
Gros Ventre, *Plains*
A figure responsible for creating the physical features of the earth. [Kroeber 1908a]

Nkamwin
Delaware, *Northeast*
An annual 12-day ceremony held in a large rectangular building known as the Big House. Its purpose is to ensure good health, prosperity, and blessing. The ceremony includes singing songs that people have received in dreams and visions. During Nkamwin, old men recite the events of puberty visions, a ritual meal is shared, and a man wearing a bearskin costume and large oval wooden mask (see *Masks and Masking*) impersonates Munsee, the guardian of all animals. See also *Mesing Keo*, the False Face dancers who perform during the ceremony. [Speck 1931]

Nolemahigan
Penobscot, *Northeast*
"Acting like a clown." The Indian Trading or Clown Dance (see *Clowns and Clowning Societies*). Dancers taking the role of traders were disguised with deer heads and antlers and wore birchbark masks (see *Masks and Masking*). They dressed in women's clothing and had humps on

their backs. For several nights in a row they would go to people's homes, stomping at the door like an animal and singing songs with weird cries until the people let them in. Then they would bargain for anything they saw. [Trigger 1978]

North Wind
Pawnee, *Plains*

Also known as *Ready-To-Give*. North Wind impregnates a young girl without marrying her, and the other villagers drive the girl and her family from camp as punishment. During a strong north wind storm, the girl gives birth to a boy, who grows quickly. One day the boy meets his father in the forest. North Wind teaches his son to hunt and to harvest artichokes as a food source. In the fall North Wind tells his wife he is angry at her village for banishing her. He gives his wife and son provisions for the winter and promises to return in the spring to teach them agriculture.

The next spring North Wind returns as promised. He plants seeds, giving white corn to his wife, yellow corn to her mother, red corn to her sister, and black corn to her grandmother. North Wind tells his son to make a *medicine bundle* with fire sticks, white corn, hawk skin, and sweet grass. He teaches that whenever a buffalo is killed, tobacco is to be placed as an offering in the buffalo's nostrils, at the base of its ears, and on top of its head. In the fall North Wind goes north again, after telling his family to avoid his wife's uncles, who are responsible for her banishment. One day the uncles, who are starving, come to their niece and her family for help. North Wind's son tells his mother to give meat to the starving people.

He calls buffalo, leads a successful war party, builds his tipi, hangs his medicine bundle, and marries the chief's daughter. Eventually he becomes chief himself. See also *Crow Lance Society* and *Kiwetin*. [Dorsey 1906a]

North Wind Man
Kaska, *Subarctic*

Through the cold he controls, the North Wind Man brings suffering. See also *Kiwetin* and Nooksak *Sotic,* who brings snow and cold. [Sheppard 1983]

Northern Lights
See *Aurora Borealis*.

No-Sleep (doo?iighaazh)
Navajo, *Southwest*

Reference to nightlong singing, during which no one should sleep. [Wyman 1970]

Nucil
Nootka, *Northwest Coast Potlatch*. An elaborate ceremonial event held to commemorate an important occasion, as in the coming of age of a daughter or initiation into a shamanic society such as the Wolf Society. Nucil was also held when a chief had accumulated great wealth for a *giveaway*. Generous giving was the mark of a great chief. [Kenyon 1977]

Nulayuuiniq (Eskimo), a baby who grows into a giant. Courtesy, Canadian Museum of Civilization (neg.#J 19408-3).

Nulayuuiniq
Eskimo, eastern Hudson Bay, *Arctic*

A newborn female who suddenly grows to be a *giant*. During a time of starvation, Nulayuuiniq is found by people who come by dogsled to rescue her village. Her mother's parka is wrapped around her neck. Nulayuuiniq chases after the people, but every time she comes close to them they throw old sealskin scraps at her and whip her.

She wails like a newborn and swallows the seal-skins whole because she has no teeth. Finally, exhausted, she turns into a solid rock island. It is because she is malevolent that all this happens. [Nungak and Arima 1988]

Nulmal
Kwakiutl, *Northwest Coast*
"Fool Dancer." Fool Dancers wear masks that look like distorted, dirty human faces, sometimes with long matted hair and large noses running with mucus, representing the spirit Nulmal. They keep spectators under control during the Winter Dance. Along with the Griz-zly Bear Dancers, the Nulmal Dancers become aggravated with mistakes and accidents that occur during the Winter Dance performances. The Fool Dancers carry clubs and spears, which they use to run errant spectators out of the ceremonial house. Unacceptable behaviors include talking and laughing at inappropriate times during the dances and shielding one's face from the heat of the fire. The Grizzly Bear Dancers attack misbehaving spectators and tear their blankets. If someone in the audience makes fun of a Fool Dancer, he strikes them with a club. See also *Hamatsa* and *Tsetseka*. [Boas 1930; King 1979]

Oaqol
Hopi, *Southwest*
A late October harvest ceremonial complex performed principally by *women*. See also *Marau, Muyinwa,* and *Hopi Ritual Cycle.* [Bradfield 1973; Stephen 1936; Voth 1903]

Ocasta
Yamasee, Cherokee, *Southeast*
Stonecoat, a figure known by his coat, which is made from pieces of flint. Although equally evil and good, Ocasta is considered one of the creator's helpers, sent to assist the Cherokee people. His only power is his ability to disappear, which does not work in front of humans. Although he cannot disappear in front of humans, he cannot be approached by them either. He makes witches and goes from village to village causing trouble, until people grow tired of him and plot to get rid of him.

A group of menstruating women, with power to approach him, trick Ocasta and pin him down by thrusting a basswood stick through his heart. When the men gather around, Ocasta tells them to burn his body with basswood. While he is being burned, Ocasta teaches the men songs and dances to help with hunting, winning wars, and healing the sick. Some of the men are given great power and become the first *medicine people.* [Mooney 1888]

Odogwashodo
Iroquois, *Northeast*
A type of *False Face* mask that is spoon-lipped (see *Masks and Masking).* [Fenton 1987]

Odziozo
Western Abenaki, *Northeast*
A transformer (see *Transformation)* who creates himself from dust touched by *Tabaldak* (the Owner, who created living beings). Odziozo reshapes the surface of the earth. When he is finished he changes himself into a rock that sits in the middle of Lake Champlain. [Trigger 1978]

Oehda
Iroquois, Great Lakes region, *Northeast*
Earth. The small piece of earth Muskrat brought from the bottom of the water (see *Earth Diver)* and placed on the back of *Turtle* so that *Aataentsic* (Woman-Who-Fell-from-the-Sky) could land safely. Oehda grew rapidly, first

to the size of an island and then to earth's present size. It is said that when Turtle gets tired and moves a bit, there are *earthquakes* and tidal waves. [Fenton 1987]

Ogre

The Nootka describe a *Yellow Cedar Bark Ogre.* The Hopi have rituals where ogrelike figures known as *Soyoko* frighten naughty children. See also *Cannibals, Malevolent Beings,* and *Monsters.*

Oh-gee-nay
Cree, *Subarctic*

An affliction suffered because of wrongful conduct. Illnesses that do not respond to the usual treatments are suspected of being oh-gee-nay, resulting from hidden or forgotten misconduct. Disease-causing offenses include murder, incest, deceit, and physical abuse. During *shaking tent* performances, visiting *powatakan* encourage the recollection and confession of these misdoings. Public confession often cures the sufferers or enables curing methods to work (see *Healing).* [Preston 1975]

Ohgiwe Society
Huron, *Northeast*

"Singers for the Dead." A women's medicine society (see *Medicine Societies)* whose primary purpose was the care and honoring of the *dead.* Members of the society often dreamed of the dead. [Tooker 1962]

Ohohwa
Seneca, *Northeast*

Owl, the old man who feasts on rodents and is jealous of his handsome nephew, Eagle. In one story Owl deceives two poor sisters on their way to offer themselves in marriage to Eagle, the son of their neighboring chief. The sisters are told by their mother that Eagle is a handsome young man with a hooked nose and strong power. The mother also warns her daughters that Eagle's uncle, Ohohwa, will try to seduce them.

As the sisters travel they see a man chasing mice around the stump of a tree. The man (Ohohwa,

the Owl) finally emerges with the tail of a mouse protruding from his mouth. When he asks where they are going, the sisters tell him of their journey to Eagle. Pointing out that he has a hooked nose, Owl convinces the sisters he is Eagle. They go with him to his lodge.

The sisters become suspicious of Ohohwa because he has no food. They follow him to a night dance where they see him feasting on mice. Realizing he is not Eagle, they trick him by placing rotten logs full of ants in their bed. Ohohwa lies down thinking he is between the two sisters and is severely bitten by the ants. The sisters escape to his nephew Eagle, who takes both of them as wives. [Curtin and Hewitt 1918]

Ohswedogo
Onondaga, Iroquois, *Northeast*

A black being assigned by *Sky-Holder* to live at the west side of the earth to help humans. See also *Dehotgohsgayeh* and *Twehdaigo.* [Fenton 1987]

Okabewis
Ojibwa, western Great Lakes area, *Northeast*

"Messenger." The man sent to teach many things to the first people on earth, who have no minds of their own. He teaches them how to make *fire* with a bow and stick and decayed wood; how to cook meat on a fire or by boiling it in fresh birchbark; and how to use the *corn* and *tobacco* that have been given them. He instructs the Ojibwa in fasting and teaches them how to pay attention to their dreams so they will know how to heal the sick (see *Healing).* [Landes 1968]

Okaga
Lakota, *Plains*

The South and the spirit of the South—also referred to as South Wind—that may be called upon to bring south winds and warm weather. Okaga is responsible for the production of fruits and grains. See also *Ta Tanka Lowanpi,* the girls' puberty rite. [Walker 1982]

Oke (Okewis)

Virginia Algonquians, *Northeast*

A fearful punishing *spirit* of undefinable shape, whose images were kept in a temple and carried into battle. Dead witches and priests were believed to continue on in the shape of oke (see *Witch).* [Hudson 1976]

Oki

Huron, Great Lakes area, *Northeast*

A powerful *spirit* who controls the events of daily life. People who display unusual behavior, such as *shamans,* madmen, and powerful warriors, are also called oki. Amulets are referred to as oki. The sky is considered the most powerful oki, because it controls the seasons and all natural phenomena, including winds, thunder, and lightning. See also *Arendiwane,* a powerful Huron spirit. [Tooker 1962]

Okiskimanisiw

Cree, Ojibwa, *Northeast, Subarctic*

Kingfisher, who appears in many stories as the bird who tells *Wesucechak* about the location and death of his brother *Misapos.* In some stories Wesucechak awards the bird with beautiful feathers, while in others Kingfisher is punished for attempting to eat Misapos's remains. [Preston 1975]

Oky ontatechiata

Huron, *Northeast*

"Those who kill by spells." Oky ontatechiata were sorcerers who practiced *witchcraft* by embedding a knob of hair, a piece of animal nail, or other foreign object in their victims. The victims could only be cured with the help of healers (ontetsans). Oky ontatechiata were usually identified in the dreams of their victims. [Tooker 1962]

Old Lady Salt

Zuni, *Southwest*

An alternate rendering of the Zuni name for *Salt Woman.*

Old Man

Blackfoot, *Plains*

A *trickster* figure known for his deceit, laziness, and humor. In one story Old Man convinces Fox to let him pluck out his fur everywhere except from his tail as a way to catch buffalo. Fox runs into a herd of buffalo, and the buffalo laugh so hard they fall over dead from exhaustion. Old Man skins the buffalo and cuts up the meat while Fox watches silently. Finally Old Man becomes angry with Fox for not answering his questions. He pushes him over and discovers that he is dead, frozen stiff because he had no fur to protect him from the cold. [Thomas 1986]

Old Man Coyote (Isaahkawuatte)

Crow, *Plains*

A figure credited with making the earth, human beings, animals, birds, wolves, buffalo, and deer. Old Man Coyote is also known as First-Worker. He sends ducks underwater to bring up some mud, which he uses to make the earth (see *Earth Diver).* He traces lines on the earth and makes creeks. He sends the ducks to dive to the creek bottoms and bring up more mud, which he uses to make First Man, whom he calls Cirape, and First Woman. Old Man Coyote refers to Cirape as his younger brother. When Cirape goes to follow deer tracks, Old Man Coyote tells him to bring back some mud, which Old Man Coyote uses to make First Woman's genitals. Old Man Coyote then tells Cirape to gather some earth, which he uses to make a penis for Cirape. Then he tells Cirape and First Woman to mate. The children born from this union become the earth's people (see *Humans, Origin of).*

Old Man Coyote is known for his strong sexual appetites. In one story, he sees a group of women coming to pick strawberries. He hides beneath the strawberry patch and causes his erect *penis* to travel among the strawberry plants. The women began to pick and eat the strawberries. One tries unsuccessfully to pick the head of Old Man Coyote's penis. She decides to bite it. She then invites her companions to pluck it, but none of them can. When they leave to get a knife to cut it off, Old Man Coyote escapes, laughing. In another story, he wants to marry a girl who desires a man with a small penis, so he trades penes with a mouse. When the other men see the little mouse dragging around the huge penis, they know Old Man Coyote is up to his tricks and warn the woman. Old Man Coyote takes his penis back from the mouse and kills him for telling about the exchange. See also *Ashammaleaxia, Awusek,* and *Trickster.* [Frey 1987; Linderman 1931]

Old Woman's Grandchild
Crow, *Plains*

Culture hero, son of the *Sun,* who is raised by an old woman after the death of his human mother. The child grows up quickly and undertakes the killing of *monsters.* His father, the Sun, watches over him. At the end of his adventures, he turns into the north star, and his grandmother becomes the *moon.* See also *Ahayuta* and *Monster Slayer and Born for Water.* [Lowie 1960]

Old Woman Underneath Us
See *Hayicanoko* (Tlingit).

Old-Woman-Who-Never-Dies
Mandan, *Plains*

A powerful grandmother figure who lives in a lodge. She is visited by two young men brought to her lodge by a whirlwind. They leave riding a *horned serpent* and encounter a giant serpent, which they kill and cook. Despite warnings not to, one of the young men eats part of the serpent, whereupon he turns into a large water serpent himself (see *Human-Animal Transformation*). He lives in the Missouri River and acts as a protector and spirit of the river. [Beckwith 1938]

Ololowishkia
Zuni, *Southwest*

A kachina similar to *Kokopelli.* See *Zuni Ritual Cycle.*

Omemihoetehesiwak
Cree, Northern Ojibwa, *Subarctic*

Ancient beings known as *Hairy Hearts;* they fight with *Nehanimis* (the son of *Wesucechak)* and others to live on earth but are destroyed. [Bloomfield 1930]

Omiigiwen
Ojibwa, Menominee, western Great Lakes region, *Northeast*

"Presentation." The term for offering a gift of friendship from one tribe to another. Usually used in conjunction with the word *drum* (dewei-gan), because it involves the ceremonial presentation of a drum (deweiganan omiigiwen). The drums are an intricate part of *Dance* Drum ceremonies. After they are made, they are painted with specific designs, decorated with fur, and hung on four feather-ornamented hooks.

Prior to a drum presentation, both the giving and receiving communities hold four-day preparations. Then come four days of dancing during which the drum is presented. The presentation begins with the lighting and smoking of pipes by the lead drummers, singers, and dancers. This is followed by another four days of dancing. The origin story of the drum is told, and as the drum is presented it is struck four times with a special stick.

The story of the origin of the Dance Drum is told at every Dance Drum ceremony. A woman, Tail Feather, saw her four sons killed during one of the first battles with the U.S. Army in the early 1870s. She ran away to escape the soldiers and hid for four days under some lily pads in a pond. While under the water she had a vision from gichi-manitou (the Great Creator), who taught her how to make a drum and the songs to sing while drumming. After four days the woman returned to what was left of her people and told them her vision, which revealed the only way to stop the soldiers from killing the remainder of her people. When the soldiers heard the sound of the drum, they put down their arms, stood still, and stopped the killing. This was the beginning of the Dance Drum also known as the *powwow* or drum religion. [Venum 1982]

Onanne
Zuni, *Southwest*
The "road" or "*road of life*," set for every person by the Sun Father. Obstacles that arise along the road, such as sickness, must be removed with the help of medicine societies to prevent premature death. [Tedlock 1975]

Onditachiae
Huron, *Northeast*
Part human, part turkey cock. The spirit of *thunder, lightning,* and *rain.* [Fenton 1987]

Ondoutaehte
Huron, *Northeast*
Great Lakes area, northeastern North America. The perpetrator of *war,* who appears as either a *dwarf* or an old woman. [Fenton 1987]

One Sitting Above
Creek, *Southeast*
See *Hisagita-imisi.*

One Who Drills
Eskimo, eastern Hudson Bay, *Arctic*
See *Ikuutayuuq,* who kills his victims by drilling into them.

Onenha
Seneca, *Northeast*
Corn, who brought *Gondagonwisas,* the Corn Harvest Ceremony, to the Seneca people. A man has always picked up abandoned corn, squash, and bean seeds and protected them by carefully carrying them to a safe place. The man becomes very ill. He has no family or friends, and is all alone in his lodge. One day, when he is near death, he hears the voices of women outside his lodge. One woman, Corn, tells her sisters Bean and Squash that the man has always cared for them and they must help him. That night

Onenha comes to the man in a dream and tells him he is not going to die. She instructs him to gather a container of rainwater and drink it to restore his health.

The man follows her instructions and recovers. Onenha sings and dances the Corn Dances in thanksgiving for the return of the man's health. She teaches him how to tend the corn plants more carefully when they are young. She also instructs him in the ceremony of thanksgiving he is to teach his people when corn is harvested. See also *Kanenhagenat.* [Curtin and Hewitt 1918]

Seneca Corn Husk mask. Photo Archives, Denver Museum of Natural History.

One-Standing-and-Moving
Haida, *Northwest Coast*
The most important land spirit supporting the Queen Charlotte Islands. His movement causes *earthquakes.* [Swanton 1905b]

One-Sung-Over (bikinahagha)
Navajo, *Southwest*
The one for whom a Navajo healing ceremonial is sung, commonly referred to in much of the Navajo literature as "patient." One-sung-over, the literal translation of the Navajo term, is preferred to "patient," which tends to exclude the religious dimension predominant in Navajo ceremonials.

One-Tail-Clear-of-Hair
Catawba, *Southeast*
Opossum, a prominent story character who often outwits other animals. In one story Opossum tempts Deer and Wolf with persimmons he has found in a tree. Opossum climbs up the tree and eats the fruit. Deer wants some and ends up killing himself by butting his head against the tree trunk. Opossum tricks Wolf into thinking he can have some persimmons if he leaps up into the tree. When he leaps, however, he falls back onto a sharp stick that Opossum has placed next to the tree. [Speck 1934]

Ones Who Hold Our Roads
(honaawonaawillapona)
Zuni, *Southwest*
A powerful group of *Raw People,* among whom the most important are the Sun Father *(Yatokka taccu)* and *Moonlight-Giving Mother.* In early interpretations of Zuni mythology, the singular form of the term *(aawonaawilona),* meaning the Sun Father, was misunderstood as referring to an androgynous creator. See also *Kachina.* [Cushing 1896; Stevenson 1905; Tedlock 1979]

Ongwe Ias
Seneca, *Northeast*
"He is a man eater." A *cannibal* who is eventually destroyed by *Hodadenon,* a culture hero. [Fenton 1987]

Ongwe onwe
Seneca, *Northeast*
"Human being." The term by which the Seneca identify themselves. Ongwe is used to describe both the *Seneca* themselves and beings with humanoid features and characteristics. The adjective onwe means "native, original, true, natural" to distinguish real human beings from the others. [Fenton 1987]

Ongwe?onweka
Mohawk, Oneida, Onondaga, Cayuga, Seneca, Tuscarora, *Northeast*
"Longhouse Way." A form of religious belief and way of life. Adherents often gather for social,

political, and religious purposes in the *longhouse,* also known as the dance house, a ceremonial structure. See also *Six Nations.* [Fenton 1987]

Only Faces
See *False Faces* (Iroquois).

Only One
Tsimshian, *Northwest Coast*
The name given to a young man by supernatural powers. He and his two companions travel to a deep pit on one side of the Skeena River in search of shamanic power. Each of the companions is lowered into the pit on a cedar-bark line, but both are bitten so badly by insects before they get halfway down that they have to be pulled up. Only One (i.e., the only one to make it to the bottom) is successfully lowered into the pit. At the bottom he finds a door. Passing through it he finds a great chief wearing a crown of grizzly bear claws filled with eagle down. Under the great chief's direction, many shamans come forth, take their supernatural powers out of their mouths, and put them into Only One's mouth. Then his companions pull him up and they start home.

On the way the two companions become faint and vomit blood, a sign that they have obtained shamanic power. The people find Only One in his house singing, surrounded by a terrible whistling noise, and he describes what has happened to him. As a great shaman, Only One heals the sick and revives the dead, although there is little illness because the diseases are afraid of him. Many shamans are jealous and try to kill him with their power, but Only One destroys them all. [Boas 1916]

Ononharoia
Huron, *Northeast*
"The upsetting of the brain." A three-day festival, often performed in response to the illness of a well-known village figure. During Ononharoia people pretended to be insane and demanded things they had seen in their *dreams.* At the end of the festival people went into the woods "to get

rid of their madness," in hopes that the afflicted person would recover. [Tooker 1962]

Onoqgontgowa
Seneca, *Northeast*
The great bumblebee. He is named by *Ganyadjigowa* (Mud Hen) while Ganyadjigowa is traveling about, even though the fiercely independent bumblebee does not want a name. [Fenton 1987]

Ontetsans
Huron, *Northeast*
Healers whose specialty is extracting the spells of sorcerers *(oky ontatechiata),* thus curing the diseases caused by their *witchcraft.* The ontetsans extracted the spell by giving the patient an *emetic* or by *sucking* the diseased part of the body (see also *Shaman*). Sometimes the ontetsans would make an incision in order to extract the spell. See also *Arendiwane,* the one who extracts spells. [Tooker 1962]

Orenda
Iroquois, *Northeast*
A power or force innate in all objects from stones to deities. Although it is a Huron term, it applies generally to an Iroquoian concept of mystic potence. The root of the word, ren, is associated with the power of *song,* which is a principal vehicle for communication between the Iroquois and the spiritual world. See also *Wakan* and *Otgon.* [Hewitt 1902]

Orphan(s)
For examples of orphans in Native American stories, see *Corncob Boy,* the Cochiti culture hero; *Gaha,* the Seneca orphan boy befriended by the wind; and *Kautyayuq,* the Povungnituk story of the poor orphan boy.

Orpheus
A motif identified by the classical Greek story of Orpheus, who went to the land of the *dead* to retrieve his wife. In North American stories, the journey to the land of the dead is undertaken by a relative in search of a deceased family member. The journey usually requires permission and involves prohibitions such as not looking at or touching the dead person or not looking back on the return trip. The inevitable violation of the prohibition means failure and the impossibility of the dead ever returning to life. These stories account for the permanence of death.

In a Blackfoot story a young man goes in search of his deceased wife. He is helped by an old woman who supplies him with powerful medicine and a pipe to communicate with the spirits of the dead. The spirits eventually return his wife to him, telling the couple to sweat thoroughly in a sweat lodge outside their village before seeing anyone and warning the husband against showing meanness toward his wife. Things go well until, after a number of years, he threatens to burn her with fire. She vanishes, never to be seen again.

An excellent example of an Orpheus story is the Pawnee *Whistle Dance.* See also *Ghost.* [Gayton 1935a; Hultkrantz 1957; Kroeber 1946; Ramsey 1978; Swanson 1976; Voegelin 1947]

Orpingalik
Eskimo, *Arctic*
The well-known Eskimo *angalkuq,* hunter, singer, and poet. Orpingalik shared information with the Danish explorer Knud Rasmussen during the Fifth Thule Expedition of 1921–1924.

Osimc
Nootka, *Northwest Coast*
The process of washing with hemlock branches and praying in the woods to procure *power* for success in hunting, a long life, wealth, or withstanding evil wishes of others. See also *Tihtipihin* and *Yellow Cedar Bark Ogre.* [Kenyon 1977]

Otakrendoiae
Huron, *Northeast*
The *dance* done at *Akhrendoiaen,* a curing ritual (see *Healing*) to free someone from insanity. The

dancers ritually killed one another with charms such as bears' claws, wolves' teeth, eagles' talons, certain stones, and dogs' sinews. When a dancer was "killed" by the charm, blood poured from his mouth and nostrils or was simulated by red powder. If members of the Atirenda medicine society were injured at any time, they would give poison instead of medicine to a person they had been called upon to cure, in order to get even. [Tooker 1962]

Otgon
Iroquois, Northeast
Poison or malevolent *power* that stands in opposition to *orenda*. See also *Heart Squeezing*. [Fenton 1987]

Othegwenhda
Seneca, *Northeast*
"He, the chief, flint." The youngest son of *Hagowanen* and *Hongak*. Othegwenhda's mother gives him a special flint *amulet* in the shape of a small finger. The amulet is imbued with the *orenda* of Hongak. Whenever Othegwenhda needs advice he calls on the flint finger, which becomes animated, tells him what to do or which direction to travel, and gives him the power of transformation.

Othegwenhda has many adventures. He increases his power with a gift of feathers from the Blue-Jay People and fights with the cannibal Djinidaqses until both become skeletons. The two skeletons continue to fight until they are reduced to two fighting skulls. Finally the skull of Othegwenhda crushes that of Djinidaqses. Othegwenhda's skull rolls about. The bones of his body reattach themselves, and his flesh and blood return to cover them. The chief rewards Othegwenhda by giving him the hand of his daughter in marriage. See also *Djieien*, who is killed by Othegwenhda. [Curtin and Hewitt 1918]

Our Grandmother
Shawnee, Oklahoma and *Northeast*
See *Kokumthena*.

Owl
The owl holds diverse and prominent meanings in many beliefs and story traditions. The Kiowa (northern Oklahoma) say that a medicine person becomes an owl after death, and that when an owl dies it becomes a cricket. The Cherokee and Creek (southeastern U.S.) believe that the cry of a screech owl means impending death (see *Dead*) or illness. Members of certain Creek medicine societies sing special songs to the owl to keep their villages free from disease. According to the Penobscot (northeast coast U.S.), anyone mocking a screech owl will be burned up by the owl. However, the barred owl's hooting is considered to be a warning against danger, and it is treated as a camp guardian. In a similar way the Pawnee (Nebraska) consider the owl to be protection during the night.

Owl is considered a destructive and malevolent figure who appears among all divisions of the Apache. The western Apache, along with the Jicarilla and Lipan, call him Big Owl and depict him as a blundering and slow-witted figure, one of the monsters pursued by the culture hero. The Mescalero and Chiricahua think of him as a giant.

Several Plains tribes honor the owl in an Owl Dance done by men and women who mimic the owl's behavior. The Menominee also mimic the owl while dancing; they tell stories of the gift of medicine from an owl disguised as Grandmother (Mi'aniu). The Crow (southern Montana) use the Owl Dance as a social *dance*. The Delaware (east coast U.S.) know they will have good fortune in hunting when they hear a screech owl.

The Blackfoot tell a story of Screech Owl *(Atsitsi)*, who is a warrior. *Owner-of-Bag* is an owl who frightens *Little Owl* in an Arapaho story. *Ohohwa* is the Seneca term for Owl, who appears in stories. *Skatene* (Choctaw) is an old woman who becomes an owl. *Stikini* (Seminole) are people who can become owls. *Tseguksk* (Tlingit) is the name of a shaman who predicted smallpox. It is believed he became an owl after dying. See also

Gitqada. [Bloomfield 1928b; Goodwin 1939; Herndon 1990; Opler 1938b, 1940, 1942]

Owl Dance
See *Owl.*

Owl Maker
Lakota, *Plains*
See *Hihankara,* the term used for an old woman.

Owner-of-Bag
Arapaho, *Plains*
A story figure portrayed as a large *owl* and used to frighten *children* who misbehave and refuse to be quiet at mealtimes. The children are told that Owner-of-Bag is lurking outside, and if they do not quiet down they will be given to Owner-of-Bag. See also *Little Owl* and *Bogey.* [Dorsey and Kroeber 1903]

Ozuha pejuta
Lakota, *Plains*
Medicine bag (ozuha, meaning "bag," and pejuta, meaning "medicine"). A bag that holds the medicines of the *pejuta wicasa,* medicine person. Unlike many *medicine bundles,* the bag itself has no special power; it is merely a bag for storing medicines. The ozuha pejuta holds ten medicines: Taopi Pejuta, a powder mixed with water and drunk for wounds; Keya Ta Cante, dried and powdered turtle's heart; Canli Wakan, special tobacco used for wounds, that is smoked in a pipe by all present with the pipe pointed toward the patient; Hante Pejuta, cedar medicine used as disinfectant and burned in the sweat lodge; Icahpahu Pejuta, pith of soap weed, used for swelling; Pejuta To, blue medicine, a powder used for anemia that is mixed with water and drunk; Sinkpetawote Pejuta, calamus root used for delirium, chewed by both the patient and the medicine person, who chews and then spits it on the face and head of the patient; Pejuta Skuya, sweet medicine used to initiate late menstrual periods; Wahpezizila Pejuta, yellow leaves medicine, a powdered remedy mixed with water or grease and applied to inflamed areas; and Taziyazan Pejuta, yucca made into a powder and drunk for stomach pain. [Walker 1982]

Pachavu
Hopi, *Southwest*

Dramatization of specific *migrations* of the founders of particular Hopi villages, erratically performed (no more frequently than every four years, but sometimes not for decades). [Wright 1973]

Pagazozi
Kawaiisu, *Great Basin*

The Kawaiisu term for people who lived north of them. The pagazozi were said to have originated when *Coyote* fell into a large lake. Coyote drowned and his hide floated to the surface of the water. Large worms crawled out of the hide and swam to shore. When they reached land they became the pagazozi people (see *Animal-Human Transformation*). [Zigmond 1980]

Paho(s)
Hopi, *Southwest*

Prayerstick (see *Prayer and Prayersticks),* an object made of a painted reed or stick four to six inches long, sometimes connected in pairs, with feathers and other objects attached. They represent prayer offerings. Pahos may also be thought of as messengers that deliver prayers to the deities. They are made in kivas on the day before a *kachina* dance and deposited at kachina shrines near the village. They are also made for such occasions as planting a field, building a house, and going on a hunt or a salt expedition. Pahos have specific physical designs and compositions, depending on the deity to whom they are directed. Paho is related to the "breath feather," nakwakwosi. This is a feather, associated with *cloud,* to which a length of cotton string is attached. [Bradfield 1973; Means 1960]

Pahokatawa
Pawnee, *Plains*

"Knee-Prints-on-the-Banks-of-the-Water." A wonderful being who comes to the people from the sky in the form of a meteor. Pahokatawa is a man who is killed and cut up by the enemy of the Pawnee. Coyotes and birds eat his flesh, and other animals eat his brain. The sky beings want Pahokatawa to live, so they tell the animals to put his flesh back. The animals return all of his body, but no one can find his brains. The sky beings place a soft, downy feather in Pahokatawa's skull in place of his brains and bring him

back to life. After his resuscitation Pahokatawa frequently warns the people of impending enemy attacks. He foretells that a large, multicolored meteorite shaped like a turtle will fall on the Plains. Many years later, some of the older people remember Pahokatawa's words and search for the turtle-shaped meteorite. When they find it, they put it in the *Morning Star* bundle. When the Pawnee moved from Nebraska to Oklahoma they placed the meteorite high up on a western hill. [Dorsey 1906a]

Painted-Porcupine
Arapaho, *Plains*

Arapaho women decorate many items and clothes with colored *porcupine* quills. Painted-Porcupine tells his wife to inform her mother and the other women in camp that he is happy to provide them with quills during the fall and winter, when he has an abundance of them. But during the warm months, he says, he has few to spare. See also *Quilling*. [Dorsey and Kroeber 1903]

Paiyatemu
Zuni, *Southwest*

The sun youth kachina, a great runner who has eight sisters. Every day he runs past the home of eight evil sisters. One of these sisters challenges him to a game of hide-and-seek with their lives at stake. The woman hides in a cloud and Paiyatemu is unable to find her. He hides behind the sun (or a sunflower), but she squeezes a drop of milk from her breast and sees reflected in it the tip of Paiyatemu's headdress. She cuts off his head, removes his heart, and buries his body. The blood that drips on the ground becomes tenatsali plants, a medicine flower with great healing qualities.

With the aid of animals, Paiyatemu's sisters locate his head and heart. His eldest sister plays his *flute*. At each note, a *butterfly* comes forth in one of the colors of the six directions. She sends a many-colored butterfly, Paiyatemu in disguise, to lure the evil sisters. They run after the butterfly, removing various articles of their clothing, in which they try to capture it. Eventually the evil

sisters, naked and tired from chasing the butterfly, lie down to sleep. Paiyatemu removes his disguise and he and his sisters return home. Paiyatemu plays his flute, and at each note one of the evil sisters comes forth as a small zigzag-flying butterfly comdemned to craziness (corresponding with nymphomania), that is, flying without direction. He sends the butterflies to the four directions to call for rain.

One version of this story is rendered as the origin story of the Newekwe Society, a society of clowns (see *Clowns and Clowning Societies)*. In this story, as the girls are sleeping, *Coyote* comes along and has sexual intercourse with them. He plucks hair from his mustache and "plants it like corn" between their legs (thus accounting for the origin of pubic hair). When the girls awaken, they are ashamed of their nakedness, and a Newekwe uses cornhusks to provide embroidered white blankets for them.

As a *kachina* Paiyatemu, the patron of music and flowers, appears playing a flute to accompany songs sung for vegetation and the return of warm weather. See also *Flood Subsided by Sacrifice*. [Benedict 1935; Bunzel 1933; Handy 1918]

Paiyuk
Ute, *Great Basin*

Water elk, *cannibal* animals that are mean and difficult to kill. *Shamans* who obtain some of their power from paiyuk are considered formidable. [Powell 1881]

Pakahk
Plains and Woods Cree, *Plains* and *Subarctic*

Skeletal *helping spirits* that give *hunting* and curing (see *Healing)* powers. Often associated with death (see Dead) and starvation, pakahk are believed to come from humans who starved to death. Pakahk are able to fly, and signal their arrival with a weird laugh. Each fall, pakahk are honored in a special gift-exchange dance known as the *Giveaway* Dance. The dance features their favorite food, bladders full of grease. [Bloomfield 1934]

Pakrokitat

Serrano, *California*

The name of the kind *creator* whose malevolent brother, *Kukitat,* emerges from his left shoulder. The two brothers are constantly battling with each other. Pakrokitat finally leaves the earth to his brother and goes to a world of his own, where people go after death (see *Dead).* [Kroeber 1948]

Palraiyuk

Eskimo, Alaska, *Arctic*

A type of *water monster* that lives in the marshes and creeks between the Yukon and Kuskokwim rivers. In the creation story, Raven travels with First Man and warns him not to drink out of certain streams and marshes lest he be grabbed and eaten by palraiyuk, who are waiting on the bank. Palraiyuk have two faces, two long tails with spiked backs, and three stomachs. Some Eskimos believe palraiyuk were more common in ancient times when the climate was much warmer; others think the monsters' decline is directly related to the coming of Western culture. Images of palraiyuk have been found at 2,000-year-old sites on St. Lawrence Island. [Tennant and Bitar 1981]

Palulukon

Hopi, *Southwest*

Water Snake, who appears in many stories and has close associations with water. He is the chief "pet" of *Cloud.* As huge serpents, two palulukon inhabit the sea upon which the world floats. Apparently these snakes await chances to cause earthquakes and turn the world over. Other stories tell of springs being transferred or drying up because of the movement or mistreatment of the palulukon, who are considered to be the source of all springs. A now extinct ceremony represented palulukon by means of a puppet covering a man's arm, which was extended through a hole in a screen. See also *Kolowisi.* [Bradfield 1973; Nequatewa 1936; Parsons 1925b; Stephen 1929, 1936; Titiev 1943]

Pana

Caribou Eskimo, *Arctic*

The Woman Up There. Pana lives in the sky and is responsible for keeping the souls of the *dead.* The sky is full of holes, and anything spilled in the sky comes down through the holes and reaches earth in the form of rain, snow, and hailstones. The dead are reborn in Pana's house and come back to earth, with the help of *Moon,* to live again as humans, animals, or fish. When the Moon is not visible at night it is because he is busy helping Pana bring souls back to earth.

Papago Ritual Cycle

Papago, *Southwest*

Papago rituals include the *wine feast,* the *salt pilgrimage,* ritual performances of rabbit and deer hunts, A?ada ("the sending," a rite often performed with other rituals intended to send away sicknesses), war rites, spring ceremonies, Wigita (a long and elaborate harvest ceremony), social dances, and girls' puberty rites. These public rituals are complemented by a number of Christian feasts, pilgrimages, and sacramental rites. Private rites include medicine and healing rituals (see *Mumkidag)* and the telling of the creation story, as well as Christian prayers and prayer vigils. [Underhill 1946; Underhill et al. 1979]

Pascola

Yaqui, *Southwest* and northwestern Mexico.

Masked dancers whose origins date from pre-Christian times. They *dance* at many Yaqui fiestas. The term pascola derives from the Yaqui word for fiesta (pahko), plus o?ola, which means "old man." Pascolas have long hair worn in a tuft on the top of the head. The mask, called pahko?ola mahka or kuta puhuba (wood face), is generally an adult male face carved in relief from cottonwood and painted black, with white or red decorations. A cross is always incised on the forehead or chin of the mask. The mask, barely large enough to cover the face, is held in place by a string running from each side to the back. It has a long beard of white horsehair, and eyebrows and

Yaqui Pascola Dancer arranging his cocoon rattle. He has placed the mask on the side of his head. Courtesy, Arizona State Museum, The University of Arizona, George Iacono, photographer.

tufts of hair at the upper cheek and sometimes across the top. When a pascola dancer is not dancing, the mask is worn on the side or the back of the head. The mask does not have *utea* (power) and is not to be feared (see *Masks and Masking)*. The dancer wears a cotton blanket wrapped around the waist, secured with a leather belt and bound around each knee. The torso is bare to the waist. A string of cocoon rattles is wound around each leg.

Many stories are told about the pascolas. A central theme is that the first pascola was the son of the *devil,* and that he was convinced to join the first fiesta created by God. He was given the opportunity to say whatever came into his head, provided he did not laugh or smile. Pascolas are often spoken of as clowns (see *Clowns and Clowning Societies)*. Although the pascolas most likely predate Christian influence and remain strongly associated with *Yoania,* most stories about them have strong Christian elements. At fiesta, pascolas dance solo to the accompaniment of musicians us-

Pascola mask.
Courtesy, Smithsonian Institution
(neg.#82-721).

ing both European and aboriginal instruments. See also *Deer Dancers, Seataka,* and *Yaqui Easter Ceremony.* [Griffith 1972; Painter 1986]

Pattikus
Pawnee, *Plains*
The crier, an older man who announced village ceremonies and recited instructions for rituals.

Pautiwa
Zuni, *Southwest*
Chief of *Kachina Village* (kothluwala), and the most prestigious of all Zuni deities. He illustrates Zuni virtues of dignity, beauty, and leadership. Pautiwa is benevolent and concerned for the welfare of all humans and *kachinas.* He coordinates the Zuni ceremonial calendar and directs all kachina performances; however, he appears in Zuni on only three occasions, all during the Winter Solstice rituals (see *Zuni Ritual Cycle)*. As chief of Kachina Village, he receives all the spirits of the *dead.* It is Pautiwa to whom Zuni people turn when they are in trouble or need help. Pautiwa has a role in many Zuni stories. See also *Kokkookwe* and *Rain Priest.* [Wright 1985]

Pazimora
Kawaiisu, *Great Basin*
A type of moss whose name the Kawaiisu use to describe both Coyote's hair and the name of the mountain where *Coyote* died. Pazimora resembles a moss that hangs in white pine trees on mountains. The Kawaiisu believe that picking pazimora in the summer may cause rain, and that if pazimora is placed in water, sleet and freezing weather will follow. [Zigmond 1980]

Peace
To create peace with European-Americans, the Menominee did the *Dream Dance, Drum Dance. Edzo* is a peacemaker in Dogrib stories.

Pejuta wicasa
Lakota, *Plains*
Pejuta means "medicine"; wicasa is "person." Medicine person, responsible for all the medicine

Pautiwa Kachina Chief of Kachina Village (Zuni). Painting by Duane Dishta from the collection of The Heard Museum, Phoenix, Arizona.

ceremonies. *Medicine people* usually belong to a particular medicine society and are responsible for keeping the medicine bag, *ozuha pejuta,* stocked with the necessary healing herbs and roots. See also *Mato Okolakiciye,* the Bear Dreamer Society. [Walker 1982]

Pelintsiek
Yurok, *California*
Dentalium shell money, also known as Great Dentalium. The dentalia came to the people from the north, traveling on the Klamath River. Pelintsiek, also known as Dentalium Shell, decides to travel upriver. In the places where he stops, the valuable dentalium shell is found. [Kroeber 1948]

Pemmican
Lakota, *Plains*
A mixture of dried meat, cherries, and grapes formed into patties, providing a food source that stores well and is convenient for traveling. Pemmican can be eaten cooked or dried, shredded or whole. [Walker 1982]

Penis
Characters classified as *tricksters* are often portrayed as having gigantic penes and being sexually promiscuous. There are hundreds of stories about the sexual exploits of these figures. Examples: The penis of *Old Man Coyote* (Crow) is eaten by a woman who thinks it is a strawberry; *Tavwots,* the Ute rabbit character, shatters the sun by throwing his penis at it. The sexual exploits of *Coyote* are widely told, as is the Kawaiisu story *Penis Baby.*

Penis Baby
Kawaiisu, *Great Basin*
Coyote disguises himself as a young woman with a baby, which is actually his penis, in order to get close to five young women who are Canadian geese. The young women make a fuss over Coyote's "baby," holding it and pinching it. Coyote has intercourse with all five women and they become pregnant. The babies are born while Coyote is hunting, and the mothers bake the babies and disappear into the sky. When Coyote returns, he eats the baked babies, not knowing they are his offspring. Afterward he goes to a pond to quench his thirst. As he drinks, he sees the reflection of the five Canadian geese women. He pleads with them to bring him up to the sky. The women link their feathers together, forming a chain to bring Coyote up, but halfway up they drop him. Coyote falls to the ground and is killed. [Zigmond 1980]

Pestilence
In a Haida story, *Wultcixaiya,* the son of Moon, prevents his sister from marrying Pestilence.

Peyote Religion
See *Native American Church.*

Pickwelaneokan
Delaware, *Northeast*
Nighthawk Dance. Pickwelaneokan is performed on the tenth and last night of the midwinter *Bear Ceremony,* as well as at the *Green Corn Dance* performed by the Delaware who shared land with the Grand River Iroquois. It is a *dance* of *thanksgiving* as well as a petition for health. Two to four young men, stripped to the waist, face the singer in a line. Each dancer carries a rattle in his right hand and the extended wing of a nighthawk in his left. They lunge and jump toward the singer, rippling their back muscles like hawks. In between songs, speeches are given and cornmeal cakes exchanged. [Speck 1931]

Pikagoyu
Kawaiisu, *Great Basin*
"Baldhead." Coyote's companion, a small dirtbug with a bald head. Pikagoyu becomes concerned when the first people on earth keep eating dirt because there is nothing else to eat; they are making big holes all over the earth. The people never die; when they grow old, they rejuvenate themselves by bathing and combing their hair. Pikagoyu complains to *Coyote,* and they decide that people should die so there will be enough

room on the earth. Coyote is the first to die, but then he comes back to life. His daughters beat him and stick a knife into him. Thinking he is mortally wounded, they leave him in a cave to die, but the worms in the cave revive Coyote by beating him with a stick. See also *Dead*. [Zigmond 1980]

Piki
Hopi, *Southwest*
Waferbread made of blue cornmeal. A delicacy made especially in preparation for *kachina* dances and weddings. [Bradfield 1973]

Pikavahairak
Karok, *California*
The name for the time before humans. The Ikxareyavs (the Native Americans who lived in Karok country before the Karok came) lived during this time. The Ikxareyavs now exist as animals such as coyote, lizard, long snake, spring salmon, and redfish; birds such as bluejay; and as plants, rocks, and ceremonies among the Karok. [Voegelin 1940]

Pilgrimage
See *Salt Pilgrimage*.

Pinanne
Zuni, *Southwest*
Literally *"wind,"* "spirit of dead" lodged in breath and ultimately in heart. A person's pinanne remains with the living four nights after death. On the morning of the fifth day, the door of the *dead* person's house is left open so the spirit can leave for good. The pinanne may make itself known through odd and unexplained sounds and happenings or in *dreams*. [Tedlock 1975]

Pine Root and Beaded Head
Cree, *Subarctic*
The first two beings on earth. They perform extraordinary feats of spiritual power and prepare for the coming of humans. When they finish their stay

on earth, Pine Root and Beaded Head are transformed into stars and plants. [Bloomfield 1930]

Pinessi
Ojibwa, Cree, *Northeast, Subarctic*
Thunderer, a visitor to the *shaking tent* and a spirit helper who appears as a peacock. He has to remain outside the shaking tent because his tremendous power might cause the lodge to break apart. Pinessi is associated with success in *war* and with *medicine*. [Preston 1975]

Pipe(s)
Also known as the Calumet (from the French word for reed pipe). A ritual object widely used in many contemporary Native American and pan-Indian religious activities. Archaeological evidence indicates that pipes have been used in North America for 4,000 years. The earliest recorded use of the pipe was in eastern Canada in 1575. Pipes were used to welcome seventeenth-century missionaries in eastern North America. The Lakota (Plains) introduced the pipe to many tribes in the 1870s. The ritual use of the pipe, particularly as a separate rite, has increased in nativistic as well as in pan-Indian movements.

A variety of stories recount the origin of the pipe. Some pipes were given during creation; others were given specifically for healing. For example, the pipe is found in the creation stories of the Ojibwa, Iowa, and Blackfoot, with special relationships to clan animals. Among the Blackfoot, Bear gave its skin for the wrapping of the medicine pipe. *White Buffalo Maiden* gave the Bison Calf Pipe to the Lakota (Plains). See also *Wohpe*.

Because pipes are powerful in and of themselves, they are kept and cared for by individuals (men and women known as Pipe Carriers) who have been chosen and initiated to be the keepers of a pipe. The pipe stem and bowl are usually kept separate and joined only for use in specific ritual events.

Among the most distinctive pipes are those with a bowl carved in the image of one's *guardian spirit*. In a powerful experience, the smoker looks down the pipe stem into the face of the guardian, as smoke and breath circulate through the guardian and the lungs of the smoker (see *Soulbieche,* an Alabama spirit being to whom the pipe is offered). Many pipes are made of Catlinite, the carvable pipestone. The Omaha *Ninba jide* is an example.

Pipes are used in a variety of ritual settings. Pipe ceremonies are used for healing, to promote intertribal relations, and for blessing in the subarctic, Plains, Iroquoian, Pacific coast, and southwest tribes. A pipe ceremony in which the pipe is offered to the four directions and smoked by all present opens many public and ceremonial occasions throughout the Plains. In Natchez opening ceremonies, the pipe is offered to the sun *(Uwashil).* The pipe is used in the widely practiced *Sun Dance* (see the Oglala *Hunka Lowanpi).* The Omaha feasting societies smoke the pipe. Plains tribes smoked the pipe in preparation for buffalo hunting *(Wani-sapa)* and in ceremonies to count coup (see the Blackfoot *Kanochisisin).* The Seneca smoke *magic herbs* for protection. The Kutenai story of *Bear Parent* explains that the pipe stem represents prayers. [Dorsey 1906b; Finger 1980; Matthews 1976; Murie 1989; Neihardt 1932; Walker 1982]

Pipe Stick Ceremony
Pawnee, *Plains*
The pipe stem used in this ceremony is given to a young man by a *water monster* who is also a medicine man. Stories tell about a young man who has wonderful dreams about a large body of water. After several days he journeys northeast to the water. There he meets a water monster whose breath draws him into the water, where he sees all types of animals. The water monster, who controls all the animal beings in the water, shows the young man the animal medicine lodge. He tells him to go home and remain alone in his lodge while he constructs an image of the water monster. These preparations will make it possible for the water monster to enter the young man's dreams in order to reveal songs and powers. The

Pipe Stick Ceremony teaches the young man how to prevent lightning strikes during thunderstorms, as well as how to invite dreams and decorate children for protection against malevolent powers. [Murie 1989]

Piplats
Nez Perce, *Plains*
Red Willow, a maiden who is supposed to marry a young man. Before her marriage she goes alone to vision-quest. Her fiance follows and kills her by shooting her with an arrow. As he starts to leave, he sees that the arrow is glowing bright red with Piplats's blood. He attempts to hide the arrow, but cannot find a place where the blood will stop glowing. Finally he throws it into a patch of willows and the red glow stops. He returns home and begins to grieve, certain no one will suspect him of the murder. Piplats's parents search for her and find her body, but are unable to find the arrow that killed her. They take Piplats home and bury her. Meanwhile, her blood causes the willow in the patch where the arrow was thrown to turn red, accounting for the color of red willow. [Phinny 1969]

Pisigsordleq
Eskimo, western Arctic, Alaska, *Arctic*
"Archer." A great *hunter* who always provides well for his wife and two children. One autumn Pisigsordleq kills a mother *bear* and her two cubs, carefully skinning them so that the skins are whole with noses and claws intact. During the year the bear meat keeps the family well fed. The following winter Pisigsordleq becomes ill. When he dies, his grieving wife honors his request that his bow and arrow be placed in his grave. The next spring, as Pisigsordleq's children are playing, a bird comes up and sings to them, saying that their father is in a faraway land, married to the beautiful daughter of a chief.

When the children tell their mother what they have heard, she becomes furious. She dresses herself and the children in the bearskins left by her husband and sings songs that transform them into brown bears. They travel to the distant village, where they find Pisigsordleq living with his new wife. The mother lowers her bearskin to reveal her identity. Astonished, Pisigsordleq tries to make peace with her, but she transforms back into a bear and tears him to pieces. Then she and the two bear children run into the forest and disappear. This is the reason there is such distrust between bears and humans. [Norman 1990]

Pitch

The Huron tell a tar baby story in which the character Pitch *(Sanopi)* taunts Coyote.

Pitch People

The Haida refer to uncultured people who have no family crest as Pitch People *(Qaslanas).*

Placenta

The Pawnee tell a story of *Long Tooth Boy,* who was born from his brother's placenta.

Plants, Origin of

Many stories describe the origin of plants. Cahuilla say that plants come from the burned body of the creator *Mukat.* See also *Corn.*

Plaza Dances

Hopi, *Southwest*

Public *kachina* dances performed in village plazas during the spring and summer months, culminating a longer series of secret or private rites. These events are sponsored to celebrate a special event and include feasting and socializing, as well as dances that both entertain and enact Hopi religion. The *dances* are unquestionably religious in character, presenting kachinas and emphasizing fertility, rain, health, and life. These dances are either mixed dances, where each dancer presents a different type of kachina, or line dances, where all the dancers present the same kachina. Clowns (see *Clowns and Clowning Societies)* often perform during the dances, especially in the intervals between kachina dance sets. See also *Hopi Ritual Cycle, Niman,* and *Tsuku.* [Wright 1973]

Pleasurable Sexual Intercourse

Kawaiisu, *Great Basin*

Coyote captures a woman and experiments with having sexual intercourse with her, but the experience is not pleasurable because it is too brief. He decides women should have their vaginas on the edge of their right hands between the thumb and forefinger, but he ejaculates before he can penetrate the vagina because it is so powerful in that position. He tries putting the vagina in its present anatomical position and leaves it there because intercourse lasts longer and is more pleasurable. See also *Vagina Dentata.* [Zigmond 1980]

Pleiades

Except for Ursa Major, the *Big Dipper,* this constellation appears most frequently in Native American stories. The Arapaho story of *Foot-Stuck-Child* tells the origin of the Pleiades. The Pleiades appears on the forehead of the Navajo figure Black God (see *Navajo Starlore).*

Poison

Choctaw, *Southeast*

According to the Choctaw, snakes and insects originally had no poisonous bites or stings. Their poisonous bites are attributed to a vine growing on the edge of the bayous, which appeared as a kind but extremely poisonous person. When the Choctaw bathed and swam in the bayous, the vine's poison killed them. Seeing this, the vine felt terrible. Deciding to get rid of his poison, he gave it to the chiefs of the snakes, bees, and wasps. See also *Akhrendoiaen,* a drink consumed by Huron dancers in a healing rite; and *Otgon,* an Iroquois term designating malevolent power. [Hudson 1976]

Poke

Eskimo, Bering Sea coast, Alaska, *Arctic*

A seal's *bladder,* dried and inflated for use as a storage container for oiled fish. [Riordan 1983]

Pokmis
Nootka, *Northwest Coast*
People who become wild because of cold and exposure from being in the woods or out in a canoe, or from being in water for a long time. When rescued and kept in isolation under constant attention, most pokmis gradually recover. [Sapir and Swadesh 1939]

Polar Bear Snout
Eskimo, northern Alaska, *Arctic*
A charm (aannuaq) that can be used only by the most powerful *shaman.* The *helping spirit* (tuunnuaq) of the shaman comes from the *bear* itself. In order to be worthy of this charm, a shaman must travel to the sea and personally confront the bear. All other charms, apart from bird charms such as peregrines, come from land animals, including brown bears, squirrels, and wolves. [Murdoch 1887; Norman 1990]

Police Societies
Plains cultures have police societies, such as the Lakota *Akicitas* and the Omaha *Wanace.*

Pollen
Navajo, *Southwest*
See *Tadidiin.*

Poor Boy
Pawnee, *Plains*
A figure to whom the *Loon Medicine Ceremony* is given.

Porcupine
A character often presented as a companion of Coyote or Beaver. The Micmac associate Porcupine with cold weather and believe he controls it. Beaver abandons Porcupine in the middle of a lake. Porcupine sings, and as he does so the water freezes and he is able to walk to shore. Plains tribes tell several versions of stories about Coyote and Porcupine killing buffalo, and Coyote cheating Porcupine out of his share of the meat. Porcupine gets even with Coyote by killing Coy-

ote's children and family members. See also *Anog Ite,* the Lakota figure who teaches quilling; and *Painted-Porcupine* (Arapaho), the porcupine animal character who is the source of quills. [Fisher 1946]

Posketa
A term for the *Green Corn Dance.*

Possession
Godzadowi is the Seneca term for possession.

Potlatch(es)
Northwest Coast
On special occasions—the attainment of chieftainship, the beginning of the ceremonial season *(Tsetseka),* the honoring of the dead—a huge feast and *giveaway* is held, accompanied by dramatic masked dancing. Apparently the hosts of the feast and giveaway obtain power and status in proportion to how much they give away. The most complex Haida potlatch *(Gia is su)* is the *Walal Potlatch,* given when someone becomes chief or when a child is adopted. The Nootka distinguish between *Nucil,* a potlatch, and *Litsu,* a feast. The *Great-Favorite* is a women's dance performed at Nootka potlatches. *Sisaok,* members of the Bella Coola dance society, are initiated during potlatch. *Tiotlbax* is the Puyallup term meaning wealth and generosity, as displayed in hosting a potlatch. [Blackman 1977; Clutesi 1969; Kan 1983, 1989]

Powamu
Hopi, *Southwest*
An annual complex of ritual events performed early in February and concerned centrally with the promotion of fertility for the coming season of growth; it also serves as a background for the initiation of children (see *Kachina Cult Initiation*). It is commonly known in English as the Bean Dance, because beans are planted in flats and kept warm in heated kivas to promote premature growth. The height of the bean sprouts presages the success of the coming agricultural

season. The public portion of this ritual complex is the parade of many distinct kachinas, who move from kiva to kiva in repeated circuits around the village. See also *Hopi Ritual Cycle; Muyinwa,* who is responsible for rain and growth, and appears at Powamu; and *Soyoko,* a ritualized frightening of children. [Voth 1901; Wright 1973]

Powatakan
Cree, Ojibwa, *Northeast, Subarctic*
Dream visitors who enter into long-lasting relationships with human beings. The powatakan come in dreams to give humans information, hunting help, and protection. Humans who receive such help are responsible for honoring the powatakan with tobacco and obedience. The relationship, which is one of mutual care and respect, is uncertain because of the unpredictability of the powatakan. Powatakan are important in the *shaking tent* ritual and often involved in conversations with *Mistapew,* the host of shaking tent performances. It is thought that people can have the powatakan for their entire lives as long as they believe in it. The more a person uses the powatakan, the more it does. See also *Oh-gee-nay,* the disease caused by wrongdoing. [Flannery, Chambers, and Jehle 1981]

Power
It might be said that Native American religions can be understood in terms of power. To know stories, prayers, and songs; to practice ritual; to have visions and dreams; to be able to call upon guardian spirits and helping spirits—these things mean power; they allow one to live a meaningful life. In the most general terms, power is denoted by the English term *medicine.*

In more tribally specific terms, power is called *Aliil* by the Navajo; *Baaxpee* by the Abenaki; *Inkoze* (the power of dreams) by the Chippewa; *Keskamsit* (the power of lucky objects) by the Maliseet; *Kyakyauna* by the Hopi; *Orenda* (or if malevolent, *Otgon)* by the Iroquois; *Syowoe* (the power to see) by the Nooksak; *Tonwan* and *Wakan* by the Lakota; *Utea* (ancient power) and *Seataka* (personal gift) by the Yaqui; and *Xoexoe* by the Nooksak. The Puyallup have a rich vocabulary of power terms, including *Astcatstudab* (secret power), *Ayaxaus* (malevolent power), *Sqalalitut* (a supernatural power), *Tiotlbax* (the power of wealth), *Tudab* (the most desired of powers), and *Xwaixwieda* (the power associated with birds, animals, and fish). The Puyallup consider the power of *Snake* useless because it makes the owner dislike others.

Osimc is the Nootka process of procuring power for hunting. A discussion of healing power appears in the Pawnee story of *Bear Medicine Woman.* Other aspects of the Pawnee conception of power are revealed in the stories of *Coming-Sun,* a powerful hunter, and *Long Tooth Boy.* The Tsimshian attribute the source of shamanic power to *Gutginsa. Hawichyepam Maapuch* (Chemehuevi) is Old Woman power. The spirit *Kwanokasha* puts Choctaw children to tests. If they pass these tests, they grow up with power. See also *Manitou.* [Elmendorf 1977]

Power-of-the-Shining-Heavens
Haida, *Northwest Coast*
A *guardian spirit* who lives on top of the sky, which is understood to be in the form of an inverted bowl. This spirit decides when people will die. When people are afraid, they appeal to Power-of-the-Shining-Heavens for protection. [Swanton 1905b]

Powwow
A social and religious dance occasion, often including representatives of several cultures. Although similar events have likely been conducted whenever peoples came together for discussion, treaty, or trade, the powwow has taken on special significance in recent decades. Powwows are often performed in cities with large concentrations of Native Americans representing many tribes. In such urban settings, the powwow is one of the most distinctively cultural events practiced by these people.

The contemporary powwow features dance contests, group dances, and *giveaways.* The dancing is performed to the accompaniment of groups (called "drums") of singers, who sit around a large drum on which they beat out the rhythms. Prayers are offered for many things. Powwows often have a distinctive tone of American patriotism, including the use of the American flag in costume and decoration. See also *Omiigiwen,* the Ojibwa drum religion.

Prayer and Prayersticks

The occasions and methods of prayer are numerous in native North America. A song, a dance, or a gesture may be considered a prayer. The strewing of cornmeal or pollen (see, for example, Navajo *Tadidiin)* is a common prayer. Some spoken prayers, as in Navajo healing ceremonials, may take hours to recite and must be done perfectly (see *Navajo Ritual Process).* Navajos also consider the creation of the present Navajo world to have been an act of prayer (see *Blessingway).*

Prayersticks are objects prepared, decorated, and often associated with symbolic offerings. Their purpose is to carry one's prayer to its intended recipient. Prayersticks may be decorated hollow reeds of varying lengths, stuffed with feathers, bits of semiprecious jewels, and pollens (see also Navajo *Keetaan* and Hopi *Paho).*

Prayer feathers, associated with *cloud,* are downy or full-sized feathers, usually attached to a cotton string. A *rainbow* may be considered the road to the spiritual world: a road of prayer. In the Hopi *Snake Dance,* snakes are danced with and then released to deliver prayers. In the Piegan *Black-Tailed Deer Dance,* prayers are said for a sick person. The Kutenai have a method of separating sincere prayers from insincere ones (see *Bear Parent). Chiwakiia* is the Crow term for prayer.

For uses of prayersticks, see also *Incest Causes Flood* (Zuni story), *Acoma Emergence and Migration, Corn Maidens* (Zuni story), *Flood Subsided by Sacrifice* (Zuni story), *Iatiku* (Keresan female creator), *Kiaklo* (Zuni kachina), *Kyakyauna* (Hopi power), *Shalako* (Zuni ritual), *Tih-kuyi-*

wuhti (the mother of game animals, to whom a prayerstick is offered prior to a hunt), and *Zuni Emergence.*

Prophecy

Many Native American mythologies, especially in the southwestern United States, include prophecies. These may once have told of the coming of Europeans or other significant events. Today many develop an apocalyptic theme, correlating imminent doom with various events in recent history such as the explosion of nuclear weapons, the building of large cities, airplane flight, or space travel.

The Jicarilla Apache believe that once this world becomes uninhabitable they will ascend to a third place above the present world. This will be a repeat of the emergence onto this world (see *Apache Creation and Emergence).* They hold that this will happen two times, with the world being destroyed once by water and once by fire. The materials from which the new worlds will be created are being kept covered by a mountain under the protection of *White Painted Woman.* The old people know which mountain this is and what it is called. [Opler 1938b]

Prophet

The history of Native American religions includes a number of prophets who, upon receiving visions, initiated *crisis cults* or *millenarian movements.* Among the best-known are Neolin (Delaware); *Kanakuk* (Kickapoo); *Tenskwatawa* (Shawnee); Wovoka (Paiute), who inspired the *Ghost Dance of 1890;* and *Smohalla* (Sahaptin).

Prophet Dance Movement
Great Basin

Early-nineteenth-century religious movement that taught that the world was coming to an end and that the *dead* would return. These impending events were to be signaled by earthquakes, volcanoes, and falling stars. The movement was advanced by prophets who claimed to have talked directly with the Christian God (see *Christianity)* or to have recently returned from the dead with specific messages. By the 1820s Christian biblical teachings had been integrated into its philosophy. During the mid-1830s, the Christianized elements of living a religious life merged with advocacy of strict rules concerning native dress and lifestyle. These were thought to ensure one's participation in the "final coming." See also *Millenarian Movements* and *Smohalla Cult*. [Beckham, Toepel, and Minor 1984]

Prostitutionway
Navajo, *Southwest*
A perhaps inappropriate rendering of *Ajilee*.

Pubic Hair
Zuni, *Southwest*
For a story of the origin of pubic hair, see *Paiyatemu*.

Pueblo Emergence and Migration
Pueblo, *Southwest*
Consistent among the origin stories of all Pueblo cultures is the idea of *emergence,* with little if any regard for the creation of the world. Origin stories usually begin with the world already in existence, the people living in worlds below this one. They emerge, often led by heroic figures, onto this world and begin journeys *(migrations)* to the south or east in search of suitable homes. Numerous times the people stop and settle, but quarrels or misfortune force them to move on until they find their final location, the place they are now living. Through this simple framework are woven many other stories and incidents that give each Pueblo culture its distinctiveness. Despite their simple outline, most emergence and migration narratives are long and complex. See also *Masau?u* and *Sipofene*. [Parsons 1930a]

Pueblos Superior to Navajos
Cochiti, *Southwest*
Soon after creation, the mother of the Navajos challenges the mother of the Pueblos to a contest. Being taller, the mother of the Navajos proclaims that whomever the sun strikes first wins. The children of the winner will be valuable, while those of the loser will be worthless. The mothers stand side by side awaiting sunrise. As the sun rises, it falls first on the hair of the mother of the Pueblos and continues to shine more on her than on the mother of the Navajos. Although the mother of the Navajos cannot understand why she is in shadow, she accepts the plight of her people. She turns into a large wood rat and runs into a crevice. Pueblo people tell this story as the basis for what they consider to be their superiority to Navajo people, not only in war but in all areas of life. Sometimes this story is told featuring a contest between "Indians" and "Whites." [Benedict 1931]

Pukjinskwes
Maliseet-Passamaquoddy, *Northeast*
A *witch* capable of appearing as either a man or woman. In some stories, she is a female black cat who attempts to trick a local chief named Pogumk. But Pogumk is really *Glooscap,* the culture hero, and he outsmarts Pukjinskwes with the help of Sable. Because of her dislike for humans, Pukjinskwes decides to transform herself (see *Transformation)* into a *mosquito*. All the mosquitoes are her offspring. [Prince 1921]

Pulekukwerek
Yurok, *California*
"Downstream Sharp." A much-admired *culture hero* born in the far north. Pulekukwerek's many adventures include killing *monsters* and *cannibal* women. He is also credited with bringing starlight (see *Stars and Starlore)* to dark nights by stealing the boy, Night, and then finding a man who weaves the sky and places the stars. Pulekukwerek disappears from earth and goes to a land far away where there is constant dancing. [Kroeber 1948]

Puppets
Native Americans have sometimes used puppets to dramatize storytelling. This practice took on grand proportions in the *Inviting-In Feasts* of the

Bearing Sea coast in Alaska. The Hopi also occasionally use puppets in *Night Dances*. [Geertz and Lomatuway'ma 1987]

Puuciigiigibi
Kawaiisu, *Great Basin*
Puucii—meaning "star" (see *Stars and Starlore)*, the name of a bird that acts as a weather *shaman*. In story traditions Puuciigiigibi is asked to bring snow and does. This bird is identified alternatively as a titmouse and a pinyon jay, both species found in the area. [Zigmond 1980]

Puwo-win
Micmac, *Northeast*
A man or woman, sometimes called a *witch*, who holds an assortment of powers including spells, potions, and the abilities to predict the future, walk on water, protect individuals or communities from malevolence, and cause harm or illness in others. [Fisher 1946]

Pyuykonhoya
Hopi, *Southwest*
The elder of two brothers who are war deities. The younger brother is Palunhoya. A story of the Sun-Eagle clan grouping tells of the journey of these twins to their father, *Sun,* and how they are able to slay Kwatoko, a giant bird. Pyuykonhoya is associated with the male initiation rites, *Wuwutcim.* See also *Ahayuta, Masewa and Uyuyewa, Monster Slayer and Born for Water,* and *Twins' Journey to Sun Father.* [Stephen 1929]

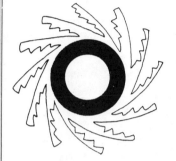

Qahopi

Hopi, *Southwest*

The word "hopi," when used as an adjective, means good, well-behaved, peaceable. The term qahopi means un-Hopi, that is, bad, mischievous, bold. [Bradfield 1973]

Qanekelak

Bella Bella, *Northwest Coast*

The *killer whale* who lives when the earth is nothing but water and ice. Qanekelak's upper body is human, but his lower body is that of a whale. One day he passes his hands over his entire body and becomes human (see *Animal-Human Transformation*). Qanekelak is the ancestor of the Killer Whale clan. He creates the *dog* and gives it to all the people. He also travels about giving names to all the animals and people. [Boas 1916]

Qasgiq (alt. kasgig)

Eskimo, Bering Sea coast, Alaska, *Arctic*

Written as "kashim" in the early literature. Traditionally, a large half-underground building used for most public ceremonies and games. It had a dual-tunnel entrance that opened in the middle of the floor. Light and ventilation came from a single window in the roof with a removable gutskin cover. Eskimo men and boys ate, slept, worked, and bathed in this communal building, where each man had his own place. Choice seats in the back corner beside the seal-oil lamp were usually reserved for the elderly men. The communal qasgiq is no longer built in Alaska. [Murdoch 1887; Nelson 1899]

Qaslanas

Haida, *Northwest Coast*

The Pitch People, looked upon as uncultured because they did not have any *crests* such as Raven, Eagle, Sea Lion, or Beaver. [Swanton 1905b]

Qaxdascidi

Tanaina, *Subarctic*

A malevolent being (see *Malevolent Creatures*), known by the mysterious noise it makes. [Norman 1990]

Qiqirn

Eskimo, Baffinland, central Canada, western Hudson Bay, *Arctic*

A mythological creature that looks like a giant *dog* but is hairless except for its mouth, feet, ears, and the tip of its tail. The Qiqirn is greatly feared because proximity to it causes seizures in humans and dogs. Nonetheless, the Qiqirn is terrified of humans and runs away the minute it hears one. [Boas 1888a]

Qisaruatsiaq
Eskimo, eastern Hudson Bay, *Arctic*

An old woman who transforms into a wolf (see *Human-Animal Transformation*). Qisaruatsiaq refuses her two sons' offers to care for her, preferring to live alone in the snowhouse she built herself. She keeps herself alive with fish, some of which she steals. One day she does not return from her fishing spot. One of her sons follows her tracks, which lead to the interior of the tundra. At dusk, he sees that one of her tracks has become a wolf track. [Nungak and Arima 1988]

Qolqalg Odai
Haida, *Northwest Coast*

Moldy-Forehead, a boy taken by two beings in a canoe to meet Half-Rock Woman. Half-Rock Woman teaches Qolqalg Odai the taboos pertaining to catching and eating *salmon*. When Moldy-Forehead returns to his people, his mother mistakes him for a grounded salmon and clubs him to death. The village holds a four-night wake. By the fourth night, Moldy-Forehead's salmon skin has been washed away by the rain, which is how a person who has almost been turned into an animal conventionally recovers human senses.

Qolqalg Odai becomes a shaman. The next spring he breaks a taboo and spears a salmon. The salmon dies, but so does Moldy-Forehead, because the salmon is his soul. The villagers sit Moldy-Forehead's body up and beat his drum, sing, and dance before him for four nights. Following the directions he has left, they lower his body into a pool where fresh and salt water mingle. Since that time, whenever a drum is heard in the deep pool, salmon are plentiful. [Swanton 1905b]

Qoluncotun,
Okanagon, Salish, *Plateau*

The *creator* of the universe and all the animals in it. Since the advent of *Christianity* the term refers to the Christian God. [Smith 1940]

Qisaruatsiaq, having become a wolf, eating her remaining boot. This sculpture illustrates a moment in an Eskimo story. Courtesy, Canadian Museum of Civilization (neg.#J 8637).

Quawteaht
Nootka, *Northwest Coast*

The first person, the *creator* of the earth and all the animals. Missing fire, Quawteaht meets with all the animals. They decide to go and search for fire, which they find at the house of Tee-thoop, the octopus, who lives both on land and sea. Mow-ach, the deer, steals the fire and carries it away in the joint of his leg. In another story, Quawteaht kills himself. He lies rotting on the ground until a helping spirit comes and rids his corpse of the vermin crawling over it, putting the vermin in a box and reviving Quawteaht. Eventually the helping spirit marries Quawteaht and they have a son, who becomes the forefather of all the Nootka people (see *Humans, Origin of*). [Sapir and Swadesh 1939]

Qudlivun (Qudliparmuit)
Eskimo, Baffinland, central Canada, western Hudson Bay, *Arctic*
A spirit land referred to in stories, where the dead are well fed and play games (see *Dead, Land of*). People who have shared food, suffered starvation, been murdered, died in childbirth, or committed suicide go to Qudlivun. [Boas 1888a]

Quilling
Arapaho, Lakota, Blackfoot, *Plains*
A technical art requiring dexterity, used to decorate clothing, shields, tipis, and utilitarian items. Porcupine quills (see also *Painted-Porcupine*) are gathered, dyed, and softened by being held in the mouth. Quilling is used to decorate buffalo robes worn for dress and special occasions. Quill designs on robes often designate the age and sex of the wearer.

Among the Arapaho, when a person is ill, sees a bad vision, or has an intuition of trouble, a friend may vow to make and quill for him or her a shirt, moccasins, buffalo robe, and leggings. Making these items also brings purity, strength, health, and prosperity to the quiller. A pregnant woman may vow to do tipi designs with quills in order to ensure an easy delivery. See also *Owner-of-Bag*.

According to the Oglala, Double Woman *(Anog Ite)* is the originator of quilling. The Arapaho attribute quilling's origin to *Nayaanxtisei*. See also *Gender Crossing*. [Dorsey and Kroeber 1903]

Quiyoughcosuck
Virginia Algonquians, *Northeast*
The term used for both priests (ritual leaders) and *helping spirits*. Their malevolent counterparts were called tagkanysough. [Hudson 1976]

Qumuʔuc
Ute, *Great Basin*
Hot rock *medicine* owned by *Bear* that gives him strength. Bear hides the qumuʔuc in the hollow of a tree, and dances and sings around it. In one story Bear has been killing people in the village of *Sunawavi* (Wolf), the culture hero. Chief Sunawavi directs some men to follow Bear, find out where the qumuʔuc is hidden, and throw water on it. When they do, the qumuʔuc turns black. Then the villagers invite Bear to a dance and tell him to sing a song. Bear asks his medicine for help, expecting it to give him a song to sing and the power to kill. But the qumuʔuc has been extinguished and nothing happens, so the people beat Bear over the head and disable him. [Lowie 1924]

R

Ra hikucu
Pawnee, *Plains*
The *warrior* assistant who made sure the chief's decisions were carried out. He also kept order in the village and helped prepare for ceremonies.

Rabbit

A common character in Native American mythology, most grandly as Hare or Great Hare *Winabojo*. Rabbit also appears very commonly as a *trickster* and culture hero; for example, see *Missapos* (Ojibwa), and *Tavwots* (Ute), who fights Sun. [Dorsey 1879, 1880]

Rabbit Dance
Menominee, *Northeast;* Creek, Yuchi, Seminole, *Southeast* and Oklahoma

A humorous circular *dance* in which men and women imitate crouching, hopping rabbits while putting food in their mouths. The Rabbit Dance is performed as part of the *Green Corn Dance*. Originally it may have been done to cheer up certain little spirits who specifically wait for food at feasts. [Hudson 1976]

Rabbit's Thin Skin
Kathlamet, *Northwest Coast*

Rabbit, the child of Deer, collects sticks while his mother gathers roots and berries. Rabbit ties the sticks together to look like people and puts them in his canoe. Then he sends the canoe down the river to a town to make the people think a war party is coming. The village people run away, and Rabbit steals all the salmon in the village. Despite his mother's warning, he repeats this deception several times. The fifth time, the village people catch and kill him, skinning him and throwing his body into the water. His mother finds his body and resuscitates him. Because he is cold, he returns to the village to ask for his blanket, that is, his skin. The people are afraid of him because he has come back to life. They offer him a variety of skins, but he accepts only what is left of his own skin, which he stretches to fit him. This explains why Rabbit's skin is so thin. [Boas 1901b]

Raccoon
Raccoon is a fascinating character who appears frequently in Native American mythology. He has many characteristics that identify him as a *trickster*. In a Kathlamet

story Raccoon, who lives with his grandmother, eats all her stored acorns. Crow tattles on him, and the grandmother hits Raccoon in the face with a fire poker (which explains the distinctive markings on Raccoon's face). Raccoon flees up a tree for safety. His grandmother asks him to throw fruit down to her, but instead he throws thorns in her mouth. She grows wings, turns into a bird, and flies away. Raccoon then visits Grizzly Bear and tells him that somebody painted his face so he would be pretty. Grizzly Bear asks Raccoon to paint his face too, but instead Raccoon pours pitch over Grizzly Bear's face. Raccoon escapes and hides in Coyote's fireplace. When Grizzly Bear comes to Coyote's house to look for Raccoon, Coyote and Raccoon trick him and eat him. Raccoon gathers fruits for Coyote, but Coyote becomes envious of Raccoon and kills him. For other stories about Raccoon, see *Azeban* (Abenaki), *Djoeaga* (Seneca), and an Achumawi story in which *Lightning* takes the form of Raccoon. [Dorsey 1884]

Rain

A false stereotypical image portrays Native American religions as consisting primarily of rain dances. Nonetheless, rain is a major concern of Native American religions, particularly in the southwestern United States. Although the purposes of their numerous dancing ceremonials are many and varied, Pueblo people will often say, if asked, "We dance for rain." A life-giving substance vital to southwestern desert survival, rain takes on dense and complex religious meanings in ritual and mythology. It often appears in a symbol complex associated with *cloud,* thunder, and lightning.

The presence of rain is often interpreted as the sign that migration journeys should cease and the travelers should settle, as in the *Acoma emergence and migration* stories and the Zuni migration stories. Although the Pima people (see *Tcu-unny-ikita*) are created last, they are distinguished by having the power to make rain. The powers of the various pairs of warrior twins in southwestern

cultures are enhanced by their ability to make rain (see *Ahayuta* and *Masewa and Uyuyewa).* The lightning weapons of these figures are associated with making rain. Other powerful figures are distinguished in terms of their ability to make rain (see the Hopi *Muyinwa* and Zuni Beast Gods, *Wemaawe)* or their association with rain, such as Spider Woman (Hopi *Kokyan wuhti),* whose web is like rain cloud. Many Pueblo ceremonial dances are associated with rain (see *Hopi Ritual Cycle, Tewa Ritual Cycle, Snake Dance,* and *Zuni Ritual Cycle),* as is the Navajo ceremonial *Blessingway.* The *Shiwanna* or Rain Makers are an important Pueblo religious society. See also *Onditachiae,* the Huron figure responsible for rain, and the Pawnee *Flint Man,* who has the power to bring rain, as well as *Flood Subsided by Sacrifice,* for an account of what happened when the Zuni rain priests made too much rain. [Underhill et al. 1979]

Rain Priest(s) (uwanammi or uwanam aasiwani)
Zuni, *Southwest*

Rain priests are associated with each of the six directions, that is, the four cardinal directions plus zenith and nadir. They live on the shores of oceans and in springs. They come to Zuni on the winds in the form of *clouds,* rainstorms, fog, and dew.

Pautiwa, chief of *kachinas,* summons people from Zuni to *Kachina Village* to gamble with the kachinas. They bring goods with them to stake on the game. The kachinas win, and the six men who lose are trapped under the floor. Realizing that anyone else who loses to the kachinas will become trapped also, the people send a young man, despised by all, to gamble with them. They consider his loss of no consequence. However, the despised young man has allied himself with *Spider Woman* by giving her an offering. He challenges the kachinas and, with Spider Woman's help, wins every time. At each loss, one of the kachinas drops beneath the floor. The kachinas soon stop gambling and pay in deer for their losses. They tell the people that the six men they have lost will remain at Kachina Village.

The people soon discover that mist and fog come from the place where the lost men sit. The men tell the people they have become Rain Priests. Whenever the people want anything they are to come and make prayer offerings, and the Rain Priests will help them. In accounting for the origin of the Rain Priests, this story explains why the men who personify the Rain Priests go on pilgrimage to the lake under which Kachina Village lies, and why people go to Kachina Village upon death (see *Dead).* [Tedlock 1979]

Rainbow(s)

Many stories tell of the origins and powers of rainbows. Algonquian tribes believe that a rainbow is formed from the vapors of a great unknown body of water in the sky. Some southeastern tribes believe a rainbow foretells dry weather because it stretches across the sky and catches the rain, preventing it from falling. For some southeastern tribes, a rainbow means a girl is menstruating for the first time or that something evil is about to happen. Stories from tribes in the western subarctic and along the Pacific northwest coast portray the rainbow as a bridge to another world. Among northern California tribes, children are cautioned not to count the colors of the rainbow because their fingers will become crooked and fall off. Walking through a rainbow will bring great healing powers to a medicine person. According to Shasta (northwestern California) stories, the Sun uses the colors of the rainbow to paint himself when he performs as a shaman.

The Navajo often associate rainbows (naatsiilid) with the bridge or the capability of moving between the human world and the world of the *diyin dine?e,* "the other side." The rainbow commonly carries heroes between these domains. In ritual, rainbows encircle and guard *sandpaintings,* with an opening on the east side. Such rainbows form the torso of an elongated figure with head and arms on one end and lower body on the other.

Short, straight rainbows also appear in sandpaintings, often at the feet of a figure, to indicate power of movement. Because rainbows designate the movement between human and other-than-human spheres, they are also inseparable from prayer (see *Prayer and Prayersticks).* See also *Shipap,* the Pueblo emergence place; *Kiaklo,* a Zuni kachina with a rainbow imprint on his cheek; *Whirling Logs' Sandpainting,* in which the Navajo hero travels between worlds on a rainbow; and the Navajo *Waterway,* where the rainbow bridges the sky. [Goddard 1933; Matthews 1887; Newcomb and Reichard 1937; Wheelwright 1942]

Rattle(s)

Percussion instruments carried in the hand or worn around the waist or leg, used in singing and dancing. Often rattles have special significance. The Hopi consider the rattle used by kachinas to be the heart. For other examples of the significance of rattles, see the Pawnee *Whistle Dance* and the Seminole rattles known as *Locv-saukv.*

Rattlesnake

A poisonous snake inhabiting large areas of North America. The rattlesnake appears widely in Native American mythology and ritual. According to the Pima story of creation, *Tcu-unnyikita,* Rattlesnake is reponsible for introducing death. The Seneca call the rattlesnake *Hagonsadji.* Hopis dance with rattlesnakes in their *Snake Dance.*

Rattlesnake-of-the-North
Okanagon, *Plateau*

A rattlesnake who lives in a house with his wife, Bow Snake, his many sons, and his brothers, Wasp and Bee. Rattlesnake-of-the-North has two sets of teeth, a new pair and an old pair. He keeps the new pair for himself and gives the old ones to his brothers. He tells them they can use the old teeth as their fangs; however, people they bite will not die but will only have pain and swelling. Rattlesnake-of-the-North will bite to kill, but promises he will never bite anyone who treats him with respect, and he will not bite anyone without first warning them with his rattle. Because Rattle-snake-of-the-North decides it is not right for a woman to be a killer, bow snakes are harmless. [Smith 1940]

Raven

Northwest Coast, Arctic

An important figure in a variety of story cycles. Raven is responsible for bringing light to the dark world, creating and transforming parts of the earth, teaching animals, and naming plants. He has an insatiable appetite for food and sex, is very deceptive, and cannot be trusted. In many stories he is a scapegoat who loses the conflicts he instigates. In Alaska, English-speaking Eskimos call Raven "Crow."

In a Tsimshian story about Raven, the parents of a dead boy invite all the animals to the wake they hold for their son. The boy's father, the chief, orders the corpse's intestines removed and burned. The next morning when the mother goes to mourn her son, she finds a young man, bright as firelight, where the corpse had been. The young man says he is the dead son come back to life, and the entire village rejoices. One day, while the young man is out walking, the chief discovers his son's corpse in the young man's room. Still, the chief continues to love his new son.

At first the young man eats very little, which concerns his parents. But after tasting scabs from the shinbones of two of the chief's slaves, he becomes ravenously hungry. He soon eats not only all his father's provisions, but everything in the village that is not hidden. The chief decides to send his son away before he consumes all the food. He gives the young man a stone to rest on, a blanket decorated with raven feathers, and a sea lion bladder filled with berries, telling him to scatter the berries so he will never be hungry. He also gives his son the name *Giant*.

Giant puts on his raven blanket and flies over the sea. He has trouble finding food because the world is still in darkness. When he realizes that light, which is sometimes described as a large piece of copper called ma, is locked away, he

disguises himself as Raven and steals it. When other animals refuse to share their food with him, he breaks the ma in a tantrum, and *light* comes to the world. At this, the frogs change Giant's name to Txamsem, i.e., Raven. This begins the adventures of Raven, who is credited with bringing daylight to the world, placing the moon in the sky, and originating fresh water and sea tides. He also makes people from the elderberry tree (see *Humans, Origin of),* scatters fish through the streams and rivers, and gives many animals their characteristic markings. From Oil Woman (Tsowatz), he learns how to cook fish. In other Tsimshian stories Raven marries *Bright-Cloud Woman,* creates animal creatures *(Hauhau),* and has a brother named *Logobola.*

Many Native American cultures have stories about Raven. He appears in the Nooksack story of the North Wind People *(Sotic).* In a Nootka story, Raven takes water from Crow *(Keninqas).* Some stories hold that Raven comes from *ghosts. Guguyni* is the Tanaina name for Raven. In Alaska, Raven can change his form because of the power of his *inua.* In Salish stories, Raven has a sister *(Whut).* The Tillamook and Coos recount stories about *Blue-Jay* similar to northwest coast stories of Raven.

The Haida of the Pacific northwest call Raven Nankilslas ("he-whose-voice-is-obeyed"). In stories he is referred to as "the-one-who-is-going-to-order-things." He is adopted by his father, "Looking-Downward"; his mother is "Flood-Tide Woman." In Haida stories, Raven's activities involve transforming things into their present condition (see *Transformation).* This includes land forms, natural phenomena, tastes, passions, and habits, as well as the customs of animals and human beings.

Raven is often the *culture hero* who journeys to steal *fire* or *light.* He is often classified as a *trickster.* [Beck 1979; Boas 1901b, 1916, 1921; Deans 1888b-1889; Driver 1977; Herndon 1990; Jensen 1980; Newton 1973; Reid and Bringhurst 1984; Rooth 1957; Sapir and Swadesh 1939; Turner and Edmonds 1968]

Raw Gums
Arapaho, *Plains*

A *cannibal* infant who sleeps all day. At night he crawls out of his cradle without disturbing his parents so he can kill and eat all the chiefs of the area. One morning his parents notice fresh human flesh in his mouth and become suspicious. That night they trick him and follow him to confirm their suspicions. Then Raw Gums's father holds a feast and informs the people his son is a cannibal. The people allow the parents to decide how to dispose of Raw Gums. They roll him in fat, throw him outdoors, and tell the dogs to eat him.

When Raw Gums hits the ground, he becomes a young man. He dances about, calling for the skeletons of all the people he has eaten. The relatives of the victims discover the skeletons and everyone moves the camp, leaving Raw Gums behind. Later he meets *White Owl Woman,* who challenges him to contests of power and intelligence. He wins all the contests and strikes White Owl Woman on the head, causing her brains to spill out. The brains are the type of *snow* that melts slowly. [Dorsey and Kroeber 1903]

Raw People (kapin aahoi)
Zuni, *Southwest*

One of the two kinds of people that live in the Zuni world. Raw People can change their forms and are considered "people" in that one of their potential forms is anthropomorphic. One group of Raw People consists of the powerful mythic figures "the *Ones Who Hold Our Roads*" (honaawonaawillapona), most important among whom are the Sun Father *(Yatokka taccu)* and *Moonlight-Giving Mother* (yaonakka citta). See also *Cooked People, Kokkookwe,* and *Sipofene.* [Tedlock 1979]

Ready-To-Give
Pawnee, *Plains*

Also known as *North Wind,* one of the *Four Beings of the North* (responsible for sending buffalo for hunts and rain for crops) who existed with the creator *Tirawahat.* Ready-To-Give is especially helpful to hunters and is believed to be the leader of the other three beings. When hunters need help finding game, they ask Ready-To-Give to send game so there will be food for the people. [Dorsey 1906a]

Red Old Man
See *Mikapi.*

Red-Spider-Woman
Pawnee, *Plains*

An old woman whose death leads to the origin of *squash medicine* and the release of buffalo from their confines in the north to roam over the earth. She lives in the center of the earth with her many daughters, controlling the growth of beans and corn (see also *Spider Woman).* The buffalo chief sends his son, Curly-Eyes, with some other buffalo to look for better land to live on. On their journey Curly-Eyes meets one of Red-Spider-Woman's daughters and falls in love with her.

The buffalo chief informs his son they must buy the daughter of Red-Spider-Woman in order for him to marry her. Delegations of buffalo are sent to the old woman with offerings for her daughter. First they offer her a valley full of buffalo, which she refuses. They offer two valleys full of buffalo, then half a land full, and finally an entire land full of buffalo, but Red-Spider-Woman refuses each time. The buffalo decide to move to her country. They travel south for many years. One day Curly-Eyes sees the girl he loves. The buffalo trample old Red-Spider-Woman's fields. She is killed and her body sinks into the prairie. The buffalo chief announces that her body will remain in the ground as a medicinal root of the squash vine. From this point on, buffalo cover the earth. [Dorsey 1906a]

Red Willow *(Piplats)*
Nez Perce, Plateau

This story tells how red willow got its name and why it is red in color.

Reversal

The purpose of many stories and rites is to establish the way of life, the shape of the world. All created things have a place, and to engage meaning means to be in that place. This primacy of place means that a great deal of power and affect can be accomplished by turning the order and expectations upside down. This is commonly done by Clowns and Clowning Societies (see also *Heyoka,* the Lakota figure whose character and behavior are based on reversals). In challenging the given order, these figures suffer the consequences and thus demonstrate through their experience the wisdom, power, and meaning of an ordered life way. What is remarkable about many Native American religions is their incorporation of the reversal of order into their most important rites and most fundamental stories.

Revitalization Movement

Encounters with Americans of European ancestry have often led to depletion and degradation of Native American cultures. The response has sometimes been an effort to revitalize the threatened culture. Encouragement of specifically Native American practices has often been accompanied by the explicit rejection of items and practices associated with White Americans, such as Christianity, formal schooling, and the use of alcohol. Revitalization movements are associated with *crisis cults* and *millenarian movements.* For examples of revitalization movements, see *Ghost Dance of 1870, Ghost Dance of 1890,* and *Shaker Religion.*

Ring and Javelin Game

See *Hoop and Pole Game.*

River-Woman

Arapaho, *Plains*

The second wife of a *water monster (hiintcabiit).* After she gives birth to a son, she is drowned by the water monster's jealous first wife, Crow-Woman. Her brother Beaver-Foot wanders along the river, grieving and carrying his sister's newborn child. Another water monster hears his grief and lifts River-Woman to the surface of the water so she can nurse her crying child. Then both mother and child disappear under the water. Beaver-Foot builds a *sweat lodge* in hopes they will resurface. A hunter appears, saying he is hunting for horned water monsters. When the water monster comes to the surface with River-Woman on his back, the hunter spears him and River-Woman is thrown to the bank. Beaver-Foot takes his sister to the sweat lodge and resuscitates her, and together they return to the lodge of Crow-Woman. [Dorsey and Kroeber 1903]

Road of Life

The way of life prescribed by many Native American cultures is expressed through the concept of a road of life. The Pima and Papago conceive of the road as a labyrinth that moves back and forth from center to periphery, eventually leading to the center if one follows the culture hero *I?itoi.* The Oglala describe it as the good red road running from north (the direction associated with purity) to south (the direction associated with the source of life). In the Delaware Big House ceremony *(Nkamwin),* participants dance the road of life. The Hopi road of life is oriented from west to east. The Native American Church (Peyote Religion) designates the Peyote Road as a line spanning the crescent-shaped altar. See also the Zuni road of life, *Onanne.*

Roasting-Dead-People

Takelma, *Northwest Coast*

The name of an insect responsible for the origin of death. When Roasting-Dead-People's child dies, he asks Coyote to lend him a blanket to bury the child. Coyote refuses, because he wants to know where *dead* people would live if they came back. Then Coyote's child dies and he asks Roasting-Dead-People to lend him a blanket to bury his child. Roasting-Dead-People refuses, reminding Coyote that he would not give him a blanket earlier and that his own child was therefore rotting. It is said that because of this, dead people do not return when they die. [Sapir 1909a]

Robin, Origin of Red Breast
Kathlamet, *Northwest Coast*
Robin kills her sister, Salmon-Berry. Salmon-Berry's children retaliate by attempting to kill Robin's children. The children escape across a river using Crane's leg as a bridge. Robin follows them, but as she is crossing the river Crane turns his leg and she falls into the water. Robin drifts ashore and Crow picks at her body. When Robin recovers, she smears the blood from her wounds over her belly. She flies to all the trees and asks them if they like her new look. Robin causes the trees that admire her red breast to be useful to humans, but those that do not are useless to humans. [Boas 1901b]

Rock(s)
Plains
Inyan, a powerful Lakota figure. See also the story theme *Rolling Rock.*

Rolling Rock
Pawnee, *Plains;* Eskimo, central Canada, Hudson Bay, *Arctic;* Ute, *Great Basin*
A story theme usually involving a figure who lends his coat to a rock to warm it up. When the person returns to get his coat, the rock is upset at having a gift taken back and chases him. The person asks many animals for help, but the rock rolls over them and kills them. The person finally escapes. The Pawnee tell a story about *Coyote* giving Rock a knife in return for helping him find food. Coyote travels to a village and is given food. He takes the knife from Rock to cut the meat. Rock becomes angry and rolls after Coyote. Bears, mountain lions, and buffalo try to help Coyote, but all get killed by Rock as Coyote escapes.

The Hudson Bay Eskimos tell a story in which *Wolverine* makes fun of Rock until Rock starts chasing him. Rock catches Wolverine and rolls over him. Wolverine screams to the wolves and foxes for help, but they tell Wolverine it serves him right for teasing Rock. Finally, lightning and thunder help Wolverine by splitting Rock in two. Rock's splitting causes strips of skin to be taken off Wolverine's back.

In a southern Ute story, *Sunawavi* (the *trickster*) urinates on Little Rock. When Big Rock comes home, Little Rock tells him what happened. Big Rock angrily rolls after Sunawavi, chasing him up and down mountains. Sunawavi calls on other animals to help him, but they are all killed by Big Rock. Sunawavi finally hides behind a small boulder that becomes as large as Big Rock. Big Rock rolls into the boulder and shatters. Sunawavi thanks the boulder by telling it that while animals will die, the boulder will last until the end of the world. [Boas 1888a; Dorsey 1906a; Lowie 1924]

Rotten-Feathers
Tsimshian, *Northwest Coast*
A young man with a special feather that allows him to melt mountains and overcome any obstacle. Rotten-Feathers desires to marry the beautiful daughter of Chieftainess Knife-Hand, who cuts off the heads of her daughter's suitors with her hands. Rotten-Feathers deceives Knife-Hand into killing her own daughter. He removes the labret from the decapitated head of Knife-Hand's daughter, and thereafter is known by the name Labret. He travels to the house of the supernatural being Sleep, and abducts his beautiful wife. Sleep pursues them, placing many obstacles such as deep crevices and thick fog in their way, but Labret overcomes each obstacle by using his special feather. [Boas 1916]

Round Dance
Iroquois, *Northeast*
A dance performed by the medicine society *Hadidos.* See also *False Faces.*

Rubbing Medicines
Nootka; *Northwest Coast*
Used in rituals for healing and as part of the *osimc* (ritual bathing) process. Rubbing medicines consist of four bundles, each having four kinds of branches. The branches may be actual branches about three or four inches long, or may consist of small fish, salmon heads, and seaweed. Different branches are used by different families, depending on their application. [Sapir and Swadesh 1939]

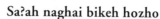

Sa?ah naghai bikeh hozho
Navajo, *Southwest*
"An all-encompassing environment of beauty." A frequent phrase in Navajo song, prayer, and story, expressing the Navajo goal of life, which is to live surrounded by beauty until dying of old age. Sa?ah naghai is identified as male, the personification of thought, and is often referred to in English as Long Life Boy. Bikeh hozho is identified as female, the personification of speech, and is often referred to in English as Happiness Girl (see also *Blessingway*). In the Navajo story of creation, these two appear in human-like form, incomparably beautiful and with long, flowing, luminescent hair. They identify themselves as the means by which all will have life. They become the inner forms *(Biigistiin)* of the earth and are identified with the inner forms of all living things. Navajos also identify Long Life Boy and Happiness Girl as the parents of *Changing Woman,* one of the central Navajo mythic figures. See also *Hozho* (beauty) and *Nilchi?i* (wind). [Witherspoon 1974, 1975, 1977]

Sacrifice(s)
Ceremonial killing of animals or human beings as sacrifices is rare in North America, even in mythology. The Zuni (as do a few other cultures) tell stories about the sacrifice of children in order to cause a flood to subside (see *Incest Causes Flood* and *Flood Subsided by Sacrifice*). The only accounts of ritual sacrifice are those of the Pawnee (see *Morning Star*). Northern Plains cultures offer sacrifices of pieces of flesh in the *Sun Dance* as part of carrying out a vow. An attitude of sacrifice is maintained in the Lakota practices of vision-questing *(Hanmdepi).*

Sagapgia
Tsimshian, *Northwest Coast*
The human princess who is captured by sea foam while traveling in a canoe with other women from her village. Sagapgia is taken to the supernatural being's underwater house in Sandy Bay at the mouth of the Skeena River because the being's son wants to marry her. For the wedding, the princess's uncle makes a great sacrifice of grease, crabapples, cranberries, dried berries, elk skins, copper, garments of sea otter and marten, abalone shells, canoes, and slaves.

The couple has a son whom the chief names Wa-medi-aks, "down the useless river." After Wa-medi-aks is born, his grandfather, the supernatural being of Sandy Bay, pulls the boy's forehead, legs, hands, and body to make him grow quickly. Later Sagapgia gives birth to a daughter who is pulled and stretched in the same manner as her brother. When the children are grown, their grandfather invites all the supernatural beings to his home for a feast. Many of the beings have been responsible for multiple drownings on the Skeena River, and the grandfather wants them to agree to let his grandchildren live. Then the chief tells his son it is time to let the princess and her children go home. Upon their return, the princess's uncle gives a great feast. [Boas 1902, 1916]

Sakaskantawe
Ojibwa, *Subarctic*

"Flying squirrel." A dream visitor who is known to arrive in the *shaking tent* speaking in opposites; for example, what is hot is cold, where there is plenty of game there is really none. His arrival at shaking tent ceremonies is associated with poor hunting. [Preston 1975]

Salmon
Northwest Coast

The dietary staple for these tribes, where salmon can be caught in great quantities at certain times of the year. Many stories are told about salmon, the culture hero Salmon Boy, Salmon Village, and the freeing of trapped salmon. *Coyote* often figures prominently in stories about salmon. In one story, a group of women has trapped all the salmon. Coyote disguises himself as a baby so the women will adopt him. He then releases the salmon so they can swim upstream and be caught. Coyote is also responsible for releasing salmon into various streams and rivers.

The Kathlamet tell a story about Salmon as he travels up river rapids to the Cascades. Along the way he meets many plants that have kept people alive during a time of famine. Salmon rewards each plant as it acknowledges his journey upriver. Then, the birds and Fish Crow, Blue-Jay, and Flounder canoe up the river. They say Salmon goes up the river with the flood tide and comes back with the ebb tide, and that he does not have the ability to swim upstream. This lie infuriates Salmon, and he twists the necks and faces of Flounder, Fish Crow, and Blue-Jay. He decides that future generations of salmon will take five days to migrate to the Cascades so they cannot be accused of traveling with the daily tides.

The Tsimshian learned to fish for salmon from *Gispawaweda*. The Tsimshian *Bright-Cloud Woman* is a salmon. The Nootka *Great-Favorite* Dance was taught by Salmon. The Haida tell a story of *Qolqalg Odai,* a salmon boy. *Tkahyal* is the Tillamook master of the salmon. [Boas 1901b; Brotherston 1979b]

Salt Pilgrimage
Papago, *Southwest*

A week-long complex ritual pilgrimage to collect salt from the northeast shore of the Gulf of California. The pilgrimage is usually taken in the hottest part of the summer. It involves fasting, the use of ritual speech, the making of prayer offerings to the ocean, running along the shore to acquire visions, the collection of salt, and a period of isolation for returning pilgrims. Pilgrimage leaders must be veterans of many pilgrimages. Novices endure additional initiatory restrictions. The ritual is conducted not only to procure needed salt, but also to bring rain and life to the desert people. See also *Papago Ritual Cycle* and *Salt Woman.* [Underhill 1946; Underhill et al. 1979]

Salt Woman or Old Lady Salt (malokatsiki)
Zuni, *Southwest*

Salt Woman and Turquoise Man live near Zuni, where the people easily supply themselves with salt and turquoise. The people become careless, soiling and wasting Salt Woman's flesh. Offended, she and Turquoise Man depart for a distant place. Finding themselves without salt, the priests hold council, make prayersticks, and send two priests after Salt Woman. They follow her trail, which they are able to do because it is salty, and finally find her far away at Salt Lake south of Zuni. As punishment for the misuse of salt, the priests' feet are badly cut as they try to gather salt, and they have difficulty finding their way back home. Salt Woman gives the priests salt and tells them how she should be approached, thus establishing the manner in which the Zuni conduct the *salt pilgrimage.*

Salt Woman is sister to the Sun Father, *Yatokka taccu.* [Benedict 1935; Bunzel 1932; Stevenson 1905; Tedlock 1979]

Sand Lizards
Lakota, *Plains*

Amulets made by the mothers of pregnant women for their prospective grandchildren. They are fashioned in the shapes of either sand lizards or tortoises, animals revered because they are difficult to kill. The amulets are made in pairs, one to hold the newborn's umbilical cord, the other to act as a decoy. It is thought that any harm directed against a child will be directed at the umbilical cord, which is believed to hold the child's spirit. Since malevolent forces will not know which amulet carries the umbilical cord, the child will be protected. The amulet is put on the child's clothing when the child begins to walk. As the child grows older, the amulet is put away and kept by the child's mother. [Walker 1982]

Sandpainting(s) (iikaah)
Navajo, *Southwest*

A rite commonly performed in Navajo healing ceremonials and essential to those classified as *Holyway.* Refers also to the object made in preparation for this rite. Sandpainting is performed on the last four days of an eight-day, nine-night healing rite. A clean sand base is prepared in the center of the ceremonial hogan. On this base, colored crushed minerals are strewn to construct pictures or patterns associated with the mythol-

ogy of the ceremonial. Each ceremonial has a variety of different specific designs that may be used for the sandpainting.

The completed painting is blessed (thereby bringing the figures depicted in it to life) by strewing *cornmeal* or pollen *(tadidiin)* on it from the four cardinal directions: east, south, west, and north. The person for whom the ceremonial is being performed, the *one-sung-over,* walks on the painting and sits in the middle of it. The one-sung-over is then identified with the sandpainting and all the figures on it by having it applied to her or his body in the ritual sequence: feet, legs, body, and head. The singer *(hataalii)* or a masked *ye?ii* moistens his hands with a medicine infusion and uses this moisture to transfer sands from the figures in the painting to the corresponding body parts of the one-sung-over, in the process destroying the sandpainting.

Through this identification with the sandpainting and with the stories recalled by songs sung during the rite, the one-sung-over's suffering is identified with that of the great Navajo heroes and with the way of the world. The rite concludes with the sands being scraped together and carried out of the hogan to be deposited in an appropriate location. See also *Apache Creation and Emergence,* in which sandpainting is used as an instrument of creation; *Rainbow,* who serves as a personified guardian surrounding sandpaintings; *Shootingway; Whirling Logs' Sandpainting; Navajo Starlore;* and *Yenaldlooshi,* the Navajo skinwalker who misuses sandpaintings. [Gill 1979b; Matthews 1885a; Newcomb 1964; Stevenson 1891; Wyman 1959, 1983]

Sanopi
Kawaiisu, *Great Basin*

"Pitch." Pitch lives in a tree and taunts *Coyote* by calling his name. Coyote tries to find Pitch and kill him, but succeeds only in getting his paws stuck in the tarlike Pitch. He tries to bite Pitch and gets his teeth stuck. Unable to move, Coyote dies. [Zigmond 1980]

Saokata

Huron, *Northeast*

"One who examines another by seeing." *Diagnosticians* who, through certain feasts, songs, and dances, used their sight to penetrate into the sick person's soul to see what he or she was desiring, and therefore what was causing the illness. Often the afflicted person would desire something in a *dream* and forget about it upon awakening. This unrealized desire was believed to cause illness. By finding out what had happened in the sick person's dreams, the Saokata could help the *Arendiwane,* medicine person, cure the person. Sometimes a group of Saokata would sweat together to increase collective power in order to help cure someone. See also *Awataerohi,* a Huron healing dance. [Tooker 1962]

Sapiya

Creek, *Southeast;* Seminole, Oklahoma and *Southeast*

Animated red, blue, and yellow *stones* that bring success in love and war. Sapiya move about like hopping fleas, and they breed and reproduce. They are controlled with special songs, and must be fed squirrel blood and watered at regular intervals lest they cause their owners to get skin diseases. They are kept in a special container with vermilion paint. When this paint is used on the Sapiya owner's face, it causes the skin to sparkle. The owner acquires the specific power of one of the stones, such as stength in battle, protection against enemies, or enchanting beauty in a love pursuit. See also *Soup Dance.* [Howard 1984; Sturtevant 1987]

Sapling

Onondaga, *Northeast*

One of the Iroquoian terms for *creator.* See also *False Faces, Hawenniyo,* and *Sky-Holder.* [Fenton 1987]

Sapu igye

Crow, *Plains*

Seven stars, also known as the *Big Dipper* (see *Stars and Starlore).* Originally the seven stars live on earth and wonder how they can achieve immortality. One of them suggests that if they become part of the earth they will live forever. They try, but cannot become part of earth. Nor are they successful at becoming trees, stones, or mountains. Finally they decide to become stars in the sky, succeeding because now they are where they are meant to be. [Lowie 1960]

Sati

Tlingit, *Northwest Coast*

The master of a dead shaman's personal *helping spirits* (yek). When a *shaman* dies, his or her family gathers to ask the spirit helpers to select a new sati. The dead shaman's successor, who cannot refuse the position on pain of illness or death, goes to the grave to get the shaman's equipment, which has been placed in the grave house with the shaman's uncremated body.

The new shaman goes to the woods with one or two more-experienced shamans and remains there until visited by the sati in the form of an animal. When the animal falls dead at the new shaman's feet, he or she cuts off a slice of the animal's tongue and places it in a small pouch, along with other pieces of the animal. The shaman wears this *medicine bundle* pouch as a necklace during healing rituals. Tongue slices signify the shaman's most powerful spirit helpers, which are all under the control of sati. As a shaman's career progresses, more tongue slices could be gathered, up to a maximum of eight slices from different animals (eight slices signify the limit of power). Each spirit is represented by an anthropomorphic mask (see *Masks and Masking).* During seances, the shaman dons different masks, depending on which spirit is being called. While wearing the masks, the shaman often becomes possessed and speaks in spirit language. [Swanton 1909]

Saya

Dunne-za (Beaver), *Subarctic*

A *culture hero* of the *Dunne-za,* the first Dreamer (see *Naachin).* Saya undertakes the first vision quest and by so doing demonstrates the empowerment of such an experience for the Dunne-za people. Prior to the completion of his vision quest and other tests, Saya's name was Swan. He is also known as Wabashu in the Cree language. Saya orbits the earth like the sun, flies with the ducks and geese, and follows the trails of animals. He flies between the seasons and knows the Trail to Heaven *(Yagatunne).*

When Swan is still a small boy, his widowed father takes a new wife, the setting sun woman, who kills animals by crushing them between her legs but does not cook them. She lies to Swan's father, saying Swan raped her. The angry father tells his son they are going hunting; instead he takes the boy to the edge of the earth where the sun sets and leaves him there. In this isolated place, Swan enters a vision quest and achieves an alliance with a helping spirit, who teaches him how to hunt ducks and geese and helps him remember powers he already has. Swan also learns the power that puts the leaves on the trees at the change of seasons.

Swan returns to his stepmother and kills her with fiery arrows that boil her alive. After more adventures with the *cannibal* monster Onli Nachi, whom he eventually kills, Swan changes his name to Saya, having discovered and claimed his power and become a man. He rids the world of all the *monsters* and then turns to *stone,* stating that when the world ends he will return. Saya is credited with working in the world so that humans can live on the earth. [Ridington 1988]

Scalping

The act of slicing the scalp from the skull. This practice was first recorded among the Hurons of the northeast before the 1600s. It was also found among the Creek in the southeast and was common to several Plains and Great Basin tribes (e.g., Pawnee, Assiniboin, Cheyenne, Blackfoot, Crow, Plains Cree). In warfare (see *War),* scalping was closely associated with retaliation. A scalp was considered a badge of honor and a sign of victory. It symbolized life and holding the power of one's

conquered enemy because it was held that the human spirit resided in human hair.

Seventeenth-century accounts tell of Huron warriors scalping and sometimes beheading their enemies. The heads and scalps were kept as trophies and displayed outside camps to intimidate intruders. Early Iroquoian tribes engaged in scalping as part of blood revenge tactics. Retaliation was not complete until an enemy was captured, or a scalp or head presented to the murdered victim's family as a replacement for the tribal member who had been killed. When Montagnais warriors returned by canoe from a battle, female relatives swam out to meet them and claimed the heads and scalps they had brought back. The women later wore the scalps suspended around their necks as decorations for dances they performed.

When a Lakota warrior presented an enemy scalp to the relatives of a man killed in battle, he gave back both the spirit of the enemy warrior and that of the lost relative to the surviving family members. Some tribes had highly ritualized uses for scalps. The Pawnee brought scalps home from battle and hung them on poles. The scalps were later tanned and worn on dance costumes; some were decorated. Others were consecrated to *Tirawahat* and placed in *medicine bundles* used by warrior societies.

Because it was believed that life and the human spirit were contained in the hair, locks of hair fringed the shirts of the *Shirt Wearers* and the *Wakincuzas,* "the ones who decide." The locks of hair on these shirts represented the people of the tribe for whom the Shirt Wearer was responsible. See also *Gender Crossing, Small Dose, Coup,* and *Mikapi* (a Blackfoot warrior). [Grinnell 1962; Lowie 1956; Murie 1989; Neihardt 1932; Wissler 1913]

Sea Woman

Eskimo, Alaska, Canada, Greenland, *Arctic*
Also known as *Sedna,* meaning "the one far down there," in Arctic Alaska; as Kannakapfaluk by the Copper Eskimos of Canada; as Nuliayok, "the

ever-copulating one" in northwest Hudson Bay; as Avilayoq in the Cumberland Sound area of Baffin Bay; and as Takanaluk arnaluk, "the woman down there" or Unigumisuitok, "the one who doesn't want a husband" in Arctic Quebec. Sea Woman controls the sea mammals (see *Master/Mistress of Animals*). She lives under the sea, usually alone but sometimes with a *dwarf* or a great *dog* that guards the entry to her house.

Several versions of the Sea Woman story are told in Arctic Canada and Greenland, but none is found among the Yupik Eskimos of the Bering Sea coast of Alaska. Essential elements in all the stories are the marriage of a human girl to an animal, usually a dog (see also *Dog Husband);* the birth of children who become founders of the Native American and White people; and the chopping off of Sedna's fingers, joint by joint, as she tries to save herself from drowning while clinging to a kayak. The joints of her fingers become sea mammals, and she drowns and becomes "the woman down there."

Because she has no fingers, Sedna cannot care for herself. It is the duty of *shamans (angalkuq)* to come to her, comb her hair, and make her happy so that she will not keep the sea mammals locked up in her house. Only the most experienced shaman can make the journey under the sea to placate her. Sea Woman is not to be confused with Ikalu nappa, "half-fish," a half-woman, half-fish creature who

also lives under the sea. [Boas 1888a; Damas 1984; Lantis 1947; Nelson 1888; Norman 1990; Nungak and Arima 1988; Sabo and Sabo 1985]

Seasons, Origin of
See *Winds, Four Great.*

Seataka
Yaqui, *Southwest*
Literally "flower body," suggestive of a kind of *power,* although Yaqui people hold that the English word "power" is inadequate. Yaqui believe that individuals are born with specialized gifts. Seataka, the most important of these gifts, is said to be fundamental to Yaqui thought and life. Seataka is the channel between human beings and the rest of nature. It is associated with the ancient world *Yoania*. A person born without seataka is thought to be poor. Seataka may be used for either good or evil (see also *Morea).* Seataka is closely associated with activities inherited from the *Surem,* such as the arts of the *pascola* and *Deer Dancers,* the composition of music and songs, and curing. The possession of seataka is also important for success in hunting, gambling, finding lost objects, and even forms of work. People with seataka are thought to be lucky, to have precognition, and to be clairvoyant. See also *Hitebi* (curer) and *Utea,* a different kind of power. [Painter 1986]

Ikalu nappa, the Eskimo half woman, half fish. Courtesy, Canadian Museum of Civilization (neg.#J 19431).

Seatco
Puyallup-Nisqually, Southern Puget Sound, *Northwest Coast*

A malevolent, larger-than-human figure (see *Malevolent Creatures*) known for his stealth and quickness. Seatco lives in the darkest parts of the forest. He sleeps all day, and at night he roams around robbing traps, breaking canoes, stealing food, and killing lost travelers. He also steals *children* and brings them up as slaves. [Smith 1940]

Sedna
Eskimo, Canada, *Arctic*

As a young woman, Sedna resists her human suitors and chooses instead to live on an island with a dog who becomes her spouse. Every day the dog swims to the girl's father to bring food back for her and their puppies. One day the father puts heavy weights in the food sack, and the *dog husband* drowns. Seeing this, the girl tells her puppy offspring to kill her father. In another version, as the father returns from the island after retrieving his widowed daughter, a terrible storm arises, threatening disaster. The father throws his daughter from the boat as an offering to try to calm the storm, but she clings to the boat. As the storm rages on, the father cuts off her fingers joint by joint in his attempt to give her to the sea. Eventually she falls into the sea and drowns. Her finger joints are transformed into sea animals, and she lives beneath the sea as their keeper (see *Master/Mistress of Animals*). See also *Adlivun,* the underworld; *Anguta,* who lives with Sedna; and *Sea Woman.* [Boas 1888a; Fisher 1975; Murdoch 1887; Wardle 1900]

Selu
Cherokee, *Southeast*

"Corn," the wife of Kanati, the hunter (see also *Kanati and Selu),* and mother of twin Thunder Boys. Selu produces corn in secret by rubbing her stomach or by defecating. Her sons observe this activity and, believing she is a witch, plot to kill her. Knowing their intentions, Selu instructs them to clear a large piece of ground and, after killing her, drag her body around it seven times. The boys kill Selu and cut off her head. Instead of clearing a large area, they clear seven small spots and drag her body twice around each small area. Wherever her blood falls, corn grows. For this reason, corn grows only in certain areas instead of everywhere in the world. The two brothers stay up all night watching the corn grow. In the morning the corn is completely ripe. See also *Corn Woman.* [Mooney 1888]

Semacha
Yavapai, *Southwest*

Deities that live in the east and visit *shamans* at night. They look like human beings, although they are visible only to shamans. They talk and travel through the air. Two semacha, Komwidapokuwia and Skatakaamcha, established many features of Yavapai culture and became patron deities of shamans, providing them with medicine power and teaching the songs for curing rituals. Shamanic rituals are the predominant form of religion among the Yavapai. A variety of stories feature the actions of Komwidapokuwia and Skatakaamcha. [Gifford 1933]

Sendeh
Kiowa, *Plains*

Also known as Sendeh Old Man. Sendeh is capable of transforming into a *coyote* or any other animal as he pleases. His mischievous nature, insatiable sexual appetite, and constant hunger suggest he is a *trickster* figure. [Voegelin 1933]

Seneca
Northeast

The Seneca call themselves *Ongwe onwe.*

Separation of Men and Women
Navajo, *Southwest*

An episode that is often part of the *Navajo emergence* stories. It usually takes place in the fourth world, the one immediately below the present world. Domestic strife, adultery, and quarreling between the sexes characterizes the relationship between men and women throughout the emergence journey. It is finally decided that men and women must separate and get along without one another. The men cross the river, leaving the women on one side while they go to live on the other.

At first all goes well. The women live by agriculture, the men by hunting. Eventually the women experience crop failure and begin to starve, while the men realize they are all growing older and that their existence is threatened because they cannot reproduce themselves. In some versions of the story, the women grow desperate. Some drown as they attempt to swim the river to rejoin the men. Others try to fill their unmet sexual desires by having intercourse with stones and other objects, thereby producing monsters. In time, each sex realizes that its existence is interdependent with the other and they are happily reunited.

Hopi and other tribes have similar stories. [Goddard 1933; Haile 1981b; Matthews 1897; Parsons 1930a; Wheelwright 1942]

Serpent
See *Horned Serpent* and *Snake*.

Seven Drums Religion
See *Smohalla Cult.*

Shadahgeah
Seneca, *Northeast*
Large, high-flying, vulture-type bird who lives above the clouds and mists and is chief of all the birds. See also *Small Dose*. [Fenton 1987]

Shaker Religion
Northwest Coast
A Native American *revitalization movement* with extensive Christian influences (see *Christianity),* started by John and Mary Slocum in the Puget Sound area of western Washington during the early 1880s. John Slocum's apparent

death and revival in 1881 lent authority to his claim that he was to carry the Christian way of life to Native American people. When John was near death during a second severe illness, his wife Mary prayed over him, crying, convulsing, and sobbing hysterically. His improvement was attributed to her seizurelike activities. As John's message spread, this style of praying and healing became the "shaking" activity practiced with this religion.

The Shaker religion lacked the anti-White feelings found in the *Smohalla Cult.* It incorporated Christian, especially Roman Catholic, elements such as the iconography of the trinity, the crucifix, and Christ as Redeemer. Shaker religion also incorporated strong puritanical codes from Protestant Christianity. Shaker religious activities included Sunday worship, *healing,* divination, burial, and thanksgiving. Healing rites took place either during Sunday worship or in patients' homes. The Shaker religion eventually spread to tribes in western Washington, southern British Columbia, the Oregon coast, and northern California. By the 1930s it was firmly established on some reservations in western Oregon. Many members later abandoned the church over differences of opinion over the role of the Bible in the religion. By 1945 its numbers had dwindled so that only a few practitioners were left. See also *Ghost Dance of 1870* and *Ghost Dance of 1890.* [Beckham, Toepel, and Minor 1984; Lenhood 1982]

Shaking Tent
Eastern Hudson Bay Cree and Boreal Subarctic Algonquians, *Subarctic;* Menominee, *Northeast;* Blackfoot and Gros Ventre, *Plains;* and *Plateau*
In the *conjuring* ritual, a conjurer's *helping spirits* communicate with him or her by shaking the structure where the rite is performed. Among the eastern Cree, one can become a conjurer only with the permission of the spirit *Mistapew,* master of ceremonies to all the other helping spirits. He is not met in dreams, but appears only during times of isolation in the bush.

The shaking tent ritual takes place at night. The conjurer, who is often hired for a set fee by a person or group of people, is bound and hidden in a small barrel-shaped lodge or tent erected on the day of the performance. As people gather outside the tent to watch, the conjurer sings and drums to call the invisible airborne spirits. When the spirits arrive, they cause the tent to shake and move from side to side. The spirits release the conjurer from his bonds, then talk among themselves, with the conjurer, and with the audience in their native tongue, as well as in foreign languages that require translation.

The shaking tent rite, with the help of the spirits, is used to obtain information about persons or events. It can also protect against sorcery by revealing its source. Questions can be asked about the diagnosis and treatment of illness. Through the rite people can attempt to locate game animals, lost articles, absent relatives, and missing people. Spirits may be addressed by individuals or groups in the audience. The spirits can point out an individual or speak to the group spontaneously. The conjurer or his or her spouse translates the unintelligible spirit conversations for the audience. All the following are spirit visitors to the shaking tent: *Assin, Crazy Woman, Mank, Miskinahk, Mostos, Nacwapew, Oh-gee-nay, Pinessi, Powatakan, Sakaskantawe,* and *Witiko.* The Menominee Thunder Cult *(Waipanows)* works in a shaking tent structure. [Densmore 1929; Hallowell 1942; Preston 1975]

Shalako
Zuni, *Southwest*

An early December ceremonial distinctive for the tall birdlike figures who give their name to its series of rituals. See also *Zuni Ritual Cycle.* Four days before the Shalako appear, a group of six figures, known as the Council of the Gods, begins a four-day retreat. This group consists of Shulawitsi (the Fire God), Saiyatasha (the Rain Priest of the North and the leader of the group), Hututu (Saiyatasha's deputy and a Rain Priest of the South), and two Yamuhakto (Wood Carriers).

On the day the six pairs of Shalako come, the Council of the Gods enters Zuni Village, sprinkling cornmeal and depositing prayer plumes in holes at six shrines throughout the village. This ritual process aligns Zuni Village with the six cosmic directions. The group goes to the Saiyatasha house, where they will remain for the night performing chants and dancing. In the evening, six identical Shalako (and an alternate dancer for each) associated with the six directions enter the village and head for six houses specially built each year for their performances. During the early part of the evening they chant prayers. Around midnight they begin their distinctive dance, lasting until morning, that includes the clacking of their long snouts and birdlike swoops from one end of the room to the other. The final performance of the Shalako is a relay race in which the figures run back and forth between 12 holes, in which they plant prayersticks (see *Prayer and Prayersticks). Koyemshi,* the mudhead clowns (see *Clowns and Clowning Societies),* are also important to Shalako.

Many of the Zuni people who perform in Shalako as Saiyatasha and his council, as well as the 12 Shalako, are chosen during the Winter Solstice Ceremonies nearly a year in advance of their Shalako performance. During this year these men must live exemplary lives. They must make many prayer offerings, often requiring a journey to distant shrines, and learn the long prayers they will chant. See also *Corn Maidens.* [Stevenson 1905; Wright 1985]

Shalikun
Salish, *Northwest Coast*

The boy whose appearance is changed by the bird Thunder and becomes associated with thunder and lightning. Thunder removes the boy's eyes, replacing them with lightning. Shalikun becomes very powerful and frightening to the village people. Eventually he is destroyed by two brothers from the village of Cowichan, who fight him with magic swords made of elk horn. [Smith 1940]

Zuni Shalako figures. Courtesy, Museum of New Mexico, Ben Wittick, photographer.

Shaman(s)

A *healer* or medicine person (see Medicine People). In the strict sense, a shaman uses ecstatic techniques to call upon spiritual help, although the term (adapted from a Siberian culture) is commonly used to refer generally to healers and medicine people. Although *healing* is clearly the most common shamanic activity, shamans also perform rituals related to hunting and agriculture, and they may conduct the dead to the other world.

See the following for information on shamans in various Native American cultures: *Angalkuq* (Yupik); *Basamacha* (Yavapai); *Caskyet* (Potawatomi); *Dream Doctor* (Atna); *Medawlinno* (Abenaki); *Nanandaw* (Ojibwa); *Oki* and *Ontetsans* (Huron); *Si?atcokam* (Pima), who treat sickness *(Mumkidag)*; *Tudab* (Puyallup); *Wapno* (Potawatomi); and *Ivivarshuk and Nisguvaushaq* (Inupiaq).

Shamans appear frequently in Native American stories. A Lakota shaman learns to play *Big Twisted Flute* from buffalo. *Big-Tail* is an important Haida shaman. *Hummingbird* was the Kawaiisu's first shaman. The Tsimshian figure *Only One* is initiated as a shaman. The Kawaiisu bird *Puuciigiigibi* is the weather shaman. Moldy-Forehead *(Qolqalg Odai)* becomes a Haida shaman. Others include *Anerneq* (Yupik); *Tcisaki,* a prominent Ojibwa shaman; and *Tseguksk,* a historical Tlingit shaman who predicted the coming of smallpox.

Spirit beings often visit or assist shamans, or are visited by shamans on spirit journeys. *Lagua* and *Tcaawunkl* are Tlingit spirits who speak through Haida shamans, and Sati is a Tlingit shaman's helping spirit. Alaskan shamans take spirit journeys to *Moon Man* and *Sea Woman.* *Semacha* are the spirits that visit Yavapai shamans. Shamans in Labrador visit and copulate with *Superguksoak* to release game. The Ute hold that a shaman is very powerful if his power comes from *Paiyuk,* a cannibal animal.

Shamans perform on many ritual occasions. These include the Alaskan *Doll Festival;* the Yokut *Heshwash Ceremony,* which includes a sha-man contest; and the Eskimo *Inviting-In Feast.* See also *Master of Sickness,* a Tlingit witch who gains power by drinking from a shaman's skull; *Polar Bear Snout,* a charm used by powerful shamans; *Spirit Powers,* for a discussion of Kalapuya shamanism; *Gender Crossing,* which may be associated with shamanism; and *Dead, Resuscitation of.* [Boas 1888a, 1916, 1930; Damas 1984; Elmendorf 1977; Golder 1903; Landes 1968; Lantis 1947; Matthews 1976; Morrow 1984; Nelson 1899; Nungak and Arima 1988; Opler 1985; Riordan 1983; Swanton 1909; Tennant and Bitar 1981; Underhill 1946]

Shape Shifting

The ability to change shape or appearance. Shape shifting is most commonly associated with malevolence and witchcraft, as in Yaqui *Morea,* the Navajo skinwalker *Yenaldlooshi,* and *Coyote,* who trades skins with hunters in order to sleep with their wives. However, shape shifting may also be an attribute of a culture hero's power.

Shell-Covered-One

Ojibwa, *Northeast, Subarctic*

One of the originators of the *Midewiwin,* also known as Shell. Concerned about the disease and death brought by *Winabojo,* Shell sends Bear to the creator with the plan for the Midewiwin. All the helping spirits meet and agree that Bear will organize the Midewiwin. They give Bear the "pack of life," a medicine bundle, to take to earth and leave at different places. Bear's path is described in Mide lore; it is said to go from the depths of the earth to the surface of the water, from the east near Niagara Falls and west to the prairies. [Landes 1968]

Shi-tsukia

Zuni, *Southwest*

One of the White *Kachinas.* The hunting skill of Shi-tsukia is affirmed each night, as he always brings home a deer. Wanting Shi-tsukia as their son-in-law, the kachinas hide all the deer so that he must come to *Kachina Village* in search of them. Every

Shi-tsukia, one of the Zuni White Kachinas. He brings the New Year. Painting by Duane Dishta from the collection of The Heard Museum, Phoenix, Arizona.

day Shi-tsukia searches for something to eat, but finds nothing. Near starvation, he finally sees two women, kachina girls, washing a buckskin. He accepts food from them and accompanies them to their village. In Kachina Village, *Pautiwa,* the chief kachina, hears Shi-tsukia's story about the absence of game and the starvation of his people. Pautiwa says that if Shi-tsukia will marry his daughter, he will give him the deer to take back to his people. Shi-tsukia marries the daughter and stays in Kachina Village through the spring, then returns to his village. There he lives with his grandmother until the winter solstice. After the days of the fire taboo during the ceremonial period, *itiwana,* Shi-tsukia comes from the east bringing the *New Year.* That same day Pautiwa comes from his house in the west to meet his son-in-law Shi-tsukia in the dance plaza, and takes him back to Kachina Village.

This story accounts for the ceremonial appearances of Shi-tsukia and Pautiwa during the Winter Solstice Ceremonies (see *Zuni Ritual Cycle).* It also indicates the significance of the little deer tails that hang as earrings from the Shi-tsukia mask. During the time when the kachinas hid the deer, Shi-tsukia remained alive by eating his ears, the little deer tails. [Benedict 1935; Bunzel 1932; Stevenson 1905; Wright 1985]

Shipap

Keres, *Southwest*

Also known as Shipapolima (Cochiti), *Sipofene* (Tewa), and *Sipapu* (Hopi). Preemergence place, home of the dead and the supernaturals. The four subterranean rooms that comprise shipap are guarded by Mountain Lion. The *emergence* was led by *Masewa and Uyuyewa,* followed by *Iatiku,* the corn mother and mother of all the people, and then by all her people. A *rainbow* formed the gateway through which the peoples entered this world. As they emerged, each tribe or group received an ear of corn and was told by Masewa where to settle. See also *Acoma Emergence and Migration, Fotease* (Jemez), and *Heluta* (Cochiti). [Benedict 1931]

Shirt Wearers

Lakota, *Plains*

The official mediators and counselors of the tribe, appointed by the tribal leaders, *Naca Ominicia.* To each shirt wearer the people present a shirt fringed with hair locks, painted blue and yellow or red and green. Blue represents the sky, yellow the rocks, red the sun, and green the earth. The fringed hair locks represent all the people of the tribe for whom the Shirt Wearer is responsible.

The Shirt Wearers reconcile quarrels between individuals and families within the tribe and act as negotiators in diplomatic relations with other nations. Their primary responsibility is the welfare of their people. They must provide bountiful hunting and good campgrounds. When a Shirt Wearer no longer feels capable of fulfilling these obligations, he trains a younger person for the position. Shirt Wearer candidates are required to go through four ceremonies: the *Hunka Lowanpi,* the Ball-Throwing or Buffalo Rite, the Ghost-Owning, and the White Buffalo Ceremony. Because only the wealthy can afford the performance of these rites, the office of Shirt Wearer is usually limited to the sons of tribal chiefs. A Shirt Wearer father bestows this honor upon his son when he is no longer able to carry out the duties of Shirt Wearer. See also *Scalping.* [Walker 1982]

Shiwanna

Pueblo, *Southwest*

Cloud People, storm spirits, what one becomes after death (see *Dead).* At Acoma, Shiwannakwe is a medicine society, the Thunder Cloud Society, that treats persons shocked by lightning and sets broken bones. At Zuni, Shiwannakwe is the Rain Makers Society, the most important of the 12 to 14 ritual societies of the Zuni. At Zuni the Shiwanna do not appear masked. [Parsons 1930a; Wright 1985]

Shodieonskon

Seneca, *Northeast*

"He abuses people by craft often." Shodieonskon delights in deceiving and abusing people. He tells people that the only way to avoid a terrible plague is for all married persons to sleep with other people's spouses. In another village he tells people that the only way to avoid the plague is to defecate in their lodges. Shodieonskon deceives people into thinking that his urine is really powerful bear oil, which they must drink with their food. In one story he tricks an entire village into believing that he is a great friend of the deceased chief and therefore must be buried with him. He then resurrects himself and tells the people the chief commanded him to marry the chief's two widows. In some stories Shodieonskon is thought to be the brother of death (see *Dead)*. In other accounts he is killed by Dahdahwat. Shodieonskon is often categorized as a *trickster* figure. [Curtin and Hewitt 1918]

Shootingway

Navajo, *Southwest*

A myth and ritual healing complex that rivals *Nightway* as the most complex and elaborate of Navajo ceremonials. It has both a male and female branch (a Navajo method of complementary classification), but little is known of the female branch. The Shootingway ceremonial includes both *Holyway* and *Uglyway* versions.

Shootingway mythology is a complex of stories centering on the travels and adventures of twin brothers, Holy Man and Holy Boy. It often begins with a series of stories that parallel the adventures of *Monster Slayer and Born for Water,* including extensive contact with *Changing Woman* and *Sun.* These stories serve to equip the twins with powers and to establish their knowledge of the world as it was created and prepared by the monster-slaying twins and Changing Woman. The balance of Shootingway mythology proceeds through a series of stories that recount the travels of Holy Man and Holy Boy. Each adventure describes the twins getting into difficulty, their rescue by *diyin dineʔe,* and the resulting ritual knowledge they gain. The composite of this knowledge amounts to Shootingway ritual.

In one adventure the twins visit the home of Arrow People who, angered by their intrusion, emerge from quivers hanging in the four directions and threaten them. The twins save themselves with prayersticks *(keetaan)* given them by Changing Woman. They learn a *sandpainting,* and Coyote *(Maʔii)* teaches them songs to help overcome their injuries.

While hunting, the twins approach a place of habitation. Holy Man sends Holy Boy home and goes on alone to investigate. He finds the home of *Big Snake,* who greets him as a son-in-law. In the exchange of tobacco gifts, Holy Man deceives and kills Big Snake by giving him poisoned tobacco. Big Snake's wife pleads with Holy Man to revive him, which he finally does in exchange for four sandpaintings. Big Snake asks Holy Man to become his son-in-law. Desiring more knowledge, Holy Man visits the homes of other Snake peoples—Grinding Snakes, Endless Snakes, and Snakes with Striped Bodies—despite Big Snake's warnings. From each group Holy Man obtains more Shootingway knowledge.

Coyote wants Big Snake's daughter, whom Holy Man has repeatedly refused to marry. He exchanges skins with Holy Man, debilitating him, and in the guise of Holy Man marries Big Snake's daughter. But the daughter has been warned by Wind *(Nilchiʔi)* and recognizes Coyote by his smell of coyote urine. The snake family finds Holy Man and restores him in a *Hoop Transformation Rite.*

In another episode the twins are hunting separately. Holy Man is picked up by lightning and transported to the home of thunders in the sky. His transgression is the use, without permission, of grebe feathers belonging to the Arrow People. In the home of Big Thunder, Holy Man is shown sandpaintings and taught the proper use of his power. Meanwhile, Holy Boy searches for Holy Man, visiting all the places he knows Holy Man has been. At one place Holy Boy finds, in the center of a pool, a cornstalk with two eagle feathers attached. When he reaches for the feathers, he falls in the pool and is immediately swallowed by a *fish,* who takes him through four homes of Water People. In each home Holy Boy frees himself from the fish by cutting it open with a flint and healing the opening. The Water People teach Holy Boy sandpaintings and knowledge of ritual powers.

Together the twins visit the home of the Translucent Rock People, who teach them songs. Joined by two Translucent Rock People, the twins visit people who cannot see their faces. One of the Rock People commits adultery with the wife of the chief of these people, and the group is sent away with a curse. Soon after, Holy Man is torn to shreds by dogs and bears, only to be restored by Ant, Sun, Moon, and Wind peoples. Another encounter leaves Holy Man shot full of arrows by White Weasel, but this time he is restored by Cactus People. Finally Holy Man travels to 12 mountaintops and spends a night on each, concluding that he has found all that is beautiful. See also *Navajo Wind Way.* [Newcomb and Reichard 1937; Reichard 1934, 1939]

Short Faces
Kutenai, *Plateau*
Twin lynxes who, while searching for their father, become the *Sun* and the *Moon.* See also *Skinkuts.* [Boas and Chamberlain 1918]

Si?atcokam
Pima, *Southwest*
Medicine people, both male and female, the most powerful members of the Pima community. They are responsible for health and healing. Their powers are inherited. See also *Makai* and *Shaman.* [Russell 1908]

Siats
Southern Ute, *Great Basin*
Cannibals that kidnap *children.* Female siats, called bapets, are large and stout, with huge breasts filled with poison milk. Kidnapped children who nurse from these breasts die instantly. A siat can be killed only with an obsidian-tipped arrow. [Lowie 1924]

Sicun
Lakota, *Plains*
The intellect, considered to be one of the manifestations of *Wakan Tanka.* [Walker 1982]

Sikuliasuituq
Eskimo, Eastern Hudson Bay, *Arctic*
"The one who does not go on ice." A giant, fearsome man who lives with his sister and steals seals from hunters. He follows the hunters only on solid ice, not on the thin ice where the seal holes are. If the hunters' wrists are clean, Sikuliasuituq will steal their catch, but if the hunters' wrists are dirty their seals will be left alone. Sikuliasuituq finally spends a night out on the ice, but he does not know how to keep warm. Some hunters tell him to tie up his legs and then cover them. When he does, the hunters stab him to death. His sister, left alone without food, dies. [Nungak and Arima 1988]

Silver Fox
Achumawi, *California*
Creator who appears out of nothing as a small cloud that condenses into the form of Silver *Fox.* Then a fog appears and condenses to become *Coyote.* Together Silver Fox and Coyote prepare the earth for the first humans, disappearing just before the humans arrive. [Dixon 1909a]

Sin
Haida, *Northwest Coast*
Day, a *culture hero* also known as "Shining Heavens." Sin's mother has been banished by her father for her indiscretion with a slave. Only Fine-Weather Woman, the wife of her youngest uncle, brings food to her. One day she discovers the infant Sin in a cockleshell. The baby grows quickly, and his mother makes him a bow and arrows from her copper bracelets. He hunts cormorants, geese, and wrens for his mother, who skins the birds and uses the skins to make coats for her son. Sin gives his mother power to make the winds blow. Before he returns to the sky, Sin tells his mother he will provide food for his

people, and she promises to send them his feathers. She settles in the woods by the bed of a creek. Whenever Sin hovers over the ocean in the morning, his mother lets fall small flakes of snow: the promised feathers. [Swanton 1905b]

Singer
Navajo, *Southwest*
The common English rendering of the term *hataalii,* referring to one who conducts ritual and is responsible for religious knowledge, including mythology.

Sipapu
Hopi, *Southwest*
The entrance to the *underworld,* the place of *emergence.* Represented as a covered hole in the floor of *kivas.* See also *Shipap.* [Bradfield 1973]

Sipofene
Tewa, *Southwest*
The dark world in which the Tewa lived before the *emergence.* Sipofene is located beneath Sandy Place Lake, north of the Tewas' present home (see also *Shipap* and *Pueblo Emergence and Migration).* In Sipofene, animals, supernaturals, and humans live together without knowing death. Winter Mother and Summer Mother, supernaturals living in Sipofene, ask one man to explore and find out how the people might leave this place. The man finally emerges onto the present surface of the earth. Having been accepted by the animals he finds there, he becomes the Hunt Chief and returns to the lower world in the form of Mountain Lion. He is the first "made person," that is, the first member of Tewa society.

Returning to Sipofene, he tells the people they will be accepted in the world above. He designates Winter and Summer Chiefs and tells them their duties. He sends six pairs of brothers called Towa?e (persons) to explore the new world in every direction. Each pair returns with the report that the earth remains soft. However, the last pair finally reports that the earth has hardened somewhat. The people prepare to leave Sipofene. They emerge and begin their journey to the south, encountering many obstacles along the way. They stop 12 times ("make 12 steps"), each time establishing a village where they remain for a time. On the twelfth stop they establish a village near present-day Ojo Caliente. There they prosper, until an epidemic hits the village and forces them to leave. They divide into six groups who go forth to found the six Tewa villages known today.

The Tewa refer to the world before emergence as ochu, meaning green, moist, and unripe (see also *Raw People).* Metaphorically it refers to being not yet Tewa, not yet human. Ochu designates the supernaturals who did not emerge, along with unborn and deceased human beings. The world after emergence is seh ta, meaning dry, hardened, or ripe (see also *Cooked People).* Seh ta designates all who appear on the earth after emergence, including human beings and supernaturals represented in ritual. See also *Tewa Ritual Cycle.* [Ortiz 1969]

Sisaok
Bella Coola, Bella Bella, *Northwest Coast*
A member of a dancing society composed of individuals who have received special names through inheritance or in visions (see *Names and Naming).* A sisaok name entitles its owner to act out in dance drama stories of mythical characters and the animal of his or her family *crest.* A person may have several sisaok names.

New members are initiated into the society during a three-night *potlatch.* Prior to the potlatch the new members are secluded. On the first night, they dance their first public dances, wearing small forehead masks (see *Masks and Masking).* New members are also responsible for donating food to the potlatch feast. On the second and third nights, the sisaok dancers act out stories, wearing masks of grizzly bears, eagles, and wasps. The dancers carry rattles carved with the images of their crests. See also *Kusiut.* [Boas 1916]

Sitec

Nooksack, Salish, *Northwest Coast*

The sitec, or *soul,* is considered to be so light that it is easily dislodged from its owner. Soul loss can occur in three different ways: sudden fright, intentional or unintentional theft, and being drawn away because of the owner's strong attachment to a distant person, place, or thing. The soul can be seen only by those with a special gift of sight. It is described as a tiny *doll* in the image of its owner.

Whenever soul loss is suspected, a *syowoe* (seer) or medium is called to examine the sufferer and determine whether the soul is missing. If the syowoe diagnoses soul loss, the medium sends his or her ghost partner to retrieve the soul. A soul that flies away because of sudden fright will go to a nearby person. Soul loss is dangerous not only to the soul's owner but also to the person who has unwittingly attracted the soul. People have no way of coping with foreign souls, which must be removed by a *shaman.*

Untreated soul loss is fatal. Death (see *Dead*) is usually slow, starting with unusual behavior and sometimes insanity. Soul loss is more common in people who are weakened physically, emotionally, or ritually, as well as in children. Therefore special precautions are taken to protect children from soul loss. Parents make their children stay off the floor during winter dances because of the proximity of ghosts near the ground at this time. They also teach children to avoid burnt food offerings meant for ghosts. [Amoss 1978]

Siwin

Nooksack, Salish, *Northwest Coast*

Spells that involve calling on one's ancestors to influence events. Siwin are used to convince people to do things they would not ordinarily do, and can even be used to influence the weather and the scarcity or plentitude of game animals. For a love spell the practitioner calls his or her dead parents and grandparents, then names the person whose emotions he or she wants to influence. Siwin are also used to numb animals so they cannot run from the hunter, paralyze enemies, and deaden the feet of runners in a footrace. In order for the siwin to be most effective, special names are used for the person or object to be influenced. The spells can be used for the benefit of either the community or an individual. Only legitimate heirs can have knowledge passed on to them through siwin. [Amoss 1978]

Six Nations

Northeast

The tribes that comprise the Iroquois. The Mohawk, Oneida, Onondaga, Cayuga, and Seneca tribes were the original Confederacy of Five Nations. They were joined in the early eighteenth century by the Tuscarora, making an association of Six Nations. [Fenton 1987]

Skahnowa

Seneca, *Northeast*

Great *turtle,* the servant of *Doonongaes,* the horned serpent, who lives in a lake. Skahnowa patrols his master's home by swimming around the lake and keeping away intruders. [Fenton 1987]

Skan

Lakota, *Plains*

The *Sky,* who created *Tate,* the *Wind,* to be his companion. Skan is considered to be an all-powerful spirit. *Wohpe* is the daughter of Skan. See also *Day, Following Night.* [Walker 1982]

Skatene

Choctaw, *Southeast*

The old woman who could transform herself into an *owl* (see *Human-Animal Transformation*). Skatene ingratiates herself with young children in order to enter their household, then beheads their father while the family sleeps. She is known by the animals and birds for her nocturnal killings. After decapitating a victim, she flees with the head in her basket. If an animal meets her and asks to see what is in the basket, she threatens it with blindness, so all the animals leave her alone.

Skawehe

Finally the old woman meets some wildcats, who insist on seeing what is in her basket even at the risk of loosing their sight. When they see the human head, the wildcats know they have found Skatene. One wildcat holds her down while the others get a club with which to kill her, but she tricks the wildcat holding her and flies away as an owl. [Hudson 1976]

Skawehe

Penobscot, *Northeast*

"Greeting." A greeting or election *dance,* performed when the neighboring tribes (Passamaquoddy, Malecite) come to witness the election of a new chief. [Trigger 1978]

Skin Pouch

Seneca, *Northeast*

Pouch made from the entire skin of a rare animal and used to hold a sorcerer's charms, fetishes, and medicines. Every reputable sorcerer possesses a skin pouch. See also *Medicine Bundle.* [Fenton 1987]

Skinkuts

Kutenai, *Plateau*

A figure whose brothers are Moose and Kingfisher. *Coyote* is married to Dog and has two children, Misqolo'wum and Q!ota'ptsek!. He travels with *Yaukekam* to make the *Sun,* but Lynx (see also *Short Faces)* becomes the Sun instead. Angry, Coyote tries to shoot Sun, but it burns his arrows and causes a fire to pursue him. He outwits the fire by wrapping himself in his blanket and lying down across the trail on which the fire is chasing him. The blanket burns but Coyote is unharmed. This is why a fire will not burn a trail. [Boas and Chamberlain 1918]

Skinwalker

See *Shape Shifting* and *Yenaldlooshi.*

Sky-Holder

Iroquois, *Northeast*

One of the names for the *creator* (Te hara Liawago). He assigns *Ohswedogo* to the west and

Twehdaigo to the east to help human beings. See also *False Faces, Hawenniyo,* and *Sapling,* another name for creator. [Fenton 1987]

Sleep

Ojibwa, *Northeast, Subarctic*

A large *cat,* with Moon's help, brings sleep to the *Midewiwin* so that dignity, peace, and order will always reign in the Mide Lodge. Members of the Midewiwin believe that after a good night's sleep, disagreements can be handled by discussion rather than by force. Sleep also allows people to *dream* and meet *helping spirits.* [Landes 1968]

Small Dose (Nigahnegaha)

Seneca, *Northeast*

Medicine made by the animals to resuscitate their human friend Bloody Hand, a famous hunter and war chief. Small Dose was then entrusted to Bloody Hand for *healing* people injured by falls, blows, or arrow wounds.

Bloody Hand has great love for birds and animals. Whenever he kills a deer he shares some of the meat with all the animals. During an intense battle, Bloody Hand is scalped (see *Scalping)* and killed, and his body left naked in the forest. All the birds of the air see the battle and the mutilation of their friend. They hold a council to figure out how to bring Bloody Hand back to life. They decide that first they must recover Bloody Hand's scalp. Black Hawk is sent to recover the scalp, because his sharp beak and claws can untie the cords that hold it. Then they make the Small Dose medicine. First each animal puts a small piece of its flesh into a pot. Then they mix the pieces with squash seeds and blood from a cornstalk grown without seeds.

The animals choose the chief of the crows to notify Shadahgeah, chief of all the birds, of their intention to rescuscitate Bloody Hand with medicine made of their flesh. When the medicine is strong enough, Chickadee is appointed to drink it. He then enters Bloody Hand's body through his mouth, travels to his stomach, and regurgitates the medicine. The rest of the animals sing and rub Bloody Hand's body with medicine, without stopping, for two days and two nights. Gradually Bloody Hand's body warms and life returns to it.

Bloody Hand is instructed that whenever the medicine is used a feast must be given in its honor, tobacco must be burned, and the animals should be remembered. The giving of feasts and the burning of tobacco is necessary to keep the medicine strong. The person in possession of the powerful medicine is to sing the songs that activate the medicine.

Small Dose medicine was extremely potent, and only a *Hochinagen,* a medicine person, could administer it. A small portion of the medicine was mixed with water. If it did not dissolve, it was understood that the patient would die, and the medicine was not given. If the medicine dissolved, it was then administered. The patient was forbidden to eat anything that had color in it; doing so would break the power of the Nigahnegaha and cause him or her to die. The patient could eat only pure white beans or white cob corn. The patient was kept isolated for four days, attended only by the Hochinagen. In cases where more than one dose of Nigahnegaha was needed, the Hochinagen would summon other medicine people to assist. They cooked a kettle of white beans for themselves and for the singers who were also called upon to help. *Tobacco* was burned to increase the strength of the medicine.

If the patient was cured, he or she celebrated by preparing a feast of a great kettle of hulled corn seasoned with meat cut into small pieces. The Hochinagen who administered the medicine came to sing and dance in honor of the medicine. Only the Hochinagen was allowed to sing at the feast of thanksgiving honoring Nigahnegaha. [Curtin and Hewitt 1918]

Smohalla
Sahaptin, *Plateau*
Founder of the *Smohalla Cult,* also known as the Dreamers. Smohalla, a Sahaptin-speaking man, was wounded and left for dead in 1860. While recovering he had a vision experience. When he returned to his people, he taught the message he had received concerning the destruction of the world, the return of the dead, and the restoration of a clean and perfect world. [Beckham, Toepel, and Minor 1984]

Smohalla Cult
Sahaptin, Cayuse, Spokane, Wasco, Wishram, Nez Perce, *Plateau*
Also known as the *Dreamers.* A cult founded by *Smohalla* about 1860 that advocated preparing for the end of the world and fostered an attitude of hostility toward intrusive European-Americans. Followers of Smohalla held their meetings in churchlike buildings. The message of resistance to European-Americans helped unite the Nez Perce and Bannock peoples for their battle against the U.S. government in the late 1870s. A modified version of Smohalla teachings, known as the Feather Religion or Seven Drums Religion, is still practiced by some native peoples along the Columbia River. See also *Ghost Dance of 1890* and *Prophet Dance Movement.* [Beckham, Toepel, and Minor 1984]

Smoking-with-the-Bear
Pawnee, *Plains*
A powerful medicine person who is given *power* by a bear to open people and eat their livers. Smoking-with-the-Bear also rids his village of malevolent *medicine people* and can produce a live bear in his curing lodge when healing a person. Smoking-with-the-Bear learns his medicine as a young boy when Magpie, errand carrier of the medicine people, takes him to Bear to be cured of a critical illness caused by a jealous medicine man. Bear revives the unconscious Smoking-with-the-Bear by blowing his breath into the boy's nostrils. He also gives the boy a bear claw, which becomes a powerful medicine. From this point on, Smoking-with-the-Bear has great healing powers and, consistent with his name, always offers smoke to the rising sun and to the bears. [Murie 1989]

Snake
Puyallup-Nisqually, Southern Puget Sound, *Northwest Coast*
A *power* (see *Sqalalitut*) considered to be useless because it causes its owner to dislike other people and to be disliked by them. Thus a man with snake power ends up living alone. [Smith 1940]

Snake(s)
Snakes are numerous in Native American mythology and ritual. *Horned serpents* appear widely. Northwest coast stories describe snakes with heads on both ends. Snakes may eat humans or turn into humans, as in the Navajo *Big Star Way* and Seminole *Human Snakes*. A snake steals a girl in the *Apache Bear Dance*. *Hinon,* the Seneca Thunderer, cures a woman made ill by a snake. *Zuzeca* (Lakota) is a snake spirit responsible for sly activities. The Pueblo *Water Snake* is associated with springs and water sources. Hopi dancers hold rattlesnakes in their mouths in the *Snake Dance*. See also *Rattlesnake*.

Snake Dance
Hopi, *Southwest*
A nine-day summer ceremony conducted jointly by the Snake and Antelope societies of several Hopi villages, alternating every other year with the *Flute Dance*. This ceremony is among the most widely recognized, although not well understood, of all Native American rituals because it features the capturing of live snakes, which the dancers hold in their mouths. The whole ceremonial complex emphasizes *rain* and the accompanying fertility, and is directed particularly to such garden (as opposed to field) crops as beans, sweet corn, squash, and melons. The captured snakes are released at the end of the ceremony, taking the prayers (see *Prayer and Prayersticks)* and wishes of the Hopi to the deities. See also *Hopi Ritual Cycle*. [Bradfield 1973; Fewkes 1888a, 1892, 1894b; Hodge 1896; Parsons 1936; Stephen 1888, 1936; Titiev 1944; Voth 1902]

Snake People
Navajo, *Southwest*
Snakes in human form. See *Beautyway*.

Snee-nee-iq
Northwest Coast
A harmful *narnauk* (animal-person of ancient time) who carries off *children* in a big basket on her back, taking them to her mountain home so she can eat them. See also *Dzoo-noo-qua*. [Boas 1916]

Snow
The Arapaho figure *Raw Gums* creates snow by bashing out the brains of White Owl Woman *(Nankubacein)*. The Haida attribute the origin of snow to feathers shed by the culture hero *Sin*. [Keshena 1911]

Snowats
Yoncalla, Kalapuya, *Northwest Coast, Plateau*
First Woman, who grows out of jellylike matter located on a stone table atop a mountain. She holds a male child. When Snowats is fully grown, she comes down the mountain with her child. They are met by a wolf (Quartux). Snowats straps her son to the wolf's back, and the two travel together as the world becomes filled with people. [Beckham, Toepel, and Minor 1984]

Societies
Most Native American cultures have societies dedicated to a variety of purposes and activities. Many of these are ritual societies that do *healing* (see *Black-Tailed Deer Dance)* or prepare for war (e.g., *Wakincuzas,* the Lakota Soldier Society) or the hunt (Omaha *Hethuska)*. Some societies are gender-restricted, such as *Ikonnokatsiyiks,* the Blackfoot men's societies. Some are dancing societies, like the Blackfoot Grass Dance Society *(Ka?espai)*. The Pawnee have the *Crow Lance Society* and the *Crow-Water Society*. Several Iroquois healing and dancing societies are associated with the *False Faces*. Membership in societies is usually restricted and requires a rite of initiation. Societies often maintain secret knowledge.

Soft Goods
Navajo, *Southwest*
See *Yodi and Ntliz.* Soft goods, yodi, is a major classification of material objects, contrasting with jewels or hard goods, ntliz.

Solar Eclipses
The infrequent solar eclipse is an awesome event. In Native American mythology the solar eclipse is frequently presented as an ominous event, as in the *Apache creation and emergence* stories, where it is attributed to incessant arguing by the early people. A solar eclipse may authenticate a vision or prophecy.

Song(s)
Many Native American rites and ceremonies are performed according to patterns established in mythology or are based on mythological events. The mythic story is sometimes told at the ritual performance. More commonly, however, the elements of the story are captured in songs sung throughout the ritual. Song is therefore almost inseparable from mythology: it is mythology ritualized. Many cultures consider songs to be property. Some, like the Navajo, would consider anyone who owns no songs to be poor.

The following provides a sampling of mythological and ritual references to songs. Special songs are sung during the Piegan *Black-Tailed Deer Dance.* In the Navajo *Blessingway,* the creation of the world is effected through song. The Nootka *Changing Masks Song* cues the dancers when to change masks. Songs tell stories in the Eskimo *Inviting-In Feast,* and song duels take place in the *Messenger Feast.* Songs are given to an initiate upon his entrance into the Pawnee *Crow-Water Society. Iniskim* (Blackfoot) is a fossil rock that teaches songs.

Songs are also sung as *medicine* in healing rites. Virtually all Navajo rites are healing rites, and each has hundreds of songs. In the Navajo *Nightway* mythology, a character's crying turns to song. The songs of the Omaha *Hethuska* society keep memories of bravery. *Nana csyak* are Nootka divining songs. *Naachin* (Beaver) are dreamers who grab songs in their dreams. *Orenda,* an Iroquoian concept of power, may be associated with songs. The Nooksack have traditions of inherited *spirit songs.* [Eckert and Newmark 1980]

Song Duels
Eskimo, Northern Alaska, Central Canadian Arctic, Greenland, *Arctic*
A ritual for airing grievances and dealing with interpersonal conflict. In central Canada, song duels were part of song and dance festivals. Other Arctic communities incorporated song duels within the intercommunity joking-avoidance relationship (see *Joking Relationships).* Song duels were held in different seasons, often outdoors, as part of boxing and head-butting activities. In a duel, the two persons involved in the conflict would sing humorous songs. Each song was intended to affirm the singer's goodness and his opponent's lack of it. Such attacks were to be received with good *humor.* The song exchange would continue until one person was either laughed down by the audience or completely humiliated.

Song Woman
Tsimshian, *Northwest Coast*
Woman who gives wonderful songs to worthy people. The songs, which come from every part of Song Woman's body, are sung in the feast houses. [Boas 1916]

So?oda
Kawaiisu, *Great Basin*
Tobacco, personified as a whirlwind traveling around the world. So?oda has neither father nor mother; it just grows on the earth. Because it lacks parents, so?oda is believed to be powerful *medicine.* [Zigmond 1980]

Sorcerer(s)
One who uses power for malevolent ends. The techniques and actions of a sorcerer are often indistinguishable from those of a *shaman* or medi-

cine person (see *Medicine People),* the principal distinction being the object to which the power or actions are directed. Synonymous with *witch.*

Sotic
Nooksack, Salish, *Northwest Coast*
"North Wind People." Supernatural guests who visit villages in winter, bringing snow and dropping temperatures. Showing disrespect to the North Wind People leads to misfortune. To show respect, the people of the village remain quiet and keep their children from playing when the North Wind People are visiting. When the North Wind People are not visiting during the winter, the villagers play drums, sing, and make offerings of berries and meat.

One time *Raven,* who has been left at home to watch the children of the North Wind People, carelessly allows a child to fall into the fire. When the North Wind People learn of the tragedy, they leave immediately. The Nooksack say this is why the North Wind People always leave suddenly. [Amoss 1978]

Soul
A term that, due to its Christian implications, may be insufficient to accurately reflect Native American conceptions. Generally its interpretation should be limited to "life force," although sometimes this force may be personified. For Native American conceptions of "soul," see *Anerneq* (Yupik), *Biigistiin* (Navajo), and *Sitec* (Nooksack). Illness may be attributed to the loss or theft of the "soul," in which case a *shaman* may be called to retrieve the soul through a spirit journey. [Elmendorf 1967; Haile 1943b]

Soulbieche
Alabama, *Southeast*
"Spirit-That-Dwells." The spirit being to whom the *pipe* is offered at all ceremonies. Soulbieche is responsible for all life. [Hudson 1976]

Soup Dance
Seminole, Oklahoma and *Southeast*
Also known as the Horned Owl Dance, it is the final event of the ceremonial year, beginning in May and ending in September. Married women are ritually selected to be the cooks for this event held at the *Square Ground.* While the women cook cornbread and a soup made from wild game, the men hunt. When the men return, everyone feasts on the soup, after which the Soup Dance continues throughout the night. The dance closes with the Drunken Dance, Hajo Opvnka. In this dance, men dressed as women act as clowns (see *Clowns and Clowning Societies),* while the women remove their *locv-saukv* (turtle leg rattles) and holler like men. The songs of the Hajo Opvnka are passionate *love* songs. It is also said that the *sapiya* (animate love stones) sing during the Soup Dance. [Sturtevant 1987]

Soyal
Hopi, *Southwest*
Winter solstice ceremony. The *Hopi Ritual Cycle* is an annual cycle divided roughly in half. The period beginning with the winter solstice and lasting until a few weeks past the summer solstice is distinguished by the frequent appearance of *kachinas,* masked messenger spirit beings. Soyal is a winter solstice ritual designed to turn the sun back in its course. Combined with this may be a ritual in which medicine is prepared and either drunk or rubbed on the body to promote health and strength. The first kachina to appear, thereby opening the kachina season, is Soyal, a shabbily dressed figure who totters along in the movements of an old man. He makes his way to *kivas,* placing prayer feathers *(paho)* and sprinkling cornmeal. Other Soyal actions include the preparation of prayer feathers for relatives, crops, animals, houses, cars, and personal well-being. In some Hopi villages, a kachina known as Mastop appears and symbolically fertilizes all the women in a ritualized gesture of copulation. [Dorsey and Voth 1901; Voth 1905b; Wright 1973]

Soyoko
Hopi, *Southwest*
A ritualized frightening by horrible-looking *kachina* figures (Soyok) in an effort to discipline

Mastop, a Hopi Kachina, symbolically fertilizes all the women during Soyal. Painting by Cliff Bahnimptewa from *Kachinas: A Hopi Artist's Documentary,* by Barton Wright, copyright © 1973 by the Heard Museum. Published by Northland Publishing, Flagstaff, Arizona, with The Heard Museum, Phoenix, Arizona. Painting from the collection of The Heard Museum, Phoenix, Arizona.

naughty *children*. The event occurs during *Powamu*. Upon a parent's request, several of these ogre figures appear at the home of the naughty child. They demand impossible tasks of the children, warning them they will be back to check on them in several days. Of course, when they return the children have not accomplished the assigned tasks and are usually hiding somewhere in the house. The parents present the children to account for their actions. The Soyok kachinas, hideous in appearance and equipped with cleavers and saws, demand that the child be turned over to be eaten. The parents refuse to release the child, but the process ends up costing the family all its stores of food. The Soyok kachinas, loaded with food, host a feast for the community and, it is hoped, the child's behavior improves. See also *Zuni Ritual Cycle* for a comparable example. [Wright 1973]

Speaker
See *Hadentheni and Hanigongendatha.*

Speech
Navajo, *Southwest*
Navajos personify speech as Long Life Girl (see *Sa?ah naghai bikeh hozho*). Speech is also associated with Wind *(Nilchi?i).*

Spider
A figure that appears often in Native American mythology. Examples include *Djieien,* the Seneca monster spider, and *Iktomi,* the Lakota *trickster.* See also *Spider Woman.*

Spider Woman
Spider appears as a woman in many mythologies. The Pawnee identify her as *Red-Spider-Woman* in their account of the origin of squash medicine, in which she becomes the root. They also know her by the name *Witch Woman.* She assists the Keresan female creator *Iatiku* by helping plant seeds. As *Kokyan wuhti,* she plays a major role in Hopi emergence, and she assists the Zuni *Pautiwa* (see *Rain Priest*). For the Navajo, Spider Woman

(na?ackjeii esdzaa) is one of those who travels through the lower worlds during the emergence journey.

Spider Woman consistently plays dual roles of helper and one who is dangerous. She is responsible for teaching *weaving* to human beings. See also *Water Monster.* [Haile 1943a; Matthews 1897; Reichard 1974; Stephen 1930]

Spirit(s)
The term "spirit" is widely used to refer to entities thought to be other than human who are insubstantial, who are named and possess characters and attributes, who have powers that influence the human world, and who are recognized, contacted, and communicated with by Native Americans. The term is inadequate, and its implications probably only vaguely approximate Native American conceptions. English is remarkably limited to terms that carry a specifically western and Christian heritage. *Inua* (Eskimo) and *nagi* (Lakota) are but two of the hundreds of Native American terms that might be translated as "spirit."

Spirit Dancing
Salish, *Northwest Coast*
Night ceremonials held between November and April, where people gather to help each other sing and dance individual spirit songs, validate the giving of family-owned names (see *Names and Naming),* initiate new dancers into spirit dancing, and affirm relationships. Public validation of names begins with the inviting of guests, who are thanked for their support with gifts given by the host. After a large feast and the distribution of gifts, the spirit singing and dancing begins.

Each person who has been initiated as a spirit dancer sings his or her own song and performs the accompanying dance, having previously received the song and dance during a *vision quest.* New initiates dance first. The dancers are in altered states of consciousness because their spirits have taken possession of them. Therefore it is important to have close friends and family ready to help them sit down when they finish, lest they fall.

Tahaum Soyoko (Hopi), as beautiful as he is frightening. He appears at Powamu to frighten naughty children.
Painting by Cliff Bahnimptewa from *Kachinas: A Hopi Artist's Documentary,* by Barton Wright, copyright ©1973 by
the Heard Museum. Published by Northland Publishing, Flagstaff, Arizona, with The Heard Museum, Phoenix,
Arizona. Painting from the collection of The Heard Museum, Phoenix, Arizona.

Spirit visions, unlike vision quests of the Plains, come without warning from deceased relatives to those who are ready to receive them. Many Salish people, however, believe that most new dancers will receive songs under the tutelage of special teachers, rather than spontaneously from deceased relatives. Families or spouses may arrange for relatives to be initiated into spirit dancing. Family support during initiation is crucial to ensuring the dancer a good relationship with his or her helping spirit. Close relatives can arrange to have family members who are exhibiting dangerous or destructive behavior initiated against their will. It is thought that gaining a helping spirit will aid the person in whatever is troubling him or her and will provide protection from harmful influences. Because of this power, initiation is handled by specialists, who agree to a nonconsenting initiation if there is no other way to help the individual. [Amoss 1978]

Spirit Journey(s)

A journey taken by an entranced *shaman* to rescue a lost or stolen life force, or to appease a *Master/Mistress of Animals*.

Spirit Keeping Ceremony

Lakota, *Plains*

An elaborate ceremony with serious tribal significance that honors the spirit of a deceased person, usually a child. Only a few people can afford to undertake the year of preparation necessary for this ceremony, which is considered the highest expression of devotion to one's family and tribe.

After a child's death and burial (see *Dead*), family members mourn for four days (see *Wacekiyapi*). The men wail and the women slash their arms. At the end of this time a small quilled pouch containing a lock of the child's hair is placed in the Ghost Lodge, a portable tipi specially constructed for this purpose. The Ghost Lodge is then placed in front of the parents' tipi, and all mourning ceases because the spirit of the dead child is present with the parents. Before a gathering of other families who have kept spirits, the

Wicasa Itacan (executive leader) smokes a red-painted pipe and instructs the parents on the gravity of keeping a spirit. To acknowledge the sanctity of this responsibility, the parents keep their faces painted red for a year. The Wicasa Itacan places food in a special bowl at the back of the ghost lodge to feed the spirit. Each day, a family member fills the bowl to keep the spirit fed.

Over the next year the parents engage skilled craftspeople to make beautiful clothes. The more beautiful and intricate the design and decorations, the more honor is given to the spirit of the deceased. If the camp is moved during the year, a specially selected horse moves the spirit and the ghost tipi. When the new camp is made, the ghost tipi is set up first. At the end of the year, when the family has accumulated enough clothing to honor the spirit, a day is chosen for its release. A Wicasa Itacan is asked to prepare the spirit and preside at the ceremony. On the day of the ceremony, the Wicasa Itacan paints a likeness of the deceased on a small piece of tanned skin. The portrait is attached to the top of a cottonwood pole about the height of the deceased. This spirit pole is placed in the rear of the ghost tipi. A taller pole, with vines entwined around its base, is placed at the front of the tipi. The family sits behind the spirit pole, and all the specially made items are brought in and placed opposite them. After the opening prayer with the pipe, the dead child's mother dresses the spirit pole in the beautiful garments. The people feast together, and the most beautiful robe is placed over the vine-wrapped pole at the tipi entrance to represent a live buffalo. A warbonnet is placed on its head, along with all the articles of clothing and goods gathered by the parents. The Wicasa Itacan then announces the people chosen to receive gifts, including the poor, the needy, and those who have helped the family during the year. All the gifts are given in the name of the honored spirit.

The Wicasa Itacan closes the ceremony by unwrapping the spirit bundle, which is done in four stages. Then he walks out of the tipi so that the spirit will be properly released and can journey on the Spirit Road, the *Milky Way*. The spirit release is an occasion of great joy. The parents then invite people to take everything that remains, leaving the opened bundle and the spirit post as their only possessions. Now the parents are destitute and ready to start anew. Friends and relatives set up a new tipi for them and bring them food. Wealthy or highly respected parents might be invited by the Wicasas or tribal leaders to perform the *White Buffalo Ceremony* in conjunction with the Spirit Keeping Ceremony. [Walker 1982]

Spirit of Dead
See *Pinanne.*

Spirit Powers
Kalapuya, *Northwest Coast*
Spirits that live in the forests and act as guardians for the people. Anyone can obtain spirit powers, but having strong spirit powers makes one a *shaman*. Shamans can be either male or female. Spirit powers are strengthened during winter dances, and shamans often give winter dances to strengthen their powers. Shamans have important community responsibilities as healers and ceremonial leaders. A shaman who falls under the power of negative guardian spirits could end up killing people by poisoning them or by stealing their spirit power. Therefore a shaman suspected of being under the power of negative spirit powers might be killed by the community. Some of the more common spirit powers are Eagle Spirit, with power to give wealth and wives, and in the past, slaves and shaman power; Coyote Spirit, for transvestite power; North Wind Spirit, for blizzard and snow power; Grizzly Bear Spirit, considered a negative power for killing people; and Grouse Spirit, for snow power.

A shaman's dress tells of his or her spirit powers and status in the village. This dress, which often reaches the ground, consists of belts decorated with beads, shells, feathers, and hair. The shaman's spirit powers are symbolized by painted canes and by a headdress made of the scalp of a large black- or red-headed woodpecker. [Beckham, Toepel, and Minor 1984]

Spirit Song(s)
Nooksack, Salish, *Northwest Coast*
The word syowen refers to the Spirit Song, the source of the song, and often the vision experience of the dancers who dance the song (see also *Spirit Dancing*). Spirit Songs are inherited from within families. The helping spirit of a deceased relative lingers, waiting to go to another member of the family. The helping spirit picks out and troubles its human partner until he or she dances and sings the Spirit Song. People who do not cooperate with the helping spirits and ignore the Spirit Song become troubled and depressed. They may be captured for initiation at the Spirit Dance and helped to develop the song that has been troubling them.

If the Spirit Song comes to a sick person, the illness is usually one that does not respond to Western medicine. In such cases a *shaman* is consulted to diagnose and cure the problem. Spirit Songs also come to people who are grieving. The bereaved person weeps constantly until the sound of weeping changes to the groans of a spirit dancer in possession.

A relationship with a Spirit Song is a constant challenge. The owner of a Spirit Song is responsible for making sure it is given adequate expression by dancing in the winter ceremonial, observing the style of face painting and costume as directed by the Spirit Song, and avoiding alcohol. Unhappy Spirit Songs make their human partners suffer, and a neglected Spirit Song will leave. People with a newly acquired Spirit Song must learn to control feelings of anger so that their Spirit Song does not take unknown action against an enemy. [Amoss 1978]

Spitting-Horn-Shell and Split-Rump
Arapaho, *Plains*
Spitting-Horn-Shell is a handsome young man whom all the girls desire as a marriage partner.

Split-Rump is a small bird that lives in the abandoned nests of geese and does not fly very high. Split-Rump convinces a young girl that he is Spitting-Horn-Shell by spitting out cut bone shells. The girl agrees to go with him to the *Sun Dance,* where Spitting-Horn-Shell dances on the back of Split-Rump, and the girl realizes she has been deceived. She leaves Split-Rump and sits beside Spitting-Horn-Shell, who takes her as his wife. Furious, Split-Rump kills Spitting-Horn-Shell. The villagers chase him to a river and then a lake, where they drag the bottom unsuccessfully for his body. Split-Rump is cursed to remain close to the lake. [Dorsey and Kroeber 1903]

Split-Faced Being
Northeast
The Iroquois giant *Dehotgohsgayeh.*

Sqalalitut
Puyallup-Nisqually, Southern Puget Sound, *Northwest Coast*
Power that comes from the supernatural and is both personal (used privately) and ceremonial (used in public), affecting every aspect of life. The amount and quality of an individual's power(s) varies depending on his or her personality. Sqalalitut power(s) are related to ceremonies that include competition for prestige through gambling, wealth, or even eating.

New power(s) may come to anyone at any age, although puberty is considered the most active time. Powers are as eager to make contact with humans as humans are to have them, because a power's appetites and pleasures can only be satisfied through its human contacts. Throughout life, people quest for new powers while striving to keep their current ones satisfied. Entire villages work to keep the powers of village members intact. Some powers are identified with certain geographical areas. Sqalalitut should not be confused with the *helping spirits* of other tribes. For other terms designating Puyallup conceptions of power, see *Astcatstudab, Ayaxaus, Swoxqwad, Tiotlbax, Tudab,* and *Xwaixwieda.* [Elmendorf 1977]

Square Ground
Creek, *Southeast;* Seminole, Oklahoma and *Southeast*
Also known as Stomp Ground. The place of religious and political activity in Seminole life, where ceremonial cycles, *Green Corn Dance, Match Ball Games,* and various dances are held. All 12 bands of the Seminole tribe use square grounds, and Seminole towns are built around them. Each Seminole belongs to a particular square or stomp ground.

The square ground consists of a square within a circle enclosed by a low mounded ring, called a tajo, made up of sweepings, leaves, and dust from annual cleanings. The area inside the tajo, where the dances and ceremonies are held, is called the paskofv. No buildings are erected on the east end of the square ground. An arbor partly covers the remaining area of the square ground. See also *Soup Dance* and *Stomp Dance.* [Howard 1984; Sturtevant 1987]

Squash Medicine
Pawnee, *Plains*
Before the advent of human beings, giants powerful enough to carry buffalo roam the earth. These giants fear nothing and make fun of both the Sun and Thunder. *Tirawahat* decides to *flood* the earth in order to destroy the giants. The buffalo in the west move, and water from the rain covers the earth. When the flood comes, the giants cling to steep banks and other high places, but eventually they sink under the water, and the earth is covered with lightning and thunder. The power of the giants remains in their bones, which have healing power for the humans who are to come.

After the origin of human beings, Black Meteor Star visits the earth and tells the humans where to dig to find a powerful root that sprang from one of the giants. A man digs up the squash root, which has a horrid smell. He offers smoke to it and addresses it as "father" and "mother." While the man is praying to the root it oozes water, and the man knows the root wants to be freed from the earth. The root is ceremoniously removed, then carefully cut up and distributed among the medicine people. The man who dug up the root takes the central part.

During the night a woman, *Red-Spider-Woman*, appears to the man. She is clothed in black with soft, downy feathers, and she carries a clamshell in her left hand and ground-up root in her right hand. She sings and drops some of the powdered root in the clamshell. Then she teaches the man how to use the root for *healing*. The man realizes he has been addressed by the root herself, and he becomes a great medicine person. [Murie 1989]

Squaw Dance
Navajo, *Southwest*
A common English name for *Enemyway*.

Starisu
Pawnee, *Plains*
A woman's dance ceremony given by the creator *Tirawahat* to celebrate the gift of buffalo sent by Tirawahat when the people were hungry. Preparation for the ceremony began in the winter, when the highest-ranking young men hunted the fattest buffalo for the ceremony. The killed buffalo was taken to the chief's lodge, where the meat was dried during the winter. In the spring, after the corn had been planted but before the spring buffalo hunt began, four *kurahus* (ritual leaders or priests) and a chief entered the lodge of another chief and requested that the ceremony be held. The kurahus invited young men and women of high rank to participate. The Starisu involved opening the *medicine bundle* and relating the origin story of the ceremony. A plentiful supply of buffalo was believed to be dependent upon the correct performance of the Starisu ceremony. [Murie 1989]

Stars and Starlore
Personified stars play many roles in mythology and ritual. Pawnee religion is particularly noted for its extensive reference to stars: *Big Black Me-teoric Star, Evening Star,* and the ritual sacrifice to *Morning Star*. The Pawnee hold that their village founders were created by the stars (see *Bundle Societies),* and they tell stories of the origin of the stars (see *Warrior Bird and the Origin of Stars).* The dice in the Pawnee *Basket Dice Game* represent stars. In the Navajo *Big Star Way,* Star People assist the culture hero. The Crow culture hero *Old Woman's Grandchild* becomes the north star. Stars are sometimes partners in marriage (see Shawnee *Waupee).*

Many Native American cultures tell stories of the origin of stars and constellations. The Piman creation story, *Tcu-unnyikita,* tells how Earth Shaman creates stars from a spray of water. The Navajo *Black God* is the creator of constellations (see also *Navajo Starlore).* The Yurok figure *Pulekukwerek* brings the stars to the night sky. *Glooscap* (Micmac) is a creator of constellations. The Cree culture heroes *Pine Root and Beaded Head* become stars. The origin of Ursa Major is the subject of many stories; see *Big Dipper, Great Bear Constellation,* and *Sapu igye.* The origin of the Pleiades is told as part of the Arapaho story of *Foot-Stuck-Child.* The Milky Way is often considered to be the road followed by the dead. Coyote is sometimes held responsible for spraying the stars across the sky to form the Milky Way. The Juaneño of California believe the deceased become stars (see *Takwe).* The Penobscot *Yuneha* is a dance that represents a constellation. See also the Catawba story of a comet, *Ugni,* and the story of the origin of the Delaware men's dance, *Linkan,* in which the dancers dance until they become stars. [Carroll 1979; Chamberlain 1982; Eason 1980; Einhorn 1976; Evans 1986; Grinnell 1894, 1921; Haeberlin 1906; Haile 1947c; Hamilton 1905; Mayo 1987; Swanson 1976; Viele 1981; Wheelwright 1940, 1956; Wilson 1893; Wissler 1936; Young 1970]

Stcemqestcint
Coeur d'Alene, *Plateau*
"Tree Men." Strong-smelling males who appear as men dressed in buffalo skins. They have the

power to transform themselves into trees and bushes. If Tree Men are seen and called to by humans, they transform into trees or bushes. The power of a human being's glance is believed to prevent them from transforming back into men. [Norman 1990]

Stikini
Seminole, Oklahoma and *Southeast*

"Man-Owls." People who transform into horned owls (see *Human-Animal Transformation* and *Owl)* and keep themselves alive by stealing and eating the hearts of humans. Stikini use their powers to put people into a deep sleep, then pull the victims' hearts out through their mouths. The hearts are cooked in a special small iron kettle. To transform into an owl, a person goes to the woods and vomits up his or her inner organs. In order to become human again, the stikini must swallow the organs. The smell of the organs often warns people there are stikini about. A stikini can be killed only with a special arrow that has been rubbed with herbal medicines and has owl feathers attached to it. [Howard 1984; Sturtevant 1987]

Stomp Dance (Opvnka hajo)
Creek, *Southeast;* Seminole, Oklahoma and *Southeast*

Considered the national dance of the Seminoles and Creeks. This *dance* is one of many central to Seminole and Creek religious life. "Stomp leaders" hold high status throughout the tribe.

Stomp Dances are nighttime dances held during May and June in preparation for the *Green Corn Dance* performed in July or August. In preparation for a Stomp Dance, the men purify themselves by washing and drinking a medicinal *emetic* called hoyvniji. The dance is initiated by men at the *Square Ground.* The leader begins by walking counterclockwise around the fire, inviting other experienced male dancers to join him. Women and girls may join once there is a line of male dancers. After the singing of introductory songs, the shell-shaker girl takes her place behind

the leader. Like all Seminole dances, the Stomp Dance has the fire as its focal point. During the first Stomp Dance of the season, the fire is fed by sacrificing meat to it. See also *Human Snakes* and *Locv-saukv,* the women's leg rattles worn during the Stomp Dance. [Howard 1984; Sturtevant 1987]

Stomp Ground
See *Square Ground.*

Stone(s)
Rocks and stones occasionally appear, sometimes personified, in Native American mythology. *Assin* (Ojibwa) is a shaking tent visitor. *Saya* (Beaver) is a culture hero who turns to stone, as does *Waux,* the Tsimshian hunter.

Stonecoats (Jokao)
Seneca, Iroquois, *Northeast*

Powerful cannibalistic creatures (see *Cannibal),* said to be the offspring of Winter. They live in the north where Winter originates, and their power resides in their inpenetrable stone coats. They are frequently found in stories concerning the origin of the *False Faces.* In one story, they are divested of their stone coats, and thus of their power, shortly after creation. They are left on earth to help hunters and heal illness.

In another story, Winter is causing severe famine with freezing temperatures and deep snow. People are so hungry they start to eat one another. Seeing what is happening, some people escape southward to a milder climate, leaving their cannibal village mates, who become monsters, giants, and Stonecoats. Eventually one of the Stonecoats finds his way to the river that separates the north land from the south, but he will not cross the river because he is afraid of water. The Stonecoat calls out to a hunter on the opposite side for help. The hunter comes to the Stonecoat in a canoe and gives him hot deer fat to drink. This causes the coat to melt, and consequently the snows begin to melt. See also *Genonsgwa* and *Ocasta.* [Fenton 1987]

Storms

The existence of storms is the subject of some stories. In the Navajo *Beautyway,* storms are released by the heroine. *Hakulaq* (Tsimshian) is a monster responsible for storms. The Passamaquoddy attribute storms to the bird figure *Wuchowsen.*

Story Knife Tales

Eskimo, Alaska, *Arctic*

A type of story told to and by Eskimo girls between the ages of 5 and 16. It involves using story knives to draw pictures on wet mud, snow, or dirt. The art of telling story knife tales is passed down by grandmothers and older sisters, who use them to entertain the girls, protect them from supernatural harm, and prepare them for adult life as women. Many local variations of story knife tales exist within the Yukon-Kuskokwim region. The girls may compete with one another to guess whose house and possessions are represented in the story. Different symbols are used to represent the time of the story, the speaker, and the identities of the various characters.

The stories usually open with a grandmother and granddaughter sitting on a bed. As the story unfolds, earlier scenes are erased and new ones drawn. The female-dominated stories deal with episodes from people's lives and emphasize the importance of obeying elders. In the stories, disobedience does not harm the one who disobeys but rather someone near to her. For example, if the girl in the story disobeys, her grandmother usually dies. The stories usually end in death and/or marriage. Most plots are originated by the grandmothers.

Story knives are 4 to 15 inches long and made from ivory, bone, antler, or wood. In contemporary times, a table knife is often used. The earliest story knife dates from before 1690. [Oswalt 1964]

Story Type(s)

Many cultures have terms to distinguish among different types of stories. Stories of origin may be distinguished from stories about historical figures. Stories that are associated closely with ritual and religion may be distinguished from stories told primarily for entertainment. A few of these terms are discussed in this dictionary. Terms that designate origin stories include *Chimikyanakowa* (Zuni) and *Tcu-unnyikita* (Pima). Many cultures have terms for ancient stories or stories of long ago; among these are *Tonht onh wodihe* (Dene Dhaa), and *Unipkaat* (Inupiaq). The Nootka term *e?ican* refers to legends, whereas oyaqhmis refers to news and *Himowico* to stories of culture heroes. Ojibwa Mide stories are called *Atisokan.* Omaha call humorous stories *Higu* and stories of visions, *Wakandanacian.* Mohave stories of war and migration are called *Ich-kanava. Wodih* is the Dine Dhaa term referring to stories, lectures, and news. Tsimshian refer to stories of individual experience as *Malesk* and animal stories as *Adaox.* [Aarne and Thompson 1964; Jacobsen 1905]

Storytelling

The oral narration of story and tradition, an essential aspect of native religious traditions throughout North America. Storytelling creates bonds, heals, clarifies identity, celebrates life paradoxes, and entertains. It also presents, maintains, and critiques history, serving to reinforce cultural and religious continuity. Practically all tribes have designations of various story types in elaborate typologies. These include such distinctions as true and false stories, anecdotes, and origin stories. Many cultures have men's stories and women's stories.

Storytelling is an activity that creates as well as preserves. Stories may originate through dreams or from helping spirit encounters. They are often considered property, and may be brought or received as gifts. Some stories are told as parts of rituals and thus must be recited with precision. Storytelling may be restricted to certain seasons of the year or times of day.

A good storyteller has the ability to develop and use the many voices in a story, performing the story while narrating it. Often, individual storytellers delight in producing rich variants of well-known stories. An aspiring storyteller must often serve an apprenticeship with a recognized storyteller in order to learn extensive and highly complicated story traditions.

Stricken Twins

Navajo, *Southwest*
A version of *Nightway* mythology.

Stvkwvnaya

Seminole, Oklahoma and *Southeast*
Tie Snake, a mythical water snake whose single horn gives powerful *medicine* for hunting and love. The stkwvnaya is summoned with four special songs, and its horn scraped for the powerful medicine. People not prepared with these songs who encounter stvkwvnaya are exposed to serious illness. [Howard 1984]

Sucking

A technique used by *shamans* to cure people suffering from an illness caused by a malevolent object within their bodies. Such an object may have been "shot" into the victim by a sorcerer or *witch*. Sometimes the shaman displays the removed object for all to see. See also *Ontetsans*, Huron healers who cure by sucking.

Sukdu

Tanaina, *Subarctic*
Story cycles used to instruct children. [Norman 1990]

Suku

Alsea, *Northwest Coast*
"Black *Bear*." The *culture hero* who is one of the first people to act as a transformer (see *Transformation*). Suku travels the world, naming rivers (see *Names and Naming*) and filling them with fish, teaching humans certain skills, creating rock formations, changing people into sea gulls and trees, and ridding the world of malevolent monsters. The Alsea make clear distinctions between Suku and *Coyote* (Mo'luptsini'sla), who also names things and people but is often characterized as *trickster* because of his behavior. [Frachtenberg 1920]

Sun

Of all celestial bodies, the sun is the most commonly personified in Native American stories. Not surprisingly, the sun is often identified as the creator of the world. The Zuni call it *Yatokka taccu,* the Sun Father. The sun is Killer-of-Enemies in the *Apache creation and emergence* stories. Also not surprisingly, Sun is often associated with the moon, as in the Zuni *Moonlight-Giving Mother* and the Cree moon *Tipiskawipisim.* Often the Sun and Moon are depicted as brother and sister. In Kutenai traditions, twin lynxes known as *Short Faces* become the sun and moon.

The sun is often associated with light and fire, and, consequently, with power. The *Bear Dance* invokes the power of Sun to cure. The sun is the source of power for *Bear Medicine Woman* (Pawnee). *Cudak,* the Puyallup women's charm, comes from Sun. Pawnee *Morning Star* replenishes Sun's fire.

Sometimes Sun is trapped or his light diminished, as in the Yurok story *Sun Trapper.* In a Jemez story, Sun is clothed to prevent his heat from reaching the earth (see *Fotease*). In a Pomo story, Coyote, brother of the creator *Madumda,* steals the sun. This "theft of *light*" theme is widespread, as are stories that describe the often heroic release of the sun (see the Tanaina story of Raven, *Guguyni,* who releases Sun).

A common and rather widespread story has Sun impregnating a woman who gives birth to *warrior twins.* Not knowing who their father is, these twins set out on a journey to find him *(Twins' Journey to Sun Father).* Widapokwi (see *Widapokwi and Amchitapuka*) has a daughter conceived with Sun (Yavapai). Sun is also the father of the Crow culture hero *Old Woman's Grandchild.* The Navajo figure *Begocidi* is the son of Sun.

The Kathlamet say that Sun is carried across the sky by *Aqalax,* an old woman. To the Navajo, Sun (johoonaa?ei, "day carrier in space") is the carrier of the sun (the orb itself is sha) and the principal deity who gives life to the world. He is the husband of *Changing Woman* and the father of *Monster Slayer and Born for Water*. His adulterous relationships are often described as the source of the monsters that inhabit the world.

In Lakota stories, Sun is the friend of the great *buffalo*. Along the Pacific northwest coast, *copper* is associated with the sun. In a Coeur d'Alene story, *Sun and Moon,* Sun kills some of Coyote's children. In another story, Sun *(Tcax-qen)* replaces Robin, who made the weather too hot. Part of the body of the Pawnee figure *Long Tongue becomes the sun. In another Pawnee story, the Sun protects the child White-Sun* against Witch Woman. The Ute rabbit character *Tavwots* fights the Sun. The Piman creator, Earth Shaman, creates the sun from a block of ice (see *Tcu-unny-ikita).*

Native American terms for Sun include: *Kaahkwa* (Seneca); *Tcho* (Yuchi); *Uwashil* (Natchez); and *Wi* (Lakota). See also *Sun Dance.* [Boas 1918; Deans 1891; Evans 1986; Goddard 1933; Grinnell 1893a; Haile 1938a; Hymes 1975; Matthews 1902a; Newcomb and Reichard 1937; Oosten 1983; Parker 1910; Rayliss 1909; Reagan 1935a; Reichard 1943, 1974; Stephen 1930; Stirling 1946]

Sun and Moon

A common theme explaining solar and lunar activity. The female Sun lives in the east, while her brother, the Moon, lives in the west. Sun has a secret lover who never reveals his name or visage, coming only during the darkest part of the month when there is no moonlight. Wanting to learn her lover's identity, Sun dips her hand in the cinders of the fire in her room and strokes his face. When Moon rises in the sky the next night, his face has dark streaks on it, betraying him as the secret lover (see *Incest).* Moon is so ashamed that thereafter he keeps as far away from Sun as possible. [Boas 1888a; Mooney 1900; Nelson 1899]

Sun Dance

Lakota, Dakota, Cheyenne, Ponca, Kiowa, Mandan, Hidatsa, Arapaho, Blackfoot, Crow, Shoshone, Ute, Comanche, *Plains* and *Plateau*

A yearly summer *dance* lasting three to four days, with central religious significance for the spiritual health and strength of participants and their families. The *Sun* is believed to be one of the most consistent powers in life (see also *Wakan Tanka).* The Sun Dance began in the early nineteenth century and spread to several tribes in the western states. With the establishment of government control and Christian missions on reservations, along with U.S. regulations discouraging its practice, the Sun Dance ceased to exist. In the late 1960s the Sun Dance made a comeback, and dances are currently held on a regular basis among the Oglala, Cheyenne, Ute, Crow, and Shoshone.

The Sun Dance has various expressions among different tribes, but all share the following elements: the special preparation of participants, the searching for and raising of the center pole, the dancing of participants to fulfill vows, and the overall support and encouragement of the dancers by the gathered tribe in the Sun Dance lodge. Often a *buffalo* head and other buffalo objects are used to honor the buffalo's important religious role.

Teton Sioux participants prepare with fasting and prayers by ritual leaders and medicine people. Four young men of respectable character are sent to search for and cut down the tree that will become the Sun Dance pole at the center of the lodge. The pole is decorated, an ornamented *pipe* is smoked, and a perfectly shaped buffalo skull is positioned at the foot of the pole. When the pole is raised, tobacco is offered and the dancers dance to plead for strength to complete the Sun Dance ritual.

On the first day of the ceremony the participants perform a sweat. Then they decorate their bodies with paint, feathers, and/or deerskin. Each dancer carries in his or her mouth an eagle-bone whistle decorated with quill and beadwork. As the dancers enter the lodge, they circle the pole and salute the sun to the beat of a special drum. In order to fulfill vows and promises they have made, participants may lacerate their arms and legs. They may suspend themselves by fastening ropes to the center pole and then to gashes in their chest or back, so that only their toes touch the ground. They may suspend themselves with their feet off the ground or attach a buffalo skull to their bodies using the ropes piercing their chests. The dancers continue until they fall unconscious or tear themselves loose. At this point they may receive a *vision.* After a required period of recovery, they smoke the pipe, sweat, and finish with food and water. During the ceremony the entire tribe provides the dancers with moral support and encouragement. Children may have their ears pierced as a form of participation.

Not all tribes include the voluntary piercing of skin as part of the Sun Dance ceremony. The Shoshone, Comanche, and Ute do not. The Ute consider the dance to be a healing dance, especially for arthritic conditions. The Ute and the Cheyenne place a willow brush at the top of the center pole and refer to the dance as the Willow Dance, without the central attention and honor being directed to the sun. Participants wave feathers and dance in a circle.

Among the Crow, the Sun Dance is called the Ashkisshe. It involves the seeking of wisdom, the fulfillment of a vow, and petitioning for help with serious personal problems. Blowing decorated bone whistles, the dancers charge the pole and retreat in a rhythmic fashion. The Crow medicine person *(akbaalia)* prays *(chiwakiia)* as an essential part of the Sun Dance. Dancing *(dissuua)* is also a central action. See also *Tsisapuec,* the great Crow warrior who gained strength in the Sun Dance, and *xapaaliia,* the physical representation of spirit power gained in the Crow Sun Dance.

Among the Blackfoot, the women of the *Matoki* (Buffalo-Cow Society) hold their ceremony at the same time as the Sun Dance. Some Lakota tribes have members of the *heyoka* society perform at the same time. The Lakota term for the

Sun Dance is *Hunka Lowanpi.* It was revealed by *White Buffalo Maiden.* See also *Ear Piercing,* practiced at Sun Dance; *Man-Above,* the Arapaho medicine person who fasted at Sun Dance; *Nariniiha* (Badger), who dances in Sun Dance; and *Wazilya,* Lakota incensing. [Dorsey and Kroeber 1903; Frey 1987; Grinnell 1962; Hassrick 1964; Jorgensen 1972, 1986; Lowie 1956; Murie 1989; Neihardt 1932; Walker 1982; Wissler 1918]

Sun Father

See *Onanne,* the road of life, and *Yatokka taccu,* the Zuni term for Sun Father.

Sun-Ray
Pawnee, *Plains*

An abusive husband who puts his wife inside a rattle hanging on his belt every time she tries to escape from him. While Sun-Ray is hunting, she finally escapes to a village where she tells the people of her husband's cruelty. She travels with the villagers on their hunting trips. When Sun-Ray finds his wife gone, he locates her by consulting the rattle and imprisons her in it once again.

Sun-Ray warns his wife she will never escape him. In his anger he throws hot coals on her. She turns into a mole (see *Human-Animal Transformation),* digs out of the lodge, and goes far away to a distant village. He pursues her, entering the village as a ray of sun. He becomes human again and returns his wife to his rattle. The people of the village scold him, saying he belongs in the sky and has no right to abuse an earthly woman. Sun-Ray throws his rattle on the ground. His wife wakes up, and he repents and releases her. Then he becomes a ray of sun and returns to the sky. [Dorsey 1906a]

Sun Trapper
Yurok, Wiyot, *California;* Oto, Gros Ventre, *Plains*

A young boy who feels mistreated goes off by himself. He takes a nap under the *Sun,* which burns his robe. Angry, he makes a noose from his sister's pubic hair and traps the Sun with it. The Sun starts to choke and the earth becomes dark. Many animals work to chew through the trap. Sun is finally freed, *light* returns, and darkness disappears. [Dorsey 1880; Voegelin 1940]

Sun Youth Kachina
See *Paiyatemu.*

Sunawavi
Ute, *Great Basin*
Wolf, a *culture hero* who brings fire to humans and creates the seasons. Sunawavi argues with his brother, *Coyote,* over the nature of death. Sunawavi holds that when people die they should come back to life, but Coyote thinks that once people die they should be *dead* forever. Coyote wins the argument and is responsible for the permanence of death. Sunawavi is responsible for the theft of fire (see *Fire, Theft of*) from Rabbit, as well as for teaching people how to roast Rabbit for food. Through his exploits with other animals, Sunawavi creates the seasons and gives some animals their physical characteristics. Sunawavi is also a medicine person. By using his powers negatively he causes Woodpecker and Duck to sicken. When Duck finds out Sunawavi is the cause of his illness, he and other medicine people kill Sunawavi, thus establishing the Ute practice of killing any medicine person who causes illness. See also *Qumuuc* (hot rock medicine) and *Rolling Rock.* [Lowie 1924]

Sungmanitu
Lakota, *Plains*
Wolf, whose spirit is responsible for energy of the chase and war parties. [Walker 1982]

Sunka
Lakota, *Plains*
Dog, whose spirit is responsible for friendship, faithfulness, and cunning. [Walker 1982]

Sunrise Dance
Apache, *Southwest*
Girls' puberty rite; see *Na ih es.*

Sun's Grief
Cherokee, *Southeast*
When Sun's daughter dies from a rattlesnake bite and goes to *Tsusginagi* (ghost country), Sun hides herself in grief. The world is always dark, and Sun's tears cause a *flood.* Finally the Cherokee send their young men and women to cheer the sun by dancing and singing to her. When the drummer quickens the rhythm of the song, Sun cheers up, uncovers her face, and begins smiling. [Mooney 1888]

Superguksoak
Labrador, *Arctic*
Wife of *Torngarsoak,* a huge white bear. She is the female guardian of land animals (see *Master/Mistress of Animals*). *Shamans* visit and copulate with her, and are thus able to attract reindeer for hunting. [Fitzhugh 1985]

Surem
Yaqui, *Southwest*
The ancient people. See *Seataka; Talking Tree; Utea,* the power inherited from the ancient people; and *Yoania,* the ancient world.

Sus lika
Tanaina, *Subarctic*
The mountain-pass dog who lives under the earth. His barking can be heard, but he is never seen. [Norman 1990]

Sweat Lodge
A small enclosure constructed of bent withes covered with skins or blankets or, alternatively, of dirt-covered stacked wood, that encloses heat for a sweat bath. The Native American rites associated with the sweat bath are themselves referred to by the term "sweat" or "sweat lodge." The sweat lodge is used as a place of teaching, planning, praying, singing, and communing with others. The sweat is often done in preparation for other rites and as a means of returning to the nonritual world after the performance of great ceremonials.

In recent years, the sweat lodge has come to be widely used as a prayer ritual separate from other rites. It has achieved the status of a principal rite among many groups of Native Americans. It is sometimes a way in which Native Americans offer to share their spirituality with non–Native Americans. The Lakota term for sweat lodge is *inipi.* The Crow call it *Awusek.* The Ojibwa have a curing sweat they call *Bear Sweat Lodge.*

Many origin stories of the sweat lodge are told among various tribal groups. In the Crow version, a man transforms into a vicious reptile with sharp teeth that lives at the bottom of a lake (see *Human-Animal Transformation).* The people put on strong rawhide gloves, catch him, and place him in a small domed structure filled with hot rocks and water, which create steam. In the midst of the steam and with much *prayer,* the people restore the reptile to his human form. See also *Buffalo-Woman* and *Corn-Woman.* [Lowie 1960]

Sweet Grass (Acorus calamus L.)

Also known as calamus, myrtle flag, sweet sedge, and sweet rush root. Sweet grass is used in preparation for and during many ceremonies. When burned it gives off a pleasant smell that is offensive to malevolent spirits but pleasing to helping spir-

its. Sweet grass is used to cleanse and purify people and objects before ritual. The plant grows wild; when it is mature it is gathered, then braided for use.

Swoxqwad
Puyallup-Nisqually, Southern Puget Sound, *Northwest Coast*
Loon, an important fishing power (see *Sqalalitut)* that also made a man brave and a good hunter. A man with Swoxqwad power could own slaves and wear a loon-skin hat at ceremonial activities. See also *Xwaixwieda,* the power of material goods. [Smith 1940]

Syowoe
Nooksack, Salish, *Northwest Coast*
A word used to describe the *power* to see events happening at a distance and in the future (see *Clairvoyance),* as well as the person or seer who has this power. Syowoe is usually given to females at birth. It can also reveal itself spontaneously, taking the woman into a trance and allowing her to see what is occurring far away. Nooksack syowoe (seers) can only help people to see what is happening; they have no power to change events. See also Sitec, the soul. [Amoss 1978]

Ta Tanka
Lakota, *Plains*

Ta, meaning "beast," and tanka, meaning "great or large." Ta Tanka is the spirit of the *Buffalo* Bull, the patron of ceremonies, health, and provisions. Ta Tanka remains in the skull of the buffalo and is in constant conflict with the spirit of Coyote *(Mica)*. Ta Tanka is the guardian of young women, and women during *menstruation*. It is believed that Ta Tanka once lived on earth and was the greatest animal ever seen in a vision. The remains of the mammoth are thought to belong to Ta Tanka. [Walker 1982]

Ta Tanka Lowanpi
Lakota, *Plains*

Buffalo Bull Ceremony, *girls' puberty rite,* held to purify daughters at their first *menstruation*. This ceremony is performed by the *wicasa wakan* (religious leader) to teach young *women* the importance of their duties as women, mothers, and wives.

It is believed that prior to first menstruation, a girl is like a boy. At first menstruation, however, a *tonwan* (spiritual power) possesses her, giving her the possibility of motherhood and making her *wakan*. At puberty a girl is sent to live alone in an isnati, a lone tipi. She is instructed to save the blood of her first menstruation, wrap it in bundles, and place the bundles in a living tree, where coyotes cannot find them. The spirit of the tree is thought to provide both protection and assurance of fertility. After the girl's seclusion in the lone tipi, she receives instructions for taking a sweat bath *(inipi)*. Then she dresses in new clothes provided by her parents, who also give her a new wooden bowl, chokecherries, an eagle feather, sagebrush, a drum, a pipe, sweet grass, and food for the feast following the ceremony.

According to tradition *Iktomi,* the trickster, persuades his friend *Coyote* to search for the bundles of menstrual blood hidden in trees and and eat them so he will have power over the girl. However, if Coyote does not know which girl made which bundle, the tonwan of the bundle works against him, and he becomes lean and mangy. For this reason the products of a girl's first menstruation are protected from coyotes.

The Ta Tanka Lowanpi ceremony was originally taught to the Lakota people by *Buffalo Woman,* who belonged to *Ta Tanka,* the Great Buffalo. Anog Ite, the Double Faced Woman, attempts to lure one of the daughters of Buffalo Woman to the home of *Iya,* the malevolent giant, and Iktomi, the trickster, in hopes of tricking her into doing many foolish things. With the help of *Wi,* the Sun, and *Okaga,* the South Wind, Buffalo Woman drives Iktomi and Iya away from her daughter's lone tipi. Later, when Buffalo Woman sees the Lakota camping on the Plains while hunting buffalo, she observes Anog Ite lurking near the camp, waiting to steal the products of girls' first menstruation. She teaches the Lakota the Bull Buffalo ceremony so their daughters will be purified and considered industrious and hospitable women. See also *Anog Ite,* Double Faced Woman, who taught women crafts. [Walker 1982]

Tabaldak
Western Abenaki, *Northeast*
Also known as the owner of the world, which the Abenaki believe has always existed. Tabaldak creates all the living beings on earth, including humans (see *Humans, Origin of).* He first creates men and women from stone. Not liking his creations, he destroys the stone humans and cuts new ones from living wood. See also *Odziozo,* the transformer who reshapes the earth. [Trigger 1978]

Tadidiin
Navajo, *Southwest*
Corn pollen, the food of the *diyin dine?e,* or Holy People. Used ceremonially in all rituals, but especially in *Blessingway,* as a beautiful gift to the diyin dine?e. As a voiceless prayer (see *Prayer and Prayersticks),* a pinch of pollen is touched to the top of the head and the mouth, then strewn in a hand gesture moving away from the one offering the pollen. Pollen is synonymous with life and fertility. *Cornmeal,* more easily procured in large quantities, carries many of the same values as pollen. See also *Sandpainting* and *Unwounded Buckskin.* [Wyman 1970]

Tagkanysough
Algonquian tribes, *Northeast*
A malevolent spirit who opposes the helping spirit *Quiyoughcosuck.*

Taikomol
Yuki, *California*
"He Who Walks Alone." The *creator.* Taikomol lives alone in the universe, so he makes land and humans from sticks and gives the people a *dance.* One day the land is flooded by the water on which it is floating, and everything Taikomol has made is destroyed. Taikomol makes another world without daylight or animals. The people in this world end up eating one another and the earth burns up. Taikomol made a third earth with mountains and rivers, but this earth wobbles too much. To balance out the wobbling, Taikomol creates a giant coyote, elk, and deer and has them lie down in the north. He then creates people out of sticks once more (see *Humans, Origin of)* and gives them the dance *(Taikomol wok).* One day a human does something wrong and dies. Taikomol buries him and resurrects him the next day, but he smells so bad the rest of the people get sick. Taikomol decides not to give people the power to resurrect the *dead.* He does, however, give them the *Hulkilal wok* (the Dance of the Dead Spirits) so they will live long lives. [Voegelin 1940]

Taikomol wok
Yuki, *California*
Dance given to the people by the creator, *Taikomol,* to honor him. In the dance a man impersonates Taikomol by wearing a Big Head costume decorated with feathers. In order to participate in the Taikomol wok, dancers must first be initiated into the *Kuksu-hesi* (secret men's society). [Voegelin 1940]

Taku Skanskan
Dakota, *Plains*
"Changes things," "that which moves." A powerful and unpredictable being who resides in the

Four Winds. Taku Skanskan is believed to have strong influence over human tragedy because his four messengers are the four dark spirits of the *night*. The buzzard, raven, fox, and wolf help him bring disease and death. [Deloria 1932]

Takwe
Juaneño, *California*
"Eater." A person who ritually ate a piece of the corpse's shoulder as part of the tribal mourning ceremony. This activity saved the heart of the deceased, who was then free to travel to the sky and become a star (see *Stars and Starlore*). The precedent for this tradition was set when death (see *Dead*) came to humans as the result of the killing of the culture hero (see *Kukitat*) by Frog (see *Excrements, Swallowing of*). As the body of the culture hero was being cremated according to tradition, Coyote jumped on the funeral pyre, tore out the heart, and ate it. [Kroeber 1948]

Talking Doctors
Coos, Takelma, Alsea, Umpqua, *Northwest Coast*
Talking doctors are male *healers* who diagnose and cure minor illnesses by reciting a long *creation* story while smoking tobacco. The story is passed down to healers by members of their families. The regular *shamans* of the region are women whose power comes from *helping spirits*. Talking doctors are also responsible for reciting the creation story at ceremonies and for placing fresh food in the mouth of a person who is breaking a fast. [Beckham, Toepel, and Minor 1984]

Talking God (haashcheelti?i)
Navajo, *Southwest*
A *ye?ii (diyin dine?e* impersonated with a mask) associated with the east, the inner form *(biigistiin)* of the eastern mountain. He controls the dawn, the eastern sky, rare game, and corn. Talking God is one of the greatest of Navajo deities and among those most frequently appearing in mythology. He acts as a mentor, directing, warn-

ing, and assisting other characters. As the leader of other ye?ii, he is the *yeibichai* or grandfather of the gods. In this role he is central to *Nightway*. He is frequently paired with Calling God (hashchee?ooghaan), his counterpart in the west. See also *Big Star Way, Eagleway, Enemyway, Flintway, Mountainway, Navajo Wind Way*, and *White Hactcin*, a comparable Apache figure. [Goddard 1933; Haile 1938a; Hill 1938; Matthews 1897, Matthews 1902a; Newcomb 1940; Reichard 1939, 1974; Sapir and Hoijer 1942; Stevenson 1891]

Talking Tree (Kutanokame)
Yaqui, *Southwest*
Talking Tree is the story tradition that tells of the dawn of *Christianity*. In the forest a tree is discovered that makes a peculiar sound caused by its vibration. Believing this vibration to be significant to them, the people gather around the tree, but they cannot understand it. The wise men gather; one of them knows Wise Woman, or Flower Woman (sea hamut), who lives as a hermit in the forest. Wise Woman has anticipated that this time would come. Although she is so old that she cannot travel with the people to the tree, she has prepared her daughter for the journey. The daughter listens to the tree and tells the people what it says. She tells them about the Christian God and his power. She tells them about evil and its power. She describes the padres who will come to teach them about good and evil, baptism, godparents, death and burial, and the cultivation of grains. When the people hear what she says, there is much confusion. Some of the people like what they hear, but many do not. Those who reject the message, the Surem, host a farewell feast, then depart to a kingdom underground, taking Yoania, the ancient world, with them.

Some Yaqui hold that the Surem became the ants that live underground. Those who stay to receive the new world described to them are the ancestors of the Yaqui people. [Giddings 1959; Painter 1986; Spicer 1954]

Tall Man (Fsti capcaki)
Seminole, Oklahoma and *Southeast*
A *giant* covered with gray hair who smells like a stagnant muddy pond and who breaks the limbs off trees, killing them, in order to make the clubs he carries. [Howard 1984]

Tammatuyuq
Eskimo, Eastern Hudson Bay, *Arctic*
An infant-killing *monster* who lives in the time of the first people. Tammatuyuq pretends to help mothers, then steals their babies (see *Children*) when they are not looking. She uses a needle to pierce the babies' heads (the fontanel) and suck out their blood. When a baby dies, she closes her eyes in great satisfaction and keeps sucking. [Nungak and Arima 1988]

Tarneq
Eskimo, *Arctic*
The invisible *ghost (anerneq)* seen in the likeness of a person after he or she has died. A tarneq can be the *helping spirit* of an *angalkuq*. Early missionaries incorrectly believed tarneq to be the corollary of the *devil*. [Lantis 1947; Nelson 1899]

Tarucuhus
Pawnee, *Plains*
"Errand men." Each village had two tarucuhus, who sat near the inside entrance of the lodge during every ceremony. They were charged with keeping the fires burning, and cooking and serving food for offerings and feasts. Since the errand men were always present, they learned most of the ceremonies, including the songs and many secrets. Although they could never use their knowledge, they were officially respected by the village. [Murie 1989]

Tatahkesewen
Menominee, *Northeast*
The *power* received during a *vision quest*. Tatahkesewen must not be talked about or shown off. It increases with age. The power of menstruating and postpartum *women* is considered superior to tatahkesewen. [Bloomfield 1928a]

Tatankan gnaskinyan
Lakota, *Plains*
Crazy Buffalo, who deceives young people in their love affairs, often causing them to do harm to rivals or themselves. [Walker 1982]

Tate
Lakota, *Plains*
The *Wind,* created by *Skan,* the Sky, to be his companion. Tate takes Ite, the beautiful daughter of Wa (First Man) and Ka (First Woman) as his wife. Ite soon gives birth to quadruplets. She is pregnant again when she begins plotting to take the place of Hanwi, the Moon, as the Sun's *(Wi)* companion. Skan discovers the plot and condemns Ite to live forever with two faces, one beautiful and one horrible. She becomes Anog Ite, the Double Faced Woman. Ite's unborn child, *Yum (Whirlwind),* is condemned to leave her.

Tate loves Ite greatly. He pleads with Skan to allow him and his four sons, along with the unborn son, Yum, to live on earth so they can be near Ite. Skan agrees and commands the four sons to establish the four cardinal directions of the world. Tate builds his lodge at the center of the world and his four sons travel around the world, dividing it into four equal parts as Skan has commanded. During their travels they have many adventures. *Iktomi,* the spider, causes them trouble, but *Wazi and Kanka,* the wizard and witch, help them. When Tate's four sons return home, Skan gives each brother control of the direction he has established. He also makes a season for each direction and gives each son control of the weather for his season. The four sons are combined into one and named *Wani,* vigor. [Walker 1982]

Tavwots
Ute, *Great Basin*
The little *rabbit* who starts a fight with the *sun* (Ta-vi) for burning his back during an afternoon nap. While journeying to the sun, Tavwots has many adventures. He discovers *corn* and steals it. He meets and tricks the bear (Kwi-ats). He steals

water from women who are making water jugs and seals the women in them. He outsmarts the tarantula (Ku-mi-a-pots).

When Tavwots finally reaches the cliff where the sun rises he hurls his *penis* at it. Sun shatters into thousands of pieces, which disperse around the earth and start a huge fire. Tavwots hides under a tree for protection. Eventually, however, the massive fire covers the entire earth and Tavwots is unable to escape. His toes, legs, and body are burned off, leaving only his head, which rolls along until his swollen eyes burst open and tears gush out, creating a great *flood*. The flood spreads around the earth and extinguishes the fire. Ute stories also identify Tavwots as the father of *Cinauau* (creator brothers). [Powell 1881]

Tawiskaron
Mohawk, *Northeast*

Flint, also referred to as Winter. Tawiskaron is building a bridge of stone from an island out in a lake so that cruel, malevolent beasts will be able to come and eat humans. These beasts are associated with the famine winter can bring. Sapling and Bluebird plot a trick and frighten Tawiskaron into fleeing. The bridge disappears behind him, making it impossible for the malevolent beasts of winter to devour humans. See also *Aataentsic*. [Fenton 1987]

Taxtax
Nez Perce, *Plateau*

Locust, a newly married woman who refuses to help her old, decrepit mother-in-law dig roots for winter storage. The mother-in-law becomes angry with lazy young Taxtax. As summer goes on, the soil becomes so hard that it is impossible to get the roots out of the ground. Locust now decides she will help get the roots. Every day for the rest of the summer, she leaves in the early morning dawn and gathers roots with the help of her friends. The old mother-in-law now has an ample winter supply and ceases to be angry with Locust. [Phinny 1969]

Tcaawunkl
Tlingit, *Northwest Coast*

Both the name of a story figure (a spirit) and the name for any *shaman* through whom the spirit speaks. Tlingit spirits often speak through Haida shamans. Because the story of Tcaawunkl illustrates the development, behavior, and powers of a shaman, the name Tcaawunkl is given to a person who displays shamanistic tendencies from birth.

Tcaawunkl is left in his cradle by his supernatural parents while they gather mussels, and forgotten. When they return to get him, he is surrounded by crows who are singing to him. After this incident he begins to act like a shaman. When Tcaawunkl is a young man, people in his village begin to die, and the villagers blame him for the deaths. Although he has many elder brothers and uncles, no one likes him except the wife of his youngest uncle. The only person who cares for him is his old grandmother, with whom he lives. She is aware of his shamanic powers and teaches him how to sharpen the bill of a heron. One day while hunting he sharpens Heron's bill for her. In return Grandmother Heron teaches Tcaawunkl to set deadfall traps, which he uses to catch many black bears. Tcaawunkl's grandmother makes him a dancing apron from an old mat and pieces of a shaman's bone. She leads songs for him and he begins to perform as a shaman every night. People come secretly to look at him and he gives them food.

When the chief's son becomes ill many shamans are called, but none can cure him. Tcaawunkl's grandmother tells the chief that her grandson can cure the boy, but the chief laughs at her until the people who have secretly gone to see Tcaawunkl say that she is speaking the truth. The chief sends for Tcaawunkl, who succeeds in curing his son. As a result Tcaawunkl becomes famous. He is called upon to cure the son of the chief of the Land Otter People, and as a result gains even more shamanic power. He outsmarts all the jealous shamans by running about and throwing urine on them, which negates their power. [Swanton 1909]

Tcaxqen
Coeur d'Alene, *Plateau*
"One-eyed one." Tcaxqen is placed in the sky to be the *Sun*. He replaces Robin, originally chosen to be the sun but who makes it far too hot for the people. [Lowie 1963]

Tcho
Yuchi, *Southeast*
The *Sun,* mother of Yohah, a star, and Sharpah, the Moon. Because she is the sun, Tcho makes her two children shine brightly in the night sky. As Tcho travels east, a drop of her blood falls to the ground, creating the first humans (see *Humans, Origin of*). [Hudson 1976]

Tcikapis
Montagnais, Naskapi, *Subarctic*
A *dwarf* of great strength whose parents are killed by bears just before his birth. His sister removes him from his mother's womb and raises him. Tcikapis is considered to be a *culture hero* because of the many good things he does for people and because of his powerful skills as a healer and conjurer (see *Conjuring*). [Helm 1981]

Tcisaki
Ojibwa, *Northeast, Subarctic*
A prominent *shaman,* usually male, who divines hidden truths while in the *shaking tent.* [Hallowell 1942]

Tcu-unnyikita
Pima, *Southwest*
"Smoke talk." The *creation* story. In the beginning all is darkness. For ages the darkness gathers until it forms the spirit of Earth Shaman (variously translated as Earth Doctor and Earth Magician, Tcuwut Makai). At this time the spirit is like a fluffy bit of cotton floating upon the wind. Conscious of his power, Earth Shaman decides to create the world. He takes a bit of dust from his breast and flattens it into a cake. By singing and dancing, Earth Shaman begins to make all the things of the world: insects, plants, and animals.

He creates the sky, and after making Gray Spider he commands it to spin a web connecting the earth and sky. Earth Shaman throws blocks of ice into the sky for the *sun* and *moon,* and a spray of water becomes the stars. By taking crystals from the large stars and dipping his walking stick in ashes and drawing it across the sky, he forms the *Milky Way.*

From images in clay Earth Shaman forms human beings (see *Humans, Origin of*), and they begin to multiply. They know neither sickness nor death. Eventually they become so crowded they have nothing to eat. Finally they begin to kill and eat one another (see also *Cannibalism*). Earth Shaman pities the people, but knows he must resolve this situation. Hooking the sky with his staff, he pulls it down to the earth, crushing to death all living things.

Entering the other side of the earth through a hole, Earth Shaman begins again by creating a race of people, the Pimas. The moon gives birth to *Coyote,* who comes to the place where the Pima people live. After a time the earth gives birth to Elder Brother (Se?ehe). Elder Brother speaks roughly to Earth Shaman and shortens the lives of humans so they will not overpopulate the earth. Elder Brother is dissatisfied with the way things have been created and takes control from Earth Shaman.

Elder Brother creates a handsome youth, I?itoi, and places him among the Pimas, telling him to marry whomever he wishes and stay with her until her first child is born. Then he must go on to another woman and do likewise. A child born to I?itoi and the daughter of South Shaman (a figure comparable to Earth Shaman living in the south) is abandoned, and its tears cause a *flood* that overwhelms the earth.

Elder Brother is the ruler of the third creation, assisted by Earth Shaman and Coyote. First they find the center of the earth and dry the floodwaters. They create the animals, birds, and plants. From clay images they create people, but the first people turn out to be Apaches. Angered that these people are the first to appear, Elder Brother throws them over the mountain. This action results in making them fierce. Of the peoples created, the Pimas are last. They are given superior capabilities, including the knowledge of seasons, the power to make *rain,* and the ability to cure sickness.

Rattlesnake appears as Soft Child. People constantly prod and scratch Soft Child because they are annoyed by his rattle. Appealing to Elder Brother, Rattlesnake is given teeth. When Rabbit tries to scratch Soft Child, he is bitten. His body swells and he is racked with fever. Although many try, none are able to cure Rabbit, and his death is the first (see also *Dead*).

The people do not know what to do with Rabbit's body to protect it from Coyote. Some propose to burn it, but they do not have fire. Blue Fly makes the first fire drill and shows the people how to make *fire* so they can burn Rabbit's body. Coyote steals the heart from the burning corpse and flees with it.

Eventually the people learn how to care for themselves. Wolf begins to wonder what has happened to his brother Coyote. The aroma given off by a roasting kidney of deer attracts Coyote to the people. Coyote tricks and abuses the wife of Puma. In anger, Puma's tribe drives all the game animals into a cave where they are imprisoned. Year after year attempts are made to liberate the game, but none succeed until Coyote himself tries. He uses deception to throw open the gates and liberate the game (see *Game, Release of*). [Russell 1908]

Tenskwatawa
Shawnee, *Northeast*

"The open door." A self-proclaimed *prophet,* who at the age of 30 claimed to have a message from the "Master of Life." According to Tenskwatawa, the Master of Life had taken pity on the Native Americans and offered advice that would save them from threatened destruction. This included warnings about abandoning practices of witchcraft and returning to buckskin dress instead of wearing clothes brought into the country by the European-Americans. It was also said that Native American women should stop intermarrying with non–Native American men. Tenskwatawa's message spread quickly. Among some tribes he was believed to be a reincarnation of the culture hero *Winabojo.* [McLoughlin 1990]

Test Theme
A common theme among Native American stories involves the testing of the protagonist. The purpose of the test may be to confirm the protagonist's claimed identity. For example, in the Navajo *Monster Slayer and Born for Water* and the Apache *White Painted Woman,* the Sun tests the warrior twins to make sure they are his children. In the Navajo *Nightway,* the twins are tested to determine their kinship to Talking God. The test may be given to ascertain that a figure is worthy of marriage or sexual relations. For examples, see the Navajo *Changing Bear Maiden, Eagleway, Enemyway, Mountainway,* and *Navajo Wind Way.* Several of these involve a group of women tossing meal balls to determine which among them will marry the hero. Another example is *Evening Star,* a Pawnee account in which a boy is tested before he can have sex with a girl. See also *Kwanokasha* (Choctaw), *Underworld* (Yupik), *Winabojo* (Ojibwa), and *Winter Berries* (Kwakiutl). [Lowie 1908b]

Tewa Ritual Cycle
Tewa, *Southwest*

Nine "works" constitute the annual cycle of Tewa ritual, social, and political activities. A "work" is a daylong retreat taken by societies of Made People, during which they pray and sing in order to harmonize human and spiritual relationships to ensure that the changes in the natural world will continue. Made People (patowa) are those made beneath the lake of emergence (see *Sipofene*), charged with the control and direction of all group ritual activities. They are organized into eight groups that include both male and female members drawn from both the Winter and Summer moieties, or social divisions of the Tewa.

The Tewa ritual cycle begins about January 20 with an activity called "of moderation" or "to lessen the cold," which is initiated by the Winter chief. Its purpose is to melt the snow and prevent extreme weather. Four days after this "work" the Winter chief goes to the home of the Summer chief and asks him to seek life for all the people. At four-day intervals, each society of Made People performs a work. This same cycle of eight groups of Made People performing works at four-day intervals is repeated beginning about February 20. This time the Summer chief initiates the work "bringing the buds to life." This is the first of two "sweet" works, so called because of the preparation of a sweet drink of fermented grain. The third cycle (second of the sweet works) is "bringing the leaves to life." "Bringing the blossoms to life" follows, beginning about April 20. "Early harvest" and "late harvest" ensue in turn. In November the Winter chief initiates his first work, called "of the middle of the structure," corresponding with a time of year that is neither winter nor summer, hot nor cold. The last work of the year is "days of the sun," which occurs in midDecember at the time of the winter solstice and serves as a rite of *New Year*.

This cycle of "works," performed in private, sanctions and initiates a corresponding cycle of public *dances* and ritual activities, often involving masked and costumed dancers and clown figures. Included are the Buffalo, Eagle, and Deer Dances; the Basket and Squash Dances; Corn Dances; Rain Dances; Harvest Dances; Hunt Dances and rituals; and the widely attended Turtle Dance and Matachine Dance, which is performed at the winter solstice. These public ritual activities precede and prepare for the annual cycle of Tewa subsistence activities of hunting and agriculture. [Ortiz 1969]

Thanadelther
Dene Dhaa (Slavey), *Subarctic*
A historical female guide credited with leading the English through many miles of the remote subarctic. Thanadelther is the subject of many stories told by the Slavey people. [Helm 1981]

Thanksgiving
The Iroquois *Ash Blowing Rite* and the Delaware Nighthawk Dance *(Pickwelaneokan)* are rites of thanksgiving.

Thlakalunka
Alabama, *Southeast*
The moccasin game, a gambling game played with four square pieces of deer hide placed on a bearskin laid out with the hairy side up. In one story about Thlakalunka, a man gambles away his family fortune, including his clothes, and then all of the world's water. Everywhere in the world the streams, ponds, and rivers dry up. Everyone is thirsty until Bicici'hka (a red-headed, speckled woodpecker) pecks a hole in a big tree from which water gushes, filling all the rivers and streams.

Thought
Navajo, *Southwest*
Personified as Long Life Boy (see *Sa?ah naghai bikeh hozho)* and associated with Wind (*Nilchi?i*).

Thunder
Thunder is widely personified in Native American mythology, often as a huge *Thunderbird*. Killer-of-Enemies, the creator in the *Apache Creation and Emergence* stories, is identified as Thunderer. *Ehlaumel* is the Yuki name for Thunder. *Ishtohoollo Aba Eloa* is the Creek being responsible for thunder. *Lightning* is the Achumawi brother to Thunder. Thunder helps the Kato creator *Nagaicho*. The Huron spirit of thunder is *Onditachiae*. In Pacific northwest coast stories, a boy, *Shalikun*, is changed by thunder. *Ani Hyuntikwalaski* are the Cherokee Thunder Beings. *Misikinipik*, the Cree great horned snake, is always at war with Thunder Beings. *Mudjikiwis* (Ojibwa) is a houskeeper who lives with Thunderer. One of the Ojibwa spirits who visits the shaking tent is *Pinessi*, the Thunderer. [Dorsey 1893a]

Thunder Cult
Menominee, *Northeast*
Waipanows, the Thunder Cult, is a medicine society that makes hunting medicine, herbal remedies, and love charms.

Thunderbird(s)
The personification of thunder as a large bird or group of birds. Thunderbirds produce thunder by moving their wings. They make lightning by opening and closing their eyes. They battle with other beings, particularly *horned serpents.* In Crow stories, Thunderbirds wear capes of eagle feathers and rip open trees to find insects for food. Many east coast tribes address the Thunderbirds as "grandfathers." In Shawnee stories, Thunderbirds are young boys who speak backwards and who, although they can move mountains, are frightened of small streams.

To the Arapaho, Thunderbird is the summer bird who challenges White Owl Woman, the winter bird, to see whose powers are greater. Thunderbird stirs up great black clouds with tremendous noise and wind. White Owl Woman stirs up thick, fast-moving white clouds that blow a piercing wind. When the clouds meet, the white clouds overcome the black clouds, scattering snow with high drifts. White Owl Woman is therefore considered the more powerful of the two.

Those who become *heyoka* (Lakota) do so in response to dreams of Thunderbirds. In the Yukon, the Thunderbird *(Tinmiukpuk)* carries whales, reindeer, and even human beings. The Kutenai figure *Yaukekam* stops Thunderbirds from killing people. [Chamberlain 1890b; Deans 1885; Dorsey and Kroeber 1903; Eells 1889; Fewkes 1890b; Radin 1931; Skinner 1914a; Webber 1936]

Tih-kuyi-wuhti
Hopi, *Southwest*
Mother of Game Animals: antelope, deer, mountain sheep, and rabbits. Sometimes identified as sister to Muyinwa. Prayersticks (see Prayer and Prayersticks) are offered to her prior to every hunt (see *Hunting).* [Bradfield 1973; Parsons 1936; Stephen 1936; Titiev 1943]

Tihtipihin
Nootka, *Northwest Coast*
The younger brother of the culture hero *Kwatyat.* Tihtipihin helps Kwatyat rescue their mother from the stomach of a *monster* who has swallowed her. The two brothers allow themselves to be swallowed as well, then dissect the monster from within. In the process they become bald because they forgot to bathe (see *Osimc)* their heads when preparing to kill the monster. [Sapir and Swadesh 1939]

Tinmiukpuk
Eskimo, Yukon-Kuskokwim delta, Alaska, *Arctic*
The *Thunderbird,* a great *eagle* capable of carrying away whales and reindeer. Sometimes it preys on humans and caribou. [Norman 1990]

Tiotlbax
Puyallup-Nisqually, Southern Puget Sound, *Northwest Coast*
The *power* (see *Sqalalitut)* of wealth and generosity. Tiotlbax is the best power for a leader to have. Tiotlbax lives under the water, originally coming across Puget Sound in a canoe. Tiotlbax is often associated with people who are in the position to give a *potlatch.* [Smith 1940]

Tipiskawipisim
Cree, Ojibwa, *Northeast, Subarctic*
The *Moon.* After a flood destroys the first humans, Tipiskawipisim creates the first female (see *Humans, Origin of).* The Canadian Swampy Cree know Moon as the sister of *Sun.* [Clay 1938]

Tiponi
Hopi, *Southwest*
A distinctive ceremonial object made for every major ceremony (Wimi). Tiponi are usually made of cottonwood root wrapped with feathers. When not in use they are kept in the clan house of the clan that "owns" the ceremony. [Bradfield 1973]

Tirawahat
Pawnee, *Plains*

"This expanse." The *creator* of the sun, moon, stars, heavens, and earth. Tirawahat creates human beings (see *Humans, Origin of*) first a woman, then a mate to make her happy. He shows them how to build a lodge, make fire, and construct an earth altar on which to honor him as their creator. He gives them bows and arrows, along with a hoe made from a buffalo shoulder blade. He also gives them red, white, black, and yellow corn seeds, as well as painted sticks representing the four directions. He teaches the woman how to plant, harvest, and cook corn.

The Chaui, a Pawnee band, told Tirawahat's creation story whenever they offered buffalo meat at the opening of a *medicine bundle*, because Tirawahat is also responsible for the supply of buffalo (see *Master/Mistress of Animals*). Tirawahat is the buffalo spirit and the provider of the Pawnees' first bundle. He gave First Man and First Woman the bundle to hang above their altar, placing the woman in charge of keeping the bundle. The animals and birds gain their procreative power from the bundle. A buffalo skull placed on the altar facing east is believed to carry the spirit of the buffalo whenever the sun's rays strike it.

Tirawahat figures extensively in other Pawnee stories and topics. See *Basket Dice Game, Big Black Meteoric Star, Buffalo-Gaming Sticks, Four Beings of the North, Morning Star, Ready-To-Give, Scalping, Squash Medicine,* and *Starisu,* the women's dance to celebrate the gift of buffalo. [Murie 1989]

Tisikhpuk
Eskimo, Bering Sea coast, Alaska, *Arctic*

Worm Man. A huge worm or caterpillar who lives during a time when animals have the power to change at will into human beings. See *Animal-Human Transformation*. [Norman 1990]

Titichakyo
Nootka, *Northwest Coast*

Chief of the Wolves, an important story figure who, along with his four messengers, is imperson-

ated during the winter *Wolf Ritual* ceremonial. The four messengers are known for their quickness. Sound-of-a-Stick-Breaking-the-Ground (so called because he can reach his goal in less time than it takes a stick to break when someone steps on it) is considered the fastest and most important of the four. The others are Water-Drips-Down-from-a-Standing-Bush (who reaches his destination as quickly as a drop of water falls from a bush to the ground), Adze-Chips-Falling-Down-on-the-Ground, and Muddy-Water-That-Has-Been-Stirred-Up-Settles-Down. [Sapir and Swadesh 1939]

Tkahyal
Tillamook, *Northwest Coast*

"South Wind," called "our grandfather." Also known as Everlasting Man and Master of the *Salmon* (Tka) (see also *Master/Mistress of Animals*). South Wind was a transformer figure (see *Transformation*) who put the world into its present order. The Tillamook describe three eras of history. During the first era, Ice, Raven, Bear, Deer, and other creatures acted like humans. During the second, Tka put things in order. The third era is the recent past. [Beckham, Toepel, and Minor 1984]

Tobacco
A plant indigenous to the North American continent that, prior to European contact, was used for multiple ceremonial and religious purposes. The Seminoles used tobacco offerings to abate storms and lightning, and to give thanks for having escaped danger. Many tribes throughout North America make tobacco offerings, either by smoking it or by placing the unsmoked leaves in certain areas as offerings to helping spirits and to animals and plants used ceremonially. The Menominee placed tobacco in graves. Tobacco is also used in curing and healing. The Cherokee fried tobacco leaves and mixed them with herbs to use as a salve, and the Iroquois used the leaves as a toothache remedy. Tobacco is also smoked to induce states of trance in order to communicate

with helping spirits and to ward off malevolent spirits. Tobacco is a *medicine* often found in *medicine bundles.*

Many stories describe the origin of tobacco. The Huron-Wyandot of the Great Lakes area tell the story of a dead girl's father who finds an injured hawk that bursts into flames when he approaches it. All that is left of the hawk is a flaming coal, in which the father sees his daughter's face. She speaks to him of the precious gift of tobacco seed that she has for her people, and stays to show him how to raise and harvest the new crop. *Apikunni* is responsible for bringing tobacco to the Blackfoot, who use it on many occasions, including *Kanochisisin,* the ceremony to count coup. Deagahgweoses (Seneca) is the maker and keeper of tobacco (*Gayegwanowasgona*). In the Traveling Rite portion of the Iroquois *Longhouse Ceremony,* the *False Faces* collect tobacco (see also *Midwinter Festival* and *Magic Herbs*). *So?oda* is the Kawaiisu term for tobacco. *Hinon,* the Thunderer, teaches the Seneca people to make tobacco offerings. *Okabewis* teaches the Ojibwa people to use tobacco. *Wohpe,* the Lakota daughter of *Skan,* teaches people how to prepare tobacco. *Xowalaci* created the Joshua people from the smoke of his tobacco. [Gilmore 1929a]

Tobacco Society
Crow, *Plains*

This ritual society plants and cares for the tobacco Nicotiana multivalvis rather than the common Nicotiana quadrivalvis. Membership in the Tobacco Society carries high status, and people pay heavy initiation fees to sponsors, who give them seeds and teach them the four special songs and the care of the plants.

In the spring, members of different chapters of the society meet to discuss their dreams, which give them instructions on the site for planting the seeds. The seeds are mixed with special ingredients of water, animal feces, and roots. Women carry the seeds in specially made bags and give them to chosen runners, who race to place the bags at the end of the prepared garden site. Each chapter plants their seeds as songs are sung, pipes are smoked, and dreams are announced. When the planting is finished, husband-and-wife teams sing and dance, after which a feast is held. Members of the society lie down at the garden's edge, hoping to receive a vision and song about the tobacco. [Frey 1987; Lowie 1960]

Tocitumba
Kawaiisu, *Great Basin*

A white rock that holds fire. Bat steals the fire from White Rock during a rainstorm and puts it under his wings to keep it from going out. Another version of the story credits Yellowhammer with stealing the fire from Tocitumba with Crow's help. [Zigmond 1980]

Tonht onh wodihe
Dene Dhaa (Slavey), *Subarctic*

Stories of long ago (see *Story Types*), including all stories about animal people and culture heroes. Tonht onh wodihe are about people no longer living and events that happened many years ago. Among these are the cycle of wolverine stories (noghe wodihe) and stories about the culture hero *Yamonhdeyi.* See also *Wodih.* [Moore and Wheelcock 1990]

Tonwan
Lakota, *Plains*

Spiritual *power* that permeates everything. Tonwan is believed to be under the control of *Wakan Tanka,* the mystery that permeates everything. See also *Ta Tanka Lowanpi* (Buffalo Bull Ceremony) and *Unktehi,* powerful beings that emit tonwan. [Walker 1982]

Topati
Nootka, *Northwest Coast*

The term used to categorize ceremonially used property such as names, songs, dances, masks, and parts of a captured whale. The use of specific topati is restricted to a given family and is inherited or transferred through family lines. See also *Yellow Cedar Bark Ogre.* [Kenyon 1977]

T

Torngarsoak

Eskimo, Labrador, *Arctic*

A huge white *bear* that resides in a cave near Ungava Bay in the Hudson Strait. Torngarsoak is master of the whales and seals of Ungava Bay. See *Master/Mistress of Animals* and *Superguksoak*. [Damas 1984]

Totem Pole

Northwest Coast

Poles, often reaching gigantic proportions, into which are carved the lineages of prominent families. The carved figures represent the animals from which human families have descended. In this area's mythology, during the primordial era all beings were animals, some of whom removed their animal forms to reveal a human form. During the *Winter Ceremonial Season* (see also *Tsetseka),* the use of animal masks effects a return to this primordial era. Some masks, called transformation masks, are constructed so that they open to show a new mask beneath the first. Sometimes they can open to several layers, revealing the depth of these lineages and the transformations that have occurred. See also *Walal Potlatch* (Haida). [Harris 1975; Sampson 1939]

Toxwid

Kwakiutl, *Northwest Coast*

A powerful woman warrior whose dance is performed during the *Tsetseka* ceremonies (Winter Ceremonial Season). Nineteenth-century performances portrayed Toxwid's indestructibility as she pleaded with the audience to kill her by cutting open her stomach or beheading her. One of her attendants would "kill"

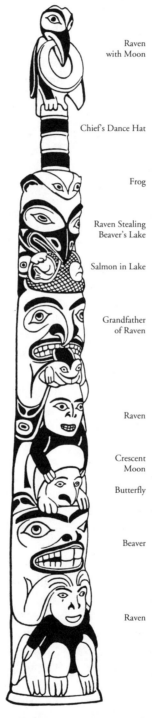

Raven with Moon

Chief's Dance Hat

Frog

Raven Stealing Beaver's Lake

Salmon in Lake

Grandfather of Raven

Raven

Crescent Moon

Butterfly

Beaver

Raven

A representation of a totem pole from the Northwest Coast.

her during the performance by driving a wedge through her head. Her elaborate costume had a fake wedge attached to her head so she could appear to be killed. To enhance this performance, the dancer broke bladders of blood carried in her mouth and dropped seals' eyes from her hair. Toxwid danced until she was fully recovered.

In contemporary Kwakiutl performances, Toxwid's actions are not as violent, although they remain quite dramatic. She may give birth to a giant frog, produce flocks of birds, or conjure a salmon. See also *Hamatsa.* [Boas 1930; Holm 1977]

Trail to Heaven

See *Yagatunne* (Dunne-za).

Transfer Ceremony

Blackfoot, *Plains*

A ceremony used to bring new members into a public society such as the Horn Society and *Matoki,* a women's society. The Transfer Ceremony takes place during the society's annual meetings. New members are secretly selected by established members whom they will replace. Alternatively, established members may sell their memberships to aspiring members for a high price. [Wissler 1913]

Transformation

The power of figures in Native American mythology is often demonstrated by their ability to change form. The power to transform may be benevolent or malevolent. Benevolent figures are known as *culture heroes, creators,* and transformers. Malevolent figures are known as witches, sorcerers, skinwalkers, and shape shifters. *Kwatyat* is a Nootka culture hero who can take many forms. *Pukjinskwes* is a Passamaquoddy witch who becomes a mosquito. The Crow figure *Akbaatatdia* has the power to transform. *Ayaxaus* (Puyallup) is a malevolent power distinguished by its ability to transform. *Coyote,* the preeminent *trickster,* is well known for his ability to transform. Sometimes this transformation takes a

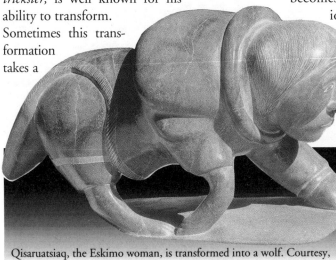

Qisaruatsiaq, the Eskimo woman, is transformed into a wolf. Courtesy, Canadian Museum of Civilization (neg.#J 14360).

highly malevolent form, as with the Navajo *Yenaldlooshi. Genonsgwa* is a Seneca figure who can change into many forms. The Eskimo notion of *inua* underlies this people's understanding of the power of transformation.

Another dimension of transformation is the ability of some figures to change aspects of the world. These figures are not so much creators, in the sense of establishing something where nothing existed previously, but instead create through making transformations that cause the world and human life to become what they now are. Some examples of these transformer figures include *Andaokut* (Nootka), *Odziozo* (Abenaki), *Suku* (Alsea), *Tkahyal* (Tillamook), *Yaukekam* (Kutenai), and *Atseemath* (Lillooet). Many figures like Coyote and *Raven,* whose classification falls into the categories of both culture hero and trickster, help shape the world by making basic transformations to the world as it was created. [Day 1976]

Transformation and Return Experience
Comanche, Arapaho, *Plains*
Eight young warriors camp under eight cottonwood trees. Over the course of 32 days, each man in turn becomes a woman (see *Women*) overnight and remains isolated, eating nothing, for four days. At the end of that time the warrior becomes male again and returns to his companions, saying nothing about what has happened. Only after all eight have transformed and observed their companions' behavior do they realize they have shared the experience. They return home and tell the other villagers of their transformations, which are blamed on the fact that they camped under cottonwood trees. [Dorsey and Kroeber 1903]

Transvestite
See *Gender Crossing, Begocidi* and *Winkte*.

Traveling Rite (Hnondowi)
Seneca, *Northeast*
"Sickness they purge." The spring and fall rite that purges illness from homes, conducted publicly by the Society of Faces. The *False Faces* go to each home, preceded by the *Husk Faces* and led by the unmasked conductor (a woman in some tribes) who carries a staff with miniature False Face and Husk Face masks hanging from it. A song is sung to quiet the *winds* because sickness is believed to be airborne. The False Faces enter the houses by crawling. They go to every room in the house, get people out of bed, and blow ashes on the household. In return they demand an offering of *tobacco,* which they collect in a basket. The Traveling Rite concludes at the *longhouse,* where the collected tobacco is offered at a special ritual in the presence of the assembled community. See also *Hadjihsa Thokste?ah* (Chief of the Husk Faces), *Longhouse Ceremony,* and *Midwinter Festival.* [Fenton 1987]

Tree

See *Talking Tree* (Yaqui).

Tribes, Origin of

For examples of stories that account for tribal origins, see *Cotsipamapot* (Moapa) and *White Painted Woman* (Apache).

Trickster(s)

A name referring to a complex character type known for his trickery, buffoonery, and crude behavior, but also as a *creator, culture hero,* and teacher. The trickster is commonly found in stories throughout native North America and is similar to figures in traditional cultures the world over.

Coyote, who has both animal and human characteristics, is unquestionably the most common trickster figure appearing in the story traditions of cultures in the southwest, Great Basin, Plateau, California, and the Great Plains (see *Badger's Limitations,* Kathlamet; *Big Dipper,* Kawaiisu; *Ma?ii,* Navajo; *Mica,* Lakota; *Old Man Coyote,* Crow; and *Sendeh,* Kiowa). But many other story characters have also been identified as tricksters. These include:

Raven, Mink, and *Blue-Jay* among Pacific northwest coast tribes; *Kwatyat,* Nootka; *Chulyen,* a crow, and *Guguyni,* a raven, of the Tanaina in central Alaska; *Winabojo* (variously Nanabush, Nanibozhu, Winebojo, *Wesucechak,* and Manabush) among some Algonquian-speaking cultures; Rabbit among southeastern tribes; Hare or Rabbit among the Lakota, Winnebago, Ponca, Omaha, and Assiniboin; Spider *(Iktomi or Inktomi, Lakota; Nihansan,* Arapaho; Vihuk or *Wihio,* Cheyenne; Nihaat, Nihehat, or Nixant, Gros Ventre); *Azeban,* a raccoon among Abenaki; *Ganyadjigowa,* a mud hen, and *Shodieonskon,* brother of death, among the Seneca; *One-Tail-Clear-of-Hair,* the opossum, Catawba; *Cunawabi,* Moapa; *Suku,* a bear, Alsea; and many others who are anthropomorphic (Wakdjunkaga, *Glooscap,* Napi, Wisaka, *Old Man,* and Widower-from-Across-the-Ocean).

The origin of the term "trickster" is commonly attributed to the 1896 edition of Daniel Brinton's *Myths of the New World,* although it does not appear in that work. In his 1885 article "The Hero-God of the Algonkins as a Cheat and Liar," Brinton cited an entry from Father Albert Lacombe's *Dictionaire de la Langue des Cris* (1878), in which Lacombe wrote that the name of the Cree figure Wisakketjak (Wesucechak) means "the trickster, the deceiver." This is probably the first time the term was used to suggest a general category.

The term "trickster" was soon embraced as a character type widely applicable in Native American mythology. Although the term seems to denote only the prankster element, it frequently identifies a character with anomalous and contradictory roles. Trickster is at once a figure elevated above human beings and a grossly erotic, gluttonous figure that seems to celebrate the most base human needs. Quite simply, throughout the history of its study, the trickster has been seen by scholars as a problem to be solved. A list of those who have attempted a resolution to the problem reads like a Who's Who in the social sciences and humanities; their explanations reflect virtually every theory of culture and mythology.

Daniel Brinton focused on what he saw as a similarity between the Algonquian terms for "light" and "white rabbit" (a similarity no others have seen). Under the influence of a "disease of language" theory (something like the party game in which a word changes as it is whispered from person to person around a circle), Brinton believed that Manabozho originated as the Great God of Light, only to degenerate through time, in part, into a lowly trickster, the Great Hare.

Franz Boas, writing late in the nineteenth century, was unconvinced by Brinton's explanation. While Brinton's theory might satisfactorily explain one anomalous figure, he wrote, it seemed unreasonable that it would similarly apply to so many figures in different cultures. Offering an alternative explanation based on a view of cultural evolution and human progress, he argued that the trickster elements are the most primitive aspects of the character and that therefore these elements existed first. As human beings and their cultures developed, the idea of culture heroes and creators arose, and in time the trickster figure began to develop these higher qualities. In many cases the culture hero and creator finally disengage from the trickster, but this has not occurred for all mythologies. Boas explains the anomalous and contradictory character of trickster figures as reflecting a stage of development where these character traits have not yet become separate.

Early in this century, Paul Radin expanded on Boas's view, centering his attention on the difference between the religious views of common people and those of religious specialists. Radin held that religious specialists are primarily interested in creators and high gods, while common people are attracted to heroes and buffoons. The trickster character reflects a combination of these interests, and cultures have developed the figure differently. Where the religious specialists were interested in deities, the trickster character may have retained his prankster character to the exclusion of higher traits. Where religious specialists have exerted more influence, the trickster tends to be a combination of prankster, culture hero, and creator.

Radin's later development of his trickster theory was more psychologically directed. He recognized in the figure something ancient, particularly in its obsession with hunger, sexuality, and self-preservation. He posited that the trickster must be the oldest of all mythological figures. Based on his study of a story cycle of the trickster Wakdjunkaga, which he collected from the Winnebago, Radin saw evidence to support the view that the trickster represents the stage in human development corresponding with the attainment of differentiation and orientation, that is, self-awareness and awareness of the world. The trickster is the symbol of the "undifferentiated psyche" in the process of transformation and differentiation.

In his study of the same body of stories, Carl Jung identified the trickster as a psychologem, that is, as an archetypal psychic structure. The extreme antiquity of the trickster corresponds with the stage of psychological development when the psyche is just leaving the animal level. In explaining why cultures have retained their reflections on this psychological development to the present, Jung saw the trickster as preservation of the "shadow" in its pristine mythological form.

A Freudian explanation has been developed by Michael Carroll, who argues that according to Freud all human beings desire both the immediate gratification of their sexual impulses and the development of civilization. According to Carroll, it is precisely the dilemma presented by these conflicting desires that trickster mythology addresses.

Mac L. Ricketts, expanding on Radin's distinction between the concerns of the common people and religious specialists, argued for the antiquity of the unity of the trickster's seemingly paradoxical characteristics, compounding the name of the character type to "trickster-transformer culture hero" or "trickster-fixer." His explanation differed from Radin's in that he argued that the trickster mythology reflects an alternative religious form held by common people—a godless humanism, a worldly religion, a religion of laughter—that celebrates human capabilities and responds to the gods by challenging them. Ricketts was most impressed by the tendencies of these various trickster characters to depend on their human qualities to resolve any problems they encounter and to satisfy their needs.

Raffaele Pettazzoni based his trickster theory on studies of Pawnee Coyote stories. Noting that the Pawnee distinguish between "true myths" and "false" ones, he identified the creation accounts as "true" and the Coyote stories as "false." Pettazzoni hypothesized that the trickster originated in an early hunting period as a kind of supreme being, a "Lord of Beasts." At the end of the primitive hunting period, the trickster was replaced or evolved into a creator figure with dominance over the whole world. Stories of this later figure are classified as "true." Meanwhile, the old

T

myths of the Lord of Beasts degenerated into "false" stories, mere legends.

In an important innovation, Barbara Babcock comes to terms with the trickster not as a problem to be solved, but as a "mess to be tolerated." By focusing on the function of paradox, of marginality, of liminality, she demonstrates that what other scholars have considered a problem is a situation that functions effectively. Among the functions Babcock identifies for trickster mythology, the most important is its role in change, criticism, and self-reflection, all stimulated and made possible by paradox and marginality. The trickster as a paradoxical and seemingly anomalous character is important to religious cultures precisely because it is the only character with the perspective to reveal and examine the meanings in all aspects of culture and life.

These are just a few of the many important trickster theories. The patterns by which this figure originated as an academic classification are clear, as are the various kinds of interpretations. Several observations are essential. First, the figure known as trickster is an academic invention intended to make more comprehensible various Native American (and other traditional cultures worldwide) figures who share some common traits. Trickster is not a term or category used by any Native American culture. Peculiarly, once invented, the trickster came to have a seductive power. The category of trickster has taken on more reality, at least for academics, than the various figures—Coyote, Raven, etc.—who are classified as tricksters. In other words, trickster is referred to as though it is a person, rather than a category invented to facilitate study. Consequently, trickster theories have focused on trickster as a figure, rather than a category, and have used actual Native American stories and figures rather sparingly, if at all, for purposes of illustration.

Many studies of trickster figures have been based exclusively on Paul Radin's book, *The Trickster: A Study in American Indian Mythology* (1956), which presents an atypical story cycle about a Winnebago character known as

Wakjunkaga. In light of the critical examination of the several trickster theories presented above, it becomes clear that trickster can be made to fit any existing body of culture theory. Essentially each of these trickster theories is a restatement of a culture theory in terms of the invented figure, the trickster.

In a provocative and powerful study, "Trickster: On Inhabiting the Space between Discourse and Story," Ann Doueihi (1984) reflects on the effect of this theorizing. She points out that we learn less from these trickster theories about Native American cultures than about the Western intellectual perspectives that inform the theories. She concludes that all this talk about trickster is "a discourse by Western culture about Western culture, with Trickster serving only in a nominal function so that the discussion may begin." When this realization is placed within the political context of a concern for relations with Native Americans, Doueihi identifies this whole academic history as driven by a "logic of domination," that is as much a part of a "discourse of power... which distorts and abuses the Indian so that he fits into an idealized image serving Western man's nostalgia and yearning, as it is in approaches that delegate the Indian to the status of primitive savage or decadent heathen."

Harsh-seeming words, but it is essential we become aware of the political and historical implications of something so apparently innocuous as studying Native American mythology. There is no easy solution. We cannot reverse the fact that the trickster has now taken on real being as a figure, at least within Western mythology, and that he is now recognized even by many contemporary Native Americans as their own. Perhaps the key is to keep clearly in mind what knowledge is desired, what subject motivates our interest. If we want to know about Western perspectives, we will direct the focus of our interest toward trickster theories. If we want to know about Native Americans and their mythologies, we will focus on the various stories and figures within specific Native American cultures. With this knowledge it may be possible to allow these choices to be of greater service to one another. See also *Bungling Host, Fecal Power,* and *Vagina Dentata.* [Abenakew 1929; Abrams and Sutton-Smith 1977; Brinton 1896; Carroll 1981; Doueihi 1984; Hubbard 1980; Hultkrantz 1984; Jung 1972; Lopez 1977; Lossiah 1976; Norman 1976; Radin 1956, 1972; Ricketts 1966; Sayre 1985; Schmerler 1931; Toelken and Scott 1981]

Tsauda and Halus

Tsimshian, *Northwest Coast*

Tsauda, the son of Sun, is the prince from the sky who wears a garment of shining light. Halus is his slave. In the dark of night, Tsauda asks a beautiful princess to marry him. She agrees, and he leaves, saying he will soon return. The following night he sends Halus to talk to the princess. Allowing her to mistake him for his master, Halus asks if her father will give his slave a good wife. She promises him a lame sister whom she wants to take with her when she marries.

Tsauda enters through the smoke hole and asks Halus what he is up to. When the slave remains silent, Tsauda curses him with bad fortune. In anger because of the deception, Tsauda marries the lame younger sister, so Halus marries the beautiful daughter. Tsauda takes his lame wife to his father in the sky and cures her by washing her. She shines almost as brightly as her husband.

Master and slave compete constantly, yet Tsauda always makes Halus look the fool. Tsauda and his wife have two beautiful daughters, Moon and Another Dear Girl, who are the beginnings of the Wolf clan. Tsauda and his wife live in the sky and never come back to earth. [Boas 1902]

Tsauz

Salish, *Northwest Coast*

A poor *crippled boy* whose mottled skin is covered with sores. One day a handsome young man comes to Tsauz's house and shakes him by the nose until all his bones fall out. The handsome young man then puts on the diseased skin of Tsauz, so that everyone believes he is Tsauz. The most beautiful woman in the village comes to love and marry him, even though she has many healthy suitors. The couple are constantly mocked, especially by Raven.

When hunting with his wife's brothers, the man secretly takes off Tsauz's skin and hangs it in a tree. He is a successful hunter, and there is always plenty to eat in the village. One day on a hunting trip, his brothers-in-law spy on him and set fire to the tree where he has hung Tsauz's diseased skin. When he returns, he puts on the charred pieces of skin that remain. The next time he goes hunting and leaves the skin in the tree, the brothers-in-law blow on it and turn it into fog. Now the husband must appear as he really is: the handsome young man. The village people are surprised and Raven is jealous. The young man and his wife are rewarded for their patience and kindness. See also *Dirty Boy.* [Boas 1902]

Tsavoojok

Paviotso, *Great Basin*

An old *giant* who challenges husbands to fight one another so he can steal their wives. Tsavoojok is defeated by a group of men who ambush and kill him. [Lowie 1924]

Tsayik

Nootka, *Northwest Coast*

The doctoring ritual, which involves curing within a feast by people who possess healing songs and have been initiated into the Tsayik. The Tsayik is held by a member of the sick person's family. A member sings all of his or her songs until he or she begins to cry, that is, until the sobbing effect in the songs gradually becomes more pronounced, at which time another person starts singing. Sometimes the feast may also include initiations into the Tsayik. In this case the initiate is believed to acquire immunity from the sick person's disease. [Clutsei 1969]

Tseguksk

Tsimshian, *Northwest Coast*

A famous *shaman* who survives an attack on his village by a jealous shaman from another village.

T

Tseguksk subsequently visits Chief Gitkstaql, a powerful shaman who lives at the bottom of the ocean. Gitkstaql enhances Tseguksk's power by giving him a club in the shape of a land otter, a small box with the lid carved in the shape of a whale fin, and a wooden chamber pot. When the club is tossed into the water it becomes animated and swims upriver, breaking the winter ice so Tseguksk can return to his village. Tseguksk takes revenge on the village of the shaman who initially attacked him, surviving multiple attempts to poison him by replacing his intestines with those of a dog. He predicts the initial devastation of *smallpox*. It is said that when he died he assumed the form of an *owl*. [Boas 1902, 1916]

Tsetseka
Kwakiutl, *Northwest Coast*
The ceremonial season, which lasts from November to March or April. The nonceremonial season, known as Bakoos, is from March to November. The four days prior to the beginning of the Tsetseka season are known as Klasila, the time to honor all who have died since the last ceremonial season. If a chief has died, he is represented by a dancer from the Atlakim Society (one of the four dance societies) who wears a mask (see *Masks and Masking*) bearing one of the chief's *crest* figures (e.g., whale, raven, bear, or wolf) on it.

During Tsetseka, the village is divided between initiated and uninitiated members of various secret and ceremonial societies. *Dances,* feasts, and *potlatches* are held to demonstrate to the uninitiated that spirit visitors are present in the village. Initiated members engage in these activities to honor the spirits.

Tsetseka is also a time for the initiation of new members into one of the four dance societies: the *Hamatsa Society,* considered to be the most complex of the dance societies; the *Winalagilis* Society, whose members dance under the guidance of the war spirit Winalagilis; the Atlakim dancers, who dance specifically to honor the dead during the four-day season of Klasila; and the Dluwakakha ("once more from heaven") dancers

who, through song and story, pass on wisdom to new initiates without using the terrifying tactics of the *Hamatsa*.

The ritually enacted dances of the taming and initiation of the Hamatsa cannibal, sometimes referred to as the Winter Dance, lasts four nights. These dances may be held to honor a deceased chief at a memorial potlatch, or as part of the dowry for a noblewoman's marriage. They are also the occasion for a person to publicly claim an inherited name (see *Names and Naming)*, which will be used at subsequent Winter Dances. The dances and names are validated by their public use in the presence of invited guests, who are given gifts of money and goods during the ceremony. When every participant claims his or her Tsetseka name, the spirits are said to be present in the village. The original dances used in the Winter Dance include specially made songs, stories, and masks, and all of them are thus highly valued possessions passed down within families or to sons-in-law. Both heirloom and newly made masks are used in contemporary Kwakiutl Winter Dances.

At the beginning of the ceremonial season, after all participants have claimed their Tsetseka names and the spirits are present, a collection of all the masks is displayed. Initiates to the various dance societies are "kidnapped" by masked dancers and removed from sight, in a reenactment of the abduction by *Cannibal-at-the-North-End-of-the-World*. While the initiates are gone, dancers act out the story of the mythic experience of the ancestor who met the helping spirit of the society. It is believed that the initiation of the kidnapped person is completed by the helping spirit who is the guardian of that particular society.

In preparation for the Winter Dance and initiation into the Hamatsa society, an initiate disappears from the village and daily life in order to learn the ways of the cannibal. When he is ready to return, the guests are invited. During the nineteenth century, Tsetseka guests stayed all winter, but today guests stay only a short time. The ceremonies begin with people gathering to mourn those who have died during the past year.

The four-night ceremony begins at sundown. At the end of the fourth night, the previously captured Hamatsa novice returns through the roof of the house. He is dressed in hemlock boughs and whistles to express wildness. Attendants try to capture the Hamatsa, but he disappears again.

On the following morning, the gathered people capture the Hamatsa and other dance initiates and return them to the ceremonial house. The Hamatsa's dances gradually become tamer. If wildness overcomes the Hamatsa during this period, he goes behind a curtain, and companions of a bird monster appear in order to calm him down. Wearing great bird masks, these dancers perform a slow dance called the HamsEmala, in which they squat, jump, and sit on the floor. When the HamsEmala dancers leave, the Hamatsa returns dressed as a tamed person, that is, wearing a blanket and apron, and dances the final dance. Finally, the female attendants and their relatives dance to symbolize the successful taming of the Hamatsa. See also *Toxwid* (woman warrior who performs), *Winter Ceremonial Season, Yagim* (a sea monster represented), and *Nulmal* (Fool Dancers). [Boas 1921, 1930; Goldman 1975; Holm 1977; Rohner and Rohner 1970]

Tsisapuec
Crow, *Plains*
Twined Tail, a Crow hero and great *warrior* who undertakes a *vision quest* to reverse the poverty caused by his brothers' gambling. Twined Tail lives with his two older brothers, Large-Inside and Eats-Like-a-Wolf. Eats-Like-a-Wolf gambles with a camp bully known as Ground-Bull. At first Eats-Like-a-Wolf wins, but Ground-Bull accuses him of cheating with help from Twined Tail. Finally the brothers have to stop gambling because they are so poor. In despair, Twined Tail goes away on a vision quest. He travels many days and finally climbs to the top of a mountain, where he cuts off his finger, offering it to the sun and praying for wisdom. He faints from the loss of blood and does not recover until late evening. He fasts and prays for three nights without dreaming. On the fourth night he dreams he is standing before a large tipi. A young woman

wearing many elk teeth invites him in to meet her father. The tipi is the Sun Dance Lodge, and Twined Tail is purified with *sweet grass* and invited to dance the *Sun Dance*. He gains strength and wisdom from the dance, where he is taught by many elders. When he awakes he becomes a great warrior. He marries well and has many children.

Tsohoqgwais
Seneca, *Northeast*
Chipmunk. [Fenton 1987]

Tsuku
Hopi, *Southwest*
Clown (see *Clowns and Clowning Societies*) who appears in many forms, commonly in groups during *Plaza Dances,* taunting *kachinas* and performing entertaining skits. Their humor is often based on reversal of norms, social criticism, gluttony, sexually explicit actions, criticism of non-Hopi, and plays on language. There are many other forms of Hopi clowns. [Sekaquaptewa 1979; Wright 1973]

Tsusginagi
Cherokee, *Southeast*
The ghost country in the darkening-land of the west. Sun's daughter goes to Tsusginagi after dying from a rattlesnake bite. See also *Sun's Grief.* [Mooney 1900]

Tudab
Puyallup-Nisqually, Southern Puget Sound, *Northwest Coast*
The most desired type of *power* (see *Sqalalitut*) because it is considered the power of strength and wealth. The word also is used to refer to a *shaman,* the shaman's powers, and the powers of warriors. A person who refuses this type of power can become quite ill and even die. If a person with this power grows tired or fatigued, the power might become detached and even leave. If the power could not be reclaimed, the person could die. Shamans have the ability to control their health and thereby their personal power.

T

Hopi Tsuku (clowns), known for gluttony, perform at many Kachina dances. Painting by Cliff Bahnimptewa from *Kachinas: A Hopi Artist's Documentary,* by Barton Wright, copyright © 1973 by the Heard Museum. Published by Northland Publishing, Flagstaff, Arizona, with The Heard Museum, Phoenix, Arizona. Painting from the collection of The Heard Museum, Phoenix, Arizona.

A Tudab (shaman) can send power, or his or her power may wander about, looking for a weaker power to overcome. If a tudab enters a person whose power is weaker, the person may become deathly ill. At the moment of death, the power speaks through the dying person's voice, taunting the weaker powers of that person. Powers are constantly struggling with each other. Revenge killing for death caused by a tudab power is considered socially acceptable. Tudab powers are widely distributed, but for the average person they are considered to be out of balance and are held in check by sqalalitut (the average individual's personal power). A person who uses power for malevolent purposes is said to be affected by *ayaxaus* (a dangerous negative power). See also *Astcatstudab,* another kind of power. [Smith 1940]

Tumanpa and Kwa?akuyi-savepone
Mohave, *Southwest*
A brother and his younger sister, the protagonists of long stories. They travel about on an adventure. Stories about them are commonly told through the singing of songs. In some versions the *incest* between brother and sister is a key feature; in other versions it is not mentioned. See also *Dreamed Stories.* [Kroeber 1948, 1972]

Tumbianoobi
Moapa, *Great Basin*
Echo, who is married to Mourning Dove. Mourning Dove is afraid of Tumbianoobi, and runs and hides when she pursues him. Eventually Tumbianoobi meets a man with a long penis, and decides to give up searching for Mourning Dove and stay with the man. They move into a group of rocks to live, but the rocks grow closer and closer together. Finally the long-penis man escapes, leaving Tumbianoobi behind. She calls to him, but at first he does not answer. When he finally speaks to her she repeats whatever he says, hence her name, Echo. [Lowie 1924]

Tunghak
Eskimo, Bering Sea coast, Alaska, *Arctic*
The most powerful of spirits, with the greatest potential for harm. Tunghak control the spirits of the animals, and therefore the fate of humans. Their home is in the moon. Tunghak appear as masked forms in *qasgiq* ceremonies. Some masks (see *Masks and Masking*) represent Tunghak as hermaphrodites; their down-turned mouths signify femaleness, while the labrets (lip and nose ornaments) in the corners of their mouths are representative of men. Other large Tunghak masks are suspended from the qasgiq ceiling so that shamans can dance behind them. See also *Inua* and *Hands.* [Lantis 1947; Nelson 1899]

Tuniit
Eskimo, Eastern Hudson Bay, *Arctic*
Legendary people who lived long ago. The strong and energetic Tuniit try constantly to outdo one another in work, hunting, and archery. They die of exhaustion from constant competition. See also *Ikuutayuuq.* [Nungak and Arima 1988]

Tunnituaqruk
Eskimo, Eastern Hudson Bay, *Arctic*
Malevolent creatures with multiple facial tattoos (tunnit). The female, *Katyutayuuq,* has big breasts on her cheeks and a vulva on her chin. Her head is much smaller than that of the male. Tunnituaqruk look for scraps of food in abandoned snow houses and hide in discarded bedding, frightening any unsuspecting passerby. [Nungak and Arima 1988]

Turning Dance
Shawnee, *Northeast*
Kaukiwawakauwa, the dance done at the one-year anniversary of a death.

Turquoise Man
See *Salt Woman.*

Turquoise Woman
See *Whiteshell Woman.*

T

Turtle

Many stories tell of Turtle. Although he is often ridiculed by humans and other animals because of his clumsiness and clowning, some cultures, such as the Maliseet-Passamaquoddy, consider Turtle to be a powerful shaman (see also *Mikchich*). In other cultures such as the Maidu, Turtle supports the world on his back (see *Earth-Initiate, Earth-Maker*) and is associated with the *Earth Diver* motif, in which animals dive for a bit of mud *(Oehda)* from which to make the earth. Stories about Turtle have been shaped by his hard shell, representing longevity, and his ability to retract into it. The Lakota turtle *(Keya)* is a guardian spirit of health.

The Seneca consider Turtle (Hahnowa) to be a warrior. Hahnowa lives alone in his own lodge. One day he decides to go on the warpath. He sings as he travels in his canoe. Hahnowa meets an elk who asks to join him. Hahnowa insists he must first see the elk run. Although the elk runs swiftly, Hahnowa says he may not come with him because he is not swift enough. Turtle then meets Senon (Skunk), who also wants to join him. At once Turtle recognizes Senon's power and grants his request. Because of his quills, Kaheda (Porcupine) is invited to join the war party, even though he trips and falls during his running test. Degiyahgon (Buffalo) fails the speed trial, but Sigwon (Rattlesnake) is invited to join.

The band of warriors decides to make war on seven sisters. Turtle tells his companions that each must choose the place best suited for his own method of fighting. Senon sits next to the fireplace, ready to attack with his odors. Kaheda hides in the woodpile to attack the person who comes for firewood.

Tuniit in battle. Courtesy, Canadian Museum of Civilization (neg.#J 14363).

Sigwaon hides in the corn bucket to attack the first person who comes for corn, and Turtle hides near the spring to fight the person who comes for water.

Senon attacks with his foul odors and fights bravely but is eventually killed and thrown aside. Kaheda attacks from the woodpile but is beaten to death by the sisters. Sigwaon bites the hand of the sister who goes for corn and kills her, but is beaten on the head by the other sisters. When one of the sisters goes to get water, Turtle bites her on the toe and will not let go. She goes back to the lodge, dragging Turtle along. The sisters' mother tells one daughter to throw Turtle in the fire and burn him up. Turtle laughs and tells her he cannot be destroyed by fire because he came from fire and enjoys nothing better than fire. The mother changes her mind and decides to take him to the creek to drown him. Turtle pleads not to be thrown into the water, but the sisters and their mother throw him in. He sinks to the bottom but a short time later rises to the surface. He holds out his claws and laughs, stating that, in truth, he is a brave warrior who lives under the water.

In another Seneca story, Mud Turtle determines the size of the world. He is sent by Bald Eagle, an old man, to determine the size of the world after other animals have failed at the task. Mud Turtle persuades members of his tribe to go in different directions and report back to him. They are gone for months. When they return they hold a council and tell Mud Turtle all they have seen. Mud Turtle pleases Bald Eagle with his report. Bald Eagle rewards Mud Turtle by making him his second chief and giving him the responsibility of supporting the world on his back. *Skahnowa* is the turtle servant of the great horned snake.

Locv-saukv, the leg rattles of Seminole and Creek women, are made from land turtles. *Miski-nahk* is the Cree term for turtle. See also the Zuni story *Worm and Turtle as Warriors.* [Curtin and Hewitt 1918; Fenton 1962; Hertzberg 1981;

Lossiah 1976; Prince 1921; Tall Bull and Weist 1971]

Turtle Dance
See *Tewa Ritual Cycle.*

Turtle Rattle(s)
Turtle shells make excellent rattles. Among the many turtle-shell rattles are those made for *kachinas.* These rattles are attached to the calf of the leg and give their sound to the dance. The Iroquois make a handheld rattle of the whole turtle. The handle appears as the outstretched head and neck of the turtle. See *False Faces; Hodigohsosga?a; Iroquois Masks, Storage of; Faces of Forests;* and *Longhouse Ceremony.*

Tuurnngaq (alt. Tuniq)
Eskimo, Eastern Hudson Bay, *Arctic*
Ancient *giant* humans who live in solid rock houses. They kill people and cause hunters to disappear. [Nungak and Arima 1988]

Twehdaigo
Onondaga, Iroquois, *Northeast*
A red being who was assigned by *Sky-Holder,* the creator, to live on the east side of earth and help humans. For Twehdaigo's counterpart who lives in the west see *Ohswedogo.* [Fenton 1987]

Twined Tail
Crow, *Plains*
The great warrior *Tsisapuec.*

Twins' Journey to Sun Father
A common theme in which twins (usually warriors) journey to their father, the Sun, to be given gifts, often weapons and armor, due them as sons of the Sun. See *Ahayuta* and *Kanaakwa* (Zuni), *Hadentheni and Hanigongendatha* (Seneca), *Iatiku* and *Masewa and Uyuyewa* (Keresan tribes), *Monster Slayer and Born for Water* and *Monsterway* (Navajo), *Pyuykonhoya* (Hopi), and *White Painted Woman* (Apache). [Wyman 1970]

T

Two-Hearts
Common Native American designation for liar or *witch*. The term "forked tongue," which is used similarly but directed more toward European-Americans, originated in the era of treaty negotiations. Speaking in Washington in 1879, Nez Perce Chief Joseph relied on both figures when he said, "What I have to say will come from the heart, and I will speak with a straight tongue."

Txamsem
The Tsimshian term for *Raven*.

Uchatngiak

Aleut, Bering Sea coast, Kodiak Island, Eskimo, Alaska, *Arctic*

The only son of a powerful chief. As a child, Uchatngiak is kept under guard in his father's hut. One day he looks out the window and sees sun, grass, and sky. He is so moved by the beauty that he cries, and his guards plead with his father to let him out. Realizing his son is grown, the chief allows him to sit outside on top of the hut.

One day Uchatngiak sees five white geese fly overhead. He follows them to the lake and discovers five beautiful young women bathing and five white goose skins lying on the shoreline. Uchatngiak hides the smallest skin. When the sisters come out of the water they quickly put on their skins, all except the youngest, who is named Agoiyuan. As her sisters wait impatiently, Uchatngiak steps out with her skin. He refuses to give it back to her, and instead dresses her in his parka and boots and brings her home to be his wife. They live together until the following spring. During the day Uchatngiak hunts, and Agoiyuan goes to the lake to eat the fine grasses she likes. Eventually Agoiyuan gives birth to a son.

Uchatngiak's sister, who dislikes Agoiyuan, gossips about her and makes fun of her strange mouth. She abuses Agoiyuan so cruelly that the goose woman puts on her goose skin and flies away, leaving her son behind. When Uchatngiak returns and finds his wife missing, he grieves. Several years pass, and Uchatngiak's son travels everywhere with him. One day the boy sees five white geese fly overhead and decides to follow them. When he does not return, Uchatngiak realizes the boy has gone with his mother, and goes looking for him.

With the help of an old woman and her brother, Uchatngiak finds his way to the village of the birds somewhere above the earth. He pleads with Agoiyuan to let him stay so he can be with his son. He is allowed to stay on the condition that he remain in his hut. Every day many birds gather in a large hut. Finally Uchatngiak's curiosity overcomes him, and he peeks into the large hut, where he sees the birds dressing and painting themselves with colored rocks. He is discovered and severely scolded, and the birds decide to move their village. Uchatngiak begs to go with them until the birds consent, and they decide Eagle will carry him. But

Raven insists on carrying Uchatngiak herself, saying that if she gets tired she will turn him over to Eagle. As they fly over the ocean, Raven tires and drops Uchatngiak. Eagle swoops down to retrieve him, but he never surfaces. Instead he becomes a white whale, while Raven becomes a large piece of drifting tree trunk. The grieving geese eventually decide to come to earth to lay their eggs and rear their young. [Golder 1903]

Ugjuknarpak
Eskimo, Alaska, *Arctic*
A giant *mouse* with skin so thick that no arrow, harpoon, or knife can penetrate it. Ugjuknarpak lives on an island and uses its long tail to lasso its prey and overturn peoples' umiaks (large skin boats). The slightest sound attracts Ugjuknarpak. [Norman 1990]

Uglyway (hochooji)
Navajo, *Southwest*
Also Ghostway and Evilway. A classification of ritual healing ceremonials intended to cure illnesses caused by the influence of ghosts, witches, and other malevolence. *Hozho* Means Beauty Or Order, As Exemplified By The Way The World Appeared When First Created. It is paired with hocho, connoting disorder and chaos or ugliness. Hocho is often the result of ghost actions or malevolence that designate, in general terms, something out of place or inappropriate. The dead are supposed to inhabit a place apart from the living. Malevolence is the use of power in an inappropriate way. Uglyway ceremonials remove and protect against the forces of chaos and disorder that give rise to illness. See also *Hoop Transformation Rite, Ma?ii, Navajo Emergence, Navajo Ritual Process,* and *Shootingway.*

Ugni
Catawba, *Southeast*
A comet, a prominent story figure who is referred to as a star with a tail (see *Stars and Starlore).* As a young boy, Ugni is stolen by a poor old woman who starves him. With the help of Woodpecker, his mother finds him and brings him food. Ugni hides his mother in the old woman's house and tricks the old woman into going out and gathering some deer meat. While she is gone Ugni sets fire to her house and escapes to the sky on a rope, along with his mother. The old woman finds the rope and pulls on the bottom of it, and Ugni and his mother start to fall. As he falls, Ugni becomes a tailed star. The old woman crashes to the ground, and Ugni and his mother escape to the sky. [Speck 1934]

Ukikunece
Omaha, *Plains*
The Ukikunece are feasting societies divided into three groups: one for married and aged men, one for younger men, and one for teenagers. The purpose of a Ukikunece is to eat and build friendships. A *pipe* is smoked at the gathering, but the ceremony does not include any singing, dancing, or business transactions. [Dorsey 1888b]

Uluaq
Eskimo, Bering Sea coast, Alaska, *Arctic*
A woman's knife, made for her by her father or uncle, used for cutting skins, meat, and fish. [Nelson 1899]

Underwater Cats
Under water cats may include lynxes, leopards, panthers, or tigers, depending on the geographical region, that live under or near water. Sometimes these animals are helpful, other times they are not. The story tradition among the Creek tells of an unmarried woman living in the town of Coosa who is impregnated by a water tiger named Wi Katca. When the woman's family wants to kill her offspring, she goes to Wi Katca for help. He causes a flood to cover the town of Coosa, so that only the main beams of the ceremonial lodge remain above water. The woman goes to live with Wi Katca, and the few flood survivors start a new town, now known as Tulsa. See also *Michi-Pichoux.* [Hudson 1976]

Underwater House
See *Gitnagunaks.*

Underworld
A world or worlds located below the present world on the earth's surface. For many cultures the underworld is the place from which the first people emerged. This motif is most common in the southwestern United States (see *Emergence).* In many cultures the underworld is the place of the *dead* (see *Adlivun);* malevolent creatures may also abide there (see, for example, the Menominee *Great White Bear). Shamans* take paths to the underworld when they communicate with the dead or retrieve lost souls.

Among the Yupik of western Alaska, the underworld where the dead reside is reached only by a pathway cluttered with obstacles. A traveler must pass many tests along the road before he or she is allowed to reach the land of the dead. A body being carried to a gravesite is set down four or five times along the way, reflecting the belief that the earth has several layers that must be crossed. A piece of wood is placed in the hand of the deceased to assist in the event he or she should need to cross a river on the journey into the underworld. Other possible obstacles along the pathway include a tree with many branches or the inner cones of fish traps.

The success of a person's journey through the underworld to the land of the dead depends on how the person has lived his or her life, as well as on the actions of his or her survivors.

Unhcegila
Lakota, *Plains*
A land *monster* resembling a dragon. Unhcegila is responsible for mysterious disappearances and death. [Walker 1982]

Unipkaat
Eskimo, Northern Alaska, *Arctic*
Legends, ancient stories. [Norman 1990]

Unktehi
Plains
A group of powerful beings that may resemble giant oxen. Their horns and tails reach the sky. Their power lies in their tails; if they lose their tails they become harmless and foolish. The Unktehi are always fighting the *Wakinyan* (Thunderbirds). The male Unktehi live primarily in deep water and under waterfalls. They are considered to be malevolent *water spirits* responsible for *floods,* drowning, and any water-related mishaps, as well as for the creation of alkali, mud, and poisonous water. The female Unktehi live primarily on earth.

The Unktehi emit power *(tonwan)* from their bodies. They feed on the spirits of human beings and on the skins of deer, dogs, and swans who are sacrificed to them in special ceremonies for the dead.

The Unktehi may be addressed as "grandfather" and "grandmother." It is believed that the Unktehi created the earth (see *Creation)* and human beings (see *Humans, Origin of),* and that they taught humans the *Wakan Wacipi,* or mystery dance. They are also thought to have taught people how to use pigments to decorate their bodies for ceremonies and war. [Powers 1975; Walker 1982]

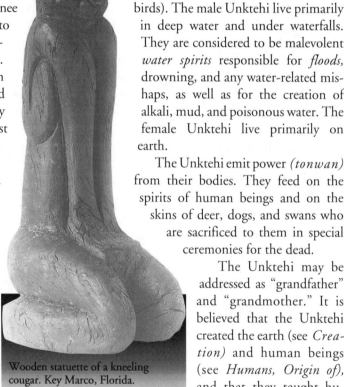
Wooden statuette of a kneeling cougar. Key Marco, Florida. Courtesy, National Museum of Natural History, Smithsonian Institution

Unktomi
Lakota, *Plains*
A variant of *Iktomi.* [Deloria 1932]

Unwilling Bride

A story motif in which a girl, often beautiful, refuses to marry any of her many suitors, even opposing her parent's wishes. She may finally wed a handsome man who, after their marriage, reveals his ugliness and cruelty. For examples of this widely used motif, see *Ahayuta, Lone Bird,* and *Marriage Test.*

Unwounded Buckskin

Navajo, *Southwest*

Many ritual objects, such as the *mountain soil bundle,* must be made of unwounded buckskin. To procure such a skin, Navajos must run down a deer. This is possible because deer, while fleet, do not have great endurance. Once the deer is caught, it is suffocated by covering its nose with pollen *(tadidiin).* The deer dies with its last breath inhaling this precious life-giving substance.

Upward Reaching Way

See *Navajo Emergence.*

Uqaluktua

Eskimo, Northern Alaska, *Arctic*

Ancestor histories. [Norman 1990]

Urine

The Nootka wash hair with urine that is stored in *cedar* containers. The Zuni *Newekwe* drink urine.

Ursa Major

See *Big Dipper* and *Great Bear Constellation.*

Utea

Yaqui, *Southwest*

A gift of *power* inherited from the ancient people, *Surem;* extraordinary strength of body and will (see also *Seataka).* It may also be acquired from powerful objects. Utea may be used for any purpose, especially matters involving the supernatural. See also *Hitebi* (curer) and *Pascola.* [Painter 1986]

Uwanammi

See *Rain Priest.*

Uwashil

Natchez, *Southeast*

"Big fire." The *Sun.* During the opening of ceremonies, smoke from the *pipe* was directed toward Uwashil to ask for blessings and health. [Hudson 1976]

Vagina Dentata

Vaginal teeth, a motif that sometimes accounts for the origin of pleasure in sexual intercourse. Stories of vagina dentata usually involve a *culture hero* or *trickster*. Women in these stories may be depicted as having in their vaginas rattlesnake's teeth, which they use to kill men who have intercourse with them. They then take the dead men's hunting equipment. These women are frequently able to hunt with their toothed vaginas. Often a culture hero, sometimes acting the role of a young husband, breaks or wears down the vaginal teeth with a wedge or stone penis, so that intercourse no longer ends in death. See also *Cotsipamapot* (Moapa), in which deer scapulae are used to file away the teeth; *Evening Star* (Pawnee), whose daughter has a toothed vagina; *Korawini?i*, the mother of the Paiutes, who has a toothed vagina; and *Pleasurable Sexual Intercourse*. [Malotki 1983]

Vasaagijik

Alaska, Yukon Territory, *Arctic*

"Greasy Mouth." The extremely unpredictable and highly changeable *culture hero* identified with the Canada Jay. His name may have derived from the Algonquian *Wesucechak*. [Norman 1990]

Ventriloquism

Potawatomi, *Northeast*

A shamanic technique (see *Caskyet*).

Venus

See *Evening Star*.

Vision(s)

A vision, often acquired through a *vision quest*, is the acquisition of power through communication with the spiritual world. Visions may also be experienced during the *Sun Dance* or by menstruating women (see *Menstrual Blood*). Only a few cultures use pharmacopia to induce visions (see *Datura* and *Native American Church*). Visions provide the authority for the creation of stories and rituals, as well as for individual and cultural action. For example, the Huron medicine person *Arendiwane* received his power in visions. The Lakota police society *(akicitas)* originated from a vision. Double Woman *(Anog Ite)* learned quilling in a vision. The Yaqui communicate with the ancient world *Yoania* through visions. [Benedict 1922]

Vision Quest(s)

A solitary fasting ritual done in quest of wisdom and power in the form of a vision, which may or may not result in the acquisition of a *helping spirit.* The site for the quest may be chosen to place the seeker in a location associated with a sought-after spirit, and is often selected by the officiating medicine person. Knowledge gained in his vision quest led *Burnt Face,* the Crow hero, to make the medicine wheel as a quest site.

Puberty is a common time to undertake a vision quest, but one may seek a vision as preparation for war, or at other times of life transition. Although the acquisition of a vision is a way for an individual to receive power and distinction, vision quests may be undertaken by the visionary's community for broader benefit. The Lakota *Horse Dance* is a performance based on an individual vision. One performance of the Horse Dance is done according to the vision of Black Elk, the famous Oglala. The Lakota term for vision quest is Hanblapi.

The great Crow warrior *Tsisapuec* undertook a vision quest to reverse the debts of his gambling brother. *Tatahkesewen* (Menominee) is the power received by a vision quester. *Xapaaliia* (Crow) is the physical representation of spirit power. The questing person may learn songs, healing knowledge, or other information, such as the dances and songs of Salish *spirit dancing.* [Amiotte 1976]

Wabasso
Ojibwa, *Northeast, Subarctic*
The brother of Winabojo.

Wabeno
Ojibwa, *Northeast, Subarctic*
"Men of the dawn sky." The brother of *Winabojo*. Fire handlers who use fire to interpret *dreams,* guide people in contacting and communicating with their helping spirits, and heal the sick. The wabeno use an herbal preparation that protects them from the fire. They formed a specific society similar to the *Midewiwin.* [Landes 1968]

Wacekiyapi
Lakota, *Plains*
A four-day period of grieving after death, during which members of the *dead* person's family walk around the camp to convey their grief. Adult men pierce their arms and legs, and women slash their limbs and may cut off their little fingers at the first joint and cut their hair short.

During Wacekiyapi the family erects a burial scaffold. At the end of the four days, the old women of the family remove the corpse from the tipi and transport it to the scaffold, using a travois pulled by the deceased's favorite horse. They use pulleys to hoist the corpse to the scaffold, where they also hang the person's belongings. A close friend of the dead person explains to the horse that its master needs it for company, then shoots it at close range so it will not suffer. The horse's tail is cut off and tied to the burial bundle that hangs from the scaffold. See also *Spirit Keeping Ceremony.* [Walker 1982]

Wacabe
Osage, *Plains*
Black *Bear,* an important *helping spirit* who symbolizes strength, courage, and old age. Wacabe is central in many ceremonies, particularly to the vigil that is also called Wacabe (alternatively spelled Wa-xo-be), in which the traditions of the Osage are recited. Wacabe is credited with originating all Osage rituals. [Dorsey 1888b]

Waipanows
Menominee, *Northeast*
The *Thunder* cult composed of *medicine people* who specialized in making *hunting* medicine, herbal remedies, and

love powders. Not to be confused with ce-sahkows, the *Buffalo Dance Cult* composed of "jugglers" who are also healers. Waipanows worked in a small birchbark lodge (see *Shaking Tent)* where spirits were consulted. [Bloomfield 1928a]

Wakan
Lakota, *Plains*
"Something mysterious." Often translated as "holy," wakan is used to preface many words and concepts. Wakan describes the potential *power* inherent in a person or animal. A wakan man or woman is a person with wisdom, especially someone in contact with the spiritual world. Wakan men and women are the ones who know prayers, songs, and rites; those who have had visions. Perhaps wakan most closely resembles the English words "wonderful" and "incomprehensible."

Animals may be wakan. Food is considered wakan because it makes life. Medicine is wakan. Anything difficult to understand is wakan. Young children and the very old are wakan. Even people who appear mentally disturbed may be considered wakan. See also *Wakan Tanka,* "the great mystery"; *Hunka Lowanpi* (the Sun Dance); *Ta Tanka Lowanpi,* the Buffalo Bull Ceremony; and *Wakanpi.* For similar concepts in other Native American cultures, see *Maxpe,* the Crow term for something mysterious, and *Orenda* (Iroquois). [Neihardt 1932; Walker 1982]

Wakan Tanka
Lakota, *Plains*
"The great mystery." Wakan Tanka represents all the spiritual beings and powers in the Oglala world. In recent times this term is commonly rendered as "Creator" or "Great Spirit," and may even be considered synonymous with the Christian God (see also *Christianity).*

The creation of the world and the sun is considered to be Wakan Tanka. The Sun, Sky, Earth, and Rock *(Inyan)* are Wakan Tanka, as are Thunderbirds, the Wind, and the Stars. The

journey taken after death is Wakan Tanka (see *Wanagi).* For related Lakota terms, see *Hanblapi* (vision quest), *Nagila* (immaterial self of inanimate objects), *Sicun* (the intellect), *Tonwan* (Lakota spiritual power), *Wakan* (power), *Wakanpi* (nonhuman things with power), *Wazilya* (the act of incensing by burning sweet grass), and *wicasa wakan* (religious leader).

Wakan Wacipi
Plains
Mystery Dance that the *Unktehi* gave to human beings shortly after the creation of the earth. The Unktehi also gave humans a *medicine bundle* that holds the skins of otter, raccoon, weasel, squirrel, loon, a variety of fish, and serpents. People who dance the Mystery Dance are the guardians of the bundle for the community. They believe the Unktehi have the greatest power of any beings. [Walker 1982]

Wakanda(s)
Omaha, Ponca, *Plains*
A group of powers that included Darkness, the Ground, the Thunder Being, the Sun, the Moon, the Morning Star, and other stars and constellations. People frequently pray to one or the other of these powers to ask for protection in serious undertakings, such as initiating a war party or departing on a long and difficult journey. [Dorsey 1888b]

Wakandagi
Omaha, Ponca, *Plains*
Long-bodied, horned *monsters* that live beneath the bluffs along the Missouri River. They are known for enticing solitary travelers and causing them to go insane. [Walker 1982]

Wakandanacian
Omaha, *Plains*
A *story type* distinguished by a focus on *visions* and secret *societies.* Prayer and fasting are required preparations for telling wakandanacian. [Dorsey 1888b]

Wakanpi

Lakota, *Plains*

All things that are not humankind and have power over all animate and inanimate beings and things on earth. There are many types of Wakanpi. *Wakan Tanka* are the superior powers among the Wakanpi.

Wakanpi watch humans constantly, and if they are not pleased they can cause harm. They are pleased by songs, ceremonies, and gifts. The songs and ceremonies of the Oglala people belong to the Wakanpi and are considered *wakan* because of this. There are malevolent Wakanpi that cause harm. The most malevolent of the evil Wakanpi is *Iya,* the giant. [Walker 1982]

Wakincuzas

Lakota, *Plains*

"The ones who decide." People chosen from among the several soldier *societies* to lead the move to a new camp. The Wakincuzas ensure an orderly move, allowing no one to wander off to hunt or lag behind. When the Wakincuzas have chosen the new campsite, they announce the decision by smoking the pipe. See also *Scalping.* [Walker 1982]

Wakinyan

Dakota, *Plains*

Thunderbirds, the flying ones, from the root "kinyan," which means to fly. Wakinyan are huge winged beings that human beings cannot see because they are shielded by thick clouds. Thunder is made by the sound of their voices, and lightning is created when they open and close their eyes. There are four kinds of Wakinyan: scarlet, black with a long beak, yellow with no beak, and blue with no ears or eyes. The Wakinyan live in the west and travel with the west wind. They protect people from *Waziya,* the North Wind. Those who become *heyoka* do so because they have dreams of Wakinyan. The Wakinyan created wild rice and a variety of prairie grasses. *Unktehi,* the powerful oxenlike beings, are always fighting with the Wakinyan. *Iktomi* is considered to be heyoka because he is always talking with the Wakinyan. [Deloria 1932]

Walal Potlatch

Haida, *Northwest Coast*

The most complex of Haida *potlatches,* by which a man became a house chief; children became yahEt (the child of a man who had given a Walal potlatch), making them eligible for important titles in their matrilineal line; and names were received (see *Names and Naming*). The Walal potlatch included a lengthy cycle of gift distribution. It was given whenever a cedar plank house was completed or a totem pole raised. The Walal potlatch included tattooing, ear and nose piercing, and the puncturing of women's lower lips to insert labrets. All these forms were indicators of rank in Haida society. The only way a husband and wife could adopt a child was by hosting a Walal potlatch at a cedar plank house-raising. The last Walal potlatch was given at the turn of the twentieth century; in contemporary society the mortuary potlatch (honoring a deceased relative) is done. See also *Gia is su.* [Blackman 1977]

Walum Olum

Delaware, *Northeast*

The account of the Delaware origin and migration, which was painted in red pictographs on sticks. The sticks helped people remember important elements of the saga, which included migrations, wars, and a listing of Delaware chiefs. [Brotherston 1979a; Leitner 1941; Voegelin and Voegelin 1954]

Wamaka nagi

Lakota, *Plains*

The animal spirit that may accompany the *wanagi,* the spirit of a human who has died, to the land of the dead. It is believed that the human spirit is happier if it has the wamaka nagi of its favorite dog or horse to accompany it. For this reason a person's dog or horse was often killed when its owner died. See also *Nagi.* [Walker 1982]

Wambli
Lakota, *Plains*
Eagle, whose spirit is responsible for councils, hunters, war parties, and battles. [Walker 1982]

Wampum
Shell beads in several colors that were gathered, drilled, dyed and used as rare objects of trade, decoration, and communication. Several stories tell of wonderful bead-spitting animals. The beads in these stories are thought to be wampum. In some stories people are tortured by having the soles of their feet burned so they will cry tears that turn to wampum beads. Wampum originated from the mouths of pipe-smoking shamans. Every time they drew on the pipe, the beads dropped from their mouths. The most powerful shaman produced black wampum; the average shaman, white beads; and the least powerful, half red and half white beads. See also *Hadjowiski; Hotgoendaqsais,* a story where wampum beads come from tears; and *Hathondas,* a poor boy who learns how to spit out wampum beads. [Ceci 1982; Slotkin and Schmitt 1949]

Wanace
Omaha, *Plains*
Young men who functioned as *Akcitas* or police-men. They surrounded buffalo on hunts and were considered to have many powers because of their bravery. The wanace acted as servants and mes-sengers for the chiefs *(Nikagahi).* Young men who had not yet proven themselves in war or on a hunt were called cenujinga. As the common people, they had no voice in tribal affairs. During a buffalo hunt they had to obey the wanace and the chiefs. The Omaha did not have a specific mili-tary or warrior group. [Dorsey 1888b]

Wanagemeswak
Penobscot, *Northeast*
Hatchet-faced and extremely thin *dwarfs* who live in rivers and small pools of water. Wanage-meswak can be seen only in profile. They make small clay *doll* figures and leave them on the riverbanks for humans to find. Finding one of these figures will bring good luck. [Trigger 1978]

Wanagi
Lakota, *Plains*
The human spirit *(nagi)* that leaves the human body after death. When this spirit is attached to a human it is life (woniya). When a human dies, this spirit becomes wanagi. See also *Wamaka nagi.* [Walker 1982]

Wani
Lakota, *Plains*
The Four *Winds,* which have power over life and the weather. Combined into one they represent vigor. See also *Tate.* [Walker 1982]

Wani-sapa
Lakota, *Plains*
A communal *buffalo hunt,* formalized by religious and political jurisdiction, which involved every member of the tribe. The *Nacas* (society of elders or former chiefs) organized a hunt whenever the tribe needed food. If the need was critical, the *shaman* joined the Nacas in controlling the Wani-sapa. The shaman would do a sweat to receive instructions about the hunt from the *helping spirit.* The helper usually told the shaman to organize the Buffalo Dance, which imitated the movement of the buffalo.

The most trustworthy scouts were chosen to locate the buffalo. If they sighted a herd, they rode back to camp and went into a special tipi that housed an altar smudged with *sweet grass,* buffalo chips, and a *pipe.* After the scouts and Nacas smoked the pipe, the entire camp moved near the herd and the hunt began. The *akicitas* (police societies) kept order during the move to ensure that no one strayed and that the buffalo were not frightened into a stampede. [Walker 1982]

Wanou
Arapaho, *Plains*
A large wart. Every morning, Wanou rolls to a riverbank to leave game for the family of a girl

named River-Woman. When he finds her hiding and watching him, Wanou becomes enraged. He swallows her family's tent, and overtakes and kills her parents and her brother, Beaver-Foot. River-Woman escapes to a woodcutter and promises to marry him if he will protect her. The woodcutter, who is a horned *water monster (hiintcabiit),* agrees. Wanou attempts to swallow him, but the woodcutter strikes the wart with his axe and splits him open. Then he revives Beaver-Foot, and takes him and River-Woman home to meet his first wife, *Crow-Woman.*

Wapno
Potawatomi, *Northeast*
A fire-handling *shaman* who amuses audiences and provides practical advice. [Densmore 1929]

War
An ancient art practiced by many Native American cultures. War is the setting for many Native American stories. Some stories are concerned with the origin of war, such as the Serrano story of *Kukitat,* who introduces war. The Huron consider *Ondoutaehte* to be the perpetrator of war.

The Yupik Eskimos of the Bering Sea coast of Alaska tell a story attributing the origins of war to the antisocial behavior of one story figure. A poor hunter from another area marries into an Alaskan coastal village group. He kills his hunting companions one by one in order to steal their catches. When his behavior is discovered, he moves north and plants seeds of distrust among the Yukon Eskimos, precipitating a war with their coastal neighbors. War finally ends when, during a great famine, a man from the Yukon and a man from the coastal community of Hooper Bay work together to stalk a seal. They share the catch to spare their families from starvation.

Various ceremonies, societies, and paraphernalia are associated with war. For examples, see *Coup; Crow Lance Society,* a society concerned with success in war and buffalo hunting; *Grain-of-Corn Bundle,* the Pawnee medicine bundle used in time of war; the *Horse Dance* done in preparation for war; *Kacale,* the Acoma clowns who have a war function; *Pinessi,* the Cree/Ojibwa Thunderer, a spirit associated with war; *Scalping;* and *Warrior.* [Dorsey 1904f, 1906b; Goldschmidt, Foster, and Essene 1939; Hill 1936; Medicine 1983]

Warrior(s)
Many Native American culture heroes and story protagonists are warriors. For a sampling see the following: *Andicicopec,* the Crow mythic figure; *Atsitsi,* the Blackfoot warrior Screech Owl; *Mikapi* (Blackfoot); Red Old Man, the warrior grandson of Pawnee *Cannibal Grandmother; Tsisapuec,* the great Crow warrior; and the many stories of *Warrior Twins.* See also *Warrior Bird and the Origin of Stars* (Pawnee). Retired Lakota warriors are known as "Big Bellies" *(Naca Ominicia).* The Pawnee had important warrior assistants *(Ra hikucu).*

Warrior Bird and the Origin of Stars
Pawnee, *Plains*
Struggles between Hawk and Fire Keeper resulting in the origin of stars. A man lives in the west with his brother, a priest, across a deep river from two Hawk brothers. The Hawk brothers use a magic log to cross the river. The older Hawk brother crosses the river and takes as his wife the priest's daughter, Fire Keeper's niece. She gives birth to a boy. Because Fire Keeper, as the girl's uncle, was not consulted about the marriage, he decides to take revenge. He captures the Hawk husband, strips his clothes from him, and burns them. In the struggle, Hawk is blinded. Fire Keeper makes him his slave.

Hawk's son cries for his father until his mother goes to search for her husband. They find the burned remnants of his clothing on the riverbank and follow his trail, which leads to Fire Keeper's tipi. Inside the tipi is a huge fire. Fire Keeper has painted both himself and her husband red, and forces the husband to stir the fire. She begs Fire Keeper to release her blind husband, and finally the uncle relents. The child stops crying

when he sees his father. Carrying Hawk's half-burned war club, the reunited family travels east for several days. One morning Hawk begs his wife to push him off a steep cliff before sunrise. Just as she is about to do so, he undergoes a transformation, becoming fully clothed with a healthy body. Hawk then takes revenge against Fire Keeper.

After killing Fire Keeper, Hawk throws fire into the sky in all directions, announcing that from now on warriors will receive help from the light of the stars. On his journey home, Hawk is thanked by the animals and birds, who give him the name Warrior Bird. The Hawk brothers inform their father-in-law, the priest who was Fire Keeper's brother, that when they die their skulls are to be kept in a bundle so the people will have protection on the warpath. They also say that the priests (see also *Kurahus*), who are also known as owls, are to remain at home as guardians of the people. [Dorsey 1906a]

Warrior-of-the-World
Kwakiutl, *Northwest Coast*
The giant *Winalagilis.*

Warrior Twins
See *Ahayuta, Masewa and Uyuyewa, Monster Slayer and Born for Water,* and *Pyuykonhoya.*

Waruxawe
Winnebago, *Northeast*
Waruxawe are *medicine bundles* that may contain a wide variety of articles such as stones, animal skins, medicines, and sometimes war clubs. Some waruxawe, such as the buffalo medicine bag, are used for healing. Other waruxawe are used to help people prepare for war. Although most waruxawe are considered to have positive power, others have malevolent power. These medicine bundles often contain bone whistles, which when blown prohibit an enemy from defending himself or from fleeing. Women are forbidden to touch the waruxawe. [Lowie 1963]

Was
Tsimshian, *Northwest Coast*
A *monster* who protects *shamans.* His head is carved on each end of the self-moving canoes of supernaturals. [Boas 1916]

Wasicun
Lakota, *Plains*
A term with multiple meanings involving mysterious power. Wasicun is used to describe the ceremonial bag owned by a *wicasa wakan* (religious leader) that carries medicines. It is also used to describe any covering—hide, cloth, fur—with which the wicasa wakan keeps a powerful spiritual object concealed. Wasicun may refer to the object itself (for example, a rock, piece of horn, or bone) that has been imbued with spiritual power. A wicasa wakan is obligated to protect the wasicun because such power is to be feared as well as respected. Through its association with the inexplicable and mysterious, the term was also used to describe the first white European-Americans. [Walker 1982]

Water
Hogan is the Lakota fish responsible for water powers. *Miqqiayuuq* (Povungnituk) is the water monster who keeps people from getting water. *Michi-Pichoux* are the Cree water lynxes who cause water dangers such as rapids. The Tsimshian water monster *Hakulaq* causes storms at sea. The Nootka figure Crow *(Keninqas)* owns fresh water. See also *Water Monster* and *Water Snake* (Pueblo).

Water Monster(s)
Among the many *monsters* and malevolent creatures in Native American stories, water monster is an important group. They are not always malevolent. In a Pawnee story, a water monster gives the pipe stem to be used in the *Pipe Stick Ceremony.* A Plains story tells of a water monster who cares for a drowned mother (see *Ghosts),* and the Arapaho figure *River-Woman* is married to a water monster.

The Navajo have a figure known as Water Monster (teehooltsoodii), "the one who grabs in deep water." He is an underworld figure resembling an otter with fine fur and horns like a buffalo. The horns designate his power. According to some stories, Water Monster's child is stolen by *Spider Woman*. In his grief, Water Monster causes a *flood* that drives people out of the fourth underworld.

The following are examples of stories about water monsters: *Emogoalekc* (Kathlamet), *Hakulaq* (Tsimshian), *Hiintcabiit* (Arapaho), *Miqqiayuuq* (Povungnituk), *Palraiyuk* (Yukon), *Hairy-Face* (Arapaho), *Paiyuk* (Ute), and Water Monster Old Man, who taught the Navajo *Waterway*. See also *Menstrual Blood* and Pueblo *Water Snake*. [Boyer 1975; Goddard 1933; Haile 1938a; Matthews 1897; Newcomb and Reichard 1937; Reichard 1974; Stephen 1930; Wheelwright 1942]

Water Monster Old Man
See *Waterway* (Navajo).

Water Snake
Pueblo, *Southwest*
Water *snakes* are associated with all springs and water sources. They sometimes appear in groups associated with the cardinal directions and their colors. The water serpent is present among all Pueblo cultures except Jemez. See also *Palulukon* and *Kolowisi*. [Parsons 1930a]

Water Spirits
See *Memekwesiwak,* the Cree water spirits.

Water Sprinkler (to ninilii)
Navajo, *Southwest*
A *ye?ii* who controls rain and waters. He is rain bringer and water carrier to the *diyin dine?e*. He appears as a clown (see *Clowns and Clowning Societies)* in the *Nightway yeibichai* dance. Dressed more poorly than the other ye?ii, he dances out of step, gets in the way of the others, is easily distracted, sits rocking on the ground holding his knees, and concentrates so hard on his dancing that he fails to realize the singing has stopped and the dancers have left. He sometimes carries the skin of a small animal as a pet. Invariably he drops the skin without noticing it. On discovering his loss he becomes frantic and searches everywhere for the skin, while its location is obvious to all. When he finds it he jumps on it as though to kill it. [Curtis 1907; Matthews 1897, 1902a; Reichard 1939; Reichard 1944a]

Waterway
Navajo, *Southwest*
A ritual curing process based on and interconnected with a complex body of mythology. Riverward Knoll Woman and Scabby Woman seek help in their plan to change things. Sunlight Boy (Sun's reflected rays in the form of a boy) is sent to help these old women. First Scabby Woman covers his skin with scabs and sends him to a ceremonial being performed nearby to see how he is received. Thinking him ugly, the people at the ceremony ridicule him. The old women rub the scabs from his skin with herbs and flowers and send him back to the ceremonial, where this time he is openly accepted. Four times the women send Sunlight Boy to be ridiculed. They also make him race around a group of plants that they identify as horses, sheep, soft goods, and jewels.

The women make Sunlight Boy exceedingly beautiful and send him once again to the nearby ceremonial performance. He is so attractive that all the women fall in love with him. Taking revenge for his treatment when he was scabby, Sunlight Boy commits adultery with the singer's *(hataalii)* 12 wives. The singer, whose name is Dark Thunder, discovers what Sunlight Boy is doing and prepares to attack him. Aided by his two old "mothers," Sunlight Boy hides on a grass clump in the middle of a lake. After a while, the winds take him as their child and agree to protect him. He journeys to the sky on crossed *rainbows*. There he learns the Waterway ritual from Water Monster Old Man. In other episodes Sunlight Boy demonstrates his power by averting an attack

by Thunder and by defeating formidable adversaries. These episodes are developed extensively in some versions of Waterway mythology. [Haile 1979; Wheelwright 1946a]

Waupee
Shawnee, Oklahoma and *Northeast*
White Hawk, a *culture hero* who tricks the youngest daughter of one of the stars (see *Stars and Starlore*) into marriage. Waupee and the Star's daughter live together on earth and have a son. The daughter misses her home in the sky and one day, with the help of Wind, returns with her son to the sky. Waupee mourns the loss of his wife and son, and the son misses his father. Seeing how much his grandson misses his father, the Star tells his daughter to take the boy to earth to visit Waupee and invite him to live in the sky with them.

Waupee is overjoyed to see his wife and son, and gladly agrees to go with them. They tell him to bring one of each kind of animal that he hunts and kills. He finds beautiful and unusual animals, preserving a tail, foot, or wing of each. When the family returns to the sky, the star chief gives a feast in their honor and invites each guest to select a gift from Waupee's trophies. Those who choose tails and claws change into animals and run off. Those who select wings or feathers become birds and fly away. Waupee, his wife, and his son each choose a white hawk's feather. They turn into hawks, spread their wings, and fly to earth.

Waux
Tsimshian, *Northwest Coast*
"Very light." The son of *Asdiwal,* a young man who can fly away like a spark. Waux is a great *hunter* who can lay his spear as a bridge across mountain valleys in order to reach the mountain goats that jump from slope to slippery slope. One day Waux goes hunting without his spear. While in pursuit of a group of mountain goats, he gets caught on a slippery, narrow mountain pass. An old mountain goat kicks the mountain angrily, opening a chasm that traps Waux. He calls to his

wife for help but she cannot hear him. He is transformed into *stone,* along with his hunting hat, blanket, pole, and dog. [Boas 1916]

Wawa
Nez Perce, *Plateau*
Mosquito, who lives alone with his grandmother. Mosquito kills his grandmother by biting her and sucking out all her blood. He takes a canoe trip to Coyote's village looking for sympathy. *Coyote* asks Mosquito why he is grieving, but is suspicious of his answers. He invites Mosquito to bring his canoe ashore and feeds him pails of blood, which Coyote gets from the villagers by having them make their noses bleed. Mosquito gorges himself on the blood. As he returns to his canoe, Coyote sets the grass on fire. Mosquito stumbles, pierces his stomach on a burnt piece of grass, and bleeds to death. [Phinny 1969]

Wazi and Kanka
Lakota, *Plains*
The wizard and *witch* condemned by *Skan* (the Sky) to live apart because of their role in helping Ite, wife of *Tate* (the Wind), replace *Hanwi* (the Moon) as the companion of *Wi* (the Sun). Initially Wazi and Kanka were Wa, First Man, and Ka, his wife. But after their participation in the deception, Skan commanded them to live apart and gave them different names. As Wazi and Kanka, wizard and witch, they may help or hinder humans as they please. [Walker 1982]

Wazilya
Lakota, *Plains*
Incensing. Making smoke by burning *sweet grass,* sage, or cedar leaves. This is done after smoking the pipe at the beginning of ceremonies. It is believed that the spirit residing in the smoke of the sweet grass is pleasing to *Wakan Tanka* and will incline Wakan Tanka to hear the ceremony with favor. Wazilya is offensive to malevolent powers and stops their activity.

Incensing is done by slowly sprinkling dried sweet grass on the hot coals of cottonwood while

a song or prayer is said. Sage usually follows the sweet grass, because malevolent powers particularly fear it and will flee from any form of the herb. Cedar is used in ceremonies involving *Wakinyan,* Thunderbird, because the cedar tree is his favorite. He never strikes it with lightning. A person who makes an offering of cedar incense when a thunderstorm is approaching will receive protection.

Buffalo chips are used as fire fuel in wazilya ceremonies for hunting or involving the buffalo because it is believed that the buffalo's spirit remains in the dried buffalo dung. When an entire tribe went on a buffalo hunt, the *wicasa wakan,* or religious leader, made the incense offering of buffalo chips when the buffalo were spotted by scouts. A wazilya of buffalo chips is also made during the *Sun Dance.* [Walker 1982]

Waziya
Lakota, *Plains*

Wa meaning "snow," zi meaning "green," ya meaning "doing something with the mouth." Wazi means "green in the snow or pines." Waziya is a mythical *giant* of the north who blows the cold north wind from his mouth. Waziya comes south during the winter and returns north in the summer. He is in a constant contest with the south winds. Waziya is responsible for snow and ice, and guards the entrance to the dance of the northern lights *(Aurora Borealis).* Waziya dresses in heavy furs, and after the coming of Christianity he was associated with Saint Nicholas. See also *Wakinyan.* [Walker 1982]

Wealth
Nootka, *Northwest Coast*

Cimmis is a supernatural figure who gives wealth.

Weather

For stories related to the weather, see *Achayongch and Achgoyan* (Aleut); the Coeur d'Alene story in which *Heat and Cold* are personified as brothers; *Hakulaq,* the Tsimshian water monster who causes storms; and the Bering Sea coast medicine man *Neshmuk,* who could control the weather. [Dorsey 1879]

Weaving
Navajo, *Southeast*

Weaving was taught to the Navajo by *Spider Woman* (see also Hopi *Kokyan wuhti).* [Gogol 1979; Reichard 1934]

Wedding
Navajo, *Southwest*

One of the functions of *Blessingway.*

Weeping of the Corn
Seneca, *Northeast*

Corn, beans, and squash begin to weep when they can no longer grow. The people go hungry and there is famine in the land. One day the old woman who is matron and chief of her clan walks near her planted field thinking about the hardship of her people. She hears bitter weeping and follows the sound. The corn, beans, and squash are all crying. Moved with compassion for them, the old woman asks why they weep. The vegetables reply that they are not properly cared for; they are not sufficiently covered with earth or given enough water, and their enemies the weeds are strangling them. They tell her they are all dying neglect.

The old woman grieves as she listens, and she begins to cry with them. She weeps all the way home and cannot stop. Her people hear her crying and come to her, asking the reason for her tears. In their distress at her weeping, they also begin to cry. The old woman chief tells them she is weeping with the corn, beans, and squash, who are dying from neglect. She instructs her people on the proper care of the vegetables and they follow her instructions. Soon the corn, beans, and squash begin to thrive.

One morning the villagers discover that corn thieves are coming in the night and carrying away the beautiful ripening green ears of corn, as well as the beans and squash. The chief calls a council to decide what to do and sends warriors to guard the fields. The warriors catch the thieves and take

them before the chief. The chief learns they live deep in the forest and that there are many in their tribe. The corn thieves are whipped daily, leaving stripes on their faces and backs. This is how the corn thieves, the raccoons, got their stripes. The chief also punishes the squash thieves by having their lips split so they cannot eat squash. This is how rabbits came to have split lips. [Curtin and Hewitt 1918]

Wegyet
Gitksan, *Northwest Coast*
"Big man." The wandering adventurer of the Gitksan people, who entertains and secretly advises people living in difficult times. Wegyet teaches the people about the dangers of overindulgence, greed, lust, and laziness (see *Culture Hero*). Stories about Wegyet are filled with *humor*. Although Wegyet resembles *Raven* in Tlingit and Haida stories, he is never credited with creating anything. He manipulates, duplicates, instigates, and disseminates, but never creates. [Angus et al. 1977]

Wemaawe (var. Wema aaciwanii),
Zuni, *Southwest*
Commonly known as the Beast Gods, these are the beasts of prey. They are considered to have a rapacious nature, although they are also identified as the priests of long life. Givers of medicine plants and curing power (see *Healing)*, they are also associated with malevolence and *witchcraft*. Their leaders are associated with the six directions: north, Mountain Lion; west, Bear; south, Badger; east, Wolf; above, Knife-Wing (a mythical monster with wings of knives); and below, Gopher. The most powerful among these, *Bear*, is invoked at curing rituals through masked impersonation. The bear paw, symbol of the Bear, is drawn on many ceremonial objects such as masks. The wemaawe are focal to 12 *medicine societies*, which use highly developed ritual to preserve and invoke the medicine powers of the wemaawe for curing and rainmaking (see *Rain*). [Bunzel 1932]

Weneyuga
A prophet of the *Ghost Dance of 1870.*

Wesucechak
Cree, *Subarctic*
The proper name of a humorous figure noted for his disguises, storytelling ability, and ravenous hunger. Although he is notoriously unscrupulous, deceitful, and ungrateful, Wesucechak's agility and quick thinking nonetheless inspire respect. He fights his antagonists the *Michi-Pichoux* (water lynxes) after the great *flood,* and he is responsible for the creation of humans (see *Humans, Origin of).*

Wesucechak is recognized by all the animals and communicates with them. He usually appears in the guise of a *wolf* or moose, but sometimes takes human form. Wesucechak's agility and transformative powers make him a character respected and talked about with *humor* by contemporary Cree people. His ability to transform himself also reflects the Cree worldview, which accepts the constant shifting of what is thought to be known. Wesucechak cannot be fully appreciated if he is regarded merely as a *trickster*.

Kisikohkew is a malevolent spirit subordinate to Wesucechak. *Kiwetin,* Wesucechak's grandfather, is the north wind. The great horned snake, *Misikinipik,* is an enemy of Wesucechak. *Misapos* is Wesucechak's younger brother; *Nehanimis* is his son. The kingfisher *Okiskimanisiw* tells Wesucechak about the death of his son. The Hairy Hearts, *Omemihoetehesiwak,* fight with Nehanimis. *Vasaagijik,* the Alaskan figure, may derive from Wesucechak. [Bloomfield 1930; Norman 1982]

Wetucks
Narragansett, *Northeast*
A mythical person who can perform feats of wonder. [Trigger 1978]

Whale(s)
Examples of stories related to whales include: *Yayu,* the Haida keeper of whales; the Povungnituk story

of the blind boy *Iumaaq;* and *Torngarsoak,* the Labrador master of whales and seals. [Deans 1892b; Lantis 1938a; Smith 1985]

Whales, Carved Wooden
Tlingit, Tsimshian, *Northwest Coast*
A hunter leaves his family for the day to go *hunting.* While he is away his brothers mistreat his wife and children. When he returns and hears what has happened, the hunter carves killer whales out of alder, cedar, spruce, and hemlock. He puts them in the water, but nothing happens until he carves a whale out of yew (yellow cedar). He paints the wooden whales with white stripes and white bellies, then shouts at them to swim. They swim out and bring back fish. When his brothers leave to go hunting, the man sends the whales out to kill them by capsizing their boats. However, he tells them to spare his youngest brother, who is not mean like the others. [Swanton 1909]

Whirling Logs' Sandpainting
Navajo, *Southwest*
A well-known *sandpainting* of the *Nightway* ceremony, accounted for by a story about Bitahatini, the hero of the "Visionary" version of Nightway mythology. Bitahatini lives with his grandmother and has a pet turkey. Having seen the whirling logs' sandpainting while learning Nightway, he is eager to visit the lake of the whirling logs to learn more. Every day he goes to the San Juan River, where he is preparing a log craft to take him on this journey. Knowing his grandmother would disapprove, he does not tell her what he is doing, and he departs in a different direction every day so as not to arouse her suspicions.

In time the log is hollowed. Bitahatini seals himself inside and launches it into the river, where it immediately sinks. In time the grandmother misses him. With help from the *diyin dine?e* she locates the sunken log and rescues Bitahatini. He begs the diyin dine?e to help him. After many refusals they finally agree, preparing a craft and assisting him on the journey. This hollow-log journey is also a major episode in the mythology of Plumeway (also known as Featherway) and *Navajo Wind Way.*

The trip involves many challenges, all of which are overcome with the help of the diyin dine?e. Eventually Bitahatini comes to the lake of the whirling logs. He is taken to a house on the shore of the lake where the sandpainting has been prepared for him, and is taught all its secrets. Finally he is taken for a ride around the lake on the whirling logs. After this, Bitahatini remains on the lakeshore where he is joined by his pet turkey. The turkey protects him and provides seeds for him to plant. The diyin dine?e teach Bitahatini about agriculture: planting, growing, harvesting, and food preparation. Eventually Bitahatini grows lonesome. The diyin dine?e transport him, along with bags full of seeds, on a *rainbow* back to his home. There he not only teaches others about the whirling logs' sandpainting, but introduces *agriculture.* [Gill 1979b]

Whirlwind
Whirlwind is often personified in Native American stories. Whirlwind assists in the creation of light in stories of the *Apache creation and emergence.* The daughter *(Dagwanoenyent)* of wind (Seneca) takes whirlwind form. In the stories of *Navajo Wind Way,* a hunter shoots at a whirlwind and it twists him into the ground. The unborn child of Wind's *(Tate)* wife is a whirlwind. The Lakota term for whirlwind is *Yum.* The Arapaho term for Whirlwind Woman is *Nayaanxtisei.* See also *Wind.* [Wissler 1905]

Whistle Dance
Pawnee, *Plains*
A *dance* originated by a man who, with the help of wind, travels to the land of the dead (see *Dead, Land of)* to find his young wife who has died (see also *Orpheus).* At the start of his journey the husband meets an old woman who lives in a tipi covered with sage, fox skins, and eagle feathers. She gives him four mud balls to use to attract his wife's attention in the land of the dead. He throws

the mud balls at his wife to remind her that people still live. When she recognizes him, she follows him home.

On their return journey the couple meet the same old woman. She tells them to keep the mud balls, and if they grow hungry on the journey home to throw one of the balls and it will become a buffalo. She teaches the man the Whistle Dance (also known as the Elk Dance because the whistle given to the man for use in the dance is made from an elk bone) to remind people of their future life in the land of the dead. She gives him red beans to take back to his people, saying that eating the beans will give people power to communicate with the dead. She also gives him a *rattle* and tells him that warriors who die on the Plains make their home in it. She instructs him to have his wife sleep each night on a bed of cactus so her nerves will become normal again. The two arrive home but stay by themselves for several days because they carry the odor of the dead.

Later the man goes on the warpath, carrying the rattle the old woman gave him. When the enemy comes near, he removes the handle of the rattle. Dust flies out and becomes armed warriors, who attack the enemy and capture many ponies. When the man holds up the rattle, the warriors become dust again and return to it. The man becomes a famous warrior, but he always travels alone. Many women want to marry him, and eventually he takes a second wife. His first wife tells him he must always remember her and be kind to her. One day while visiting his second wife, the man speaks unkindly about his first wife. When he returns home he finds her bones lying on the bed. He places the bones in a grave and mourns, but no spirit addresses him. He performs the Whistle Dance but cannot communicate with his wife. He has lost her forever.

White Buffalo Ceremony
Lakota, *Plains*
A rarely performed ceremony for one who has died, done in conjunction with the *Spirit Keeping Ceremony*. The family holding the ceremony ob-

tains the skin of a white buffalo as a special honor to the *White Buffalo Maiden*. After the Spirit Keeping Ceremony, in which all the family's possessions are given away (see *Giveaway*) and the spirit of their dead relative is released, the white buffalo skin is laid in a ghost tipi. A warbonnet is placed on its head and moccasins are put at its feet.

The ceremony opens with a consecration and prayer using the pipe, and the area is purified with sage. A bowl of water and two long carved paddles are placed next to a buffalo skull altar. A small hole at the front of the buffalo skin head is filled with charred earth and covered with a scarlet cloth. The owner of the white buffalo skin and the presiding *Wicasa Itacan* place 16 tufts of red-painted goose down at the four corners of the tipi and on the blackened earth, symbolizing the living things on earth.

After a prayer of thanksgiving for the White Buffalo Maiden, leader of the Lakota nation and source of life-giving food, all present feast on meat (representing strength) and cherries (representing truthfulness). At daybreak, four young brothers of the deceased take the buffalo skin out of the tipi and hang it in front of the lodge. Gifts of clothing and utensils prepared for this purpose are placed around the skin and given away. Then the skin is cut into three pieces. The owner keeps the inner piece, and the outer two are given to the Lakota leaders, the Wicasas, to make headdresses. These headbands are secured with a large shell and have two eagle feathers attached. Worn only in times of peace, they ensure that the teachings of White Buffalo Maiden are carried in the minds of the Wicasas.

White Buffalo Maiden
Lakota, *Plains*
Also known as White Buffalo Cow Woman or White Buffalo Calf Woman. She is credited with bringing the *pipe* to the Oglala people, as well as with giving the people several ceremonies (see *Hunkapi, Sun Dance,* and *White Buffalo Ceremony*). White Buffalo Maiden made humans relatives of all four-legged and fur-bearing beings. When a young woman goes through puberty, she

is under the special guardianship of White Buffalo Maiden.

White Buffalo Maiden first appears on the crest of a hill as a beautiful woman. Two young hunters see her. One of the men thinks of having intercourse with her, but his companion warns him against it because it is highly unusual to see a beautiful woman alone on the Plains. The men approach the woman, who can read their thoughts; she encourages the interested man to have intercourse with her. As he embraces her, they are surrounded by a cloud of white smoke. When the smoke clears, the woman emerges but all that remains of the man is his skeleton, which is covered with worms. The woman tells his companion to return to his camp, gather the leaders, and wait for her. When she appears in the village, she presents the chief with a pipe that has a bison calf carved on one side and is decorated with 12 eagle feathers. She instructs the people on the use of the pipe, then leaves. As she walks over the ridge of a hill, she transforms into a white buffalo and gallops away. [Neihardt 1932; Walker 1982]

White Faces
Miami, *Northeast*
Males who dress as and do the work of women under the direction of female spirits encountered on *vision quests*. See also *Gender Crossing.*

White Hactcin
Jicarilla Apache, *Southwest*
A figure common to Jicarilla stories, perhaps comparable to Navajo *Talking God.* See *Europeans, Origin of.* [Opler 1938b]

White Hawk
See *Waupee,* the Shawnee culture hero who marries Star.

White House Ruin
Southwest
A well-known cliff dwelling ruin in Canyon de Chelly in northeastern Arizona. See *Ye?ii.*

White Moccasins
Pawnee, *Plains*
A name of Sun, who protects *White-Sun.*

White Owl Woman *(Nankubacein)*
Arapaho, Plains
A winter bird figure who causes snow (see Raw Gums) and fights with the summer *Thunderbirds.*

White Painted Woman
Apache, *Southwest*
In the Jicarilla story, after the *emergence* from the worlds below this one (see *Apache Creation and Emergence),* the world quickly begins to fill with people who are all of the same lineage. Coyote, Raven, and Buzzard, concerned about the prospect of overpopulation, contrive the origin of death (see *Dead*). Some girls sexually abuse themselves with feathers and stones. They give birth to *monsters* who are a menace to human beings, killing and eating them.

Realizing their freedom, the people decide to move about the world. Some groups stop to play games, while the main group continues to move in a sunwise (clockwise) spiraling movement toward the center of the earth. Frequently groups break away from the main group and remain behind. Those who continue traveling and finally arrive at the center of the world are the Jicarilla Apache (see also *Tribes, Origin of).* The other groups become different tribes.

Two girls wander away and the people do not know where they are. The girls go to a mountaintop where they stay a long time, living on fruit they find there. One day while one of the girls, White Painted Woman, is sleeping, Sun comes and sleeps with her, and has sexual intercourse with her during the night. The same night Water has sexual intercourse with the other girl, White Shell Woman. Both girls become pregnant. Sun instructs them in a performance that establishes the way the Apache conduct a *girls' puberty rite* (see *Na ih es).* The women give birth to two boys who grow quickly. The women are very poor and cannot even provide toys for their sons. They tell

the boys they must visit their fathers to get something with which to play.

The boys, who when they attain manhood are known as *Killer-of-Enemies* and *Child-of-the-Water,* finally arrive at the home of Sun (see also *Twins' Journey to Sun Father* and *Monster Slayer and Born for Water).* He tests them to determine that they are indeed his sons (see also *Test Theme).* He gives them weapons, prayers, and songs. Upon their return they begin many adventures in which they seek and destroy monsters, preparing the way for human beings (see also *Monsterway).*

Apache women model their lives after White Painted Woman and White Shell Woman, who are particularly important figures in girls' puberty rites. See also Apache *Prophecy* and *Changing Woman.* [Hoijer 1938; Opler 1938b; Opler 1940; Opler 1942]

White Shell Woman (kohak oka)
Zuni, *Southwest*
Mother or maternal grandmother of the Sun Father *(Yatokka taccu),* the creator and giver of life and light. She lives in his home in the western ocean. [Matthews 1897; Newcomb 1940; Reichard 1974; Tedlock 1979]

White-Sun
Pawnee, *Plains*
A child loved and cared for by all the women in the village except an old witch, known as Witch Woman, who is jealous of him. She knows he was born under the protection of the *Sun,* also known as White Moccasins. Witch Woman decides to steal White-Sun. She blows her breath on *Clam Shell,* who turns into an old woman with a wrinkled face. The next day Witch Woman steals White-Sun from his tipi and carries him far away to the east, leaving Clam Shell to act as Witch Woman in her place. The village mourns the child's loss.

As White-Sun grows, he develops wonderful powers. He lives with Witch Woman, whom he believes to be Clam Shell, and calls her mother. One day Crow and Insect tell the boy of his true parents. Red Hawk leads White-Sun home, and Clam Shell tells him how the witch traded places with her. The power Witch Woman has given Clam Shell is gone, and she asks White-Sun to carry her to the water, where she will remain. The chief of the village wants White-Sun to marry his daughter, but the boy refuses because it is not yet time for him to marry.

White-Sun leads a successful war party and brings buffalo to the village. Then he takes a war party to the east to find the lodge of Witch Woman. As he approaches it, he transforms himself into a hawk and the rest of the war party into owls. He kills Witch Woman, but she revives and laughs at him. He becomes human again and kills her with his war club. His companions bury her before returning home. White-Sun goes to the river with a young friend, and Clam Shell rewards him with magical power. After another successful buffalo hunt, White-Sun marries the chief's daughter and becomes a great medicine man (see *Medicine People).*

Whiteshell Woman (asdzaa yoolgai)
Navajo, *Southwest*
In some stories, Whiteshell Woman and Turquoise Woman (asdzaa dootlijii) are alternative names for *Changing Woman,* although in other stories they have separate identities. In the monster-slaying stories (see *Monsterway),* Whiteshell Woman is the sister of Changing Woman and another wife of the *Sun.* In *Eagleway,* Whiteshell Woman and Turquoise Woman are created by Changing Woman from epidermis rubbed from under her breasts. Their story is a lonely one of fleeing, hiding from monsters, and trying to acquire enough food to survive. Whiteshell Woman is also an Apache figure (see *Europeans, Origin of).*

Whut
Salish, *Northwest Coast*
The thrush, *Raven's* sister. Whut has the power to dance and sing a variety of berries into existence. Her brother Raven loves berries and tries unsuccessfully to imitate her song and dance.

Wi

Lakota, *Plains*

The term designating both the *sun* and the *moon*. The moon is believed to be a representative of the sun, which is referred to as day moon (anpetu wi) or night moon (hanhepi wi). See also *Day, Following Night; Hanwi; Ta Tanka Lowanpi;* and *Tate.*

Wica Nagi

See *Nagi.*

Wicasa Itacan

Lakota, *Plains*

Leader. See *Hunkayapi, Spirit Keeping Ceremony,* and *White Buffalo Ceremony.*

Wicasa Wakan

Lakota, *Plains*

A person who knows all the ceremonies and is responsible for conducting them; a religious leader. One becomes a wicasa wakan by apprenticeship and ceremonial initiation. The ceremony for becoming a wicasa wakan is done to ensure the ability to communicate with *Wakan Tanka* ("the great mystery") and to prepare and empower the wicasa wakan's outfit and medicine objects, known as the wasicun. A wicasa wakan knows the special ritual language (iye wakan) and the spirit language (hanbloglaka). The wicasa wakan is entitled to sit at any council meeting, but may speak only to communicate the will of Wakan Tanka.

A wicasa wakan found to be deceptive will be punished, even to the point of death, by the akicitas, the marshals. A wicasa wakan who is punished and survives is no longer regarded as a religious leader but may become a wicasa hmunga, a wizard.

The wicasa wakan conducts such rites and rituals as *ear piercing, hanblapi* (vision quest), *hanbloglaka* (spirit language), *Hunka Lowanpi* (Sun Dance), *inipi* (sweat lodge), *Ta Tanka Lowanpi* (Buffalo Bull Ceremony), *wasicun* (power), and *wazilya* (incensing).

Widapokwi and Amchitapuka

Yavapai, *Southwest*

Female creator and her grandson, key figures in southeastern Yavapai mythology, as evident in the following summary of the creation story.

All the people live in the *underworld.* A tree grows to pierce the sky of the underworld, and the people emerge (see also *Emergence)* into this world. They fail to close the hole and water gushes up, flooding the world and drowning all the people.

Widapokwi is sealed in a hollow log with a number of birds and enough provisions to sustain her until the *flood* recedes. After she emerges from the log, she gives birth to a daughter conceived with *Sun* (at sunrise, water from a spring had dripped into her vagina just as the sun's rays touched her). The daughter is the firstborn in this world. See *Monster Slayer and Born for Water.*

When the daughter has grown to maturity, Widapokwi instructs her to conceive a child with the Sun in the same manner that Widapokwi conceived her (see *Incest).* But the sun refuses to rise, knowing this is his daughter. Widapokwi tricks him by lying upon her daughter until the moment the sun rises, then rolling to the side so that the sunrise water and rays enter the daughter's vagina. The girl becomes pregnant and gives birth to a son named Amchitapuka, which means "first man on earth." Shortly after giving birth to Amchitapuka, the mother is carried away and eaten by eagles.

Amchitapuka is raised by his grandmother and becomes a great man. He eventually avenges his mother's death by transforming the eagles so they no longer eat people. As an old man, Amchitapuka is a great chief. As he prepares to die, he names (see *Names and Naming)* the months and the constellations (see also Culture Hero).

In recent times, Widapokwi is equated with the Christian God (see also *Christianity)* and Amchitapuka with Jesus. Among the western Yavapai, Widapokwi is the name used for the grandmother, but the grandson has the name Nyapakaamte, meaning "man up above." [Gifford 1932]

Wife Mistreated

A common motif in which a wife, often one who provides food (such as a corn woman), is mistreated and disappears. *Bear Wife* (Carrier), who supplies food, vanishes when she is mistreated. Raven mistreats his wife *Bright-Cloud Woman* (Tsimshian). When *Grouse Girl* (Aleut) is mistreated by her potential husband, she flies away. When *Sun-Ray* (Pawnee) mistreates his wife, she turns into a mole.

Wihio

Cheyenne, *Plains*

A figure kown for his deceit, ravenous appetite, and ability to imitate humans. Wihio teams up with *Coyote* to steal his favorite food, dried elk tongue. Coyote suggests Wihio dress as a woman and carry Coyote wrapped as a baby so they will be invited into a lodge and fed dried tongue meat. They go to a lodge where a man offers Wihio all the tongue he can eat. Coyote cries like a baby and is given a small amount of tongue, but Wihio refuses to share his portion with Coyote. When they leave the lodge, Wihio fears that Coyote will tell others about his deception and stinginess, so he drowns him by throwing him into the river, still wrapped in his baby bundle. See also *Trickster*.

Wild Men

Haida, *Northwest Coast*

Gagixit are humans made wild by the Land-Otter People. See also *Pokmis* (Nootka).

Willow Dance

Ute, *Great Basin;* Cheyenne, *Plains*

Version of the *Sun Dance*.

Wilughoyuk

Eskimo, Bering Sea coast, Alaska, *Arctic*

A sea shrew mouse who gets into a hunter's clothing through a boot hole and eats him alive.

Wimi

Hopi, *Southwest*

This term designates any major ceremony in the *Hopi Ritual Cycle*. [Bradfield 1973]

Winabojo

Algonquian tribes, Ojibwa, *Northeast, Subarctic*

Also known as Nanabush or Nanabozho. Referred to as Menapus ("Big Rabbit") by the Menominee of Michigan and Wisconsin, and as Manabozho or Manabush by the Ojibwa. Both powerful and benevolent, Winabojo is also capable of deception and stupidity. He has the skill to bring all animate things into being as well as the ability to impersonate any of them. He is regarded as the first teacher of animals and plants, and specializes in teaching deception and trickery of enemies, thereby prolonging the lives of various animals.

Tribal groups differ in their understandings of Winabojo's origins. The Menominee say that Menapus is fathered by the North *Wind* when a young girl ignores her grandmother's warnings against facing north, and the fierce North Wind whirls her around and impregnates her. In some versions, the woman gives birth to triplets, Menapus and his two brothers, Little Wolf (Muhwase) and Flint Stone. When Flint Stone is delivered, he causes his mother to bleed to death. In a grief-stricken rage, the grandmother tosses Flint Stone away. He becomes a gift to humans, enabling them to start *fire*. The third triplet, Little Wolf, is killed, and Menapus has various adventures as he attempts to avenge his brother's death.

According to the Ojibwa, Winabojo has a brother known as Wabosso. The two brothers challenge each other on a number of occasions and Wabosso ends up disappearing. In another Ojibwa story, Winabojo lives shortly after the arrival of the first humans. He marries a human woman and has children. When the family is attacked by a group of unfriendly intruders, Winabojo kills all his family except his infant daughter to spare them from the attackers. He and his daughter leave the earth and live with his grandmother in the sky. When Ojibwa lifestyle begins to change due to the arrival of traders, a group of men go in search of Winabojo. They find him living with his grandmother and his daughter, now fully grown. The men ask for *healing* power, and Winabojo gives them each a

leather bag of *medicine*. He also gives his daughter to the men. She is able to keep the power of the medicine strong. Winabojo tells the men that if they do not have sexual intercourse with his daughter until they reach home, one of them can marry her. The men fail to follow his instructions and Winabojo's daughter disappears (see also *Test Theme*). Winabojo is considered to be both *trickster* and *culture hero*. Some cultures believed *Tenskwatawa*, the Shawnee prophet, was the incarnation of Winabojo. [Blackbird 1987b; Chamberlain 1891; Dorsey 1892; Helbig 1987; Leekley 1965; Makarius 1973; Marano 1985; Reid 1963]

Winalagilis

Kwakiutl, *Northwest Coast*

"Warrior-of-the-World." A *giant* who travels around in a canoe that he never leaves. He is attended by ghosts who can bring the dead to life. Winalagilis is also the name of a dance society. See also *Tsetseka*.

Wind(s)

Often personified, the Wind is a character in stories across North America. Wind *(Nilchi?i)* is depicted as creator and is a major figure in some Navajo stories; Little Winds serve as messengers (see also *Wind's Child)*. Wind is the father of the Menominee figure *Winabojo*. The Onondaga figure *Hadu?igona* controls the wind. The Seneca term for wind is *Gaha*. *Kiwetin* is the Cree term for north wind. *Tate*, the Lakota north wind, is created by *Skan*, the Sky. *Wani* (Lakota) is the power over life and weather. To the Zuni, wind (pinanne) is the spirit of the dead. The Pawnee tell stories of Wind, whose name is *Ready-To-Give*. *Nalq* (Tsimshian) travels with his wife, the North Wind. *Dagwanoenyent* (Seneca) is the daughter of Wind. Wind goes to find girls in the *Apache Bear Dance*. Songs are sung to quiet the wind in the Seneca *Traveling Rite*. See also *Achayongch and Achgoyan* (Aleut). [McNeley 1981]

Wind Bird

See *Bmola*.

Wind-Woman (Yehamiyu)

Alsea, *Northwest Coast*

Also known as Cyclone. Wind-Woman is an old woman whose five children, four boys and a girl, travel around the world. Before they leave, Wind-Woman gives her daughter a powerful stick with which to protect her brothers from harm. The brothers visit many places and win many wives by gambling. Each time they move to a new place they leave their wives behind. Eventually the brothers are tricked by some villagers. As they gamble late into the night, they are sealed up in a rock house. Terrified, their sister returns to Wind-Woman and tells her what has happened. Wind-Woman goes to her sons' rescue, splitting the rock with her powerful stick, and the family starts home. At each village where her sons have gambled, Cyclone touches her powerful stick to the ground, causing the entire village to turn over and burying the inhabitants under the earth.

Windigo

See *Witiko*.

Winds, Four Great

Tsimshian, *Northwest Coast*

Considered to be the four great chiefs of the four corners of the world (see *Cardinal Directions)*. The South, East, and West Winds gang up on North Wind because North Wind makes the world pale in winter. When South Wind starts a war against North Wind, East and West Winds join in to defeat North Wind. Finally North Wind promises that the world will be green for six months. The four winds make a law that the South Wind should sometimes blow during winter in order to bring rain to the land that the North Wind has made cold and frozen. In the spring the three winds will play together to melt the frozen ground, and during the summer West Wind is to blow softly over the land to comfort it.

The winds have children. South Wind has four boys and one girl, named Proud Rain-Wind, Excrement Face, Rain Under the Knee, Going Behind the Mountains, and Drops of a Spring

Water. West Wind has two children, Evening Clouds and Red Evening Clouds. East Wind also has two children, Clouds Falling on the Mountain Top and Red Morning Clouds. North Wind has twins, Frozen and Freezer. North Wind's son Freezer wants to marry South Wind's only daughter, but her brothers object. A year later North Wind asks South Wind for his daughter to marry his other son. The Wind Fathers agree, and Drops of a Spring Water is married to Frozen.

Living with her husband in North Wind's house, Drops of a Spring Water freezes. She sends a wild duck with a message to her father, South Wind, to rescue her. One by one, the chief sends her brothers to rescue her. The first three are driven away by the cold rains of North Wind, but Going Behind the Mountains succeeds by approaching slowly while North Wind is resting and getting his brothers to help him bring fierce rains to melt the frozen land. He rescues Drops of a Spring Water and brings her home. South Wind calls a meeting of the Four Great Winds and explains what he has done and why. The Winds decide that each will have the earth for three months. North Wind will have three months in the winter; South Wind, three months in the fall; West Wind, three months in the summer; and East Wind, three months in the spring.

Wind's Child (nilchi?i biyaji)
Navajo, *Southwest*
One of the messenger winds who inform characters, often the heroes of the stories, what is happening in the world, and who offer advice on what action to take. See also *Nilchi?i.* [Haile 1938a; Reichard 1944a, 1974]

Wine Feast (nawait i?ita)
Papago, *Southwest*
"Wine drinks." A ritual complex coinciding with the ripening of the saguaro cactus fruit, a time approximating the summer solstice. The fruit are harvested and used as the basic ingredient in making wine. The feast begins with

nights of singing and dancing, continues with a "sit and drink" night during which ritual speeches are made while the cactus wine is drunk, and concludes with several days and nights of celebration. See also *Papago Ritual Cycle.* [Underhill 1946; Underhill et al. 1979]

Winkte
Lakota, *Plains*
A male transvestite. These men adopt female roles, dress as women, and live at the edge of camp. They are expert at tanning hides and quilling. Winkte are feared because their domestic abilities are thought to be supernatural. See also *Gender Crossing.*

Winpe
Maliseet-Passamaquoddy, *Northeast*
Loon, who befriends *Glooscap* when he is traveling in Newfoundland. In payment for Loon's loyalty, Glooscap teaches him a strange howling cry. The Passamaquoddy believe that when a loon cries it is calling for Glooscap.

Winter, Origin of
Many Native American cultures have stories to explain the origin of winter. The Kathlamet (Oregon/Washington coast) tell a story of a young boy who breaks the taboo against playing with excrement (see *Excreta).* His action brings about constant cold and snowfall. The unceasing cold causes hunger in the village. The villagers try to buy the boy from his parents and place him on the ice, but the parents refuse. Eventually the parents realize that only in their village is it always cold, while other villages have fresh strawberries and catch spring salmon. The people in the neighboring villages tease the boy's father and name him Frost. At last the parents agree to sell their son to the villagers, who carry him out to the water's edge and place him on the ice. When he dies, the rain begins to fall, melting the ice and snow. Warm weather comes quickly, and soon the people are catching spring salmon and sturgeon. See also the Zuni story *Coyote and Eagle*

Steal Light, but Cause Winter; Hotho, the Seneca term for personified winter; and *Tawiskaron,* the Mohawk term for winter.

Winter Berries
Kwakiutl, Squamish, *Northwest Coast*
A young husband is told by his jealous male in-laws to go out and find berries in the dead of winter (see *Test Theme).* He invariably returns with many berries, which only serves to further irritate his in-laws. In one story version, the young husband brings back a full basket of salmon berries that never becomes depleted. In another version, he is aided by a grandfather *helping spirit* who whistles cranberries onto bare vines. Among the Squamish, the husband magically produces the berries in front of his in-laws and then summons Hummingbird, Bumblebee, and Wren to fly around them singing so that they ripen.

Winter Ceremonial Season
Bella Coola, *Northwest Coast*
A ceremonial season beginning in November and ending in February. This season begins with a 27-day event honoring the coming of Noakxnim, a supernatural responsible for weather and game. The season closes with the lifting of taboos practiced in ceremonial houses, such as the prohibition of entrance by a recently widowed person and the avoidance of certain foods. Each of the ceremonies performed throughout the season lasts four days. Ceremonies are held to initiate new members into masking societies, cut wood for the masks, make the masks, and assign masks to the newly initiated (see *Masks and Masking).* Almost every evening new members of masked societies join established members in dramatic performances that include juggling and mime. Some of the characters in the performances include *cannibals:* the Scratcher, with long dangerous claws; the Breaker, who destroys property; Winwina, who brings salmon; and Nunuoska, who gives birth to all the plants and animals following the sequence of the seasons. The person

portraying Thunder wears a bearlike mask and makes tremendous noise. The Moon is represented in a double mask (a mask with an interior face covered by a hinged exterior face), and there are many masks of birds and animals. Also included is the series of *Kusiotem* dances. A Mystery Dance may be performed that engages the audience in a guessing game. This game may continue for the entire Winter Ceremonial Season. See also *Tsetseka* and *Hamatsa Society.* [Holm 1977]

Winter Solstice Ceremony
Solstices and equinoxes are important ritual occasions. For example, see Hopi *Soyal* and the Zuni rites described in *Zuni Ritual Cycle.*

Wise One
Apache, *Southwest*
Younger brother to Killer-of-Enemies in the *Apache creation and emergence.*

Wise Woman
Yaqui, *Southwest*
The woman who could hear the *Talking Tree.*

Wiske
Potawatomi, *Northeast*
The *culture hero* who in the origin stories creates the Potawatomi *clans* and gives them bundles (see *Medicine Bundle).* Each clan has a bundle with specific rights and obligations. The Fish clan, for example, renew their medicine four times a year. The Man clan has rules regarding ritual use of the bundle before going to war. Wiske's twin brother, *Cipyapos,* guards the afterworld and receives the souls of the *dead.*

Witch(es)
Although in recent years the terms "witch" and "witchcraft" have taken on broader meanings not restricted to malevolence, the term as used by both Native Americans and ethnographers retains its negative connotation. Because of a tendency to perceive evil in most things they did not understand, some early missionaries unfortunately and

erroneously applied negative terms to much of Native American religious practice.

Reflecting Native American distinctions, the term "witch" refers to anyone who uses power to socially malevolent ends. Witches and sorcerers are synonymous; both are clearly distinguished from *medicine people* and *shamans*. Most Native American cultures have terms denoting witches; for example, *Haldawit* (Tsimshian), *Puwo-win* (Micmac), and *Oky ontatechiata* (Huron). The Tlingit call a witch the *Master of Sickness*. The term *Two-Hearts* refers broadly to witches.

Witches often appear as characters in Native American stories. *Dagwanoenyent* (Seneca), the daughter of Wind, is a witch. The Seneca figure *Haiendonnis* is a sorcerer who encourages witches. The Algonquian *Oke* is a punishing spirit associated with witches. *Pukjinskwes* (Passamaquoddy) is a shape-shifting witch. Another shape shifter is the Navajo Coyote *Yenaldlooshi*. Witches are often credited with causing illness, as in the Navajo *Enemyway* (see also *Uglyway*) tradition and the Cherokee Stonecoat *(Ocasta)*, who creates witches. See also *Witchcraft* and *Witch Woman* (Pawnee). [Blanchard 1982; Harrington 1901; Mallery 1890]

Witch Woman
Pawnee, *Plains*
Also known as *Spider Woman*. Witch Woman is capable of multiple disguises. She keeps all the buffalo locked in a cave that is guarded by snakes under her spell. The snakes are fed by a young man named *Morning Star* who hunts for them. During a time of famine, a village chief asks Morning Star to come live in his village and hunt for his starving people. The young man explains he must feed the snakes who keep the buffalo trapped in a cave. The snakes tell Morning Star that if he can overcome Witch Woman, both the snakes and the buffalo will be free.

On each of three consecutive days, the young man befriends the snakes and releases some of the buffalo for the starving village. On the third day the witch appears, wearing a robe decorated with the morning star. She threatens to make all the buffalo go back to the cave if the young man releases any more of them. She also reveals his hidden identity as Morning Star. Morning Star shoots at her robe, and the morning star picture disappears; in its place appears a figure of the new moon. Witch Woman laughs. Morning Star shoots at the picture of the new moon, and it becomes a quarter moon. He shoots twice more, and the picture becomes a three-quarter moon and then a full moon. When he shoots at the picture of the full moon, it falls to the ground and becomes a spider. Morning Star puts the spider on an arrow and shoots it to heaven, saying that it must stay in the heavens and not try to live with people. The spider lives in the heavens as the moon, and the old witch woman falls down and dies. The snakes and the buffalo are consequently released. See also *Gambler; Game, Release of; Moon Woman;* and *White-Sun*.

Witchcraft
Witchcraft is the practice of witches (see *Witch* for a discussion of terms related to witchcraft). Native American mythology includes stories of the origin of witchcraft. A full example, in this case for Navajo culture, can be found in the discussions of *Navajo Emergence, Blessingway, Hocho*, and *First Man and First Woman*. Iroquois views of witchcraft appear in stories of *False Face Medicine* and *ontetsans*, healers who cure diseases caused by witchcraft. See also *Amulets*, sometimes used to protect against witchcraft; *Morea* (Yaqui); and *Wemaawe*, the Zuni Beast Gods. [Deming 1902; Kluckhohn 1944; Prince 1899; Speck 1903; Titiev 1942]

Witi
Catawba, *Southeast*
Medicine administered by blowing through a tube of cane in order to charge it with the personal power of the medicine person. The medicine is a mixture of herbs boiled in an earthen pot. Heating the medicine is thought to create steam within the sick person and heat him or her up. The

patient drinks the medicine; then the medicine person blows the medicine over him or her with the cane tube. The administration is usually accompanied by singing.

Witiko
Northern Canada, *Subarctic*
Fearsome anthropomorphic *cannibal* beings. During famine, humans can become witiko and compulsively seek human flesh. Human witiko differ from the nonhuman northern witiko giants and the malignant transformations of the spirits Ice and North.

The nonhuman witiko are depicted as *giants* who use treetops as snowshoes and cover vast distances with every step. Their most common characteristics are a heart of ice, filthiness, a mean appearance, and the ability to transform humans into cannibals. They become witiko after being mortally wounded and subsequently eaten by the human families with whom they lived. Their power can be overcome by *conjuring,* and human *excreta* blind and confuse them.

Hunters and trappers often report sightings of giant witikos and warn about places to avoid because of them. Subarctic storytellers warn of both creatures and humans who are witiko because they have eaten human flesh, which gives them superhuman strength to overcome their victims. These people often reject food and plead for their own executions by other village members. Sometimes humans become possessed of witiko by *dreaming* of the malevolent spirits North and Ice. In these cases the condition can be overcome with conjuring (see *Shaking Tent*).

Witiko stories express the danger and isolation of living in the subarctic wilderness as well as taboos against cannibalism. The earliest written records of witiko are found in eighteenth-century Hudson Bay Company diaries. The understanding of witiko as a nonhuman giant is found among tribes in Ontario, Manitoba, Saskatchewan, North Dakota, Michigan, and Wisconsin, as well as the Naskapi and Montagnais of eastern Canada. See also *Assin* and *Maskwamiy.*

[Brightman 1988; Colombo 1982; Cooper 1933; Flannery, Chambers, and Jehle 1981; Lowei 1925b; Morrisseau 1982; Nevins 1982; Norman 1982; Preston 1980; Schoolcraft 1982; Schmarz 1982; Stevens 1982; Teicher 1969; Turner 1977]

Wiwilemekw
Maliseet-Passamaquoddy, *Northeast*
A sea *monster* often thought to be an alligator. A person who summons the courage to face a Wiwilemekw and take scrapings from its horns can gain many strengths.

Wiyohipeyata
Lakota, *Plains*
Wi meaning "sun," yo meaning "to do," hi meaning "to arrive," peya, meaning "to lie down or retire," ta meaning "the place," that is, the place where the sun retires. Thus Wiyohipeyata is the West, whose spirit is responsible for the coming of evening and everything that happens in the *night.* Wiyohipeyata is also present at the death of humans and animals (see *Dead*).

Wiyohiyanpa
Lakota, *Plains*
Wi meaning "sun," yo, meaning "to do," hi meaning "to arrive," yanpa meaning "the place," that is, the place where the sun arrives. Thus Wiyohiyanpa is the East, whose spirit is responsible for everything that happens during the day.

Wodih
Dene Dhaa (Slavey), *Subarctic*
Wo (general) plus dih (say). The category that includes all traditional and hunting stories, lectures, news, recent events, hunting stories, prophecies, and traditional stories (see *Story Type*). Any extended speech act is classified as wodih. Wodih stand in contrast to shin (songs) used to address spirits. Storytellers often mix wodih and shin. See also *Tonht onh wodihe.*

Wodziwob
A prophet of the *Ghost Dance of 1870*.

Woge

Yurok, *California*

The first people to live on earth. Woge are responsible for the present geography of the world. The woge disappeared from earth, traveling to a land across the ocean, long before the advent of human beings.

Wohpe

Lakota, *Plains*

Daughter of *Skan,* the Sky, created by him from his own being. Wohpe is the patron of harmony, beauty, and pleasure. No one is as beautiful as she. Wohpe is credited with bringing the *pipe* to the Lakota people. She taught the people how the pipe was to be smoked at the beginning of feasts and how to prepare *tobacco* for it. She also appointed caretakers for the pipe.

Wohpe lived with *Tate,* the Wind, at the center of the world. She cared for *Yum,* Whirlwind, the banished son of Ite, whom she taught to dance and play many games. Because of this, Skan made Yum responsible for dancing, games, and love.

Wohpe carefully kept count of the number of Moon's cycles that elapsed during the time Tate's four sons were gone from his lodge. She showed her father, Skan, that the four brothers were absent from Tate's lodge 12 moon cycles, so Skan decided that 12 moons would make one Wani-yetu, a year. See also *Anog Ite.*

Wolf

The wolf figures prominently in Native American mythology, sometimes as the older brother of *Coyote.* Wolf may be depicted as creator, as in the Paiute story *Wolf Creates the Earth.* He is the Ute culture hero *Sunawavi.* The Lakota identify Wolf *(Sungmanitu)* as the spirit of the chase and war.

An Aleut character, Killer Whale *(Akhlut),* takes the form of a wolf, as does the Cree figure *Wesucechak.* Sometimes the wolf is depicted as vicious even to his own family, as in the Shoshone story *Birth from Dead Mother's Uterus,* and the Inupiaq story of *Alarana and Aligunaluk.* The Nootka practice a wolf ritual during the winter ceremonial season (see *Titichakyo,* the chief of wolves, and *Yellow Cedar Bark Ogre,* both of whom are impersonated in this ritual). The Quileute have a healing society known as the *Wolf Society.* [Morgan 1936]

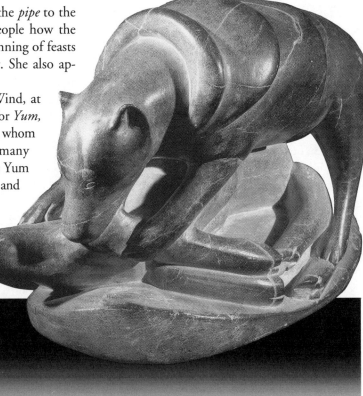

Qisaruatsiaq, the wolf, eating a caribou. This sculpture illustrates a moment in an Eskimo story. Courtesy, Canadian Museum of Civilization (neg.#J 8607).

Wolf Creates the Earth

Owens Valley Paiute, *Great Basin*

Wolf, the strongest man in the world, paddles around in a boat feeling lonely. He creates *Coyote* and calls him brother. Wolf decides they cannot spend all their time paddling around in the water.

They need to create the earth, so they both take a handful of dirt and place it on the water, where it stays as a little island. Because the earth island is shaky, they add more and more dirt until it becomes solid. Coyote runs around on the earth and declares it is too small. Wolf adds more dirt until Coyote is happy. This is how the earth was created. [Steward 1936]

Wolf Ritual
Nootka, *Northwest Coast*
A winter ceremonial ritual in which *Titichakyo* (chief of wolves) and *Yellow Cedar Bark Ogre* are impersonated.

Wolf Society
Quileute, Makah, *Northwest Coast*
A healing society that dances the Wolf *Dance* at the request of a sick person or the patient's family members. The Wolf Society originated when the Wolf chief was killed by the culture hero Changer. Changer danced in the wolf's skin and gained power for healing.

Wolverine
Dene Dhaa (Slavey), *Subarctic*
Wolverine is a central story character whose close companion is often Wolf and whose cousin is Marten. Stories about Wolverine usually highlight not only his trickery and thievery, but also his powers to resuscitate humans. He is sometimes portrayed as the pet of giants.

In one story, Wolverine steals two human children and feeds them only the fat he has stolen from animal carcasses. The children eventually discover all the meat Wolverine has stored away in his cache and they eat some. They ask Wolverine why he feeds them only fat when he has so much meat. Wolverine says he does this so they will be able to survive when they are on their own. Because the children have betrayed him, Wolverine sends them out into the world and they soon become thieves and liars. For another story involving a wolverine see *Rolling Rock*.

Woman Up There
Eskimo, *Arctic*
Pana is the woman who keeps in her sky house the souls of the dead who are to be reborn.

Woman Who Fell from the Sky
See *Aataentsic.*

Women
A great many Native American stories and rites are about women or reflect on what it means to be a woman. Among the most important rites are the puberty rites in which a girl is made into a woman. A Lakota woman may experience a vision (see *Hanblapi*) at the time of her first menstruation. In the rite *Kinaalda,* Navajo girls are made into women on the model of *Changing Woman.* The Apache girls' puberty rite is known as *Na ih es.* The Lakota girls' puberty rite is *Ta Tanka Lowanpi.*

Like many cultures, the Zuni tell a story centering on *Women's Ways.* Fertility is the concern of the Hopi ceremonial known as *Marau,* and the Hopi women's harvest ceremonial is *Oaqol.* There are a great many women's dances, such as the Nootka *Great-Favorite;* the Pawnee *Starisu,* which celebrates the gift of buffalo; and Seminole and Creek women's dances performed during the *Green Corn Dance* (see also *Locv-saukv,* the women's leg rattles). *Cudak* is a Puyallup women's charm.

Although hunting is a predominantly male activity throughout North America, women hunters do exist (see *Hunters, Female*). *Toxwid* (Kwakiutl) is a woman warrior. According to the Menominee, the power of a menstruating woman is greater than vision power *(Tatahkesewen).* The Seneca tell stories of a group of ferocious women known as *Gahondjidahonk.* They also tell stories of powerful women chiefs (see *Godasiyo* and *Godiont*). In a Pawnee story a man named *Coming-Sun* loses his power because he is attracted to women. [Herzog et al. 1984; Landes 1971; Medicine 1983; Powers 1986; Underhill 1936]

Women's Ways
Zuni, *Southwest*

While a girl is hunting rabbits—considered man's work—because she has no man to provide for her, she is caught by a *cannibal,* the female *kachina* Atoshle. The warrior twins, *Ahayuta,* rescue her. The older twin marries her and teaches her a woman's proper activities. The girl soon bears twins. While playing with their friends, the twins cut off the other children's arms, legs, and ears, and mix them up before placing them back on their friends' bodies. Because they are a danger to the other children, the twins are removed from the village and sent to live at the Ahayuta shrines. [Benedict 1935; Cushing 1896; Parsons 1930b]

Woodtick
Coeur d'Alene, *Plateau*

A female story character who magically produces food for the starving *Coyote.* Woodtick feeds Coyote because she wants him as her husband, but Coyote insults her by telling her she has no neck, and she abandons him. Near starvation, Coyote goes to Woodtick's house and persuades her to let him stay. He watches as she calls deer, and when they come she chooses two and pierces their ears. They die and become food for her and Coyote. After a while Coyote decides to call the deer, thinking he does not need Woodtick. The deer come to his call but he cannot pierce their ears the way Woodtick does. All the deer run away, even the old deer bones he has saved from previous meals. Enraged, Coyote throws Woodtick out of the house. She leaves and Coyote is left to starve. See also *Bungling Host* and *Trickster.*

Worm and Turtle as Warriors
Zuni, *Southwest*

The warrior twins, *Ahayuta,* are careless in herding their turkeys. The birds wander away and are killed for their feathers by the people of a nearby pueblo. One turkey survives and gobbles "I-wo-lo-ka," which means "murder." In preparation for their revenge, the warrior twins call upon Worm and *Turtle.* Turtle hangs onto the back of

the younger twin, his shell serving as a shield, and Worm vomits what he has eaten, covering and suffocating the pursuers. Consequently Worm is always small, having disgorged himself. The twins scalp the enemies and bring the scalps back on a pole for the scalp dance. [Benedict 1935; Cushing 1896]

Wounded Knee Massacre
The U.S. military killed some 300 people at Wounded Knee, South Dakota, late in December 1890, dealing a blow that nearly ended the *Ghost Dance of 1890.*

Wovoka
A Paiute prophet instrumental in the rise of the *Ghost Dance of 1890.*

Wry Face
Iroquois, *Northeast*

Dehotgohsgayeh, the Iroquois giant.

Wuchowsen
Maliseet-Passamaquoddy, Eastern Maine, *Northeast*

A giant *bird* who lives in the north and is responsible for *storms* and gales. Wuchowsen lives on a rock at the end of the north sky. Whenever he moves, the wind blows with great force. Eventually he is tamed by the culture hero *Glooscap.*

Wuhti
Hopi, *Southwest*

Hopi term designating a married woman. See also *Mana,* the term designating a female kachina.

Wultcixaiya (Wultcixaiya)
Haida, *Northwest Coast*

The son of *Moon.* He rescues his sister from her marriage to Pestilence. Moon's son wears a steel coat and covers his canoe with boards to protect himself from the death and disease emitted by Pestilence. He knocks down the front of Pestilence's rock house with a bone club, thus releasing not only his sister but much of the sickness stored in Pestilence's house.

Wuwutcim

Hopi, *Southwest*

The ceremonial initiation of young men ages 15 or 16 into Hopi society; formally, the initiation into one of four adult men's fraternities. The name wuwutcim is thought to come from wuwutani, "to grow up." It is a complex, four-day ceremonial performed in November to introduce initiates to the most fundamental ideas in Hopi religion and culture. Wuwutcim was brought into this world by the Bow clan. See also *Hopi Ritual Cycle* and *Pyuykonhoya*. [Bradfield 1973; Dorsey and Voth 1901; Fewkes and Stephen 1892; Parsons 1923a; Stephen 1936; Titiev 1940, 1941]

Xapaaliia
Crow, *Plains*

Medicine, the physical representation of spiritual power *(baaxpee)* obtained through a *vision quest* and dancing the *Sun Dance* (asjkisshe). The term also refers to objects found in *medicine bundles,* such as an eagle feather fan, otter skin, or buffalo effigy. People who heal (akbaalias) have special relationships with animals that enhance the healers' power. The power of this relationship is manifested in the person's medicine, the xapaaliia *(akbaalia).*

Xoexoe
Nooksack, Salish, *Northwest Coast*

An untranslatable term indicating positive and negative *power* that is both diffuse and impersonal. This power can be partially controlled by individual beings, even by the Christian God, but it does not come from any single source and is never totally under anyone's control. The quality of the power emerges when an individual being acknowledges and attempts to work with it for positive or negative gains.

Xowalaci
Joshua, *Northwest Coast*

The *creator* known as "the Giver," who had a human helper, First Man. Xowalaci and First Man live in a *sweat lodge* on the primordial waters. First Man spends most of his time outside the house with his tobacco, and Xowalaci spends most of his time inside. To relieve his boredom, Xowalaci creates land, then attempts to create human beings (see *Humans, Origin of).* His first attempt produces sea mammals and dogs. Disappointed, he tries again. The second time he comes up with snakes. Finally, First Man attempts to create people from his *tobacco* smoke. He smokes for three days. A house and a beautiful woman appear from the smoke. The woman is lonely until Xowalaci tells First Man to have intercourse with her. Xowalaci makes First Man invisible and puts the woman into a deep sleep so she will not know that First Man has had sex with her and fathered her child. The male child grows quickly.

Wanting to know who her son's father is, the woman ignores the boy, expecting the father to come to care for him. When the boy becomes ill, emaciated, and filthy, she

feels remorse and cares for him. She sings medicine songs to get milk to feed him. He recovers and grows strong and handsome.

Xowalaci finally sends First Man to the woman and she learns he is the father of her son. They live together and have 16 children who settle north and south of the Rogue River in Oregon.

Xwaixwieda
Puyallup-Nisqually, Southern Puget Sound, *Northwest Coast*
The general term applied to any animal, bird, or fish *power* (see *Sqalalitut*) that made the owner wealthy from successful hunting or fishing. The person who had xwaixwieda had many material goods. See also *Swoxqwad.* [Smith 1940]

Yagatunne
Dunne-za (Beaver), *Subarctic*

The Trail to Heaven, walked by a person's *ghost* and his or her shadow in darkness at death. The trail is made by a person while on earth. At death the person's shadow (not unlike a soul) begins to search for the trail he or she has made. The trail is walked at night until the darkness clears and there is enough light for the person to follow the trail to heaven. The ghost walking this trail can be dangerous to the deceased's shadow, because it will try to separate a good person's shadow from his or her body and prevent it from following the trail to heaven. The ghost can be particularly dangerous if, at death, there are unresolved conflicts and bad deeds holding the shadow down and preventing it from following the trail upward.

A person may shorten the Trail to Heaven by dancing to the songs of the Dreamers (those who have danced the Trail to Heaven and returned). These dances are done with relatives around a fire. It is believed that by following the tracks of the Dreamers and those of one's relatives who have walked the trail, one's mind begins to follow the Trail to Heaven.

The Dunne-za believe it is harder for people to find and follow Yagatunne since the construction of the Alaskan Highway during World War II through Dunne-za country. People who die on this highway are believed to have a difficult time finding the beginning of the Trail to Heaven they had made while living. See also *Naachin,* those who experience the Trail to Heaven, and the culture hero *Saya* (Swan), who knows the Trail to Heaven. [Ridington 1988]

Yagim (iak im)
Kwakiutl, *Northwest Coast*

"Badness." A sea *monster* responsible for bad weather, capsizing boats, and eating humans. This sharklike monster is represented at the *Tsetseka* Ceremonies (the winter festival) by a huge mask fringed with red-dyed cedar bark (see *Masks and Masking).* [Boas 1921]

Yahola and Hayuya
Creek, *Southeast*

Male deities who reside in the sky without any companionship. They are responsible for strength, physical health, and clarity of thought and vision. Medicine people often invoke the name of Yahola for help and healing. See also *Helping Spirits*. [Swanton 1928b]

Yahwera
Kawaiisu, *Great Basin*

A supernatural being associated with mountain quail but also described as looking like a hawk. His home is in the land of the dead. Yahwera can be heard but not seen, and can imitate both human speech and a dog's bark. His house is reached through a tunnel in Black Canyon, a place well known to many Kawaiisu. The way to his house is guarded by large snakes, as well as by brown and grizzly bears. Yahwera keeps many powerful medicines and is often visited by sick people. Although he does not claim to be a healer, he will give medicines to his visitors and teach them healing songs and games. He also shows his visitors how to heal themselves by washing in a spring, by sweating in a lodge, and by washing their hair. [Zigmond 1980]

Yagim, the Kwakiutl sea monster as represented by this huge, red-dyed, cedar-fringed mask. Courtesy, Thomas Burke Memorial Washington State Museum, Eduardo Calderon, photographer (catalog #1-1451).

Yai
Nootka, *Northwest Coast*

Yai are small supernatural beings who live in the woods. They are long and slim, and almost completely black in color. Because they have no skeletal structure, they turn into foam when someone attempts to catch them. They are able to marry human women. Although they are not harmful, animals are afraid of them, and so they are poor hunters. [Sapir and Swadesh 1939]

Yamonhdeyi
Dene Dhaa (Slavey), *Subarctic*

The most important *culture hero,* capable of taking many forms. He is responsible for making arrowheads and for teaching eagles to eat fish and small birds instead of human flesh. Seeking a wife, Yamonhdeyi comes to a village where a father offers him his only daughter. She is already married, but her husband is always away hunting and killing sleeping people in neighboring villages. Yamonhdeyi kills the husband with an arrow made from a wolverine tooth. He gathers eagle feathers for his arrows and teaches the eagles to eat fish, rabbits, and ducks instead of the people they had been eating.

When Yamonhdeyi returns to his wife and her family, they tell him of a huge creature sleeping in a meadow. It is a woolly mammoth. Yamonhdeyi kills it and returns to his wife's village. His father-in-law becomes concerned because Yamonhdeyi is interfering with all the animals, taking feathers and sinew for his bows. He tells his daughter to turn into a bear and chase Yamonhdeyi. She does so, but Yamonhdeyi assembles his bow and arrow and kills her. Her distraught parents chase him into a beaver pond, and he hides at the bottom. The parents call for two pelicans to drink all the water out of the pond, but when the water is nearly gone Yamonhdeyi persuades an insect to pierce the pelicans' pouches. The pond floods, killing his wife's parents, and Yamonhdeyi escapes. See also *Tonht onh wodihe,* a story type. [Moore and Wheelock 1990]

Yaqui Easter Ceremony
Yaqui, *Southwest*

The principal annual ceremonial occasion for the Yaqui peoples living in Arizona. It coincides with the Christian Lent (see also *Christianity*) and culminates in grand ritual drama during Holy Week. Early in the eighteenth century the Yaqui people, then living along rivers in Sonora, invited Jesuit missionaries to live among them. Soon most Yaquis were baptized and their life ways changed. They left their homes on scattered rancherias and built towns, which they modeled on European towns, giving them biblical names. The Yaquis creatively combined aboriginal and Christian elements. Through more than a century, ending in the late 1800s, during which Yaquis lived without the influence of Christian missionaries, they continued to practice a full ceremonial calendar that retained many Christian-like elements. Late in the nineteenth century, as the Yaqui scattered in defeat at the hands of the Mexican government, some Yaqui communities were established in Arizona near Tucson and Phoenix. Here they began to revive their religion and culture, to which the Yaqui Easter celebration became central. Although the Yaqui Easter Ceremony is clearly modeled on the Christian Passion, it contains Yaqui elements that likely originated in pre-Christian aboriginal traditions.

The kohtumbre yaura, or Lenten ceremonial officials, are responsible for the Yaqui Easter ceremony. They are composed of two societies, the caballeros (horsemen) and the fariseos (Pharisees), organized on a military model (the cavalry and the infantry). The fariseos represent the evil ones who persecuted and executed Christ. Fariseos are sometimes collectively referred to as the Soldiers of Rome. The officers appear dressed completely in black. Even their faces are largely covered with black scarves. The common soldiers are the *chapayekas,* who appear in masked costume. One chapayeka appears on the first Friday of Lent to begin the search for Jesus. Other chapayekas join him each week during Lent, so that by Holy Week there may be 20 or more. On Holy Thursday, when the chapayekas reach full strength, they capture Jesus, and on Good Friday they symbolically crucify him. On Friday night they are tricked and consequently lose possession of Jesus. The Gloria on Holy Saturday is the climax of the Easter ceremony.

On Holy Saturday the chapayekas present the threat of evil and, perhaps ironically, entertain as clowns (see *Clowns and Clowning Societies).* Along with the black-garbed fariseo officers, the chapayekas appear in the plaza before the Yaqui church, in which an effigy of Judas, their leader, has been erected. Throughout Saturday morning many Yaqui people approach Judas and tie scarves of penance to him. The evil threat of the fariseos builds throughout the morning, as women and children take positions inside the church. At the climactic moment, the church bell tolls and the fariseos rush the church in an attempt to recapture it. The women and children burst from the church, repelling the fariseos by throwing green leaves and flower petals, the transformed blood of Christ. After three such assaults, all the chapayekas have given up their masks, daggers, and swords, and have placed them around the Judas effigy. They are rushed to the church to rededicate themselves to Jesus. The Judas effigy and all the masks and rubbish are torched, creating a huge conflagration. Immediately the whole community erupts in fiesta, featuring *pascola* dancers, *deer dancers,* and a matachini dance troupe. [Painter 1986]

Yatokka taccu
Zuni, *Southwest*

The Sun Father. Along with *Moonlight-Giving Mother* (his wife, although she is always separated from him), the giver of light and life (see *Creator).* The Sun Father has homes in both the western and eastern oceans. *White Shell Woman* (kohak oka), the Sun Father's mother or maternal grandmother, lives in the western house. *Salt Woman* (or Old Salt Lady), who lives in a lake to the south of Zuni, is the Sun Father's sister. See also *Ahayuta,* the twin sons; *Kanaakwe; Ones Who*

Hold Our Roads; Raw People; and Zuni Emergence. [Tedlock 1979]

Yaukekam
Kutenai, *Plateau*

The proper name of the powerful transformer figure (see *Transformation)* who travels with *Coyote* (see also *Skinkuts)* and saves him from a giant. Yaukekam and Coyote stop the *Thunderbirds* from killing village people. They then travel to the sun. Yaukekam obtains arrow wood, the arrow straightener, sinew, flint, and the bow stave for humankind. Humans who fear Yaukekam's power attempt to drown him, but he is resuscitated by the fish. He tells his nephew Duck to be helpful to humans. Yaukekam finally retires to the east end of the world. [Boas and Chamberlain 1918]

Yayu
Haida, *Northwest Coast*

Supernatural-Being-Looking-Landwards. Keeper of *whales* (see *Master/Mistress of Animals* and *Big-Tail).* [Swanton 1905b]

Yegwe
Coos, *Northwest Coast*

A *spirit* that lives in the woods; when encountered by a human it reflects the human image like a mirror. A meeting with a yegwe that mirrors one's image means the person's life will be shortened. [Beckham, Toepel, and Minor 1984]

Yeibichai
Navajo, *Southwest*

Derived from *ye?ii* and bichai, meaning "his or its grandfather." This may refer to the lead ye?ii, *Talking God,* designating him as the grandfather of the ye?ii. According to another interpretation, the ye?ii are seen as the grandfathers to the Navajo people. Yeibichai also is a common designation for the *Nightway* ceremonial, because the ye?ii dance publicly, often to large gatherings, on the last nights of Nightway performances. [Haile 1947a]

Ye?ii
Navajo, *Southwest*

Diyin dine?e, or Holy People, who appear in Navajo ceremonials in *sandpainting* representations and masked rites and dances (see *Masks and Masking).* The ye?ii were created in a rite shortly after the emergence onto the present world. They include: *Talking God* (hashcheltii); Calling God (hashchehooghaan); Male God (hashche baka) and Female God (hashche ba?aad), of which there are six each; *Black God* (hashcheshzhini); *Monster Slayer* (naachee neezghani); Born for Water (to bajishchini); Gray God or *Water Sprinkler,* the clown (to neinilii); Hump Back (ghaa askidii); Fringed Mouth (zahadoolzhahi); Red God (hashchelchii); Destroyer or Whipping God (haadachiishii); Whistling God (hashche idiilcoos); and Shooting God (hashche oltlhi).

Upon their creation the ye?ii sat erect but were unable to speak or move. First Man performed further ritual acts to give them sinews, veins, and arteries, but they still could not move. Finally First Man blew winds into them, thereby providing them with *biigistiin,* or inner life-forms. Now the ye?ii could walk, stand, move, see, and breathe. They received their call from Corn Beetle, but they never spoke. As a result, Navajo maskers are admonished never to speak into their masks. The ye?ii may be referred to as hashche, meaning "he failed to speak."

When the ye?ii prepared to leave the Navajo world for their homes, they made face prints (niikehe) of themselves in white bead, turquoise, abalone, and jet. They directed that human beings should reproduce these faces in buckskin, establishing the origin of ye?ii masking practices. Each ye?ii is associated with a specific cardinal direction or other distinctive location, even serving as the inner form of these places. Each has a unique appearance replicated in mask and costume, along with a distinctive prayerstick *(keetaan)* and set of offerings. The ye?ii live in White House Ruin (kiniineeihai) in Canyon de Chelly, although other homes are sometimes mentioned. See also *Hactcin* for the Apache equivalent. [Haile 1947a]

Yellow Cedar Bark Ogre
Nootka, *Northwest Coast*
A supernatural being who gives power for health and long life. The mask (see *Masks and Masking*) of this being is worn in a dance on the fourth day of the Wolf Ritual. A lazy young man goes wandering in the mountains after giving his wife a quantity of yellow cedar bark with which to make a robe. While in the mountains, the young man sees an ogre, a fearsome being whose robe is covered with slime. It circles around him,

calling out his name and playing hide-and-seek with him. After the encounter, the young man stays in the mountains, fasting and bathing with hemlock (see *Osimc*). When he returns home, he makes a mask resembling the ogre. At the *Wolf Ritual* he wears the mask and imitates the ogre's dance. The Yellow Cedar Bark Dance and mask become the young man's *topati,* ceremonial property. [Sapir and Swadesh 1939]

Yellow Woman
Pueblo, *Southwest*
Corn woman or maiden who is a figure in many stories. She may appear as a *kachina* mana, that

Navajo yeibichai, or masked gods. Talking God, Gray God, and a female ye?ii, from left to right. Courtesy, Smithsonian Institution, National Anthropological Archives, Simeon Schwemberger, photographer (neg.#82-2048).

is, a female kachina. At Cochiti, for example, Yellow Woman kachina wears a green mask (see *Masks and Masking)* and has her hair done in butterfly whorls on the sides of her head. She wears an embroidered ceremonial blanket as a dress and an all-white manta over her shoulders. Yellow Woman tends to be a stock heroine in many stories, taking on a wide range of identities, including bride, witch, chief's daughter, bear woman, and ogress. [Benedict 1931]

Yenaldlooshi
Navajo, Southwest

Literally "he who trots along here and there on all fours." A human *witch* who wears *coyote* skins and travels at night, also known as a skinwalker, subject of many stories. Yenaldlooshi are said to gain their power by killing a near relative, sometimes a sibling. Navajos believe skinwalkers meet at night in caves to perform malevolent deeds. They are naked (shocking in light of Navajo modesty) save for masks and an abundance of jewelry. In their nefarious rituals they pervert every convention of Navajo tradition, including performing such unthinkable acts as creating *sandpaintings* only to spit, urinate, and defecate on them. They have intercourse with the dead. They practice *cannibalism,* sitting in circles and eating piles or basketsful of human flesh. Recognizable human heads are displayed in rows on shelves in their caves. To harm Navajos, they may climb atop a hogan containing a sleeping family and sprinkle through the smoke hole a pollen made from the ground bones of human infants. Contact with this loathsome pollen causes sickness, social problems, even death.

In stories, Navajos detect yenaldlooshi by the presence of strange noises, loud barking dogs, or dirt falling from the hogan ceiling. The skinwalker is pursued and may be shot or captured, whereupon it might plead for its life. If the skinwalker is not caught, the services of a singer *(hataalii)* or medicine person are sought for protection.

In many Navajo stories, Coyote enervates a man, often a hunter, by throwing his skin on him; in exchange Coyote receives the appearance of the hunter. Coyote is usually motivated to exchange skins by his desire to have sex with the hunter's wife. While Coyote enjoys living in the place of the hunter, the hunter is immobilized in the position of a sleeping coyote, nose to anus. Eventually the wife recognizes the man as Coyote, not her husband. Not only is he lazy, but her house soon begins to smell of coyote urine. See also *Ma?ii.* [Brady 1984]

Yenogeaunus
Seneca, *Northeast*

A witch encouraged by the sorcerer *Haiendonnis.*

Yimantuwinyai
Hupa, *California*

A *culture hero* who slays monsters and makes the world habitable for humans.

Yoania
Yaqui, *Southwest*

The ancient enchanted world, from which Yaquis believe they have inherited everything. In Yoania lived the *Surem,* little people only three feet tall. They were never sick, did not know death, and were renewed each month by the new moon. Their lives were lived in unity with all other creatures in the world. All creatures were able to communicate with one another by means of a gift called *seataka.* With the introduction of Christianity, Yoania went underground, that is, it came to exist in a world below this one (see *Talking Tree),* but it is believed to be accessible through *visions* experienced in wild and remote places. The *pascola* (masked dancers) in particular are prone to having Yoania visions. Yoania is the subject and setting of many of the old Yaqui stories, and many stories are told of Yoania visions. [Beals 1943, 1945; Painter 1986]

Yodi and Ntliz
Navajo, *Southwest*

Fabrics or "soft goods" and "jewels." Archaic terms commonly used in stories, prayers, and songs to designate soft goods, such as bows and arrows, quivers, baskets, horses and sheep, and anything soft; and jewels, including shell, turquoise, and jet as well as beads, necklaces, and earrings. [Wyman 1970]

Yona
Cherokee, *Southeast*

"Bear." The *Bear Dance* used for *healing*. Men and women *dance* as couples, imitating many of the bear's movements, such as clawing and growling. After the advent of Christian missionaries, the Yona dance became a social dance with sexual joking (see *Jokes and Joking*) between couples, ending with strong embraces, i.e., "bear hugs." [Mooney 1900]

Yum
Lakota, *Plains*

The *Whirlwind,* who has power over chance, games, and love. See also *Tate* (Wind) and *Wohpe,* daughter of Skan, who cared for Yum. [Walker 1982]

Yuneha
Penobscot, *Northeast*

The *Snake Dance,* also called permatagiposi ("coming twisting along the ground"). A long line of dancers followed a leader in a twisting path that would grow first tighter, then looser as the dancers moved through a village. The last person in the line often dragged observers into the line. The *dance* represents a serpent-shaped constellation of stars (see *Stars and Starlore).* [Trigger 1978]

Yuwipi
Plains

A rite of clairvoyance and divination in which a *shaman* is wrapped and bound in a blanket, then the room is completely darkened. As the ritual progresses, those present see the spirits, who appear as little flashes or dots of light. These spirits speak to the Yuwipi leader and assist him in freeing himself from his bonds. At the ritual's closing, when the lights are raised, the shaman is free and possesses the information sought after. [Powers 1984]

Zuni
Southwest

The name by which the Zuni call themselves is *Ashiwi.*

Zuni Emergence
Zuni, *Southwest*

Those who are to be human beings, *Cooked People* or Daylight People, exist within the earth at a dark and crowded place four levels below the present surface. The Sun Father *(Yatokka taccu)* commands that his sons *(Ahayuta,* the warrior twins) lead the *emergence* of the people into the daylight. The people have no mouth openings. Their fingers and toes are webbed, and they have horns and tails. The warrior twins slit mouth openings in the people's faces, cut their webs to form fingers and toes, and cut off their horns and tails. A priest's son and daughter are sent to find a place where the people may live. The sister and brother commit incest; their children are the *koyemshi.* The people travel about looking for a place to live. A water strider, an insect that skates on the surface tension of water, places its feet at the edges of the world. Where its heart comes to rest marks *itiwana,* the middle place, the present location of Zuni.

Some versions of the emergence story describe the origins of four *medicine bundles* essential to Zuni prayers. In some versions the Sun Father wants the people to emerge because he has no one to provide him with offerings. These versions include the development of prayersticks as prayer offerings (see *Prayer and Prayersticks).* Other versions include contests in which birds and animals of prey play games to determine which will win the privilege of hunting in the daytime. See also *Kanaakwe* and *Zuni Ritual Cycle.* [Benedict 1935; Bunzel 1932; Cushing 1896; Parsons 1923d; Stevenson 1905]

Zuni Ritual Cycle
Zuni, *Southwest*

The Zuni New Year coincides with the winter solstice. A series of rites is performed during a 20-day period known as *itiwana,* centering on the solstice, in order to clean and prepare the village for the New Year. Following the Winter Solstice Ceremonies is a period of ground cleansing (uwanaga), during which various *kachina* impersonations may take place. The most common of these are appearances of *monster* and *cannibal* figures, Natashku and

Atoshle or Suyuki (see *Soyoko* for Hopi counterpart). The performances of these figures are associated with disciplining children by frightening them. The dreadful-looking and acting monster and cannibal figures threaten naughty children.

Winter Dances begin in February and last until April. On a quadrennial basis in March, young boys are initiated in events that focus on the recounting of Zuni history and way of life. *Kiaklo,* who knows the Zuni story, is a central figure in these rites. In long ritual orations, Kiaklo recites the story of creation and history as well as the privileges and duties of being Zuni.

Summer Dances begin at the Summer Solstice and continue into September, concluding with the Oknekyanna or *Ololowishkia* performance. Ololowishkia is an ithyphallic kachina (see also *Kokopelli)* whose public performance includes filling a large bowl with a black liquid ejected from his phallus. Corn ground during the rite is mixed with this liquid to form a dough distributed throughout the audience. The dough is a prayer object for fertility and is later planted in a field or placed in the home.

Early in December after nearly a year of planning and preparation, the most widely known of Zuni ceremonials, *Shalako,* occurs. This event features the construction of six to eight Shalako houses and the appearances of the distinctive Shalako kachinas, along with the *koyemshi* and an impressive group known as the Council of the Gods.

Immediately following Shalako is Molawai, a ritual dramatization of the loss and recovery of the *Corn Maidens.* See also *Pautiwa, Shi-tsukia,* and *Zuni Emergence.* [Wright 1985]

Zuzeca

Lakota, *Plains*

Snake, whose spirit is responsible for sly activity, going about unknown and unseen, and lying. [Walker 1982]

Bibliography

Aarne, A., and S. Thompson
1964 *The Types of the Folk-tale: A Classification and Bibliography.* Helsinki: Suomalainen Tiedeakatemia, Academia Scientarium Fennica.

Abenakew, E.
1929 "Cree Trickster Tales." *Journal of American Folklore* 42: 309–354.

Aberle, D. F.
1942 "Mythology of the Navaho Stick-Dice." *Journal of American Folklore* 55: 144–155.
1966 *The Peyote Religion among the Navaho.* Chicago: Aldine.

Abrams, D. M., and B. Sutton-Smith
1977 "The Development of the Trickster in Children's Narrative." *Journal of American Folklore* 90: 29–47.

Ackerman, C.
1975 "A Tsimshian Oedipus." In *Proceedings of the 2nd Congress, Canadian Ethnology Society,* edited by J. Freedman and J. H. Barkow. 1: 65–85. Ottawa: National Museums of Canada.

Adamson, T.
1934 *Folk-Tales of the Coast Salish.* American Folklore Society. *Memoirs* 27.

Ahenakew, F.
1987 *Waskahikanowiyiniw acimowina = Stories of the House People.* Winnipeg: University of Manitoba Press.

Allaire, L.
1984 "A Native Mental Map of Coast Tsimshian Villages." In *The Tsimshian,* edited by M. Sequin, 82–98. Vancouver: University of British Columbia Press.

Altman, G. J.
1947 "Guardian-Spirit of the Salish." *Masterkey* 21(5): 155–160.

Amiotte, A.
1976 "Eagles Fly Over." *Parabola* 1(3): 28–41.

Amoss, P. T.
1977 "Strategies of Reorientation: The Contribution of Contemporary Winter Dancing to Coast Salish Identity and Solidarity." *Arctic Anthropology* 14(1): 77–83.
1978 *Coast Salish Spirit Dancing: The Survival of an Ancestral Religion.* Seattle: University of Washington Press.
1984 "A Little More than Kin, and Less than Kind: The Ambiguous Northwest Coast Dog." In *The Tsimshian and Their Neighbors of the North Pacific Coast,* edited by J. Miller and C. M. Eastman. Seattle: University of Washington Press.

Anderson, F. G.
1955 "The Pueblo Kachina Cult: A Historical Reconstruction." *Southwestern Journal of Anthropology* 11: 404–419.

Angus, C., et al.
1977 *We-gyet Wanders On: Legends of the Northwest.* Saanichton, British Columbia: Hancock House.

Aoki, H., and D. E. Walker, Jr.
1989 *Nez Perce Oral Narratives.* University of California. *Publications in Linguistics* 104.

Apakok, A.
1985 "From the Belchers to Great Whale by Kayak." *Inuktitut* 60: 4–18.

Applegate, R. B.
1978 *Atishwin: The Dream Helper in South-Central California.* Socorro, NM: Ballena Press.
1979 "The Black, the Red and the White: Duality and Unity in the Luiseño Cosmos." *Journal of California and Great Basin Anthropology* 1: 71–88.

Arizona State University
1973 *North American Indians: A Comprehensive Annotated Bibliography for the Secondary Teacher.* Tempe: Arizona State University, Indian Education Center.

Bibliography

Ashwell, R.
1978 *Coast Salish: Their Art, Culture and Legends.* Saanichton, British Columbia and Seattle, WA: Hancock House.

Astrov, M.
1950 "The Concept of Motion as the Psychological Leitmotif of Navaho Life and Literature." *Journal of American Folklore* 63: 45–56.

Aubin, G. F.
1982 "Ethnographic Notes from Golden Lake." In *Papers of the 13th Algonquian Conference,* edited by W. Cowan, 47–52. Ottawa: Carleton University.

Axtell, J.
1982 "Bronze Men and Golden Ages: The Intellectual History of Indian-White Relations in Colonial America." *Journal of Interdisciplinary History* 12: 663–675.

Babcock, B. A.
1984–1985 "We're All in There in the Clay." In *The 8th Congress for the International Society for Folk Narrative Research,* edited by R. Kvideland and T. Selberg, 29–48. June 12–17. Paper 1. Bergen, Norway: International Society for Folk Narrative Research.
1987 "Taking Liberties Writing from the Margins, and Doing It with a Difference." *Journal of American Folklore* 100(398): 390–411.

Bagley, C. B.
1930 *Indian Myths of the Northwest.* Seattle: Lowman & Hanford.

Bahr, D. M.
1975 *Pima and Papago Ritual Oratory: A Study of Three Texts.* San Francisco: Indian Historian Press.
1977 "On the Complexity of Southwest Indian Emergence Myths." *Journal of Anthropological Research* 33: 317–349.
1981 "The Whole Past in a Yavapai Mythology." *American Indian Culture and Research Journal* 5(2): 1–35.

Bahr, D. M., et al.
1974 *Piman Shamanism and Staying Sickness.* Tucson: University of Arizona Press.

Ballard, A. C.
1927–1929 "Some Tales of the Southern Puget Sound Salish." University of Washington. *Publications in Anthropology* 2(3): 57ff.

1929 "Mythology of Southern Puget Sound." University of Washington. *Publications in Anthropology* 3: 31–150.

Ballard, C. G.
1982 "The Boas Connection in American Indian Mythology: A Research Narrative on Ethnocentrism." *American Indian Culture and Research Journal* 6(3): 47–68.

Bancroft, H. H.
1875–1876 *The Native Races of the Pacific States of North America.* New York: Appleton.

Barbeau, C. M.
1915a *Huron and Wyandot Mythology.* Geological Survey of Canada. *Anthropology Series* 11.
1915b "Loucheux Myths." *Journal of American Folklore* 28: 249–257.
1915c "Wyandot Tales, Including Foreign Elements." *Journal of American Folklore* 28: 83–95.
1946 "Bear Mother." *Journal of American Folklore* 59: 1–12.

Barnes, G. F.
1975 *Tales of the High Hills: Legends of the Montauk Indians.* Sag Harbor, NY: East Hampton Town Bicentennial Committee.

Barnes, L. M.
1901, 1909 "Digger Indian Legends." *Land of Sunshine* 14: 130–134, 310–314, 397–402 (1901); 16: 130, 223, 310, 397 (1909).

Barnouw, V.
1955 "A Psychological Interpretation of a Chippewa Origin Legend." *Journal of American Folklore* 68: 73–85, 211–223, 341–355.

Barnouw, V., comp.
1977 *Wisconsin Chippewa Myths and Tales and Their Relation to Chippewa Life.* Madison: University of Wisconsin Press.

Barrett, S. A.
1906 "A Composite Myth of the Pomo Indians." *Journal of American Folklore* 19: 37–51.
1919 *Myths of the Southern Sierra Miwok.* University of California. *Publications in American Archaeology and Ethnology* 16.
1933 *Pomo Myths.* Public Museum of the City of Milwaukee. *Bulletin.*

Basso, K.
1966 *The Gift of Changing Woman.* Smithsonian Institution. Bureau of American Ethnology. *Bulletin* 196: 113–73.

1978 "The Enemy of Every Tribe: 'Bushman' Images in Northern Athapaskan Narratives." *American Ethnologist* 5: 690–709.

Bauer, G. W.
1973 *Tales from the Cree.* Cobalt, Ontario: Highway Bookshop.

Bayliss, C. K.
1909 "A Tewa Sun Myth." *Journal of American Folklore* 22: 333–335.

Beals, R. L.
1943 "The Aboriginal Culture of the Cahita Indians." *Ibero-Americana* 19.
1945 *The Contemporary Culture of the Cahita Indians.* Smithsonian Institution. Bureau of American Ethnology. *Bulletin* 142.

Beauchamp, W. M.
1888, 1889a, 1893 "Onondaga Tales." *Journal of American Folklore* 1: 44–48 (1888); 2: 261–270 (1889); 6: 173–180 (1893).
1889b "The Great Mosquito." *Journal of American Folklore* 2: 284.
1891 "Hi-a-wat-ha." *Journal of American Folklore* 4: 295–306.
1892 "Iroquois Notes." *Journal of American Folklore* 5: 223–229.
1895 "Onondaga Tale of the Pleiades." *Journal of American Folklore* 13: 281–282.
1898 "Indian Corn Stories and Customs." *Journal of American Folklore* 11: 195–202.
1976 *Iroquois Folk Lore: Gathered from the Six Nations of New York.* New York: AMS Press. Originally published by Dekler Press, Syracuse, NY (1922).

Beck, M. L.
1979 "Raven: Benefactor, Transformer, Trickster, Thief." *Indian Historian* 12(2): 50–53, 62.

Beckham, S. D., K. A. Toepel, and R. Minor
1984 *Native American Religious Practices and Uses in Western Oregon.* University of Oregon. *Anthropological Papers* 31.

Beckwith, M. W.
1930a *Myths and Hunting Stories of the Mandan and Hidatsa Sioux.* Poughkeepsie, NY: Vassar College.
1930b "Mythology of the Oglala Dakota." *Journal of American Folklore* 43: 339–442.
1932 "Myths and Ceremonies of the Mandan and Hidatsa." *Publications of the Folklore Foundation* 12: 117–267. Poughkeepsie, NY: Vassar College.

1934 "Mandan and Hidatsa Tales." *Publications of the Folklore Foundation* 14: 269–320. Poughkeepsie, NY: Vassar College.
1938 *Mandan-Hidatsa Myths and Ceremonies.* American Folklore Society. *Memoirs* 32.

Bell, J. M.
1903 "Fireside Stories of the Chippewyans." *Journal of American Folklore* 16: 73–84.

Bell, R.
1893 "Ojibway Legends and Traditions." *Journal of American Folklore* 6: 153–154.
1897 "History of the Che-che-puy-ew-tis (Legend of the Northern Crees)." *Journal of American Folklore* 10: 1–8.
1901 "Legends of the Slavey Indians of the Mackenzie River." *Journal of American Folklore* 14: 25–29.

Benally, C.
1982 *A Dineji Nakee' Naahane': A Utah Navajo History.* Monticello, UT: San Juan School District.

Benedict, R. F.
1922 "The Vision in Plains Culture." *American Anthropologist* 24: 1–23.
1923 "The Concept of the Guardian Spirit in North America." American Anthropological Association. *Memoirs* 29.
1930 "Eight Stories from Acoma." *Journal of American Folklore* 43: 59–88.
1931 "Tales of the Cochiti Indians." Smithsonian Institution. Bureau of American Ethnology. *Bulletin* 98.
1935 *Zuñi Mythology.* 2 vols. Columbia University. *Contributions to Anthropology* 21.
1968 "Introduction to Zuñi Mythology." *Studies on Mythology,* edited by R. A. Georges, 102–36. Homewood, IL: Dorsey.

Benedict, S.
1983 "The Tsioneskwenrie Plant People." *American Indian Culture and Research Journal* 7(2): 25–26.

Berckefeldt, S. V.
1977 "The Humpback Flute Player." *Masterkey* 51: 113–115.

Bierhorst, J., ed.
1976 *The Red Swan Myths and Tales of the American Indian.* New York: Farrar, Straus & Giroux.
1985 *The Mythology of North America.* New York: William Morrow.

Bingham, S., and J. Bingham, eds.
1984 *Between Sacred Mountains: Navajo Stories and Lessons from the Land.* Tucson: Sun Tracks, University of Arizona Press.

Birket-Smith, K.
1976 *Contributions to Chippewyan Ethnology.* New York: AMS Press. Originally published as *Report of the Fifth Thule Expedition, 1921–24, Vol. 6, No. 3.* Copenhagen: Gyldendalske Boghandel, Nordisk Forlag (1930).

Black Elk, C., and T. Giago.
1980 "The Ancient Legend of Iktomi the Trickster and Modern Tribal Leadership." *Wassaja: The Indian Historian* 13(1): 34–35.

Black, L. T.
1983 "Eskimo Motifs in Aleut Art and Folklore." *Etudes/Inuit/Studies* 7(1): 3–23.

Blackbird, A. J.
1987a "Ne-Naw-bo-zhoo Spoils the Sugar Trees." In *Nanabozhoo: Giver of Life,* edited by A. K. Helbig, 170. Brighton, MI: Green Oak Press.
1987b "The Origin of Ne-Naw-bo-zhoo." In *Nanabozhoo: Giver of Life,* edited by A. K. Helbig, 50. Brighton, MI: Green Oak Press.

Blackburn, T. C.
1975 *December's Child: A Book of Chumash Oral Narratives.* Berkeley: University of California Press.

Blackburn, T. C., ed.
1977 *Flowers of the Wind: Papers on Ritual, Myth, and Symbolism in California and the Southwest.* Socorro, NM: Ballena Press.

Blackman, M. B.
1977 "Ethnohistoric Changes in the Haida Potlatch Complex." *Arctic Anthropology* 14: 39–53.

Blackwood, E.
1984 "Sexuality and Gender in Certain Native American Tribes: The Case of Cross-Gender Females." *Signs* 10: 27–42.

Blanchard, D.
1982 "Who or What's a Witch? Iroquois Persons of Power." AIQ 6: 218–237.

Bloomfield, L.
1928a *Menominee Texts.* American Ethnological Society, New York. *Publications* 12.
1928b "The Story of the Bad Owl." *Proceedings of the 22nd Session of the International Congress of Americanists* 2: 23–25.

1930 *Sacred Stories of the Sweet Grass Cree.* Bulletin (National Museum of Canada) 60, Anthropological Series 11.
1934 *Plains Cree Texts.* American Ethnological Society, New York. *Publications* 14.
1956 *Eastern Ojibwa: Grammatical Sketch, Text, and Word List.* Ann Arbor: University of Michigan Press.

Blue Cloud, P.
1982 *Elderberry Flute Song: Contemporary Coyote Tales.* Trumansburg, NY: Crossing Press.

Boas, F.
1888a *The Central Eskimo.* Smithsonian Institution. Bureau of American Ethnology. *Annual Report* 6.
1888b "Gleanings from the Emmons Collection of Ethnological Materials from Alaska." *Journal of American Folklore* 1: 215–219.
1888c "Myths and Legends of the Catloltq of Vancouver Island." *American Antiquarian* 10: 201–211, 366–373.
1891a "Dissemination of Tales among the Natives of North America." *Journal of American Folklore* 4: 13–20.
1891b "Notes on the Snanaimuq." *American Anthropologist* (Old Series) 2: 321–328.
1894a *Chinook Texts.* Smithsonian Institution. Bureau of American Ethnology. *Annual Report* 20.
1894b, 1897 "Eskimo Tales and Songs." *Journal of American Folklore* 7: 45–50 (1894); 10: 109–115 (1897).
1894c "Notes on the Eskimo of Port Clarence, Alaska." *Journal of American Folklore* 7: 205–208.
1895 "Salishan Texts." *Proceedings of the American Philosophical Society* 34: 31–48.
1896 "The Growth of American Mythologies." *Journal of American Folklore* 9: 1–11.
1898a *The Mythology of the Bella Coola Indians.* American Museum of Natural History. Publication of the Jesup North Pacific Expedition 1.
1898b "Traditions of the Tillamook Indians." Journal of American Folklore 11: 23–38, 133–150.
1899 "Northern Elements in the Mythology of the Navajo." *American Anthropologist* (Old Series) 10: 371.
1901a *The Eskimo of Baffin Land and Hudson Bay.* American Museum of Natural History, New York. *Bulletin* 15.
1901b *Kathlamet Texts.* Smithsonian Institution. Bureau of American Ethnology. *Annual Report* 26.
1902 *Tsimshian Texts.* Smithsonian Institution. Bureau of American Ethnology. *Annual Report* 27.

1904 "The Folk-Lore of the Eskimo." *Journal of American Folklore* 17: 1–13.
1910 *Kwakiutl Tales*. Columbia University. *Contributions to Anthropology* 2.
1914 "Mythology and Folk-Tales of the North American Indians." *Journal of American Folklore* 27: 374–410.
1916 *Tsimshian Mythology*. Smithsonian Institution. Bureau of American Ethnology. *Annual Report* 31.
1917a *Folk-tales of Salishan and Sahaptin Tribes*. American Folklore Society. *Memoirs* 11.
1917b "The Origin of Death." *Journal of American Folklore* 30: 486–491.
1918 "Northwest Coast Theft of Sun." *Journal of American Folklore* 31: 641–648.
1921 "Ethnology of the Kwakiutl." Smithsonian Institution. Bureau of American Ethnology. *Annual Report* 35(2).
1922a "Abstract Characteristics of Keresan Folk Tales." *International Congress of Americanists* 20(1): 223–224.
1922b "Tales of Spanish Provenience from Zuñi." *Journal of American Folklore* 35: 62.
1926–1928 *Keresan Texts* (pt. 1-2). American Ethnological Society, New York. *Publications* 8.
1928 *Bella Bella Texts*. Columbia University. *Contributions to Anthropology* 5.
1930 *The Religion of the Kwakiutl Indians*. Columbia University. *Contributions to Anthropology* 10.
1932 *Bella Bella Tales*. American Folklore Society. *Memoirs* 25.
1934 "A Chehalis Text." *International Journal of American Linguistics* 8(2): 103–110.
1935 *Kwakiutl Culture as Reflected in Mythology*. American Folklore Society. *Memoirs* 28.

Boas, F., and A. F. Chamberlain
1918 "Kutenai Tales." Smithsonian Institution. Bureau of American Ethnology. *Bulletin* 59.

Boas, F., and E. C. Parsons
1924 "Spanish Tales from Laguna and Zuñi, New Mexico." *Journal of American Folklore* 33: 47–72.

Bogaras, W.
1918 *Tales of the Yukaghir, Lamut, and Russianized Natives of Eastern Siberia*. American Museum of Natural History, New York. *Anthropological Papers* 20.

Bogart, E. M. M.
1928 *Legends of Kan-yuk-sa*. Macon, GA: J. W. Burke.

Boice, L. P.
1979 "The Iroquois Sense of Place: Legends as a Source of Environmental Imagery." *New York Folklore* 5: 179–188.

Bourke, J. G.
1886 "The Urine Dance of the Zuñis." In *Proceedings of the American Association for the Advancement of Science, 34th Meeting, August 1885*. Salem, MA: Salem Press.
1889 "Cosmogony and Theogony of the Mojave Indians of the Rio Colorado, Arizona." *Journal of American Folklore* 2: 169–189.
1890 "Notes on Apache Mythology." *Journal of American Folklore* 3: 209–212.

Bowers, A. W.
1950 *Mandan Social and Ceremonial Organization*. Social Anthropological Series. University of Chicago Publications in Anthropology. Chicago: University of Chicago Press.

Boyer, L. B.
1975 "The Man Who Turned into a Water Monster. A Psychoanalytic Contribution to Folklore." *Psychoanalytic Study of Society* 6: 100–133.

Boyle, D.
1908 "The Killing of the Wa-sak-apee-quay by Pe-se-quan, and Others." *Annual Archaeological Report*, 91–121. Toronto.

Bradfield, R. M.
1973 *A Natural History of Associations. A Study in the Meaning of Community, Vol. 2*. London: Duckworth.

Brady, M. K.
1980 "Narrative Competence: A Navajo Example of Peer Group Evaluation." *Journal of American Folklore* 93: 158–181.
1984 *"Some Kind of Power": Navajo Children's Skinwalker Narratives*. Salt Lake City: University of Utah Press.

Brassard, D.
1980 "Three Montagnais Myths: A Structuralist Approach." *Anthropologica* 22: 187–202.

Brean, A.
1975 *Athabaskan Stories*. Anchorage: AMU Press.

Brenizer, M. M.
1976 *The Nantucket Indians: Legends and Accounts before 1659*. Nantucket, MA: Poets Corner Press.

Bibliography

Brescia, W., Jr.
1985 "Choctaw Oral Tradition Relation to Tribal Origin." In *The Choctaw before Removal,* edited by C. K. Reeves, 3–16. Jackson: University Press of Mississippi.

Bright, W. O.
1977 "Coyote Steals Fire (Karok)." In *Northern California Texts,* edited by V. Golla and S. Silver, 3–9. Chicago: University of Chicago Press.
1979 "A Karok Myth in 'Measured Verse': The Translation of a Performance." *Journal of California and Great Basin Anthropology* 1: 117–123.
1980 "Coyote's Journey." *American Indian Culture and Research Journal* 4(1–2): 21–48.
1981 "Literature: Written and Oral." In *Georgetown University Roundtable on Languages and Linguistics,* 271–283. Washington: Georgetown University Press.

Brightman, R. A.
1988 "The Windigo in the Material World." *Ethnohistory* 35: 337–379.

Brill, E. C.
1906 "Caughnawaga Legend." *Journal of American Folklore* 19: 127–129.

Brinton, D.G.
1870 *National Legend of the Chahta-Muskokee Tribes.* Morrisania.
1885 *The Lenape and Their Legends.* Brinton's Library of Aboriginal American Literature, vol. 5. Philadelphia: D. G. Brinton.
1896 *The Myths of the New World,* 3d ed. New York: Leypoldt & Holt.

Brito, S. J.
1989 *The Way of a Peyote Roadman.* American University Studies. New York: Peter Lang.

Brotherston, G.
1979a "Genesis According to Walam Olum." In *Image of the New World: The American Continent Portrayed in Native Texts,* edited by G. Brotherston, 176–178. London: Thames & Hudson.
1979b "How Salmon Are Lured Inland." In *Image of the New World: The American Continent Portrayed in Native Texts,* edited by G. Brotherston, 204–205. London: Thames & Hudson.

Brown, J. E.
1953 *The Sacred Pipe: Black Elk's Account of the Seven Rites of the Oglala Sioux.* Baltimore: Penguin.

1982 *The Spiritual Legacy of the American Indian.* New York: Penguin.

Brown, J. S. H., and R. Brightman, eds.
1988 *The Orders of the Dreamed: George Nelson on Cree and Northern Ojibwa Religion and Myth, 1923.* St. Paul: Minnesota Historical Society Press.

Brown, V.
1974 *Voices of Earth and Sky: The Vision Life of Native Americans and Their Culture Heroes.* Harrisburg, PA: Stackpole Books.
1985 *Native Americans of the Pacific Coast: Peoples of the Sea Wind.* Happy Camp, CA: Naturegraph.

Brown, W.
1890 "Wa-ba-ba-nal, or Northern Lights: A Wabanaki Legend." *Journal of American Folklore* 3: 213–214.

Brugge, D. M., and C. J. Frisbie, eds.
1982 *Navajo Religion and Cultures: Selected Views.* Santa Fe: Museum of New Mexico Press.

Bunnell, C. O.
1933 *Legends of the Klickitats: A Klickitat Version of the Story of the Bridge of the Gods.* Portland, OR: Metropolitan Press.

Bunzel, R. L.
1930 *The Pueblo Potter.* New York: Columbia University Press.
1932 "Introduction to Zuñi Ceremonialism, Zuñi Origin Myths, Zuñi Ritual Poetry, Zuñi Katcinas." Smithsonian Institution. Bureau of American Ethnology. *Annual Report* 47.
1933 *Zuñi Texts.* American Ethnological Society, New York. *Publications* 15.

Burns, L. M.
1901 "Digger Indian Legends." *Land of Sunshine* 14 (pt. 1–4): 130–134, 223–226, 310–314, 397, 402.

Burrows, E.
1926 "Eskimo Tales." *Journal of American Folklore* 39: 79–81.

Bushnell, D. I., Jr.
1909 *The Choctaw of Bayou Lacomb, St. Tammany Parish, Louisiana.* Smithsonian Institution. Bureau of American Ethnology. *Bulletin* 48.
1985 "Myths of the Louisiana Choctaw." In *A Choctaw Source Book,* edited by J. H. Peterson, Jr., 526–535. New York: Garland.

Bushotter, G.
1888 "Teton-Dakota Ghost Story." *Journal of American Folklore* 1: 68–71.

Caldwell, G. W.
1892 "California Indian Creation Myth." *Journal of American Folklore* 5: 73–74.
1902 "California San Joaquin Myth." *Journal of American Folklore* 15: 104–106.
1906, 1908 "California Mission Indian Myth." *Journal of American Folklore* 19: 309–321 (1906); 21: 35–42, 237–245 (1908).
1919 *Legends of Southern California.* San Francisco: Phillips & Van Orden.

Caldwell, J. R.
1945 "A Tale Actualized in a Game." *Journal of American Folklore* 58: 50.

Calhoun, F.
1946 "Four Puget Sound Folktales." *Journal of American Folklore* 59: 40–44.

Calkowski, M.
1975 "Cannibalism and Infertility: Sexual Imbalance in Interior Salish Mythology." *Proceedings of the 2nd Congress, Canadian Ethnology Society* 1: 47–64. Ottawa: National Museums of Canada.

Callaghan, C. A.
1977 "Coyote, the Imposter (Lake Miwok)." In *Northern California Texts,* edited by V. Golla and S. Silver, 10–16. Chicago: University of Chicago Press.

Callender, C., and L. M. Kochems
1983 "The North American Berdache." *Current Anthropology* 24: 443–470.

Campbell, B.
1975 "The Shining Youth in Tsimshian Mythology." In *Proceedings of the 2nd Congress, Canadian Ethnology Society,* edited by J. Freedman and J. Barkow, 1: 86–109. Ottawa: National Museums of Canada.
1977 "The Kidnapped Bride." *Anthropologica* 19: 49–62.

Campbell, S.
1916 "Two Cheyenne Stories." *Journal of American Folklore* 29: 406–408.

Canfield, W. W.
1902 *The Legends of the Iroquois, Told by "the Cornplanter."* New York: A. Wessels.

Carmichael, A.
1922 *Indian Legends of Vancouver Island.* Toronto: Musson.

Carr, H.
1986 "The Hero Twins." *New Scholar* 10(1–2): 1–17.

Carroll, M. P.
1979 "A New Look at Freud on Myth: Re-analyzing the Star-Husband Tale." *Ethos* 7(3): 189–205.
1981 "Levi-Strauss, Freud, and the Trickster: A New Perspective upon an Old Problem." *American Ethnologist* 8: 301–313.
1982 "The Rolling Head: A Revitalized Pyschoanalytic Perspective on Myth." *Journal of Psychoanalytic Anthropology* 5(1): 29–56.

Carson, W.
1917 "Ojibwa Tales." *Journal of American Folklore* 30: 491–493.

Catlin, G.
1841 *Letters and Notes on the Manners, Customs, and Conditions of the North-American Indians.* New York: Wiley and Putnam.

Ceci, L.
1982 "The Value of Wampum among the New York State Iroquois: A Case Study in Artifact Analysis." *Journal of Anthropological Research* 38: 97–107.

Chamberlain, A. F.
1889a "A Mohawk Legend of Adam and Eve." *Journal of American Folklore* 2: 228.
1889b, 1890a "Tales of the Mississaguas." *Journal of American Folklore* 2: 141–147 (1889); 3: 149–154 (1890).
1890b "The Thunder-bird amongst the Algonkins." *American Anthropologist* (Old Series) 3: 51–55.
1891 "Nanibozhu amongst the Otchipwe, Mississagas and Other Algonkian Tribes." *Journal of American Folklore* 4: 193–213.
1892 "A Mississaga Legend of Naniboju." *Journal of American Folklore* 5: 291.
1893 "The Coyote and the Owl." *Memoirs of the International Congress of Anthropologists,* 282–284.
1894 "Kootenay Legend: The Coyote and the Mountain Spirit." *Journal of American Folklore* 7: 195–196.
1900 "Some Items of Algonkian Folk-Lore." *Journal of American Folklore* 13: 271–277.

1905 "Mythology of Indian Stocks North of Mexico." *Journal of American Folklore* 18: 111–122.

Chamberlain, V. D.
1982 *When Stars Came Down to Earth: Cosmology of the Skidi Pawnee Indians of North America.* Los Altos, CA: Ballena Press.

Chance, N.
1990 *The Inupiat and Arctic Alaska: An Ethnography of Development.* Ft. Worth: Holt, Rinehart and Winston.

Chandler, K.
1905 *In the Reign of Coyote: Folklore from the Pacific Coast.* Boston, New York: Ginn & Co.

Chapin, G.
1940 "A Navajo Myth from the Chaco Canyon." *New Mexico Anthropologist* 4(4): 63–67.

Chapman, J. W.
1903 "Athapascan Traditions from the Lower Yukon." *Journal of American Folklore* 16: 180–185.
1912 "The Happy Hunting-Ground of the Ten'a." *Journal of American Folklore* 25: 66–71.
1914 *Ten'a Texts and Tales from Anvik, Alaska.* American Ethnological Society, New York. *Publications* 6.

Chapman, K. M.
1916 "The Evolution of the Bird in Decorative Art." *Art and Archaeology* 4: 307-316.
1933 *Pueblo Indian Pottery,* vol. 1. Nice, France: C. Szwedzicki.

Clay, C.
1938 *Swampy Cree Legends, Being Twenty Folk Tales from the Annals of a Primitive, Mysterious, Fast-Disappearing Canadian Race, as Told to C. Clay by Kuskapatchees, the Smoky One.* Toronto: Macmillan.

Clements, W. M., and F. M. Malpezzi
1984 Native American Folklore 1879–1979: An Annotated Bibliography. Chicago: Swallow Press.

Clutesi, G.
1969 *Potlatch.* Sidney, British Columbia: Gray's Publishing.

Codere, H.
1948 "The Swai'xwe Myth of the Middle Fraser River: The Integration of Two Northwest Coast Cultural Ideas." *Journal of American Folklore* 61: 1–17.

Cody, B. P.
1939 "A Maidu Myth of the Creation of Indian Women." *Masterkey* 13(2): 83.
1941 "Yurok Tales." *Masterkey* 15(6): 228–231.

Colby, B. N.
1973 "A Partial Grammar of Eskimo Folktales." *American Anthropologist* 75: 645–662.

Cole, D., and L. Muller-Wille
1984 "Franz Boas Expedition to Baffin Island 1883–1884." *Etudes/Inuit/Studies* 8(1): 37–63.

Coleman, B., Sr., E. Frogner, and E. Eich
1962 *Ojibwa Myths and Legends.* Minneapolis: Ross and Haines.

Colombo, J. R., ed.
1982 *Windigo: An Anthology of Fact and Fantastic Fiction.* Saskatoon, Saskatchewan: Western Producer Prairie Books.

Colton, H. S.
1947a "Hopi Deities." *Plateau* 20(1): 10–16.
1947b "What Is a Kachina?" *Plateau* 19(3): 40–47.
1959 *Hopi Kachina Dolls; with a Key to Their Identification.* Albuquerque: University of New Mexico Press.

Connelley, W. E.
1899 "Notes on the Folk-Lore of the Wyandots." *Journal of American Folklore* 12: 116–125.

Converse, H. M. C.
1908 *Myths and Legends of the New York State Iroquois.* New York State Museum. *Bulletin* 125.

Coolidge, D., and M. R. Coolidge.
1930 *The Navajo Indians.* Boston: Houghton Mifflin.

Cooper, J. M.
1933 "The Cree Witiko Psychosis." *Primitive Man* 6: 20–24.

Cornplanter, J. J.
1938 *Legends of the Longhouse.* Philadelphia: J. B. Lippincott.

Costello, J. A.
1986 *The Siwash: Their Life, Legends, and Tales. Puget Sound and the Pacific Northwest.* Fairfield, WA: Ye Galleon Press.

Courlander, H.
1987 *The Fourth World of the Hopis.* Albuquerque: University of New Mexico Press.

Courtney, R.
1985 "Indigenous Theatre: Indian and Eskimo Ritual Drama." In *Contemporary Canadian Theatre, New World Visions: A Collection of Essays,* edited by A. Wagner, 206–215. Toronto: Simon & Pierre.

Cove, J. A.
1978 "Survival or Extinction: Reflections on the Problem of Famine in Tsimshian and Kaguru Mythology." In *Extinction and Survival in Human Populations,* edited by C. D. Laughlin and I. Brady. New York: Columbia University Press.
1985 *A Detailed Inventory of the Barbeau Northwest Coast Files.* Canada National Museum of Man. Paper (Canadian Centre for Folk Culture Studies) 54. Mercury Series. Ottawa: National Museums of Canada.

Cowan, W., ed.
1976 *Papers of the Seventh Algonquian Conference.* Ottawa: Carleton University.
1982 *Papers of the Thirteenth Algonquian Conference.* Ottawa: Carleton University.
1984 *Papers of the Fifteenth Algonquian Conference.* Ottawa: Carleton University.

Cresswell, J. R.
1923 "Folk-tales of the Swampy Cree." *Journal of American Folklore* 36: 404–406.

Cruikshank, J.
1978 *When the World Began: A Teacher's Guide to Comparative and Local Mythology.* White Horse: Yukon Department of Education.
1979 *Athapaskan Women, Lives and Legends.* Canada National Museum of Man. Paper (Canadian Ethnology Service) 57. Mercury Series. Ottawa: National Museums of Canada.
1983 *The Stolen Women: Female Journeys in Tagish and Tutchone.* Canada National Museum of Man. Paper (Canadian Ethnology Service) 87. Mercury Series. Ottawa: National Museums of Canada.

Curry, J. L.
1987 *Back in the Beforetime: Tales of the California Indians.* New York: M. K. McElderry Books.

Curtin, J.
1898 *Creation Myths of Primitive America in Relation to the Religious History and Mental Development of Mankind.* Boston: Little, Brown.
1912 *Myths of the Modocs.* Boston: Little, Brown.
1922 *Seneca Indian Myths.* New York: Dutton.

Curtin, J., and J. N. B. Hewitt
1918 *Seneca Fiction, Legends, and Myths.* Smithsonian Institution. Bureau of American Ethnology. *Annual Report* 32.

Curtis, E. S.
1907–1930 *The North American Indian.* 20 vols. Seattle: E. S. Curtis.

Cushing, F. H.
1882 "Zuñi Social, Mythic and Religious Systems." *Popular Science Monthly* 21: 186–192.
1883 *Zuñi Fetishes.* Smithsonian Institution. Bureau of American Ethnology. *Annual Report* 2: 1880–1881.
1884, 1885 "Zuñi Breadstuff." *Millstone* 9: 1–12 (1884); 10: 1–4, 6–8 (1885).
1892 "A Zuñi Folk-tale of the Underworld." *Journal of American Folklore* 5: 49–56.
1893 "The Giant Cloud-Swallower." *Archaeologist* 1: 241–244.
1896 *Outlines of Zuñi Creation Myths.* Smithsonian Institution. Bureau of American Ethnology. *Annual Report* 13(6).
1901 *Zuñi Folk Tales.* London and New York: G. P. Putnam's Sons.
1923 "Origin Myth from Oraibi." *Journal of American Folklore* 36: 163–170.

Damas, D., ed.
1984 *Handbook of North American Indians.* Vol. 5: *Arctic.* Washington: Smithsonian Institution Press.

Dangel, R.
1929 "Bear and Fawns." *Journal of American Folklore* 42: 307–308.

Dauenhauer, N. M., and R. Dauenhauer, ed.
1987 *Haa Shuka, Our Ancestors: Tlingit Oral Narratives.* Seattle: University of Washington Press; Juneau, AK: Sealaska Heritage Foundation.

Dauenhauer, R. L.
1981 "Notes on Swanton Numbers 80 and 81." *Journal of American Folklore* 94: 358–364.

Davidson, D. S.
1928 "Folk Tales from Grand Lake Victoria, Quebec." *Journal of American Folklore* 41: 275–283.

Davis, J. B.
1909 "The Liver Eater: A Cherokee Story." University of Liverpool. *Annals of Archaeology and Anthropology* 2: 134–138.

Dawson, G. M.
1891 "Notes on the Shuswap People of British Columbia." Royal Society of Canada. *Proceedings and Transactions* 2: 3–44.

Day, G. M.
1976 "The Western Abenaki Transformer." *Journal of the Folklore Institute* 13(1): 75–89.

deAngulo, J.
1935 "Pomo Creation Myth." *Journal of American Folklore* 48: 203–262.
1973 *Coyote Man and Old Doctor Loon.* Edited by B. Callahan. San Francisco: Turtle Island Foundation.
1975 "The Creation." *Alcheringa* 1(1): 7.
1976 *Shabegok.* Edited by B. Callahan. Berkeley, CA: Turtle Island Foundation.

deAngulo, J., and W. R. Benson
1932 "The Creation Myth of the Pomo Indians." *Anthropos* 27: 261–274.

deAngulo, J., and L. S. Freeland
1928 "Miwok and Pomo Myths." *Journal of American Folklore* 41: 232–253.

Deans, J.
1885 "The Thunder Bird." *American Antiquarian* 7: 357–358.
1888a "What Befell the Slave Seekers." *Journal of American Folklore* 1: 123–124.
1888b–1889 "The Raven in the Mythology of Northwest Americans." *American Antiquarian,* 109–114, 273–278, 297–301, 368–369, 383.
1889 "The Story of the Bear and His Indian Wife." *Journal of American Folklore* 2: 255–260.
1891a "A Creation Myth of the Tsimshians of Northwest British Columbia." *Journal of American Folklore* 4: 34.
1891b "The Daughter of the Sun: A Legend of the Tsimshians of British Columbia." *Journal of American Folklore* 4: 32–33.
1892a "The Doom of the Katt-a-quins." *Journal of American Folklore* 5: 232–235.
1892b "Legend of the Fin-back Whale Crest of the Haidas, Queen Charlotte's Island, B.C." *Journal of American Folklore* 5: 43–47.
1899 *Tales from the Totems of the Hidery.* International Folk-lore Association. *Archives* 2.

Deloria, E.
1932 *Dakota Texts.* American Ethnological Society, New York. *Publications* 14.

DeMallie, R. J., ed.
1984 *The Sixth Grandfather.* Lincoln: University of Nebraska Press.

DeMallie, R. J., and E. A. Jahner
1980 "Walker's Outline of Oglalla Mythology." In *Lakota Belief and Ritual,* edited by J. Walker, 50–54. Lincoln: University of Nebraska Press.

DeMallie, R. J., and D. R. Parks, eds.
1987 *Sioux Indian Religion: Tradition and Innovation.* Norman: University of Oklahoma Press.

Demetracopoulou, D.
1933 "The Loon Woman Myth." *Journal of American Folklore* 46: 101–128.

Deming, E. W.
1902 "Abenaki Witchcraft Story." *Journal of American Folklore* 15: 62–63.

Denny, M. B.
1906–1907 "Orleans Indian Legends." *Out West* 25: 37–40, 161–166, 268–271, 373–375, 452–454 (1906); 26: 73–80, 168–170, 267–268 (1907).

Densmore, F.
1923 "Mandan and Hidatsa Music." Smithsonian Institution. Bureau of American Ethnology. *Bulletin* 80: 35–48.
1929 *Chippewa Customs.* Smithsonian Institution. Bureau of American Ethnology. *Bulletin* 86.

DeSmet, Fr.
1905 *Life, Letters and Travels of Father Pierre-Jean DeSmet, S.J., 1801–1873.* 4 vols. New York: F. P. Harper.

Dewdney, S.
1975 *The Sacred Scrolls of the Southern Ojibway.* Toronto: University of Toronto Press, for the Glenbow-Alberta Institute.

Dixon, J. E.
1985 "Cultural Chronology of Central Interior Alaska." *Arctic Anthropology* 22(1): 47–66.

Dixon, R. B.
1900 "Some Coyote Stories from the Maidu Indians of California." *Journal of American Folklore* 13: 267–270.
1903 "System and Sequence in Maidu Mythology." *Journal of American Folklore* 16: 32–36.
1905a *Maidu Myths.* American Museum of Natural History, New York. *Bulletin* 17.
1905b "The Mythology of the Shasta-Achomawi." *American Anthropologist* 7: 607–613.

1907–1910 *The Chimariko Indians and Language.* University of California. *Publications in American Archaeology and Ethnology* 5.

1908 "Achomawi and Atsugewi Tales." *Journal of American Folklore* 21: 159–177.

1909a "Achomawi Myths." *Journal of American Folklore* 22: 283–287.

1909b "The Mythology of the Central and Eastern Algonkins." *Journal of American Folklore* 22: 1–9.

1910 "Shasta Myths." *Journal of American Folklore* 23: 8–37, 364–370.

1912 *Maidu Texts.* American Ethnological Society, New York. *Publications* 4.

Dobkin de Rios, M.
1984 *Hallucinogens: Cross-Cultural Perspectives.* Albuquerque: University of New Mexico Press.

Dorsey, G. A.
1902, 1903a "Wichita Tales." *Journal of American Folklore* 15: 215–239 (1902); 16: 160–179 (1903).

1903b *The Arapaho Sun Dance: The Ceremony of the Offerings Lodge.* Field Columbian Museum. *Publication* 75. Anthropological Series 4.

1903c "How the Pawnee Captured the Cheyenne Medicine Arrows." *American Anthropologist* 5: 644–659.

1904a *The Mythology of the Wichita.* Carnegie Institution of Washington. *Publications* 21.

1904b *Traditions of the Arikara.* Carnegie Institution of Washington. *Publications* 17.

1904c *Traditions of the Osage.* Field Columbian Museum. *Publication* 88. Anthropological Series 7(1).

1904d *Traditions of the Skidi Pawnee.* American Folklore Society. *Memoirs* 8.

1904e "An Arikara Story-telling Contest." *American Anthropologist* 6: 240–244.

1904f "The Osage Mourning-War Ceremony." *American Anthropologist* 4: 404–412.

1905 *Traditions of the Caddo.* Carnegie Institution of Washington. *Publications* 41.

1906a *The Pawnee Mythology.* (pt. 1). Carnegie Institution of Washington. *Publications* 59.

1906b "Pawnee War Tales." *American Anthropologist* 8: 337–345.

1906c "Legend of the Teton-Sioux Medicine Pipe." *Journal of American Folklore* 1 9: 326–329.

1975 *The Cheyenne.* Fairfield, WA: Ye Galleon Press.

1986 "Traditions of the Caddo." In *The Southern Caddo,* edited by H. F. Gregory, 3–136. New York: Garland.

Dorsey, G. A., and A. L. Kroeber
1903 *Traditions of the Arapaho.* Field Columbian Museum. *Publication* 81. Anthropological Series 5.

Dorsey, G. A., and H. R. Voth
1901 *The Oraibi Soyal Ceremony.* Field Columbian Museum. *Publication* 55. Anthropological Series 3(1).

Dorsey, J. O.
1879 "How the Rabbit Killed the (Male) Winter." *American Antiquarian* 2: 128–132.

1880 "How the Rabbit Caught the Sun in a Trap." Smithsonian Institution. Bureau of American Ethnology. *Annual Report* 1: 581–583.

1884 "The Myths of the Raccoon and the Crawfish." *American Antiquarian* 6: 237–240.

1888a "Abstracts of Omaha and Ponka Myths." *Journal of American Folklore* 1: 74–78, 204–208.

1888b "Osage Traditions." Smithsonian Institution. Bureau of American Ethnology. *Annual Report* 6.

1888c "Ponka Stories, Told by Tim Potter, or Big Grizzly Bear, in 1872, at Ponka Agency, Dakota Territory." *Journal of American Folklore* 1: 73.

1888d "A Teton Dakota Ghost Story." *Journal of American Folklore* 1: 68–72.

1889 "Teton Folk-Lore Notes." *Journal of American Folklore* 2: 133–139.

1891 "Teton Folk-Lore." *American Anthropologist* (Old Series) 2: 143.

1892 "Nanibozhu in Siouan Mythology." *Journal of American Folklore* 5: 293–304.

1893a "Modern Additions to Indian Myths, and Indian Thunder Superstitions." *Journal of American Folklore* 6: 232.

1893b "Two Biloxi Tales." *Journal of American Folklore* 6: 48–50.

1894 "A Study of Siouan Cults." Smithsonian Institution. Bureau of American Ethnology. *Annual Report* 11.

Doueihi, A.
1984 "Trickster: On Inhabiting the Space between Discourse and Story." *Soundings: An Interdisciplinary Journal* 67(3): 283–311.

Dozier, E. P.
1956 "The Role of the Hopi-Tewa Migration Legend in Reinforcing Cultural Patterns and Prescribing Social Behavior." *Journal of American Folklore* 69: 176–180.

Driver, H. E.
1941 *Girls' Puberty Rites in Western North America.* University of California. *Anthropological Records* 6(2).

1969 *Indians of North America.* 2nd ed. Chicago: University of Chicago Press.

Driver, J.
1977 "The Cherokee Storyteller: The Raven Mocker." *Journal of Cherokee Studies* 2: 190–194.

DuBois, C. G.
1901 "The Mythology of the Diegueños." *Journal of American Folklore* 14: 181–185.
1904a "Mission Indian Religion: A Myth in the Making." *Southern Workman* 33: 353.
1904b "Story of the Chaup: A Myth of the Diegueños." *Journal of American Folklore* 17: 217–242.
1905a "The Mythology of the Diegueños: Mission Indians of the San Diego County, California, As Proving Their Status To Be Higher than Is Generally Believed." *Proceedings of the 13th Session of the International Congress of Americanists,* 101–107.
1905b "Religious Ceremonies and Myths of the Mission Indians." *American Anthropologist* 7: 620–629.
1906 "Mythology of the Mission Indians." *Journal of American Folklore* 19: 52–60.
1907 "Diegueño Myths and Their Connections with the Mohave, and Two Types or Styles of Diegueño Religious Dancing." *Proceedings of the 15th Session of the International Congress of Americanists* 2: 129–134, 135–138.
1908a "Across the Purple Sea: An Indian Tale." *Southern Workman* 37: 101–106.
1908b *Religion of the Luiseño Indians.* University of California. *Publications in American Archaeology and Ethnology* 8.

DuBois, C. G., and D. Demetracopoulou
1931 "Wintu Myths." University of California. *Publications in American Archaeology and Ethnology* 28: 279–403.
1932 "A Study of Wintu Mythology." *Journal of American Folklore* 45: 373–500.

Dumarest, F. N.
1919 "Notes on Cochiti." American Folklore Society. *Memoirs* 6: 212ff.

Dundes, A.
1962 "Earth-Diver: Creation of the Mythopoeic Male." *American Anthropologist* 64: 1032–1051.
1964a *The Morphology of North American Indian Folktales.* Helsinki: Suomalainen Tiedeakatemia, Academia Scientarium Fennica.
1964b "Texture, Text, and Context." *Southern Folklore Quarterly* 28: 251–265.

1979 "Heads or Tails: A Psychoanalytic Study of Potlatch." *Journal of Psychological Anthropology* 2: 395–424.
1986 "Structural Typology of North American Indian Folktales." *Journal of Anthropological Research* 42: 417–426.

Dunlop, G. M.
1934 *Tales of the Indians of the Plains.* Edmonton, Alberta: Institute of Applied Art.

Earle, E., and E. A. Kennard
1938 *Hopi Kachinas.* New York: J. J. Augustin.

Eckert, P., and R. Newmark
1980 "Central Eskimo Song Duels: A Contextual Analysis of Ritual Ambiguity." *Ethnology* 5(19): 191–211.

Edelman, S. P.
1974 "Ascension Motifs and Reversals in Tewa Narratives." *Journal of Anthropological Research* 30: 35–40.

Eells, M.
1884 "Do-ki-batt, or the God of the Puget Sound Indians." *American Antiquarian* 6: 389–393.
1889 "The Thunder Bird." *American Anthropologist* (Old Series) 2: 329–336.
1890 "Myths of the Puget Sound Indians." *American Antiquarian* 12: 160–165.

Eggan, D.
1971 "The Personal Use of Myth in Dreams." In *Myth: A Symposium,* edited by T. A. Sebeok, 107–121. Bloomington: Indiana University Press.

Eggan, F.
1950 *Social Organization of the Western Pueblos.* Chicago: University of Chicago Press.

Ehrlich, C.
1937 "Tribal Culture in Crow Mythology." *Journal of American Folklore* 50: 307–409.

Elliott, W.C.
1939 "Lake Lillooet Tales." *Journal of American Folklore* 44: 166–182.

Elmendorf, W. W.
1967 "Soul Loss Illness in Western North America." In *Indian Tribes of Aboriginal America,* edited by S. Tax, 104–111. New York: Cooper Square.
1977 "Coastal and Interior Salish Power Concepts: A Structural Comparison. *Arctic Anthropology* 14(1): 64–76.

Emmons, G. T.
1911 *The Tahltan Indians.* University of Pennsylvania. *Publications in Anthropology* 4.

Erdoes, R., and A. Ortiz, eds.
1984 *American Indian Myths and Legends.* New York: Pantheon Books.

Espinosa, A. M.
1918 "All Soul's Day at Zuñi, Acoma and Laguna." *Journal of American Folklore* 31: 550–552.
1936 "Pueblo Indian Folk Tales." *Journal of American Folklore* 4: 69–134.

Evans, G.
1986 "In the Alignment of the Sun and the Stars, Scholars Read the History of the Sioux." *Chronicle of Higher Education* 33(5): 7, 9.

Evers, L.
1983 "People of the Sacred Mountain: Restoration, Recreation, Veneration." *Western American Literature* 18(2): 151–154.

Evers, L., and F. S. Molina
1987 *Yaqui Deer Songs: Maso Bwikam.* Tucson: University of Arizona Press.

Farella, J. R.
1984 *The Main Stalk: A Synthesis of Navajo Philosophy.* Tucson: University of Arizona Press.

Faris, J. C.
1990 *The Nightway.* Albuquerque: University of New Mexico Press.

Farrand, L.
1900 "Traditions of the Chilcotin Indians." American Museum of Natural History. *Memoirs* 4: 1–54.
1916 "Myths of the Bellabella." Smithsonian Institution. Bureau of American Ethnology. *Annual Report* 31: 883–888.

Farrand, L.; and L. J. Frachtenberg, ed.
1915 "Shasta and Athapascan Myths from Oregon." *Journal of American Folklore* 28: 207–242.

Farrand, L. and W. S. Kahnweiler
1902 "Traditions of the Quinault Indians." American Museum of Natural History. *Memoirs* 4: 77–102.

Farrand, L., and T. Mayer
1917a *Sahaptin Tales.* American Folklore Society. *Memoirs* 11: 135–179.

1917b "Quileute Tales." *Journal of American Folklore* 32: 251–279.

Feer, M.
1973 "The Skunk and the Smallpox: Mythology and Historical Reality." *Plains Anthropology* 18(59): 33–39.

Fenton, W. N.
1947 "Iroquois Indian Folklore." *Journal of American Folklore* 60: 383–397.
1962 "'This Island, the World on the Turtle's Back.'" *Journal of American Folklore* 75: 283–300.
1975 "The Lore of the Longhouse: Myth and Ritual and Red Power." *Anthropology Quarterly* 48: 131–147.
1978 "Cherokee and Iroquois Connections Revisited." *Journal of Cherokee Studies* 3: 239–249.
1987 *The False Faces of the Iroquois.* Norman: University of Oklahoma Press.

Fenton, W. N., and G. P. Kurath
1951 "The Feast of the Dead, or Ghost Dance, at Six Nations Reserve, Canada." In *Symposium on Local Diversity in Iroquois Culture,* edited by W. N. Fenton. Smithsonian Institution. Bureau of American Ethnology. *Bulletin* 149: 143–165.

Fewkes, J. W.
1890 "Contribution to Passamaquoddy Folk-Lore." *Journal of American Folklore* 3: 257–280.
1891, 1892 "A Few Summer Ceremonials at Zuñi Pueblo." *Journal of American Ethnology and Archaeology* 1: 1–62 (1891); 2: 1–160 (1892).
1892a "A Few Tusayan Pictographs." *American Anthropologist* 5: 9–26.
1893 "A-wa-to-bi: An Archaeological Verification of a Tusayan Legend." *American Anthropologist* 6: 363–377.
1894a "Dolls of the Tusayan Indians." *Internationales Archiv fur Ethnographie* 7: 45–73.
1894b "The Snake Ceremonials at Walpi." *Journal of American Ethnology and Archaeology* 4: 1–126.
1895 "The Destruction of the Tusayan Monsters." *Journal of American Folklore* 8: 132–137.
1896 "The Tusayan Ritual: A Study of the Influence of Environment on Aboriginal Cults." Smithsonian Institution. *Annual Report* 683–700.
1897a "The Sacrificial Element in Hopi Worship." *Journal of American Folklore* 10: 187–201.

Bibliography

1897b "Tusayan Katchinas." Smithsonian Institution. Bureau of American Ethnology. *Annual Report* 15: 245–313.
1900a "The New-Fire Ceremony at Walpi." *American Anthropologist* 2: 80–138.
1900b "A Theatrical Performance at Walpi." Washington Academy of Sciences. *Proceedings* 2: 605–629.
1901 *Archaeological Expedition to Arizona in 1895.* Smithsonian Institution. Bureau of American Ethnology. *Annual Report* 17(2).
1902 *Tusayan Migration Traditions.* Smithsonian Institution. Bureau of American Ethnology. *Annual Report* 19.
1903 "Hopi Katchinas Drawn by Native Artists." Smithsonian Institution. Bureau of American Ethnology. *Annual Report* 21: 3–126.
1904 *Two Summers' Work in Pueblo Ruins.* Smithsonian Institution. Bureau of American Ethnology. *Annual Report* 22.
1910 "The Butterfly in Hopi Myth and Ritual." *American Anthropologist* 12: 576–594.

Fewkes, J. W., and A. M. Stephen.
1892 "The Na-Ác-Nai-Ya: A Tusayan Initiation Ceremony." *Journal of American Folklore* 5: 189–217.

Fiddler, T., and J. R. Stevens, eds.
1985 *Legends from the Forest.* Told by Chief T. Fiddler. Moonbeam, Ontario: Penumbra Press.

Fienup-Riordan, A.
1987 "Robert Redford, Apanuugpak, and the Invention of Tradition." *Etudes/Inuit/Studies* 11(1): 135–148.

Fine Day
1973 *My Cree People.* Invermere, British Columbia: Good Medicine Books.

Finger
1980 "Wohpe and the Gift of the Pipe." In *Lakota Belief and Ritual,* edited by J. R. Walker, 109–112. Lincoln: University of Nebraska Press.

Fisher, J. F.
1975 "An Analysis of the Central Eskimo Sedna Myth." *Temenos* 11: 27–42.

Fisher, M. W.
1946 "The Myths of North and Northeastern Algonquians in Reference to Algonquian Mythology as a Whole." In *Man in Northeastern North America,* edited by F. Johnson. Peabody Foundation for Archaeology. *Papers* 3.

Fitzhugh, W. W.
1985 "The Nulliak Pendants and Their Relation to Spiritual Traditions in Northeast Prehistory." *Arctic Anthropology* 22(2): 87–109.

Flannery, R., M. E. Chambers, and P. Jehle
1981 "Witiko Accounts from the James Bay Cree." *Artic Anthropology* 18(1): 57–77.

Fogelson, R. D.
1980 "The Conjuror in Eastern Cherokee Society." *Journal of Cherokee Studies,* 60–87. Fall.

Ford, R. I., ed.
1985 *The Ethnographic American Southwest: A Source Book. Southwestern Society in Myth, Clan, and Kinship.* New York: Garland.

Forde, C. D.
1931 "Ethnography of the Yuma Indians." University of California. *Publications in American Archaeology and Ethnology* 28(4): 83–278.

Foster, G. M.
1944 *A Summary of Yuki Culture.* Berkeley: University of California Press.

Frachtenberg, L. J.
1914a *Coos Texts.* Columbia University. *Contributions to Anthropology* 1.
1914b *Lower Umqua Texts and Notes on the Kusan Dialects.* Columbia University. *Contributions to Anthropology* 4.
1920 *Alsea Texts and Myths.* Smithsonian Institution. Bureau of American Ethnology. *Bulletin* 67.

Frey, R.
1987 *The World of the Crow Indians: As Driftwood Lodges.* Norman: University of Oklahoma Press.

Frisbie, C.
1967 *Kinaalda: A Study of the Navajo Girl's Puberty Ceremony.* Middletown; CT: Wesleyan University Press.
1987 *Navajo Medicine Bundles or Jish.* Albuquerque: University of New Mexico Press.

Frisbie, C., ed.
1980 *Southwest Indian Ritual Drama.* Albuquerque: University of New Mexico Press.

Frost, H. K.
1912 "Two Abnaki Legends." *Journal of American Folklore* 25: 188–190.

Gatschet, A. S.
1884 *A Migration Legend of the Creek Indians, with a Linguistic, Historic and Ethnographic Introduction.* Library of Aboriginal American Literature 4. Philadelphia: D. G. Brinton.
1888 "Tchikilli's Kasi'hta Legend in the Creek and Hitchiti Languages." Academy of Science of St. Louis. *Transactions* 5: 33–239.
1890 *The Klamath Indians of Southwestern Oregon.* Smithsonian Institution. *Contributions to North American Ethnology* 2.
1891a "Modoc Tales." *Journal of American Folklore* 4: 139–141.
1891b "A Mythic Tale of the Isleta Indians, New Mexico." *Proceedings of the American Philosophical Society* 29: 208–217.
1891c "Oregonian Folk-Lore." *Journal of American Folklore* 4: 139–143.
1895 "Some Mythic Tales of the Yuchi Indians." *American Anthropologist* (Old Series) 6: 279.
1897 "Mythologic Text in the Klamath Language of Southern Oregon." *American Antiquarian* 1: 161–166.

Gayton, A. H.
1935a "The Orpheus Myth in North America." *Journal of American Folklore* 48: 263–291.
1935b "A Real Affiliation of California Folktales." *American Anthropologist* 37: 582–599.

Gayton, A. H., and S. S. Newman
1940 "Yokuts and Western Mono Myths." University of California. *Anthropological Records* 5(1): 1–109.

Geertz, A. W.
1987 "Hopi Coyote: Trickster, Corpse, or God?" *History of Religions* 27: 89–92.

Geertz, A. W., and M. Lomatuway'ma
1987 *Children of the Cottonwood: Piety and Ceremonialism in Hopi Indian Puppetry.* American Traditional Religions 12. Lincoln: University of Nebraska Press.

George, W., et al.
1979 *Origin of the Pine Nuts and Other Stories from the Walker River Paiute Reservation. Adapted from an original story as told by W. George and retold by H. Cook.* Schurz, NV: Walker River Paiute Tribe.

Getchell, A.
1924 *Bibliography of Oregon Indian Myths.* Salem, OR.

Gibbs, J. F.
1929 "Moshoquop the Avenger as Loyal Friend." *Utah Historical Quarterly* 2(1): 3–8.

Giddings, R. W.
1959 "Yaqui Myths and Legends." *Anthropological Papers of the University of Arizona* 2. Tucson: University of Arizona Press.

Gifford, E. W.
1917 *Miwok Myths.* University of California. *Publications in American Archaeology and Ethnology* 12.
1923 "Western Mono Myths." *Journal of American Folklore* 36: 301–367.
1932 "The Southeastern Yavapai." University of California. *Publications in American Archaeology and Ethnology* 29(8): 177–252.
1933 "Northeastern and Western Yavapai Myths." *Journal of American Folklore* 46: 347–415.
1937 "Coast Yuki Myths." *Journal of American Folklore* 50: 115–173.

Gill, S. D.
1977 "Hopi Kachina Cult Initiation: The Shocking Beginning to the Hopi's Religious Life." *Journal of the American Academy of Religion,* 45(2) supplement A: 447–464.
1979a *Songs of Life: An Introduction to Navajo Religious Culture.* Leiden: E. J. Brill.
1979b "Whirling Logs and Colored Sands." In *Native Religious Traditions,* edited by E. Waugh and R. Prithipaul, 151–163. Waterloo, Ontario: Wilfrid Laurier University Press for Canadian Corporation for Studies in Religion.
1983a *Native American Traditions: Sources and Interpretations.* Belmont, CA: Wadsworth.
1983b "Navajo Views of Their Origin." In *Handbook of North American Indians. Vol. 9: Southwest,* edited by A. Ortiz, 502–505. Washington: Smithsonian Institution Press.
1987a "Native American Mythology: North America." In *The Encyclopedia of Religion,* 157–166. New York: Macmillan.
1987b *Native American Religious Action: A Performance Approach to Religion.* Columbia: University of South Carolina Press.

Gilliland, H.
1972 *The Flood.* 2d ed. Billings: Montana Council for Indian Education.

Gilmore, M. R.
1926 "Arikara Genesis and Its Teachings." Museum of the American Indian, New York. *Indian Notes* 3: 188–193.
1929a "Arikara Account of the Origin of Tobacco and Catching Eagles." Museum of the American Indian, New York. *Indian Notes* 6: 26–32.
1929b "The Arikara Book of Genesis." Michigan Academy of Science, Arts and Letters. *Papers* 12: 95–120.

1929c *Prairie Smoke: A Collection of Lore of the Prairies.* New York: Columbia University Press.

Goddard, P. E.
1904 *Hupa Texts.* University of California. *Publications in American Archaeology and Ethnology* 10.
1906 "Lassik Tales." *Journal of American Folklore* 19 133–140.
1907 "Navaho Myths, Prayers and Songs, with Texts and Translations, by W. Matthews." University of California. *Publications in American Archaeology and Ethnology* 5(2): 21–63.
1909 *Kato Texts.* University of California. *Publications in American Archaeology and Ethnology* 5.
1911 *Jicarilla Apache Texts.* American Museum of Natural History, New York. *Anthropological Papers* 8.
1912 *Chipewyan Texts.* American Museum of Natural History, New York. *Anthropological Papers* 10.
1914 *Chilula Texts.* University of California. *Publications in American Archaeology and Ethnology* 10.
1915 *Sarsi Texts.* University of California. *Publications in American Archaeology and Ethnology* 11.
1916 *The Beaver Indians.* American Museum of Natural History, New York. *Anthropological Papers* 10.
1919 "San Carlos Apache Texts." American Museum of Natural History, New York. *Anthropological Papers* 24: 141–367.
1920a *Myths and Tales from the White Mountain Apache.* American Museum of Natural History, New York. *Anthropological Papers* 24.
1920b *Myths and Tales of the San Carlos Apache.* American Museum of Natural History, New York. *Anthropological Papers* 24.
1933 "Navajo Texts." American Museum of Natural History, New York. *Anthropological Papers* 34.

Gogol, J. M.
1979 "Klickitat Indian Legend: Origin of Basket Weaving." *American Indian Basketry Magazine* 1(1): 31–34.

Golder, F. A.
1903 "Tales from Kodiak Island." *Journal of American Folklore* 16: 16–31, 85–103.
1905 "Aleutian Stories." *Journal of American Folklore* 18: 215–222.
1907a "A Kodiak Island Story." *Journal of American Folklore* 20: 296–299.

1907b "Songs and Stories of the Aleuts, with Transcriptions from Veniaminov." *Journal of American Folklore* 20: 132–142.
1907c "Tlingit Myths." *Journal of American Folklore* 20: 290–295.
1909 "Eskimo and Aleut Stories from Alaska." *Journal of American Folklore* 22: 10–24.

Goldfrank, E. S.
1948 "The Impact of Situation and Personality on Four Hopi Emergence Myths." *Southwestern Journal of Anthropology* 4: 241–262.

Goldman, I.
1975 *The Mouth of Heaven: An Introduction to Kwakiutl Religious Thought.* New York: Wiley.

Goldschmidt, W., G. Foster, and F. Essene
1939 "War Stories from Two Enemy Tribes." *Journal of American Folklore* 52: 141–154.

Golla, V., and S. Silver, eds.
1977 *Northern California Texts.* Chicago: University of Chicago Press.

Goodwin, G.
1939 *Myths and Tales of the White Mountain Apache.* American Folklore Society. *Memoirs* 33.
1945 "A Comparison of Navaho and White Mountain Apache Ceremonial Forms and Categories." *Southwestern Journal of Anthropology* 1: 498–506.

Gordon, G. B.
1918 "Legends of the Kit-selas." *Museum Journal* 9: 39–49.

Gordon, H. L.
1881 *Legends of the Northwest.* St. Paul, MN: St. Paul Book and Stationery.

Gould, M. K.
1917a *Okanagon Tales.* American Folklore Society. *Memoirs* 11.
1917b *Sanpoil Tales.* American Folklore Society. *Memoirs* 11.
1921 "Two Legends of the Mojave-Apache, Told by Captain Jim of That Tribe." *Journal of American Folklore* 34: 319–320.

Graber, R. B.
1983 "The 'Rolling Head' Revisited: Towards a Psychocultural Materialism." *Journal of Psychoanalytic Anthropology* 6(3): 331–337.

Grant, R. V.
1946 "The Koni Killah. A Kwakiutl Tale." *Journal of American Folklore* 59: 194–196.

Graves, C. S.
1929   *Lore and Legends of the Klamath River Indians.* Yreka, CA: Press of the Times.

Graves, M. D.
1935   *Manitou and the Animals: An Indian Legend.* Albany: L. L. Fuller.

Green, J.
1979   *Zuñi: Selected Writings of Frank H. Cushing.* Lincoln: University of Nebraska Press.

Green, R. D. R.
1978   "Culturally Based Science: The Potential for Traditional People, Science and Folklore." In *Folklore Studies in the Twentieth Century,* edited by V. J. Newall, 204–212. Woodbridge, England: Rowman and Littlefield, and Totowa, NJ: Brewer.

Greenlee, R. F.
1945   "Folk Tales of the Florida Seminole." *Journal of American Folklore* 58: 138–144.

Gridley, M. E.
1939   *Indian Legends of American Scenes.* Chicago: M. A. Donahue and Co.

Griffin, G. H.
1934   *Legends of the Evergreen Coast.* Vancouver, British Columbia: Clark & Stuart.

Griffith, J. S.
1972   "Pascola Masks." *The Kiva* 4: 185–198.

Grinnell, G. B.
1889   *Pawnee Hero Stories and Folk-tales.* New York: Forest & Stream.
1891   "The Young Dog's Dance." *Journal of American Folklore* 4: 307–313.
1892a   *Blackfoot Lodge Tales.* New York: Forest & Stream.
1892b   "Development of a Pawnee Myth." *Journal of American Folklore* 5: 127–134.
1893a   "A Blackfoot Sun and Moon Myth." *Journal of American Folklore* 6: 44–47.
1893b   "Pawnee Mythology." *Journal of American Folklore* 6: 113–130.
1894   "A Pawnee Star Myth." *Journal of American Folklore* 7: 197–200.
1903   "A Cheyenne Obstacle Myth." *Journal of American Folklore* 16: 108–115.
1907, 1908   "Some Early Cheyenne Tales." *Journal of American Folklore* 20: 169–194 (1907); 21: 269–320 (1908).
1910   "The Great Mysteries of the Cheyenne." *American Anthropologist* 12: 542–576.
1913   *Blackfoot Indian Stories.* New York: C. Scribner's Sons.

1921   "Falling-Star." *Journal of American Folklore* 34: 308–315.
1926   *By Cheyenne Campfires.* New Haven, CT: Yale University Press.
1962   *The Cheyenne Indians: Their History and Ways of Life.* New York: Cooper Square.

Gualtieri, A. R.
1984   *Christianity and Native Traditions: Indigenization and Syncretism among the Inuit and Dene of the Western Arctic.* Notre Dame, IN: Cross Cultural Publications.

Gunn, J.
1917   *Schat-chen: History, Traditions and Narratives of the Queres Indians of Laguna and Acoma.* Albuquerque, NM: Albright & Anderson.

Gunther, E.
1925   "Klallam Folk Tales." University of Washington. *Publications in Anthropology* 1: 113–169.

Haeberlin, H. K.
1924   "Mythology of Puget Sound." *Journal of American Folklore* 37: 371.
1985   "The Idea of Fertilization in the Culture of the Pueblo Indians." In *The Ethnographic American Southwest: A Source Book. Southwestern Society in Myth, Clan, and Kinship,* edited by R. I. Ford, 1–55. New York: Garland.

Hagar, S.
1895   "Micmac Customs and Traditions." *American Anthropologist* 8(1): 31–42.
1896   "Micmac Magic and Medicine." *Journal of American Folklore* 9: 170–177.
1897   "Weather and the Seasons in Micmac Mythology." *Journal of American Folklore* 10: 101–105.
1900   "The Celestial Bear." *Journal of American Folklore* 13: 92–103.
1906   "Cherokee Star Lore." *Boas Anniversary Volume,* 354. New York: G. E. Stechert.

Haile, B.
1933   "Navaho Games of Chance and Taboo." *Primitive Man* 6: 35–40.
1938a   *Origin Legend of the Navaho Enemy Way.* Yale University. *Publications in Anthropology* 17.
1938b   "Navaho Chantways and Ceremonials." *American Anthropologist* 40: 6–52.
1940   "A Note on the Navaho Visionary." *American Anthropologist* 42: 359.
1942   "Navaho Upward-Reaching Way and Emergence Place." *American Anthropologist* 44: 407–420.

1943a *Origin Legend of the Navaho Flintway.* University of Chicago. Publications in Anthropology, Linguistic Series.

1943b "Soul Concepts of the Navaho." *Annali Lateranensi* 7: 59–94..

1947a *Head and Face Masks of the Navaho.* St. Michaels, AZ: St. Michaels Press.

1947b *Navaho Sacrificial Figurines.* Chicago: University of Chicago Press.

1947c *Starlore among the Navaho.* Santa Fe, NM: Museum of Navajo Ceremonial Art.

1978 *Love-Magic and Butterfly People: The Slim Curly Version of the Ajilee and Mothway Myths,* edited by K. Luckert. Flagstaff: Museum of Northern Arizona Press.

1979 *Waterway: A Navajo Ceremonial Myth as Told by the Black Mustache Circle.* Flagstaff: Museum of Northern Arizona Press.

1981a *The Upward Moving and Emergence Way: The Gishin Brye Version.* Lincoln: University of Nebraska Press.

1981b *Women versus Men: A Conflict of Navajo Emergence.* Lincoln: University of Nebraska Press.

1984 *Navajo Coyote Tales: The Curly To Aheedliinii Version.* Lincoln: University of Nebraska Press.

Halbert, H. S.

1894 "A Choctaw Migration Legend." *American Antiquarian* 16: 215–216.

1985 "The Choctaw Robin Goodfellow." In *A Choctaw Source Book,* edited by J. H. Peterson, Jr., 215–216. New York: Garland.

Hale, H.

1888 "Huron Folklore." *Journal of American Folklore* 1: 177–183.

Hall, C. F.

1879 *Narrative of the Second Arctic Expedition.* Washington: Government Printing Office.

Hallowell, A. I.

1926 "Bear Ceremonialism in the Northern Hemisphere." *American Anthropologist* 28: 1–176.

1934 "Some Empirical Aspects of Northern Saulteaux Religion." *American Anthropologist* 36: 389–404.

1936 "The Passing of the Midewiwin in the Lake Winnipeg Region." *American Anthropologist* 38: 32–51.

1939 "Some European Folk Tales of the Berens River Saulteaux." *Journal of American Folklore* 52: 155–179.

1940 "Magic: The Role of Conjuring in Saulteaux Society." *Papers Presented Before the Monday Night Group, 1939–1940,* edited by M. A. May, 94–115. New Haven, CT.

1942 *The Role of Conjuring in Saulteaux Society.* Philadelphia Anthropological Society. *Publications* 2.

1946 "Concordance of Ojibwa Narratives in the Published Works of Henry R. Schoolcraft." *Journal of American Folklore* 59: 136–153.

1947 "Myth, Culture and Personality." *American Anthropologist* 49: 544–556.

1960 "Ojibwa Ontology, Behavior, and World View." In *Culture in History: Essays in Honor of Paul Radin,* edited by S. Diamond, 19–52. New York: Columbia University Press.

Hamilton, J. C.

1894 "Two Algonquin Legends. The Loon and the Ka-Kakè." *Journal of American Folklore* 7: 201–204.

1905 "Stellar Legends of the American Indians." Royal Astronomical Society of Canada. *Transactions* 47–50.

Handy, E. L.

1918 "Zuñi Tales." *Journal of American Folklore* 31: 451–471.

Harrington, J. P.

1908 "A Yuma Account of Origins." *Journal of American Folklore* 21: 324–348.

1932 *Karuk Indian Myths.* Smithsonian Institution. Bureau of American Ethnology. *Bulletin* 107.

Harrington, J. P., and H. H. Roberts

1928 "Picuris Children's Stories, with Text and Songs." Smithsonian Institution. Bureau of American Ethnology. *Annual Report* 43: 289–447.

Harrington, M. R.

1901 "An Abenaki 'Witch Story.'" *Journal of American Folklore* 14: 160.

1906 "Da-ra-sá-kwa: A Caughnawaga Legend." *Journal of American Folklore* 19: 127–129.

Harris, C.

1975 *Sky Man on the Totem Pole.* Toronto: McClelland and Stewart.

Harris, M.

1976 "Lévi-Strauss et la Palourde: Réponse à la Conférence Gildersleeve de 1972." *L'Homme* 16(2–3): 5–22.

Harrison, C.

1892 "Religion and Family among the Haidas." *Journal of the Anthropological Institute of Great Britain and Ireland* 21: 14–29.

Harrison, M., and J. Williams
1977 "How Everything Began and How We Learned To Live Right." *The Yavapai of Fort McDowell: An Outline of Their History and Culture,* edited by Sigrid Khera. Fountain Hills, AZ: Fort McDowell Mohave-Apache Indian Community.

Harrod, H. L.
1987 Renewing the World: Plains Indian Religion and Morality, 14. Tuscon: University of Arizona Press.

Harvey, B. III
1972 "An Overview of Pueblo Religion." In New Perspectives on the Pueblos, edited by A. Ortiz, 197–217. Albuquerque: University of New Mexico Press.

Hassrick, R. B.
1964 *The Sioux Life and Customs of a Warrior Society.* Norman: University of Oklahoma Press.

Hatcher, M. A.
1927 "Myths of the Tejas Indians." TFSP 6: 107–118.

Hauser, R. E.
1990 "The Berdache and the Illinois Indian Tribe during the Last Half of the Seventeenth Century." *Ethnohistory* 37: 45–64.

Hawkes, E. W.
1916 *The Labrador Eskimos.* Geological Survey of Canada. *Anthropology Series* 14.

Haywood, C.
1961 *A Bibliography of North-American Indian Folklore and Folksong.* Revised ed. New York: Dover.

Hearne, S.
1911 *A Journey from Prince of Wales' Fort in Hudson's Bay to the Northern Ocean.* Toronto: Champlain Society.

Hedrick, B. C., J.C. Kelley, and C. L. Riley, eds.
1974 *The Classic Southwest: Readings in Archaeology, Ethnohistory, and Ethnology.* Carbondale: Southern Illinois University Press.

Heizer, R. F.
1974 "Miscellany: Some Costanoan Songs, Place Names, Sample Sentences, the Lord's Prayer and Mythology." In *The Costanoan Indians,* 69–75. Cupertino: California History Center.
1978 "Mythology: Regional Patterns and History of Research." In *Handbook of North American Indians. Vol. 8: California,* 654–657. Washington: Smithsonian Institution Press.

Helbig, A. K., ed.
1987 *Nanabozhoo: Giver of Life.* Brighton, MI: Green Oak Press.

Helm, J., ed.
1981 *Handbook of North American Indians. Vol. 6: Subarctic.* Washington: Smithsonian Institution Press.

Henshaw, H. W.
1972 "The Luiseño Creation Myth." *Masterkey* 46: 93–100.

Herndon, M.
1980 "Fox, Owl and Raven." In *Traditional Music of North American Indians,* edited by C. Heth, 175–192. Los Angeles: University of California, Music Department.

Hertzberg, H. W.
1981 "The World on the Turtle's Back: An Iroquois Creation Myth." In *The Indian Peoples of Eastern America: A Documentary History of the Sexes,* edited by J. Axtell, 173–179. New York: Oxford University Press.

Herzog, K., et al.
1984 "Women, Religion, and Peace in an American Indian Ritual." *Explorations in Ethnic Studies* 7(1): 16–38.

Hewett, E. L.
1930 *Ancient Life in the American Southwest.* Indianapolis: Bobbs-Merrill.

Hewitt, J. N. B.
1892 "Legend of the Founding of the Iroquois League." *American Anthropologist* 5: 131–148.
1894 "Raising and Falling of the Sky in Iroquois Legends." *American Anthropologist* (Old Series) 5: 344.
1902 "Orenda and a Definition of Religion." *American Anthropologist* 4: 33–46.
1903 *Iroquoian Cosmology.* Smithsonian Institution. Bureau of American Ethnology. *Annual Report* 21.
1959 "Mythology." In *Handbook of American Indians North of Mexico,* edited by F. W. Hodge, 1: 964–972. New York: Pageant.
1987 "Notes on the Creek Indians." Edited by J. R. Swanton. In *A Creek Source Book,* edited by W. C. Sturtevant, 119–159. New York: Garland.

Hickerson, H.
1962 "Notes on the Post-contact Origin of the Midewiwin." *Ethnohistory* 9: 404–426.

1963 "The Sociohistorical Significance of Two Chippewa Ceremonials." *American Anthropologist* 65: 67–85.

Hieb, L. A.
1972 "Meaning and Mismeaning: Toward an Understanding of the Ritual Clown." In *New Perspectives on the Pueblos,* edited by A. Ortiz, 163–195. Albuquerque: University of New Mexico Press.

Hilbert, V.
1985 *Haboo: Native American Stories from Puget Sound.* Seattle: University of Washington Press.

Hilder, F. F.
1899 "A Texas Indian Myth." *American Anthropologist* 1: 592–594.

Hilger, M. I., Sr.
1951 *Chippewa Child Life and Its Cultural Background.* Smithsonian Institution. Bureau of American Ethnology. *Bulletin* 146.

Hill, G.
1976 "The Cherokee Storyteller: The Giant Inchworm." *Journal of Cherokee Studies* 1: 55–58.

Hill, K.
1963 *Glooscap and His Magic: Legends of the Wabanaki Indians.* London: Gollancz.
1978 *More Glooskap Stories: Legends of the Wabanaki Indians.* Toronto: McClelland and Stewart.

Hill, W. W.
1935a "The Hand Trembling Ceremony of the Navaho." *El Palacio* 38: 65–69.
1935b "The Status of the Hermaphrodite and Transvestite in Navaho Culture." *American Anthropologist* 37: 273–279.
1936 "Navaho Warfare." Yale University. *Publications in Anthropology* 5.
1938 "The Agricultural and Hunting Methods of the Navaho Indians." Yale University. *Publications in Anthropology* 18.

Hill, W. W., and D. W. Hill
1943a *Navaho Humor.* General Series in Anthropology (Menasha) 9.
1943b "The Legend of Navajo Eagle-Catching-Way." *New Mexico Anthropologist* 6–7: 31–36.
1943c "Two Navajo Myths." *New Mexico Anthropologist* 6–7: 111–114.
1945 "Navaho Coyote Tales and Their Position in the Southern Athabascan Group." *Journal of American Folklore* 58: 317–343.

Hill-Tout, C.
1897 "Notes on the Cosmogony and History of the Squamish Indians." Royal Society of Canada. *Proceedings and Transactions* series 2, 3: 85–90.
1898 "Haida Stories and Beliefs." In *Report of the 68th Meeting of the British Association for the Advancement of Science,* 700–708.
1907 *British North America. Vol. 1: The Far West, the Home of the Salish and the Dene.* London: Constable.
1921a "Report on the Ethnology of the Siciatl of British Columbia." *Journal of the Anthropological Institute of Great Britain and Ireland* 34.
1921b "Report on the StsEelis and Sk'aulits Tribes of the HalkomelEm Division of the Salish of British Columbia." *Journal of the Anthropological Institute of Great Britain and Ireland* 34.
1922 "Report on the Ethnology of the StlatlumH of British Columbia." *Journal of the Anthropological Institute of Great Britain and Ireland* 35.
1924 "Report on the Ethnology of the Southeastern Tribes of Vancouver Island, British Columbia." *Journal of the Anthropological Institute of Great Britain and Ireland* 37.

Hillyer, W. H.
1931 *The Box of Daylight.* New York: Knopf.

Hines, D. M.
1976 "The History and Traditional Lore of the Inland Pacific Northwest: Archival Materials." *Journal of the Folklore Institute* 13: 91–103.

Hinton, L. L., ed.
1984 "Havasupai Literature." In *Spirit Mountain,* edited by L. Hinton and L. J. Watahomigie, 99–162. Tucson: Sun Tracks and the University of Arizona Press.

Hodge, F. W.
1896 "Pueblo Snake Ceremonials." *American Anthropologist* 9: 133–136.
1937 "A Zuñi Folktale of the Maximilian Jay." *Masterkey* 2(3): 89.

Hoebel, A.
1978 *The Cheyennes.* Ft. Worth and Chicago: Holt, Rinehart and Winston.

Hoebel, E. A.
1941 "The Asiatic Origin of a Myth of the Northwest Coast." *Journal of American Folklore* 54: 1–9.

Hoffman, C.
1974 *Drum Dance; Legends, Ceremonies, Dances and Songs of the Eskimos.* Agincourt, Ontario: Gage.

Hoffman, W. J.
1880 "An Absaroka Myth." *Journal of the Anthropological Institute of Great Britain and Ireland* 10: 239–240.
1883 "Selish Myths." *Bulletin of the Essex Institute* 15: 24–40. Salem, MA.
1891 *The Midewinin or "Grand Medicine Society" of the Ojibwa.* Smithsonian Institution. Bureau of American Ethnology. *Annual Report* 7.
1892a "Mythology of the Menomini Indians." *American Anthropologist* (Old Series) 3: 243–258.
1892b "The Water Babies, an Arickaree Story." *American Antiquarian* 14: 167–169.
1896 *The Menomini Indians.* Smithsonian Institution. Bureau of American Ethnology. *Annual Report* 14.

Hoijer, H.
1938 *Chiricahua and Mescalero Apache Texts by Harry Hoijer, with Ethnological Notes by M. E. Opler.* University of Chicago Publications in Anthropology. Linguistics Series. Chicago: University of Chicago Press.

Holden, M. M.
1976 "Making All the Crooked Ways Straight: The Satirical Portrait of Whites in Coast Salish Folklore." *Journal of American Folklore* 89: 271–293.

Holm, B.
1977 "Traditional and Contemporary Kwakiutl Winter Dance." *Arctic Anthropology* 14(1): 5–24.

Holm, G.
1980 "Moon Myths in North America." In *The Alaska Seminar,* edited by Anna Birgitta Rooth, 108–125. Stockholm: Almqvist & Wiksell International.

Hooper, L.
1920 *The Cahuilla Indians.* University of California. *Publications in American Archaeology and Ethnology* 16.

Howard, J. H.
1984 *Oklahoma Seminole Medicines, Magic, and Religion.* Norman: University of Oklahoma Press.

Hubbard, P.
1980 "Trickster, Renewal and Survival." *American Indian Culture and Research Journal* 4(4): 113–124.

Hudson, C.
1976 *The Southeastern Indians.* Knoxville: University of Tennessee Press.

1984 *Elements of Southeastern Indian Religion.* Leiden: E. J. Brill.

Hudson, D. T.
1977 *The Eye of the Flute: Chumash Traditional History and Ritual as Told by Fernando Librado Kitsepawit to John P. Harrington.* Santa Barbara, CA: Santa Barbara Museum of Natural History.

Hudson, J. W.
1901 "An Indian Myth of the San Joaquin Basin." *Journal of American Folklore* 15: 104–106.

Hudson, T.
1978 "The Integration of Myth and Ritual in South-Central California: The 'Northern Complex.'" *Journal of California Anthropology* 5: 25–250.

Huges, J. D.
1977 "Havasupai Traditions." *Southwest Folklore* 1(2): 35–52.

Hultkrantz, A.
1957 *The North American Indian Orpheus Tradition.* Monograph Series 2. Stockholm: Ethnographic Museum of Sweden.
1972 "An Ideological Dichotomy: Myths and Folk Beliefs among the Shoshoni Indians of Wyoming." In *History of Religions* 11: 339–353.
1979 "Myths in Native North American Religions." In *Native Religious Traditions,* edited by E. H. Waugh and K. D. Prithipaul. Studies in Religion 8: 77–97. Waterloo, Ontario,: Wilfred Laurier University Press.
1981 *Belief and Worship in Native North America,* edited by C. Vecsey. Syracuse, NY: Syracuse University Press.
1983 "A Shoshone Storyteller." *Temenos* 19: 44–54.
1984 "The Myths of the Trickster and Cultural Hero." In *Anthropology as a Historical Science: Essays in Honour of Stephen Fuchs,* edited by M. Bhuriy and S. M. Michael, 113–26. Indore, India: San Prakashan Sanchar Kendra.

Hunt, G.
1906 "The Rival: A Kwakiutl Story." In *Boas Anniversary Volume,* 108–137. New York: G. E. Stechert.
1916 "Myths of the Nootka." Smithsonian Institution. Bureau of American Ethnology. *Annual Report* 31: 888–935.

Hymes, D. H.
1975 "Folklore's Nature and the Sun's Myth." *Journal of American Folklore* 88: 345–369.

1981 *"In Vain I Tried To Tell You": Essays in Native American Ethnopoetics.* Philadelphia: University of Pennsylvania Press.
1990 "Mythology." In *Handbook of North American Indians. Vol. 7: Northwest Coast.* Washington: Smithsonian Institution Press.

Ives, E. D., ed.
1964 "Malecite and Passamaquoddy Tales." *Northeast Folklore* 6: 16–18.

Jack, E.
1895 "Maliseet Legends." *Journal of American Folklore* 8: 193–208.

Jacobs, M.
1939 "Coos Narrative and Ethnologic Texts." University of Washington. *Publications in Anthropology* 8(1).
1940 "Coos Myth Texts." University of Washington. *Publications in Anthropology* 8(2).
1952 "Psychological Inferences from a Chinook Myth." *Journal of American Folklore* 65: 121–137.
1959 *The Content and Style of an Oral Literature.* Chicago: University of Chicago Press.
1960 *The People Are Coming Soon: Analyses of Clackamas Chinook Myths and Tales.* Seattle: University of Washington Press.

Jacobsen, J. A.
1905 "Types of Haida and Tlingit Myths." *American Anthropologist* 7: 94–104.

Jahner, E. A.
1983 "Finding the Way Home: The Interpretation of American Indian Folklore." In *Handbook of American Folklore,* edited by Richard M. Dorson, et al., 11–17. Bloomington: Indiana University Press.

James, G. W.
1902 "A Saboba Origin-Myth." *Journal of American Folklore* 15: 36–39.
1903 "The Legend of Tauquitch and Algoot." *Journal of American Folklore* 16: 153–159.

Jenks, A. E.
1902 "The Bear-Maiden." *Journal of American Folklore* 15: 33–35.

Jenness, D.
1924a "Eskimo Folklore." In *Report of the Canadian Arctic Expedition, 1913–1918.* Ottawa: F. A. Acland.
1924b "Myths and Traditions from Northern Alaska, the Mackenzie Delta and Coronation Gulf." In *Report of the Canadian Arctic Expedition, 1913–1918.* Ottawa: F. A. Acland.
1934 "Myths of the Carrier Indians of British Columbia." *Journal of American Folklore* 47: 97–269.
1935 *The Ojibwa Indians of Parry Island, Their Social and Religious Life.* Ottawa: Canada Department of Mines, Bulletin 78, Anthropological Series 17.

Jensen, A.
1980 "A Structural Approach to the Tsimshian Raven Myths: Levi-Strauss on the Beach." *Anthropologica* 22: 159–186.

Jewell, D. P.
1987 *Indians of the Feather River: Tales and Legends of the Concow Maidu of California.* Menlo Park, CA: Ballena Press.

Jewett, J. R.
1967 *Narrative of the Adventures and Sufferings of John R. Jewett.* Fairfield, WA: Ye Galleon Press.

Jimmie, R.
1974 "Choctaw Tales and Legends by Randy and Leonard Jimmie." *Nanih Waiya* 1(3): 6–11.

Jochelson, W.
1895 "The Mythology of the Koryak." *American Anthropologist* 6: 413–425.
1908 *The Koryak.* American Museum of Natural History. Publication of the Jesup North Pacific Expedition 6.

Johnson, B. H., and S. Cheechoo
1981 *Tales the Elders Told: Ojibway Legends.* Royal Ontario Museum.

Johnson, E. P. (Tekahionwake)
1911 *Legends of Vancouver.* Vancouver, British Columbia: Saturday Sunset Press.

Johnston, B.
1982a "A Man Named Weendigo." In *Windigo: An Anthology of Fact and Fantastic Fiction,* edited by J. R. Colombo, 201–203. Saskatoon, Saskatchewan: Western Producer Prairie Books.
1982b *Ojibway Ceremonies.* Toronto: McClelland and Stewart.

Jones, W.
1901 "Episodes in the Culture Hero Myth of the Sauks and Foxes." *Journal of American Folklore* 14: 225–239.
1907 *Fox Texts.* American Ethnological Society, New York. *Publications* 1.

1911 "Notes on the Fox Indians." *Journal of American Folklore* 24: 209–237.
1915 *Kickapoo Tales.* American Ethnological Society, New York. *Publications* 9.
1916 "Ojibwa Tales from the North Shore of Lake Superior." *Journal of American Folklore* 29: 368–391.

Jones, W., and T. Michelson
1919 *Ojibwa Texts.* 2 vols. American Ethnological Society, New York. *Publications* 7.

Jorgensen, J. G.
1972 *The Sun Dance Religion.* Chicago: University of Chicago Press.
1986 "Ghost Dance, Bear Dance, and Sun Dance." In *Handbook of North American Indians. Vol. 11: Great Basin.* Washington: Smithsonian Institution Press.

Jose, V.
1980 "I'toi and Ho'ok'oks." In *The South Corner of Time: Hopi Navajo, Papago, Yaqui Tribal Literature,* edited by L. Evers, et al., 110–121. Tucson: University of Arizona Press.

Josselin de Jong, J. P. B. de
1913 *Original Odzibwe-Texts, with English Translation, Notes and Vocabulary.* Leipzig, Berlin: B. G. Teubner.

Judkins, R. A.
1975 "Iroquois Images of Death." In *Actas del XLI Congreso Internacional de Americanistas* 3: 190–193. Cordoba, Mexico: Instituto Nacional de Anthropologia e Historia.

Judson, E. Z. C.
1858 *Thayendanegea, the Scourge, or the War-Eagle of the Mohawks.* New York: F. A. Brady.

Judson, K. B.
1910 *Myths and Legends of the Pacific Northwest.* Chicago: A. C. McClung.
1911 *Myths and Legends of Alaska.* Chicago: A. C. McClung.
1913 *Myths and Legends of the Great Plains.* Chicago: A. C. McClung.
1914 *Myths and Legends of the Mississippi Valley and the Great Lakes.* Chicago: A. C. McClung.
1917 *Myths and Legends of British North America.* Chicago: A. C. McClung.

Jung, C.
1972 "On the Psychology of the Trickster Figure." In *The Trickster,* edited by P. Radin. New York: Schocken Books.

Kan, S.
1983 "Words That Heal the Soul: Analysis of the Tlingit Potlatch Oratory." *Arctic Anthropology* 20(2): 47–59.
1989 *Symbolic Immortality: The Tlingit Potlatch of the Nineteenth Century.* Washington: Smithsonian Institution Press.

Keaveney, M. M.
1983 "Humor in Navajo Coyote Tales." In *Proceedings of Seminar/Conference on Oral Traditions,* edited by I. Crouch and G. Owen, 44–57. Las Cruces: New Mexico State University.

Kelly, I. T.
1939 "Northern Paiute Tales." *Journal of American Folklore* 51: 363–438.

Kelly, W. H.
1977 "Cocopa Ethnography." *Anthropology Papers of the University of Arizona.* Tucson.

Kendall, M. B.
1978 "Five Coyote Anecdotes (Yavpe)." In *Coyote Stories,* edited by W. Bright, 155–161. Chicago: University of Chicago Press.
1979 "Wolf and Coyote: An Upland Yuman Text." *Amerindia* 4: 127–147.

Kendall, M. B., and E. Sloane
1976 "Skara K?a mca: The Lofty Wanderer (Yavapai)." In *Yuman Texts,* edited by M. Langdon. *International Journal of American Linguistics* Native American Text Series 1(3): 68–83. Chicago: University of Chicago Press.

Kenyon, S. M.
1977 "Traditional Trends in Modern Nootka Ceremonies." *Arctic Anthropology* 14(1): 25–38.

Keppler, J.
1929 "Some Seneca Stories." Museum of the American Indian, New York. *Indian Notes* 6: 372–376.

Kercheval, G. T.
1893 "An Otoe and an Omaha Tale." *Journal of American Folklore* 6: 199–204.

Kerst, C. H.
1986 *Ethnic Folklife Dissertations from the U.S. and Canada 1960–1980: A Selected Annotated Bibliography.* Washington, DC: American Folklife Center, Library of Congress.

Keshena, E.
1911 "How the Hunter Punished the Snow." *Carlisle Arrow* 7(37): 4. Carlisle, PA.

Bibliography

Kidder, A. V.
1931, 1936 *Pottery of Pecos*. 2 vols. New Haven, CT: Yale University Press.

King, D. H., and L. H. King
1975 "The Mythico-religious Origin of the Cherokees. *Appalachian Journal* 2(4): 258–264.

King, J. C. H.
1979 *Portrait Masks from the Northwest Coast of America*. New York: Thames and Hudson.

Kinietz, V.
1939 "Birch Bark Records among the Chippewa." Indiana Academy of Science. *Proceedings* 49: 38–40.

Kinnaman, J. O.
1910 "Chippewa Legends." *American Antiquarian* 32: 96–102, 137–144.

Kissell, Mary L.
1916 *Basketry of the Papago and Pima*. American Museum of Natural History, New York. *Anthropological Papers* 17.

Klah, H.
1942 *Navajo Creation Myth*. Sante Fe, NM: Museum of Navajo Ceremonial Art.

Kleivan, I., and B. Sonne
1985 *Eskimos: Greenland and Canada*. Leiden: E. J. Brill.

Kluckhohn, C.
1942 "Myths and Rituals: A General Theory." *Harvard Theological Review* 35: 45–79.
1944 *Navajo Witchcraft*. Peabody Museum of American Archaeology and Ethnology, Harvard University. *Papers* 22.
1969 "Navaho Categories." In *Primitive Views of the World*, edited by S. Diamond, 95–128. New York: Columbia University Press.

Kluckhohn, C., and L. C. Wyman
1940 *An Introduction to Navaho Chant Practice*. American Anthropological Association. *Memoirs* 53.

Knight, J.
1913 "Ojibwa Tales from Sault Ste. Marie, Michigan." *Journal of American Folklore* 26: 91.

Knight, M. F.
1925 "Wampanoag Indian Tales." *Journal of American Folklore* 38: 134–137.

Knox, R. N.
1923 "Blackfoot Version of the Magic Flight." *Journal of American Folklore* 36: 401–403.

Kobrinsky, V. H.
1979 "The Mouths of Earth: The Dialectical Allegories of the Kwakiutl Indians." *Dialectical Anthropology* 4: 163–177.

Kohl, J. G.
1860 *Kitchi Gami: Wanderings Round Lake Superior,* transcribed by L. Wraxall. London: Chapman and Hall.

Köngäs, E. K.
1960 "The Earth-Diver (Th. A 812)." *Ethnohistory* 7: 151–180.

Kootenai Culture Committee for the Federated Salish and Kootenai Tribes
1984 *Kootenai Legends*. Elmo, MT: The Committee.

Krappe, A. H.
1946 "A Solomon Legend among the Indians of the North Pacific." *Journal of American Folklore* 59: 309–314.

Kroeber, A. L.
1899a "Animal Tales of the Eskimo." *Journal of American Folklore* 12: 17–23.
1899b "Tales of the Smith Sound Eskimo." *Journal of American Folklore* 12: 166–182.
1900 "Cheyenne Tales." *Journal of American Folklore* 13: 161–190.
1901 "Ute Tales." *Journal of American Folklore* 14 252–285.
1902 "Preliminary Sketch of the Mohave Indians." *American Anthropologist* 4: 276–285.
1905 "Wishosk Myths." *Journal of American Folklore* 18: 85–107.
1906 "Mission Indian (Luiseño) Myths." *Journal of American Folklore* 19: 309–321.
1907 *Indian Myths of South Central California*. University of California. *Publications in American Archaeology and Ethnology* 4(4).
1908a *Gros Ventre Myths and Tales*. American Museum of Natural History, New York. *Anthropological Papers* 1.
1908b "Catch-words in American Mythology." *Journal of American Folklore* 21: 222–227.
1919 "Sinkyone Tales." *Journal of American Folklore* 32: 346–351.
1923 "American Culture and the Northwest Coast." *American Anthropologist* 25: 1–20.
1925 *Handbook of the Indians of California*. Smithsonian Institution. Bureau of American Ethnology. *Bulletin* 78.

1932 "Yuki Myths." *Anthropos* 27: 905–940.
1935 *Walapai Ethnography.* American Anthropological Association. *Memoirs* 42.
1946 "A Karok Orpheus Myth." *Journal of American Folklore* 59: 13–19.
1948 "Seven Mohave Myths." University of California. *Anthropological Records* 11 (1): 1–70.
1951 "A Mohave Historical Epic." University of California. *Anthropological Records* 11(1): 71–176.
1972 "More Mohave Myths." University of California. *Anthropological Records* 27: 1–160.
1976 *Yurok Myths.* Berkeley: University of California Press.

Kroeber, A. L., and E. W. Gifford
1980 *Karok Myths.* Berkeley: University of California Press.

Kroeber, H. R.
1908 "Pima Tales." *American Anthropologist* 10: 231–236.
1909 "Papago Coyote Tales." *Journal of American Folklore* 22: 339–342.
1912 "Traditions of the Papago Indians." *Journal of American Folklore* 25: 95–105.

Kroeber, H. R., and H. Rothschild
1908 "Wappo Myths." *Journal of American Folklore* 21: 321–323.

Kroeber, K., ed.
1981 *Traditional American Indian Literatures: Texts and Interpretations.* Lincoln: University of Nebraska Press.

Kroul, M.
1974 "Definitional Domains of the Koyukon Athapaskan Potlatch." *Arctic Anthropology* 11, supplement.

Laidlaw, G. E.
1920 "Ojibwa Myths and Tales." *Ontario Provincial Museum, Annual Archaeological Report, 1920* 32: 66–85.

Laird, C.
1974 "The Buffalo in Chemehueir Folklore." *Journal of California Anthropology* 1: 220–224.
1975 "Two Chemehuevi Teaching Myths." *Journal of California Anthropology* 2: 18–24.
1976 *The Chemehuevis.* Banning, CA: Malki Museum Press.
1977 "Behavioral Patterns in Chemehuevi Myths." In *Flowers of the Wind,* edited by L. J. Bean and T. C. Blackburn. Anthropological Papers 8: 97–103. Socorro, NM: Ballena Press.

1978a "The Androgynous Nature of Coyote." *Journal of California Anthropology* 5(1): 67–72.
1978b "Origin of the Horse." *Journal of California Anthropology* 5(2): 251–255.
1984 *Mirror and Pattern: George Laird's World of Chemehuevi Mythology.* Banning, CA: Malki Museum Press.

Landes, R.
1968 *Ojibwa Religion and the Midewiwin.* Madison: University of Wisconsin Press.
1971 *The Ojibwa Woman.* New York: W. W. Norton.

Langdon, M., ed.
1976 *Yuman Texts.* Chicago: University of Chicago Press. *International Journal of American Linguistics* Native American Texts Series 1(3).

Lankford, G. E. III
1980 "Pleistocene Animals in Folk Memory." *Journal of American Folklore* 93: 293–304.
1983 The Unfulfilled Promise of North American Indian Folklore. In *Handbook of American Folklore,* edited by R. Dorson, et al., 18–23. Bloomington: Indiana University Press.

Lankford, G. E. III, ed.
1987 *Native American Legends: Southeastern Legends* Tales from the Natchez, Caddo, Biloxi, Chickasaw, and Other Nations. Little Rock, AR: August House.

Lantis, M.
1938a "The Alaskan Whale Cult and Its Affinities." American Anthropologist 40: 438–464.
1938b "The Mythology of Kodiak Island, Alaska." Journal of American Folklore 51: 123–172.
1947 *Alaskan Eskimo Ceremonialism.* American Ethnological Society, New York. *Monographs* 11.
1953 "Nunivak Eskimo Personality as Revealed in the Mythology." University of Alaska. *Anthropological Papers* 2: 109–174.

LaPena, F. R.
1982 "Legends of the Yosemite Miwok." *Four Winds* 2(4): 66–72.

LaPointe, J.
1976 *Legends of the Lakota.* San Francisco: Indian Historian Press.

Lasley, M.
1902 "Sak and Fox Tales." *Journal of American Folklore* 15: 170–178.

Lavrischeff, T. I.
1928 "Two Aleut Tales." *American Anthropologist* 30: 121–124.

Lawton, H. W.
1974 "Agricultural Motifs in Southern California Indian Mythology." *Journal of California Anthropology* 1: 55–79.

Lee, G.
1977 "Chumash Mythology in Paint and Stone." *Pacific Coast Archaeological Quarterly* 13(3): 1–14.

Lee, R.
1982 "Politics, Sexual and Non-sexual, in an Egalitarian Society." In *Politics and History in Band Societies.* New York: Cambridge University Press.

Leekley, T. B.
1965 *The World of Manabozho: Tales of the Chippewa Indians.* New York: Vanguard.

Leeson, B. W.
1933 "A Quatsino Legend." *Canadian Geographical Journal* 7(1): 23–39.

LeFlesche, F.
1912 "Wakondagi." *American Anthropologist* 14: 106–109.
1918 "Tribal Rites of Osage Indians." *Smithsonian Miscellaneous Collections* 68(pt. 12): 84–90.
1920 "Osage Tribal Rites." *Smithsonian Miscellaneous Collections* 72(pt. 1): 71–73
1925a "The Osage Tribe: Rite of the Chiefs. Sayings of the Ancient Men." Smithsonian Institution. Bureau of American Ethnology. *Annual Report* 36: 43–559.
1925b "The Osage Tribe: Rite of Vigil." Smithsonian Institution. Bureau of American Ethnology. *Annual Report* 39: 31–631.
1928 "The Osage Tribe: Two Versions of the Child-Naming Rite." Smithsonian Institution. Bureau of American Ethnology. *Annual Report* 43: 23–164.
1930 "The Osage Tribe: Rite of the Wa-xo-be." Smithsonian Institution. Bureau of American Ethnology. *Annual Report* 45: 523–833.

Leitner, L.
1941 *The Walum-Olum: A Legend of the Lenape Indians.* Brooklyn, NY.

LeJeune, P.
1634 "Relation of What Occurred in New France in the Year 1633." *Jesuit Relations* 5: 81. Paris.
1635 "Relation of What Occurred in New France in the Year 1634." *Jesuit Relations* 6: 97. Paris.

Leland, C. G.
1884 *The Algonquin Legends of New England; or, Myths and Folk Lore of the Micmac, Passamaquoddy, and Penobscot Tribes.* Boston: Houghton Mifflin.

Leland, C. G., and J. D. Prince
1902 *Kuloskap the Master, and Other Algonkin Poems.* New York: Funk and Wagnalls.

Lenhood, P.
1982 "Indian Shaker Religion." AIQ 6: 283–290.

Lerman, N.
1976 *Legends of the River People.* Vancouver, British Columbia: November House.

Lesser, A.
1928 "Bibliography of American Folklore, 1915–1928." *Journal of American Folklore* 41: 1–60.

Levi-Strauss, C.
1967 "Four Winnebago Myths: A Structural Sketch." In *Myth and Cosmos,* edited by J. Middleton, 15–26. Austin: University of Texas Press.
1976 "The Story of Asdiwal." In *The Structural Study of Myth and Totemism,* edited by E. Leach, 1–47. London: Tavistock.
1982 *The Way of the Masks.* Seattle: University of Washington Press.

Levine, G. S., ed.
1980 *Languages and Lore of the Long Island Indians.* Readings in Long Island Archaeology and Ethnohistory 4. Stony Brook, NY: Suffolk County Archaeological Association.

Linderman, F. B.
1915 *Indian Why Stories: Sparks from War Eagle's Lodge-Fire.* New York: C. Scribner's Sons.
1920 *Indian Old Man Stories.* New York: C. Scribner's Sons.
1926 *Kootenai Why Stories.* New York: C. Scribner's Sons.
1931 *Old Man Coyote.* New York: C. Scribner's Sons.
1932 *Red Mother.* New York: C. Scribner's Sons.

Lofthouse, J.
1913 "Chipewyan Stories." Royal Canadian Institute, Toronto. *Transactions* 10: 43–51.

Lopez, B. H.
1977 *Giving Birth to Thunder, Sleeping with His Daughter: Coyote Builds North America.* Kansas City, KS: Sheed Andrews and McMeel.; New York: Avon Books.

Lopez, F.
1980 "Frank Lopez and the Papago Origin Story." In *The South Corner of Time: Hopi, Navajo, Papago, Yaqui Tribal Literature,* edited by L. Evers et al., 128–149. Tucson: University of Arizona Press.

Lossiah, B.
1976 "The Cherokee Storyteller: The Trickster Turtle." *Journal of Cherokee Studies* 1: 110–112.

Lowie, R. H.
1908a "Catch-words for Mythological Motifs." *Journal of American Folklore* 21: 24–27.
1908b "The Test-Theme in North American Mythology." *Journal of American Folklore* 21: 97–148.
1909 *The Northern Shoshone: Part 2, Mythology.* American Museum of Natural History, New York. *Anthropological Papers* 2.
1910 *The Assiniboine.* American Museum of Natural History, New York. *Anthropological Papers* 4.
1912 *Chipewyan Tales.* American Museum of Natural History, New York. *Anthropological Papers* 10.
1918 *Myths and Traditions of the Crow Indians.* American Museum of Natural History, New York. *Anthropological Papers* 25.
1924 "Shoshonean Tales." *Journal of American Folklore* 37: 1–242.
1925a "A Crow Woman's Tale." In *American Indian Life,* edited by E. C. Parsons, 35–40. New York: B. W. Huebsch.
1925b "Windigo, a Chipewyan Story." In *American Indian Life,* edited by E. C. Parsons, 325–336. New York: B. W. Huebsch.
1930 "A Crow Text." University of California. *Publications in American Archaeology and Ethnology* 29: 155–175.
1939 "Hidatsa Texts." *Prehistory Research Series.* Indiana Historical Society 1: 173–239. Indianapolis.
1942 *Studies in Plains Indian Folklore.* University of California. *Publications in American Archaeology and Ethnology* 40(1). 1–28.
1956 *The Crow Indians.* New York: Reinhart.
1960 *Crow Texts.* Berkeley: University of California Press.
1963 *Indians of the Plains.* New York: American Museum Science Books.

Luckert, K. W.
1975 *The Navajo Hunter Tradition.* Tucson: University of Arizona Press.

1978 *A Navajo Bringing-Home Ceremony: The Claus Chee Sonny Version of Deerway Ajilee.* Flagstaff: Museum of Northern Arizona Press.
1979 *Coyoteway.* Tucson: University of Arizona Press.

Luomala, K.
1940 "Oceanic, American-Indian, and African Myths of Snaring the Sun." Bernice P. Bishop Museum Bulletin 168. Honolulu.
1977 "The Ear-Sleeper Motif in Navajo Mythology." *Journal of American Folklore* 90: 467–471.

Lyman, W. D.
1904 "Myths and Superstitions of the Oregon Indians." *American Antiquarian Society. Proceedings* 16: 221–251.
1915 "Indian Myths of the Northwest." American Antiquarian Society. *Proceedings* 25: 375–395.

McAllister, D. P.
1949 *Peyote Music.* Viking Fund Publications in Anthropology 13. New York.

McClintock, W.
1910 *The Old North Trail, or Life, Legends and Religion of the Blackfeet Indians.* London: Macmillan.
1933 "Blackfoot Legends: The Twin Brothers: The Story of Belly Fat." *Masterkey* 3: 41–46; 5: 70–73.

McDermott, L.
1901 "Folk-Lore of the Flathead Indians of Idaho." *Journal of American Folklore* 14: 240–251.

MacDonald, G. F.
1984 "Painted Houses and Woven Blankets; Symbols of Wealth in Tsimshian Art and Myth." In *The Tsimshian and Their Neighbors of the North Pacific Coast,* edited by J. Miller and C. M. Eastman, 109–136. Seattle: University of Washington Press.

McElwain, T.
1978 *Mythological Tales and the Allegany Seneca.* Stockholm Studies in Comparative Religion 17. Stockholm: Acta Universitatis Stockholmiensis.
1980 "Methods on Mask Morphology: Iroquoian False Faces in the Ethnographical Museum, Stockholm." *Temenos* 16: 68–83.

Macfarlan, A. A., and P. J. Macfarlan
1974 *Fireside Book of North American Indian Folktales.* Harrisburg, PA: Stackpole Books.

McIlwraith, T. F.
1948 *The Bella Coola Indians.* 2 vols. Toronto: University of Toronto Press.

Maclean, J.
1890 "Blackfoot Indian Legends." *Journal of American Folklore* 3: 296(196298.
1893 "Blackfoot Mythology." *Journal of American Folklore* 6: 165–172.

McLendon, S.
1982 "Meaning, Rhetorical Structure, and Discourse in Myth." In *Georgetown University Round Table on Languages and Linguistics,* edited by D. Tannen, 284–305. Washington: Georgetown University Press.

McLoughlin, W. G.
1976 "A Note on African Sources of American Indian Racial Myths." *Journal of American Folklore* 89: 331–335.
1990 "Ghost Dance Movements: Some Thoughts on Definition Based on Cherokee History." *Ethnohistory* 37: 25–44.

McNeary, S. A.
1984 "Image and Illusion in Tsimshian Mythology." In *The Tsimshian and Their Neighbors of the North Pacific Coast,* edited by J. Miller and C. M. Eastman, 3–15. Seattle: University of Washington Press.

McNeil, W. K.
1975 "Mary Henderson Eastman: Pioneer Collector of American Folklore." *Southern Folklore Quarterly* 39: 171–189.
1980 "Mary Alicia Owen: Collector of Afro-American and Indians Lore in Missouri." *Missouri Folklore Society Journal* 2: 1–14.

McNeley, J. K.
1981 *Holy Wind in Navajo Philosophy.* Tucson: University of Arizona Press.

McTaggart, F. E.
1976 *Wolf That I Am: In Search of the Red Earth People.* Boston: Houghton Mifflin.

McWhorter, L. V.
1983 *Hear Me, My Chiefs: Nez Perce History and Legend.* Caldwell, ID: Caxton Printers.

Major, M., and T. M. Pearce
1972 *Southwest Heritage: A Literary History with Bibliographies.* 3d ed. Albuquerque: University of New Mexico Press.

Makarius, L.
1970 "Ritual Clowns and Symbolical Behavior." *Diogenes* 69: 44–73.
1973 "The Crime of Manabozo." *American Anthropologist* 75: 663–665.

Mallery, G.
1890 "The Fight with the Giant Witch." *American Anthropologist* (Old Series) 3: 65–70.

Malotki, E.
1983 "The Story of the 'Tsimonamamant' or Jimson Weed Girls: A Hopi Narrative Featuring the Motif of the Vagina Dentata." In *Smoothing the Ground: Essays on Native American Oral Literature,* edited by B. Swann, 204–220. Berkeley: University of California Press.
1987a *Earth Fire: A Hopi Legend of the Sunset Crater Eruption.* Flagstaff, AZ: Northland Press.
1987b *Stories of Maasaw: A Hopi God.* Lincoln: University of Nebraska Press.

Malouf, C., and E. R. Smith
1947 "Some Gosiute Mythological Characters and Concepts." *Utah Humanities Review* 1(4): 369–377.

Manzo, J. T.
1982 "Native Americans, Euro-Americans: Some Shared Attitudes toward Life in the Prairies." *American Studies* 23(2): 39–48.

Marano, L.
1985 "Windigo Psychosis: The Anatomy of an Emic-Etic Confusion." *Current Anthropology* 23: 385–397.

Marriott, A. L.
1947 *Winter-Telling Stories.* New York: Crowell.

Marriott, A. L., and C. K. Rachlin
1972 *American Indian Mythology.* New York: New American Library.
1975 *Plains Indian Mythology.* New York: Crowell.

Martin, C.
1980 "Subarctic Indians and Wildlife." In *American Indian Environments,* edited by C. Vecsey and R. W. Venables, 38–45. Syracuse, NY: Syracuse University Press.

Martin, H. N.
1977 *Myths and Folktales of the Alabama-Coushatta Indians of Texas.* Austin, TX: Encino Press.

Martin, I.
1978 "The Cherokee Story-teller: The Deer's Blunt Teeth." *Journal of Cherokee Studies* 3: 45–48.

Mason, J. A.
1910 "Myths of the Uintah Utes." *Journal of American Folklore* 23: 299–363.
1912 *The Ethnology of the Salinan Indians.* University of California. *Publications in American Archaeology and Ethnology* 10(4).
1921 "The Papago Migration Legend." *Journal of American Folklore* 34: 254–268.

Mason, P. F., et al.
1976 *Indian Tales of the Northwest.* Vancouver, British Columbia: CommCept Publishing.

Matthews, W.
1877 *Ethnography and Philology of the Hidatsa Indians.* U.S. Geological and Geographical Survey. *Miscellaneous Publications* 7.
1883 "A Part of the Navajo's Mythology." *American Antiquarian* 5: 207–224.
1885a "Mythic Dry-Painting of the Navajos." *American Naturalist* 19(10): 931–939.
1885b "The Origin of the Utes: A Navajo Myth." *American Antiquarian* 7: 271–274.
1886 "Some Deities and Demons of the Navajos." *American Naturalist* 20: 841–850.
1887 *The Mountain Chant: A Navajo Ceremony.* Smithsonian Institution. Bureau of American Ethnology. *Annual Report* 5.
1889 "Naqoilpi, the Gambler: A Navajo Myth." *Journal of American Folklore* 2: 89–94.
1894a "Navajo Rite-Myths." *Journal of American Folklore* 7: 249–250.
1894b "Some Illustrations of the Connections between Myth and Ceremony." *Memoirs of the International Congress of Anthropology,* 246–251. Chicago.
1897 *Navaho Legends.* American Folklore Society. *Memoirs* 5.
1902a *The Night Chant, a Navaho Ceremony.* New York: Knickerbocker Press.
1902b "Myths of Gestation and Parturition." *American Anthropologist* 4: 734–743.
1907 *Navaho Myths, Prayers, and Songs.* University of California. *Publications in American Archaeology and Ethnology* 5(2).

Matthews, Z. P.
1976 "Huron Pipes and Iroquoian Shamanism." *Man in the Northeast* 12: 15–31.

Mayo, G. W.
1987 *Star Tales: North American Indian Stories about the Stars.* New York: Walker.

Means, F. C.
1960 "The Hopi Religion and Dry Farming." In *Sunlight on the Hopi Mesas,* 119–128. Philadelphia: Judson.

Mechling, W. H.
1913 "Maliseet Tales." *Journal of American Folklore* 26: 219–258.
1914 *Malecite Tales.* Geological Survey of Canada. *Anthropology Series* 49.

Medicine, B.
1983 "Warrior WomenSex Role Alternatives for Plains Indian Women." In *The Hidden Half: Studies of Plains Indian Women.* New York: University Press of America.

Meeker, L. L.
1901 "Siouan Mythological Tales." *Journal of American Folklore* 14: 161–164.
1902 "White Man: A Siouan Myth." *Journal of American Folklore* 15: 84–87.

Melody, M. E.
1977 "Maka's Story: A Study of Dakota Cosmogony." *Journal of American Folklore* 90 149–167.
1980 "Lakota Myth and Government: The Cosmos as the State." *American Indian Culture and Research Journal* 4(3): 1–19.

Melton, A.
1911 "The Legend of Black Snake." *Carlisle Arrow* 8(10): 1.

Merriam, C. H.
1930 "The Em'-tim'-bitch, a Shoshonean Tribe." *American Anthropologist* 32: 469–499.

Michelson, G.
1976 "The Legend of Teharahsahkwa." *Man in the Northeast* 12: 3–13.

Michelson, T.
1911a "Menominee Tales." *American Anthropologist* 13: 68–88.
1911b "Ojibwa Tales." *Journal of American Folklore* 24: 249–250.
1911c "Piegan Tales." *Journal of American Folklore* 24: 238–248.
1913 "Notes on the Folklore and Mythology of the Fox Indians." *American Anthropologist* 15:699–700.
1915 "Micmac Tales." *Journal of American Folklore* 28: 59–69.
1916 "A Piegan Tale." *Journal of American Folklore* 29: 408–409.
1917 "Notes on Peoria Folk-Lore and Mythology." *Journal of American Folklore* 30: 493–495.
1931 "Three Ottawa Tales." *Journal of American Folklore* 44: 191–196.
1933 "Narrative of an Arapaho Woman." *American Anthropologist* 35: 595–610.

1938 "What Happened to the Green Bear Who Was Blessed with a Sacred Pack." Smithsonian Institution. Bureau of American Ethnology. *Bulletin* 119: 161–176.

Milford, S. J.
1941 "Why the Coyote Has a Black Spot on His Tail." *El Palacio* 48(4): 83–84.

Millman, L.
1987 *A Kayak Full of Ghosts: Eskimo Tales.* Santa Barbara, CA: Capra.

Mindeleff, C.
1900 *Localization of Tusayan Clans.* Smithsonian Institution. Bureau of American Ethnology. *Annual Report* 19(pt. 2).

Mindeleff, V.
1891 *A Study of Pueblo Architecture: Tusayan and Cibola.* Smithsonian Institution. Bureau of American Ethnology. *Annual Report* 8.

Mishler, C. W.
1984 "Telling about Bear: A Northern Athapaskan Men's Riddle Tradition." *Journal of American Folklore* 97: 61–68.
1990 "Missionaries in Collision: Anglicans and Oblates among the Gwich-in, 1861–5." *Arctic,* 43(2): 121–126.

Mitchell, C.
1979 "Ceremony as Ritual." AIQ 5: 27–35.

Mitchell, F.
1978 *Navajo Blessingway Singer: The Autobiography of Frank Mitchell, 1881–1967,* edited by C. J. Frisbie and D. P. McAllester. Tucson: University of Arizona Press.

Mooney, J.
1888 "Myths of the Cherokees." *Journal of American Folklore* 1: 97–108.
1889 "Cherokee and Iroquois Parallels." *Journal of American Folklore* 2: 67.
1891 "The Sacred Formulas of the Cherokees." Smithsonian Institution. Bureau of American Ethnology. *Annual Report* 7.
1896 "The Ghost Dance Religion and the Sioux Outbreak of 1890." Smithsonian Institution. Bureau of American Ethnology. *Annual Report* 14(2).
1898a *The Calendar History of the Kiowa Indians.* Smithsonian Institution. Bureau of American Ethnology. *Annual Report* 17.
1898b "The Jicarilla Genesis." *American Anthropologist* (Old Series) 11: 197–209.
1900 *Myths of the Cherokee.* Smithsonian Institution. Bureau of American Ethnology. *Annual Report* 19.

1982 "Cherokee Plant Lore." *Journal of Cherokee Studies* 7: 37.

Moore, J. H.
1975 "Asdiwal, Boas, and Henry Tate: A Note on Structuralist Methodology." *Anthropos* 70: 926–930.
1987 *The Cheyenne Nation: A Social and Demographic History.* Lincoln: University of Nebraska Press.

Moore, P., and A. Wheelcock, eds.
1990 *Wolverine Myths and Visions: Dene Tradition from Northern Alberta.* Lincoln: University of Nebraska Press.

Moquin, W., and C. Van Doren, eds.
1973 *Great Documents in American Indian History.* New York: Praeger.

Morgan, W.
1936 *Human-Wolves among the Navajo.* Publications in Anthropology 11. New Haven, CT: Yale University Press.
1945 "The Organization of a Story and Tale." *Journal of American Folklore* 58: 169–194.

Morice, A. G.
1892 "Are the Carrier Sociology and Mythology Indigenous or Exotic?" Royal Society of Canada. *Proceedings and Transactions* series 1, 10(pt. 2): 109–126.
1895 "Three Carrier Myths." Royal Canadian Institute, Toronto. *Transactions* 5: 1.

Morrow, R.
1984 "It Is Time for Drumming: A Summary of Recent Research on Yup'ik Ceremonialism." *Etudes/Inuit/Studies* 8: 113–140.

Morris, C. P.
1976 "Bears, Juniper Trees, and Deer: The Metaphors of Domestic Life. An Analysis of a Yavapai Variant of the Bear Maiden Story." *Journal of Anthropological Research* 32: 246–254.
1986 "'Monster Slayer' among the Upland Yumans: A Folk Theory on the Evolution of Hunting Cultures." *American Indian Quarterly* 10: 199–211.

Morrison, K. M.
1979 "Towards a History of Intimate Encounters: Algonkian Folklore, Jesuit Missionaries, and Kiwake, the Cannibal Giant." *American Indian Culture and Research Journal* 3(4): 51–80.
1984 *The Embattled Northeast: The Elusive Ideal of Alliance in Abenaki-Euramerican Relations.* Berkeley: University of California Press.

Morrisseau, N.
1965 *Legends of My People, the Great Ojibway.* Edited by S. Dewdney. Toronto: Ryerson.
1982 "The Death of Windigo." In *Windigo: An Anthology of Fact and Fantastic Fiction,* edited by J. R. Colombo, 204–205. Saskatoon, Saskatchewan: Western Producer Prairie Books.

Mourning Dove
1933 *Coyote Stories.* Caldwell, ID: Caxton, Printers.

Murdoch, J.
1886 "A Few Legendary Fragments from the Point Barrow Eskimos." *American Naturalist* 19: 594.
1887 *Ethnological Results of the Point Barrow Expedition.* Smithsonian Institution. Bureau of American Ethnology. *Annual Report* 9(1).

Murie, J. R.
1989 *Ceremonies of the Pawnee.* Lincoln: University of Nebraska Press.

Nabokov, P.
1967 *Two-Leggings: The Making of a Crow Warrior.* New York: Crowell.

Neff, M. L.
1912 "Pima and Papago Legends." *Journal of American Folklore* 25: 51–65.

Neihardt, J. G.
1932 *Black Elk Speaks.* New York: William Morrow.

Nelson, E. W.
1899 *The Eskimo about Bering Strait.* Smithsonian Institution. Bureau of American Ethnology. *Annual Report* 18.

Nelson, R. K.
1974 "Relationships between Eskimo and Athapaskan Cultures in Alaska: An Ethnographic Perspective." *Arctic Anthropology* 11 (supplement): 48–53.
1980 *Shadow of the Hunter: Stories of Eskimo Life.* Chicago: University of Chicago Press.

Nequatewa, E.
1936 *Truth of a Hopi and the Clan Stories of Shungopovi.* Bulletin 8. Flagstaff: Museum of Northern Arizona.
1980 "Dr. Fewkes and Masauwu." In *The South Corner of Time: Hopi, Navajo, Papago, Yaqui Tribal Literature,* edited by Larry Evers et al., 36–37. Tucson: University of Arizona Press.

Nevins, J. B.
1982 "A Tale of the Windego." In *Windigo: An Anthology of Fact and Fantastic Fiction,* edited by J. R. Colombo, 22–25. Saskatoon, Saskatchewan: Western Producer Prairie Books.

Newcomb, F. J.
1940 "Origin Legend of the Navajo Eagle Chant." *Journal of American Folklore* 53: 50–77.
1964 *Hosteen Klah: Navaho Medicine Man and Sand Painter.* Norman: University of Oklahoma Press.

Newcomb, F. J., S. Fishler, and M. C. Wheelwright
1956 *A Study of Navajo Symbolism.* Peabody Museum of Archaeology and Ethnology, Harvard University. *Papers* 32(3).

Newcomb, F. J., and G. A. Reichard
1937 *Sandpaintings of the Navajo Shooting Chant.* New York: J. J. Augustin.

Newell, W. W.
1896 "Navaho Legends." *Journal of American Folklore* 9: 211–218.
1901 "Dakota Legend of the Head of Gold." *Journal of American Folklore* 14: 138–139.

Newton, N.
1973 *Fire in the Raven's Nest: The Haida of British Columbia.* Toronto: New Press.

Nichols, J. D., ed.
1983 *Nookomis Gaa-inaajimotawid = What My Grandmother Told Me.* St. Paul: Minnesota Archaeological Society.

Norman, H. A.
1976 *The Wishing Bone Cycle: Narrative Poems from the Swampy Cree Indians.* New York: Stonehill.
1982 *Where the Chill Came From: Cree Windigo Tales and Journeys.* San Francisco: North Point Press.
1990 *Northern Tales: Traditional Stories of Eskimo and Indian Peoples.* New York: Pantheon.

Nowlan, A.
1983 *Nine Micmac Legends.* Hantsport, Nova Scotia: Lancelot Press.

Nungak, Z., and E. Arima
1988 *Inuit Stories.* Ottawa: National Museums of Canada.

Nusbaum, M. A. B.
1923 "Origin Myth from Zuñi." *Journal of American Folklore* 36: 135–162.

1925 "Another Tower of Babel." *El Palacio* 18(1): 9–12.
1926 *The Seven Cities of Cibola.* New York: G. P. Putnam's Sons.
1930 "Zuñi Tales." *Journal of American Folklore* 43: 1–59.

O'Bryan, A.
1956 *The Dine: Origin Myths of the Navaho Indians.* Smithsonian Institution. Bureau of American Ethnology. *Bulletin* 163.

Olden, S. E.
1923 *Shoshone Folk Lore, As Discovered from the Rev. John Roberts, a Hidden Hero, on the Wind River Indian Reservation in Wyoming.* Milwaukee, WI: Morehouse.

Oman, L. K.
1975 *Eskimo Legends.* Anchorage: Alaska Methodist University Press.

Omidsalar, M.
1983 "Oedipus in Kansas: A Version of Aarne-Thompson 569 (Grimm No. 54) among the Potawatomi Indians." *American Imago* 40(2): 159–174.

O'Neill, P.
1976 *Legends of a Lost Tribe: Folk Tales of the Beothuck Indians of Newfoundland.* Toronto: McClelland and Stewart.

Oosten, J. G.
1983 "The Incest of Sun and Moon: An Examination of the Symbolism of Time and Space in Two Iglulik Myths." *Etudes/Inuit/Studies* 7(1): 143–151.

Opler, M. E.
1936 "A Summary of Jicarilla Apache Culture." *American Anthropologist* 38: 202–223.
1938a *Dirty Boy: A Jicarilla Tale of Raid and War.* American Folklore Society. *Memoirs* 52.
1938b *Myths and Tales of the Jicarilla Apache.* American Folklore Society. *Memoirs* 31.
1940 *Myths and Legends of the Lipan Apache Indians.* American Folklore Society. *Memoirs* 36.
1941 *An Apache Life-Way.* Chicago: University of Chicago Press.
1942 *Myths and Legends of the Chiricahua Apache Indians. With Comparative Notes by David French.* American Folklore Society. *Memoirs* 37.
1943 "The Origins of Comanche and Ute." *American Anthropologist* 45: 155–158.
1947 "Mythology and Folk Belief in the Maintenance of Jicarilla Apache Tribal Endogamy." *Journal of American Folklore* 60: 126–129.

1985 "The Creative Role of Shamanism in Mescalero Apache Mythology." In *The Ethnographic American Southwest: A Source Book. Southwestern Society in Myth, Clan, and Kinship,* edited by R. I. Ford, 268–281. New York: Garland.

Ortiz, A.
1969 *The Tewa World: Space, Time, Being, and Becoming in a Pueblo Society.* Chicago: University of Chicago Press.
1972 "Ritual Drama and the Pueblo World View." *New Perspectives on the Pueblos,* edited by A. Ortiz, 135–161. Albuquerque: University of New Mexico Press.

Oswalt, W. H.
1964 "Traditional Story Knife Tales of Yuk Girls." *Proceedings of the American Philosophical Society* 108(4).

Overholt, T., and J. B. Callicott
1982 *Clothed-in-Fur, and Other Tales: An Introduction to an Ojibwa World View.* Washington: University Press of America.

Owl, K. F.
1981 "Cherokee Heritage and Folklore." In *The Cherokee Perspective,* edited by L. French and J. Hornbuckle, 117–122. Boone, NC: Appalachian Consortium Press.

Packard, R. L.
1891 "Notes on the Mythology and Religion of the Nez Percés." *Journal of American Folklore* 4: 327–330.

Painter, M. T.
1986 *With Good Heart: Yaqui Beliefs and Ceremonies in Pascua Village.* Tucson: University of Arizona Press.

Palmer, V. W.
1925 *Honne, the Spirit of the Chehalis: The Indian Interpretation of the Origin of the People and Animals.* Geneva, NY: W. F. Humphrey.

Palmer, W. R.
1946 *Pahute Indian Legends.* Salt Lake City: Deseret.

Pandey, T. N.
n.d. "Some Reflections on Zuñi Religion." In *The Religious Character of Native American Humanities,* edited by S. Gill, 184–207. Tempe, AZ: Department of Humanities and Religious Studies.

Parker, A. C.
1910 "Iroquois Sun Myths." *Journal of American Folklore* 23: 473–479.
1912 "Certain Iroquois Tree Myths and Symbols." *American Anthropologist* 14: 608–620.
1924 *Seneca Myths and Folk-tales.* Buffalo Historical Society. *Publications* 27.

Parker, S.
1962 "Motives in Eskimo and Ojibwa Mythology." *Ethnology* 1: 516–523.

Parkhill, T.
1992 "'Of Kluskap's Birth, and of His Brother Malsum, the Wolf': The Story of Charles Godfrey Leland's 'Purely American Creation.'" *American Indian Culture and Research Journal* 16(1): 45–69.

Parkman, F.
1963 *The Jesuits of North America in the Seventeenth Century.* Boston: Little, Brown.
1982 "Legendary Lore." In *Windigo: An Anthology of Fact and Fantastic Fiction,* edited by J. R. Columbo, 26. Saskatoon, Saskatchewan: Western Producer Prairie Books.

Parks, D. R., ed.
1977 *Caddoan Texts.* Chicago: University of Chicago Press.
1984 *Arikara Coyote Tales: A Bilingual Reader = Naa'iikawis Sahnis.* Roseglen, ND: White Shield School District #89.

Parmentier, R. J.
1979 "The Mythological Triangle: Poseyemu, Montezuma, and Jesus in the Pueblos." In *Handbook of North American Indians. Vol. 9: Southwest,* edited by A. Ortiz, 609–622. Washington: Smithsonian Institution Press.

Parsons, E. C.
1916 "The Zuñi Mo'lawia." *Journal of American Folklore* 29: 392–399.
1917a "All Souls Day at Zuñi, Acoma, and Laguna." *Journal of American Folklore* 30: 495–496.
1917b "Notes on Zuñi." American Anthropological Association. *Memoirs* 4: 149–327.
1918a "Acoma Tales." *Journal of American Folklore* 31: 216–255.
1918b "The Antelope Clan in Keresan Custom and Myth." *Man.* 17: 190–193.
1918c "Nativity Myth at Laguna and Zuñi." *Journal of American Folklore* 31: 256–263.
1918d "Pueblo-Indian Folk-Tales, Probably of Spanish Provenience." *Journal of American Folklore* 31: 216–255.

1919 "Folklore of the Cherokee." *Journal of American Folklore* 32: 384–393.
1920 "Notes on Ceremonialism, Laguna." American Museum of Natural History, New York. *Anthropological Papers* 19(4): 97ff.
1921–1922 "A Narrative of the Ten'a of Anvik, Alaska." *Anthropos* 17: 51–71.
1923a "The Hopi Wowochim Ceremony in 1920." *American Anthropologist* 25: 156–187.
1923b "Navaho Folk-Tales." *Journal of American Folklore* 36: 368–375.
1923c "Origin Myth from Oraibi." *Journal of American Folklore* 36: 163–170.
1923d "Origin Myth of Zuñi." *Journal of American Folklore* 36: 135–162.
1925a "Micmac Folklore." *Journal of American Folklore* 38: 55–133.
1925b *A Pueblo Indian Journal 1920–21.* American Anthropological Association. *Memoirs* 32: 1–123.
1928 *Tewa Tales.* American Folklore Society. *Memoirs* 19.
1929a *Kiowa Tales.* American Folklore Society. *Memoirs* 22.
1929b "On the Travels of Folk Tales, and One Tale from the State of Puebla." *Mexican Folkways* 5: 71–77.
1930a *Pueblo Indian Religion.* Chicago.
1930b "Zuñi Tales." *Journal of American Folklore* 43: 1–58.
1931 "Laguna Tales." *Journal of American Folklore* 44: 137–143.
1933 "Hopi and Zuñi Ceremonialism." American Anthropological Association. *Memoirs* 39: 1–108.
1940 *Taos Tales.* American Folklore Society. *Memoirs* 34.
1974 "Tsaidetali." *Indian America* 8(7): 33–34.
1985 "Ceremonial Organization." In *The Ethnographic American Southwest: A Source Book. Southwestern Society in Myth, Clan, and Kinship,* edited by R. I. Ford, 108–167. New York: Garland.

Parsons, E. C., and R. L. Beals
1934 "The Sacred Clowns of the Pueblo and Mayo-Yaqui Indians." *American Anthropologist* 36: 491–514.

Parsons, E. C., and F. Boas
1920 "Spanish Tales from Luguna and Zuñi, N. Mex." *Journal of American Folklore* 33: 47–72.

Peet, S. D.
1909 "Mythology of the Menominees." *American Antiquarian* 31: 1–14.

Pepper, G. H.
1908 "Ah-jih-lee-hah-neh: A Navajo Legend." *Journal of American Folklore* 21: 178–183.

Peri, D. W., et al.
1982 *Ethnobotanical Mitigation, Warm Springs Dam–Lake Sonoma, California.* San Francisco: U.S. Army Corps of Engineers.

Perrot, N.
1981 "The First Ottawas (c. 1720)." In *The Indian Peoples of Eastern America,* edited by J. Axtell, 179–181. New York: Oxford University Press.

Peterson, J. H., Jr., ed.
1985 *A Choctaw Source Book.* New York: Garland.

Peterson, P.
1980 "Ethnological and Social Background as Reflected in the Myths." In *The Alaska Seminar,* edited by Anna Birgitta Rooth. Acta Universitatis Upsaliensis, Studia Ethnologica Upsaliensia 6: 192–221. Stockholm: Distribution Almqvist & Wiksell.

Pettitt, G. A.
1946 *Primitive Education in North America.* University of California. *Publications in American Archaeology and Ethnology* 43(1).

Phinney, A.
1969 *Nez Perce Texts.* New York: AMS Press.

Pitkin, H.
1977 "Coyote and Bullhead (Wintu)." In *Northern California Texts,* edited by V. Golla and S. Silver. *International Journal of American Linguistics.* Native American Texts Series 2(2): 82–104. Chicago: University of Chicago Press.

Pontiac
1973 "A Visit to the 'Master of Life': A Delaware Legend." In *Great Documents in American Indian History,* edited by W. Moquin and C. Van Doren, 27–30. New York: Praeger.

Potts, W. J.
1892 "Creation Myth of the California Indians." *Journal of American Folklore* 5: 73–74.

Powell, J. W.
1881 *Sketch of the Mythology of the North American Indians.* Smithsonian Institution. Bureau of American Ethnology. *Annual Report* 1.

Powell, P. J.
1969 *Sweet Medicine: The Continuing Role of the Sacred Arrows, the Sun Dance, and the Sacred Buffalo Hat in Northern Cheyenne History.* Norman: University of Oklahoma Press.

Powers, M. N.
1980 "Menstruation and Reproduction: An Oglala Case." *Signs* 6: 54–65.
1986 *Oglala Women: Myth, Ritual, and Reality.* Chicago: University of Chicago Press.

Powers, S.
1877 *Tribes of California.* Smithsonian Institution. *Contributions to North American Ethnology* 3.
1882 "North American Indian Legends and Fables of the California Indians." *Folk-lore Record* 5.

Powers, W. K.
1977 *Oglala Religion.* Lincoln: University of Nebraska Press.
1982 *Yuwipi, Vision and Experience in Oglala Ritual.* Lincoln: University of Nebraska Press.
1986 *Sacred Language: The Nature of Supernatural Discourse in Lakota.* Norman: University of Oklahoma Press.

Pradt, G. H.
1902 "Shakok and Miochin: Origin of Summer and Winter." *Journal of American Folklore* 15: 88–90.

Preston, R. J.
1975 *Cree Narrative: Expressing the Personal Meanings of Events.* Canada National Museum of Man. Paper (Canadian Ethnology Service) 30. Mercury Series. Ottawa: National Museums of Canada.
1980 "The Witiko: Algonkian Knowledge and Whitemen Knowledge." In *Manlike Monsters on Trial: Early Records and Modern Evidence,* edited by M. Halpin and M. Ames, 111–131. Vancouver: University of British Columbia Press.

Prince, J. D.
1899 "Some Passamaquoddy Witchcraft Tales." *Proceedings of the American Philosophical Society* 38: 181–189.
1902 "A Modern Delaware Tale." *Proceedings of the American Philosophical Society* 41: 20, 34.
1905 "A Tale in the Hudson River Indian Language." *American Anthropologist* 7: 74–84.
1921 *Passamaquoddy Texts.* American Ethnological Society, New York. *Publications* 10.

Quinn, W. W., Jr.
1983 "Something Old, Something True: A Hopi Example of the Need for Cosmology." *South Dakota Review* 21(2): 20–55.

Radin, P.
1909 "Winnebago Tales." *Journal of American Folklore* 22: 288–313.

1913 "Personal Reminiscences of a Winnebago Indian." *Journal of American Folklore* 26: 293–318.

1914 *Some Myths and Tales of the Ojibwa of Southeast Ontario.* Geological Survey of Canada. *Anthropology Series* 2. Ottawa.

1924 *Wappo Texts. First Series.* University of California. *Publications in American Archaeology and Ethnology* 19.

1926a "Literary Aspects of Winnebago Mythology." *Journal of American Folklore* 39: 18–52.

1926b "Winnebago Myth Cycles: Their Significance and Function. Part 1: The Trickster Cycle." *Primitive Culture* 1: 8–86.

1931 "The Thunderbird Warclub: A Winnebago Tale." *Journal of American Folklore* 44: 143–166.

1945 *The Road of Life and Death: A Ritual Drama of the American Indians.* Bollingen Series 5. New York: Pantheon Books.

1950 *Winnebago Culture as Described by Themselves: The Origin Myth of the Medicine Rite; Three Versions.* Baltimore: Waverly Press.

1972 *The Trickster: A Study in American Indian Mythology.* New York: Schocken Books.

1973 *Literary Aspects of North American Mythology.* Norwood, PA: Norwood Editions.

Radin, P., and A. B. Reagan
1928 "Ojibwa Myths and Tales." *Journal of American Folklore* 41: 61–146.

Rae, J.
1850 *Narrative of an Expedition to the Shores of the Arctic Sea in 1846 and 1847.* London: T. & W. Boone.

Ramsey, J.
1977 "The Bible in Western Indian Mythology." *Journal of American Folklore* 90: 442–454.

1978 "From 'Mythic' to 'Fictive' in a Nez Perce Orpheus Myth." *Western American Literature* 13: 119–132.

Ramsey, J., ed.
1977 *Coyote Was Going There: Indian Literature of the Oregon Country.* Seattle: University of Washington Press.

Rand, S. T.
1894 *Legends of the Micmacs.* Wellesley Philological Publications. New York: Longman's, Green.

Randle, M. C.
1952 "Psychological Types from Iroquois Folktales." *Journal of American Folklore* 65: 13–21.

Randolf, R.
1937 *Sweet Medicine and Other Stories of the Cheyenne Indians.* Caldwell, ID: Caxton Printers.

Ransom, J. E.
1947 "Stories, Myths and Superstitions of Fox Island Aleut Children." *Journal of American Folklore* 60: 62–72.

Rasmussen, K.
1921 *Eskimo Folk-tales.* Edited by W. Worster. London: Gyldendal.

1932 *The Eagle's Gift: Alaska Eskimo Tales.* New York: Doubleday, Doran.

Rau, V. E., and N. Olney, Jr.
1975 *Pushapmi Stories (Grandfather's Stories).* Toppenish, WA: Kamiakin Research Institute.

Ray, C., and J. Stevens
1984 *Sacred Legends of the Sandy Lake Cree.* Toronto: McClelland and Stewart.

Ray, V. F.
1933 "Sanpoil Folk Tales." *Journal of American Folklore* 46: 129–187.

Reagan, A. B.
1919 "The Flood Myth of the Chippewa." Indiana Academy of Science. *Proceedings* 347–352.

1921 "Flood Myths of the Bois Fort Chippewas." Kansas Academy of Science. *Transactions* 30: 437–443.

1935a *Sun God, Moccasin Tales.* Provo, UT: Graham Printing.

1935b "Some Myths of the Hoh and Quillayute Indians." Kansas Academy of Science. *Transactions* 38: 43–85.

Reagan, A. B., and L. V. M. Walters
1933 "Tales from the Hoh and Quileute." *Journal of American Folklore* 46: 297–346.

Reichard, G. A.
1921 "Literary Types and Dissemination of Myths." *Journal of American Folklore* 34: 269–307.

1930 "The Style of the Coeur d'Alene Mythology." *Proceedings of the 24th Session of the International Congress of Americanists,* 242–253.

1934 *Spider Woman: A Story of Navajo Weavers and Chanters.* New York: Macmillan.

1939 *Navajo Medicine Man.* New York: J. J. Augustin.

1943 "Good Characters in Myth: The Navaho Sun God." *Journal of American Folklore* 56: 141–143.
1944a *The Story of the Navajo Hail Chant.* New York: G. A. Reichard.
1944b "Individualism and Mythological Style." *Journal of American Folklore* 57: 16–25.
1947 *An Analysis of Coeur d'Alene Indian Myths.* American Folklore Society. *Memoirs* 41.
1974 *Navaho Religion: A Study of Symbolism.* Bollingen Series 18. Princeton, NJ: Princeton University Press.

Reid, A. P.
1873 "Religious Beliefs of the Ojibois or Saulteaux Indians." *Journal of the Royal Anthropological Institute of Great Britain and Ireland* 3: 106–113.

Reid, D. M.
1963 *Tales of Nanabozho.* New York: H. Z. Walck.

Reid, S.
1977 "Four Kwakiutl Themes on Isolation." *British Columbia Monthly* 3.
1979 "The Kwakiutl Man Eater." *Anthropologica* 21: 247–275.

Reid, W., and R. Bringhurst
1984 *The Raven Steals the Light.* Vancouver, British Columbia: Douglas & McIntyre.

Richards, C. E.
1920 "Indian Legends of Colorado." American Library Association. *Bulletin* 14: 203–210.

Ricketts, M. L.
1966 "The North American Indian Trickster." *History of Religions* 5(2): 327–350.

Rider, C. D.
1982 "Folklore and Educational Administration in Alaska: An Ethnographic Study of Rural School Administration. *Research in Rural Education* 1(1): 15–20.

Rides at the Door
1979 *NAPI Stories.* Browning, MT: Browning School District 9.

Ridington, R.
1988 *Trail to Heaven: Knowledge and Narrative in a Northern Native Community.* Iowa City: University of Iowa Press.

Riggs, S. R.
1883 "Mythology of the Dakotas." *American Antiquarian* 5: 147–149.

Rink, H.
1974 *Tales and Traditions of the Eskimo.* Montreal: Queen's University Press.

Rink, H., and F. Boas
1889 "Eskimo Tales and Songs." *Journal of American Folklore* 2: 123–131.

Rink, S.
1900 "The Girl and the Dog: An Eskimo Tale with Comments." *American Anthropologist* (Old Series) 11: 181, 209.
1902 "A Comparative Study of Two Indian and Eskimo Legends." International Congress of Americanists. *Proceedings* 8: 279.

Riordan, A.
1983 *The Nelson Island Eskimo.* Anchorage: Alaska Pacific University Press.

Rios, R.
1976 "A Legend of Taquish Peak." In *A Collection of Enthnographical Articles on the California Indians,* edited by R. F. Heizer, 61–62. Ramona, CA: Ballena Press.

Rios, T.
1980 "The Egg." In *The South Corner of Time: Hopi, Navajo, Papago, Yaqui Tribal Literature,* edited by L. Evers et al., 151–154. Tucson: University of Arizona Press.

Risser, A.
1941 "Seven Zuñi Folk Tales." *El Palacio* 48: 215–226.

Robins, R. H.
1985 "The Young Man from Serper: A Yurok Folktale." In *Collectanea Philologica: Festschmitter für Helmut Gipper zum 65,* 2 vols., edited by G. Heinz and P. Schmitter, 633–644. Baden-Baden: Valentin Koerner.

Rockwell, D.
1991 *Giving Voice to Bear.* Niwot, Colorado: Roberts Rinehart.

Roessel, R. A., Jr., and P. Dillon
1974 *Coyote Stories of the Navajo People.* Phoenix: Navajo Curriculum Press.

Rogers, B. T., and A. H. Gayton
1944 "Twenty-seven Chuckchansi Yokuts Myths." *Journal of American Folklore* 57: 190–207.

Rohner, R. C., and E. C. Rohner
1970   *The Kwakiutl Indians, Indians of British Columbia.* New York: Holt, Rinehart and Winston.

Romalis, S.
1983   "The East Greenland Tupilaq Image: Old and New Visions." *Etudes/Inuit/Studies* 7(1): 152–159.

Rooth, A. B.
1957   "The Creation Myths of the North American Indians." *Anthropos* 52: 497–508.
1962   *The Raven and the Carcass. An Investigation of a Motif in the Deluge Myth in Europe, Asia and North America.* Folklore Fellows Communications 186, Academia Scientarium Fennica. Helsinki: Suomalainen Tiedeakatemia.
1980a   "The Giants' Wrestling." In *The Alaska Seminar,* edited by A. B. Rooth, 39–83. Stockholm: Distribution Almqvist & Wiksell.
1980b   "The Wolverine's Trap: An Attempt at Folkloristic and Biocultural Epistemology." In *The Alaska Seminar,* edited by A. B. Rooth, 5–38. Stockholm: Distribution Almqvist & Wiksell.

Rooth, A. B., ed.
1980   *The Alaska Seminar.* Stockholm: Distribution Almqvist & Wiksell.

Rosman, A., and P. G. Rubel
1971   *Feasting with Mine Enemy: Rank and Exchange among Northwest Coast Societies.* New York: Columbia University Press.

Ross, J.
1979   "Mescalero Traditions." *Arkansas Amateur* 18(7): 5–9.

Rossiter, H.
1925   *Indian Legends from the Land of Al-ay-ek-sa.* Ketchikan, AK: Ketchikan Alaska Chronicle.

Ruby, R. H., and J. A. Brown
1986   *A Guide to the Indian Tribes of the Pacific Northwest.* Norman: University of Oklahoma Press.

Rush, E. M.
1930   "Legend of the Paiutes of the Owens River Valley in California." *El Palacio.* March. Sante Fe, NM.

Russell, F.
1889   "Myths of the Jicarilla Apache." *Journal of American Folklore* 11: 253–271.
1898   *Explorations in the Far North.* Iowa City: University of Iowa Publications.

1900   "Athabascan Myths." *Journal of American Folklore* 13: 11–18.
1908   *The Pima Indians.* Smithsonian Institution. Bureau of American Ethnology. *Annual Report* 26.
1985   "Sophiology." In *The Ethnographic American Southwest: A Source Book. Southwestern Society in Myth, Clan, and Kinship,* edited by R. I. Ford, 206–238. New York: Garland.

Sabo, G., and D. Sabo
1985   "Belief Systems and Ecology of Sea Mammal Hunting among the Baffinland Eskimo." *Arctic Anthropology* 22(2): 77–86.

St. Clair, H. H., and L. J. Frachtenberg
1909   "Traditions of the Coos Indians of Oregon." *Journal of American Folklore* 22: 25–41.

St. Clair, H. H., and R. H. Lowie
1909   "Shoshone and Comanche Tales." *Journal of American Folklore* 22: 265–282.

Sampson, M. J.
1939   *The Swinomish Totem Pole; Tribal Legends.* Bellingham, WA: Union Printing.

Sandoval (Hastin Tlo'tsihee)
1980   "The Beginning." In *The South Corner of Time: Hopi, Navajo, Papago, Yaqui Tribal Literature,* edited by L. Evers, et al., 53–62. Tucson: University of Arizona Press.

Sapir, E. A.
1907   "Preliminary Report on the Language and Mythology of the Upper Chinook." *American Anthropologist* 9: 533–545.
1909a   *Takelma Texts.* University of Pennsylvania. *Publications in Anthropology* 11(1).
1909b   *Wishram Texts, by Edward Sapir; Together with Wasco Tales and Myths, Collected by Jeremiah Curtin and Edited by Edward Sapir.* American Ethnological Society, New York. *Publications* 2.
1910a   *Yana Texts, Together with Yana Myths Collected by Roland B. Dixon.* University of California. *Publications in American Archaeology and Ethnology* 9(1).
1910b   "Song Recitative in Paiute Mythology." *Journal of American Folklore* 23: 455–472.
1910c   "Two Paiute Myths." *Museum Journal of University of Pennsylvania* 1: 15–18.
1919   "A Flood Legend of the Nootka Indians of Vancouver Island." *Journal of American Folklore* 32: 351.
1930   "Tales of the Ute Indians." PAAA 65: 297–535.

Sapir, E. A., and H. Hoijer
1942 *Navaho Texts.* Iowa City, IA: Linguistic
Society of America.

Sapir, E. A., and M. Swadesh
1939 *Nootka Texts: Tales and Ethnological
Narratives.* Philadelphia: Linguistic Society of
America, University of Pennsylvania.

Sapir, J.
1928 "Yurok Tales." *Journal of American Folklore*
41: 253–261.

Saxton, D., and L. Saxton
1973 *O'othham Hoho'ok A'agitha; Legends and
Lore of the Papago and Pima Indians.* Tucson:
University of Arizona Press.

Sayre, R. F.
1985 "Trickster." *North Dakota Quarterly* 53(2):
68–81.

Schaeffer, C.
1947 "The Bear Foster Parent Tale: A Kutenai
Version." *Journal of American Folklore* 60:
286–288.

Schmerler, H.
1931 "Trickster Marries His Daughter." *Journal of
American Folklore* 44: 196–207.

Schmidt, W.
1948 "The Central-Algonkin Flood Myth."
*Actes du XXVIII Congres International des
Americanistes, Paris 1947,* 317–319. Paris:
Musée de l'Homme.

Schmitter, F.
1910 *Upper Yukon Native Customs and
Folk-Lore. Smithsonian Miscellaneous
Collections* 56(4).
1982 "The Weendigoes." In *Windigo: An
Anthology of Fact and Fantastic Fiction,*
edited by J. R. Colombo, 14–20.
Saskatoon, Saskatchewan: Western
Producer Prairie Books.

Schwarz, H. T.
1982 "Windigo." In *Windigo: An Anthology
of Fact and Fantastic Fiction,* edited by
J. R. Colombo, 191–193. Saskatoon,
Saskatchewan: Western Producer
Prairie Books.

Scobie, A.
1975 "The Battle of the Pygmies and Cranes
in Chinese, Arab and North American
Indian Sources." *Folklore* 86: 122–132.

Sekaquaptewa, E.
1979 "One More Smile for a Hopi Clown."
Parabola 4(1): 6–9.
1981 "Hopi: 'Wunuuqam,' Ones Who Stand."
Plateau 53(2): 18–23.

Seymour, P. J.
1985 *The Golden Woman: The Colville Narrative
of Peter J. Seymour.* Tucson: University of
Arizona Press.

Shaul, D. L.
1987 "The Hopi Coyote Story as Narrative."
*Journal of Pragmatics: An Interdisciplinary
Bi-monthly of Language Studies* 11(1): 3–25.

Sheppard, J.
1983 "The Dog Husband: Structural Identity and
Emotional Specificity in Northern Athapaskan
Oral Narrative." *Arctic Anthropology* 20(1).

Shotridge, L.
1922 "Land Otter-Man." *Museum Journal* 13: 55–59.
1930 "How Ats-ha Followed the Hide of His
Comrade to Yek Land." *Museum Journal* 21:
215–226.

Sides, D. S.
1961 *Decorative Art of the Southwestern Indians.*
New York: Dover.

Silver, S., and C. Wicks
1977 "Coyote Steals the Fire (Shasta)." In
Northern California Texts, edited by V. Golla
and S. Silver, 121–131. Native American Texts
Series 2(2). *International Journal of American
Linguistics.* Chicago: University of Chicago Press.

Simmons, W. S.
1982 "Return of the Timid Giant: Algonquian
Legends of Southern New England." In *Papers
of the Thirteenth Algonquian Conference,* edited
by W. Cowan, 237–242. Ottawa: Carleton
University.
1984 "Genres in New England Indian Folklore."
In *Papers of the Fifteenth Algonquian Conference,*
edited by W. Cowan, 69–80. Ottawa: Carleton
University.

Simms, S. C.
1903 *Traditions of the Crows.* Field Columbian
Museum. *Publication* 85. Anthropological Series
2(6).
1904 "Traditions of the Sarcee Indians." *Journal
of American Folklore* 17: 180–182.
1906 "Myths of the Bungees or Swampy Indians
of Lake Winnipeg." *Journal of American Folklore*
19: 334–340.

Skinner, A.
1911 "Notes on the Eastern Cree and Northern Saulteaux." American Museum of Natural History, New York. *Anthropological Papers* 9.
1913 "European Folk-Tales Collected among the Menominee Indians." *Journal of American Folklore* 26: 64–80.
1914a "Algonquin and the Thunderbird." *American Museum Journal* 14: 71–72.
1914b "Some Aspects of the Folk-Lore of the Central Algonkin." *Journal of American Folklore* 27: 97–100.
1916a "European Tales from the Plains Ojibwa." *Journal of American Folklore* 29: 330–340.
1916b "Plains Cree Tales." *Journal of American Folklore* 29: 341–367.
1919 "Plains Ojibwa Tales." *Journal of American Folklore* 32: 280–305.
1920a "The Iowa Origin Myth." Museum of the American Indian, New York. *Indian Notes and Monographs* 4: 189–192.
1920b "Medicine Ceremony of the Menomini, Iowa and Wahpeton, Dakota." Museum of the American Indian, New York. *Indian Notes and Monographs* 4.
1920c "Wahpeton Dakota Origin Myths." Museum of the American Indian, New York. *Indian Notes and Monographs* 4: 273–278.
1928 "Sauk Tales." *Journal of American Folklore* 41: 147–183.

Skinner, A., and J. V. Satterlee.
1915 *Folklore of the Menomini Indians.* American Museum of Natural History, New York. *Anthropological Papers* 8.

Skye, M. L.
1911 "Origin of the Green Corn." *Red Man* 4: 28–29.

Slobodin, R.
1971, 1975 "Without Fire: A Kutchin Tale of Warfare, Survival, and Vengeance." In *Proceedings: Northern Athapaskan Conference* 1, edited by A. M. Clark (1971). Ottawa: National Museums of Canada: 259–301 (1975).

Slotkin, J. S., and C. Schmitt
1949 "Studies of Wampum." *American Anthropologist* 51: 223-236.

Smith, D.
1985 "Big Stone Foundations: Manifest Meaning in Chipewyan Myths." *Journal of American Culture* 18: 73–77.

Smith, E. A.
1883 "Myths of the Iroquois." Smithsonian Institution. Bureau of American Ethnology. *Annual Report* 2: 51–112.

Smith, H. I.
1894 "Notes on Eskimo Traditions." *Journal of American Folklore* 7: 209–216.
1897 "The Monster in the Tree: An Ojibwa Myth." *Journal of American Folklore* 10 324–325.
1906 "Some Ojibwa Myths and Traditions." *Journal of American Folklore* 19: 215–230.

Smith, K. N.
1960 "A Penobscot Indian Story of Colonial Maine." *Northeast Folklore* 3(1): 10–11.
1985 "Whales in Pacific Northwest Culture and Mythology." *Northwest Folklore* 4(1): 31–42.

Smith, L. H.
1906 *The Indian Story of the Creation and Flood.* Denver.

Smith, M.
1940 *The Puyallup-Nisqually.* New York: Columbia University Press.

Snelling, W. J.
1830 *Tales of the Northwest.* Boston: Hilliard, Gray, Little and Wilkins.

Spalding, A.
1979 "Eight Inuit Myths/Inuit Unipkaaqtuat Pingasuniarvinilit." Paper (Canadian Ethnology Service) 59. Canada National Museum of Man. Mercury Series. Ottawa: National Museums of Canada.

Sparkman, P. S.
1908 "Notes on California Folk-Lore." *Journal of American Folklore* 21: 35–36.

Speck, F. G.
1903 "A Pequot-Mohegan Witchcraft Tale." *Journal of American Folklore* 16: 104–106.
1904 "Some Mohegan-Pequot Legends." *Journal of American Folklore* 17: 183–184.
1909 *Ethnology of the Yuchi Indians.* University of Pennsylvania. *Publications in Anthropology* 1.
1910 "An Algonkian Myth." *University of Pennsylvania Museum Journal* 1: 49ff.
1913a "European Tales among the Chickasaw Indians." *Journal of American Folklore* 26: 292.
1913b "European Folk-tales among the Penobscot." *Journal of American Folklore* 26: 81–84.

1913c "Some Catawba Texts and Folk-Lore." *Journal of American Folklore* 29: 319–330.

1915a *Myths and Folk-lore of the Timiskaming Algonquin and Timagami Ojibwa.* Geological Survey of Canada. *Anthropology Series* 9. Ottawa.

1915b "Some Naskapi Myths from Little Whale River." *Journal of American Folklore* 28: 70–77.

1915c "Penobscot Tales." *Journal of American Folklore* 28: 52–58.

1915d "Some Micmac Tales from Cape Breton Island." *Journal of American Folklore* 28: 59–69.

1917 "Malecite Tales." *Journal of American Folklore* 30: 479–485.

1918 "Penobscot Transformer Tales." *International Journal of American Linguistics* 1(3).

1925a "Montagnais and Naskapi Tales from the Labrador Peninsula." *Journal of American Folklore* 38: 1–32.

1925b "Wawenock Myth Texts from Maine." Smithsonian Institution. Bureau of American Ethnology. *Annual Report* 43: 165–197.

1931 "A Study of the Delaware Big House Ceremony." Pennsylvania Historical Commission. *Publications* 2: 5–192.

1934 *Catawba Texts.* New York: Columbia University Press.

1935a "Mammoth or 'Stiff-Legged Bear.'" *American Anthropologist* 37: 159–163.

1935b "Penobscot Tales and Religious Beliefs." *Journal of American Folklore* 48: 1–107.

1987a "The Creek Indians of Taskigi Town." In *A Creek Source Book,* edited by W. C. Sturtevant, 99–164. New York: Garland.

1987b "Nenebuc, the Transformer." In *Nanabozhoo: Giver of Life,* edited by A. K. Helbig, 28–37. Brighton, MI: Green Oak Press.

Speck, F. G., and L. G. Carr
1908 "Catawba Potters and Their Work." *American Anthropologist* 10: 399–408.

Speck, F. G., and G. Herzog
1942 *The Tutelo Spirit Adoption Ceremony.* Harrisburg: Pennsylvania Historical Commission.

Spence, L.
1975 *The Myths of the North American Indians.* Blauvelt, NY: Multimedia.

Spencer, J.
1909 "Shawnee Folk-Lore." *Journal of American Folklore* 22: 319–326.

Spencer, K.
1947 *Reflection of Social Life in the Navaho Origin Myth.* University of New Mexico Publications in Anthropology 3. Albuquerque: University of New Mexico Press.

1957 *Mythology and Values: An Analysis of Navaho Chantway Myths.* American Folklore Society. *Memoirs* 48.

Spencer, P. U.
1983 *Who Speaks for Wolf: A Native American Learning Story as Told to Turtle Woman Singing by Her Father, Sharp-Eyed Hawk.* Austin, TX: Tribe of Two Press.

Spicer, E. H.
1954 *Potam: A Yaqui Village in Sonora.* American Anthropological Association. *Memoirs* 77, 56(4), pt. 2.

Spinden, H. J.
1908 "Myths of the Nez Percé." *Journal of American Folklore* 21: 13–23, 149–158.

1917 *Nez Perce Tales.* American Folklore Society. *Memoirs* 11.

Squier, E. G.
1848 "Ne-she-kay-be-nais; or, the Lone Bird. An Ojibway Legend." *American Review* 2(3): 255–259.

Stamp, H.
1915a "A Malecite Tale (Adventures of Bukschinskwuk)." *Journal of American Folklore* 28: 243–248.

1915b "Water Fairies." *Journal of American Folklore* 28: 310–316.

Standing Bear, L.
1934 *Stories of the Sioux.* Boston: Houghton Mifflin.

Stephen, A. M.
1888 "Legend of the Snake Order of the Moqui, As Told by Outsiders." *Journal of American Folklore* 1: 109–114, 165.

1929 "Hopi Tales." *Journal of American Folklore* 42: 1–72.

1930 "Navajo Origin Legend." *Journal of American Folklore* 43: 88–104.

1936 *Hopi Journal of Alexander M. Stephen,* edited by E. C. Parsons. Columbia University. *Contributions to Anthropology* 23.

1940 "Hopi Indians of Arizona." *Southwest Museum Leaflets* 14: 1–47.

Stern, T.
1963 "Ideal and Expected Behavior As Seen in Klamath Mythology." *Journal of American Folklore* 76: 21–30.

Stevens, J. R.
1982 "Stories of the Windigo." In *Windigo: An Anthology of Fact and Fantastic Fiction,* edited

by J. R. Colombo, 193–200. Saskatoon, Saskatchewan: Western Producer Prairie Books.

Stevens, J. R., and C. Ray
1971   *Sacred Legends of the Sandy Lake Cree.* Toronto: McClelland and Stewart.

Stevenson, J.
1883   "Illustrated Catalogue of the Collections Obtained from the Indians of New Mexico and Arizona in 1879." Smithsonian Institution. Bureau of American Ethnology. *Annual Report* 2: 407-422.
1891   *Ceremonies of the Hasjelti Dailjis and Mythical Sand Painting of the Navajo Indians.* Smithsonian Institution. Bureau of American Ethnology. *Annual Report* 8.

Stevenson, M. C.
1887   *The Religious Life of the Zuñi Child.* Smithsonian Institution. Bureau of American Ethnology. *Annual Report* 5.
1894   *The Sia.* Smithsonian Institution. Bureau of American Ethnology. *Annual Report* 11.
1905   *The Zuñi Indians: Their Mythology, Esoteric Fraternities and Ceremonies.* Smithsonian Institution. Bureau of American Ethnology. *Annual Report* 23.

Steward, J. H.
1930, 1931a   "The Ceremonial Buffoon of the American Indian." Michigan Academy of Science, Arts and Letters. *Papers* 14 (1930); 187–207 (1931).
1931b   "Notes on Hopi Ceremonies in Their Initiatory Form in 1927–1928." *American Anthropologist* 33: 56–79.
1936   "Myths of the Owens Valley Paiute." University of California. *Publications in American Archaeology and Ethnology* 34(5).

Stewart, G. W.
1906   "A Yokuts Creation Myth." *Journal of American Folklore* 19: 322.

Stewart, O. C.
1986   "The Peyote Religion." In *Handbook of North American Indians. Vol. 11: Great Basin.* Washington: Smithsonian Institution Press.
1987   *Peyote Religion: A History.* Norman: University of Oklahoma Press.

Stirling, M. W.
1942   *Origin Myth of Acoma and Other Records.* Smithsonian Institution. Bureau of American Ethnology. *Bulletin* 135.

1946   "Concepts of Sun among American Indians." In *Smithsonian Report for 1945,* 387–400.

Stross, B.
1971   "Serial Order in Nez Perce Myths." *Journal of American Folklore* 84: 104–113.

Sturtevant, W., ed.
1987   *A Seminole Source Book.* New York: Garland.

Sullivan, L. E.
1982   "Multiple Levels of Religious Meaning in Culture: A New Look at Winnebago Sacred Texts." *Canadian Journal of Native Studies* 2(2): 221–247.

Swadesh, M., and M. H. Swadesh
1933   "Nitinat Texts." *International Journal of American Linguistics* 7: 195–208.

Swan, J. G.
1868   *The Indians of Cape Flattery.* Smithsonian Institution. *Contributions to Knowledge* 220.

Swanson, E. H., ed.
1970   *Languages and Cultures of Western North America: Essays in Honor of Sven S. Liljeblad.* Pocatello: Idaho State University Press.

Swanson, G. E.
1976   "Orpheus and Star Husband: Meaning and Structure of Myths." *Ethnology* 15: 115–133.

Swanton, J. R.
1905a–1909   *Contributions to the Ethnology of the Haida.* American Museum of Natural History. Publication of the Jesup North Pacific Expedition 5.
1905b   *Haida Texts and Myth.* Smithsonian Institution. Bureau of American Ethnology. *Bulletin* 29.
1905c   "Types of Haida and Tlingit Myths." *American Anthropologist* 7: 94–104.
1907   "Mythology of the Indians of Louisiana and the Texas Coast." *Journal of American Folklore* 20: 285–289.
1908   *Haida Texts, Masset Dialect.* American Museum of Natural History. Publication of the Jesup North Pacific Expedition 10.
1909   *Tlingit Myths and Texts.* Smithsonian Institution. Bureau of American Ethnology. *Bulletin* 39.
1913   "Animal Stories from the Indians of the Muskhogean Stock." *Journal of American Folklore* 26: 193–218.
1917   "Some Chitimacha Myths and Beliefs." *Journal of American Folklore* 30: 474–478.

1928a *Religious Beliefs and Medical Practices of the Creek Indians.* Smithsonian Institution. Bureau of American Ethnology. *Annual Report* 42.

1928b *Social Organization and Social Usages of the Indians of the Creek Confederacy.* Smithsonian Institution. Bureau of American Ethnology. *Annual Report* 42.

1928c *Social and Religious Beliefs and Usages of the Chickasaw Indians.* Smithsonian Institution. Bureau of American Ethnology. *Annual Report* 44.

1929 *Myths and Tales of the Southeastern Indians.* Smithsonian Institution. Bureau of American Ethnology. *Bulletin* 88.

1946 *The Indians of the Southeastern United States.* Smithsonian Institution. Bureau of American Ethnology. *Bulletin* 137.

Swindlehurst, F.
1905 "Folk-Lore of the Cree Indians." *Journal of American Folklore* 18: 139–143.

Sylvester, N. B.
1884 *Indian Legends of Saratoga and of the Upper Hudson Valley.* Troy, NY: N. B. Sylvester & Co.

Talamantez, I. M.
1982 "Dance and Ritual in the Study of Native American Religious Traditions." *New Scholar* 8: 535–549.

Talashoma, H.
1980 "How Maasaw and the People of Oraibi Got Scared to Death Once." In *The South Corner of Time: Hopi, Navajo, Papago, Yaqui Tribal Literature,* edited by L. Evers, 29–34. Tucson: University of Arizona Press.

Talayesva, D. C.
1971 *Sun Chief: The Autobiography of a Hopi Indian.* New Haven, CT: Yale University Press.

Tall Bull, H., and T. Weist
1971 *The Turtle Went to War: Northern Cheyenne Folktales.* Billings: Montana Council for Indian Education.

Taylor, A.
1933 "A Classification of Formula Tales." *Journal of American Folklore* 46: 77–88.

Taylor, A. R.
1977 "Arikara Texts." In *Caddoan Texts,* edited by D. R. Parks. Chicago: University of Chicago Press.

Tedlock, B.
1975 "The Clown's Way." In *Teachings from the American Earth,* edited by D. Tedlock and B. Tedlock, 105–120. New York: Liveright.

1983 "Zuñi Sacred Theater." AIQ 7: 93–110.

Tedlock, D.
1972a *Finding the Center: Narrative Poetry of the Zuñi Indians.* New York: Dial.

1972b "On the Translation of Style in Oral Narrative." In *Toward New Perspectives in Folklore,* edited by A. Paredes and R. Bauman. Bibliographical and Special Series 23: 114–133. Publications of the American Folklore Society. Austin: University of Texas Press.

1972c "Pueblos Literature: Style and Verisimilitude." *New Perspectives on the Pueblos,* edited by A. Ortiz, 219–242. Albuquerque: University of New Mexico Press.

1975 "An American Indian View of Death." In *Teachings from the American Earth,* edited by D. Tedlock and B. Tedlock, 248–271. New York: Liveright.

1979 "Zuñi Religion and World View." In *Handbook of North American Indians. Vol. 9: Southwest,* edited by A. Ortiz, 499–508. Washington: Smithsonian Institution Press.

1983 "The Spoken Word and the Work of Interpretation in American Indian Religion." In *The Spoken Word and the Work of Interpretation,* edited by D. Tedlock, 45–63. Philadelphia: University of Pennsylvania Press.

Teicher, M. I.
1960 *Windigo Psychosis: A Study of a Relationship between Belief and Behavior among the Indians of Northeastern Canada.* Seattle: University of Washington Press.

Teit, J. A.
1898 *Traditions of the Thompson River Indians.* American Folklore Society. *Memoirs* 6.

1900–1909a *The Shuswap.* American Museum of Natural History. *Publication of the Jesup North Pacific Expedition* 2.

1909b "Two Tahltan Traditions." *Journal of American Folklore* 22: 314–318.

1912a *Mythology of the Thompson River Indians.* American Museum of Natural History. Publication of the Jesup North Pacific Expedition 8.

1912b "Traditions of the Lillooet Indians of British Columbia." *Journal of American Folklore* 25: 292–371.

1916 "European Tales from the Upper Thompson Indians." *Journal of American Folklore* 29: 301–329.

1917a "Folk–tales of the Salishan Tribes." American Folklore Society. *Memoirs* 11.

1917b "Okanagon Tales." American Folklore Society. *Memoirs* 11.

1917c "Pend d'Oreille Tales." American Folklore Society. *Memoirs* 11.

1917d "Tales from the Lower Fraser River." American Folklore Society. *Memoirs* 11.

1917e "Thompson Tales." American Folklore Society. *Memoirs* 11.

1917f "Coeur d'Alene Tales." American Folklore Society. *Memoirs* 11.

1917g "Kaska Tales." *Journal of American Folklore* 30: 427–473. .

1919, 1921a "Tahltan Tales." *Journal of American Folklore* 32: 198–250 (1919); 34: 223–253, 335–356 (1921).

1921b "Two Plains Cree Tales." *Journal of American Folklore* 34: 320–321.

1937 "More Thompson Indian Myths." *Journal of American Folklore* 50: 173–190.

ten Kate, H. F. C.
1917 "A Zuñi Folk-tale." *Journal of American Folklore* 30: 496–499.

Tennant, E., and J. Bitar, eds.
1981 *Yupik Lore: Oral Traditions of an Eskimo People.* Bethel, AK: Lower Kuskokwim School District.

Terrell, J. W.
1892 "The Demon of Consumption: A Legend of Cherokees of North Carolina." *Journal of American Folklore* 5: 125–126.

Thayer, J. S.
1980 "The Berdache of the Northern Plains: A Socioreligious Perspective. *Journal of Anthropological Research* 36: 287–293.

Thomas, D.
1986 *A Blackfoot Source Book (Papers by Clark Wissler).* New York: Garland.

Thomas, L. L., J. Z. Kronenfeld, and D. B. Kronenfeld
1976 "Asdiwal Crumbles: A Critique of Levi-Straussian Myth Anaylsis." *American Ethnologist* 3: 147–173.

Thompson, L.
1945 "Logico-Aesthetic Integration in Hopi Culture." *American Anthropologist* 47: 540–553.

Thompson, L., and A. Joseph
1965 *The Hopi Way.* New York: Russell & Russell.

Thompson, S.
1919 *European Tales among the North American Indians: A Study in the Migration of Folk-Tales.* Colorado Springs: Colorado College.

1922a "The Indian Legend of Hiawatha." Modern Language Association. *Publications* 37: 128-140.

1922b "The Transmission of Folk-tales." *Gayley Anniversary Volume.* Berkeley.

1946 *The Folk-tale.* New York: Holt, Rinehart and Winston.

1955–1958 *Motif-Index of Folk-literature.* 6 vols. Bloomington: Indiana University Press.

1968 *Tales of the North-American Indians.* Cambridge, MA: Harvard University Press.

1971 "Myth and Folktales." In *Myth: A Symposium,* edited by T. A. Sebeok, 169–180. Bloomington: Indiana University Press.

Ticasuk (E. I. Brown)
1981 *The Longest Story Ever Told. Qayaq: The Magical Man.* Anchorage: Alaska Pacific University Press.

Titiev, M.
1939 "The Story of Kokopele." *American Anthropologist* 41: 91–98.

1940 "A Hopi Visit to the Afterworld." Michigan Academy of Science, Arts, and Letters. *Papers* 26: 495–504.

1942 "Notes on Hopi Witchcraft." Michigan Academy of Science, Arts, and Letters. *Papers* 28: 549–557.

1943 "Two Hopi Tales from Oraibi." Michigan Academy of Science, Arts, and Letters. *Papers* 29: 425–437.

1944 *Old Oraibi: A Study of the Hopi Indians of Third Mesa.* Peabody Museum of American Archaeology and Ethnology, Harvard University. *Papers* 22(1).

1948 "Two Hopi Myths and Rites." *Journal of American Folklore* 61: 31–43.

1950 "The Religion of the Hopi Indians." In *Forgotten Religions,* edited by V. Ferm, 365–378. New York: Philosophical Library.

1971 "Some Aspects of Clowning among the Hopi Indians." *Themes in Culture (Essays in Honor of Morris E. Opler),* edited by M. D. Zamora, J. M. Mahar, and H. Orenstein, 326–336. Quezon City, Philippines: Kayumanggi.

1972 *The Hopi Indians of Old Oraibi. Change and Continuity.* Ann Arbor: University of Michigan Press.

Toelken, J. B., and T. Scott
1981 "Poetic Retranslation of the 'Pretty Languages' of Yellowman." In *Traditional*

Literatures of the American Indians: Texts and Interpretations, edited by K. Kroeber, 65–116. Lincoln: University of Nebraska Press.

Tooker, E.
1962 *An Ethnography of the Huron Indians, 1615–1649.* Smithsonian Institution. Bureau of American Ethnology. *Bulletin* 190.

Townsend, A. L.
1977 "Shoshone-Bannock Legend." *Idaho Heritage* 1(10).

Trejo, J.
1974 "Coyote Tales: A Paiute Commentary." *Journal of American Folklore* 87: 66–71.

Trigger, B. G., ed.
1978 *Handbook of North American Indians. Vol. 15: Northeast.* Washington: Smithsonian Institution Press.

Trimble, S., ed.
1981 "Stories from the Land." *Plateau* 53(2). Flagstaff: Museum of Northern Arizona Press.

Trowbridge, C. C.
1986 *Indian Tales of C. C. Trowbridge: Collected from Wyandots, Miamis, and Shawanoes,* edited by C. E. Schorer. Brighton, MI: Green Oak Press.

Turenne, L. de
1924 "Ute Legend of Creation." *El Palacio* 4(7): 104–105.

Turner, D. H.
1977 "Windigo Mythology and the Analysis of Cree Social Structure." *Anthropologica* 19: 63–73.
1978 "Dialectics in Tradition: Myth and Social Structure in Two Hunter-Gatherer Societies." Royal Anthropological Institute of Great Britain and Ireland. *Occasional Paper* 36.
1979 "Behind the Myths: An Introduction to the Structural Study of Myth and Folklore." In *Challenging Anthropology,* edited by D. H. Turner and G. A. Smith, 17–26. Toronto: McGraw-Hill Ryerson.

Turner, H. G.
1987 "The Race of the Fox and the Turtle." In *Nanabozhoo: Giver of Life,* edited by A. K. Helbig, 127. Brighton, MI: Green Oak Press.

Turner, H. J., and H. Edmonds
1968–1969 "St. Michael Eskimo Myths and Tales." University of Alaska. *Anthropology Papers* 14(1): 43-83.

Turner, L. M.
1894 *Ethnology of the Ungava District, Hudson Bay Territory.* Smithsonian Institution. Bureau of American Ethnology. *Annual Report* 11.

Tyhurst, R.
1975 "Comparative Analysis of Northern and Southern Athapaskan 'Slayer of Monsters' Myth." In *Proceedings of the Second Congress, Canadian Ethnology Society,* edited by J. Freedman and J. H. Barkow. Paper (Canadian Ethnology Service) 28(1): 150–153. Mercury Series. Ottawa: National Museums of Canada.

Ullom, J. C.
1969 *Folklore of the North American Indians: An Annotated Bibliography.* Washington: Library of Congress.

Underhill, R. M.
1936 *The Autobiography of a Papago Woman.* American Anthropological Association. *Memoirs* 46.
1938 *Singing for Power: The Song Magic of the Papago Indians of Southern Arizona.* Berkeley: University of California Press.
1946 *Papago Indian Religion.* New York: Columbia University Press.

Underhill, R. M., et al.
1979 *Rainhouse and Ocean: Speeches for the Papago Year.* Flagstaff: Museum of Northern Arizona Press.

Utley, F. L.
1974 "The Migration of Folktales: Four Channels to the Americas." *Current Anthropology* 15: 5–27.

VanEtten, T.
1987 *Ways of Indian Wisdom: Stories Retold by Teresa VanEtten.* Santa Fe, NM: Sunstone Press.

Vecsey, C. T.
1983a "The Emergence of the Hopi People." *American Indian Quarterly* 7(3): 69–92.
1983b *Traditional Ojibwa Religion and Its Historical Changes.* Philadelphia: American Philosophical Society.
1984 "Midewiwin Myths of Origin." In *Papers of the Fifteenth Algonquian Conference,* edited by W. Cowan, 445–467. Ottawa: Carleton University.

Vecsey, C. T., and J. F. Fisher
1984 "The Ojibwa Creation Myth: An Analysis of Its Structure and Content." *Temenos* 20: 66–100.

Velten, H. V.
1939 "Two Southern Tlingit Tales." *International Journal of American Linguistics* 10: 65–74.
1944 "Three Tlingit Stories." *International Journal of American Linguistics* 10: 168–180.

Vennum, T., Jr.
1978 "Ojibwa Origin-Migration Songs of the *Mitewiwin.*" *Journal of American Folklore* 91: 753–791.
1982 *The Ojibwa Dance Drum.* Smithsonian Folk Studies 2. Washington: Smithsonian Institution Press.

Vick, A., ed.
1983 *The Cama-i Book: Kayaks, Dogsleds, Bear Hunting, Bush Pilots, Smoked Fish, Mukluks, and Other Traditions of Southwestern Alaska.* Garden City, NY: Doubleday.

Viele, C. W., ed.
1981 "Paiute: Why the North Star Stands Still." *Plateau* 53(2): 8–11.

Vizenor, G. R.
1981 *Summer in the Spring; Ojibwe Lyric Poems and Tribal Stories.* Minneapolis: Nodin Press.
1984 *People Named the Chippewa: Narrative Histories.* Minneapolis: University of Minnesota Press.

Voegelin, C. F.
1936 *The Shawnee Female Deity.* Yale University. *Publications in Anthropology* 10.

Voegelin, C. F., and E. W. Voegelin
1944 "The Shawnee Female Deity in Historical Perspective." *American Anthropologist* 46: 370–375.
1954 *Walam Olum or Red Score: The Migration Legend of the Lenni Lenape or Delaware Indians.* Indianapolis: Indiana Historical Society.

Voegelin, E. W.
1933 "Kiowa-Crow Mythological Affiliations." *American Anthropologist* 35: 470–474.
1940 "Culture Element Survey: Northeast California." *Anthropological Records* 10.
1944 "Mortuary Customs of the Shawnee and Other Eastern Woodlands Tribes." *Prehistory Research Series* 2(4).
1947 "Three Shasta Myths, Including 'Orpheus.'" *Journal of American Folklore* 60: 52–58.

Voth, H. R.
1901 *The Oraibi Powamu Ceremony.* Field Columbian Museum. *Publication* 61. Anthropological Series 3(2).

1902 *Oraibi Summer Snake Ceremony.* Field Columbian Museum. *Publication* 83. Anthropological Series 3(4).
1903 "The Oraibi Oaqol Ceremony." Field Columbian Museum. *Publication* 84. Anthropological Series 6(1).
1905a *Four Hopi Tales.* Field Columbian Museum. Anthropological Series 9.
1905b *The Traditions of the Hopi.* Field Columbian Museum. *Publication* 96. Anthropological Series 8.
1912a "Arapaho Tales." *Journal of American Folklore* 25: 43–50.
1912b "The Oraibi Marau Ceremony." Field Columbian Museum. *Publication* 156. Anthropological Series 11(1).

Wagner, G.
1931 *Yuchi Tales.* American Ethnological Society, New York. *Publications* 13.

Wake, C. S.
1907 "A Widespread Boy-Hero Story." *Journal of American Folklore* 20: 216–219.

Walens, S. G.
1981 *Feasting with Cannibals: An Essay on Kwakiutl Cosmology.* Princeton, NJ: Princeton University Press.

Walker, J. R.
1982 *Lakota Belief and Ritual.* Edited by R. DeMallie and E. Jahner. Lincoln: University of Nebraska Press.
1983 *Lakota Myth.* Lincoln: University of Nebraska Press.

Wallace, A. F. C.
1972 *The Death and Rebirth of the Seneca.* New York: Random House.

Wallis, W. D.
1923 "Beliefs and Tales of the Canadian Dakota." *Journal of American Folklore* 36: 36–101.
1936 "Folk Tales from Shumopovi, Second Mesa." *Journal of American Folklore* 49: 1–68.

Wallis, W. D., and M. Titiev
1944 "Hopi Notes from Chimopovy." Michigan Academy of Science, Arts, and Letters. *Papers* 30: 523–555.

Wardle, H. N.
1900 "The Sedna Cycle: A Study in Myth Evolution." *American Anthropologist* 2: 568–603.

Warren, W.
1885 *History of the Ojibways. Based upon Traditions and Oral Statements.* St. Paul: Minnesota Historical Society.

Watahomigie, L. J.
1981 "Hualapai: Origin of the People." *Plateau* 53(2): 24–27.

Waterman, T. T.
1908–1910 *Religious Practices of the Diegueño Indians.* University of California. *Publications in American Archaeology and Ethnology* 8.
1909 "Analysis of the Mission Indian Creation Story." *American Anthropologist* 11: 41–55.
1914 "The Explanatory Element in the Folk-Tales of the North American Indians." *Journal of American Folklore* 27: 1–54.

Webber, W. L.
1936 *The Thunderbird "Tootooch" Legends: Folk Tales of the Indian Tribes of the Pacific Northwest Coast.* Seattle: Ace Printing.

Weigand, P. C.
1975 "Possible References to La Quemada in Huichol Mythology." *Ethnohistory* 22: 15–20.

Weigle, M.
1987 "Creation and Procreation, Cosmogony and Childbirth: Reflections on Ex Nihilo, Earth Diver, and Emergence Mythology." *Journal of American Folklore* 100: 426–435.

Weitlaner, R. J.
1915 "Seneca Tales and Beliefs." *Journal of American Folklore* 28: 309–310.

Welch, L.
1977 "The Cherokee Story-teller: The Red and Green Crayfish." *Journal of Cherokee Studies* 2: 246–249.

Weltfish, G.
1936 "The Vision Story of a Fox-Boy, a South Bend Pawnee Text." *International Journal of American Linguistics* 9(1): 44–76.

Wetherell, B.
1941 "A Zuñi Legend." *Masterkey* 12(5): 196–198.

Wetherill, L. W., and B. Cummings
1922 "A Navaho Tale of Pueblo Bonito." *Art and Archaeology* 14: 132–136.

Wheeler-Voegelin, E., and R. W. Moore
1957 "The Emergence Myth in Native North America." In *Studies in Folklore in Honor of Distinguished Service Professor Stith Thompson,* edited by W. E. Richmond, 66–91. Bloomington: Indiana University Press.

Wheelwright, M. C.
1938 "Tleji or Yehbechai Myth." Museum of Navajo Ceremonial Art. *Bulletin* 1.
1940 "Myth of Sontso (Big Star)." Museum of Navajo Ceremonial Art. *Bulletin* 2.
1942 *Navajo Creation Myth: The Story of the Emergence.* Navajo Religion Series 1. Santa Fe, NM: Museum of Navajo Ceremonial Art.
1945 "Eagle Catching Myth and Bead Myth." Museum of Navajo Ceremonial Art, *Bulletin* 3.
1946a *Hail Chant and Water Chant.* Navajo Religion Series 2. Santa Fe, NM: Museum of Navajo Ceremonial Art.
1946b "Nilth Chiji Bakaji (Wind Chant) and Feather Chant." Museum of Navajo Ceremonial Art. *Bulletin* 4.
1949 *Emergence Myth According to the Hanelthnayhe or Upward-Reaching Rite.* Navajo Religion Series 3. Santa Fe, NM: Museum of Navajo Ceremonial Art.
1951 "Myth of Mountain Chant and Myth of Beauty Chant." Museum of Navajo Ceremonial Art. *Bulletin* 5.
1956 *The Myth and Prayers of the Great Star Chant, and the Myth of the Coyote Chant.* Navajo Religion Series 4. Santa Fe, NM: Museum of Navajo Ceremonial Art.

White, L.
1932 *The Acoma Indians.* Smithsonian Institution. Bureau of American Ethnology. *Annual Report* 47.
1962 *Pueblo of Sia, New Mexico.* Smithsonian Institution. Bureau of American Ethnology. *Bulletin* 184.

Whitehead, H.
1981 "The Bow and the Burden Strap: A New Look at Institutionalized Homosexuality in Native North America." In *Sexual Meanings, the Cultural Construction of Gender and Sexuality,* edited by S. B. Ortner and H. Whitehead. New York: Cambridge University Press.

Wickersham, J.
1898 "Nusqually Mythology." *Overland Monthly* 32: 345–351.

Will, G. F.
1912 "Some Hidatsa and Mandan Tales." *Journal of American Folklore* 25: 93–94.
1913 "No-Tongue, a Mandan Tale." *Journal of American Folklore* 26: 331–337.

1916 "The Story of No-Tongue." *Journal of American Folklore* 29: 402–406.

Will, G. F., and H. J. Spinden
1906 *The Mandans: A Study of Their Culture, Archaeology and Language.* Peabody Museum of American Archaeology and Ethnology, Harvard University. *Papers* 3(4).

Williamson, R. A.
1984 *Living the Sky: The Cosmos of the American Indian.* Boston: Houghton Mifflin.

Willis, H.
1975 "Hollisso Inchuwa & Beliefs." *Nanih Waiya* 2(4): 47–54.

Wilson, G.
1929 "Hidatsa Eagle-Trapping Ceremonies." American Museum of Natural History, New York. *Anthropological Papers* 30(4): 187–194.

Wilson, R. N.
1893 "Blackfoot Star Myths." *American Antiquity* 15: 149–150, 200–203.

Wilson, T.
1900 "Dakota Legend of the Head of Gold." *Journal of American Folklore* 13: 294–296.

Winter, K.
1975 *Shananditti: The Last of the Beothucks.* North Vancouver, British Columbia: J. J. Douglas.

Wissler, C.
1905 "The Whirlwind and the Elk in the Mythology of the Dakota." *Journal of American Folklore* 18: 257–268.
1907 "Some Dakota Myths." *Journal of American Folklore* 20: 121–131, 195–206.
1910 *Material Culture of the Blackfoot Indians.* American Museum of Natural History, New York. *Anthropological Papers* 5(1).
1911 *The Social Life of the Blackfoot Indians.* American Museum of Natural History, New York. *Anthropological Papers* 7(1).
1913 *Societies and Dance Associations of the Blackfoot Indians.* American Museum of Natural History, New York. *Anthropological Papers* 11(4).
1914 "Material Cultures of the North American Indians." *American Anthropologist* 16: 447–505.
1918 "Sun Dance of the Blackfoot Indians." American Museum of Natural History, New York. *Anthropological Papers* 16(3).
1936 *Star Legends among the American Indians.* New York: American Museum of Natural History.

Wissler, C., and D. C. Duvall
1909 *Mythology of the Blackfoot Indians.* American Museum of Natural History, New York. *Anthropological Papers* 2(1).

Witherspoon, G.
1974, 1975 "Central Concepts of Navajo World View." *Linguistics* 159: 41–59 (1974) and 161: 69–87 (1975).
1977 *Language and Art in the Navajo Universe.* Ann Arbor: University of Michigan Press.

Wittfogel, K. A., and E. S. Goldfrank
1943 "Some Aspects of Pueblo Mythology and Society." *Journal of American Folklore* 56: 17–30.

Witthoft, J.
1949 *Green Corn Ceremonialism in the Eastern Woodlands.* University of Michigan. Museum of Anthropology. *Occasional Contributions* 13.

Wood, C. E. S.
1929 *A Book of Indian Tales.* New York: Vanguard.

Wood, N., ed.
1981 "Ute: Creation Legend." *Plateau* 53(2): 4–7.

Woodward, J.
1981 "Historical Notes on the Legend of Nojoqui Falls." *Masterkey* 55: 110–113.

Woosley, D. J.
1908 "Cahuilla Tales." *Journal of American Folklore* 21: 239–240.

Wright, B.
1973 *Kachinas: A Hopi Artist's Documentary.* Flagstaff, AZ: Northland Press.
1985 *Kachinas of the Zuñi.* Flagstaff, AZ: Northland Press.

Wyman, L. C.
1925 *The Mountainway of the Navajo.* Tucson: University of Arizona Press.
1936a "The Female Shooting Life Chant: A Minor Navaho Ceremony." *American Anthropologist* 38: 634–653.
1936b "Origin Legends of Navaho Divinatory Rites." *Journal of American Folklore* 49: 134–142.
1947 "Review of Wheelright's *Hail Chant and Water Chant.*" *American Anthropologist* 49: 633-637.
1957 *Beautyway: A Navaho Ceremonial.* Princeton, NJ: Princeton University Press.

Bibliography

1959   *Navaho Indian Painting: Symbolism, Artistry, and Psychology* Boston: Boston University Press.
1962   *The Windways of the Navaho.* Colorado Springs: Taylor Museum of the Colorado Springs Fine Arts Center.
1970   *Blessingway.* Tucson: University of Arizona Press.
1983   *Southwest Indian Drypainting.* Albuquerque: University of New Mexico Press.

Wyman, L. C., and F. L. Bailey
1943   *Navaho Upward Reaching Way: Objective Behavior, Rationale and Sanction.* University of New Mexico. *Bulletin* 389.
1945   "Idea and Action Patterns in Navaho Flintway." *Southwestern Journal of Anthropology* 1: 356–377.

Wyman, L. C, W. W. Hill, and I. Osanai
1942   *Navajo Eschatology.* University of New Mexico. *Bulletin* 377.

Wyman, L. C., and C. Kluckhohn
1938   *Navaho Classification of Their Song Ceremonials.* American Anthropological Association. *Memoirs* 50.

Yava, A.
1980   "Way Back in the Distant Past." In *The South Corner of Time: Hopi, Navajo, Papago, Yaqui Tribal Literature,* edited by L. Evers et al., 8–13. Tucson: University of Arizona Press.

Young, F. W.
1970   "A Fifth Analysis of the Star Husband Tale." *Ethnology* 9: 389–413.

Young, K., and T. D. Cutsforth
1928   "Hunting Superstitions in the Cow Creek Region of Southern Oregon." *Journal of American Folklore* 41: 283–285.

Young Bull
1973   "The End of the World: A Pawnee Myth." In *Great Documents in American Indian History,* edited by W. Moquin and C. Van Doren, 97–99. New York: Praeger.

Zigmond, M. L.
1980   *Kawaiisu Mythology.* Socorro, NM: Ballena Press.

Zolbrod, P. G.
1981   "From Performance to Print: Preface to a Native American Text." *Georgia Review* 35(3): 465–509.
1983   "Poetry and Culture: The Navajo Example." In *Smoothing the Ground: Essays on Native American Oral Literature,* edited by B. Swann, 221–244. Berkeley: University of California Press.
1984   *Dine bahane': The Navajo Creation Story.* Albuquerque: University of New Mexico Press.

Zolbrod, P. G., ed.
1981   "Navajo: How High Desert Formed." *Plateau* 53(2): 12–17.

Zumwalt, R. L.
1976, 1978   "Henry Rowe Schoolcraft 1793–1864: His Collection and Analysis of the Oral Narratives of American Indians." Kroeber Anthropological Society. *Papers.* Pp. 53–54 (1976); 44–57 (1978).

Zuñi People
1972   *The Zuñis: Self-Portrayals.* Albuquerque: University of New Mexico Press.

Index by Tribe

Abenaki
Brown 1890; Cowan 1976; Cowan 1984; Day 1976; Deming 1902; Frost 1912; Harrington)01; Hill 1963; Hill 1978; Mallery 1890; Morrison 1984; Speck 1925b; Stamp 1915b

Acnumawi
Silver Fox
Demetracopoulou 1933; Dixon 1908; Dixon 1909a

Acoma
Acoma Emergence and Migration; Honani; Kacale; Kobictaiya; Masewa and Uyuyewa
Benedict 1930; Mitchell 1979; Parsons 1917a; Parsons 1918a; Stirling 1942; White 1932

Ahtna
Dream Doctor

Alabama
Bead Spitter; Big Man-Eater; Soulbieche; Thlakalunka
Martin 1977

Aleut
Achayongch and Achgoyan; Grouse Girl; Uchatngiak
Black 1983; Golder 1903; Golder 1905; Golder 1907b; Golder 1909; Lavrischeff 1928; Ransom 1947

Algonquian tribes (Northeast)
Beaver; Maskwa; Tagkanysough

Algonquian tribes (Subarctic)
Aurora Borealis; Maskwa; Shaking Tent; Winabojo

Alsea
Asin; Cyclone; Suku; Talking Doctors; Wind-Woman
Beckham, Toepel, and Minor 1984; Frachtenberg 1920

Apache
Animals, Creation of; Apache Bear Dance; Apache Creation and Emergence; Black Hactcin Creates Animals and Humans; Child-of-the-Water; Crown Dancers;
Europeans, Origin of; Hactcin; Hactcin, Departure of; Killer-of-Enemies; Mountain Spirits; Na ih es; Naayenezgane; Sunrise Dance; White Hactcin; White Painted Woman; Wise One
Basso 1966; Bourke 1890; Caldwell 1945; Goddard 1919; Goddard 1920a; Goddard 1920b; Goodwin 1939; Goodwin 1945; Opler 1941

Arapaho
Cawacnenitan; Crow-Woman; Foot-Stuck-Child; Found-in-Grass; Ghost Dance of 1890; Hairy-Face; Hantceciitehi; Hantitaeinici; Hiintcabiit; Hixtcaba Nihancan; Lime Crazy; Little Owl; Man-Above; Moon, Origin of Shadows on; Nankubacein; Nariniiha; Nayaanxatisei; Nihansan; Owner-of-Bag; Painted-Porcupine; Quilling; Raw Gums; River-Woman; Spitting-Horn-Shell and Split-Rump; Sun Dance; Transformation and Return Experience; Wanou; White Owl Woman
Dorsey 1903b; Dorsey and Kroeber 1903; Michelson 1933; Voth 1912a

Arctic (culture area)
Eskimo; Ikalu nappa; Raven; Superguksoak; Vasaagijik
Judson 1911; Norman 1990

Arikara
First Creator and Lone Man; Kawenho
Dorsey 1904b; Dorsey 1904e; Gilmore 1926; Gilmore 1929a; Gilmore 1929b; Hoffman 1892b; Parks 1984; Taylor 1977

Assiniboin
Lowie 1910; Reagan 1935a

Athapaskan tribes (Subarctic)
Inkoze; Knowledge
Mishler 1984

Atsugewi
Dixon 1908

Bannock
Ghost Dance of 1890

Index by Tribe